MODERN SPOKEN CAMBODIAN

MAP OF CAMBODIA

North ←

National Boundaries
Provincial Boundaries
Rivers and Shores
Provincial Capitals
Phnom Penh
Railways

THAILAND

LAOS

DANGREK MOUNTAINS

Preah Vihear

(Phnom Kreng Mean Chey)

Siem Reap

Battambang

Pursat

Tonlé Sap

Ratanakiri

(Lomphat)

Stung Treng

Mondulkiri

(Sen Monorom)

Kratié

Mekong

Tonlé Mekong

Kampong Thom

Kampong Cham

Kampong Chhnang

Kampong Speu

Koh Kong

(Khemarak-Phoumnville)

CARDAMOM MOUNTAINS

Kampot

Takéo

Kandal

Prey Veng

Svay Rieng

SOUTH VIETNAM

Mekong

Tonlé Bassac

GULF OF THAILAND

វគ្គខេមរភាសា

MODERN SPOKEN CAMBODIAN

by Franklin E. Huffman

with the assistance of
Charan Promchan and
Chhom-Rak Thong Lambert

Cornell University, Southeast Asia Program
Ithaca, New York 14853

Cornell Southeast Asia Program Publications
640 Stewart Avenue, Ithaca, NY 14850-3857

ISBN 978-0-87727-521-3

PREFACE

This book is an outgrowth of three years of study of the Cambodian language at the School of Oriental and African Studies of the University of London, in Southeast Asia, and at Cornell University, and of three years of teaching Cambodian at Yale University.

It would be impossible to mention all those who have had a hand in bringing this work to completion. Thanks are especially due to Professor Fang-kuei Li of the University of Washington, who first suggested the Cambodian language as a field of study; Mrs. Judith M. Jacob of the London School of Oriental and African Studies, who gave me the first practical introduction to Cambodian; Professor Robert B. Jones of Cornell University, for his help and guidance during the preparation of a dissertation on Cambodian grammar; Mr. Charan Promchan, who provided the material on which the Dialogues are based; Mrs. Chhom-Rak Thong Lambert, who assisted with the testing and revision of the materials; and Mr. Im Proum, who provided the Cambodian voice on the accompanying tapes.

I also wish to thank the Cambodians who served as informants in the course of my research in London, Thailand, Cambodia, and New Haven; the Department of East and South Asian Languages and Literatures of Yale University, which kindly granted me sufficient time from teaching duties to complete the work; and the Yale University Press, which dealt patiently with the many problems involved in printing a language textbook.

F. E. H.

September, 1969

CONTENTS

INTRODUCTION

THE LANGUAGE

Cambodian, also known as Khmer, is the official language of the Kingdom of Cambodia. It is spoken by some 5,000,000 people in Cambodia, and mutually intelligible dialects are spoken by approximately 400,000 inhabitants of the provinces of Buriram, Surin, and Srisaket in northeastern Thailand, and by approximately 450,000 people in the Mekong Delta of South Vietnam.

Cambodian is the major modern representative of the Mon-Khmer language family, which includes, besides Mon in Lower Burma, also hundreds of related dialects scattered over most of mainland Southeast Asia, such as the Palaung, Wa, and Riang in Burma, the Khmu, Lamet, and Sô in Laos, the Kuy, Chong, and Lawa in Thailand, the Stieng, Biet, and Samre in Cambodia, the Bahnar, Halang, and Sre in Vietnam, and possibly the Semang and Sakai in Malaya.[1] No wider affiliation for the Mon-Khmer family has been conclusively demonstrated, although most linguists now think that Vietnamese is related to Mon-Khmer. Pater Wilhelm Schmidt's hypothesis of an Austroasiatic language family on the Southeast Asian mainland, including, besides Mon-Khmer, also the Munda languages of northeastern India, Khasi in Assam, the Cham group in South Vietnam and Cambodia, Nicobarese, and Semang and Sakai in the Malay peninsula,[2] is unwarranted by present evidence, and his further grouping of Austroasiatic with the Austronesian languages of island Southeast Asia to form an Austric superstock is even more speculative, although many of Schmidt's assumptions have been proven correct by later research.

As for foreign influences on the language, the Cambodians have borrowed much of their administrative, military, and literary vocabulary from Sanskrit. With the advent of Theravada Buddhism at the beginning of the 15th century, Cambodians began to borrow Pali words, and continue to use Pali as a major source of neologisms today. Although Cambodian and Thai are not, so far as we know, genetically related, a high percentage of their vocabularies stem from a common source, as the result both of mutual borrowing over a long period of historical contact, and of common borrowing of learned terminology from Pali and Sanskrit. During the period of French domination, many French words were borrowed into the language and have become a part of the colloquial language, especially in urban areas. There is also a smattering of Chinese and Vietnamese loanwords in colloquial speech.

Unlike its neighbors Thai and Vietnamese, which are tonal and essentially monosyllabic, Cambodian is non-tonal and has a high percentage of disyllabic words. Like the Malayo-Polynesian languages, it has a relatively complex morphology, forming disyllabic derivatives from monosyllabic bases by prefixation and infixation, although these processes are rarely productive in the language.

---

1. Frank M. LeBar, Gerald D. Hickey, and John K. Musgrave, Ethnic Groups of Mainland Southeast Asia (New Haven, Human Relations Area Files, 1964), pp. 287–88.

2. P. Wilhelm Schmidt, "Les peuples mon-khmêr; trait d'union entre les peuples de l'Asie centrale et de l'Austronésie," Bulletin de l'École Française d'Extrême-Orient 7 (1907): 213-63.

The typical stress pattern in such disyllables is an unstressed presyllable followed by a stressed main syllable. Even polysyllabic loanwords from Pali and Sanskrit tend to be assimilated to this pattern of alternation between an unstressed and a stressed syllable.

THE COURSE

The aim of this course is to provide the student with a thorough command of the basic structures of standard spoken Cambodian. Standard Cambodian is the dialect taught in the schools, used for mass communication, and spoken by educated Cambodians; it is also the dialect which corresponds more closely than any other with the writing system. Although some colloquial dialects, notably that of Phnom Penh and the immediately surrounding area, differ considerably from the standard at the phonological level, standard Cambodian is virtually identical with the dialect spoken by the majority of the people in the central Provinces, and would be understood throughout the country.

This course does not purport to be a "painless" or "easy" approach to speaking Cambodian; no such approach exists for any language. It is well known that a poorly motivated student will not learn to speak a foreign language, regardless of the approach, and that a highly motivated student will usually do well in learning a foreign language, also regardless of the approach, which leads some language teachers to the conclusion that the teaching method used is irrevelant. However, it stands to reason that if a highly motivated student can make progress in spite of a poor method, he should make much more rapid and efficient progress with an efficient approach to language learning.

This course is based on the audio-oral method of language teaching developed by the Intensive Language Program of the American Council of Learned Societies and used so successfully during World War II, as modified by advances in language teaching techniques since that time. This method assumes that (1) to learn to speak a language, you must use it; and (2) to use a language correctly, you must hear it. Since the best authority on what the language sounds like is a native speaker, this book is designed to be used with the help of a native speaker of Cambodian. If a native speaker of Cambodian is unavailable to the student, he must rely solely on the tapes that accompany each lesson and that are designed to provide supplementary practice for the student outside the classroom.

In working with a native speaker, the following points should be remembered:

1. The job of the native speaker is to act as a drillmaster, to provide a model for the student to imitate, and to correct the student's pronunciation and usage. It is not his job to "explain" the language; that is the job of this book or of the linguist. The student should ask the native speaker only how something is said, never why it is said in such and such a way. Language structures are arbitrary, and there is no answer to the question why.

2. The drillmaster's models, and the student's repetitions, should always be spoken at normal speed. To speak at an abnormally slow speed, which is the tendency with most language teachers, simply distorts pronunciation and intonation. Furthermore, although the student might be able to make himself understood at a slow speed, he would be unable to comprehend the reply. It is just as easy to learn a phrase at normal speed as at a slow speed, and much more useful.

3. The native speaker should ideally be a speaker of standard Cambodian. However, if his speech differs from that presented in this book, the student should in all cases imitate the speech of the native speaker.

Lesson 1 of this book is devoted to Pronunciation Drills. These drills should be repeated until the student has mastered the sounds of the language. The sound system of a language is finite, and can be learned in a relatively short time if properly presented. The student who does not master the pronunciation of a language at the beginning of the course will usually make the same mistakes throughout his study of the language. Where possible, words used in the pronunciation drills are actual words that occur frequently in ordinary speech, and they represent all of the sound combinations in the language that are likely to cause trouble for speakers of English. Once these words have been mastered, they can serve as mnemonic aids for all other words having the same sound combinations.

All subsequent lessons are based on dialogues dealing with common situations and topics. Each of these lessons is divided into four sections—Dialogue, Grammar and Drills, Comprehension, and Conversation.

A. Dialogues

The aim of this section is to relate the students' learning to authentic situations, and to provide the student with a repertory of useful sentences from the very beginning of his study. Frequently the range of meaning of a Cambodian word does not coincide with the range of meaning of any particular word in English. Such discrepancies are much more frequent than is commonly imagined, no matter what two languages are involved, so that word-for-word translations are often inaccurate and misleading. Thus it is important for the student to learn the complete utterance required by a given social situation rather than to try to establish equivalences between individual words of the target language and those of his native language. These complete utterances are represented in this text by the sentences of the Dialogues, which are translated by the utterance in English which would be required in the same situation. Thus they are seldom word-for-word translations, since the two utterances may differ both as to the order (syntax) and the semantic range (meaning) of their constituent elements. In the English equivalents of the Cambodian sentences, words that occur in the Cambodian sentence but not in the English equivalent are enclosed in parentheses ( ); words that occur in the English equivalent but not in the Cambodian sentence are enclosed in brackets [ ].

The list of words preceding each complete utterance (the "build-up") contains all vocabulary items not previously encountered, and has the purpose of acquainting the student with the pronunciation and approximate meaning of the elements contained in the following utterance.

Some of the vocabulary items in the build-ups are followed by alternative pronunciations; e.g.:

sapbaay (səpbaay, səbaay)   happy, pleasant

These alternative forms are reduced forms that occur in normal colloquial speech. The unstressed presyllables of disyllabic words are most subject to this reduction. In the build-ups, the drillmaster will give the pronunciation only of the first form, which is the form that occurs in careful speech, and by which all words are listed in the Glossary. He will not be called upon to pronounce the reduced forms in isolation, since it is unlikely that he would be able to do so, just as it would be difficult for an English speaker to reproduce in isolation the reduced pronunciation /gɔ́nə/ of the words "going to" in the utterance "I'm going to go." However, in the complete utterance which follows, vocabulary items will be represented in the forms in which they normally occur in the style of speech being represented. If the pronunciation used by the drillmaster differs from that represented in the transcription, the student should imitate the pronunciation of the drillmaster. Specific patterns of reduction will be discussed in the Grammar and Drills sections of later lessons.

The following procedure should be followed in learning the Dialogues:

1. The students should read, or have read to them, the English equivalent of the word or utterance to be pronounced.

2. With the books closed, the students repeat the utterance after the drillmaster in unison. This should be done twice, or until the students can repeat the entire utterance at normal speed. In the case of long utterances, the teacher may want to break them at first into appropriate shorter phrases, building up to the complete utterance.

3. After having repeated all the utterances of the Dialogue with the books closed, the same procedure should be repeated with the students looking at the transcription of the sentences in order to associate the sounds with their transcriptions.

Note: It is absolutely essential that the words and sentences be repeated first with the books closed, for two reasons: (a) to force the student to rely on his ears rather than his eyes, and thus to develop the aural ability so necessary to learning a foreign language, and (b) to prevent the students from making false associations with familiar-looking symbols.

4. As an assignment, the student should practice the sentences of the Dialogue with tapes, or if tapes are not available, with the mnemonic aid of the transcription, until he can without hesitation give the Cambodian sentence when supplied with the English equivalent, and vice versa. He should be prepared to demonstrate this mastery at the next class session.

B. Grammar and Drills

Children learn to speak their native language by the age of five or six without being told anything about grammar; they internalize grammatical patterns subconsciously from the speech they hear around them. Similarly it would not, strictly speaking, be necessary to say anything about grammar in learning a second language, provided that the grammatical patterns were properly presented by the lesson material. But second language learning differs from native language learning in several important ways:

1. It is possible, in second language learning, to shorten the five or six years it takes a child to learn his native language by analyzing and extracting the basic patterns of a target language for drill and reinforcement. This is much more efficient than the random reinforcement that takes place in first language learning.

2. As we grow older we are less receptive to learning by imitation than in early childhood, although this varies from student to student. The experience of formal education instills in advanced students the desire to analyze, to label, and to verbalize what they are studying. Thus if not provided with a correct analysis, the student will invariably make his own analysis, frequently incorrect because of inadequate information.

3. The mind of the student of a second language is no longer a linguistic tabula rasa; he will inevitably try to force the categories and patterns of the target language into the mould of his native language. Thus it is important to contrast the structure of the target language with that of the student's native language (contrastive grammar).

Thus while a student must have internalized the structure of the target language through practice in order to use it successfully, he also has a psychological need to know about it. Furthermore, we can assume that the student who is sufficiently motivated to embark on the study of a rare language is intelligent enough to apply a conscious knowledge of the structure of a language to his competence in the use of the language.

Speaking a language, whether one's native language or a second language, is a skill; like any skill, it can be acquired only by practice. The rules that govern the flow of our native speech are automatic and unconscious; if we had to stop and think of the rules by which we speak we would be unable to speak. Likewise the rules of a second language must be learned until they become as automatic as those of our native language. This is the purpose of the drills. Each drill selects a basic syntactic construction and provides for its repetition until it becomes automatic and unconsciously productive for the student. Some drills vary the words that may occur in one syntactic position (substitution drills). The student thus becomes aware of word classes, or "parts of speech," based on syntactic position. Other drills show the relationship between two or more different syntactic patterns (transformation and response drills), at the same time providing reinforcement of each pattern.

Thus each grammar note, which is intended to help the student "know about" Cambodian grammar, is followed by one or more drills, which are intended to help the student "know" Cambodian grammar. If the student is limited by time, he should emphasize the drills to the neglect of the grammar notes, since it is more important to "know" the grammar than to "know about" it.

Experience has shown that the following approach to the Drills is most successful:

1. The students should have studied (or have explained to them) each grammatical point before proceeding with the drills. Since each grammatical point is immediately followed by the relevant drill(s), the sentences of the drills can serve as further illustrative examples for the grammatical note.

2. The teacher should read each sentence of the drill, particularly those in the Student column, to be translated by individual students as an exercise in comprehension. The drill can be effective only if the student is fully aware of the significance of the pattern being drilled.

3. The teacher should read each sentence in the Student column for repetition by the students in unison.

4. The teacher reads the sentence or cue in the Teacher column; the students perform the substitution, expansion, transformation, or response called for by the drill. If the response is short and simple, the students should respond in unison. However, if the response called for is long and/or complicated, the students should respond individually the first time; then the drill should be repeated with the students responding in unison.

Experience has shown that to attempt to go directly to Step 4, which is the ultimate objective of each drill, without the preliminary steps outlined above, is confusing to the student and therefore counterproductive. Remember: the more times a student hears, imitates, or produces a particular pattern, the better.

C. Comprehension

This section consists of a number of conversations and dialogues which involve, so far as possible, only the vocabulary and grammatical patterns already introduced in the Dialogue of the same lesson. Its purpose is to provide practice in understanding and using the vocabulary and patterns already introduced. These conversations can be used in the following ways: (1) to test the student's comprehension of vocabulary and patterns already introduced by having him give the correct English translation on hearing the sentences pronounced; (2) as an assignment, with the student memorizing the conversations and being prepared to take the role of any of the conversants in repeating the conversations in class; (3) for dictation exercises to test the student's mastery of the transcription system, and, at a later point, of the writing system.

D. Conversation

This section represents the primary aim of the course—to enable the student to use correct conversational Cambodian in actual situations of give and take. Suggested conversation outlines are provided. It is important, particularly in the early lessons, to adhere closely to these outlines, which are designed to evoke only those phrases and patterns with which the student is already familiar. Attempts at free conversation in the early stages are counterproductive, since the student invariably gets into vocabulary and patterns that he is not equipped to handle. More freedom can be allowed in later lessons, when the student has a larger repertory of vocabulary and patterns on which to draw.

SCOPE OF THE BOOK

Since the aim of this book is to develop competence in spoken Cambodian, it does not deal with the writing system. Although it is entirely possible to learn to read without knowing what a language sounds like, the student can learn to read much more quickly and efficiently once he is familiar with the underlying sound system and vocabulary represented by the writing system. This is the sequence in which we learn to read our native language. Thus it is recommended that the student begin his study of the writing system only after having mastered the sound system, and that his first reading texts should involve vocabulary and structures which have already been encountered. The author's Cambodian Writing System and Beginning Reader (New Haven, Yale University Press, 1970) is designed for use concurrently with Modern Spoken Cambodian, and should be begun after the first few weeks of Modern Spoken Cambodian have been covered. It is anticipated that about 225 classroom hours should be required for the completion of Modern Spoken Cambodian, and that about 75 classroom hours should be devoted to the Cambodian Writing System and Beginning Reader, for a total of about 300 hours of classroom instruction.

TAPE RECORDINGS

The Pronunciation Drills and the Dialogue and Comprehension sections of each lesson are recorded on 53 consecutive tapes; each section of the text is provided with the number of its corresponding tape. Tapes may be purchased at cost from Foreign Language Laboratory, Yale University, 111 Grove Street, New Haven, Connecticut 06510.

LESSON 1. PRONUNCIATION DRILLS

The following drills provide practice in producing and distinguishing between the sounds of Cambodian. Most of the examples involve <u>actual words</u> arranged in <u>minimal pairs</u>, i.e. pairs of words which differ only with regard to one sound, thus establishing the phonetic distinction as a structural, or <u>phonemic</u>, one. The meanings of actual words are provided as an aid to the teacher. Nonsense words are preceded by an asterisk.

Since Cambodian vowels present more difficulty to English speakers than do Cambodian consonants, most of the drills involve vowel contrasts. Each vowel is contrasted with its phonetically closest neighbor, and short vowels are contrasted with their long counterparts. As for consonant sounds, only those points which are likely to cause trouble are dealt with.

The procedure to be followed in the pronunciation drills is as follows:

1) <u>Imitation drill</u> (with books closed)

Teacher	Student
a) phaa	a) phaa
b) paa	b) paa
c) phaa, paa	c) phaa, paa

This procedure should be repeated for each contrast until the teacher is satisfied that the students have mastered the contrast involved.

2) <u>Association drill</u> (with books open)

Repeat the above drill with the students looking at their books in order to associate the sounds with their transcriptions.

3) <u>Comprehension drill</u>

The teacher should repeat the two (or more) contrasting words in a random order, and the student should identify the sounds and write them in the proper order. If the students are unable to do this, steps 1 and 2 above should be repeated until the students have no difficulty in distinguishing aurally between the sounds.

<u>Sample:</u> Teacher (speaking)	Student (writing)
thaa	th
taa	t
taa	t
thaa	th
taa	t
taa	t
taa	t
thaa	th
thaa	th

<u>NOTE:</u> If the teacher speaks a non-standard dialect of Cambodian, he may not maintain all of the vowel contrasts presented in the section on VOWELS. If the teacher makes no distinction between two vowel representations, the two should be treated as equivalent throughout the book.

A. CONSONANTS

Aspirated vs. Unaspirated Initials

The Cambodian initial sequences ph, th, ch, and kh are pronounced like the English p, t, ch, and k in the words pin, tin, chin, and kin, but with slightly more aspiration, so that such sequences cause no difficulty for speakers of English. However, the unaspirated initials p, t, c, and k are more difficult for English speakers, although they will cause no difficulty for speakers of French, Spanish, or Italian, which have similar sounds. The letters p, t, and k have an unaspirated pronunciation in English when they occur as the second member of an initial consonant sequence, as in the words spy, sty, and sky, but this pronunciation never occurs in initial position. These sounds can be produced simply by holding one's breath, producing simultaneous closure of the glottis. It is sometimes helpful to students to say that the Cambodian sounds p, t, c, and k are midway between English b and p, d and t, j and ch, and g and k respectively, although such a description is not very accurate phonetically. The foregoing comments are intended to aid the student in his imitation of the native speaker, which is the best way to learn to produce new sounds.

1. /ph/ vs. /p/
      /phaa/ silk cloth vs. /paa/ father
      /phii/ proudly vs. /pii/ from

2. /th/ vs. /t/
      /thaa/ to say vs. /taa/ old man
      /thuu/ relaxed vs. /tuu/ chest

3. /ch/ vs. /c/
      /chaa/ to fry vs. /caa/ to mark off
      /chuu/ sound of a downpour vs. /cuu/ sour

4. /kh/ vs. /k/
      /khuu/ sound of whistling vs. /kuu/ pair
      /khae/ month vs. /kae/ to repair

Voiced vs. Voiceless Unaspirated vs. Voiceless Aspirated Initials

The Cambodian voiced initials b and d are similar to the English b and d in bay and day, but are more tense and are frequently preceded by slight prevoicing. The same effect can sometimes be produced by preceding the English word by the unstressed article a: a bay, a day, then gradually reducing the vocalism of the preceding article.

1. /b/ vs. /p/ vs. /ph/
      /biə/playing cards vs. /piə/ to brush against vs. /phiə/ a gift
      /baɑŋ/ older sibling vs. /paɑŋ/ to expect vs. /phaɑŋ/ too

2. /d/ vs. /t/ vs. /th/
      /dae/ also vs. /tae/ but vs. /thae/ to care for
      /dou/ to exchange vs. */tou/ vs. /thou/ vase.

Initial Nasals

Cambodian has four initial nasal sounds: m, n, ñ, and ŋ. Of these only ñ and ŋ pose any difficulty for English speakers. ñ is similar to the ny in canyon. ŋ occurs in English words having a final ng, as in sing, but it never occurs initially in

English. For students who have difficulty with this sound it is sometimes helpful to pronounce the word <u>singing</u>, repeating the second syllable until he can iso-
late the syllable -<u>nging</u>, e.g.:

    singinginginging . . . nging

1. /ñ/ vs. /ŋ/
    */ñaa/ vs. */ŋaa/
    /ñiət/ relative vs. /ŋiət/ salted

2. /m/ vs. /n/ vs. /ñ/ vs. /ŋ/
    */maa/ vs. /naa/ where vs. */ñaa/ vs. */ŋaa/
    /miət/ size vs. /niət/ master vs. /ñiət/ relative vs. /ŋiət/ salted

B. VOWELS

Long Vowels and Diphthongs

1. /ii/ vs. /ee/
    /liiŋ/ to fry vs. /leeŋ/ to play
    /tii/ place vs. /tee/ negative auxiliary

2. /ee/ vs. /ei/[1]
    /kee/ they vs. /kei/ heritage
    /leeŋ/ to play vs. /leiŋ/ a personal name
    /ceeh/ June vs. /ceih/ thread

3. /ii/ vs. /ei/
    /miiŋ/ aunt vs. /meiŋ/ a personal name
    /liiw/ unmarried vs. /leiw/ button

4. /ei/ vs. /ɛɛ/
    /kei/ heritage vs. /kɛɛ/ craw
    /leiŋ/ a personal name vs. /lɛɛŋ/ to quit
    /ceik/ banana vs. /cɔcɛɛk/ to discuss

5. /ei/ vs. /ae/
    /kei/ heritage vs. /kae/ to correct
    /keiw/ to funnel vs. /kaew/ glass

6. /ɛɛ/ vs. /ae/
    /kɛɛ/craw vs. /kae/ to correct
    /prɛɛ/ silk cloth vs. /prae/ to translate
    /pnɛɛk/ eye vs. /pnaek/ section

7. /ee/ vs. /ei/ vs. /ɛɛ/ vs. /ae/
    /kee/ they vs. /kei/ heritage vs. /kɛɛ/ craw vs. /kae/ to correct
    /leeŋ/ to play vs. /leiŋ/ a name vs. /lɛɛŋ/ to divorce vs. /kɑnlaeŋ/ place

8. /ɨɨ/ vs. /əə/
    /lɨɨ/ to hear vs. /ləə/ on
    /chɨɨ/ sick vs. /chəə/ wood
    /plɨɨ/ bright vs. /pləə/ stupid

---

1. This contrast is not maintained in some dialects.

9. /əə/ vs. /əɨ/[1]
   /ləə/ on vs. */ləɨ/
   /khəəñ/ to see vs. /məɨn/ 10,000

10. /əɨ/ vs. /aə/
    /məɨn/ 10,000 vs. */maən/
    */kəɨt/ vs. /kaət/ to be born

11. /əə/ vs. /aə/
    /təə/ ensnared vs. /taə/ question particle
    /cəəŋ/ foot vs. */caəŋ/

12. /uu/ vs. /oo/
    /kuu/ pair vs. /koo/ ox
    /ruuŋ/ hole vs. /rooŋ/ hall

13. /oo/ vs. /ou/[1]
    /koo/ ox vs. /kou/ to stir
    /tooc/ gibbon vs. /touc/ small

14. /uu/ vs. /oo/ vs. /ou/
    /kuu/ pair vs. /koo/ ox vs. /kou/ to stir
    /tuuc/ small vs. /tooc/ gibbon vs. /touc/ small

15. /ou/ vs. /ao/
    /cou/ please vs. /cao/ thief
    /kou/ to stir vs. /kao/ to shave
    /coul/ to enter vs. /caol/ to abandon

16. /aa/ vs. /ɑɑ/
    /kaa/ work vs. /kɑɑ/ neck
    /kaaŋ/ to extend vs. /kɑɑŋ/ bracelet
    /caap/ sparrow vs. /cɑɑp/ spade, hoe

17. /aa/ vs. /ae/
    /kaa/ work vs. /kae/ to repair
    /khaat/ to lose vs. /khaet/ province
    /kaaw/ earring vs. /kaew/ glass

18. /aay/ vs. /ae/
    /caay/ to spend vs. /cae/ a hook
    /baay/ cooked rice vs. /bae/ to turn
    /mdaay/ mother vs. /dae/ also

19. /aa/ vs. /aə/
    /taa/ grandfather vs. /taə/ question particle
    /kaat/ map vs. /kaət/ to be born
    /cŋaay/ far vs. /cŋaəy/ in disorder

20. /ou/ vs. /ɔɔ/
    /kou/ to stir vs. /kɔɔ/ mute
    /souk/ to bribe vs. /sɔɔk/ to insert

---

1. This contrast is not maintained in some dialects.

21. /aɑ/ vs. /ɔɔ/
     /kaɑ/ neck vs. /kɔɔ/ mute
     /kaɑŋ/ bracelet vs. /kɔɔŋ/ gong
     /chaɑ/ 7th letter of the alphabet vs. /chɔɔ/ to stand

22. /oo/ vs. /ɔɔ/
     /koo/ ox vs. /kɔɔ/ mute
     /rook/ disease vs. /rɔɔk/ to seek
     /rooy/ to shed vs. /rɔɔy/ hundred

23. /aɑ/ vs. /ao/
     /kaɑ/ neck vs. /kao/ to shave
     /qaɑn/ tender vs. /qaon/ to bow
     /thaɑy/ to withdraw vs. */thaoy/

24. /oo/ vs. /ou/ vs. /ɔɔ/ vs. /aɑ/ vs. /ao/
     /koo/ ox vs. /kou/ to stir vs. /kɔɔ/ mute vs. /kaɑ/ neck vs. /kao/ to shave

25. /ae/ vs. /aə/
     /tae/ but vs. /taə/ question particle
     /prae/ to translate vs. /praə/ to use

26. /aə/ vs. /ao/
     /baək/ to open vs. /baok/ to beat
     /kaət/ to be born vs. /kaot/ to respect
     /haəy/ already vs. */haoy/

27. /ɔɔ/ vs. /ɔə/
     /pɔɔ/ benediction vs. /pɔə/ color
     /cɔɔ/ embroidery vs. /cɔə/ resin

28. /ɨɨ/ vs. /ɨə/
     /rɨɨ/ or vs. /rɨə/ mature, old
     /lɨɨ/ to hear vs. /lɨəŋ/ yellow

29. /ii/ vs. /iə/
     /lii/ to carry on the shoulder vs. /liə/ to take leave
     /cii/ a plant vs. /ciə/ to be
     /liiw/ unmarried vs. /liəw/ Lao

30. /uu/ vs. /uə/
     /kuu/ pair vs. /kuə/ proper
     /ruup/ form vs. /ruəp/ to collect

31. /iə/ vs. /ɨə/ vs. /uə/
     /liəŋ/ to wash vs. /lɨəŋ/ yellow vs. /luəŋ/ king
     /ciə/ to be vs. /cɨə/ to believe vs. /cuə/ a row
     /riəy/ to distribute vs. /rɨəy/ continuously vs. /ruəy/ tired

32. /iə/ vs. /eə/[1]
     /tiən/ candle vs. /teən/ gift
     /riəp/ to arrange vs. /reəp/ flat

---

1. This contrast occurs only in certain non-standard dialects; in this text the vowel in both words is transcribed /iə/.

Summary of Long Vowels and Diphthongs

/ii/ : /sii/ to eat	/iə/: /ciə/ to be
/ee/: /kee/ they	/ɨə/: /cɨə/ to believe
/ɛɛ/: /kɛɛ/ craw	/uə/: /cuə/ row
/ɨɨ/: /lɨɨ/ to hear	/ei/: /kei/ heritage
/əə/: /ləə/ on	/əɨ/: /məɨn/ 10,000
/aa/: /kaa/ work	/ou/: /kou/ to stir
/ɑɑ/: /kɑɑ/ neck	/ae/: /kae/ to repair
/uu/: /kuu/ pair	/aə/: /daə/ to walk
/oo/: /koo/ ox	/ao/: /kao/ to shave
/ɔɔ/: /kɔɔ/ mute	/ɔə/: /pɔə/ color

Short Vowels and Diphthongs

1. /i/ vs. /e/
    /cih/ to ride vs. /ceh/ to know
    /nih/ this vs. /neh/ (variant form of /nih/)

2. /i/ vs. /ɨ/
    /rih/ to ridicule vs. /rɨh/ root
    */tih/ vs. /tɨh/ direction

3. /ɨ/ vs. /ə/
    /cɨt/ near vs. /cət/ heart
    /lɨc/ to sink vs. /ləc/ west
    /tɨñ/ to buy vs. /dəñ/ to chase
    /plɨw/ thigh vs. /pləw/ road
    /prɨy/ forest vs. /prəy/ thatching grass

4. /ə/vs. /a/
    /cət/ heart vs. /cat/ to order
    /kən/ to thresh vs. /kan/ to hold
    /cəñ/ to exit vs. /cañ/ to be defeated
    /mdəc/ how vs. /sdac/ king
    */təw/ vs. /taw/ bushel
    /dəy/ ground vs. /day/ hand
    /prəy/ thatching grass vs. /pray/ salty

5. /ɨw/ vs. /əw/ vs. /aw/
    /tɨw/ to go vs. */təw/ vs. /taw/ bushel
    /plɨw/ thigh vs. /pləw/ road vs. */plaw/

6. /ɨy/ vs. /əy/ vs. /ay/
    /cɨy/ victory vs. */cəy/ vs. /cay/ louse
    /prɨy/ forest vs. /prəy/ thatching grass vs. /pray/ salty

7. /a/ vs. /ɑ/
    /kat/ to cut vs. /kɑt/ to jot down
    /cap/ to begin vs. /cɑp/ to finish

8. /ɑ/ vs. /o/
    /cɑŋ/ to want vs. /coŋ/ end
    /kɑt/ to jot down vs. /kot/ monks' quarters

9. /u/ vs. /o/
    /kun/ merit vs. /kon/ film
    /thum/ to smell vs. /thom/ big

10. /e/ vs. /eə̆/
    /teh/ to ridicule vs. /teə̆h/ to slap
    */neq/ vs. /neə̆q/ person

11. /a/ vs. /eə̆/
    /taŋ/ to establish vs. /teə̆ŋ/ all
    /tah/ to totter vs. /teə̆h/ to slap

12. /u/ vs. /uə̆/
    /puh/ to boil vs. /puə̆h/ snake
    /kampuŋ/ in the process of vs. /kampuə̆ŋ/ port[1]

13. /o/ vs. /oə̆/
    /kot/ monks' quarters vs. /koə̆t/ 3rd person pronoun
    /pon/ equal to vs. /poə̆n/ thousand

14. /ɑ/ vs. /oə̆/
    /kɑt/ to jot down vs. /koə̆t/ 3rd person pronoun
    /cɑp/ to finish vs. /coə̆p/ attached

Summary of Short Vowels and Diphthongs

/i/:	/cih/ to ride	
/e/:	/ceh/ to know	/teə̆h/ to slap
/ɨ/:	/cɨt/ near	
/ə/:	/cət/ heart	
/a/:	/kat/ to cut	
/ɑ/:	/kɑt/ to jot down	
/u/:	/puh/ to boil	/puə̆h/ snake
/o/:	/kot/ monks' quarters	/koə̆t/ 3rd person pronoun

[Tape 2]   Short vs. Long Vowels

1. /i/ vs. /ii/
   /cih/ to ride vs. */ciih/
   */ciq/ vs. /ciik/ to dig

2. /e/ vs. /ee/
   /ceh/ to know vs. /ceeh/ June

3. /e/ vs. /ei/
   /ceh/ to know vs. /ceih/ thread

4. /ɨ/ vs. /ɨɨ/
   /rɨt/ to tighten vs. /rɨɨt/ to knead
   /yɨt/ to stretch vs. /yɨɨt/ slow

5. /ə/ vs. /əə/
   */cəŋ/ vs. /cəəŋ/ foot

6. /ə/ vs. /əɨ/
   /bət/ to close vs. /bəɨt/ to inhale

7. /a/ vs. /aa/
   /kap/ to hack vs. /kaap/ poetry
   /cah/ old vs. /caah/ response particle

---

1. In many dialects the /u/ vs. /uə̆/ contrast is maintained only before
/-h/.

/cam/ to wait vs. /caam/ Cham
/can/ moon vs. /caan/ plate
/caw/ grandson vs. /caaw/ evenly matched
/cay/ louse vs. /caay/ to spend

8. /aw/ vs. /aaw/ vs. /ao/
/caw/ grandson vs. /caaw/ evenly matched vs. /cao/ thief

9. /ay/ vs. /aay/ vs. /ae/
/cay/ louse vs. /caay/ to spend vs. /cae/ a hook

10. /ɑ/ vs. /ɑɑ/
/cɑp/ to finish vs. /cɑɑp/ spade
/cɑm/ exact vs. /cɑɑm/ peak
/kɑŋ/ bicycle vs. /kɑɑŋ/ bracelet

11. /u/ vs. /uu/
/tuk/ to keep vs. /tuuk/ boat
/puk/ decayed vs. /puuk/ mattress
/nuh/ that vs. /muuh/ a fly

12. /o/ vs. /oo/
/cok/ to stop up vs. /cook/ fortune
/kok/ heron vs. /kook/ land

13. /o/ vs. /ou/
/kon/ film vs. /koun/ child
/qoh/ firewood vs. /qouh/ to drag
/bok/ to collide vs. /bouk/ to add

14. /ŭə/ vs. /uə/[1]
/lŭəŋ/ to be overcome vs. /luəŋ/ king
/cŭəl/ to bump vs. /cuəl/ to rent
/lŭəh/ to redeem vs. /luəh/ wire

C. INITIAL CONSONANT SEQUENCES

Two-place Initial Consonant Sequences

There are 85 different two-place initial consonant sequences in Cambodian
words. Although these 85 sequences fall into different phonetic categories on the
basis of the ways in which they are pronounced, no sequence is pronounced in two
different ways (although the category in which a particular sequence falls may
differ from speaker to speaker). Thus they are in complementary distribution
and can all be analyzed as sequences of only two consonants, /CC-/.

1. Initial /p t c k/ in two-place sequences.
a) Initial /p t c k/ are unaspirated before /r s h/. First contrast all the examples in each row, then all the examples in each column.

/prəə/ to use	/trəw/ correct	/craən/ much	/kruu/ teacher
/psaa/ market			/ksae/ string
/phək/ to drink	/thaa/ to say	/chaa/ to fry	/khae/ month

---

1. In some dialects this contrast is not maintained.

b) Initial /p t c k/ are pronounced with slight aspiration, but no voicing before /p t c k m n ñ ŋ w y l/. First contrast all the examples in each row, then all the examples in each column.

	/tpo̊əl/ cheek	/cpůəh/ toward	/kpůəh/ high
/pte̊əh/ house			/kte̊əh/ skillet
/pco̊əp/ attach			/kcəy/ to borrow
/pkaa/ flower	/tkaəŋ/ illustrious	/ckae/ dog	
	/tməy/ new	/cmaa/ cat	/kmae/ Khmer
/pnum/ mountain	/tnam/ medicine	/cnaŋ/ pot	/knoŋ/ in
/pñaə/ to send			/kñom/ I
/pŋuut/ bathe (tr.)	/tŋay/ day	/cŋaay/ far	
	/twiə/ door	/cweiŋ/ left	/kwaq/ blind
/pyuə/ to hang	/tyuuŋ/ charcoal		/kyɑl/ wind
/plae/ fruit	/tlay/ expensive	/claəy/ to answer	/kliən/ hungry

c) Initial /p t c k/ are usually released with slight vocalism before /q b d/ and in the sequence /kŋ-/. First contrast all the examples in each row, then all the examples in each column.

/pqaem/ sweet	/tqouñ/ to complain	/cqəŋ/ bone	/kqaek/ crow
	/tbaañ/ to weave	/cbah/ clear	/kbaal/ head
/pdəy/ husband		/cdao/ lingot	/kdaw/ hot
			/kŋaan/ swan

2. Initial /m l q/ in /CC-/ sequences are released with slight vocalism as in 1c above. Contrast the examples by columns.

/mteeh/ a pepper	/lpəñ-lpoñ/ irresponsible
/mcul/ needle	/lkɨk-lkɨk/ noisily
/mqɑɑm/ an herb	/lqɑɑ/ good, pretty
/mdaay/ mother	/lbaeŋ/ game
/mno̊əh/ pineapple	/lmɔɔm/ sufficient
/mñae-mñɑɑ/ wheedling	/lŋiəc/ afternoon
/mlup/ shade	/lwɛɛŋ/ compartment
/mriəm/ finger	/lhoŋ/ papaya
/msaw/ flour	/qwəy/ what
/mhoup/ food	

3. Initial /s/ in /CC-/ sequences is pronounced with slight vocalism before /q b d/ (as in 1c above), and, before all other consonants, like English s in stop. Contrast the following examples by columns.

/sqaek/ tomorrow	/spɨy/ cabbage	/sñaeñ/ to fear
/sbaek/ skin	/stɨŋ/ river	/sŋiəm/ quiet
/sdap/ to listen	/sko̊əl/ know	/swaa/ monkey
	/smaw/ grass	/slap/ to die
	/snaa/ crossbow	/srəy/ woman

Three-place Initial Consonant Sequences

There are only two three-place initial consonant sequences in Cambodian, and in both cases the third member is /-h-/.

/sthaanii/ station   /lkhaon/ drama

D. DISYLLABLES

Minor Disyllables

Minor disyllables are quite common in Cambodian, and consist of an unstressed presyllable of shape CV+, CrV+, CVN+, or CrVN+, followed by a
stressed syllable. In rapid speech the vowels of all minor disyllables are reduced to /ə/. The following examples of minor disyllables are all transcribed
in their careful speech forms; the reduced forms are treated in a later unit. In
the drills below imitate carefully the native speaker's pronunciations.

1. Presyllables of shape CV+

/kɑkaay/ to scratch about   /sɑsei/ to write
/cɔcɛɛk/ to discuss   /mənuh/ human
/tɔtuəl/ to receive   /mədaaŋ/ one
/pɔpɔɔk/ cloud   /rəbɑh/ thing
/bɑbuəl/ to agree   /qayuq/ age
/dɑdael/ same   /rɔliiŋ/ smooth

2. Presyllables of shape CrV+

/prɑkan/ to object   /crɑqouh/ lazy
/prɑdap/ instrument   /krɑbəy/ water buffalo
/trɑciəq/ ear   /srɑlañ/ to like
/crɑmoh/ nose   /srɑmaoc/ ant

3. Presyllables of shape CVN+

/bɑŋkaət/ to originate   /cumwiñ/ around
/damlouŋ/ potato   /tumpiə/ to chew
/cɑŋkaa/ chin   /tuənlee/ river
/kɑnlaeŋ/ place   /puənlɨɨ/ light
/sɑndaek/ beans   /kuənlɔɔŋ/ furrow

4. Presyllables of shape CrVN+

/prammuəy/ six   /prambəy/ eight
/prampɨl/ seven   /prambuən/ nine

Major Disyllables

Major disyllables consist of two stressed syllables in close juncture. The
first three examples below are morphologically simple, i.e. they do not contain
more than one meaningful element; the last three are compounds.

/siəwphɨw/ book   /muəy-muəy/ slowly
/phiəsaa/ language   /buəŋ-suəŋ/ to pray
/kawqəy/ chair   /sduəc-sdaəŋ/ insignificant

E. POLYSYLLABLES

Polysyllables tend to conform in normal speech to the stress pattern typical
of minor disyllables, i.e. alternation of an unstressed with a stressed syllable.
Imitate the native speaker's pronunciation of the following examples.

1. Three syllables

/thŏəmmədaa/ usually   /koo-krɑbəy/ livestock
/rŏət-mŭəntrəy/ minister   /qaamerɨc/ America

2. Four syllables

/puttəsahsnaa/ Buddhism   /qathaathibaay/ commentary
/bɑntəc-bɑntuəc/ somewhat   /tumniəm-tumlŏəp/ customs

3. Five syllables

/rattənaqkirii/ Ratanakiri (province)
/phoocəniiyəthaan/ restaurant
/riəc-rŏətthaaphibaal/ royal government

4. Six syllables

/prɑthiəniəthɨppədəy/ president
/wicaarənaqkəthaa/ editorial

For a summary statement of Cambodian phonology, see the author's
Cambodian System of Writing and Beginning Reader (New Haven, Yale University Press, 1970), Chapter II, "Phonology."

LESSON 2. USEFUL WORDS AND PHRASES

A. DIALOGUE

[Part One]

cumriəp (cəmriəp)	to inform
suə	to question
1. cumriəp-suə.	Good-day, Greetings, Hello!
look	Sir, or you (polite)
2. cumriəp-suə look.	Good-day, Sir.
look-srəy	Madam, or you (polite)
3. cumriəp-suə look-srəy.	Good-day, Madam.
sok	to be happy, well
sapbaay (səpbaay, səbaay)	to be happy, pleasant
sok-səpbaay	to be well and happy
ciə	to be well
tee? (teh?)	final question word
4. look sok-səpbaay ciə tee?	Are you well? (addressing a man)
baat	polite response word used by men
kñom	I, me, my
tee (teh)	emphatic final particle
5. baat, kñom sok-səpbaay ciə tee.	Yes, I'm quite well.
6. look-srəy sok-səpbaay ciə tee?	Are you well? (addressing a woman)
caah (cah)	polite response word used by women
7. caah, kñom sok-səpbaay ciə tee.	Yes, I'm quite well.
qɑɑ-kun	to thank; thank you
craən	much, many
nah	very, very much
8. qɑɑ-kun craən nah.	Thank you very much.
coh	and what about. . . ?, and how about. . . ?
9. coh, look?	And how about you?
10. kñom sok-səpbaay ciə tee.	I'm fine.
11. soum-tooh (som-tooh).	Excuse me; I'm sorry.
mɨn (m-)	negative auxiliary
qəy	anything, something
tee (teh)	final negative particle
12. mɨn-qəy tee.	Don't mention it; you're welcome.
13. baat.	Yes (man speaking).
14. baat, tee.	No (man speaking).
15. caah.	Yes (woman speaking).
16. caah, tee.	No (woman speaking).

qɑñcəəñ (qəñcəəñ, ñcəəñ)	word of polite invitation
tɨw	to go
naa?	where?, which?
17. look qəñcəəñ tɨw naa?	Where are you going?
salaa-riən (salaa, səlaa)	school
18. kñom tɨw salaa.	I'm going to school.
nɨw	to be situated, reside, remain
qae-naa? (qinaa?)	where?
19. salaa nɨw qae-naa?	Where is the school?
phoocəniiyəthaan	restaurant (formal)
(phoocniithaan)	
20. phoocəniiyəthaan nɨw qae-naa?	Where is the restaurant?
pteə̆h	house, shop, building
sɑmnaq (səmnaq)	to rest, stay
pteə̆h-səmnaq	hotel
21. pteə̆h-səmnaq nɨw qae-naa?	Where is the hotel?
bɑŋkuə̆n (bəŋkuə̆n)	toilet
22. bəŋkuə̆n nɨw qae-naa?	Where is the toilet?
khaaŋ (khaŋ-)	side, direction
sdam	right (side)
day	hand
sdam-day	to be on the right
khaaŋ-sdam-day	the right-hand side
23. nɨw khaŋ-sdam-day.	It's on the right.
cweiŋ	left (side)
cweiŋ-day	to be on the left
khaaŋ-cweiŋ-day	the left-hand side
24. nɨw khaŋ-cweiŋ-day.	It's on the left.
muk	in front of
khaaŋ-muk	front, in front
25. nɨw khaŋ-muk.	It's in the front.
kraoy	behind, after
khaaŋ-kraoy	back, in back
26. nɨw khaŋ-kraoy.	It's in the back.
qae-nih (qinih)	here
27. nɨw qae-nih.	It's here.
qae-nuh (qinuh)	there
28. nɨw qae-nuh.	It's there.
mɛɛn	to be right, true
haəy (həy, qəh)	already, indeed
29. mɛɛn haəy.	That's right.
30. mɨn mɛɛn tee.	That's not right.

trəw-kaa	to need, to want
qwəy (qəy)	what?
31. look/look-srəy trəw-kaa qəy?	What would you like?
baarəy (barəy, pərəy)	cigarette
32. kñom trəw-kaa barəy.	I want some cigarettes.
cɑŋ	to want, want to
baan	to have, to get
cɑŋ baan	to want to have
chəə-kuh (chəkuh)	match(es)
33. look/look-srəy cɑŋ baan	Do you want some matches?
chəə-kuh tee?	
nih	here is/are
nɨŋ	and, with
34. nih barəy nɨŋ chəə-kuh.	Here are the cigarettes and matches.
tɔtuəl-tiən (tətuəl-tiən)	to eat (with reference to oneself)
baay	cooked rice; food
35. kñom cɑŋ tətuəl-tiən baay.	I'd like to have some food.
tɨk	water
tae	tea (plant)
tɨk-tae	tea (liquid)
tɨk-dɑh-koo	milk
kaafei (kafei)	coffee
skɑɑ	sugar
numpaŋ	bread
pɔɔŋ-moǎn	(chicken) egg(s)
36. look/look-srəy trəw-kaa	Would you like some tea?
tɨk-tae tee?	
kaew	a glass
muəy kaew (məkaew)	one glass, a glass (of)
37. baat, tee; kñom trəw-kaa kafei	No; I want a glass of coffee.
məkaew.	
38. nih look/look-srəy.	Here you are.
tlay	to cost, to be expensive
ponmaan? (pənmaan, pəmaan)	how much?, how many?
39. tlay ponmaan?	How much is it? ([It] costs how much?)
bəy	three
riəl	riel (Cambodian monetary unit)
40. tlay bəy riəl.	It's three riels.
maoŋ	hour, time
41. maoŋ ponmaan?	What time is it?
pii	two
42. maoŋ pii haəy.	It's two o'clock.
dɑl	to reach, arrive at
peel	time, occasion
ñam	to eat or drink (informal)
ñam baay	to have a meal
43. dɑl peel ñam baay haəy.	It's time to eat (already).

rɔteh (rəteh)	car, cart
pləəŋ	fire, light
rɔteh-pləəŋ (rəteh-pləəŋ)	train
cəñ	to leave, exit
qaŋkal (qəŋkal, ŋkal)	when? (in the future)

44. rəteh-pləəŋ cəñ qaŋkal? — When does the train leave?

dɑp	ten

45. rəteh-pləəŋ cəñ maoŋ dɑp. — The train leaves at ten o'clock.

kon	film, movie
cap	to begin (to)
leeŋ	to play
pii	from, since
pii-qaŋkal (pii-qəŋkal, pii-ŋkal)	when? (in the past)

46. kon nih cap leeŋ pii-qəŋkal? — When did this movie start?

niətii	minute(s)

47. kon nih cap leeŋ dɑp niətii haəy. — This film started ten minutes ago.

tŋay	day, sun
tŋay-nih (ŋay-nih)	today
kdaw	hot

48. tŋay-nih kdaw nah. — It's very hot today.

sqaek	tomorrow

49. kñom tɨw sqaek. — I'm going tomorrow.

mɔɔk (mɔɔ)	to come
msəl-məñ	yesterday
pii-msəl-məñ	(on) yesterday

50. knom mɔɔk pii-msəl-məñ. — I came yesterday.

soum (som)	please
liə	to take leave, to say good-by

51. soum liə haəy. — Good-by.

52. baat. /caah. — Good-by. (as a response).

Numbers

1.	muəy (mə-)	one
2.	pii	two
3.	bəy	three
4.	buən	four
5.	pram	five
6.	prammuəy (pəmmuəy)	six (five + one)
7.	prampɨl (pəmpɨl)	seven (five + two)
8.	prambəy (pəmbəy)	eight (five + three)
9.	prambuən (pəmbuən)	nine (five + four)
10.	dɑp	ten
11.	dɑp-muəy	eleven
12.	dɑp-pii	twelve
16.	dɑp-prammuəy	sixteen
20.	məphɨy (mphɨy)	twenty
21.	məphɨy-muəy	twenty-one

30.	saamsəp	thirty
40.	saesəp	forty
50.	haasəp	fifty
60.	hoksəp	sixty
70.	cətsəp	seventy
80.	paetsəp	eighty
90.	kawsəp	ninety
100.	muəy-rɔɔy (mərɔɔy)	one hundred

B. GRAMMAR AND DRILLS

1. General Discussion

You will notice that Cambodian words are not inflected for such categories as tense, number, and gender; i.e. they are invariable in shape, except for phonological changes which take place as a result of rapid pronunciation (called reduction; this will be dealt with later). For example, the verb tɨw can mean 'go, goes, going, went, or gone', while the noun barəy can mean either 'cigarette' or 'cigarettes'. This lack of inflection has led some people to the assumption that such languages are 'simple', 'imprecise', or 'have no grammar'. Nothing could be farther from the truth. Languages do differ as to which grammatical categories are compulsory, i.e. must be stated, and which are optional. For example, while the categories of number, gender, and tense must be stated in English but are optional in Cambodian, they may nevertheless be unambiguously specified in Cambodian by the use of expanded phrases involving additional auxiliaries and particles, on the level of syntax. Similarly, with the word 'carry' in English, the specification of 'mode of carrying' is optional, although it may be specified by the use of expanded phrases, such as 'carry in the hand', 'carry on the back', etc. In Cambodian, however, there is no general word meaning 'to carry', and the semantic category 'mode of carrying' is compulsory; e.g.:

> yuə 'to carry in the hand'
> lii   'to carry on the back'
> rɛɛk 'to carry on a pole across the shoulder'
> bəy 'to carry in the arms'
> tuul 'to carry on the head'
> Etc.

As your study of Cambodian progresses, you will find that when it is deemed necessary, Cambodian possesses the grammatical machinery for being explicit. It is axiomatic that all languages are mutually translatable, but they may rely on different mechanisms for the expression of ideas.

Cambodian has two major morphological (pertaining to word structure rather than to sentence structure) mechanisms: 1) the derivation of related (mostly disyllabic) words from monosyllabic words by the use of prefixes and infixes (although these prefixes and infixes do not have a constant meaning and are not generally productive, i.e. may not be applied to just any word), and 2) compounding (both of which will be discussed at a later point).

Cambodian thus relies more heavily on syntactic (pertaining to word order) mechanisms than on morphological mechanisms. In Lesson 1 you have seen a number of constructions (syntactic patterns) which seem quite similar to English, e.g.: Subject-Verb-Object (SVO):

kñom tɨw səlaa.   I'm going to school.
kñom trəw-kaa barəy.   I need some cigarettes.
kñom tətuəl-tiən baay.   I am eating rice.

Others, however, are quite different; e.g. modifiers generally follow the words they modify in Cambodian but precede them in English, e.g.:

pteə̆h thom   large house
srəy lqɑɑ   pretty girl
barəy pii   two cigarettes

Another striking difference between Cambodian and English is the relative independence of the verb. In English a predication or statement usually includes both a subject (actor or topic) and a predicate of some kind. In Cambodian, however, once a subject has been introduced, or is clear from context, it may be omitted from the predication. A predication in Cambodian, then, is defined as 'any verb or verb phrase, with or without a subject or topic'. Thus the "sentence" tɨw. may have a variety of meanings, depending on the context: 'I'm going', 'He went.', 'They've gone.', 'Let's go.', etc.

1-A. Substitution Drill

[In a substitution drill, the student substitutes one of a class of grammatically equivalent words or phrases in a specific frame provided by the teacher.]

Model:

Teacher	Student
1. kñom tɨw səlaa.	kñom tɨw səlaa.
I'm going to school.	I'm going to school.
2. pteə̆h.	kñom tɨw pteə̆h.
home.	I'm going home.

Teacher	Student
kñom tɨw səlaa.	kñom tɨw səlaa.
pteə̆h.	kñom tɨw pteə̆h.
pteə̆h-səmnaq.	kñom tɨw pteə̆h-səmnaq.
phoocəniiyəthaan.	kñom tɨw phoocəniiyəthaan.
bəŋkuə̆n.	kñom tɨw bəŋkuə̆n.
səlaa-riən.	kñom tɨw səlaa-riən.

1-B. Substitution Drill

Teacher	Student
kñom trəw-kaa barəy.	kñom trəw-kaa barəy.
chəə-kuh.	kñom trəw-kaa chəə-kuh.
pɔɔŋ-moə̆n.	kñom trəw-kaa pɔɔŋ-moə̆n.
numpaŋ.	kñom trəw-kaa numpaŋ.
skɑɑ.	kñom trəw-kaa skɑɑ.
baay.	kñom trəw-kaa baay.
kafei.	kñom trəw-kaa kafei.

1-C. <u>Substitution Drill</u>

<u>Teacher</u>	<u>Student</u>
səlaa nɨw qae-naa?	səlaa nɨw qae-naa?
bəŋkŭən	bəŋkŭən nɨw qae-naa?
ptĕəh-səmnaq	ptĕəh-səmnaq nɨw qae-naa?
phoocəniiyəthaan	phoocəniiyəthaan nɨw qae-naa?
ptĕəh	ptĕəh nɨw qae-naa?
səlaa-riən	səlaa-riən nɨw qae-naa?

2. Intonation

Cambodian intonation is not fully understood. However a few general statements can be made.

1) Statements are normally accompanied by a falling contour on the last word of the sentence, as in

    kñom sok-səbaay ciə tee.⌒   I'm quite well.

However, rising instead of falling contour may also occur at the end of statements, in which case it seems to carry the secondary implication that the statement is obvious or anticipated, as in

    kñom sok-səbaay ciə tee.⌐   I'm fine [of course].

2) Questions are usually accompanied by rising contour on the last word of the sentence. However, falling contour may also occur in questions. Falling contour with a question seems to carry a secondary implication of superiority or familiarity of the speaker to the addressee, while rising contour with a question reflects deference, politeness, or formality. The following examples are translated freely in order to illustrate the semantic nuances.

    look qəncəəñ tɨw naa?⌐   Where are you going, Sir?
    look tɨw naa?⌄   Where in the world are you going?

In this book, the falling intonation normally associated with statements will be represented by a period, and the rising intonation normally associated with questions will be represented by a question mark. However, the student should always imitate the intonation used by the native speaker, both in the classroom and on the tapes.

2-A. <u>Intonation Drill</u>

Imitate the teacher's pronunciation of the following questions and answers, paying particular attention to the contrast in intonation.

<u>Teacher</u>	<u>Student</u>
look tɨw naa?⌐	look tɨw naa?
kñom tɨw səlaa.⌄	kñom tɨw səlaa.
səlaa nɨw qae-naa?⌐	səlaa nɨw qae-naa?
səlaa nɨw qae-nuh.⌄	səlaa nɨw qae-nuh.
maoŋ pəmaan haəy?⌐	maoŋ pəmaan haəy?
maoŋ dɑp haəy.⌄	maoŋ dɑp haəy.

3. The Use of Response Particles

The function of the response particles <u>baat</u> (used by men) and <u>caah</u> (used by women) is <u>polite acknowledgment of a previous utterance</u> by another speaker, whether the previous utterance was a statement or a question. Following a question, the occurrence of a response particle as the sole constituent of the response implies affirmation. A negative reply is indicated by a response particle followed by the negative final particle <u>tee</u>, or by <u>tee</u> alone. In exchanges between equals, response particles tend to be discontinued after the initial exchanges. However, in exchanges between a superior and an inferior, response particles tend to be used throughout the exchange by the inferior, but may be discontinued (or not used at all) by the superior party in the exchange.

Response particles usually occur with a falling intonational contour. Such internal contours will be indicated in this text by a comma. The student should imitate the intonation of the native speaker in all cases.

3-A. <u>Response Drill</u>

1) Respond affirmatively to the following questions, using only the appropriate response particle:

Teacher	Student
look/look-srəy sok-səbaay ciə tee?	baat/caah.
look/look-srəy tɨw səlaa tee?	baat/caah.
look/look-srəy trəw-kaa barəy tee?	baat/caah.

2) Respond negatively to the following questions, using the appropriate response particle and the final negative particle <u>tee</u>.

look/look-srəy sok-səbaay ciə tee?	baat, tee. /caah, tee.
look/look-srəy tɨw səlaa tee?	baat, tee. /caah, tee.
look/look-srəy trəw-kaa barəy tee?	baat, tee. /caah, tee.

3) Give the response indicated, preceded by the appropriate response particle.

look/look-srəy sok-səbaay ciə tee?	baat/caah, kñom sok-səbaay ciə tee.

4) Have each student address the question in 3 above to another student.

4. The Modal Verbs <u>caŋ</u> and <u>cap</u>

The verbs <u>caŋ</u> 'to want to' and <u>cap</u> 'to begin to' belong to the class of <u>modal verbs</u> which immediately precede, and in some way modify, a following main verb. [This class will be treated more fully later.] Examples:

look <u>caŋ</u> baan chəə-kuh tee?	Do you <u>want</u> (to have) some matches?
kon nih <u>cap</u> leeŋ pii-qəŋkal?	When did this film <u>start</u> (to play)?

4-A. <u>Substitution Drill</u>

Teacher	Student
kñom caŋ baan <u>barəy</u>.	kñom caŋ baan <u>barəy</u>.
<u>skaa</u>.	kñom caŋ baan <u>skaa</u>.
<u>chəə-kuh</u>.	kñom caŋ baan <u>chəə-kuh</u>.
<u>baay</u>.	kñom caŋ baan <u>baay</u>.
<u>kafei</u>.	kñom caŋ baan <u>kafei</u>.
<u>pɔɔŋ-moən</u>.	kñom caŋ baan <u>pɔɔŋ-moən</u>.

5. The Verb nɨw

The verb nɨw means 'to reside, remain, be located at', and therefore is frequently followed by a word or phrase which is descriptive of a location; e.g.
A nɨw B.

5-A. Progressive Substitution Drill

[In a progressive substitution drill the student is required to make substitution in more than one slot or frame. The slot for which the substitution is intended should be clear from the context.]

Model:

Teacher	Student
səlaa nɨw qae-nih.	səlaa nɨw qae-nih.
pteəh	pteəh nɨw qae-nih.
khaŋ-muk	pteəh nɨw khaŋ-muk.

In the following drill there are 6 substitutions for each slot, so that there are
6 × 6 = 36 possible sentences.

səlaa-riən	nɨw qae-nih.
phoocəniiyəthaan	nɨw qae-nuh.
pteəh	nɨw khaŋ-muk.
pteəh-səmnaq	nɨw khaŋ-kraoy.
bəŋkuən	nɨw khaaŋ-sdam-day.
səlaa	nɨw khaaŋ-cweiŋ-day.

6. Interrogative Words

The following interrogative words have been encountered in the Dialogue:

naa?	where?
qae-naa?	(at) where?
ponmaan?	how much?, how many?
qwəy?	what?
qɑŋkal?	when? (in the future)
pii-qɑŋkal?	when? (in the past)

Notice that the question word occurs at the end of the question, and is replaced
in the answer by the information requested.

look qəñcəəñ tɨw naa?	kñom tɨw pteəh.
salaa nɨw qae-naa?	salaa nɨw khaaŋ-sdam-day.
look trəw-kaa qəy?	kñom trəw-kaa barəy.
tlay ponmaan?	tlay bəy riəl.
look cəñ qəŋkal?	kñom cəñ sqaek.
look mɔɔk pii-qəŋkal?	kñom mɔɔk pii-msəl-məñ.

6-A. Response Drill

Model:

Teacher	Student
1) look tɨw naa? (pteəh)	kñom tɨw pteəh.
2) nih tlay ponmaan? (bəy riəl)	nih tlay bəy riəl.

Teacher	Student
look trəw-kaa qəy? (kafei)	kñom trəw-kaa kafei.
look tɨw naa? (səlaa)	kñom tɨw səlaa.
səlaa nɨw qae-naa? (khaŋ-muk)	səlaa nɨw khaŋ-muk.
nih tlay ponmaan? (pram riəl)	nih tlay pram riəl.
look cəñ qəŋkal? (sqaek)	kñom ceñ sqaek.
look mɔɔk pii-qəŋkal? (pii-msəl-məñ)	kñom mɔɔk pii-msəl-məñ.
look caŋ baan qəy? (barəy)	kñom caŋ baan barəy.
look ñam qwəy? (baay)	kñom ñam baay.

6-B. Response Drill

Teacher	Student
look trəw-kaa qəy? (tɨk-tae)	kñom trəw-kaa tɨk-tae.
look trəw-kaa qəy? (barəy)	kñom trəw-kaa barəy.
look trəw-kaa qəy? (kafei)	kñom trəw-kaa kafei.
look trəw-kaa qəy? (chəə-kuh)	kñom trəw-kaa chəə-kuh.
look trəw-kaa qəy? (pɔɔŋ-moӗn)	kñom trəw-kaa pɔɔŋ-moӗn.
look trəw-kaa qəy? (tɨk-dah-koo)	kñom trəw-kaa tɨk-dah-koo.
look trəw-kaa qəy? (kafei məkaew)	kñom trəw-kaa kafei məkaew.

6-C. Question-Response Drill

Have each student direct the question in 6-B above to a second student, who supplies an answer and directs the question to a third student, and so on.

Model: 1st Student: look trəw-kaa qəy?
         2nd Student: kñom trəw-kaa kafei məkaew.
                       look trəw-kaa qəy?
         3rd Student: kñom trəw-kaa tɨk-tae.

6-D. Response Drill

Teacher	Student
səlaa nɨw qae-naa? (qae-nih)	səlaa nɨw-qae-nih.
(khaŋ-muk)	səlaa nɨw khaŋ-muk.
(khaŋ-kraoy)	səlaa nɨw khaŋ-kraoy.
(qae-nuh)	səlaa nɨw qae-nuh.
(khaŋ-sdam-day)	səlaa nɨw khaŋ-sdam-day.
(khaŋ-cweiŋ-day)	səlaa nɨw khaŋ-cweiŋ-day.

6-E. Question-Response Drill

Have each student direct the question in 6-D above to a second student, who supplies an answer and directs the question to a third student, and so on.

7. qəŋkal vs. pii-qəŋkal

Notice that qəŋkal means 'when in the future?' as in

rəteh-pləəŋ cəñ qəŋkal?	When does (will) the train leave?

pii-qəŋkal, on the other hand, means 'when in the past?' as in

kon nih cap leeŋ pii-qəŋkal?	When did this movie start?

7-A. Transformation Drill

[In a transformation drill, the student changes the sentences given by the
teacher to sentences of a different form; e.g. from affirmative to negative.]
Change the questions below from 'when in the future' to 'when in the past'.

Teacher	Student
look mɔɔk qəŋkal?	look mɔɔk pii-qəŋkal?
kon nih cap leeŋ qəŋkal?	kon nih cap leeŋ pii-qəŋkal?
rəteh-pləəŋ cəñ qəŋkal?	rəteh-pləəŋ cəñ pii-qəŋkal?
look ñam baay qəŋkal?	look ñam baay pii-qəŋkal?
look tɨw pteˇəh qəŋkal?	look tɨw pteˇəh pii-qəŋkal?
look tɨw səlaa qəŋkal?	look tɨw səlaa pii-qəŋkal?

8. The Verb qəñcəəñ

qəñcəəñ is a verb of polite invitation which precedes the main verb or verb
phrase in utterances in which the speaker wishes to show respect for the status
of the addressee; e.g.:

look qəñcəəñ tɨw naa?   Where are you going, Sir?

When the action referred to is obvious from the context, the main verb may be
omitted. In the context of having a meal, it would mean 'Please go ahead (and
have some food).' and so on. As a main verb, however, qəñcəəñ means 'to invite'.

8-A. Response Drill

The following responses should be preceded by the appropriate response
particle.

Teacher	Student
look/look-srəy qəñcəəñ tɨw naa? (səlaa)	baat/caah, kñom tɨw səlaa.
(phooceniiyəthaan)	phoocəniiyəthaan.
(pteˇəh)	pteˇəh.
(pteˇəh-səmnaq)	pteˇəh-səmnaq.
(bəŋkuˇən)	bəŋkuˇən.
(səlaa-riən)	səlaa-riən.

8-B. Question-Response Drill

Have each student pose the question in 8-A above to a second student, who
gives one of the replies above.

9. The Perfective Particle haəy

The perfective particle haəy can in most occurrences be translated by the
English word 'already', e.g.:

koˇət tɨw haəy.	He's already gone.
rəteh-pləəŋ cəñ haəy.	The train has already left.
maoŋ dɑp haəy.	[It's] already ten o'clock.

In other cases, however, haəy seems to have a purely emphatic or confirmatory
function, such as 'indeed' or 'of course', e.g.:

<pre>
        mɛɛn haəy.   That's so; Yes, I agree.
     (look miən barəy tee?)   (Do you have cigarettes?)
        baat, miən haəy.   Yes, I have (of course).
</pre>

The fact that haəy must be translated by at least two different words in English does not mean that there are two homophonous words in Cambodian both pronounced haəy; it means rather that the semantic boundaries of haəy do not coincide with those of any single word in English. The situation can be represented graphically as follows:

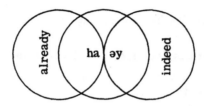

haəy, then, can most satisfactorily be described as a perfective particle. [The class of final particles will be dealt with more fully later.]

9-A. Response Drill

Teacher	Student
maoŋ pənmaan haəy? (bəy)	maoŋ bəy haəy.
(buən)	maoŋ buən haəy.
(prammuəy)	maoŋ prammuəy haəy.
(prambəy)	maoŋ prambəy haəy.
(dɑp)	maoŋ dɑp haəy.
(dɑp-pii)	maoŋ dɑp-pii haəy.

9-B. Substitution Drill

Teacher	Student
dɑl peel ñam baay haəy.	dɑl peel ñam baay haəy.
tɨw ptěəh	dɑl peel tɨw ptěəh haəy.
tɨw səlaa	dɑl peel tɨw səlaa haəy.
cəñ	dɑl peel cəñ haəy.
liə	dɑl peel liə haəy.
tətuəl-tiən baay	dɑl peel tətuəl-tiən baay haəy.

10. The Word tee

Notice that the word tee has three functions, or uses:

1) As a negative particle, as in

<pre>
     baat, tee. (or simply tee.)   No.
</pre>

tee also occurs as the second element in the discontinuous negative mɨn . . . tee, as in

<pre>
     mɨn mɛɛn tee.   [That's] not right.
     kñom mɨn trəw-kaa kafei tee.   I don't want any coffee.
</pre>

2) As a final question particle, as in

      look sok-sapbaay ciə <u>tee</u>?   Are you well?

In this use it is comparable to the Spanish question word <u>no</u>? In very formal speech the compound question word <u>rɨɨ-tee</u>? 'or not?' occurs, as in

      look sok-sapbaay ciə <u>rɨɨ-tee</u>?   Are you well?

3) As an emphatic particle, as in

      kñom sok-sapbaay ciə <u>tee</u>.   I'm <u>quite</u> well.

In all such cases, however, <u>tee</u> has a connotation of negation, limitation, or disparagement, as in

      kñom kroən-tae mɔɔk daə-leeŋ <u>tee</u>.   I just came for fun [<u>that's all</u>].

Thus it can be seen that all three functions of the form <u>tee</u> share a semantic bond —that of some form of negation.

10-A. Transformation Drill

Convert the following affirmative sentences to negative sentences.

Teacher	Student
kñom tɨw.	kñom <u>mɨn</u> tɨw <u>tee</u>.
kñom ñam.	kñom <u>mɨn</u> ñam <u>tee</u>.
tŋay-nih kdaw.	tŋay-nih <u>mɨn</u> kdaw <u>tee</u>.
kñom tɨw pteəh.	kñom <u>mɨn</u> tɨw pteəh <u>tee</u>.
kñom ñam baay.	kñom <u>mɨn</u> ñam baay <u>tee</u>.
kñom trəw-kaa barəy.	kñom <u>mɨn</u> trəw-kaa barəy <u>tee</u>.
mɛɛn.	<u>mɨn</u> mɛɛn <u>tee</u>.
səlaa nɨw khaŋ-sdam-day.	səlaa <u>mɨn</u> nɨw khaŋ-sdam-day <u>tee</u>.
kñom caŋ baan chəə-kuh.	kñom <u>mɨn</u> caŋ baan chəə-kuh <u>tee</u>.

10-B. Transformation Drill

Convert the following statements to questions, using the final question particle <u>tee</u>?.

Teacher	Student
look tɨw.	look tɨw <u>tee</u>?
look ñam.	look ñam <u>tee</u>?
look trəw-kaa barəy.	look trəw-kaa barəy <u>tee</u>?
look caŋ baan chəə-kuh.	look caŋ baan chəə-kuh <u>tee</u>?
tŋay-nih kdaw.	tŋay-nih kdaw <u>tee</u>?
rəteh-pləəŋ cəñ.	rəteh-pləəŋ cəñ <u>tee</u>?
sqaek look mɔɔk.	sqaek look mɔɔk <u>tee</u>?
look tɨw pteəh.	look tɨw pteəh <u>tee</u>?

11. Cambodian Numerals

Notice that the names of the numerals 1–9 are based on a system of five. The names of the numerals 6–9 are compounds which consist of the word for five plus the word for the appropriate additional numeral.

muəy	one	prammuəy	six
pii	two	prampii (prampɨl)	seven
bəy	three	prambəy	eight
buən	four	prambuən	nine
pram	five	dɑp	ten

(The form prampɨl 'seven' occurs in all levels of colloquial speech, prampii occurring only in a formal reading pronunciation.)

The names of the numerals 11-19 consist of the word dɑp 'ten' plus the word for the appropriate additional numeral from 1-9. (Alternative forms of the numerals 11-19 are discussed in Lesson 6.)

dɑp-muəy	eleven	dɑp-prammuəy	sixteen
dɑp-pii	twelve	dɑp-prampɨl	seventeen
dɑp-bəy	thirteen	dɑp-prambəy	eighteen
dɑp-buən	fourteen	dɑp-prambuən	nineteen
dɑp-pram	fifteen	məphɨy	twenty

The names of the tens from 30-90 are borrowed from Thai, and, although they are multiplicative compounds in Thai, they are simple forms from the point of view of Cambodian numerals, since their individual elements are meaningless in Cambodian.

saamsəp	thirty	cətsəp	seventy
saesəp	forty	paetsəp	eighty
haasəp	fifty	kawsəp	ninety
hoksəp	sixty		

The names of the numerals intermediate between the tens are compounds consisting of the appropriate ten plus the appropriate additional numeral 1-9.

məphɨy-muəy	21	məphɨy-prampɨl	27
məphɨy-pii	22	məphɨy-prambəy	28
məphɨy-bəy	23	məphɨy-prambuən	29
məphɨy-buən	24	saamsəp	30
məphɨy-pram	25	saamsəp-muəy	31
məphɨy-prammuəy	26	Etc. up to 99	

11-A. Repetition Drill

Teacher	Student
muəy, pii, bəy, buən, pram	muəy, pii, bəy, buən, pram
prammuəy, prampɨl, prambəy,	prammuəy, prampɨl, prambəy,
prambuən, dɑp	prambuən, dɑp

11-B. Counting Drill

Have students count from 1-99, each student in turn supplying the successively higher numeral.

11-C. Response Drill

Teacher	Student
nih tlay ponmaan? (pram)	nih tlay pram riəl.
(prampɨl)	nih tlay prampɨl riəl.
(prambuən)	nih tlay prambuən riəl.

Teacher	Student
(dɑp-pram)	nih tlay dɑp-pram riəl.
(məphɨy-muəy)	nih tlay məphɨy-muəy riəl.
(saamsəp-pram)	nih tlay saamsəp-pram riəl.
(saesəp-prambəy)	nih tlay saesəp-prambəy riəl.
(Etc.)	

11-D. Substitution Drill

Teacher	Student
maoŋ dɑp dɑp niətii.	maoŋ dɑp dɑp niətii.
dɑp-pram	maoŋ dɑp dɑp-pram niətii.
məphɨy	maoŋ dɑp məphɨy niətii.
saesəp-pram	maoŋ dɑp saesəp-pram niətii.
haasəp-prambuən	maoŋ dɑp haasəp-prambuən niətii.
saamsəp-pii	maoŋ dɑp saamsəp-pii niətii.
məphɨy-pram	maoŋ dɑp məphɨy-pram niətii.

11-E. Translation Drill

Have the students give the English equivalents of Cambodian numerals selected in random order from the names of the numerals 1–99.

11-F. Translation Drill

Have the students give the Cambodian equivalents of English numerals selected in random order from 1–99.

[Tape 5]   C. COMPREHENSION[1]

1. Meeting on the Street

A: cəmriəp-cuə look.
    look sok-səpbaay ciə tee?

B: baat, kñom sok-səpbaay ciə tee.
    coh, look?

A: kñom sok-səpbaay ciə tee, qɑɑ-kun craən.
    look qəñcəəñ tɨw naa?

B: kñom tɨw pteəh.
    coh, look?

A: kñom tɨw səlaa.
    soum liə haəy.

B: baat.

---

1. The masculine forms of the pronouns and response particles have been used throughout; they should be replaced by the feminine forms when appropriate.

2. Asking for Directions

Bill:	soum-tooh look.
	pteˑəh-səmnaq nɨw qae-naa?
Stranger:	baat, pteˑəh-səmnaq nɨw khaŋ-muk.
Bill:	nɨw khaŋ-sdam-day mɛɛn tee?
Stranger:	mɨn mɛɛn tee.
	nɨw khaŋ-cweiŋ-day.
Bill:	qɑɑ-kun look craən nah.
Stranger:	mɨn qəy tee.

3. In the Restaurant

Waiter:	look trəw-kaa qəy?
Bill:	baat, kñom caŋ baan pɔɔŋ-moˑən nɨŋ numpaŋ.
Waiter:	look trəw-kaa tɨk-tae tee?
Bill:	baat, tee.
	kñom caŋ baan kafei tɨk-dɑh-koo məkaew.
Waiter:	look trəw-kaa skɑɑ tee?
Bill:	tee, qɑɑ-kun.
	maoŋ ponmaan haəy?
Waiter:	baat, maoŋ prambuən haəy.
Bill:	qɑɑ-kun craən.

4. Getting Ready to Leave

Bill:	kñom trəw-kaa barəy.
Waiter:	nih look.
	look trəw-kaa chəə-kuh tee?
Bill:	baat, tee.
	baay nɨŋ barəy tlay ponmaan?
Waiter:	baat, tlay saamsəp-pram riəl.
Bill:	nih look.
Waiter:	qɑɑ-kun craən.

D. CONVERSATION

1. Greetings

   a) A greets B.
   b) B greets A and asks if he is well.
   c) A replies that he is well and returns the question.
   d) B replies that he is well and thanks A.
   e) A says good-by to B.
   f) B responds appropriately.

2. <u>Asking Directions</u>

   a) A approaches B, excuses himself, and asks him where the restaurant is.
   b) B replies that it is straight ahead.
   c) A asks if it's on the right.
   d) B replies that it <u>is</u> on the right.
   e) A asks B what time it is.
   f) B replies that it is 10 o'clock.
   g) A thanks B.
   h) B responds appropriately.

3. <u>In the Restaurant</u>

   a) A asks B what he wants.
   b) B replies that he wants a glass of coffee with milk, and bread.
   c) A asks B if he wants cigarettes.
   d) B answers affirmatively that he wants cigarettes and matches.
      Then he asks how much it costs.
   e) A answers that it comes to 25 riels, then thanks B.

4. <u>Two Friends Meet on the Street</u>

   a) A greets B.
   b) B greets A and asks him when he came.
   c) A replies that he came yesterday.
   d) B asks A where he is going.
   e) A replies that he is going to a restaurant.
   f) B asks A at what time he is going to eat.
   g) A replies that he is going to eat at 7:30.

LESSON 3. IN THE CLASSROOM

A. DIALOGUE

miən
siəwphɨw (səphɨw)
1. look miən siəwphɨw tee?

to have, to exist
book(s)
Do you have a book?

2. baat, miən.

Yes, [I] have.

baək
3. soum look baək siəwphɨw.

to open
Please open your books.

tumpɔə (təmpɔə, təpɔə)
tii-
tii-ponmaan? (-pəmaan?)
4. baək tumpɔə tii-ponmaan?

page
ordinalizing prefix
the how-many'th?
What page (should we open to)?

tii-pram
5. tumpɔə tii-pram.

fifth
Page five. (The fifth page.)

bət
6. soum bət siəwphɨw.

to close; to affix
Please close your books.

thaa
taam
7. soum thaa taam kñom.

to say
to follow; according to, after
Please say after me.

trəw
8. trəw haəy.

to be correct, exact
That's right. (That's correct.)

9. mɨn trəw tee.

That's not right. (That's not correct.)

teə̆ŋ-qɑh (təŋ-qɑh)
kniə
teə̆ŋ-qɑh kniə
10. soum thaa teə̆ŋ-qɑh kniə.

all
together
all together
Please say [it] all together.

sdap
baan
sdap baan
11. look sdap baan tee?

to listen, hear, obey
to be able to
to be able to hear or to understand
Do you understand? (Can you understand?)

12. kñom sdap mɨn baan tee.

I don't understand. (I can't understand.)

məc?
13. look thaa məc?

how?, what?
What (how) did you say?

mədɑɑŋ
tiət
14. soum thaa mədɑɑŋ tiət.

one time, once
again, further
Please say [it] again.

niyiəy (nyiəy)
muəy-muəy
15. soum niyiəy muəy-muəy.

to speak, to talk
slowly, deliberately
Please speak slowly.

nih   this, here (demonstrative pro-
                                         noun)
sqəy   what?
16. nih sqəy?   What's this? (This [is] what?)

nuh   that, there (demonstrative pro-
                                         noun)
17. nuh sqəy?   What's that?

kɨɨ   is, being, as follows
ciə   to be
18. nuh kɨɨ ciə siəwphɨw.   That's a book.

rɔbɑh (rəbɑh)   thing
nih   this, these (demonstrative adj.)
kee   3rd person pronoun
haw   to call
thaa   that, saying, as follows
19. rəbɑh nih kee haw thaa qwəy?   What's this thing called? (This thing
                                       they call saying what?)

nuh   that, those (demonstrative adj.)
kmaw-day (~ day-kmaw)   pencil
cɔə-lup   eraser
dəy-sɑɑ   chalk
kdaa-khiən   blackboard
kawqəy   chair
tok   table
20. rəbɑh nuh kee haw thaa kmaw-day. That's called a pencil.

piəq   word
məəl   to read, to pronounce
21. piəq nuh məəl thaa məc?   How is that word pronounced? (That
                                       word reads how?)

22. piəq nuh məəl thaa kawqəy.   That word is pronounced "kawqəy".

sɑsei (səsei, təsei)   to write
ləə   on, above
23. soum səsei piəq nih nɨw ləə   Please write this word on the black-
    kdaa-khiən.   board.

kliə   sentence, phrase; space
24. soum məəl kliə nuh.   Please read that sentence.

naa   which? (interrogative adj.)
25. som-tooh, kliə naa?   Excuse me, which sentence?

dɑdael (dədael, tədael)   the same
26. kliə dədael?   The same sentence?

bɑntŏəp (bəntŏəp, pətŏəp)   next, following in succession
27. mɨn mɛɛn tee; kliə bəntŏəp.   No, the next sentence.

prae   to translate
28. kliə nuh prae thaa məc?   How is that sentence translated?
                                       (That sentence translates as what?)

nɨŋ future auxiliary: will, about to
suə to ask
sɑmnuə (səmnuə) question

29. kñom nɨŋ suə səmnuə. I will ask [some] questions.

claəy to answer

30. soum claəy səmnuə kñom. Please answer my question(s).

məc kɑɑ (kɑ-) why?, how is it that?

31. məc kɑ-claəy mɨn baan? Why can't you answer?

klah some
yuəl to understand (the meaning)

32. piəq klah kñom mɨn yuəl tee. I didn't understand some of the words.

qañcəŋ (qəñcəŋ, ñcəŋ) then, in that case
puənyuəl (pənyuəl) to explain
cbah to be clear
qaoy cbah clearly, making [it] clear

33. qəñcəŋ kñom nɨŋ pənyuəl qaoy Then I'll explain it clearly.
    cbah.

cou let's; go ahead and, please
twəə (thəə) to make, to do
nɨŋ with

34. cou twəə kliə nɨŋ piəq nih. Please make a sentence with this word.

B. GRAMMAR AND DRILLS

1. The Verb miən

When the verb miən occurs after a subject, it can be conveniently translated 'to have'. However, when it occurs without a subject or after a topic, its meaning is 'there is, there exists', which is probably its more general meaning. (This use is taken up in Lesson 4.)

1-A. Substitution Drill

Teacher	Student
look miən siəwphɨw tee?	look miən siəwphɨw tee?
kmaw-day	look miən kmaw-day tee?
dəy-sɑɑ	look miən dəy-sɑɑ tee?
cɔə-lup	look miən cɔə-lup tee?
kawqəy	look miən kawqəy tee?
tok	look miən tok tee?

2. The Auxiliaries soum and cou

soum is a polite auxiliary which may precede either a verb or a subject plus verb with the meaning 'please', as in

soum look baək siəwphɨw. Please open your books.
soum thaa taam knom. Please repeat after me.

cou occurs in the same syntactic position as soum, but is more imperative, and is confined to pedagogical or prescriptive admonitions on the part of a teacher or parent, such as

<table>
<tr><td>cou twəə kliə nɨŋ piəq nuh.</td><td>(Would you) make a sentence with this word.</td></tr>
</table>

2-A. Substitution Drill

Teacher	Student
soum look baək siəwphɨw.	soum look baək siəwphɨw.
bət siəwphɨw.	soum look bət siəwphɨw.
thaa taam kñom.	soum look thaa taam kñom.
thaa mədaaŋ tiət.	soum look thaa mədaaŋ tiət.
niyiəy muəy-muəy	soum look niyiəy muəy-muey.
məəl kliə bəntoŏp.	soum look məəl kliə bəntoŏp.
claəy səmnuə kñom.	soum look claəy səmnuə kñom.
twəə kliə nɨŋ piəq nih.	soum look twəə kliə nɨŋ piəq nih.

2-B. Transformation Drill

Teacher	Student
soum baək siəwphɨw.	cou baək siəwphɨw.
soum bət siəwphɨw.	cou bət siəwphɨw.
soum thaa taam kñom.	cou thaa taam kñom.
soum thaa mədaaŋ tiət.	cou thaa mədaaŋ tiət.
soum niyiəy muəy-muəy.	cou niyiəy muəy-muəy.
soum məəl kliə bəntoŏp.	cou məəl kliə bəntoŏp.
soum claəy səmnuə kñom.	cou claəy səmnuə kñom.
soum twəə kliə nɨŋ piəq nih.	cou twəə kliə nɨŋ piəq nih.

3. Ordinal Numerals

Ordinal numerals in Cambodian are formed by prefixing the ordinalizing prefix tii- 'place' to the numeral.

muəy	one	tii-muəy	first
bəy	three	tii-bəy	third
məphɨy-pram	twenty-five	tii-məphɨy-pram	twenty-fifth

The question-word ponmaan 'how many, how much' may also be preceded by the ordinalizing prefix: tii-ponmaan? 'the how-many-eth?', as in

baək tumpɔə tii-ponmaan?	Open to which page?
tumpɔə tii-pram.	Page five. (The fifth page.)

3-A. Substitution Drill

Teacher	Student
baək tumpɔə tii-muəy.	baək tumpɔə tii-muəy.
tii-pram.	baək tumpɔə tii-pram.
tii-dɑp-pram.	baək tumpɔə tii-dɑp-pram.
tii-bəy.	baək tumpɔə tii-bəy.
tii-prambuən.	baək tumpɔə tii-prambuən.

Teacher	Student
tii-saamsəp.	baək tumpɔə tii-saamsəp.
tii-haasəp-prampɨl.	baək tumpɔə tii-haasəp-prampɨl.
tii-saesəp-pii.	baək tumpɔə tii-saesəp-pii.

3-B. Response Drill

Teacher	Student
baək tumpɔə tii-ponmaan? (tii-bəy)	baək tumpɔə tii-bəy.
tŋay-nih kɨɨ ciə tŋay tii-ponmaan? (tii-prampɨl)	tŋay-nih kɨɨ ciə tŋay tii-prampɨl.
nih kɨɨ ciə siəwphɨw tii-ponmaan? (tii-dɑp-pii)	nih kɨɨ ciə siəwphɨw tii-dɑp-pii.
pteᵉh nih kɨɨ ciə pteᵉh tii-ponmaan? (tii-pram)	pteᵉh nih kɨɨ ciə pteᵉh tii-pram.
tŋay-nih kɨɨ ciə tŋay tii-ponmaan? (tii-məphɨy)	tŋay-nih kɨɨ ciə tŋay tii-məphɨy.
məəl kliə tii-ponmaan? (tii-prambəy)	məəl kliə tii-prambəy.
nih kɨɨ ciə kawqəy tii-ponmaan? (tii-kawsəp-prambuən)	nih kɨɨ ciə kawqəy tii-kawsəp-prambuən.

4. The Adverbial Phrase teᵉəŋ-qah kniə

teᵉəŋ-qah kniə is an adverbial phrase meaning 'all together, all at once', as in

soum thaa teᵉəŋ-qah kniə.	Please say [it] all together.

4-A. Substitution Drill

Teacher	Student
soum thaa teᵉəŋ-qah kniə.	soum thaa teᵉəŋ-qah kniə.
tɨw	soum tɨw teᵉəŋ-qah kniə.
niyiəy	soum niyiəy teᵉəŋ-qah kniə.
twəə	soum twəə teᵉəŋ-qah kniə.
məəl	soum məəl teᵉəŋ-qah kniə.
səsei	soum səsei teᵉəŋ-qah kniə.
claəy	soum claəy teᵉəŋ-qah kniə.

5. mədaaŋ tiət

mədaaŋ tiət is another adverbial phrase; it means 'once again, over again', as in

soum thaa mədaaŋ tiət.	Please say [it] again.

5-A. Substitution Drill

Teacher	Student
soum thaa mədaaŋ tiət.	soum thaa mədaaŋ tiət.
məəl	soum məəl mədaaŋ tiət.
səsei	soum səsei mədaaŋ tiət.
twəə	soum twəə mədaaŋ tiət.
sdap	soum sdap mədaaŋ tiət.
claəy	soum claəy mədaaŋ tiət.
pənyuᵉəl	soum pənyuᵉəl mədaaŋ tiət.

6. Adverbial Phrases

The following adverbs and adverbial phrases have been encountered:

tèəŋ-qah kniə:	soum thaa tèəŋ-qah kniə.	Please say it all together.
mədaaŋ tiət:	soum thaa mədaaŋ tiət.	Please say it again.
muəy-muəy:	soum niyiəy muəy-muəy.	Please speak slowly.
taam kñom:	soum thaa taam kñom.	Please repeat after me.
qaoy cbah:	kñom nɨŋ pənyuəl qaoy cbah.	I'll explain it clearly.

6-A. Progressive Substitution Drill

In the following drill there are five substitutions for each slot, so that there are 5 × 5 = 25 possible sentences.

soum thaa tèəŋ-qah kniə.
    məəl muəy-muəy.
    twəə taam kñom.
    səsei mədaaŋ tiət.
    claəy qaoy cbah.

7. nih and nuh

The demonstratives nih and nuh, like English this and that, function both as demonstrative pronouns and as demonstrative adjectives; e.g.:

Demonstrative pronouns:

    nih sqəy? What's this?   nuh sqəy? What's that?

Demonstrative adjectives:

    rəbah nih   this thing   rəbah nuh   that thing

7-A. Response Drill

Teacher	Student
nih sqəy? (kmaw-day)	nuh kɨɨ ciə kmaw-day.
(siəwphɨw)	nuh kɨɨ ciə siəwphɨw.
(cɔə-lup)	nuh kɨɨ ciə cɔə-lup.
(tok)	nuh kɨɨ ciə tok.
(kawqəy)	nuh kɨɨ ciə kawqəy.
(barəy)	nuh kɨɨ ciə barəy.
(kdaa-khiən)	nuh kɨɨ ciə kdaa-khiən.

7-B. Question-Response Drill

Have each student direct the above question to a second student, indicating an object. The second student gives the correct reply, then directs the question to a third student, and so on.

8. thaa (Verb) vs. thaa (Quotative Conjunction)

Notice that the word thaa occurs with two functions:

a) as a transitive verb meaning 'to say', as in

    look thaa məc?   What did you say?

b) as a quotative conjunction after certain verbs, with the meaning 'that, saying, as follows', as in

rəbɑh nih kee haw <u>thaa</u> qwəy?	What's this thing called?
	(This thing they call <u>saying</u> what?)
kliə nuh prae <u>thaa</u> məc?	How is that sentence translated?
	(That sentence translates <u>as</u> how?)

(This second use of <u>thaa</u> will be treated more fully later.)

8-A. Substitution Drill

Teacher	Student
rəbɑh nih kee haw thaa <u>kmaw-day.</u>	rəbɑh nih kee haw thaa <u>kmaw-day.</u>
<u>kawqəy.</u>	rəbɑh nih kee haw thaa <u>kawqəy.</u>
<u>siəwphɨw.</u>	rəbɑh nih kee haw thaa <u>siəwphɨw.</u>
<u>dəy-sɑɑ.</u>	rəbɑh nih kee haw thaa <u>dəy-sɑɑ.</u>
<u>tok.</u>	rəbɑh nih kee haw thaa <u>tok.</u>
<u>kdaa-khiən.</u>	rəbɑh nih kee haw thaa <u>kdaa-khiən.</u>
<u>barəy.</u>	rəbɑh nih kee haw thaa <u>barəy.</u>

8-B. Response Drill

In this drill, the teacher should indicate, but not name, the object shown in parentheses.

Teacher		Student
rəbɑh nih kee haw thaa qwəy?	(kmaw-day)	rəbɑh nuh kee haw thaa <u>kmaw-day.</u>
	(dəy-sɑɑ)	rəbɑh nuh kee haw thaa <u>dəy-sɑɑ.</u>
	(kawqəy)	rəbɑh nuh kee haw thaa <u>hawqəy.</u>
	(siəwphɨw)	rəbɑh nuh kee haw thaa <u>siəwphɨw.</u>
	(tok)	rəbɑh nuh kee haw thaa <u>tok.</u>
	(kdaa-khiən)	rəbɑh nuh kee haw thaa <u>kdaa-khiən.</u>

8-C. Question-Response Drill

Have each student direct the question in 8-B above to a second student, indicating an object. The second student gives the correct reply, then directs the question to a third student, and so on.

9. <u>thaa</u> vs. <u>niyiəy</u>

Notice that <u>thaa</u> as a verb means 'to say', while <u>niyiəy</u> means 'to talk, to speak', as contrasted in the following two sentences:

soum <u>thaa</u> mədɑɑŋ tiət.	Please <u>say</u> [it] again.
soum <u>niyiəy</u> muəy-muəy.	Please <u>speak</u> slowly.

9-A. Translation Drill

Translate the following sentences, using <u>thaa</u> or <u>niyiəy</u> as required.

Teacher	Student
What did you say?	look <u>thaa</u> məc?
I speak slowly.	kñom <u>niyiəy</u> muəy-muəy.
Please say it again.	soum <u>thaa</u> mədɑɑŋ tiət.

Teacher	Student
Please speak slowly.	soum niyiəy muəy-muəy.
Please speak all together.	soum niyiəy teّəŋ-qɑh kniə.
Please say [it] all together.	soum thaa teّəŋ-qɑh kniə.

10. nɨw ləə

In the expression nɨw ləə, nɨw is a verb meaning 'to be located, to reside, to remain', and ləə is a preposition meaning 'on, above', as in

siəwphɨw nɨw ləə tok.	The book is on the table.

In the above example, nɨw ləə is somewhat similar to the English expression 'is on'. In some sentences, however, nɨw ləə can be translated by 'on' alone, as in

səsei piəq nih nɨw ləə kdaa-khiən.	Write this word on the blackboard.

10-A. Progressive Substitution Drill

Teacher	Student
kmaw-day nɨw ləə tok.	kmaw-day nɨw ləə tok.
kawqəy.	kmaw-day nɨw ləə kawqəy.
siəwphɨw.	kmaw-day nɨw ləə siəwphɨw.
kdaa-khiən.	kmaw-day nɨw ləə kdaa-khiən.
cɔə-lup	cɔə-lup nɨw ləə kdaa-khiən.
kawqəy.	cɔə-lup nɨw ləə kawqəy.
tok.	cɔə-lup nɨw ləə tok.
siəwphɨw.	cɔə-lup nɨw ləə siəwphɨw.

11. məəl and prae as Passive Verbs

Although there is no class of passive verbs as such in Cambodian, most active verbs occur also in a passive function. In the following sentences, məəl 'to read' and prae 'to translate' are active verbs and are followed by direct objects.

kñom məəl siəwphɨw.	I'm reading a book.
kñom nɨŋ prae kliə nih.	I'll translate this sentence.

In the following sentences, however, they are passive.

piəq nih məəl thaa məc?	How is this word pronounced?
	(This word reads saying how?)
kliə nih prae thaa məc?	How is this sentence translated?
	(This sentence translates as what?)

11-A. Response Drill

Teacher		Student
piəq nih məəl thaa məc?	(siəwphɨw)	piəq nih məəl thaa "siəwphɨw".
	(kawqəy)	piəq nih məəl thaa "kawqəy".
	(sɑsei)	piəq nih məəl thaa "sɑsei".
	(kmaw-day)	piəq nih məəl thaa "kmaw-day".
	(baək)	piəq nih məəl thaa "baək".
	(rɔbɑh)	piəq nih məəl thaa "rɔbɑh".

11-B. Response Drill

Teacher	Student
"siəwphɨw" prae thaa <u>məc</u>?	"siəwphɨw" prae thaa "<u>book</u>".
"kawqəy" prae thaa <u>məc</u>?	"kawqəy" prae thaa "<u>chair</u>".
"sɑsei" prae thaa <u>məc</u>?	"sɑsei" prae thaa "<u>to write</u>".
"cɔə-lup" prae thaa <u>məc</u>?	"look-kruu" prae thaa "<u>eraser</u>".
"bɑək" prae thaa <u>məc</u>?	"bɑək" prae thaa "<u>to open</u>".
"rəbɑh" prae thaa <u>məc</u>?	"rəbɑh" prae thaa "<u>thing</u>".

12. <u>naa</u> as an Interrogative Adjective

In Lesson 2 <u>naa</u> occurred as an interrogative pronoun meaning 'where?', in

look qəñcəəñ tɨw naa?	<u>Where</u> are you going?

When <u>naa</u> follows a noun, it functions as an interrogative adjective, as in

som-tooh, kliə <u>naa</u>?	Excuse me, <u>which</u> sentence?

12-A. Transformation Drill

Teacher	Student
soum məəl kliə nuh.	som-tooh, kliə naa?
soum bɑək siəw-phɨw.	som-tooh, siəwphɨw naa?
soum prae piəq nuh.	som-tooh, piəq naa?
soum bɑək tumpɔə tii-pram.	som-tooh, tumpɔə naa?
soum claəy səmnuə kñom.	som-tooh, səmnuə naa?
soum səsei kliə nuh.	som-tooh, kliə naa?

13. <u>dɑdael</u> and <u>bɑntoə̆p</u>

In the following exchange, <u>dɑdael</u> and <u>bɑntoə̆p</u> function as adjectives meaning 'the same ____' and 'the next ____' respectively.

kliə dədael?	The <u>same</u> sentence?
mɨn mɛɛn tee; kliə bəntoə̆p.	No, the <u>next</u> sentence.

13-A. Transformation Drill

Teacher	Student
kliə dədael?	mɨn mɛɛn tee; kliə bəntoə̆p.
tumpɔə dədael?	mɨn mɛɛn tee; tumpɔə bəntoə̆p.
siəwphɨw dədael?	mɨn mɛɛn tee; siəwphɨw bəntoə̆p.
piəq dədael?	mɨn mɛɛn tee; piəq bəntoə̆p.
səmnuə dədael?	mɨn mɛɛn tee; səmnuə bəntoə̆p.

13-B. Transformation Drill

Teacher	Student
kliə bəntoə̆p?	mɨn mɛɛn tee; kliə dədael.
tumpɔə bəntoə̆p?	mɨn mɛɛn tee; tumpɔə dədael.
piəq bəntoə̆p?	mɨn mɛɛn tee; piəq dədael.
səmnuə bəntoə̆p?	mɨn mɛɛn tee; səmnuə dədael.
siəwphɨw bəntoə̆p?	mɨn mɛɛn tee; siəwphɨw dədael.

14. The Future Auxiliary nɨŋ

The word nɨŋ has been met as a conjunction, as in

nih barəy nɨŋ chəə-kuh.   Here are the cigarettes and matches.

It has also occurred as a preposition meaning 'with', as in

cou twəə kliə nɨŋ piəq nih.   Make a sentence with this word.

When it occurs as a preverbal auxiliary, it indicates future or incipient action, as in

kñom nɨŋ suə səmnuə.   I will ask some questions.

14-A. Transformation Drill

Teacher	Student
kñom suə səmnuə.	kñom nɨŋ suə səmnuə.
kñom tɨw ptẽəh.	kñom nɨŋ tɨw ptẽəh.
kñom thaa mədaaŋ tiət.	kñom nɨŋ thaa mədaaŋ tiət.
kñom məəl siəwphɨw.	kñom nɨŋ məəl siəwphɨw.
kñom tətuəl-tiən baay.	kñom nɨŋ tətuəl-tiən baay.
kñom tɨw sqaek.	kñom nɨŋ tɨw sqaek.
kñom prae kliə nih.	kñom nɨŋ prae kliə nih.
rəteh-pləəŋ cəñ maoŋ dɑp.	rəteh-pləəŋ nɨŋ cəñ maoŋ dɑp.

15. The Completive Verb baan

In the following sentence, baan functions as a completive verb, which follows, and expresses the completion or possibility of achievement of, a preceding main verb. (The class of completive verbs will be discussed more fully later.)

kñom sdap baan.   I can understand. (I hear able.)

When a completive verb phrase is negated, the negative auxiliary precedes the second, or completive, verb, rather than the first verb as in other kinds of verb phrases:

kñom sdap mɨn baan tee.   I can't understand.
                                          (I hear not able fin.-neg.)

By contrast, the negative auxiliary in a modal verb phrase precedes the first, or modal, verb of the phrase, as in

·   kñom mɨn caŋ nam baay tee.   I don't want to eat.

15-A. Transformation Drill

Teacher	Student
kñom sdap baan.	kñom sdap mɨn baan tee.
kñom twəə baan.	kñom twəə mɨn baan tee.
kñom məəl baan.	kñom məəl mɨn baan tee.
kñom səsei baan.	kñom səsei mɨn baan tee.
kñom claəy baan.	kñom claəy mɨn baan tee.
kñom prae baan.	kñom prae mɨn baan tee.

16. məc and məc kɑɑ

The question word məc in final position can usually be translated 'how?', as in

piəq nuh məəl thaa məc?   How is that word pronounced?

məc also occurs in the question look thaa məc?, which in English must be translated 'What did you say?'. However, məc kɑɑ (in rapid speech shortened to məc kɑ- or simply məc) at the beginning of a question means 'why?, how is it that. . . ?', as in

məc kɑ-claəy mɨn baan?   Why can't you answer?
                                   (How is it that you can't answer?)

16-A. Substitution Drill

Teacher	Student
məc kɑɑ prae mɨn baan?	məc kɑɑ prae mɨn baan?
məəl	məc kɑɑ məəl mɨn baan?
claəy	məc kɑɑ claəy mɨn baan?
twəə	məc kɑɑ twəə mɨn baan?
sdap	məc kɑɑ sdap mɨn baan?
niyiəy	məc kɑɑ niyiəy mɨn baan?
suə	məc kɑɑ suə mɨn baan?
thaa	məc kɑɑ thaa mɨn baan?

16-B. Substitution Drill

Teacher	Student
məc kɑɑ claəy mɨn baan?	məc kɑɑ claəy mɨn baan?
sdap mɨn baan?	məc kɑɑ sdap mɨn baan?
səsei nɨw ləə kdaa-khiən?	məc kɑɑ səsei nɨw ləə kdaa-khiən?
məəl siəwphɨw?	məc kɑɑ məəl siəwphɨw?
baək siəwphɨw?	məc kɑɑ baək siəwphɨw?
mɨn yuəl?	məc kɑɑ mɨn yuəl?
look niyiəy muəy-muəy?	məc kɑɑ look niyiəy muəy-muəy?
bət siəwphɨw?	məc kɑɑ bət siəwphɨw?

17. sdap baan vs. yuəl

Both sdap baan and yuəl can be translated 'to understand', but sdap baan means to understand in the sense of being able to hear, or to catch, an unfamiliar sound, such as a sentence in a foreign language, as in

look thaa məc?; knom sdap mɨn   What did you say?; I didn't understand.
baan tee.

yuəl, on the other hand, means to understand in the sense of learning or comprehending the meaning of the principle of a question or problem, as in

piəq klah knom mɨn yuəl tee.   I don't understand (the meaning of)
                                   some of the words.

17-A. Completion Drill

Complete the following sentences, using the negative form of <u>sdap baan</u> or <u>yuəl</u> as appropriate.

Teacher	Student
look thaa məc?;	kñom <u>sdap mɨn baan</u> tee.
soum thaa mədaaŋ tiət;	kñom <u>sdap mɨn baan</u> tee.
soum pəñyuəl mədaaŋ tiət;	kñom <u>mɨn yuəl</u> tee.
soum niyiəy muəy-muəy;	kñom <u>sdap mɨn baan</u> tee.
piəq nuh prae thaa məc?;	kñom <u>mɨn yuəl</u> tee.
kliə nuh kñom prae mɨn baan;	kñom <u>mɨn yuəl</u> tee.

18. Topic-Comment Sentences

A very common type of sentence in Cambodian is one in which a topic, usually the object of the main verb of the sentence, is announced first, and is then followed by a comment about it, as in

| <u>piəq klah</u>, kñom mɨn yuəl tee. | <u>Some words</u>, I didn't understand. |
| <u>kliə nuh</u>, kñom prae mɨn baan tee. | <u>That sentence</u>, I can't translate. |

Such sentences usually have an alternative form with the object following the verb, as in

| kñom prae <u>kliə nuh</u> mɨn baan tee. | I can't translate <u>that sentence</u>. |

A preposed object indicates that the object, rather than the subject, of the main verb is the primary topic of the sentence; in other words, it emphasizes the object.

18-A. Transformation Drill

Teacher	Student
kñom mɨn yuəl <u>piəq nuh</u> tee.	<u>piəq nuh</u> kñom mɨn yuəl tee.
kñom prae <u>kliə nuh</u> mɨn baan tee.	<u>kliə nuh</u> kñom prae mɨn baan tee.
kñom məəl <u>piəq nuh</u> mɨn baan tee.	<u>piəq nuh</u> kñom məəl mɨn baan tee.
kñom yuəl <u>piəq nuh</u> haəy.	<u>piəq nuh</u> kñom yuəl haəy.
kñom sdap <u>kliə nuh</u> mɨn baan tee.	<u>kliə nuh</u> kñom sdap mɨn baan tee.
kñom sdap <u>kliə nuh</u> baan haəy.	<u>kliə nuh</u> kñom sdap baan haəy.
kñom prae <u>kliə nuh</u> baan.	<u>kliə nuh</u> kñom prae baan.
kñom səsei <u>piəq nuh</u> baan.	<u>piəq nuh</u> kñom səsei baan.
kñom claəy <u>səmnuə nuh</u> mɨn baan tee.	<u>səmnuə nuh</u> kñom claəy mɨn baan tee.

[Tape 7]   C. COMPREHENSION

1. Teacher: look (look-srəy) miən siəwphɨw tee?

    Student: baat (caah), miən.

    Teacher: cou look (look-srəy) baək siəwphɨw.

    Student: baək tumpɔə tii-ponmaan?

    Teacher: tumpɔə tii-dɑp.

Student: som-tooh, kñom sdap mɨn baan tee.
           soum thaa mədɑɑŋ tiət.

Teacher: tumpɔə tii-dɑp.

Student: qɑɑ-kun.

2. Teacher: soum bət siəwphɨw.
              thaa taam kñom.

Student: qəñcəŋ məəl siəwphɨw mɨn baan tee?

Teacher: trəw haəy.

Student: qəñcəŋ soum niyiəy muəy-muəy.

Teacher: rəteh-pləəŋ cəñ maoŋ dɑp.
           sdap baan tee?

Student: baat (caah), sdap baan.

3. Teacher: rəbɑh nih kee haw thaa qwəy?

Student: rəbɑh nuh kee haw thaa "kawqəy".

Teacher: trəw haəy.
           nuh sqəy?

Student: baat (caah), nuh kɨɨ ciə kdaa-khiən.

Teacher: "pencil" prae thaa məc?

Student: "pencil" prae thaa kmaw-day.

Teacher: trəw haəy.
           soum twəə kliə nɨŋ piəq nuh.

Student: kñom miən kmaw-day.

Teacher: trəw haəy.

4. Teacher: piəq nih məəl thaa məc?

Student: baat (caah), piəq nuh məəl thaa pteə̆h-səmnaq.

Teacher: look (look-srəy) yŭəl piəq nuh tee?

Student: kñom mɨn yŭəl tee.
           soum twəə kliə nɨŋ piəq nuh.

Teacher: kee səmnaq nɨw pteə̆h-səmnaq.
           yŭəl tee?

Student: baat (caah), kñom yŭəl haəy, qɑɑ-kun.

D. CONVERSATION

1. Finding the Page
   a) The teacher asks a student if he has a book.
   b) The student answers that he does.
   c) The teacher tells the student to open his book.

d) The student asks which page.

e) The teacher replies that it is page 10.

2. Finding the Sentence

   a) The teacher asks a student to read the first sentence.

   b) The student reads: "look miən siəwphɨw tee?".

   c) The teacher asks the student if he understands that sentence.

   d) The student replies affirmatively that he understands it.

   e) The teacher asks the student to read again.

   f) The student asks if he is to read the same sentence.

   g) The teacher answers negatively, and says that it's the next sentence.

3. Translating A Sentence

   a) The teacher tells a student to repeat after him, then says:
"rəbɑh nih kee haw thaa kdaa-khiən."

   b) The student repeats the sentence.

   c) The teacher asks the student to translate that sentence.

   d) The student replies that he can't translate it.

   e) The teacher says that, in that case, he will explain it.

4. Answering A Question

   a) The teacher tells the students to close their books, then says he will ask a question.

   b) The student asks the teacher to speak slowly.

   c) The teacher asks "What time will you leave?", then asks the student if he can answer.

   d) The student replies that he can't answer, and that he didn't understand some of the words, then asks the teacher to say it again.

   e) The teacher repeats the question.

   f) The student replies: "I will leave at 10 o'clock."

LESSON 4. AT THE MARKET

[Tape 8]   A. DIALOGUE

meiŋ

qei!	interjection to attract attention: hey!
saraan	Saran (a personal name)
tɨñ	to buy
1. qei, saraan; mɔɔk tɨñ qəy?	Hey, Saran; what did [you] come to buy?

saraan

trəw	to have to, must
qaŋkaa (qəŋkaa, ŋkaa)	uncooked (husked) rice
kilou	kilogram
2. kñom trəw tɨñ qəŋkaa pii kilou.	I have to buy two kilos of rice.
haəy	then, and then
daəm	specifier for long slender objects, such as trees, pencils, cigarettes
phaaŋ	too, in addition
3. haəy kñom trəw tɨñ kmaw-day bəy daəm phaaŋ.	And I have to buy three pencils (pencils three ones) too.
meiŋ	you (personal name used as a pronoun)
qaeŋ	reflexive pronoun: you, yourself
dae	also, as well; nevertheless
4. coh, meiŋ-qaeŋ mɔɔk tɨñ qəy dae?	Say, Meng, what are you buying?

meiŋ

krŏən-tae	only, just
daə	to walk, to go
daə-ləəŋ	to stroll, to amuse oneself
5. kñom krŏən-tae mɔɔk daə-leeŋ tee.	I just came to amuse myself.
coul-cət	to like (to)
məəl	to look at, to see
pseiŋ	to be different
pseiŋ-pseiŋ	various, different
6. kñom coul-cət daə məəl rəbah pseiŋ-pseiŋ.	I like to walk [around and] look at various things.
psaa	market
mɔnuh (mənuh, mnuh)	person(s), human being(s)
7. nɨw psaa nih miən mənuh craən nah.	There are a lot of people at this market.

43

saraan

kɑnlaeŋ (kənlaeŋ, kəlaeŋ)	place
luəq	to sell
plae-chəə	fruit

8. nih kənlaeŋ luəq plae-chəə.   Here's a place [where they] sell fruit.

meiŋ

krouc	orange(s), citrus fruit
touc	to be small
touc-touc	to be quite small (plural)

9. krouc nih touc-touc naḥ.   These oranges are quite small.

tae	but (conjunction)
thom	to be large
lqaa	to be good, pretty

10. tae krouc nih thom haəy lqaa phaaŋ.   But these oranges are large and pretty too.

[To Shopkeeper]   saraan

lou	dozen
muəy lou (məlou)	a dozen, per dozen

11. krouc thom-thom nih məlou tlay ponmaan?   How much are these big oranges per dozen?

Shopkeeper

12. krouc nuh məlou tlay məphɨy-pii riəl.   Those oranges are twenty-two riels per dozen.

13. look trəw-kaa ponmaan?   How many do you want?

saraan

tae	but, only (preposition)
kɑnlah (kənlah, kəlah)	half

14. kñom trəw-kaa tae kənlah lou tee.   I want only a half-dozen.

ceik	banana(s)
tum	to be ripe
rɨɨ	or
nɨw	yet, still
haəy-rɨɨ-nɨw (haəy-rɨnɨw, haəy-nɨw)	yet? (already or not yet?)

15. ceik nih tum haəy-rɨnɨw?   Are these bananas ripe yet?

Shopkeeper

16. mɨn-toən (m-toən)   not yet
    ceik nuh mɨn-toən tum tee.   Those bananas aren't ripe yet.

17. tae ceik nih tum haəy.   But these bananas are ripe (already).

snət	specifier for hands of bananas
muəy snət (məsnət)	one hand, per hand (of bananas)

18. məsnət tlay prambəy riəl.   They're eight riels per hand.

saraan

yɔɔk (yɔɔ)	to take

19. kñom yɔɔk ceik tum pii snət nih.   I'll take these two ripe bunches.

te̊əŋ-qɑh (təŋ-qɑh)   all, everything (pronoun)
20. te̊əŋ-qɑh tlay ponmaan?   How much for everything?

Shopkeeper

tlay   price, cost
21. tlay te̊əŋ-qɑh saesəp-muəy riəl.   It's forty-one riels all together.

meiŋ

som   to request, ask for
mɔɔk (mɔɔ, məh)   orientation of action toward the
                                       speaker
22. som barəy muəy mɔɔk.   Could I have a cigarette?

sarɑɑn

kmiən   not have, not exist
23. som-tooh, kñom kmiən barəy tee.   I'm sorry, I don't have any cigarettes.

meiŋ

baə   if
24. baə kmiən, kñom tɨw tɨñ.   If [you're] out, I'll go buy [some].

[To Shopkeeper]

qaoy   to give
kañcap (kəñcap, kəcap)   specifier for small packages
haəy-nɨŋ   and
prəqap (prəqap, pəqap)   specifier for small boxes
25. qaoy barəy mə-kəñcap mɔɔk haəy-   Give me a pack of cigarettes and two
    nɨŋ chəə-kuh pii prəqap phaaŋ.   boxes of matches too.

klian   to be hungry (for)
sarɑɑn   you (personal name used as a
                                       pronoun)
26. sarɑɑn kliən baay tee?   Are you hungry, Saran?

sarɑɑn

27. baat, kliən dae.   Yes, I am hungry.

meiŋ

mɔɔk   hortatory auxiliary: come on and
haaŋ   shop, store
muəy plɛɛt (məplɛɛt)   awhile, one moment, for awhile
sən   polite imperative: first; do
28. mɔɔk tɨw ñam baay nɨw haaŋ nih   Let's get something to eat in this shop
    məplɛɛt sən.   for awhile, [shall we?].

sarɑɑn

kɑɑ (kɑ-)   auxiliary: so, then, accordingly
29. tɨw, kɑ-tɨw.   Let's go then. (We'll go if you wish.)

[Later]

tralap (trəlap, təlap)   to reverse, to turn around
kaa   work
twəə-kaa   to work
30. dɑl maoŋ kñom trəlap tɨw twəə-   It's time for me to go back to work.
    kaa haəy.

mei ŋ

31. kñom kɑɑ trəw tɨw twəə-kaa dae.   I have to go to work too.

saraɑn

wɨñ   contrastive particle: back, again
ciə-muəy (cə-muəy)   with, along with
ciə-muəy kniə   together

32. qəñcəŋ daə tɨw wɨñ ciə-muəy kniə.   Then [let's] walk back together.

B. GRAMMAR AND DRILLS

1. Question and Answers

Questions are formed in three ways in Cambodian, all of which normally involve the typical rising question intonation (See Lesson 2, B, 2).

1) In questions requesting specific information, a specific question word is
used (see Lesson 2, B, 6); e.g.:

look qəñcəəñ tɨw naa?   Where are you going?
look mɔɔk tɨñ qwəy?   What did you come to buy?
rəteh-pləəŋ cəñ qəŋkal?   When does the train leave?

2) In questions requiring a yes-or-no answer, a final question particle is
used. The full form of the final question particle tee? is rɨɨ-tee?, which occurs
only in written Cambodian or in formal speech, and which is shortened in colloquial speech to rɨ-tee? or to tee? alone. This tee? may be shortened in rapid
speech to teh? or qeh?, or may be represented solely by a rising intonational contour following the last word of the question.

An affirmative response to a yes-or-no question may consist only of a repetition of the main verb of the question, or of a full repetition of the question in affirmative form. It is usually preceded in polite speech by the appropriate form
of the response particle, baat for men and caah for women. In the following examples, the optional fuller responses are shown in parentheses.

look sok-səpbaay ciə tee?   baat, (kñom) sok-səpbaay (ciə tee).
    Are you well?   Yes, (I'm quite) well.
look sdap baan tee?   baat, (kñom sdap) baan.
    Can you understand?   Yes, (I) can (understand).
look trəw-kaa chəə-kuh tee?   baat, (kñom) trəw-kaa (chəə-kuh).
    Do you want matches?   Yes, (I) want (matches).
look kliən baay tee?   baat, (kñom) kliən (baay dae).
    Are you hungry?   Yes, (I am) hungry.
look miən pɔɔŋ-moăn tee?   baat, (kñom) miən (pɔɔŋ-moăn).
    Do you have eggs?   Yes, (I) have (eggs).

A negative response to a yes-or-no question may consist of the negative
particle tee alone, but tee is usually followed by the negative form of the main
verb. In polite speech tee may be preceded by the appropriate form of the response particle, and followed by the full negative transform of the question. In
the following examples, the optional portions of the replies are enclosed in
parentheses.

look tɨw tee?	(baat) tee, (kñom) mɨn tɨw tee.
Are you going?	(Resp.) no, (I'm) not going.
look sdap baan tee?	(baat) tee, (kñom) sdap mɨn baan tee.
Can you understand?	(Resp.) no, (I) don't understand.
look tɨn barəy tee?	(baat) tee, (kñom) mɨn tɨn (barəy) tee.
Are you buying cigarettes?	(Resp.) no, (I'm) not buying (cigarettes).
look kliən baay tee?	(baat) tee, (kñom) mɨn kliən (baay) tee.
Are you hungry?	(Resp.) no, (I'm) not hungry (for rice).
look miən pɔɔŋ-moˇən tee?	(baat) tee, (kñom) kmiən (pɔɔŋ-moˇən) tee.
Do you have eggs?	(Resp.) no, (I) don't have (eggs).

3) Certain questions occur without a final question particle or question word. Such questions are always truncated forms of questions already introduced in the conversation, and have the general meaning 'What about _____ [with regard to the question under discussion]?', as in the following exchanges:

look sok-səpbaay ciə tee?	How are you?
baat, qɑɑ-kun.	Fine, thank you.
coh, look?	How about you?
look kliən baay tee?	Are you hungry?
baat, kñom kliən.	Yes, I am.
coh, look?	And you?

1-A. Transformation Drill

Convert the following statements to questions with the use of the final question particle tee?; change kñom 'I' to look 'you'.

Teacher	Student
kñom tɨw psaa.	look tɨw psaa tee?
kñom tɨñ barəy.	look tɨñ barəy tee?
kñom yɔɔk kafei.	look yɔɔk kafei tee?
kñom kliən baay.	look kliən baay tee?
kñom coul-cət daə-leeŋ.	look coul-cət daə-leeŋ tee?
psaa nih thom.	psaa nih thom tee?

1-B. Response Drill

Supply the fullest affirmative answer to each of the following questions.

Teacher	Student
look sok-səpbaay ciə tee?	baat, kñom sok-səbaay ciə tee.
look sdap baan tee?	baat, kñom sdap baan.
look trəw-kaa barəy tee?	baat, kñom trəw-kaa barəy.
look tɨw psaa tee?	baat, kñom tɨw psaa.
look kliən baay tee?	baat, kñom kliən baay.
look yɔɔk kafei tee?	baat, kñom yɔɔk kafei.
look miən plae-chəə tee?	baat, kñom miən plae-chəə.
look coul-cət daə-leeŋ tee?	baat, kñom coul-cət daə-leeŋ.
look tɨñ baay tee?	baat, kñom tɨñ baay.

1-C. Response Drill

Supply a short affirmative answer to the following questions.

Model: Teacher: look sok-səbaay ciə tee?   Are you well?
        Student: baat, sok-səbaay.   Yes, [I'm] well.

Teacher	Student
look sok-səpbaay ciə tee?	baat, sok-səpbaay.
look sdap baan tee?	baat, (sdap) baan.
look trəw-kaa barəy tee?	baat, trəw-kaa.
look tɨw psaa tee?	baat, tɨw.
look kliən baay tee?	baat, kliən.
look yɔɔk kafei tee?	baat, yɔɔk.
look miən plae-chəə tee?	baat, miən.
look coul-cət daə-leeŋ tee?	baat, (kñom) coul-cət.
look tɨñ baay tee?	baat, tɨñ.

1-D. Response Drill

Supply a full negative answer, preceded by the appropriate response particle, to each of the following questions.

Teacher	Student
look sdap baan tee?	baat tee, kñom sdap mɨn baan tee.
look trəw-kaa barəy tee?	baat tee, kñom mɨn trəw-kaa barəy tee.
look tɨw psaa tee?	baat tee, kñom mɨn tɨw psaa tee.
look kliən baay tee?	baat tee, kñom mɨn kliən baay tee.
look yɔɔk tɨk-tae tee?	baat tee, kñom mɨn yɔɔk tɨk-tae tee.
look miən ceik tee?	baat tee, kñom kmiən ceik tee.
look tɨñ barəy tee?	baat tee, kñom mɨn tɨñ barəy tee.
look cɑŋ baan kafei tee?	baat tee, kñom mɨn cɑŋ baan kafei tee.

1-E. Response Drill

Supply a short negative answer to each of the following questions.

Model: Teacher: look tɨw tee?
        Student: tee, mɨn tɨw tee.

Teacher	Student
sdap baan tee?	tee, sdap mɨn baan tee.
trəw-kaa barəy tee?	tee, mɨn trəw-kaa tee.
tɨw psaa tee?	tee, mɨn tɨw tee.
kliən baay tee?	tee, mɨn kliən tee.
yɔɔk tɨk-tae tee?	tee, mɨn yɔɔk tee.
miən plae-chəə tee?	tee, kmiən tee.
coul-cət daə-leeŋ tee?	tee, mɨn coul-cət tee.
miən ceik tee?	tee, kmiən tee.
tɨñ barəy tee?	tee, mɨn tɨñ tee.
cɑŋ baan kafei tee?	tee, mɨn cɑŋ baan tee.

1-F. Transformation Drill

Convert the following full answers to short answers.

Teacher	Student
baat tee, kñom mɨn tɨw tee.	tee, mɨn tɨw tee.
baat tee, kñom sdap mɨn baan tee.	tee, sdap mɨn baan tee.
baat tee, kñom mɨn trəw-kaa baay tee.	tee, mɨn trəw-kaa tee.
baat tee, kñom kmiən ceik tee.	tee, kmiən tee.
baat tee, kñom mɨn tɨw psaa tee.	tee, mɨn tɨw tee.
baat tee, kñom mɨn kliən baay tee.	tee, mɨn kliən tee.
baat tee, psaa nih mɨn thom tee.	tee, mɨn thom tee.
baat tee, krouc nih mɨn tum tee.	tee, mɨn tum tee.

2. Specifiers

Specifiers (S) are words which follow numerals (X) in numerical noun phrases (NXS), and which specify the size, shape, amount, or kind of unit being counted. The following specifiers have been encountered so far in numerical noun phrases:

lou:	krouc məlou	a dozen oranges
snət:	ceik pii snət	two hands of bananas
kilou:	qaŋkaa bəy kilou	three kilos of rice
kañcɑp:	barəy pii kəñcɑp	two packs of cigarettes
prəqɑp:	chəə-kuh pii prəqɑp	two boxes of matches
kaew:	kafei məkaew	a glass of coffee
daəm:	kmaw-day bəy daəm	three pencils (three "sticks" of pencils)

These specifiers differ only in word order from the partitive words which occur with mass nouns in English, e.g.:

a glass of water	a sheaf of wheat
a pound of butter	a bottle of beer
a lump of sugar	a pack of cigarettes
a piece of candy	a rubber of bridge

The difficulty in translating daəm into English in the example above stems from the fact that 'pencil' can be used as a mass noun in Cambodian, but is a specific noun in English. [This topic is treated more fully in Lesson 5.]

2-A. Substitution Drill

Teacher	Student
kñom trəw-kaa krouc məlou.	kñom trəw-kaa krouc məlou.
pɔɔŋ-moăn	kñom trəw-kaa pɔɔŋ-moăn məlou.
siəwphɨw	kñom trəw-kaa siəwphɨw məlou.
kmaw-day	kñom trəw-kaa kmaw-day məlou.
kawqəy	kñom trəw-kaa kawqəy məlou.

2-B. Substitution Drill

Teacher	Student
kñom caŋ baan tɨk məkaew.	kñom caŋ baan tɨk məkaew.
tɨk-tae	kñom caŋ baan tɨk-tae məkaew.
kafei	kñom caŋ baan kafei məkaew.
tɨk-dah-koo	kñom caŋ baan tɨk-dah-koo məkaew.
tɨk	kñom caŋ baan tɨk məkaew.

2-C. Substitution Drill

Teacher	Student
kñom tɨñ skaa pii kilou.	kñom tɨñ skaa pii kilou.
krouc	kñom tɨñ krouc pii kilou.
qəŋkaa	kñom tɨñ qəŋkaa pii kilou.
kafei	kñom tɨñ kafei pii kilou.
tae	kñom tɨñ tae pii kilou.
skaa	kñom tɨñ skaa pii kilou.

2-D. Substitution Drill

Teacher	Student
kñom miən barəy pii daəm.	kñom miən barəy pii daəm.
chəə-kuh	kñom miən chəə-kuh pii daəm.
dəy-saa	kñom miən dəy-saa pii daəm.
kmaw-day	kñom miən kmaw-day pii daəm.

2-E. Transformation Drill

In colloquial speech, the numeral muəy 'one' has the reduced form mə- before specifiers. In the following sentences replace the careful form by the reduced form.

Teacher	Student
kñom trəw-kaa krouc muəy lou.	kñom trəw-kaa krouc məlou.
kñom trəw-kaa kafei muəy kaew.	kñom trəw-kaa kafei məkaew.
kñom trəw-kaa barəy muəy kəñcap.	kñom trəw-kaa barəy mə-kəñcap.
kñom trəw-kaa chəə-kuh muəy prəqap.	kñom trəw-kaa chəə-kuh mə-prəqap.
kñom trəw-kaa kmaw-day muəy daəm.	kñom trəw-kaa kmaw-day mədaəm.
kñom trəw-kaa qəŋkaa muəy kilou.	kñom trəw-kaa qəŋkaa mə-kilou.
kñom trəw-kaa ceik muəy snət.	kñom trəw-kaa ceik məsnət.

3. Demonstrative Noun Phrases

The order of elements in a demonstrative noun phrase (of the kind so far encountered) is as follows:

1) Noun (N)
2) Adjective (A)
3) Numeral (X)
4) Specifier (S)
5) Demonstrative (D)

Example:

N	A	X	S	D
ceik	tum	pii	snət	nih
banana	ripe	two	hands	this

'these two bunches of ripe bananas'

The following abbreviations of the basic pattern occur:

ceik nih   this (these) banana(s)
ceik tum nih   this (these) ripe banana(s)
ceik pii snət nih   these two bunches of bananas

Notice that the demonstrative element occupies final position in any noun phrase in which it occurs.

If the noun to be counted is a <u>specific noun</u> (i.e. requires no specifier) the specifier position is unoccupied.

Example:

N	A	X	D
pteə̆h	thom	bəy	nih
house	big	three	this

'these three big houses'

3-A. Expansion Drill

Teacher	Student
pteə̆h nih (pram)	pteə̆h <u>pram</u> nih
ceik nih (pii)	ceik <u>pii</u> nih
kawqəy nih (buən)	kawqəy <u>buən</u> nih
krouc nih (pram)	krouc <u>pram</u> nih
barəy nih (pii)	barəy <u>pii</u> nih
siəwphɨw nih (bəy)	siəwphɨw <u>bəy</u> nih

3-B. Expansion Drill

Teacher	Student
pteə̆h pram nih (thom)	pteə̆h <u>thom</u> pram nih
ceik pii nih (tum)	ceik <u>tum</u> pii nih
kawqəy buən nih (touc)	kawqəy <u>touc</u> buən nih
krouc pram nih (thom)	krouc <u>thom</u> pram nih
barəy pii nih (tlay)	barəy <u>tlay</u> pii nih
siəwphɨw bəy nih (lqɑɑ)	siəwphɨw <u>lqɑɑ</u> bəy nih

3-C. Translation Drill

Compose the noun phrases called for from the chart below.

N	A	X	D
pteə̆h	thom	pii	nih
siəwphɨw	touc	bəy	nuh
krouc	lqɑɑ	buən	
ceik	tlay	pram	
barəy	tum		
pɔɔŋ-moə̆n			
kawqəy			

Teacher	Student
1. this house	pteǝh nih
2. this big house	pteǝh thom nih
3. these three houses	pteǝh bǝy nih
4. these three big houses	pteǝh thom bǝy nih
5. that book	siǝwphɨw nuh
6. that little book	siǝwphɨw touc nuh
7. those two books	siǝwphɨw pii nuh
8. those two little books	siǝwphɨw touc pii nuh
9. those bananas	ceik nuh
10. those ripe bananas	ceik tum nuh
11. those four ripe bananas	ceik tum buǝn nuh
12. these eggs	pɔɔŋ-moǝn nih
13. these three eggs	pɔɔŋ-moǝn bǝy nih
14. these three little eggs	pɔɔŋ-moǝn touc bǝy nih
15. that pretty chair	kawqǝy lqaa nuh
16. those five pretty chairs	kawqǝy lqaa pram nuh
17. this cigarette	barǝy nih
18. these two cigarettes	barǝy pii nih
19. those four pretty houses	pteǝh lqaa buǝn nuh
20. those expensive oranges	krouc tlay nuh
21. those three expensive oranges	krouc tlay bǝy nuh
22. these three chairs	kawqǝy bǝy nih
23. those three chairs	kawqǝy bǝy nuh
24. those two bananas	ceik pii nuh
25. those two ripe bananas	ceik tum pii nuh

3-D. Expansion Drill

Teacher	Student
ceik nih (tum)	ceik tum nih
pteǝh nih (thom)	pteǝh thom nih
krouc nih (lqaa)	krouc lqaa nih
kafei nih (tlay)	kafei tlay nih
qǝŋkaa nih (lqaa)	qǝŋkaa lqaa nih
krouc nih (touc)	krouc touc nih
kmaw-day nih (lqaa)	kmaw-day lqaa nih
barǝy nih (tlay)	barǝy tlay nih

3-E. Expansion Drill

Teacher	Student
ceik nih (pii snǝt)	ceik pii snǝt nih
krouc nih (mǝlou)	krouc mǝlou nih
qǝŋkaa nih (pii kilou)	qǝŋkaa pii kilou nih
barǝy nih (pii kǝñcap)	barǝy pii kǝñcap nih.
kmaw-day nih (bǝy daǝm)	kmaw-day bǝy daǝm nih
kafei nih (mǝkaew)	kafei mǝkaew nih
pɔɔŋ-moǝn nih (pii lou)	pɔɔŋ-moǝn pii lou nih
chǝǝ-kuh nih (bǝy prǝqap)	chǝǝ-kuh bǝy prǝqap nih

3-F. Expansion Drill

Teacher	Student
ceik tum nih (pii snət)	ceik tum pii snət nih
krouc thom nih (pii lou)	krouc thom pii lou nih
barəy tlay nih (mə-kəñcap)	barəy tlay mə-kəñcap nih
kafei tlay nih (buən kaew)	kafei tlay buən kaew nih
pɔɔŋ-moŏn touc nih (məlou)	pɔɔŋ-moŏn touc məlou nih
kmaw-day lqaa nih (bəy daəm)	kmaw-day lqaa bəy daəm nih

3-G. Expansion Drill

Teacher	Student
skaa pii kilou nih (tlay)	skaa tlay pii kilou nih
krouc məlou nih (thom)	krouc thom məlou nih
ceik məsnət nih (lqaa)	ceik lqaa məsnət nih
barəy mə-kəñcap nih (tlay)	barəy tlay mə-kəñcap nih
pɔɔŋ-moŏn bəy lou nih (touc)	pɔɔŋ-moŏn touc bəy lou nih
kafei buən kaew nih (tlay)	kafei tlay buən kaew nih
chəə-kuh mə-prəqap nih (touc)	chəə-kuh touc mə-prəqap nih

3-H. Translation Drill

Compose the noun phrases called for from the chart below:

N	A	X	S	D
krouc	thom	muəy (mə-)	lou	nih
barəy	touc	pii	kilou	nuh
chəə-kuh	lqaa	bəy	snət	
pɔɔŋ-moŏn	tlay	buən	kəñcap	
ceik		pram	prəqap	
kmaw-day			kaew	
kafei			daəm	
skaa				
qəŋkaa				

Teacher	Student
1. this orange	krouc nih
2. this big orange	krouc thom nih
3. these two dozen oranges	krouc pii lou nih
4. these two dozen big oranges	krouc thom pii lou nih
5. this coffee	kafei nih
6. this expensive coffee	kafei tlay nih
7. these three glasses of expensive coffee	kafei tlay bəy kaew nih
8. this pretty rice	qəŋkaa lqaa nih
9. these five kilos of pretty rice	qəŋkaa lqaa pram kilou nih
0. those five (sticks of) pencils	kmaw-day pram daəm nuh
1. those five pretty pencils	kmaw-day lqaa pram daəm nuh
2. these two packs of cigarettes	barəy pii kəñcap nih

13. these two packs of expensive cigarettes	barəy tlay pii-kəñcap nih
14. those two hands of bananas	ceik pii snət nuh
15. those two hands of ripe bananas	ceik tum pii snət nuh
16. those two boxes of matches	chəə-kuh pii prəqap nuh
17. those two boxes of little matches	chəə-kuh touc pii prəqap nuh
18. these eggs	pɔɔŋ-moən nih
19. these little eggs	pɔɔŋ-moən touc nih
20. these two dozen eggs	pɔɔŋ-moən pii lou nih
21. these two dozen little eggs	pɔɔŋ-moən touc pii lou nih
22. that sugar	skaa nuh
23. that expensive sugar	skaa tlay nuh
24. that kilo of sugar	skaa mə-kilou nuh
25. that expensive kilo of sugar	skaa tlay mə-kilou nuh

4. miən without a Subject

The verb miən frequently occurs without a subject with the meaning 'there is/ are, there exist/s', as in:

nɨw psaa nih, miən mənuh craən nah.
There are a lot of people at this market.

4-A. Substitution Drill

Teacher	Student
nɨw psaa nih, miən mənuh craən nah.	nɨw psaa nih, miən mənuh craən nah.
rəbah	nɨw psaa nih, miən rəbah craən nah.
plae-chəə	nɨw psaa nih, miən plae-chəə craən nah.
haaŋ	nɨw psaa nih, miən haaŋ craən nah.
kee daə-leeŋ	nɨw psaa nih, miən kee daə-leeŋ craən nah.
mənuh	nɨw psaa nih, miən mənuh craən nah.

5. məplɛɛt

məplɛɛt is a contraction of muəy plɛɛt, and frequently occurs as an adverbial element with the meaning 'one moment, a little bit, awhile', as in

mɔɔk tɨw ñam baay nɨw haaŋ nih məplɛɛt sən.
Let's get something to eat in this shop for a while, shall we?

5-A. Substitution Drill

Teacher	Student
mɔɔk tɨw daə-leeŋ məplɛɛt sən.	mɔɔk tɨw daə-leeŋ məplɛɛt sən.
ñam kafei	mɔɔk tɨw ñam kafei məplɛɛt sən.
tɨñ barəy	mɔɔk tɨw tɨñ barəy məplɛɛt sən.
məəl kon	mɔɔk tɨw məəl kon məplɛɛt sən.
ñam baay	mɔɔk tɨw ñam baay məplɛɛt sən.
twəə-kaa	mɔɔk tɨw twəə-kaa məplɛɛt sən.
tɨñ rəbah	mɔɔk tɨw tɨñ rəbah məplɛɛt sən.

6. <u>trəw</u> and <u>coul-cət</u> as Modal Verbs

The verbs <u>trəw</u> and <u>coul-cət</u> occur as main verbs, as in

trəw haəy.   That's <u>right</u>.
kñom <u>coul-cət</u> kafei.   I <u>like</u> coffee.

They also occur as <u>modal verbs</u> (i.e. as preposed modifiers of main verbs) with the meanings 'must' and 'like to' respectively, as in

kñom <u>trəw</u> tɨw twəə-kaa.   I <u>have to</u> go to work.
kñom <u>coul-cət</u> mɔɔk nih.   I <u>like to</u> come here.

When a sentence containing a modal verb is negated, the negative auxiliary <u>pre-</u>cedes the <u>modal verb</u>, as in

kñom <u>mɨn</u> trəw tɨw pteəh tee.   I <u>don't have to</u> go home.
kñom <u>mɨn</u> coul-cət twəə-kaa tee.   I <u>don't like to</u> work.

6-A.   Progressive Substitution Drill

Teacher	Student
kñom trəw tɨñ barəy.	kñom trəw <u>tɨñ barəy</u>.
tɨw psaǎ.	kñom trəw <u>tɨw psaǎ</u>.
coul-cət	kñom <u>coul-cət</u> tɨw psaǎ.
mɔɔk leeŋ.	kñom coul-cət <u>mɔɔk leeŋ</u>.
tɨw psaa.	kñom coul-cət <u>tɨw psaa</u>.
trəw	kñom <u>trəw</u> tɨw psaa.
ñam baay.	kñom trəw <u>ñam baay</u>.
coul-cət	kñom <u>coul-cət</u> ñam baay.
daə-leeŋ.	kñom coul-cət <u>daə-leeŋ</u>.
tɨñ rəbah.	kñom coul-cət <u>tɨñ rəbah</u>.
trəw	kñom <u>trəw</u> tɨñ rəbah.
tɨw pteəh.	kñom trəw <u>tɨw pteəh</u>.

6-B.   Transformation Drill

Teacher	Student
kñom trəw tɨñ barəy.	kñom <u>mɨn</u> trəw tɨñ barəy <u>tee</u>.
kñom trəw tɨw pteəh.	kñom <u>mɨn</u> trəw tɨw pteəh <u>tee</u>.
kñom coul-cət tɨw psaa.	kñom <u>mɨn</u> coul-cət tɨw psaa <u>tee</u>.
kñom coul-cət mɔɔk ləəŋ.	kñom <u>mɨn</u> coul-cət mɔɔk leeŋ <u>tee</u>.
kñom trəw tɨw psaa.	kñom <u>mɨn</u> trəw tɨw psaa <u>tee</u>.
kñom trəw ñam baay.	kñom <u>mɨn</u> trəw ñam baay <u>tee</u>.
kñom coul-cət ñam baay.	kñom <u>mɨn</u> coul-cət ñam baay <u>tee</u>.
kñom coul-cət daə-leeŋ.	kñom <u>mɨn</u> coul-cət daə-leeŋ <u>tee</u>.
kñom coul-cət tɨñ rəbah.	kñom <u>mɨn</u> coul-cət tɨñ rəbah <u>tee</u>.
kñom trəw tɨñ rəbah.	kñom <u>mɨn</u> trəw tɨñ rəbah tee.

7. <u>phɑɑŋ</u> vs. <u>dae</u>

The word <u>phɑɑŋ</u> means 'too, in addition to, along with', while <u>dae</u> means 'too, as well, at the same time'. <u>phɑɑŋ</u> has been met in the following sentence:

qaoy barəy pii kəñcap mɔɔk haəy-nɨŋ chəə-kuh pii prəqap <u>phɑɑŋ</u>.
Give me two packs of cigarettes and two boxes of matches <u>too</u>.

dae has been met in the following sentences:

    coh meiŋ qaeŋ, mɔɔk tɨñ qəy dae?
       How about you, Meng; what are you buying?
    kñom kɑ-trəw tɨw twəə-kaa dae.
       I have to go to work too.

The difference between the two can be illustrated with the following two sentences:

kñom som tɨw phaaŋ.	May I go along [with you]?
kñom trəw tɨw dae.	I have to go too (but not necessarily along with you).

7-A. Translation Drill

Teacher	Student
kñom tɨw _____. (along)	kñom tɨw phaaŋ.
kñom tɨw _____. (as well)	kñom tɨw dae.
kñom trəw tɨñ plae-chəə _____. (in addition)	kñom trəw tɨñ plae-chəə phaaŋ.
kñom trəw tɨñ plae-chəə _____. (as well)	kñom trəw tɨñ plae-chəə dae.
kñom trəw tɨñ krouc haəy-nɨŋ ceik _____. (in addition)	kñom trəw tɨñ plae-chəə haəy-nɨŋ ceik phaaŋ.
kñom som tɨw _____. (along)	kñom som tɨw phaaŋ.
kñom kɑ-trəw tɨw twəə-kaa _____. (as well)	kñom kɑ-trəw tɨw twəə-kaa dae.
kñom tɨw psaa _____. (along with you)	kñom tɨw psaa phaaŋ.

8. Adjectival Verbs

    There are three kinds of verbs which may occur as main verbs in Cambodian sentences. [NOTE: A verb may be defined as any word which can be preceded by the negative auxiliary mɨn.] The first two kinds of verbs are similar to English verbs, and should present no problem.

  1) Transitive verbs (or verbs which may be followed by a direct object)

kñom tɨñ barəy.	I buy cigarettes.
kñom ñam baay.	I eat rice.

  2) Intransitive verbs (or verbs which are never followed by an object)

kñom daə tɨw psaa.	I walk to [go to] the market.
qəñcəəñ qəŋkuy.	Please sit down.

  3) Adjectival verbs have no direct equivalent in English. They function as noun modifiers (English adjectives), as verb modifiers (English adverbs), and as main verbs (in which case they are equivalent to English be + adjective).

As adjective:	srəy lqaa	pretty girl
As adverb:	srəy nuh twəə-kaa lqaa.	That girl works well.
As main verb:	srəy nuh lqaa.	That girl is pretty.

They are marked as verbs (rather than simply adjectives) by the fact that they may be preceded by the negative mɨn:

srəy nuh mɨn lqaa tee.	That girl is not pretty.

As a sub-class of verbs, adjectival verbs may be defined as any verb which may be followed by the intensifying adverb nah 'very'.

> srəy nuh lqɑɑ nah. That girl is very pretty.

Following are some of the adjectival verbs which have been met so far:

lqɑɑ	to be pretty, good
thom	to be large
touc	to be small
tlay	to be expensive
sapbaay	to be happy
tum	to be ripe

8-A. Progressive Substitution Drill

Teacher	Student
krouc nih lqɑɑ nah.	krouc nih lqɑɑ nah.
touc	krouc nih touc nah.
tum	krouc nih tum nah.
tlay	krouc nih tlay nah.
thom	krouc nih thom nah.
pteəh nuh	pteəh nuh thom nah.
ceik nuh	ceik nuh thom nah.
siəwphɨw nuh	siəwphɨw nuh thom nah.
lqɑɑ	siəwphɨw nuh lqɑɑ nah.
mənuh nuh	mənuh nuh lqɑɑ nah.
səpbaay	mənuh nuh səpbaay nah.

8-B. Transformation Drill

Teacher	Student
krouc nih lqɑɑ nah.	krouc nih mɨn lqɑɑ tee.
ceik nuh thom nah.	ceik nuh mɨn thom tee.
krouc nih touc nah.	krouc nih mɨn touc tee.
siəwphɨw nuh lqɑɑ nah.	siewphɨw nuh mɨn lqɑɑ tee.
ceik nuh tum nah.	ceik nih mɨn tum tee.
krouc nih thom nah.	krouc nih mɨn thom tee.
siəwphɨw nih thom nah.	siəwphɨw nih mɨn thom tee.
pteəh nuh thom nah.	pteəh nuh mɨn thom tee.
mənuh nuh səpbaay nah.	mənuh nuh mɨn səpbaay tee.
krouc nih tlay nah.	krouc nih mɨn tlay tee.

9. The Compound Question Particle haəy-rɨɨ-nɨw?

The compound question particle haəy-rɨɨ-nɨw? may be shortened in rapid speech to haəy-rɨnɨw? or haəy-nɨw?. Literally it means 'already-or-not-yet?' and can best be translated 'yet?'.

> look tɨw psaa haəy-rɨnɨw?
> you go market already-or-not-yet?
> Have you gone to the market yet?

An affirmative answer involves the use of one of the completive particles haəy, ruəc, or ruəc-haəy 'already' after the verb:

> baat, kñom tɨw psaa ruəc-haəy.   Yes, I've already been to the market.

A negative answer involves the discontinuous negative mɨn-toən . . . tee 'not yet' before and after the verb:

> baat, kñom mɨn-toən tɨw psaa tee.   No, I've not yet been to the market.

9-A. Transformation Drill

Teacher	Student
look tɨw psaa.	look tɨw psaa haəy-rɨnɨw?
look tɨñ barəy.	look tɨñ barəy haəy-rɨnɨw?
look twəə-kaa.	look twəə-kaa haəy-rɨnɨw?
rəteh-pləəŋ cəñ.	rəteh-pləəŋ cəñ haəy-rɨnɨw?
ceik nih tum.	ceik nih tum haəy-rɨnɨw?
look tɨw məəl kon.	look tɨw məəl kon haəy-rɨnɨw?

9-B. Response Drill

Supply an affirmative answer to the following questions:

Teacher	Student
look tɨw psaa haəy-rɨnɨw?	baat, kñom tɨw haəy.
look tɨñ barəy haəy-rɨnɨw?	baat, kñom tɨñ haəy.
look tɨw məəl kon haəy-rɨnɨw?	baat, kñom tɨw haəy.
rəteh-pləəŋ cəñ haəy-rɨnɨw?	baat, rəteh-pləəŋ cəñ haəy.
look məəl siəwphɨw nih haəy-rɨnɨw?	baat, kñom məəl haəy.
ceik nih tum haəy-rɨnɨw?	baat, ceik nih tum haəy.
look twəə-kaa haəy-rɨnɨw?	baat, kñom twəə-kaa haəy.

9-C. Response Drill

Supply a negative answer to the following questions:

Teacher	Student
look tɨw psaa haəy-rɨnɨw?	baat, kñom mɨn-toən tɨw psaa tee.
look tɨñ barəy haəy-rɨnɨw?	baat, kñom mɨn-toən tɨñ barəy tee.
look tɨw məəl kon haəy-rɨnɨw?	baat, kñom mɨn-toən tɨw məəl kon tee.
rəteh-pləəŋ cəñ haəy-rɨnɨw?	baat, rəteh-pləəŋ mɨn-toən cəñ tee.
look məəl siəwphɨw nih haəy-rɨnɨw?	baat, kñom mɨn-toən məəl siəwphɨw nih tee.
ceik nih tum haəy-rɨnɨw?	baat, ceik nih mɨn-toən tum tee.
look twəə-kaa haəy-rɨnɨw?	baat, kñom mɨn-toən twəə-kaa tee.

10. mɔɔk as a Directional Verb

mɔɔk has already been met as a primary verb with the meaning 'to come', e.g.:

> kñom mɔɔk pii-msəl-məñ.   I came yesterday.

mɔɔk also frequently occurs after the main verb as one of a small class of directional verbs (of which more will be said later) with the meaning 'orientation of action toward the speaker', as in

kñom som barəy muəy <u>mɔɔk</u>.
I ask-for cigarette one <u>come</u>   Could I have a cigarette?

10-A. <u>Substitution Drill</u>

<u>Teacher</u>	<u>Student</u>
kñom som <u>barəy muəy</u> mɔɔk.	kñom som <u>barəy muəy</u> mɔɔk.
<u>siəwphɨw nuh</u>	kñom som <u>siəwphɨw nuh</u> mɔɔk.
<u>kmaw-day muəy</u>	kñom som <u>kmaw-day muəy</u> mɔɔk.
<u>dəy-sɑɑ mədaəm</u>	kñom som <u>dəy-sɑɑ mədaəm</u> mɔɔk.
<u>kafei məkaew</u>	kñom som <u>kafei məkaew</u> mɔɔk.
<u>chəə-kuh muəy</u>	kñom som <u>chəə-kuh muəy</u> mɔɔk.
<u>kawqəy nuh</u>	kñom som <u>kawqəy nuh</u> mɔɔk.
<u>barəy muəy</u>	kñom som <u>barəy muəy</u> mɔɔk.

11. The Auxiliary <u>kɑɑ</u>

kɑɑ (ka-) is a preverbal auxiliary whose function is to indicate that the clause in which it occurs is related to, or is a consequence of, some preceding clause or utterance. It can usually be translated 'so, then, accordingly', as in

tɨw, <u>ka-tɨw</u>.   [If you want to] go, <u>then</u> [let's] go.

In some environments, however, it has no equivalent in English, and is not translated, as in

kñom <u>kɑɑ</u> trəw tɨw twəə-kaa dae.   I have to go to work too.

Its sole function here is to refer back to the previous utterance (sentence 30 in the Dialogue):

dɑl maoŋ kñom trəlɑp tɨw twəə-kaa haəy.
It's time for me to go back to work.

11-A. <u>Transformation Drill</u>

<u>Teacher</u>	<u>Student</u>
kñom trəw tɨw psaa.	kñom <u>kɑɑ</u> trəw tɨw psaa <u>dae</u>.
kñom kliən baay.	kñom <u>kɑɑ</u> kliən baay <u>dae</u>.
kñom trəw tɨw twəə-kaa.	kñom <u>kɑɑ</u> trəw tɨw twəə-kaa <u>dae</u>.
kñom coul-cət kafei.	kñom <u>kɑɑ</u> coul-cət kafei <u>dae</u>.
kñom coul-cət tɨw daə-leeŋ.	kñom <u>kɑɑ</u> coul-cət tɨw daə-leeŋ <u>dae</u>.
kñom trəw tɨw pteˀəh.	kñom <u>kɑɑ</u> trəw tɨw pteˀəh <u>dae</u>.
krouc nih thom.	krouc nih <u>kɑɑ</u> thom <u>dae</u>.
pteˀəh nuh lqɑɑ.	pteˀəh nuh <u>kɑɑ</u> lqɑɑ <u>dae</u>.

12. <u>soum</u> vs. <u>som</u>

The word <u>soum</u> 'please' is sometimes shortened in rapid speech until it becomes homophonous with <u>som</u> 'to ask for'. <u>soum</u>, however, is always an auxiliary, as in

<u>soum</u> thaa mədaɑŋ tiət.   <u>Please</u> say [it] again.
<u>soum</u> look baək siəwphɨw.   <u>Please</u> open your books.
<u>soum</u> qəŋkuy.   <u>Please</u> sit down.

som, on the other hand, is a verb meaning 'to ask for, to request', as in

   kñom som barəy muəy mɔɔk.   Could I have a cigarette?

13. The Contrastive Particle wɨñ

   wɨñ is a contrastive particle which means 'back again, on the other hand, in the reverse direction'. It occurs in:

   coh, look wɨñ?   And how about you (on the other hand)?

Here its function is to turn attention back to the initiation of the exchange. In this lesson it occurs in:

   qəñcəŋ daə tɨw wɨñ ciə-muəy kniə.   Then [let's] walk back together.

13-A. Substitution Drill

Teacher	Student
kñom trəw trəlap tɨw pteəh wɨñ.	kñom trəw trəlap tɨw pteəh wɨñ.
twəə-kaa	kñom trəw trəlap tɨw twəə-kaa wɨñ.
psaa	kñom trəw trəlap tɨw psaa wɨñ.
salaa	kñom trəw trəlap tɨw salaa wɨñ.
ñam baay	kñom trəw trəlap tɨw ñam baay wɨñ.
tɨñ rəbɑh	kñom trəw trəlap tɨw tɨñ rəbɑh wɨñ.
pteəh kñom	kñom trəw trəlap tɨw pteəh kñom wɨñ.

14. Use of Personal Names as 2nd Person Pronouns

   There is no equivalent of English 'you' in Cambodian. look is used only in formal or polite speech. Between equals, the name of the person addressed is frequently used in place of a second person pronoun, as in

   sarɑɑn kliən baay tee?   Are you (Saran) hungry?

Frequently the use of a name in this capacity is softened further by the addition of the reflexive pronoun qaeŋ 'yourself, oneself' after the name, as in

   coh, meiŋ qaeŋ tɨñ qəy dae?   Say, what are you buying (Meng)?

14-A. Expansion Drill

Teacher	Student
sarɑɑn tɨw naa?	sarɑɑn qaeŋ tɨw naa?
meiŋ mɔɔk tɨñ qəy?	meiŋ qaeŋ mɔɔk tɨñ qəy?
seiŋ twəə-kaa qae-naa?	seiŋ qaeŋ twəə-kaa qae-naa?
saŋ kliən baay tee?	saŋ qaeŋ kliən baay tee?
sarɑɑn caŋ tɨñ qəy?	sarɑɑn qaeŋ caŋ tɨñ qəy?
meiŋ caŋ ñam kafei tee?	meiŋ qaeŋ caŋ ñam kafei tee?
seiŋ miən barəy tee?	seiŋ qaeŋ miən barəy tee?

15. The Interjection coh

   The interjection coh occurs with a contrastive function before questions which shift attention to a second person, as in the following exchanges:

   kñom sok-sapbaay ciə tee.   I'm quite well.
      coh, look?   And you?

    kñom mɔɔk tɨn qaŋkɑɑ.   I've come to buy some rice.
      coh, meiŋ qaeŋ mɔɔk tɨn qəy dae?   What are <u>you</u> buying, Meng?

15-A. <u>Transformation-Response Drill</u>

<u>Teacher</u>	<u>Student</u>
kñom sok-sapbaay ciə tee.	coh, look?
kñom mɔɔk tɨñ qaŋkɑɑ.	coh, look mɔɔk tɨñ qəy dae?
kñom tɨw psaa.	coh, look tɨw naa dae?
kñom twəə-kaa qae-nih.	coh, look twəə-kaa qae-naa dae?
kñom kliən baay.	coh, look kliən baay tee?
kñom kmiən barəy tee.	coh, look miən barəy tee?

[Tape 9]   C. COMPREHENSION

1. <u>Friends Meet on the Street</u>

cɑmraən: qei, meiŋ tɨw naa?

meiŋ: kñom tɨw psaa.
         cəmraən cɑŋ tɨw ciə-muəy kñom tee?

cɑmraən: maoŋ ponmaan haəy?

meiŋ: maoŋ prambəy kənlah haəy.

cɑmraən: kñom tɨw mɨn baan tee.
         kñom trəw tɨw twəə-kaa maoŋ prambuən.

2. <u>In a Food Store</u>

Salesman: look trəw-kaa qəy?

meiŋ: qəykɑɑ mə-kilou tlay ponmaan?

Salesman: qəŋkɑɑ mə-kilou dɑp-bəy riəl.
         look trəw-kaa ponmaan kilou?

meiŋ: kñom trəw-kaa tae bəy kilou tee.
         miən tae tee?

Salesman: baat, miən.

meiŋ: qaoy kñom mə-kəñcɑp mɔɔk.

Salesman: look trəw-kaa kafei tee?
         haaŋ kñom miən kafei lqɑɑ nah.

meiŋ: baat, kñom mɨn trəw-kaa kafei tee.
         teəŋ-qɑh tlay ponmaan?

Salesman: teəŋ-qɑh tlay saesəp-buən riəl.

3. <u>Having a Cup of Coffee</u>

phɑɑn: tŋay-nih tɨw twəə-kaa maoŋ ponmaan?

kuəŋ: maoŋ prambuən.
      maoŋ ponmaan haəy?

phɑɑn: maoŋ prambəy məphɨy niətii haəy.
            mɔɔk ñam kafei ciə-muəy knom sən.

kuəŋ: tɨw, kɑ-tɨw.

phɑɑn: kuəŋ qaeŋ trəw-kaa tɨk-dɑh-koo nɨŋ skɑɑ tee?

kuəŋ: yɔɔk tae skɑɑ tee.

phɑɑn: cɑŋ baan numpaŋ tee?

kuəŋ: tee, kñom mɨn-toˀən kliən tee.

phɑɑn: kñom kɑɑ mɨn kliən dae.

4. Asking for a Cigarette

kuəŋ: kñom som barəy muəy mɔɔk.

phɑɑn: soum qəñcəəñ.
            som-tooh, kñom kmiən chəə-kuh tee.

kuəŋ: qəñcəŋ mɔɔk tɨw tɨñ nɨw haaŋ nuh.

Salesman: look trəw-kaa qəy?

kuəŋ: kñom trəw-kaa barəy mə-kəñcap haəy-nɨŋ chəə-kuh pii prəqap.

Salesman: nih, look.

kuəŋ: teˀəŋ-qɑh tlay ponmaan?

Salesman: teˀəŋ-qɑh tlay prampɨl riəl.
            qɑɑ-kun craən.

D. CONVERSATION

1. Going to the Market

a) A greets B, and asks him where he is going.
b) B replies that he is going to the market.
c) A says that he has to go to the market too.
d) B suggests that they walk to the market together.
e) A replies that it's fine with him, then asks B what he has to buy.
f) B replies that he has to buy some fruit and some rice, and then asks A what he has to buy.
g) A replies that he wants to buy a book and three pencils.

2. At the Market

a) A remarks to B that this is a very big market.
b) B agrees, and says that there are a lot of people at this market.
c) A asks B for a cigarette.
d) B says he's sorry, but he doesn't have any cigarettes.
e) A says that in that case he'll go buy some in that shop.
f) B asks A if he has matches.
g) A replies that he has two boxes of matches.

3. Buying Fruit

a) A points out a place where they sell fruit.
b) The salesman asks B what he wants.
c) B asks him how much these big oranges are per dozen.
d) The salesman tells him that those big oranges aren't ripe yet, but says that these little oranges are ripe and good, and that they are 20 riels per dozen.
e) B says he wants only a half dozen.
f) A asks the salesman if these little bananas are ripe yet.
g) The salesman answers that they are ripe, and that they cost three riels per bunch.
h) A says he'll take two bunches.

4. In A Food Store

a) The salesman asks A what he would like.
b) A says he needs five kilos of rice and a kilo of sugar.
c) The salesman asks him what else he wants.
d) A replies that he wants a dozen eggs and two boxes of matches.
e) The salesman asks if he wants some coffee, and adds that his shop has very good coffee.
f) A answers that he doesn't need coffee, but that he'll take a package of tea, then asks how much it is all together.
g) The salesman replies that all together it's fifty-five riels.

5. Having A Cup of Coffee

a) A greets B, and asks him where he is going.
b) B replies that he is going to work.
c) A invites B to go have some coffee for a while first.
d) B says it's fine with him.
e) B asks A if he takes milk.
f) A replies that he does.
g) A tells the waiter to bring two glasses of coffee with milk.
h) B exclaims that it's time for him to go to work already.
i) A says he has to go to work too.
j) B says in that case they'll walk back together.

LESSON 5. GETTING ACQUAINTED

[Tape 10]   A. DIALOGUE

cɑmraən

skoŏl	to know, be acquainted with
puəq-maaq	friend(s)
neə̆q	specifier for ordinary persons

1. look skoŏl puəq-maaq kñom pii   Do you know these two friends of mine?
   neə̆q nih tee?

John

mɨn-dael (m-dael)	never (to have done something)

2. baat, tee; kñom mɨn-dael skoŏl tee.   No, I've never met (gotten acquainted
                                            with) them.

cɑmraən

srok	country, district
baaraŋ (baraŋ, praŋ)	French; France
srok-baraŋ	France

3. nɨh kɨɨ look Paul Dumet, mɔɔk   This is Mr. Paul Dumet, from France.
   pii srok-baraŋ.

cən	Chinese; China
srok-cən	China

4. nɨh kɨɨ look Lim Sieng, mɔɔk pii   This is Mr. Lim Sieng, from China.
   srok-cən.

Sieng

cmuə̆h	name; to have the name of

5. som-tooh, look cmuə̆h qəy?   Excuse me, what is your name?

John

6. baat, kñom cmuə̆h John Carter.   My name is John Carter.

Paul

qaamerikaŋ	American
qɑŋglee	English; Englishman

7. som-tooh, look ciə qaamerikaŋ   Excuse me, are you American or
   rɨɨ qɑŋglee?   English?

John

8. baat, kñom ciə qaamerikaŋ.   I'm an American.

cɑmraən

twəə (thəə)	to work as
tiəhiən (təhiən)	soldier
cumnuəñ	commerce
neə̆q-cəmnuəñ	merchant, businessman

9. look Paul twəə tiəhiən; look Sieng   Paul is a soldier; Sieng is a business-
   ciə neə̆q-cəmnuəñ.   man.

64

niqsət (nihsət)   university student
10. look John ciə nihsət.   John is a student.

Paul

riən   to study, to learn
kmae   to be Cambodian; a Cambodian
srok-kmae   Cambodia
rɨɨ   final question particle in either-
                                                 or questions
11. look mɔɔk riən nɨw srok-kmae rɨɨ?   Did you come to study in Cambodia?

John

teehsəcaa   tourist; tourism
12. baat, tee; kñom ciə teehsəcaa.   No, I'm a tourist.

khəəñ   to see
qaŋkɔɔ (qəŋkɔɔ, ŋkɔɔ)   Angkor
woət   wat, temple
qaŋkɔɔ-woət   Angkor Wat
yuu   to be long (in time)
mɔɔk   aspectual particle: toward
                                                 speaker in time
ciə yuu nah mɔɔk haəy   for a long time now
13. kñom caŋ khəəñ qaŋkɔɔ-woət   I've wanted to see Angkor Wat for a
    ciə yuu nah mɔɔk haəy.   long time now.

[To Paul]

dael   to have ever
14. look dael tɨw məəl qəŋkɔɔ-woət   Have you ever been to see Angkor Wat?
    tee?

Paul

baan   to have (done something), to have
                                                 had the opportunity to
daaŋ   time, occasion, occurrence
15. baat, kñom baan tɨw khəəñ qəŋkɔɔ-   Yes, I've been to see Angkor Wat twice.
    woət pii daaŋ haəy.

cnam   year
16. kñom baan nɨw srok-kmae muəy   I've lived in Cambodia for a year now.
    cnam mɔɔk haəy.

Sieng

17. look mɔɔk nɨw srok-kmae yuu   Have you been in (lived in) Cambodia
    haəy rɨɨ?   long?

John

prɑhael (prəhael, pəhael)   about, approximately; perhaps
prɑhael ciə   about, approximately; perhaps
khae   month
ponnoh   only, only to that extent
18. mɨn yuu tee; prəhael ciə bəy khae   Not long; only about three months.
    ponnoh.

Sieng

ceh	to know; to know how to
phiəsaa	language
phiəsaa-kmae	the Cambodian language; Cambodian

19. look ceh niyiəy phiəsaa-kmae
    lqɑɑ nah.

You speak Cambodian very well.

John

bɑntəc (bəntəc, ntəc)	some, a little
bɑntəc-bɑntuəc (bəntəc- bəntuəc, ntəc-ntuəc)	a little bit, somewhat
sahaqroə̆t (səhaqroə̆t)	union, confederation
qaamerɨc	America
sahaqroə̆t-qaamerɨc	the United States

20. kñom baan riən phiəsaa-kmae
    bəntəc-bəntuəc nɨw sahaqroə̆t-
    qaamerɨc.

I studied Cambodian a little in the
United States.

cɑmraən

pibaaq (pəbaaq)	to be difficult

21. phiəsaa-kmae pibaaq riən tee?

[Did you find] Cambodian difficult to
learn?

John

ponmaan (pənmaan, pəmaan)	much, to any extent
mɨn . . . ponmaan tee	not so very, not to any extent

22. mɨn pibaaq ponmaan tee.

[It's] not so difficult.

ñoə̆p	fast, quick
peek	too much, excessively

23. tae baə look niyiəy ñoə̆p peek,
    kñom sdap mɨn baan tee.

But if you speak too fast, I can't
understand.

[To Sieng]

puukae (pukae)	to be good (at), skillful (at)

24. look kɑɑ pukae niyiəy phiəsaa-
    kmae dae.

You're (reference-to-preceding-state-
ment) good at speaking Cambodian too.

kroŋ	city
pnum-pɨñ (num-pɨñ, m-pɨñ)	Phnom Penh

25. look nɨw kroŋ pnum-pɨñ baan
    ponmaan cnam haəy?

How long have you lived in Phnom
Penh?

Sieng

26. kñom nɨw pnum-pɨñ baan prəhael
    pram cnam haəy.

I've lived in Phnom Penh for about
five years.

cɑmraən

kraw	outside
kraw pii	outside of, besides
phiəsaa-qɑŋglee	the English language

27. kraw pii kmae nɨŋ cən,   Besides Cambodian and Chinese,
    ceh niyiəy phiəsaa-qaŋglee phaaŋ.   Sieng can speak English too.

Sieng

28. kñom niyiəy baan bəntəc-   I can speak it a little.
    bəntuəc.

29. phiəsaa-qaŋglee pibaaq nah.   English is very difficult.

John

    douc   as, like
30. phiəsaa-qaŋglee mɨn pibaaq   English isn't as hard as Chinese.
    douc phiəsaa-cən tee.

Paul

    sruəl   to be easy, comfortable
31. phiəsaa-cən sruəl niyiəy, tae   Chinese is easy to speak, but difficult
    pibaaq səsei nah.   to write.

32. camraən kaa niyiəy phiəsaa-baraŋ   Chamroeun speaks French quite well
    lqaa dae.   too.

B. GRAMMAR AND DRILLS

1. The Specifier neəq

The specifier neəq is used in all numerical noun phrases involving the counting of ordinary persons, such as students, friends, teachers, etc., e.g.:

kñom skoəl tiəhiən bəy neəq.   I know three soldiers.

1-A. Substitution Drill

kñom skoəl menuh bəy neəq.	kñom skoəl menuh bəy neəq.
nihsət	kñom skoəl nihsət bəy neəq.
tiəhiən	kñom skoəl tiəhiən bəy neəq.
puəq-maaq	kñom skoəl puəq-maaq bəy neəq.
kmae	kñom skoəl kmae bəy neəq.
neəq-cumnuən	kñom skoəl neəq-cumnuən bəy neəq.
cən	kñom skoəl cən bəy neəq.
teehsəcaa	kñom skoəl teehsəcaa bəy neəq.

2. Nouns and Noun Specifiers

Cambodian nouns can be divided into two subclasses on the basis of the ways in which they are counted.

1) **Mass nouns** are nouns which, when counted, always occur in numerical noun phrases with the word order noun + numeral + specifier (NXS). Specifiers are words which specify the size, shape, amount, or kind of unit being counted. Some specifiers encountered so far are:

lou in krouc muəy lou   one dozen oranges
kaew in kafei buən kaew   four glasses of coffee
kilou in qaŋkaa muəy kilou   a kilo of rice

These specifiers differ only in word order from the partitive words which occur
with mass nouns in English, e.g.:

a glass of water	a sheaf of wheat
a pound of butter	a bottle of beer
a lump of sugar	a pack of cigarettes

In short, there are as many specifiers as there are nouns denoting containers,
aggregates, or units in the language. Cambodian nouns differ from English nouns
primarily in that many nouns which are specific nouns in English are mass nouns
in Cambodian. This accounts for the difficulty of translating the specifiers which
accompany them, and which have no counterparts in English. Examples of such
nouns, with their specifiers, are:

kmaw-day pii daəm	(pencils + two + long cylindrical object) two pencils
mənuh pii neǎq	(humans + two + person) two persons

Just as you cannot say in English 'three dynamites', but must say 'three sticks/
boxes/pounds of dynamite' because 'dynamite' is a mass noun, likewise you cannot say *mənuh bəy 'persons three' in Cambodian, but must say mənuh bəy neǎq
'three persons', since mənuh is a mass noun.

Some nouns which occur as mass nouns followed by a specifier in careful
speech occur as specific nouns without a specifier in more colloquial speech, e.g.:

Careful	Colloquial	
kmaw-day pii daəm	kmaw-day pii	two pencils
puəq-maaq pii neǎq	puəq-maaq pii	two friends

Once the head noun of a numerical noun phrase has been introduced, the specifier phrase may occur in second reference without the noun head, e.g.:

kñom miən puəq-maaq pii neǎq.	I have two friends.
pii neǎq nuh twəə tiəhiən.	They (those two persons) are soldiers.

2) Specific nouns are nouns which may occur in numerical noun phrases with
the word order noun + numeral (NX), i.e. without a specifier. Specific nouns may
also occur as mass nouns. The great majority of Cambodian nouns belong to this
class. The following are examples of general nouns which have been encountered
so far:

As specific nouns		As mass nouns	
ceik pii	two bananas	ceik pii snət	two hands of bananas
barəy pii	two cigarettes	barəy pii kəñcap	two packs of cigarettes
chəə-kuh pii	two matches	chəə-kuh pii prəqap	two boxes of matches

3) Independent specifiers are specifiers which characteristically occur after
numerals (in first reference) without a preceding noun head. Such specifiers are
units of time, money, or distance. Independent specifiers encountered so far are:

riəl in tlay bəy riəl.	It costs three riels.
cnam in kñom baan niw srok-kmae muəy cnam mɔɔk haəy.	I've been in Cambodia for a year.
khae in prəhael-ciə bəy khae ponnoh.	Only about three months.

2-A. Translation Drill

From the chart below, construct the numerical noun phrases or specifier phrases called for by the teacher. Numberical noun phrases involving mass nouns, or specific nouns used as mass nouns, will have the structure NXS. Noun phrases involving specific nouns will have the structure NX. Specifier phrases involving an independent specifier will have the structure XS.

Nouns (N)	Numerals (X)	Specifiers (S)
Specific nouns	muəy (mə-)	Dependent specifiers
siəwphɨw	pii	lou
tok	bəy	snət
kawqəy	buən	kilou
barəy	pram	kəñcap
chəə-kuh	prammuəy	prəqap
ceik	dap	neəq
krouc	məphɨy	kaew
kmaw-day	craən*	daəm
	kanlah*	
Mass nouns		Independent specifiers
qaŋkɑɑ		cnam
skɑɑ		khae
tɨk		tŋay
kafei		maoŋ
mənuh		niətii
puəq-maaq		riəl
tiəhiən		

* In numerical noun phrases, the words craən 'many' and kanlah 'half' function like numerals.

1) Numerical noun phrases involving mass nouns (NXS)

Teacher	Student
two kilos of sugar	skɑɑ pii kilou
a dozen oranges	krouc məlou
three glasses of water	tɨk bəy kaew
two boxes of matches	chəə-kuh pii prəqap
two hands of bananas	ceik pii snət
a pack of cigarettes	barəy mə-kəñcap
many kilos of oranges	krouc craən kilou
three kilos of rice	qaŋkɑɑ bəy kilou
four glasses of coffee	kafei buən kaew
three persons	mənuh bəy neəq
two friends	puəq-maaq pii neəq
a dozen books	siəwphɨw muəy lou
two cigarettes	barəy pii daəm
twenty soldiers	tiəhiən məphɨy neəq

Teacher	Student
a half-dozen oranges	krouc kənlah lou
many persons	mənuh craən nĕəq
five pencils	kmaw-day pram daəm
many packs of cigarettes	barəy craən kəñcap
a half-pack of cigarettes	barəy kənlah kəñcap
two matches	chəə-kuh pii daəm

2) Numerical noun phrases involving specific nouns (NX)

Teacher	Student
two tables	tok pii
four chairs	kawqəy buən
a cigarette	barəy muəy
three oranges	krouc bəy
two bananas	ceik pii
five pencils	kmaw-day pram
three books	siəwphɨw bəy
two matches	chəə-kuh pii
three friends	puəq-maaq bəy
two cigarettes	barəy pii

3) Numerical phrases involving independent specifiers (XS)

Teacher	Student
three years	bəy cnam
twenty minutes	məphɨy niətii
two hours	pii maoŋ
six months	prammuəy khae
three days	bəy tŋay
ten riels	dɑp riəl
five minutes	pram niətii
many days	craən tŋay

3. Position of ordinal numerals

Ordinal numerals, being adjectives, follow rather than precede independent specifiers, e.g.:

bəy tŋay 'three days', but tŋay tii-bəy 'the third day'
pram cnam 'five years', but cnam tii-pram 'the fifth year'
dɑp khae 'ten months', but khae tii-dɑp 'the tenth month'

With the independent specifier maoŋ 'hour', however, ordinalization is indicated solely by shifting the position of the numeral, and the ordinalizing particle tii- is not used; e.g.:

bəy maoŋ 'three hours', but maoŋ bəy 'three o'clock'
dɑp maoŋ 'ten hours', but maoŋ dɑp 'ten o'clock'

3-A. Transformation Drill

Teacher	Student
kñom trəw twəə-kaa bəy maoŋ.	kñom trəw twəə-kaa maoŋ bəy.
kñom trəw twəə-kaa pram tŋay.	kñom trəw twəc-kaa tŋay tii-pram.
kñom trəw twəə-kaa pii khae.	kñom trəw twəə-kaa khae tii-pii.
kñom trəw twəə-kaa bəy cnam.	kñom trəw twəə-kaa cnam tii-bəy.
kñom trəw twəə-kaa prambəy maoŋ.	kñom trəw twəə-kaa maoŋ prambəy.
kñom trəw twəə-kaa dɑp tŋay.	kñom trəw twəə-kaa tŋay tii-dɑp.

4. ponmaan as a Numeral

The word ponmaan 'how much, how many' functions like a numeral in numerical noun phrases; i.e. it occupies the same syntactic position as a numeral. In answers to questions involving ponmaan, it is replaced by a numeral; e.g.:

look tɨñ skɑɑ ponmaan kilou?	How many kilos of sugar did you buy?
kñom tɨn skɑɑ bəy kilou.	I bought three kilos of sugar.
look ñam ceik ponmaan?	How many bananas did you eat?
kñom ñam ceik bəy.	I ate three bananas.
look mɔɔk pnum-pɨñ baan ponmaan khae haəy?	How many months have you been in Phnom Penh?
kñom mɔɔk pnum-pɨñ baan bəy khae haəy.	I've been in Phnom Penh for three months.

4-A. Response Drill (NXS)

Teacher	Student
look miən krouc ponmaan lou?	kñom miən krouc pram lou.
look miən qəŋkɑɑ ponmaan kilou?	kñom miən qəŋkɑɑ pram kilou.
look miən kmaw-day ponmaan daəm?	kñom miən kmaw-day pram daəm.
look miən kafei ponmaan kaew?	kñom miən kafei pram kaew.
look miən barəy ponmaan kəñcɑp?	kñom miən barəy pram kəñcɑp.
look miən barəy ponmaan daəm?	kñom miən barəy pram daəm.
look miən chəə-kuh ponmaan prəqap?	kñom miən chəə-kuh pram prəqap.
look miən ceik ponmaan snət?	kñom miən ceik pram snət.
look miən puəq-maaq ponmaan neəq?	kñom miən puəq-maaq pram neəq.

4-B. Response Drill (NX)

Teacher	Student
look miən tok ponmaan?	kñom miən tok bəy.
look miən kmaw-day ponmaan?	kñom miən kmaw-day bəy.
look miən puəq-maaq ponmaan?	kñom miən puəq-maaq bəy.
look miən barəy ponmaan?	kñom miən barəy bəy.
look miən siəwphɨw ponmaan?	kñom miən siəwphɨw bəy.
look miən kawqəy ponmaan?	kñom miən kawqəy bəy.
look miən ceik ponmaan?	kñom miən ceik bəy.

4-C. Response Drill (XS)

Teacher	Student
look twəə-kaa nih baan ponmaan cnam haəy?	kñom twəə-kaa nih baan bəy cnam haəy.
look twəə-kaa nih baan ponmaan khae haəy?	kñom twəə-kaa nih baan bəy khae haəy.
look twəə-kaa nih baan ponmaan tŋay haəy?	kñom twəə-kaa nih baan bəy tŋay haəy.
look twəə-kaa nih baan ponmaan maoŋ haəy?	kñom twəə-kaa nih baan bəy maoŋ haəy.
look twəə-kaa nih baan ponmaan niətii haəy?	kñom twəə-kaa nih baan bəy niətii haəy.

4-D. Response Drill (XS)

Teacher	Student
look miən ponmaan riəl? (bəy)	kñom miən bəy riəl.
look miən ponmaan riəl? (pram)	kñom miən pram riəl.
look miən ponmaan riəl? (məphɨy)	kñom miən məphɨy riəl.
look miən ponmaan riəl? (saamsəp-bəy)	kñom miən saamsəp-bəy riəl.
look miən ponmaan riəl? (haasəp-pii)	kñom miən haasəp-pii riəl.
look miən ponmaan riəl? (mərɔɔy)	kñom miən mərɔɔy riəl.
look miən ponmaan riəl? (mərɔɔy-haasəp)	kñom miən mərɔɔy-haasəp riəl.

5. Possessive Modifiers

Possessive modifiers, like other modifiers in Cambodian, follow the word they modify; e.g.:

puəq-maaq kñom (friend my) my friend
pteəh look   (house your) your house (speaking to look)

Frequently a phrase contains two possessive modifiers in succession:

pteəh puəq-maaq kñom (house friend my) my friend's house

5-A. Substitution Drill

Teacher	Student
pteəh nih ciə pteəh kñom.	pteəh nih ciə pteəh kñom.
look.	pteəh nih ciə pteəh look.
mənuh nuh.	pteəh nih ciə pteəh mənuh nuh.
puəq-maaq kñom.	pteəh nih ciə pteəh puəq-maaq kñom.
look Paul.	pteəh nih ciə pteəh look Paul.
look-srəy.	pteəh nih ciə pteəh look-srəy.

6. Optional Subject

As pointed out in Lesson 2, B, 1, when the subject of a Cambodian sentence is clear from the context, it may be omitted. In other words, in many sentences the use of a subject is optional where it would be compulsory in English.

6-A. Transformation Drill

Teacher	Student
look tɨw naa?	tɨw naa?
kñom kroͤən-tae daə-leeŋ tee.	kroͤən-tae daə-leeŋ tee.
look mɔɔk tɨñ qwəy?	mɔɔk tɨñ qwəy?
kñom mɔɔk tɨn barəy.	mɔɔk tɨn barəy.
kñom sok-səpbaay ciə tee.	sok-səpbaay ciə tee.
kñom tɨw psaa.	tɨw psaa.
psaa nɨw qae-naa?	nɨw qae-naa?
psaa nɨw khaŋ-muk.	nɨw khaŋ-muk.
kon nih leeŋ qəŋkal?	leeŋ qəŋkal?
kñom trəw tɨw sqaek.	trəw tɨw sqaek.
krouc nih thom nah.	thom nah.

7. The Position of Possessive Adjectives in Noun Phrases

The order of elements in noun phrases was pointed out in Lesson 4, B, 3. When a possessive adjective, such as <u>kñom</u> 'my' occurs in a noun phrase, it follows the nouns and precedes the numeral; e.g.:

<u>N</u> <u>A</u> <u>X</u> <u>S</u> <u>D</u>
puəq-maaq kñom pii neͤəq nih   'these two friends of mine'
friend my two person this

[If, however, the A position is preempted by a descriptive attribute such as <u>touc</u> 'small', the possessive attribute may occur as a phrasal attribute <u>rəbɑh kñom</u> 'of mine' immediately preceding the X position; e.g.:

<u>N</u> <u>A1</u> <u>A2</u> <u>X</u> <u>S</u> <u>D</u>
puəq-maaq touc rəbɑh kñom pii neͤəq nih   'these two small friends of mine']
friend small of mine two person this

7-A. Expansion Drill

	Teacher	Student
1)	puəq-maaq	puəq-maaq
	nih	puəq-maaq nih.
	pii neͤəq	puəq-maaq pii neͤəq nih
	kñom	puəq-maaq kñom pii neͤəq nih
2)	pteͤəh	pteͤəh
	nih	pteͤəh nih
	bəy	pteͤəh bəy nih
	kñom	pteͤəh kñom bəy nih
3)	ceik	ceik
	nuh	ceik nuh
	pii snət	ceik pii snət nuh
	look	ceik look pii snət nuh
4)	barəy	barəy
	nuh	barəy nuh
	pii	barəy pii nuh
	look	barəy look pii nuh

7-B. Expansion Drill

Teacher	Student
pteə̆h pii nih (kñom)	pteə̆h kñom pii nih
puəq-maaq bəy neə̆q nih (kñom)	puəq-maaq kñom bəy neə̆q nih
pɔɔŋ-moə̆n bəy lou nuh (look)	pɔɔŋ-moə̆n look bəy lou nuh
pteə̆h pram nuh (look)	pteə̆h look pram nuh
ceik pii snət nuh (look)	ceik look pii snət nuh
kawqəy buən nuh (look)	kawqəy look buən nuh
siəwphɨw bəy nih (kñom)	siəwphɨw kñom bəy nih
kmaw-day muəy daəm nuh (look)	kmaw-day look muəy daəm nuh
krouc nih (kñom)	krouc kñom nih
skɑɑ pram kilou nuh (look)	skɑɑ look pram kilou nuh

8. The Adverbial Phrase ciə yuu nah mɔɔk haəy

The adverbial phrase ciə yuu nah mɔɔk haəy means 'for a long time now (up to the present)', as in

kñom cɑŋ khəə̆ñ qəŋkɔɔ-woə̆t ciə yuu nah mɔɔk haəy.	I've wanted to see Angkor Wat for a long time now.

8-A. Substitution Drill

Teacher	Student
kñom cɑŋ khəə̆ñ qəŋkɔɔ-woə̆t ciə yuu nah mɔɔk haəy.	kñom cɑŋ khəə̆ñ qəŋkɔɔ-woə̆t ciə yuu nah mɔɔk haəy.
riən phiəsaa-kmae	kñom riən phiəsaa-kmae ciə yuu nah mɔɔk haəy.
baan nɨw srok-kmae	kñom baan nɨw srok-kmae ciə yuu nah mɔɔk haəy.
twəə-kaa qae-nih	kñom twəə-kaa qae-nih ciə yuu nah mɔɔk haəy.
cɑŋ tɨw srok-kmae	kñom cɑŋ tɨw srok-kmae ciə yuu nah mɔɔk haəy.
cɑŋ məəl kon nuh	kñom cɑŋ məəl kon nuh ciə yuu nah mɔɔk haəy.
cɑŋ tɨw psaa	kñom cɑŋ tɨw psaa ciə yuu nah mɔɔk haəy.

9. The Functions of baan

The word baan has occurred in three different syntactic positions and with three different functions:

1) As a primary verb meaning 'to have, to get':

look cɑŋ baan chəə-kuh tee?	Do you want (to have) some matches?

2) As a modal verb meaning 'to have been able to, to have had a chance to':

kñom baan tɨw pii dɑɑŋ.	I've gone (been able to go) twice.

In this function, baan can conveniently be translated by the English present perfect phrase 'to have (done something)', but in fact its meaning is more precisely 'to have had the chance (to do something)'.

In sentences involving past time and a numerical phrase, as in the example above, baan may occur after the primary verb and before the numerical phrase, with little or no change in meaning; e.g.:

kñom tɨw baan pii daaŋ.	I've gone twice.
kñom nɨw pnum-pɨñ baan prəhael pram cnam haəy.	I've lived in Phnom Penh for about five years.

3) As a completive verb meaning 'to be able to', in which case it always follows the primary verb which it complements:

kñom sdap baan.	I can understand.
kñom sdap mɨn baan tee.	I can't understand.

Since in each of its occurrences baan belongs to a well-defined syntactic class, we say that baan belongs to three different 'parts of speech' or 'word classes'. Nevertheless its three functions are semantically related, all having to do with 'getting' or 'achieving'.

9-A. Substitution Drill (baan as a primary verb)

Teacher	Student
kñom caŋ baan kafei pii kaew.	kñom caŋ baan kafei pii kaew.
barəy muəy.	kñom caŋ baan barəy muəy.
krouc məlou.	kñom caŋ baan krouc məlou.
tɨk-tae məkaew.	kñom caŋ baan tɨk-tae məkaew.
ceik pii snet.	kñom caŋ baan ceik pii snət.
qəŋkaa bəy kilou.	kñom caŋ baan qəŋkaa bəy kilou.
barəy mə-kəñcap.	kñom caŋ baan barəy mə-kəñcap.

9-B. Transformation Drill (Modal verb, or past time)

Teacher	Student
kñom baan tɨw pii daaŋ.	kñom tɨw baan pii daaŋ.
kñom baan nɨw srok-kmae muəy cnam.	kñom nɨw srok-kmae baan muəy cnam.
kñom baan tɨw məəl qəŋkɔɔ-woăt pii daaŋ.	kñom tɨw məəl qəŋkɔɔ-woăt baan pii daaŋ.
look baan mɔɔk qae-nih ponmaan daaŋ haəy?	look mɔɔk qae-nih baan ponmaan daaŋ haəy?
look baan nɨw pnum-pɨñ ponmaan cnam?	look nɨw pnum-pɨñ baan ponmaan cnam?
look baan mɔɔk nɨw srok-kmae ponmaan khae haəy?	look mɔɔk nɨw srok-kmae baan ponmaan khae haəy?
kñom baan tɨw psaa bəy daaŋ.	kñom tɨw psaa baan bəy daaŋ.

9-C. Substitution Drill (Completive Verb)

Teacher	Student
kñom sdap baan.	kñom sdap baan.
tɨw	kñom tɨw baan.

Teacher	Student
niyiəy phiəsaa-kmae	kñom niyiəy phiəsaa-kmae baan.
mɔɔk sqaek	kñom mɔɔk sqaek baan.
səsei kmae	kñom səsei kmae baan.
tɨw məəl kon	kñom tɨw məəl kon baan.
tɨw tŋay-nih	kñom tɨw tŋay-nih baan.

9-D   Transformation Drill

Teacher	Student
kñom sdap baan.	kñom sdap mɨn baan tee.
kñom tɨw baan.	kñom tɨw mɨn baan tee.
kñom niyiəy phiəsaa-kmae baan.	kñom niyiəy phiəsaa-kmae mɨn baan tee.
kñom məəl siəwphɨw baan.	kñom məəl siəwphɨw mɨn baan tee.
kñom səsei kmae baan.	kñom səsei kmae mɨn baan tee.
kñom tɨw məəl kon baan.	kñom tɨw məəl kon mɨn baan tee.
kñom tɨw tŋay-nih baan.	kñom tɨw tŋay-nih mɨn baan tee.

10. Modal Verbs

Modal verbs precede, and in some way limit or modify, a following main verb or another modal verb, as in the utterance:

kñom trəw tɨw pteəh.   I must go home.

Some modal verbs occur also as full verbs, e.g.:

trəw haəy.   That's right.

and some occur only as modal verbs, e.g.:

kñom caŋ tɨw psaa.   I want to go to the market.

The following modal verbs have been encountered so far:

caŋ	to wish to	dael	to have ever
trəw	to have to, must	ceh	to know how to
coul-cət	to like to	pukae	to be good at
baan	to have been able to	cap	to begin (to)

10-A. Substitution Drill

Teacher	Student
kñom caŋ riən phiəsaa-kmae.	kñom caŋ riən phiəsaa-kmae.
trəw	kñom trəw riən phiəsaa-kmae.
coul-cət	kñom coul-cət riən phiəsaa-kmae.
dael	kñom dael riən phiəsaa-kmae.
pukae	kñom pukae riən phiəsaa-kmae.
caŋ	kñom caŋ riən phiəsaa-kmae.
kñom caŋ niyiəy phiəsaa-kmae.	kñom caŋ niyiəy phiəsaa-kmae.
ceh	kñom ceh niyiəy phiəsaa-kmae.

11. dael vs. baan

The modal verb dael precedes main verbs with the meaning 'to have ever',
as in: look dael tɨw məəl qəŋkɔɔ-woət tee?
          Have you ever gone to see Angkor Wat?

When preceded by the negative auxiliary mɨn, it means 'never', as in

kñom min-dael trəw tee.   I never win (I've never hit [it]).
kñom min-dael tɨw məəl qəŋkɔɔ-   I've never gone to see Angkor Wat.
  woət tee.

The modal verb baan, on the other hand, means 'to have been able to, to have had the opportunity to, etc.', and thus is not directly equivalent to the English perfect auxiliary 'have'; e.g.:

kñom baan tɨw khəəñ qəŋkɔɔ-woət   I've been (had the opportunity of going)
  pii dααŋ.   to see Angkor Wat twice.
kñom baan nɨw srok-kmae muəy   I've lived (had the opportunity to live)
  cnam haəy.   in Cambodia for a year.

11-A. Transformation Drill

Teacher   Student

kñom dael tɨw.   kñom min-dael tɨw tee.
kñom dael məəl kon nuh.   kñom min-dael məəl kon nuh tee.
kñom dael tɨw məəl qəŋkɔɔ-woət.   kñom min-dael tɨw məəl qəŋkɔɔ-woət tee.
kñom daəl riən phiəsaa-kmae.   kñom min-dael riən phiəsaa-kmae tee.
kñom dael tɨw kroŋ pnum-pɨñ.   kñom min-dael tɨw kroŋ pnum-pɨñ tee.
kñom dael ñam baay qae-nuh.   kñom min-dael ñam baay qae-nuh tee.
kñom dael twəə tiəhiən.   kñom min-dael twəə tiəhiən tee.

12. The Question Particle rɨɨ

The question particle rɨɨ is used instead of tee in any question involving one of a number of alternatives, while tee is used in questions where a yes or no answer is anticipated. The contrast can be illustrated by the following pair of examples:

look qəñcəəñ tɨw psaa tee?
  Are you going to the market? (Is there a possibility that you will go to the market? [No prior assumption on the part of the speaker.])

look qəñcəəñ tɨw psaa rɨɨ?
  Are you going to the market? (Is it the market you're going to [or somewhere else]?)

An affirmative response to a question ending in rɨɨ may involve only the appropriate response particle, or it may involve a response particle plus a confirmation of the alternative mentioned in the question.

Examples

look qəñcəəñ tɨw psaa rɨɨ?   baat, (tɨw psaa).
  Are you going to the market?   Yes, ([I'm] going to the market).
look mɔɔk pii-msəl-məñ rɨɨ?   baat, (pii-msəl-məñ).
  Did you come yesterday?   Yes, (yesterday).
nih tlay hoksəp riəl rɨɨ?   baat, (hoksəp).
  Does this cost sixty riels?   Yes, (sixty).
look ciə baraŋ rɨɨ?   baat, (baraŋ).
  Are you French?   Yes, (French).

A negative response to an either-or question may consist of the negative tee, or, more politely, baat tee, but it will usually be followed by the correct alternatives.

Examples:

look qəñcəəñ tɨw psaa rɨɨ?	baat tee, (knom tɨw salaa).
Are you going to the market?	No, (I'm going to school).
look mɔɔk pii-msəl-məñ rɨɨ?	baat tee, (kñom mɔɔk tŋay-nih).
Did you come yesterday?	No, (I came today).
nih tlay hoksəp riəl rɨɨ?	baat tee, (tlay cətsəp).
Does this cost sixty riels?	No, ([it] costs seventy).
look ciə baraŋ rɨɨ?	baat tee, (qaamerikaŋ).
Are you French?	No, (American).

12-A. Response Drill

Supply an affirmative answer to each of the following either-or questions, confirming the alternative mentioned in the question.

Model: Teacher	Student
look qəñcəəñ tɨw psaa rɨɨ?	baat, tɨw psaa.
Are you going to the market?	Yes, [I'm] going to the market.

Teacher	Student
look qəñcəəñ tɨw pteəh rɨɨ?	baat, tɨw pteəh.
look mɔɔk pii-msəl-məñ rɨɨ?	baat, pii-msəl-məñ.
nih tlay hoksəp riəl rɨɨ?	baat, hoksəp.
look ciə baraŋ rɨɨ?	baat, baraŋ.
pteəh look nɨw khaŋ-sdam-day rɨɨ?	baat, nɨw khaŋ-sdam-day.
look tɨñ qəŋkɑɑ rɨɨ?	baat, tɨñ qəŋkɑɑ.
salaa-riən nɨw khaŋ-muk rɨɨ?	baat, nɨw khaŋ-muk.
look trəw-kaa muəy kilou rɨɨ?	baat, muəy kilou.

12-B. Response Drill

Supply a negative answer plus the correct alternative to each of the following either-or questions.

Teacher	Student
look qəñcəəñ tɨw pteəh rɨɨ? (psaa)	tee, kñom tɨw psaa.
look mɔɔk pii-msəl-məñ rɨɨ? (tŋay-nih)	tee, kñom mɔɔk tŋay-nih.
nih tlay hoksəp riəl rɨɨ? (cətsəp)	tee, tlay cətsəp.
look ciə baraŋ rɨɨ? (qaamerikaŋ)	tee, kñom ciə qaamerikaŋ.
pteəh look nɨw khaŋ-sdam-day rɨɨ?	tee, nɨw khaŋ-cweiŋ-day.
(khaŋ-cweiŋ-day)	
look tɨñ qəŋkɑɑ rɨɨ? (tae)	tee, kñom tɨñ tae.
salaa-riən nɨw khaŋ-muk rɨɨ? (khaŋ-kraoy)	tee, nɨw khaŋ-kraoy.
look trəw-kaa muəy kilou rɨɨ? (pii kilou)	tee, pii kilou.

12-C. Transformation Drill

Convert the following statements to questions, choosing the proper question particle — either rɨɨ or tee. Without a context, however, some of the following examples may lend themselves to either interpretation.

Model: Teacher   Student

    kñom kliən baay.   look kliən baay tee?
      I'm hungry.   Are you hungry?
    kñom mɔɔk pii-msəl-məñ.   look mɔɔk pii-msəl-məñ rɨɨ?
      I came yesterday.   Did you come yesterday?

     Teacher   Student

    kñom sdap baan.   look sdap baan tee?
    look nuh ciə baraŋ.   look nuh ciə baraŋ rɨɨ?
    pteʾəh nuh lqɑɑ.   pteʾəh nuh lqɑɑ tee?
    kñom miən barəy.   look miən barəy tee?
    səlaa-riən nɨw khaŋ-muk.   səlaa-riən nɨw khaŋ-muk rɨɨ?
    kñom yɔɔk muəy kilou.   look yɔɔk muəy kilou rɨɨ?
    look nuh twəə tiəhiən.   look nuh twəə tiəhiən rɨɨ?
    kñom caŋ baan kafei.   look caŋ baan kafei tee?
    kñom coul-cət daə-leeŋ.   look coul-cət daə-leeŋ tee?
    nih tlay dɑp riəl.   nih tlay dɑp riəl rɨɨ?
    kñom ciə nihsət.   look ciə nihsət rɨɨ?
    kñom ceh phiəsaa-cən.   look ceh phiəsaa-cən tee?
    kñom ciə teehsəcɑɑ.   look ciə teehsəcɑɑ rɨɨ?
    siəwphɨw nih ciə siəwphɨw kñom.   siəwphɨw nih ciə siəwphɨw look rɨɨ?
    kñom skoʾəl look chɨən.   look skoʾəl look chɨən tee?
    kñom yɔɔk tɨk-tae.   look yɔɔk tɨk-tae tee?
    kñom tɨw sqaek.   look tɨw sqaek rɨɨ?

[Tape 11]   C. COMPREHENSION

1. Introducing a Friend

    seiŋ: nih puəq-maaq kñom, cmuʾəh chɨən.
            nih cmuʾəh Paul.

    Paul: cumriəp-suə look chɨən.

    chɨən: cumriəp-suə look Paul.
            look ciə qaamerikaŋ rɨɨ?

    Paul: baat, mɨn mɛɛn tee; kñom baraŋ.

    chɨən: look twəə-kaa qəy nɨw srok-kmae?

    Paul: kñom ciə neʾəq-cəmnuəñ.
            coh look?

    chɨən: kñom twəə tiəhiən.

2. More Introductions

    seiŋ: look chɨən, nih kɨɨ puəq-maaq kñom, cmuʾəh naat.

    chɨən: cumriəp-suə look naat.

    naat: cumriəp-suə look chɨən.

    chɨən: look qəñcəəñ tɨw naa?

seiŋ: tɨw ñam baay.
           look caŋ tɨw tee?

chɨən: baat, qɑɑ-kun.
           kñom kliən baay dae.
           look trəw-kaa barəy tee?

naat: baat, som muəy mɔɔk.

chɨən: look miən chəə-kuh tee?

naat: qɑɑ-kun, kñom miən haəy.

3. Studying English

seiŋ: chɨən qaeŋ thəə qəy?

chɨən: baat, kñom riən phiəsaa-qaŋglee.

seiŋ: riən phiəsaa-qaŋglee thəə qəy?

chɨən: kñom nɨŋ tɨw riən nɨw sahaqrɔət-qaamerɨc.

seiŋ: qəñcəŋ? tɨw qəŋkal?

chɨən: kñom nɨŋ tɨw cnam kraoy.

seiŋ: tɨw riən qəy?

chɨən: kñom nɨŋ riən twəə cumnuəñ.

4. A Friend from France

samɨt: look skoəl look Paul Dumet tee?

heiŋ: cumriəp-suə look Paul.
           look mɔɔk pii naa?

Paul: kñom mɔɔk pii srok-baraŋ.

heiŋ: look twəə-kaa qəy nɨw srok-kmae?

Paul: kñom ciə neəq-cumnuəñ.

samɨt: look mɔɔk nɨw srok-kmae baan ponmaan cnam haəy?

Paul: kñom mɔɔk mə-cnam haəy.
           look dael tɨw srok-baraŋ tee?

samɨt: baat, kñom tɨw mədɑɑŋ.

D. CONVERSATION

1. Three Friends Meet

   a) Nath (naat) greets Sieng, then asks him if he knows (Mr.) Paul.
   b) Sieng replies that he knows him, then greets Paul.
   c) Paul asks Sieng where he is going.
   d) Sieng replies that he is just walking.
   e) Paul asks him if he would like to have some coffee in that shop.
   f) Sieng replies that it's fine with him.

g) Nath tells the waiter to bring three glasses of coffee.

h) Sieng asks Paul how many days he's been in Phnom Penh.

i) Paul replies that he's been in Phnom Penh for three days.

2. Discussing Angkor Wat

a) Sieng asks Paul what country he comes from.

b) Paul replies that he comes from France.

c) Sieng asks Paul if he has come to study in Cambodia.

d) Paul replies negatively, and says that he is a tourist.

e) Nath asks Paul if he has been to see Angkor Wat yet.

f) Paul answers that he has not yet gone to see Angkor Wat.

g) Sieng says that he has lived in Cambodia for five years, but that he has never had the chance to go to see Angkor Wat.

h) Nath says that he has been to see Angkor Wat twice.

3. Discussing Vocations

a) John asks Sieng where he comes from.

b) Sieng replies that he comes from China.

c) Nath asks Sieng how long he has been in Cambodia.

d) Sieng replies that he has been in Cambodia for three years.

e) John asks Sieng what he does in Cambodia.

f) Sieng replies that he is a merchant.

g) Nath asks John if he's French or American.

h) John replies that he is an American.

i) Nath asks John if he's a tourist.

j) John replies that he's a student, then asks Nath what work he does.

k) Nath replies that he is a soldier, then asks John if he's been in Cambodia long.

l) John replies that it hasn't been long; only about two months.

4. Discussing Languages

a) Sieng tells John he speaks Cambodian very well.

b) John replies that he speaks it a little, but that if you speak too fast, he can't understand.

c) Nath asks John if he knows how to speak French.

d) John replies that he studied French a little in America.

e) Nath says that, besides Cambodian and Chinese, Sieng speaks English too.

f) Sieng says that English is very difficult.

g) John says English isn't as difficult as Chinese.

h) Nath says Chinese is difficult to write, but easy to speak.

LESSON 6. RELATIVES

[Tape 12]   A. DIALOGUE

                    phaan

1. cumriəp-suə look Robert.   Hello, Mr. Robert.

   khaan   to miss, to lack
   cuəp   to meet
2. khaan baan cuəp kniə yuu haəy.   We haven't seen (met) each other in
                                         a long time.

                    Robert

   qou   interjection
   rɔwŭəl (rəwŭəl, ləwŭəl)   to be busy
3. qou, kñom rəwŭəl nah.   Oh, I've been very busy.

                    naat

   qaŋkuy (qəŋkuy, ŋkuy)   to sit down
4. qəñcəəñ qəŋkuy, look.   Please, sit down.

   yəəŋ   we (familiar)
   kampuŋ-tae (kəmpuŋ-,   in the process of
     kəpuŋ-)
   niyiəy kniə leeŋ   to chat, to visit together
5. yəəŋ kəmpuŋ-tae niyiəy kniə leeŋ.   We're just chatting.

                    Robert

   qampii (qəmpii, mpii)   about, of
6. niyiəy qəmpii qwəy?   What are you talking about?

                    phaan

   kruəsaa   family
7. niyiəy qəmpii kruəsaa.   [We're] talking about [our] families.

                    Robert

   teə̆ŋ-pii (təŋ-pii)   both
   prəpŭən (prəpŭən, pəpŭən)   wife
8. look teə̆ŋ-pii neə̆q miən prəpŭən   Are both of you married?
   haəy-rɨnɨw?

                    naat

   phaan   Phân; a personal name
   kaa   to get married
   kaa prəpŭən   to marry a wife
   ruəc-haəy   already
9. phaan kaa prəpŭən ruəc-haəy.   Phân is married already.

   camnaek (cəmnaek)   part, share; as for, on the part of
10. cəmnaek kñom wɨñ, mɨn-toə̆n   But I'm not married yet.
    miən prəpŭən tee.

                         82

Robert

qaayuq (qayuq)   age; to be of the age . . .
11. phaan qayuq ponmaan haəy?   How old are you, Phân?

phaan

12. baat, kñom qayuq saamsəp-pram   I'm already thirty-five.
haəy.

Robert

koun   offspring, child(ren)
13. look miən koun ponmaan ne̊əq?   How many children do you have?

phaan

proh   man, male
koun-proh   son
srəy   woman, female
koun-srəy   daughter
14. kñom miən koun pii ne̊əq; koun-   I have two children; a son three years
proh qayuq bəy cnam, haəy-niŋ   old and a daughter one year old.
koun-srəy qayuq mə-cnam.

15. coh, look?   How about you?

Robert

niw   to be still . . . , to remain
kamlah (kəmlah, kəlah)   to be a bachelor
niw-laəy   still, up to the present
16. baat, kñom niw kəmlah niw-laəy   No, I'm still a bachelor.
tee.

qəwpuk   father
mdaay   mother
qəwpuk-mdaay   father and mother, parents
17. kñom niw ciə-muəy qəwpuk-mdaay.   I live with [my] parents.

naat

baaŋ   older brother or sister
pqoun   younger brother or sister
baaŋ-pqoun   brothers and sisters (older and
                                         younger siblings)
18. look miən baaŋ-pqoun craən ne̊əq   Do you have many brothers and sisters?
tee?

Robert

19. min craən ponmaan tee.   Not so many.

baaŋ-proh   older brother
20. kñom miən baaŋ-proh pii ne̊əq.   I have two older brothers.

pqoun-srəy   younger sister
məne̊əq (muəy ne̊əq)   one person; alone
dael   relative pronoun: that, which, who
21. haəy kñom miən pqoun-srəy   Then I have a younger sister who is
məne̊əq dael niw riən niw-laəy.   still in school (is still studying).

naat

cieŋ	more than

22. kñom mien bɑɑŋ-pqoun craən cieŋ look. — I have more brothers and sisters than you [do].

23. kñom mien bɑɑŋ-pqoun prammuəy neəq. — I have six brothers and sisters. (The speaker includes himself, and the verb mien means 'there are'.)

24. bɑɑŋ-proh məneəq twəə cumnuəñ. — One older brother is in business.

bɑɑŋ-srəy	older sister
pdəy	husband

25. bɑɑŋ-srəy kñom mien pdəy haəy. — My older sister is married (has a husband) already.

koət	respectful 3rd person pronoun
kruu	teacher, master
bəŋrien (bəŋrien, pəŋrien)	to teach, cause to learn
kruu-bəŋrien	teacher

26. pdəy koət twəə kruu-bəŋrien. — Her husband is a teacher.

pqoun-proh	younger brother
srok-qaamerɨc	America

27. haəy kñom mien pqoun-proh məneəq dael rien nɨw srok-qaamerɨc. — Then I have a younger brother who is studying in America.

koun-səh	student

28. pqoun-srəy pii neəq tiət cie koun-səh. — Two other younger sisters are school-children.

taa	grandfather, old man
look-taa	Grandfather (polite)
yiəy	grandmother, old woman
look-yiəy	Grandmother (polite)
mdaay-thom	older sister of either parent
miiŋ	younger sister of either parent
mdaay-miiŋ	Aunt (younger sister of either parent)

29. kraw pii nuh, mien look-taa, look-yiəy, mdaay-thom, haəy-nɨŋ mdaay-miiŋ tiət. — Besides that, there's Grandfather, Grandmother, an older aunt, and a younger aunt.

Robert

yii!	interjection of surprise or mild annoyance
ñiət-sɑndaan (-səndaan)	relatives, family

30. yii, look mien ñiət-səndaan craən nah! — Say, you have a lot of relatives!

phɑɑn

bəŋkaət (bəŋkaət, pəkaət)	to create, give birth to
bɑɑŋ-pqoun-bəŋkaət	full siblings

31. kñom kmien bɑɑŋ-pqoun-bəŋkaət tee. — I don't have any full brothers or sisters.

cii-doun-muəy	1st cousin (of one grandmother)
pqoun-cii-doun-muəy	younger first cousin
pqoun-cii-doun-muəy-srəy	younger female first cousin
cuəy	to help (to)
thae-reə̆qsaa	to care for, take care of

32. miən tae pqoun-cii-doun-muəy-srəy
    dael cuəy thae-reə̆qsaa koun kñom.

There's only a younger (female) cousin
who helps take care of my children.

wiə	familiar or derogatory 3rd person pronoun
pram-dɑndɑp (-dəndɑp, -ndɑp)	fifteen

33. wiə qayuq pram-dəndɑp cnam.

She's fifteen years old.

ruəc	then, or besides
qəwpuk-thom	older brother of either parent
qəwpuk-miə	younger brother of either parent

34. ruəc kñom miən qəwpuk-thom
    məneə̆q haəy-nɨŋ qəwpuk-miə
    məneə̆q nɨw ciə-muəy kñom phɑɑŋ.

Then I have an older uncle and a younger uncle living with me too.

B. GRAMMAR AND DRILLS

1. Kinship Terminology

Some Cambodian kinship terms are of a type usually referred to as "classificatory"; i.e. they are based on some wider criterion than that of specific biological
relationship, on which kinship terms are based in English. The primary criterion
in Cambodian is that of relative age; for example, bɑɑŋ may be used to refer to any
relative or friend who is older than the speaker but of the same generation, while
pqoun means 'younger relative or friend of same generation'. Thus bɑɑŋ might
refer to an older brother, older sister, older cousin, or older friend. bɑɑŋ-pqoun,
which can be conveniently translated 'brothers and sisters', means literally 'older
and younger relatives'. When it is necessary to specify a biological relationship,
such terms may be followed by bɑŋkaət (bəŋkaət, pəkaət) 'to give birth to'; for example:

bɑɑŋ-pqoun-bəŋkaət 'older full siblings'

Since relative age is the primary criterion, such terms are non-specific as to
sex. Sex may be specified by adding the word proh 'male' or srəy 'female' to non-
sex-specific terms, e.g.:

bɑɑŋ-proh	'older brother'	koun-proh	'son'
bɑɑŋ-srəy	'older sister'	koun-srəy	'daughter'
pqoun-prɔh	'younger brother'		
pqoun-srəy	'younger sister'		

Other terms, such as qəwpuk 'father' and mdaay 'mother' are unambiguous as to
sex, but are classificatory as to generation, and are included in compounds which
refer to siblings of one's parents, e.g.:

qəwpuk-thom	'uncle (older than one's parents)'
qəwpuk-miə	'uncle (younger than one's parents)'
mdaay-thom	'aunt (older than one's parents)'
mdaay-miiŋ	'aunt (younger than one's parents)'

Likewise the terms taa 'grandfather' and yiəy 'grandmother' are sex-specific, but may refer either to one's biological grandparents, or to old people of one's grandparents' generation. The more respectful terms are look-taa and look-yiəy, which are usually used in referring to one's biological grandparents, but may also refer to non-related but respected elders.

Terms referring to specific relatives of one's own generation must include the terms baaŋ or pqoun as appropriate, e.g.:

baaŋ-cii-doun-muəy-proh   'older male first cousin'
baaŋ-cii-doun-muəy-srəy   'older female first cousin'
    (cii-doun-muəy 'of one grandparent')
pqoun-cii-doun-muəy-proh   'younger male first cousin'
pqoun-cii-doun-muəy-srəy   'younger female first cousin'

1-A. Composition Drill

From the chart below, construct the kinship term called for, whether simple or compound.

baaŋ pqoun baaŋ-pqoun koun qəwpuk mdaay	cii-doun-muəy thom miə miiŋ	proh srəy	baŋkaət

father	full siblings	older male cousin	younger full brother
younger sibling	younger full sister	older uncle	younger cousin
older brother	offspring	younger aunt	older sibling
brothers and sisters	daughter	mother	younger sibling
older aunt	older cousin	younger uncle	full older brother
son	cousins	older female cousin	younger male cousin

1-B. Substitution Drill

Teacher	Student
kñom miən baaŋ-pqoun bəy neăq.	kñom miən baaŋ-pqoun bəy neăq.
baaŋ-proh	kñom miən baaŋ-proh bəy neăq.
pqoun-srəy	kñom miən pqoun-srəy bəy neăq.
koun-proh	kñom miən koun-proh bəy neăq.
koun-srəy	kñom miən koun-srəy bəy neăq.
qəwpuk-thom	kñom miən qəwpuk-thom bəy neăq.
mdaay-miiŋ	kñom miən mdaay-miiŋ bəy neăq.
qəwpuk-miə	kñom miən qəwpuk-miə bəy neăq.
mdaay-thom	kñom miən mdaay-thom bəy neăq.
baaŋ-pqoun-bəŋkaət	kñom miən baaŋ-pqoun-bəŋkaət bəy neăq.
baaŋ-cii-doun-muəy-proh	kñom miən baaŋ-cii-doun-muəy-proh bəy neăq.
baaŋ-cii-doun-muəy-srəy	kñom miən baaŋ-cii-doun-muəy-srəy bəy neăq.
pqoun-cii-doun-muəy-srəy	kñom miən pqoun-cii-doun-muəy-srəy bəy neăq.

Teacher	Student
baaŋ-proh-bəŋkaət	kñom miən baaŋ-proh-bəŋkaət bəy neə̆q.
pqoun-srəy-bəŋkaət	kñom miən pqoun-srəy-bəŋkaət bəy neə̆q.
ñiət-səndaan	kñom miən ñiət-səndaan bəy neə̆q.

1-C. Translation-Substitution Drill

Teacher	Student
qəwpuk kñom tɨw psaa haəy.	qəwpuk kñom tɨw psaa haəy.
(mother)	mdaay kñom tɨw psaa haəy.
(grandfather)	look-taa kñom tɨw psaa haəy.
(grandmother)	look-yiəy kñom tɨw psaa haəy.
(wife)	prəpuən kñom tɨw psaa haəy.
(husband)	pdəy kñom tɨw psaa haəy.
(older sister)	baaŋ-srəy kñom tɨw psaa haəy.
(younger brother)	pqoun-proh kñom tɨw psaa haəy.
(parents)	qəwpuk-mdaay kñom tɨw psaa haəy.
(older cousin)	baaŋ-cii-doun-muəy kñom tɨw psaa haəy.
(younger female cousin)	pqoun-cii-doun-muəy-srəy kñom tɨw psaa haəy.
(older uncle)	qəwpuk-thom kñom tɨw psaa haəy.
(younger aunt)	mdaay-miiŋ kñom tɨw psaa haəy.
(father)	qəwpuk kñom tɨw psaa haəy.

2. qayuq and cmuə̆h

The words qayuq 'age' and cmuə̆h 'name' (Lesson 5) are nouns which can best be translated as verbs in English in the following sentences:

mənuh nuh qayuq məphɨy-pram cnam.	That man [is] 25 years old.
mənuh nuh cmuə̆h phaan.	That man [is] named Phân.

In fact, however, the above sentences are examples of the topic-comment sentence-type (described in Lesson 3, B, 19) in which a topic is announced and made about it with no verb present. The nominal nature of the words can more clearly be seen in the following examples:

mənuh nuh miən qayuq saamsəp cnam.	That man is 30 years old.
mənuh nuh miən cmuə̆h wɛɛŋ.	That man has a long name.

2-A. Translation-Response Drill

Teacher		Student
look qayuq ponmaan?	(twenty-five)	kñom qayuq məphɨy-pram.
	(eighteen)	kñom qayuq dap-prambəy.
	(thirty-two)	kñom qayuq saamsəp-pii.
	(forty-one)	kñom qayuq saesəp-muəy.
	(seventeen)	kñom qayuq dap-prampɨl.
	(twenty-nine)	kñom qayuq məphɨy-prambuən.
	(thirty-six)	kñom qayuq saamsəp-prammuəy.
	(twenty-three)	kñom qayuq məphɨy-bəy.

2-B. Response Drill

Teacher		Student
look cmuəh qwəy?	(phɑɑn)	kñom cmuəh phɑɑn.
	(Robert)	kñom cmuəh Robert.
	(naat)	kñom cmuəh naat.
	(siəŋ)	kñom cmuəh siəŋ.
	(John)	kñom cmuəh John.
	(cɑmraən)	kñom cmuəh cɑmraən.
	(Paul)	kñom cmuəh Paul.
	(Bill)	kñom cmuəh Bill.
	(meiŋ)	kñom cmuəh meiŋ.

2-C. Response Drill

Have each student address the questions in A and B above to a second student.

3. kampuŋ(-tae) 'in the process of'

kampuŋ(-tae) is one of a class of aspectual auxiliaries which precede all verbs in a verb phrase, and in some way modify a following verb or verb phrase. kampuŋ(-tae) denotes the progressive aspect, and can be translated something like 'in the process of, in the act of', as in:

yəəŋ kəmpuŋ-tae niyiəy kniə leeŋ.   We're just (in the process of) chatting.

3-A. Substitution Drill

Teacher	Student
yəəŋ kəmpuŋ-tae niyiəy kniə leeŋ.	yəəŋ kəmpuŋ-tae niyiəy kniə leeŋ.
ñam baay.	yəəŋ kəmpuŋ-tae ñam baay.
məəl kon.	yəəŋ kəmpuŋ-tae məəl kon.
məəl siəwphɨw.	yəəŋ kəmpuŋ-tae məəl siəwphɨw.
daə-leeŋ.	yəəŋ kəmpuŋ-tae daə-leeŋ.
twəə-kaa.	yəəŋ kəmpuŋ-tae twəə-kaa.
qəŋkuy leeŋ.	yəəŋ kəmpuŋ-tae qəŋkuy leeŋ.
ñam kafei.	yəəŋ kəmpuŋ-tae ñam kafei.

3. Expansion Drill

Teacher	Student
kñom riən phiəsaa-qaŋglee.	kñom kəmpuŋ-tae riən phiəsaa-qaŋglee.
kñom məəl kon.	kñom kəmpuŋ-tae məəl kon.
kñom daə-leeŋ.	kñom kəmpuŋ-tae daə-leeŋ.
kñom qəŋkuy leeŋ.	kñom kəmpuŋ-tae qəŋkuy leeŋ.
kñom məəl siəwphɨw.	kñom kəmpuŋ-tae məəl siəwphɨw.
kñom twəə-kaa.	kñom kəmpuŋ-tae twəə-kaa.
kñom ñam baay.	kñom kəmpuŋ-tae ñam baay.

4. mɨn . . . ponmaan tee

In most contexts the word ponmaan is a question word meaning 'how much?' or 'how many?', e.g.:

nih tlay <u>ponmaan</u>?	How much does this cost?
maoŋ <u>ponmaan</u>?	What time is it?
look trəw-kaa <u>ponmaan</u>?	How many do you need?
look miən baaŋ-pqoun <u>ponmaan</u> neəq?	How many brothers and sisters do you have?

However, when <u>ponmaan</u> occurs in the frame <u>mɨn (V) ponmaan tee</u>, it has the meaning 'not so (V)', 'not (V) to any extent', e.g.:

mɨn craən ponmaan tee.	not so much, not so many
mɨn tlay ponmaan tee.	not so expensive
kñom mɨn kliən ponmaan tee.	I'm not so hungry.

4-A. Transformation Drill

Teacher	Student
kñom mɨn kliən tee.	kñom mɨn kliən <u>ponmaan</u> tee.
kñom mɨn kdaw tee.	kñom mɨn kdaw <u>ponmaan</u> tee.
srəy nuh mɨn lqaa tee.	srəy nuh mɨn lqaa <u>ponmaan</u> tee.
pteəh nuh mɨn touc tee.	pteəh nuh mɨn touc <u>ponmaan</u> tee.
krouc nih mɨn tlay tee.	krouc nih mɨn tlay <u>ponmaan</u> tee.
mənuh nuh mɨn thom tee.	mənuh nuh mɨn thom <u>ponmaan</u> tee.
kmiən craən tee.	kmiən craən <u>ponmaan</u> tee.

4-B. Response Drill

look kliən tee?	<u>mɨn</u> kliən <u>ponmaan tee</u>.
look miən baaŋ-pqoun craən neəq tee?	<u>mɨn</u> craən <u>ponmaan tee</u>.
srəy nuh lqaa tee?	<u>mɨn</u> lqaa <u>ponmaan tee</u>.
mənuh nuh thom tee?	<u>mɨn</u> thom <u>ponmaan tee</u>.
pteəh nuh touc tee.	<u>mɨn</u> touc <u>ponmaan tee</u>.
kafei nuh kdaw tee?	<u>mɨn</u> kdaw <u>ponmaan tee</u>.
phiəsaa kmae pibaaq tee?	<u>mɨn</u> pibaaq <u>ponmaan tee</u>.

5. nɨw . . . nɨw-laəy

When <u>nɨw</u> occurs preceding a main verb, it is a modal verb with the meaning 'still, now, at present', as in

koət <u>nɨw</u> riən nɨw srok-qaamerɨc.	He's <u>still</u> studying in America.

Frequently <u>nɨw</u> as a modal verb is reinforced by the final adverbial phrase <u>nɨw-laəy</u> 'still, up to the present time', which is redundant in the English translation; e.g.:

kñom <u>nɨw</u> kəmlah <u>nɨw-laəy</u>.	I'm <u>still</u> a bachelor (<u>still</u>).
kñom <u>nɨw</u> twəə-kaa qae-nuh <u>nɨw-laəy</u>.	I'm <u>still</u> working there (<u>up to the present</u>).

When <u>nɨw-laəy</u> follows <u>nɨw</u> as a primary verb, its translation as 'still' is not redundant; e.g.:

baaŋ-proh kñom nɨw pteəh <u>nɨw-laəy</u>.	My older brother is <u>still</u> living at home.

5-A. Transformation Drill

Teacher	Student
kñom twəə-kaa qae-nuh.	kñom nɨw twəə-kaa qae-nuh nɨw-laəy.
kñom riən phiəsaa-kmae.	kñom nɨw riən phiəsaa-kmae nɨw-laəy.
kñom twəə-kaa nɨw pteəh.	kñom nɨw twəə-kaa nɨw pteəh nɨw-laəy.
pqoun-srəy kñom riən.	pqoun-srəy kñom nɨw riən nɨw-laəy.
baaŋ-proh kñom twəə tiəhiən.	baaŋ-proh kñom nɨw twəə tiəhiən nɨw-laəy.
kñom twəə kruu-bəŋriən.	kñom nɨw twəə kruu-bəŋriən nɨw-laəy.
pqoun-proh kñom ciə nihsət.	pqoun-proh kñom nɨw ciə nihsət nɨw-laəy.
kñom kəmlah.	kñom nɨw kəmlah nɨw-laəy.

6. ciəŋ as a Preposition

When ciəŋ is followed by an object, it functions as a preposition meaning 'more than', or '-er than', as in:

kñom miən baaŋ-pqoun craən ciəŋ look.	I have more brothers and sisters than you [do].
pteəh nih thom ciəŋ pteəh nuh.	This house is larger than that house.

6-A. Substitution Drill

Teacher	Students
kñom miən baaŋ-pqoun craən ciəŋ look.	kñom miən baaŋ-pqoun craən ciəŋ look.
siəwphɨw	kñom miən siəwphɨw craən ciəŋ look.
rəbah	kñom miən rəbah craən ciəŋ look.
koun	kñom miən koun craən ciəŋ look.
kmaw-day	kñom miən kmaw-day craən ciəŋ look.
barəy	kñom miən barəy craən ciəŋ look.
qayuq	kñom miən qayuq craən ciəŋ look.

6-B. Translation Drill

From the chart below, construct the comparative statement called for:

pteəh nih	thom	ciəŋ	pteəh nuh
psaa nih	touc		psaa nuh
siəwphɨw nuh	tlay		siəwphɨw nih
krouc nih	pibaaq		krouc nuh
kafei	lqaa		tae
srəy nih	sruəl		srəy
phiəsaa-kmae			phiəsaa-cən
barəy nih			barəy
daəm-chəə nih			daəm-chəə nuh

Teacher	Student
This house is larger than that house.	pteəh nih thom ciəŋ pteəh nuh.
Coffee is more expensive than tea.	kafei tlay ciəŋ tae.
These cigarettes are more expensive than those cigarettes.	barəy nih tlay ciəŋ barəy nuh.
That book is smaller than this book.	siəwphɨw nuh touc ciəŋ siəwphɨw nih.

Teacher	Student
This girl is prettier than that girl.	srəy nih lqaa ciəŋ srəy nuh.
This house is more expensive than that house.	pteəh nih tlay ciəŋ pteəh nuh.
Cambodian is more difficult than Chinese.	phiəsaa-kmae pibaaq ciəŋ phiəsaa-cən.
This market is larger than that market.	psaa nih thom ciəŋ psaa nuh.
These oranges are larger than those oranges.	krouc nih thom ciəŋ krouc nuh.
That book is more expensive than this book.	siəwphɨw nuh tlay ciəŋ siəwphɨw nih.
This tree is prettier than that tree.	daəm-chəə nih lqaa ciəŋ daəm-chəə nuh.
This market is more expensive than that market.	psaa nih tlay ciəŋ psaa nuh.
These oranges are prettier than those oranges.	krouc nih lqaa ciəŋ krouc nuh.
That book is prettier than this book.	siəwphɨw nuh lqaa ciəŋ siəwphɨw nih.
This tree is larger than that tree.	daəm-chəə nih thom ciəŋ daəm-chəə nuh.
This girl is smaller than that girl.	srəy nih touc ciəŋ srəy nuh.
This house is prettier than that house.	pteəh nih lqaa ciəŋ pteəh nuh.
These oranges are smaller than those oranges.	krouc nih touc ciəŋ krouc nuh.
Cambodian is easier than Chinese.	phiəsaa-kmae sruəl ciəŋ phiəsaa-cən.

7. dael as a Relative Pronoun

dael has been met as a modal verb meaning 'to have ever' or, after the negative auxiliary mɨn, 'never', as in

| look dael tɨw məəl qəŋkɔɔ-woət tee? | Have you ever been to see Angkor Wat? |
| tee, kñom mɨn-dael tɨw tee. | No, I've never gone. |

dael also occurs as a general relative pronoun which relates attributive clauses to nouns, much like the English relative pronouns 'who, that, which', as in

| kñom miən pqoun-srəy məneəq dael nɨw riən nɨw-laəy. | I have a younger sister who is still studying. |
| miən tae pqoun-cii-doun-muay-srəy məneəq dael cuəy thae-reəqsaa koun kñom. | There's only a younger (female) cousin who helps take care of my children. |

7-A. Substitution Drill

Teacher	Student
kñom miən pqoun-srəy məneəq dael nɨw riən nɨw-laəy.	kñom miən pqoun-srəy məneəq dael nɨw riən nɨw-laəy.
pqoun-proh	kñom miən pqoun-proh məneəq dael nɨw riən nɨw-laəy.
baaŋ-proh	kñom miən baaŋ-proh məneəq dael nɨw riən nɨw-laəy.
baaŋ-srəy	kñom miən baaŋ-srəy məneəq dael nɨw riən nɨw-laəy.

Teacher	Student
koun-proh	kñom miən <u>koun-proh</u> məneə̆q dael nɨw riən nɨw-laəy.
koun-srəy	kñom miən <u>koun-srəy</u> məneə̆q dael nɨw riən nɨw-laəy.
pqoun-cii-doun-muəy-proh	kñom miən <u>pqoun-cii-doun-muəy-proh</u> məneə̆q dael nɨw riən nɨw laəy.
bɑɑŋ-cii-doun-muəy-srəy	kñom miən <u>bɑɑŋ-cii-doun-muəy-srəy</u> məneə̆q dael nɨw riən nɨw-laəy.

7-B. Transformation Drill

Change each of the following pairs of sentences into a complex sentence with a dependent attributive clause introduced by <u>dael</u>.

Model: Teacher   Student

kñom miən pqoun-srəy məneə̆q.   kñom miən pqoun-srəy məneə̆q
kŏə̆t nɨw riən nɨw-laəy.   <u>dael</u> nɨw riən nɨw laəy.

Teacher	Student
kñom miən koun-proh məneə̆q. kŏə̆t nɨw riən nɨw-laəy.	kñom miən koun-proh məneə̆q <u>dael</u> nɨw riən nɨw-laəy.
kñom miən bɑɑŋ-proh məneə̆q. kŏə̆t riən nɨw srok-qaamerɨc.	kñom miən bɑɑŋ-proh məneə̆q <u>dael</u> riən nɨw srok-qaamerɨc.
kñom miən bɑɑŋ-srəy məneə̆q. kŏə̆t miən pdəy haəy.	kñom miən bɑɑŋ-srəy məneə̆q <u>dael</u> miən pdəy haəy.
kñom miən qəwpuk-thom məneə̆q. kŏə̆t twəə tiəhiən.	kñom miən qəwpuk-thom məneə̆q <u>dael</u> twəə tiəhiən.
kñom miən koun-srəy məneə̆q. wiə nɨw ciə koun-səh nɨw-laəy.	kñom miən koun-srəy məneə̆q <u>dael</u> nɨw ciə koun-səh nɨw-laəy.
kñom miən pqoun-proh məneə̆q. kŏə̆t miən prəpuə̆n haəy.	kñom miən pqoun-proh məneə̆q <u>dael</u> miən prəpuə̆n haəy.
kñom miən qəwpuk-miə məneə̆q. kŏə̆t riən nɨw srok-barɑŋ.	kñom miən qəwpuk-miə məneə̆q <u>dael</u> riən nɨw srok-barɑŋ.
kñom miən koun-srəy məneə̆q. wiə qayuq prammuəy cnam.	kñom miən koun-srəy məneə̆q <u>dael</u> qayuq prammuəy cnam.
kñom miən mdaay-miiŋ məneə̆q. kŏə̆t nɨw ciə-muəy kñom.	kñom miən mdaay-miiŋ məneə̆q <u>dael</u> nɨw ciə-muəy kñom.

8. Alternate Forms for the Numerals 11–19

The numerals 11–19 (introduced in Lesson 2) have alternate forms which occur in more colloquial speech. These alternate forms are composed of the numerals 1–9 plus the bound form <u>-dɑndɑp</u> (dəndɑp, tədɑp) '-teen', as follows:

	Formal	Colloquial
11	dɑp-muəy	muəy-dəndɑp (mə-tədɑp)
12	dɑp-pii	pii-dəndɑp
13	dɑp-bəy	bəy-dəndɑp
14	dɑp-buən	buən-dəndɑp
15	dɑp-pram	pram-dəndɑp
16	dɑp-prammuəy	prammuəy-dəndɑp
17	dɑp-prampɨl	prampɨl-dəndɑp
18	dɑp-prambəy	prambəy-dəndɑp
19	dɑp-prambuən	prambuən-dəndɑp

8-A. Transformation Drill

Teacher	Student
kñom qayuq dɑp-muəy cnam.	kñom qayuq muəy-dəndɑp cnam.
kñom qayuq dɑp-pii cnam.	kñom qayuq pii-dəndɑp cnam.
kñom qayuq dɑp-bəy cnam.	kñom qayuq bəy-dəndɑp cnam.
kñom qayuq dɑp-buən cnam.	kñom qayuq buən-dəndɑp cnam.
kñom qayuq dɑp-pram cnam.	kñom qayuq pram-dəndɑp cnam.
kñom qayuq dɑp-prammuəy cnam.	kñom qayuq prammuəy-dəndɑp cnam.
kñom qayuq dɑp-prampɨl cnam.	kñom qayuq prampɨl-dəndɑp cnam.
kñom qayuq dɑp-prambəy cnam.	kñom qayuq prambəy-dəndɑp cnam.
kñom qayuq dɑp-prambuən cnam.	kñom qayuq prambuən-dəndɑp cnam.

8-B. Translation-Substitution Drill

In the following drill use the colloquial forms of the numerals 11-19.

Teacher	Student
kñom qayuq məphɨy cnam.	kñom qayuq məphɨy cnam.
(eleven)	kñom qayuq muəy-dəndɑp cnam.
(thirty-seven)	kñom qayuq saamsəp-prampɨl cnam.
(nineteen)	kñom qayuq prambuən-dəndɑp cnam.
(twenty-six)	kñom qayuq məphɨy-prammuəy cnam.
(fifty-three)	kñom qayuq haasəp-bəy cnam.
(sixty-eight)	kñom qayuq hoksəp-prambəy cnam.
(thirteen)	kñom qayuq bəy-dəndɑp cnam.
(eighteen)	kñom qayuq prambəy-dəndɑp cnam.
(forty-four)	kñom qayuq saesəp-buən cnam.
(fourteen)	kñom qayuq buən-dəndɑp cnam.
(twenty-nine)	kñom qayuq məphɨy-prambuən cnam.
(twelve)	kñom qayuq pii-dəndɑp cnam.
(seventy-two)	kñom qayuq cətsəp-pii cnam.
(seventeen)	kñom qayuq prampɨl-dəndɑp cnam.

[Tape 13]   C. COMPREHENSION

1. Discussing One's Family

mɨən: som-tooh, kruəsaa look mɨən mənuh ponmaan neˇəq?

thɨm: baat, teəŋ-qɑh mɨən prammuəy neˇəq, kɨɨ qəwpuk-mdaay kñom, bɑɑŋ-
      proh məneˇəq, pqoun-srəy pii neˇəq, haəy-nɨŋ kñom.

mɨən: bɑɑŋ-proh look qayuq ponmaan haəy?

thɨm: bɑɑŋ-proh knom qayuq məphɨy-pii haəy.
pqoun-srəy məneəq qayuq pram-dəndɑp, haəy-nɨŋ pqoun-srəy məneəq
tiət qayuq prambuən cnam.

mɨən: coh look, qayuq ponmaan haəy?

thɨm: kñom qayuq prambəy-dəndɑp cnam haəy.

2. Discussing a Wedding

sɑɑŋ: cumriəp-suə, suən.
khaan baan cuəp kniə yuu nah mɔɔk haəy.
suən qaeŋ mɔɔk pnum-pɨñ twəə qəy?

[New Vocabulary]

[qəywan 'things, provisions, luggage']
suən: kñom mɔɔk tɨñ qəywan.
[riəp-kaa 'to have a wedding, to get married']
pqoun-srəy kñom riəp-kaa khae nih.

[neəq-naa 'who?']
sɑɑŋ: koət kaa ciə-muəy neəq-naa?

suən: kaa ciə-muəy look bun sok.
sɑɑŋ qaeŋ skoəl koət tee?

sɑɑŋ: baat, kñom mɨn skoəl tee.
tae kñom skoəl pqoun-proh koət, pipruəh riən nɨw səlaa ciə-muəy kñom.
look sok twəə-kaa qəy?

suən: koət twəə tiəhiən.

3. An Introduction

chɨn: cumriəp-suə qaat.

qaat: cumriəp-suə chɨn.

chɨn: nih kɨɨ pqoun-srəy kñom, cmŭəh narii.

narii: cumriəp-suə, look qaat.

qaat: look qəñcəəñ tɨw naa?

chɨn: kñom nɨŋ tɨw ñam baay, ruəc tɨw məəl kon.
look cɑŋ tɨw ciə-muəy kñom tee?

qaat: narii, cɑŋ tɨw tee?

narii: tɨw, kɑ-tɨw.

4. Looking for a Friend

John: som-tooh, pteəh look sambou nɨw qae-naa?

Stranger: baat, pteəh tii-bəy nɨw khɑŋ-sdam-day.

John: soum qɑɑ-kun.
kñom skoəl look sambou peel nɨw riən nɨw srok-qaamerɨc.

Stranger: kñom ciǝ baaŋ-pqoun-cii-doun-muǝy niŋ look sɑmbou.
            qǝwpuk koǝt niŋ qǝwpuk kñom ciǝ baaŋ-pqoun-bǝŋkaǝt.
            som-tooh, look cmüǝh qwǝy?

John: kñom cmüǝh John.

Stranger: look tɨw pteǝh look sɑmbou qǝylǝw-nih rɨɨ?

John: baat.

            [cuun 'to accompany']
Stranger: qǝñcǝŋ kñom niŋ cuun look tɨw.

John: qɑɑ-kun.

D. CONVERSATION

1. Discussing Families

   a) A greets B and C, and asks them what they are doing.
   b) B replies that they're just chatting, and invites A to sit down.
   c) A asks them what they're talking about.
   d) C replies that they're talking about their families, then asks A if he is
      married yet.
   e) A replies that he is married.
   f) B asks A how many children he has.
   g) A replies that he has two children; a girl four years old and a boy two
      years old; then A asks C if he is married yet.
   h) C replies that he is still a bachelor.

2. Brothers and Sisters

   a) A asks B how many brothers and sisters he has.
   b) B replies that he has four brothers and sisters; his older brother has a
      wife already, and is a businessman; his older sister is a teacher.
   c) A asks B if his older sister is married yet.
   d) B replies that his older sister doesn't have a husband yet; then he says
      that he has one more younger sister who is still a school-girl.
   e) A asks B how old his younger sister is.
   f) B replies that she is twelve years old.

3. Extended Families

   a) A asks B if his family has many people.
   b) B replies that there are not so many, and says that he has no full brothers
      or sisters; besides his parents, there are his grandfather, his grandmother,
      and one older uncle living with him too.
   c) A says that one younger uncle and one younger aunt live with him.
   d) B asks him who else there is besides that.
   e) A replies that he has a younger female cousin who lives with him, and that
      she helps take care of his children.

4. Discussing a Wedding

    a) A asks B and C what they are talking about.

    b) B replies that they are talking about his older sister, and that she is going to have a wedding this month.

    c) A asks B whom his sister is marrying.

    d) B replies that she is marrying Mr. Nath, and asks C if he knows him.

    e) C replies that he doesn't know him, and asks B what work Mr. Nath does.

    f) B replies that he is a businessman.

    g) C asks B how old Mr. Nath is.

    h) B replies that he is 30 years old.

LESSON 7. REVIEW OF LESSONS 2-6

A. Review of Dialogues

In preparation for the review lesson, review the Dialogues of Lessons 2-6. To test yourself, cover the English column and provide the English equivalents of the Cambodian sentences; then cover the Cambodian column and provide the Cambodian equivalents of the English sentences. If you cannot give the Cambodian equivalents quickly and smoothly, review the relevant sections of the Grammar and Drills.

B. Review of Comprehension

The teacher will read selected conversations from the Comprehension sections of Lessons 2-6, calling on individual students for English translations of the sentences.

C. Questions

Provide an appropriate answer to each of the following oral questions. Make the answers factual when possible. Every response should be preceded by the appropriate response particle, baat or caah. "Yes" or "No" answers should be followed by an affirmation or negation of the content of the question, in either the full form or an appropriate abbreviated form, e.g.:

look tɨw psaa tee?	baat, mɨn tɨw tee.
Are you going to the market?	No, I'm not (going).

Answers may be either written or oral; if oral, every student should have an opportunity to answer every question. If a test for grading purposes is desired, the answers may be written, but in either case the questions should be oral. The teacher will repeat each question twice. Listen to the question in its entirety the first time; an unfamiliar word may be cleared up by the context in which it occurs.

1. look (look-srəy) sok-sapbaay ciə tee?
2. look (look-srəy) yɔɔk kafei tee?
3. look (look-srəy) miən siəwphɨw tee?
4. krouc nih tum haəy-rɨɨ-nɨw?
5. pteəh-səmnaq nɨw qae-naa?
6. look (look-srəy) ceh niyiəy phiəsaa-kmae tee?
7. look (look-srəy) niyiəy qəmpii qwəy?
8. look (look-srəy) miən bɑɑŋ-pqoun ponmaan neəq?
9. maoŋ ponmaan haəy?
10. rəteh-pləəŋ cəñ maoŋ ponmaan?
11. look mɔɔk pii-qəŋkal?
12. look (look-srəy) cmuəh qwəy?
13. psaa nuh thom tee?
14. baək tumpɔə tii-ponmaan?
15. phoocəniyəthaan nɨw qae-naa?
16. chair prae thaa məc?
17. look (look-srəy) qəñcəəñ tɨw naa?
18. look (look-srəy) sdap baan tee?
19. teəŋ-qɑh tlay ponmaan?
20. piəq nuh məəl thaa məc?

97

21. piəq dədael?
22. qəŋkaɑ nih mə-kɨlou tlay ponmaan?
23. look (look-srəy) mɔɔk riən nɨw srok-kmae rɨɨ?
24. phiəsaa-cən pibaaq riən tee?
25. look (look-srəy) mɔɔk tŋay-nih rɨɨ?
26. look (look-srəy) mɔɔk pii srok naa?
27. look (look-srəy) qayuq ponmaan?
28. look (look-srəy) yuəl kliə nuh tee?
29. look (look-srəy) ciə baraŋ rɨɨ qaŋglee?
30. look (look-srəy) tɨw qəŋkal?
31. kon nih cap ləəŋ pii-qəŋkal?
32. look (look-srəy) twəə-kaa qwəy?
33. look (look-srəy) trəw tɨw twəə-kaa maoŋ ponmaan?
34. look (look-srəy) coul-cət məəl siəwphɨw tee?
35. look (look-srəy) kaa haəy-rɨnɨw?
36. look (look-srəy) miən koun ponmaan neəq?
37. look (look-srəy) kliən baay tee?
38. look (look-srəy) caŋ tɨw daə-ləəŋ tee?
39. look (look-srəy) trəw-kaa cəə-kuh tee?
40. look (look-srəy) miən bɑɑŋ-pqoun-bəŋkaət ponmaan neəq?
41. rəbɑh nih kee haw thaa qwəy?
42. look (look-srəy) claəy səmnuə kñom baan tee?
43. look (look-srəy) trəw tɨñ qwəy?
44. ceik tum nih mə-snət tlay ponmaan?
45. look (look-srəy) nɨw srok-kmae baan ponmaan cnam haəy?
46. look (look-srəy) skoəl puəq-maaq kñom tee?
47. look (look-srəy) niyiəy phiəsaa-baraŋ baan tee?
48. look (look-srəy) kaa ciə-muəy neəq-naa?
49. look (look-srəy) dael tɨw sahaqroət-qaamerɨc tee?
50. look (look-srəy) tɨw məəl qəŋkɔɔ-woət baan ponmaan dɑɑŋ haəy?

D. Translation

1. It's very hot today.
2. I came yesterday.
3. I have to go to the market.
4. My house is on the left.
5. My friend comes from China.
6. Please close your books.
7. I know how to speak English.
8. There are many people at this market.
9. These oranges aren't ripe yet.
10. Please say it all together.
11. That man is a tourist.
12. I have many brothers and sisters.
13. Paul is a (university) student and John is a soldier.
14. I'm still a bachelor.
15. I don't understand this sentence.
16. I want to buy four dozen eggs.
17. This house is larger than that house.
18. Write this sentence on the blackboard.
19. I've lived in Cambodia for five years.
20. I've never gone to see Angkor Wat.
21. They sell fruit at that shop.
22. This film started (to play) ten minutes ago.
23. I bought three pencils yesterday.
24. I want (to have) two kilos of rice.
25. I have to go to work at eight o'clock.
26. Open your books to page 26.
27. Cambodian (language) is easier than Chinese.

28. I have four full brothers and sisters.
29. One of my older brothers is a schoolteacher.
30. Could I have a cigarette?
31. There are a lot of people at this market today.
32. Give me a pack of cigarettes and a box of matches.
33. My older aunt and my younger aunt live with me too.
34. I've been to England twice.
35. I've wanted to see that movie for a long time now.
36. French isn't as difficult as Cambodian.
37. Cambodian is easy to speak, but difficult to write.
38. My older uncle is a businessman.
39. My younger sister helps take care of my children.

40. My son is five years old and my daughter is three years old.
41. I have a younger brother who is studying in France.
42. We're (in the process of) talking about our families.
43. I can't answer; I don't understand that question.
44. Let's (come) go get something to eat in that shop for a little while.
45. I studied Chinese a little bit in France.
46. Tomorrow I have to buy various things at the market.
47. My older (male) cousin works in a hotel.
48. My grandfather and my grandmother live with my parents.
49. That girl isn't so pretty.
50. My older sister isn't married (doesn't have a husband) yet.

LESSON 8. VOCATIONS

            A. DIALOGUE

chuən

dɑl	when
chup	to stop
chup riən	to stop studying; to finish school
taə	question particle (formal)
kɨt	to think (about), to plan (to)

1. dɑl look chup riən, taə, kɨt twəə-kaa qwəy? — What do you plan to do when you finish school?

samrac

dəŋ	to know
praakɑt (prakɑt, prəkɑt)	to be sure, exact
ciə prakɑt	surely, for sure

2. kñom mɨn-tŏən dəŋ ciə prakɑt tee. — I don't yet know for sure.

pontae (pəntae, pənnae)	but
meethiəwii	lawyer

3. pontae kñom cɑŋ twəə məəthiəwii. — But I'd like to be a lawyer.

chuən

pɛɛt	medicine (as a science); doctor
kruu-pɛɛt	doctor
ciəŋ	comparative adverb: more

4. kñom kɨt thaa twəə kruu-pɛɛt lqɑɑ ciəŋ. — I think it would be better to be a doctor.

samrac

weeliə (weliə)	time
peel-weliə	time
qɑh	to use up, consume
qɑh peel-weliə	to be time-consuming

5. riən twəə kruu-pɛɛt qɑh peel-weliə yuu nah. — It takes a long time to study to be a doctor.

wɨcciə	science, study
wɨcciə-pɛɛt	medicine (as a study)
sɑp	every
sɑp-tŋay-nih	these days, at the present time

6. baaŋ-proh kñom kəmpuŋ-tae riən wɨcciə-pɛɛt sɑp-tŋay-nih. — My older brother is studying medicine at present.

cɑmnuən (cəmnuən)	number, total
təəp	then, after which

7. kŏət trəw riən cəmnuən bəy cnam tiət, təəp cəñ twəə-kaa. — He has to study for three more years, after which [he can] go out and practice.

8. som-tooh, qəwpuk look twəə-kaa   Excuse me, what work does your
   qwəy?   father do?

   chuən

   riəcckaa   government service
   kaa-riəcckaa   government service (as a profes-
                                             sion)
9. baat, qəwpuk kñom twəə   My father is in (does) government
   kaa-riəcckaa.   service.

10. coh, qəwpuk look twəə qwəy dae?   What does your father do?

    samrac

    caaŋ-waaŋ   director, manager
    rooŋ   hall, building, factory
    dɑmbaañ (dəmbaañ)   weaving
    rooŋ-dəmbaañ   weaving mill
11. baat, kŏət ciə caaŋ-waaŋ   He's the manager of a weaving mill.
    rooŋ-dəmbaañ.

    chuən

    neə̆q-twəə-kaa   worker(s)
12. nɨw kənlaeŋ nuh miən   How many workers are there there?
    neə̆q-twəə-kaa ponmaan neə̆q?

    samrac

    smiən   clerk, secretary
    dou   to trade, exchange
    luə̆q-dou   to do trade
    neə̆q-luə̆q-dou   salesman
    kammәkɑɑ   workers, laborers
13. teə̆ŋ-qɑh miən prəhael mərɔɔy   Altogether there are about a hundred,
    neə̆q, kɨɨ smiən, neə̆q-luə̆q-dou,   including clerks, salesmen, and
    haəy-nɨŋ kammәkɑɑ.   laborers.
14. look cəñ pii salaa, taə, kɨt   Tell me, when you get out of school,
    twəə-kaa qwəy?   what do you plan to do?

    chuən

15. kñom cɑŋ twəə kruu-bəŋriən.   I want to be a teacher.

    samrac

    tnaq   class, level
    qwəy?   what? (interrogative adjective)
16. look cɑŋ bəŋriən tnaq qwəy˘   What level do you want to teach?

    chuən

    wɨttyiəlay (~ wɨccialay)   secondary school, lycée
    piipruə̆h (pipruə̆h)   because
    praq   money; silver
    praq-khae   salary
17. kñom cɑŋ bəŋriən nɨw wɨttyiəlay   I want to teach in a secondary school
    pipruə̆h baan praq-khae craən.   because one gets more salary.

səmrac

luy   money
18. baə look caŋ baan luy craən,   If you want a lot of money, it would
    twəə cəmnuəñ lqaa ciəŋ.   be better to go into business.

               chuən

lmɔɔm   enough, adequate (to)
cəñcəm   to support, maintain, raise
ciiwɨt (ciwɨt)   life
cəñcəm ciwɨt   to support oneself, to make a
                                                   living
19. kñom mɨn caŋ baan luy craən peek   I don't want too much money; just
    tee; lmɔɔm cəñcəm ciwɨt baan haəy.   enough to live on.

baək   to drive
taqsii   taxi
neəq-baək-taqsii   taxi-driver
rɔɔk   to seek, to earn
krup-krŏən   adequate, complete, full
20. neəq-baək-taqsii kaa rɔɔk praq   Even a taxi-driver can earn enough
    baan krup-krŏən dae.   money.

               səmrac

tumnee   to be free, vacant, at leisure
laan   automobile
cih   to mount, to ride
kaa-baan (ka-baan)   to be a possibility
21. mɛɛn haəy; nɨw peel tumnee, kee   Right; and in his free time, he can
    cih laan daə-leeŋ ka-baan dae.   use the car for pleasure too.

               chuən

rɔbah (rəbah)   of, belonging to
srae   rice field
twəə-srae   to farm (raise rice)
neəq-twəə-srae   rice farmer
22. qəwpuk-miə rəbah kñom ciə   My (younger) uncle is a rice farmer.
    neəq-twəə-srae.

               səmrac

kaal   time
mun   before
kaal-mun   before, at first
ciəŋ   skilled laborer
chəə   wood
ciəŋ-chəə   carpenter
23. qəwpuk-thom kñom, kaal-mun twəə   My (older) uncle was formerly a
    ciəŋ-chəə.   carpenter.

qəyləw-nih   now
krɨəŋ   thing, accessory
tuu   cabinet
krɨəŋ-tok-tuu   furniture
neəq-luəq-krɨəŋ-tok-tuu   furniture salesman

24. qəyləw-nih koə̆t ciə   Now he's a furniture salesman.
    neə̆q-luə̆q-kriəŋ-tok-tuu.

                          chuən

25. haaŋ rəbɑh koə̆t nɨw qae-naa?   Where is his shop?

                      sɑmrac

      cɨt   near
      rooŋ-twəə-barəy   cigarette factory
26. haaŋ koə̆t nɨw cɨt rooŋ-twəə-   His shop is near the cigarette
    barəy.   factory.

      kat   to cut
      sɑq   hair
      haaŋ-kat-sɑq   barbershop
27. som-tooh, kñom trəw tɨw   Excuse me, I must go to the barber-
    haaŋ-kat-sɑq sən.   shop.

28. soum liə sən haəy.   I must say good-by.

                          chuən

29. baat, soum liə.   O.K., good-by.

B. GRAMMAR AND DRILLS

1. Noun Compounds

As pointed out in Lesson 5, the specifier neə̆q 'person' is used in counting nouns whose referents are ordinary persons, e.g.:

      mənuh bəy neə̆q   three persons
      kruu-bəŋriən bəy neə̆q   three teachers

neə̆q also combines with verbs and nouns to form noun compounds whose referents are persons who characteristically perform the action of the verb, or who are categorized by the noun. Such compounds encountered so far are:

   a) neə̆q + verb or verb phrase

      neə̆q + luə̆q-dou 'to trade': neə̆q-luə̆q-dou 'salesman'
      neə̆q + twəə-kaa 'to work': neə̆q-twəə-kaa 'worker'
      neə̆q + twəə-srae 'to farm': neə̆q-twəə-srae 'farmer'
      neə̆q + baək taqsii 'to drive a taxi': neə̆q-baək-taqsii 'taxi-driver'

   b) neə̆q + noun

      neə̆q + cəmnuəñ 'commerce': neə̆q-cəmnuəñ 'merchant'
      neə̆q + riəcckaa 'government service': neə̆q-riəcckaa 'civil servant'

The words ciəŋ 'artisan', kruu 'teacher, master', haaŋ 'shop, store', and rooŋ 'building, factory' have also been encountered as heads of compounds formed in a similar way:

      ciəŋ 'artisan' + chəə 'wood': ciəŋ-chəə 'carpenter'
      kruu 'teacher' + bəŋriən 'to teach': kruu-bəŋriən 'teacher'
      kruu 'teacher' + pɛɛt 'medicine': kruu-pɛɛt 'doctor'

haaŋ 'shop' + <u>kat sɑq</u> 'to cut hair': <u>haaŋ-kat-sɑq</u> 'barbershop'
<u>rooŋ</u> 'factory' + <u>twəə barəy</u> 'to make cigarettes': <u>rooŋ-twəə-barəy</u>
    'cigarette factory'
<u>rooŋ</u> 'factory' + <u>dəmbaañ</u> 'weaving': <u>rooŋ-dəmbaañ</u> 'weaving mill'

1-A. Composition Drill

From the chart below compose the compounds indicated.

Head Word	Attribute
neə̆q 'person' ciəŋ 'artisan' kruu 'teacher' haaŋ 'shop' rooŋ 'building'	luə̆q-dou 'to do trade' twəə-kaa 'to work' twəə-srae 'to farm' cəmnuəñ 'commerce' baək taqsii 'to drive a taxi' luə̆q krɨəŋ-tok-tuu 'to sell furniture' teehsəcɑɑ 'tourism' pɛɛt 'medicine' bəŋriən 'to teach' twəə barəy 'to make cigarettes' chəə 'wood' kat sɑq 'to cut hair' riəcckaa 'government service' luə̆q siəwphɨw 'to sell books'

Teacher	Student
worker	neə̆q-twəə-kaa
taxi-driver	neə̆q-baək-taqsii
carpenter	ciəŋ-chəə
teacher	kruu-bəŋriən
salesman	neə̆q-luə̆q-dou
barbershop	haaŋ-kat-sɑq
doctor	kruu-pɛɛt
merchant	neə̆q-cəmnuəñ
farmer	neə̆q-twəə-srae
tourist	neə̆q-teehsəcɑɑ
weaving mill	rooŋ-dəmbaañ
barber	ciəŋ-kat-sɑq
book-salesman	neə̆q-luə̆q-siəwphɨw
bookstore	haaŋ-luə̆q-siəwphɨw
furniture store	haaŋ-luə̆q-krɨəŋ-tok-tuu
furniture salesman	neə̆q-luə̆q-krɨəŋ-tok-tuu
cigarette factory	rooŋ-twəə-barəy
civil servant	neə̆q-riəcckaa

2. twəə with Vocations

In Cambodian, as in English, a subject can be related to a noun complement by means of a copulative, such as <u>ciə</u> 'be, is', e.g.:

qəwpuk kñom <u>ciə</u> neə̆q-twəə-srae.   My father <u>is</u> a farmer.

However, when the noun complement is the name of a vocation which doesn't involve the head-word neǝq 'person', it is normally connected with the subject by means of the verb twǝǝ 'to make, to do', in which case it means 'work as' or 'follows the profession of'; e.g.:

qǝwpuk kñom twǝǝ kruu-pɛɛt.

My father is (follows the profession of) a doctor.

kñom cɑŋ twǝǝ kruu-bǝŋriǝn.

I want to be (work as) a teacher.

2-A. Substitution Drill

Teacher	Student
puǝq-maaq kñom ciǝ kruu-pɛɛt.	puǝq-maaq kñom ciǝ kruu-pɛɛt.
ciǝŋ-chǝǝ.	puǝq-maaq kñom ciǝ ciǝŋ-chǝǝ.
neǝq-baǝk-taqsii.	puǝq-maaq kñom ciǝ neǝq-baǝk-taqsii.
neǝq-twǝǝ-srae.	puǝq-maaq kñom ciǝ neǝq-twǝǝ-srae.
meethiǝwii.	puǝq-maaq kñom ciǝ meethiǝwii.
neǝq-cǝmnuǝñ.	puǝq-maaq kñom ciǝ neǝq-cǝmnuǝn.
smiǝn.	puǝq-maaq kñom ciǝ smiǝn.
neǝq-luǝq-dou.	puǝq-maaq kñom ciǝ neǝq-luǝq-dou.
kruu-bǝŋriǝn.	puǝq-maaq kñom ciǝ kruu-bǝŋriǝn.

2-B. Substitution Drill

Teacher	Student
qǝwpuk kñom twǝǝ kruu-pɛɛt.	qǝwpuk kñom twǝǝ kruu-pɛɛt.
smiǝn.	qǝwpuk kñom twǝǝ smiǝn.
meethiǝwii.	qǝwpuk kñom twǝǝ meethiǝwii.
kruu-bǝŋriǝn.	qǝwpuk kñom twǝǝ kruu-bǝŋriǝn.
ciǝŋ-kat-sɑq.	qǝwpuk kñom twǝǝ ciǝŋ-kat-sɑq.
ciǝŋ-chǝǝ.	qǝwpuk kñom twǝǝ ciǝŋ-chǝǝ.
tiǝhiǝn.	qǝwpuk kñom twǝǝ tiǝhiǝn.

3. Unmarked Subordinate Clauses

In the sentence: dɑl look chup riǝn, taǝ, kɨt twǝǝ-kaa qwǝy? 'When you get out of school, what work do you plan to do?', the subordinate clause is introduced, as in English, by a subordinating conjunction dɑl 'when'. Alternatively, however, a prior subordinate clause whose action precedes or is a prerequisite for that of the main clause may occur without a subordinating conjunction, e.g.:

look cǝñ pii salaa, taǝ, kɨt twǝǝ-kaa qwǝy? (you exit from school, say plan work what?)

[When] you get out of school, what work do [you] plan to do?

kñom kmiǝn kaa twǝǝ, kñom coul-cǝt mɔɔk mǝǝl rǝbah pseiŋ-pseiŋ. (I not-have work do, I like-to come see things various.)

[When] I have nothing to do, I like to come and see the various things.

3-A. Substitution Drill

Teacher	Student
kñom cǝñ pii salaa, kñom cɑŋ twǝǝ kruu-bǝŋriǝn.	kñom cǝñ pii salaa, kñom cɑŋ twǝǝ kruu-bǝŋriǝn.

Teacher	Student
riən pɛɛt.	kñom cəñ pii salaa, kñom caŋ riən pɛɛt.
tɨw sahaqrŏət-qaamerɨc.	kñom cəñ pii salaa, kñom caŋ tɨw sahaqrŏət-qaamerɨc.
baək taqsii.	kñom cəñ pii salaa, kñom caŋ baək taqsii.
twəə-srae.	kñom cəñ pii salaa, kñom caŋ twəə-srae.
twəə kaa-riəcckaa.	kñom cəñ pii salaa, kñom caŋ twəə kaa-riəcckaa.
twəə smiən.	kñom cəñ pii salaa, kñom caŋ twəə smiən.
kñom kmiən kaa twəə, kñom coul-cət tɨw psaa.	kñom kmiən kaa twəə, kñom coul-cət tɨw psaa.
tɨw daə-leeŋ.	kñom kmiən kaa twəə, kñom coul-cət tɨw daə-leeŋ.
tɨw rɔɔk puəq-maaq.	kñom kmiən kaa twəə, kñom coul-cət tɨw rɔɔk puəq-maaq.
tɨw ñam baay.	kñom kmiən kaa twəə, kñom coul-cət tɨw ñam baay.
tɨw məəl kon.	kñom kmiən kaa twəə, kñom coul-cət tɨw məəl kon.
tɨw kat sɑq.	kñom kmiən kaa twəə, kñom coul-cət tɨw kat sɑq.

4. The Question Particle taə

The question particle taə frequently occurs at the beginning of an interrogative clause in polite speech, or in formal questions such as those addressed by a teacher to a student in the classroom situation. It signals the fact that a question follows, and is roughly equivalent to the polite 'Tell me . . .' which may preface a question in English. A falling intonation typically separates taə from the interrogative clause which follows.

Examples:

look cəñ pii salaa, taə, kɨt twəə-kaa qwəy?	[When] you get out of school, what work do you plan to do?
taə, look qəñcəəñ tɨw naa?	Excuse me, where are you going?

4-A. Transformation Drill

Convert the following questions to formal questions preceded by the polite question particle taə.

Teacher	Student
look qəñcəəñ tɨw naa?	taə, look qəñcəəñ tɨw naa?
look cmŭəh qwəy?	taə, look cmŭəh qwəy?
ptĕəh look nɨw qae-naa?	taə, ptĕəh look nɨw qae-naa?
look mɔɔk pii srok naa?	taə, look mɔɔk pii srok naa?
look caŋ twəə qwəy?	taə, look caŋ twəə qwəy?
look mɔɔk rɔɔk nĕəq-naa?	taə, look mɔɔk rɔɔk nĕəq-naa?
look riən nɨw qae-naa?	taə, look riən nɨw qae-naa?
look nɨw srok-kmae yuu haəy rɨɨ?	taə, look nɨw srok-kmae yuu haəy rɨɨ?

5. ciəŋ as a Comparative Adverb

When ciəŋ follows a verb or verb phrase, it functions like a comparative adverb, e.g.:

kñom kɨt thaa twəə kruu-pɛɛt lqaa ciəŋ.	I think it would be better to be a doctor.

5-A. Transformation Drill

Teacher	Student
srəy nih lqaa. (srəy nuh)	srəy nuh lqaa ciəŋ.
twəə meethiəwii lqaa. (kruu-pɛɛt)	twəə kruu-pɛɛt lqaa ciəŋ.
ptĕəh nih thom. (ptĕəh nuh)	ptĕəh nuh thom ciəŋ.
ceik nih tum. (ceik nuh)	ceik nuh tum ciəŋ.
phiəsaa-kmae pibaaq. (cən)	phiəsaa-cən pibaaq ciəŋ.
phiəsaa-baraŋ sruəl. (kmae)	phiəsaa-kmae sruəl ciəŋ.
kñom miən baaŋ-pqoun craən. (kñom)	kñom miən baaŋ-pqoun craən ciəŋ.
krouc nih touc. (krouc nuh)	krouc nuh touc ciəŋ.
barəy nih tlay. (barəy nuh)	barəy nuh tlay ciəŋ.

6. The Conjunction təəp

təəp is a conjunction which relates the second of two coordinate clauses to a preceding clause which is both a logical and temporal prerequisite for the second; it can be translated 'then, and then, after which', e.g.:

kŏət trəw riən cəmnuən bəy cnam tiət, təəp cəñ twəə-kaa.
He has to study (for a period of) three more years, after which [he can] go out and practice.

6-A. Substitution Drill

Teacher	Student
kñom trəw riən bəy cnam tiət, təəp cəñ twəə-kaa.	kñom trəw riən bəy cnam tiət, təəp cəñ twəə-kaa.
trəlap tɨw ptĕəh.	kñom trəw riən bəy cnam tiət, təəp trəlap tɨw ptĕəh.
twəə kaa-riəcckaa.	kñom trəw riən bəy cnam tiət, təəp twəə kaa-riəcckaa.
cəñ twəə tiəhiən.	kñom trəw riən bəy cnam tiət, təəp cəñ twəə tiəhiən.

Teacher	Student
twəə kruu-bəŋriən.	kñom trəw riən bəy cnam tiət, təəp twəə kruu-bəŋriən.
chup.	kñom trəw riən bəy cnam tiət, təəp chup.

6-B. Substitution Drill

Teacher	Student
kñom ñam baay sən, təəp tɨw məəl kon.	kñom ñam baay sən, təəp tɨw məəl kon.
tɨw salaa.	kñom ñam baay sən, təəp tɨw salaa.
tɨw daə-leeŋ.	kñom ñam baay sən, təəp tɨw daə-leeŋ.
məəl siəwphɨw.	kñom ñam baay sən, təəp məəl siəwphɨw.
tɨw pteəh.	kñom ñam baay sən, təəp tɨw pteəh.
tɨw twəə-kaa.	kñom ñam baay sən, təəp tɨw twəə-kaa.
tɨw psaa.	kñom ñam baay sən, təəp tɨw psaa.

7. The Verb lmɔɔm

As an adjectival verb, lmɔɔm means 'to be adequate, enough, comfortable, suitable', as in:

| praq-khae nuh lmɔɔm tee? | Is that salary adequate? |
| look baan kafei lmɔɔm tee? | Have you had enough coffee? |

Like other adjectival verbs, lmɔɔm also modifies nouns and other verbs, with the meaning 'enough, adequately, suitably', as in:

| krouc nih tlay lmɔɔm. | These oranges are moderately priced. |
| pteəh nuh thom lmɔɔm. | That house is comfortably large. |

lmɔɔm also occurs as a modal verb preceding other verbs, with the meaning 'enough to, adequate for', as in:

| praq-khae kñom lmɔɔm cəñcəm ciwɨt. | My salary is adequate to live on. |
| koun kñom thom lmɔɔm tɨw riən haəy. | My child is big enough to go to school. |

7-A. Expansion Drill

Teacher	Student
pteəh nih thom.	pteəh nih thom lmɔɔm.
krouc nih tlay.	krouc nih tlay lmɔɔm.
kafei nih kdaw.	kafei nih kdaw lmɔɔm.
srəy nuh lqɑɑ.	srəy nuh lqɑɑ lmɔɔm.
phiəsaa-kmae sruəl.	phiəsaa-kmae sruəl lmɔɔm.

7-B. Substitution Drill

Teacher	Student
kñom miən luy lmɔɔm cəñcəm ciwɨt.	kñom miən luy lmɔɔm cəñcəm ciwɨt.
tɨn siəwphɨw nih.	kñom miən luy lmɔɔm tɨn siəwphɨw nih.
tɨw məəl kon.	kñom miən luy lmɔɔm tɨw məəl kon.
ñam baay mədɑɑŋ.	kñom miən luy lmɔɔm ñam baay mədɑɑŋ.

Teacher	Student
koun kñom thom lmɔɔm <u>tɨw riən haəy</u>.	koun kñom thom lmɔɔm <u>tɨw riən haəy</u>.
<u>cuəy kñom twəə-kaa</u>.	koun kñom thom lmɔɔm <u>cuəy kñom twəə-kaa</u>.

8. The Completive Verb <u>kaa-baan</u>

The completive verb <u>baan</u> 'to be able' was discussed in Lesson 3, B, 15; e.g.:

kñom tɨw <u>baan</u>.	I <u>can</u> go.
kñom tɨw <u>mɨn baan</u> tee.	I <u>can't</u> go.

<u>kaa-baan</u> is also a completive verb, but with the specialized meaning 'to be feasible, to be a possibility'. The contrast between <u>baan</u> and <u>kaa-baan</u> can be seen in the following pair of examples:

kñom niyiəy phiəsaa-kmae <u>baan</u>.	I <u>can</u> (am able to) speak Cambodian.
kñom niyiəy phiəsaa-kmae <u>kaa-baan</u>.	I <u>can</u> speak Cambodian, (if you like).

8-A. Substitution Drill

Teacher	Student
yəəŋ tɨw məəl kon ka-baan.	yəəŋ tɨw məəl kon ka-baan.
tɨw ñam baay	yəəŋ tɨw ñam baay ka-baan.
niyiəy phiəsaa-baraŋ	yəəŋ niyiəy phiəsaa-baraŋ ka-baan.
tɨw pnum-pɨñ	yəəŋ tɨw pnum-pɨñ ka-baan.
cuəy twəə-kaa	yəəŋ cuəy twəə-kaa ka-baan.
tɨw daə-leeŋ	yəəŋ tɨw daə-leeŋ ka-baan.
tɨn barəy tiət	yəəŋ tɨn barəy tiət ka-baan.
tɨw pteəh nuh	yəəŋ tɨw pteəh nuh ka-baan.

9. Reduction

Cambodian words, like the words of any language, are subject to reduction or contraction in rapid speech. In English, attempts are frequently made to represent these reduced forms orthographically, as in the sentences "Whaddaya mean?" and "I'm gonna go." In most languages, it is unstressed or weakly stressed syllables which tend to get slighted in rapid speech. Likewise in Cambodian, the unstressed presyllables of disyllabic words are the least stable, and tend to undergo change in rapid speech. Certain definite patterns of reduction can be established:

1) In disyllables whose stressed syllable has an initial stop, unstressed presyllables of shape CVN- (Consonant-Vowel-Nasal) tend to be reduced in colloquial speech to CəN-, and in still more rapid speech to N-; e.g.:

qañcəəñ > qəñcəəñ > ñcəəñ	'polite invitation'
qaŋkuy > qəŋkuy > ŋkuy	'to sit down'
bantəc-bantuəc > bəntəc-bəntuəc > ntəc-ntuəc	'a little'

2) In disyllables whose stressed syllable has an initial continuant, unstressed syllables of shape CVN- tend to be reduced first to CəN-, and then to Cə-; e.g.:

kanlaeŋ > kənlaeŋ > kəlaeŋ	'place'
ponmaan > pənmaan > pəmaan	'how much, how many'
kanlah > kənlah > kəlah	'half'

The reduced form kəlah 'half' nevertheless contrasts with the word klah 'some'.

3) Presyllables of shape CrV- are reduced to Crə- or simply Cə-:

prɑhael > prəhael > pəhael	'perhaps, about'
prɑpuˇən > prəpuˇən > pəpuˇən	'wife'
prɑteeh > prəteeh > pəteeh	'country'

4) Presyllables of shape CVV- are shortened to CV-:

piipruˇəh > pipruˇəh	'because'
qaayuq > qayuq	'age'
baaraŋ > baraŋ (> praŋ)	'French'

5) Presyllables of shape CV- are reduced to Cə-:

rɔbɑh > rəbɑh	'thing; of'
rɔteh > rəteh	'cart'
mɔnuh > mənuh	'human'

6) The presyllables dɑ- and sɑ- change first to Cə- and then to tə-; bɑ- changes first to bə- and then to pə-:

dɑdael > dədael > tədael	'same'
sɑsei > səsei > təsei	'to write'
bɑbuəl > bəbuəl > pəbuəl	'to persuade'

7) When the word muəy 'one' precedes a specifier, it is characteristically reduced to mə-. In fact many words involving the presyllable mə- almost never occur with the full form muəy-, and have standardized spellings in the writing system, much like the English contractions "don't" and "I'll":

muəy-plɛɛt > məplɛɛt	'an instant, awhile'
muəy-phɨy > məphɨy	'twenty'
muəy-neˇəq > məneˇəq	'one person'
muəy-rɔɔy > mərɔɔy	'one hundred'

8) Some words which end in a nasal are shortened to N- when they occur as unstressed elements in compounds:

prambəy	> pəmbəy	> mbəy	'eight'
khaaŋ-kraoy	> khaŋ-kraoy	> ŋ-kraoy	'behind, the back'
pnum-pɨñ	> num-pɨñ	> m-pɨñ	'Phnom Penh'

9) The negative auxiliary mɨn may be reduced in unstressed position to m-:

mɨn dael > m-dael	'never'
mɨn mɛɛn > m-mɛɛn	'not really'
mɨn qəy tee > m-qəy tee	'never mind'

10) The future auxiliary nɨŋ is reduced in rapid speech to a nasal homorganic with the initial of the following word; e.g.:

nɨŋ mɔɔk > m-mɔɔk	'will come'
nɨŋ tɨw > n-tɨw	'will go'
nɨŋ kat > ŋ-kat	'will cut'

11) Some monosyllabic words have variant forms whose occurrence is not conditioned by loss of stress, but seems to be a matter of degree of colloquialism (and perhaps of dialect):

twəə	>	thəə	'to do'	rɔɔk > rɔɔ	'to search'
tŋay	>	ŋay	'day'	məəl > məə	'to watch'
mɔɔk	>	mɔɔ	'to come'	qwəy > qəy	'what'
yɔɔk	>	yɔɔ	'to take'		

9-A. Repetition Drills

Repeat the following sentences after the teacher, first in a slow careful pronunciation, then in a rapid pronunciation. Ideally the first repetition should involve the full unreduced forms of the underlined words, and the second repetition the shortest, most reduced, forms. In fact, however, both of the teacher's pronunciations may fall between the two extremes. Furthermore, the rapid pronunciations may involve some changes not discussed above, as well as the addition of some particles which occur in rapid speech but which are not appropriate to more formal speech. The student should in all cases imitate the teacher's pronunciation as closely as possible.

Model: Teacher   Student

Careful

qañcəəñ qaŋkuy qae-nih.   qañcəəñ qaŋkuy qae-nih.

Rapid

ñcəəñ ŋkuy qinih.   ñcəəñ ŋkuy qinih.

Careful   Rapid

1) qañcəəñ mɔɔk khaaŋ-nih.   ñcəəñ mɔɔ ŋ-nih.
   qañcəəñ qaŋkuy qae-nih.   ñcəəñ ŋkuy qinih.
   mɔɔk ñam baay bantəc-bantuəc tɨw. mɔɔ ñam baay ntəc-ntuəc təh.

2) look twəə-kaa kanlaeŋ naa?   look thəə-kaa kəlaeŋ naa?
   qəyləw-nih maoŋ ponmaan?   qələw maoŋ pəmaan?
   qəyləw-nih maoŋ prambəy kanlah.   qələw maoŋ mbəy kəlah.

3) kŏət qaayuq prahael məphɨy-pram.   kŏət qayuq pəhael məphɨy-pram.
   kñom mɨn-tŏən miən prapuən tee.   kñom m-tŏən miən pəpuən teh.
   kñom mɨn-dael tɨw prateeh-baaraŋ   kñom m-dael tɨw pəteeh-baraŋ teh.
   tee.

4) sap-tŋay-nih kñom rɔwŭəl nah.   sap-ŋay-nih kñom ləwŭəl nəh.
   mɔnuh nuh tɨñ rɔbah craən nah.   mənuh nuh tɨñ rəbah craən nəh.
   kñom nɨŋ cih rɔteh-pləəŋ tɨw.   kñom ñ-cih rəteh-pləəŋ tɨw.

5) look qaayuq ponmaan?   look qayuq pəmaan?
   kñom nɨŋ tɨñ kaafei muəy kaew.   kñom n-tɨñ kafei məkaew.
   kñom caŋ riən phiəsaa-baaraŋ   kñom caŋ riən phiəsaa-baraŋ
   piiprŭəh·sruəl sasei.   piprŭəh sruəl təsei.

6) qañcəəñ ñam kaafei muəy-plɛɛt sən. ñcəəñ ñam kafei məplɛɛt sən.
   siəwphɨw nih tlay muəy-rɔɔy riəl. səphɨw nih tlay mərɔɔy riəl.
   kñom baan tɨw məəl qaŋkɔɔ-wŏət   kñom baan tɨw məə ŋkɔɔ-wŏət
   muəy daaŋ.   mədaaŋ.

7) koun kñom qaayuq prambəy cnam.   koun kñom qayuq mbəy cnam.
   prampɨl tŋay tiət kñom tɨw pnum-pɨñ. mpɨl ŋay tiət, kñom tɨw m-pɨñ.
   kñom mɨn-dael tɨw pnum-pɨñ tee.   kñom m-dael tɨw m-pɨñ teh.
   mɨn-qəy tee.   m-qəy teh.

<u>Careful</u>   <u>Rapid</u>

8) kñom niŋ tɨw <u>pnum-pɨñ</u> sqaek.   kñom <u>n-tɨw</u> <u>m-pɨñ</u> sqaek.
   tŋay-nih kñom niŋ tɨw <u>məəl</u> kon.   ŋay-nih kñom <u>n-tɨw</u> <u>məə</u> kon.
   koət <u>twəə-kaa</u> nɨw <u>khaaŋ-kraoy</u>.   koət <u>thəə-kaa</u> nɨw <u>ŋ-kraoy</u>.

[Tape 15]   C. COMPREHENSION

1. <u>Discussing Vocations</u>

    thuən: baaŋ-proh look qəyləw-nih twəə-kaa qwəy?

    sun: baat, koət twəə-kaa nɨw haaŋ-luəq-laan.

    thuən: koət coul-cət kaa nuh tee?

    sun: baat, koət mɨn coul-cət ponmaan tee, tae baan praq-khae lmɔɔm
                 cəñcəm ciwɨt.

    thuən: coh, baaŋ-srəy look twəə-kaa qwəy dae?

    sun: baat, koət twəə smiən nɨw rooŋ-dəmbaañ.

    thuən: koət twəə-kaa nɨw kanlaeŋ nuh yuu haəy rɨɨ?

    sun: baat, prəhael pram khae haəy.

2. <u>Two Friends Go Out Together</u>

    Servant: look miən kaa qwəy?

    ceiŋ: look siduu nɨw pteəh tee?

    Servant: caah, look nɨw pteəh.
                 som-tooh, look cmuəh qwəy?

    ceiŋ: kñom cmuəh ceiŋ, ciə puəq-maaq look siduu mɔɔk pii pnum-pɨñ.

[Servant calls siduu]

    siduu: cumriəp-suə ceiŋ.
                 yii, khaan baan cuəp kniə yuu haəy!
                 ceiŋ ñam baay haəy-rɨnɨw?

    ceiŋ: baat, mɨn-toən ñam tee.

    siduu: mɔɔk tɨw ñam baay ciə-muəy kñom sən.
                 ñam baay haəy, yəəŋ tɨw psaa.

    ceiŋ: tɨw ka-tɨw; kñom trəw tɨñ siəwphɨw phaaŋ.
                 cih taqsii tɨw rɨɨ?

    siduu: baat tee; kñom miən laan.

3. <u>Discussing an Older Brother</u>

    kuŋ: cumriəp-suə camraən.
                 (look) qəñcəəñ tɨw naa?

    camraən: kñom tɨw leeŋ pteəh baaŋ-proh kñom.
                 koət ciə meethiəwii.

kuŋ: koǒt twəə meethiəwii baan ponmaan cnam haəy?

camraən: koǒt twəə baan bəy cnam haəy.

kuŋ: koǒt miən prəpuǒn haəy-riniw?

camraən: baat, koǒt miən prəpuǒn haəy.

kuŋ: koǒt miən koun haəy rii?

camraən: baat, koǒt miən koun-proh pii neǒq dael ciə koun-səh.

4. A New Car

riən: qou, look tiñ laan rii?

chaem: baat.

riən: yii, laan nih lqɑɑ nah!
look tiñ pii-qəŋkal?

chaem: kñom tiñ baan bəy tŋay haəy.

riən: look tiñ kənlaeŋ naa?

chaem: kñom tiñ mɔɔk pii haaŋ qəwpuk-thom kñom.
baə tumnee, mɔɔk tiw cih laan daə-leeŋ.

riən: tiw kɑ-tiw.

D. CONVERSATION

1. Plans for the Future

   a) A asks B what he plans to do when he gets out of school.
   b) B replies that he doesn't know yet for sure, but that he'd like to be a doctor.
   c) A says he thinks it would be better to be a schoolteacher.
   d) B comments that schoolteachers don't get much money.
   e) A replies that schoolteachers get enough money to live on, then says that if you want a lot of money, it would be better to be a lawyer.
   f) B agrees, but says that he doesn't want much money.

2. Discussing Jobs

   a) A asks B what work he does in Phnom Penh.
   b) B replies that he is a taxi-driver, then says that formerly he helped his father, who is a rice-farmer. B then asks A what he does.
   c) A replies that he is a clerk in a cigarette factory.
   d) B asks A where he lives.
   e) A replies that he lives with his older brother, who is a schoolteacher.
   f) B asks A what level his brother teaches.
   g) A replies that his brother teaches in a secondary school.

3. Discussing Professions

   a) A asks B if he has finished school (stopped studying) yet.
   b) B answers that he hasn't finished yet.
   c) A asks B what he plans to do when he gets out of school.

d) B replies that he wants to go into government service, then asks A the same question.
e) A says he wants to be a lawyer.
f) B objects that it takes a very long time to study to be a lawyer.
g) A agrees, but says that lawyers get a lot of money.

4. The Furniture Shop

a) A asks B where he works.
b) B replies that he is a salesman in a furniture shop.
c) A asks B where the furniture shop is.
d) B replies that it is near the weaving mill.
e) A asks B if it is a large shop.
f) B replies that it is not so big, and says that there are about 20 workers, including salesmen, carpenters, and laborers.
g) A says he is going to the movies, and asks B if he can go with him.
h) B replies that he can go (if he likes), since his father is the manager of the shop.

LESSON 9. THE WEATHER

A. DIALOGUE

Robert

pliəŋ	rain; to rain
tleə̆q	to fall
klaŋ	strong, hard, extreme

1. qei, pliəŋ tleə̆q klaŋ nah!   Hey, [it's] really raining hard!

chααŋ

crɔɔk	to take shelter
kraom	under
daəm-chəə	tree

2. mɔɔk tɨw crɔɔk nɨw kraom daəm-   Let's go take shelter under that tree.
    chəə nuh sən.

bαntəc-tiət (bəntəc-, ntəc-)	soon, in a little while
muk-tae	probably, likely to
reə̆ŋ	to dry up (here: to quit)

3. bəntəc-tiət muk-tae reə̆ŋ haəy.   [It will] probably quit soon.

Robert

plɨc	to forget
chat	umbrella
qəyləw (qaaləw, qələw)	now
tɔtɨk (tətɨk)	to be wet
qαh	entirely, completely

4. kñom plɨc yɔɔk chat mɔɔk; qəyləw   I forgot to bring an umbrella; now
    kñom tətɨk qαh.   I'm all wet.

chααŋ

pruə̆h	because
qaaw	shirt, coat
qaaw-pliəŋ	raincoat

5. kñom mɨn tətɨk pənmaan tee, pruə̆h   I didn't get so wet, because I have
    kñom miən qaaw-pliəŋ.   a raincoat.

Robert

rɔdəw (rədəw)	season
rədəw-pliəŋ	the rainy season

6. rədəw-pliəŋ miən pənmaan khae?   How many months are there in the
                                         rainy season?

chααŋ

taŋ-pii	from, starting from
miqthonaa (mithonaa)	June
khae-mithonaa	the month of June
rɔhout (rəhout, ləhout)	throughout, all the way to
dαl	to, until, reaching to

toqlaa (tolaa)   October
khae-tolaa   the month of October

7. baat, rədəw-pliəŋ miən pram khae,   The rainy season lasts (has) five
kɨɨ taŋ-pii khae-mithonaa rəhout   months, (that is) starting from the
dɑl khae-tolaa.   month of June up to the month of Oc-
                                        tober.

Robert

roʾəl   every
roʾəl-tŋay   every day

8. taə, nɨw rədəw-pliəŋ miən pliəŋ   Say, does it rain every day in the
roʾəl-tŋay rɨɨ?   rainy season?

chaaŋ

thoʾəmmedaa   usual, usually
taam-thoʾəmmədaa   usually

9. baat, taam-thoʾəmmədaa pliəŋ   Yes, usually it rains every day.
roʾəl-tŋay.

Robert

pɨñ   throughout, fully; to be full
pɨñ muəy tŋay (pɨñ mə-tŋay)   all day

10. pliəŋ pɨñ mə-tŋay rɨɨ?   Does it rain all day?

chaaŋ

cuən-kaal   sometimes
rɔsiəl (rəsiəl)   early afternoon
tŋay-rəsiəl   in the early afternoon

11. cuən-kaal pɨñ mə-tŋay, tae   Sometimes [it rains] all day, but
thoʾəmmədaa pliəŋ tae   usually it rains only in the early
tŋay-rəsiəl tee.   afternoon.

12. nɨw srok-qaamerɨc miən buən   There are four seasons in America,
rədəw, mɛɛn tee?   right?

Robert

nɨŋ haəy   that's it, you've got it

13. baat, nɨŋ haəy.   Yes, that's right.

chaaŋ

rɔŋiə (rəŋiə)   cold, chilly
rədəw-rəŋiə   the cold season
rədəw-kdaw   the hot season

14. nɨw nih, miən tae bəy rədəw tee,   Here there are only three seasons—
kɨɨ rədəw-pliəŋ, rədəw-rəŋiə,   the rainy season, the cold season,
haəy-nɨŋ rədəw-kdaw.   and the hot season.

wɨccəkaa   November
khae-wɨccəkaa   the month of November
kumpheʾəq   February
khae-kumpheʾəq   the month of February
tɨw   to, up to

15. rədəw-rəŋiə kɨɨ pii khae-wɨccəkaa   The cold season is from November
tɨw khae-kumpheʾəq.   to February.

minaa	March
khae-minaa	the month of March
quhsəphiə	May
khae-quhsəphiə	the month of May

16. rədəw-kdaw kɨɬ pii khae-minaa tɨw khae-quhsəphiə.

The hot season lasts from March to May.

Robert

traceˇəq (trəceˇəq, təceˇəq)	to be cool

17. rədəw-rəŋiə trəceˇəq nah tee?

Is the cold season very cool?

chaaŋ

18. mɨn rəŋiə douc srok-qaameric tee; krŏən-tae trəceˇəq lmɔɔm ponnoh.

It's not as cold as [in] America; it's just comfortably cool, that's all.

kɑɑq	frozen, congealed
tɨk-kɑɑq	ice; ice water; snow

19. kmiən tɨk-kɑɑq tleˇəq tee.

[We] don't have any snow. (There is no falling of snow.)

kyɑl (~kcɑl)	wind
bɑq	to blow
cəəŋ	north
khaaŋ-cəəŋ (khaŋ-cəəŋ)	the north

20. miən tae kyɑl bɑq mɔɔk pii khaŋ-cəəŋ.

There's just a wind blowing from the north.

yup	night, evening

21. tae yup klah rəŋiə bəntəc dae.

But some nights are rather cold.

Robert

sɑh	(not) at all

22. kñom mɨñ coul-cət rədəw-kdaw sɑh.

I don't like the hot season at all.

chaaŋ

23. kñom kɑɑ mɨñ coul-cət dae.

I don't like [it] either.

trɑŋ	to be straight
tŋay-trɑŋ	(at) midday, noon
naa	anywhere, somewhere (indefinite pronoun)
tɨw naa mɔɔk naa	to go anywhere, to go and come

24. tŋay-trɑŋ, tɨw naa mɔɔk naa pibaaq nah.

At midday, it's uncomfortable (difficult) to go anywhere.

tlŏəp	to be accustomed (to)
peel-yup	at night
keeŋ	to sleep, recline
luˇəq	to fall asleep
keeŋ luˇəq	to sleep
keeŋ mɨn luˇəq	to be unable to sleep

25. peel-yup, baə mɨn tlŏəp, keeŋ mɨn luˇəq tee.

At night, if [you're] not used to [it], [you] can't sleep.

Robert

ciəŋ-kee	the most, the most of all
26. look coul-cət rədəw naa ciəŋ-kee?	What season do you like best?

chaaŋ

27. kñom coul-cət rədəw-rəɲiə ciəŋ-kee.	I like the cold season the most.
qaakaah (qakaah)	air, weather
28. miən qakaah lqaa.	The weather's nice.
29. mɨn rəɲiə, mɨn kdaw; sruəl lmɔɔm.	It's not cold, it's not hot; it's just pleasant.

Robert

cɨt	nearly, almost
30. qəyləw pliəŋ cɨt reəŋ haəy.	The rain has almost stopped now.
taa	to continue
tɨw	orientation of action away from speaker in time
taa tɨw tiət	on, further
31. mɔɔk daə taa tɨw tiət.	Let's continue walking. (Let's walk on.)

Names of Months Not Mentioned Above

meˇəqkəraa (maqkəraa)	January
meesaa (mesaa)	April
kaqkədaa	July
səyhaa	August
kaññaa	September
tnuu	December

B. GRAMMAR AND DRILLS

1. The Names of the Months

There are three sets of names for the months in Cambodia. Those listed in the first column below are the official names as presently taught in the schools and used in modern publications, and are the names used in the preceding Dialogue. These months coincide with the months of the Western calendar, and are sometimes referred to by the French names (column 2) by those educated during French administration. The set of names listed in the third column below refer to the traditional lunar system of months, and correspond roughly to the last half of one month and the first half of the next month of the Western calendar; e.g. miəq 'January-February'. These names are still widely used by older people in the countryside, and by the clergy. In this text the student will be required to memorize only the standard set of names; the other two systems are included for reference.

Standard	French	Lunar	
meə̆qkəraa	saŋwiyee	miəq	January
kumpheə̆q	feewriyee	phɑlkun (phəkun)	February
minaa	mah	caet	March
meesaa	qaawriil	pisaaq	April
quhsəphiə	mee	ceeh	May
mithonaa	swaŋ	qasaat	June
kaqkədaa	suyyee	sraap	July
səyhaa	quut	phattəbot	August
kaññaa	seittɑɑm	qaasoc (qasoc)	September
tolaa	qoktoup	katdək (kədək)	October
wɨccəkaa	nɨwwɑɑm	mɨkkəsei	November
tnuu	deisɑɑm	boh	December

1-A. Response Drill

Looking at the chart above, answer the following questions.

Teacher	Student
baə khae nih ciə khae-meə̆qkəraa, khae kraoy ciə khae qwəy?	baə khae nih ciə khae-meə̆qkəraa, khae kraoy ciə khae-kumpheə̆q.
baə khae nih ciə khae-kaññaa, khae kraoy ciə khae qwəy?	baə khae nih ciə khae-kaññaa, khae kraoy ciə khae-tolaa.
baə khae nih ciə khae-tnuu, khae kraoy ciə khae qwəy?	baə khae nih ciə khae-tnuu, khae kraoy ciə khae-meə̆qkəraa.
baə khae nih ciə khae-quhsəphiə, khae kraoy ciə khae qwəy?	baə khae nih ciə khae-quhsəphiə, khae kraoy ciə khae-mithonaa.
baə khae nih ciə khae-meesaa, khae kraoy ciə khae qwəy?	baə khae nih ciə khae-meesaa, khae kraoy ciə khae-quhsəphiə.
baə khae nih ciə khae-tolaa, khae kraoy ciə khae qwəy?	baə khae nih ciə khae-tolaa, khae kraoy ciə khae-wɨccəkaa.
baə khae nih ciə khae-səyhaa, khae kraoy ciə khae qwəy?	baə khae nih ciə khae-səyhaa, khae kraoy ciə khae-kaññaa.
baə khae nih ciə khae-minaa, khae kraoy ciə khae qwəy?	baə khae nih ciə khae-minaa, khae kraoy ciə khae-meesaa.
baə khae nih ciə khae-kaqkədaa, khae kraoy ciə khae qwəy?	baə khae nih ciə khae-kaqkədaa, khae kraoy ciə khae-səyhaa.
baə khae nih ciə khae-mithonaa, khae kraoy ciə khae qwəy?	baə khae nih ciə khae-mithonaa, khae kraoy ciə khae-kaqkədaa.
baə khae nih ciə khae-kumpheə̆q, khae kraoy ciə khae qwəy?	baə khae nih ciə khae-kumpheə̆q, khae kraoy ciə khae-minaa.
baə khae nih ciə khae-wɨccəkaa, khae kraoy ciə khae qwəy?	baə khae nih ciə khae-wɨccəkaa, khae kraoy ciə khae-tnuu.

1-B. Response Drill

Repeat the above drill, using the following formula:

Teacher	Student
baə khae nih ciə khae-meə̆qkəraa, khae mun ciə khae qwəy?	baə khae nih ciə khae meə̆qkəraa, khae mun ciə khae-tnuu.

1-C. Response Drill

Repeat Drills 1-A and 1-B above, without referring to the chart.

2. Confirmatory Questions and Answers

Confirmatory questions usually take the form of a statement, followed by mɛɛn tee? 'isn't that right?, isn't that so?, right?'; e.g.:

niw srok-qaameric miən buən rədəw, In America, there are four seasons,
mɛɛn tee?   right?

In rapid speech mɛɛn tee? may be shortened to mɛɛn teh? or mɛɛn qeh? The common affirmative response to a confirmatory question is niŋ haəy (in some dialects nəŋ haəy), shortened in rapid speech to niŋ qəh. A contradictory response consists of min mɛɛn tee (m-mɛɛn qəh) 'that's not right', followed optionally by the correct statement, e.g.:

look miən baaŋ-pqoun buən neə̆q, You have four brothers and sisters,
mɛɛn tee?   right?

min mɛɛn tee; miən tae bəy neə̆q tee. No; [I] have only three.

2-A. Transformation Drill

Convert the following statements to confirmatory questions.

Teacher	Student
niw srok-qaameric miən buən rədəw.	niw srok-qaameric miən buən rədəw, mɛɛn tee?
look miən baaŋ-pqoun buən neə̆q.	look miən baaŋ-pqoun buən neə̆q, mɛɛn tee?
look tiw srok-qaameric.	look tiw srok-qaameric, mɛɛn tee?
khae nih kii khae-minaa.	khae nih kii khae-minaa, mɛɛn tee?
look twəə kruu-bəŋriən.	look twəə kruu-bəŋriən, mɛɛn tee?
rədəw-pliəŋ miən pram khae.	rədəw-pliəŋ miən pram khae, mɛɛn tee?
mənuh nuh ciə kruu-pɛɛt.	mənuh nuh ciə kruu-pɛɛt, mɛɛn tee?
pteə̆h look niw khaŋ-cweiŋ-day.	pteə̆h look niw khaŋ-cweiŋ-day, mɛɛn tee?
qəwpuk look twəə meethiəwii.	qəwpuk look twəə meethiəwii, mɛɛn tee?
look qayuq məphiy-pram.	look qayuq məphiy-pram, mɛɛn tee?
look cmuə̆h phaan.	look cmuə̆h phaan, mɛɛn tee?

2-B. Reciprocal Response Drill

Have each student address a confirmatory question to a second student, who replies baat, niŋ haəy, then addresses another confirmatory question to a third student, and so on.

Model: 1st Student: nɨw srok-qaamerɨc miən buən rədəw, mɛɛn tee?

        2nd Student: baat, nɨŋ haəy.
                 look miən bɑɑŋ-pqoun buən nĕəq, mɛɛn tee?

        3rd Student: baat, nɨŋ haəy. [Etc.]

2-C. Response Drill

Give a negative response to each of the following questions, followed by the alternative supplied by the teacher.

Teacher	Student
nɨw srok-kmae miən buən rədəw, mɛɛn tee? (miən tae bəy rədəw tee)	mɨn mɛɛn tee; miən tae bəy rədəw tee.
look miən bɑɑŋ-pqoun buən nĕəq, mɛɛn tee? (miən tae pii nĕəq tee)	mɨn mɛɛn tee; miən tae pii nĕəq tee.
look tɨw srok-qaamerɨc, mɛɛn tee? (kñom tɨw srok-barɑŋ)	mɨn mɛɛn tee; kñom tɨw srok-barɑŋ.
khae nih kɨɨ khae-minaa, mɛɛn tee? (khae nih kɨɨ khae-meesaa)	mɨn mɛɛn tee; khae nih kɨɨ khae-meesaa.
look twəə kruu-bəŋriən, mɛɛn tee? (kñom twəə tiəhiən)	mɨn mɛɛn tee; kñom twəə tiəhiən.
rədəw-pliəŋ miən pram khae, mɛɛn tee? (miən prammuəy khae)	mɨn mɛɛn tee; miən prammuəy khae.
mənuh nuh ciə kruu-pɛɛt, mɛɛn tee? (kŏət ciə kruu-bəŋriən)	mɨn mɛɛn tee; kŏət ciə kruu-bəŋriən.
ptĕəh look nɨw khaŋ-cweiŋ-day, mɛɛn tee? (nɨw khaŋ-sdam-day)	mɨn mɛɛn tee; nɨw khaŋ-sdam-day.
qəwpuk look twəə meethiəwii, mɛɛn tee? (kŏət twəə kaa-riəcckaa)	mɨn mɛɛn tee; kŏət twəə kaa-riəcckaa.
look qayuq məphɨy-pram, mɛɛn tee? (məphɨy-prampɨl)	mɨn mɛɛn tee; məphɨy-prampɨl.
look cmŭəh phɑɑn, mɛɛn tee? (kñom cmŭəh naat)	mɨn mɛɛn tee; kñom cmŭəh naat.

3. tae 'but, only'

tae is one of a class of words which occur both as conjunctions and as prepositions. As a conjunction, tae has been encountered in the following sentences:

ceik nuh mɨn-tŏən tum tee, tae ceik nih tum haəy.	Those bananas aren't ripe yet, but these bananas are ripe already.
phiəsaa-cən sruəl niyiəy, tae pibaaq səsei.	Chinese is easy to speak, but difficult to write.

As a preposition, tae has occurred in the following sentences:

kñom trəw-kaa tae kənlah lou tee.	I need only a half-dozen.
nɨw nih, miən tae bəy rədəw tee.	Here, there are only three seasons.
thoëmmədaa, pliəŋ tae tŋay-rəsiəl ponnoh.	Usually it rains only in the afternoon, that's all.

When tae occurs as a preposition, it is usually followed at the end of the sentence by a second limiting element, such as tee or ponnoh, which is redundant in English.

3-A. Transformation Drill

Teacher	Student
nɨw nih miən bəy rədəw.	nɨw nih, miən tae bəy rədəw tee.
kñom miən dap riəl.	kñom miən tae dap riəl tee.
kñom trəw-kaa bəy kilou.	kñom trəw-kaa tae bəy kilou tee.
koët baan nɨw pii tŋay.	koët baan nɨw tae pii tŋay tee.
kñom niyiəy phiəsaa-kmae.	kñom niyiəy tae phiəsaa-kmae tee.
kñom miən baaŋ-pqoun bəy neëq.	kñom miən baaŋ-pqoun tae bəy neëq tee.
pliəŋ tleëq tŋay-rəsiəl.	pliəŋ tleëq tae tŋay-rəsiəl tee.
kñom tɨw baan mədaaŋ.	kñom tɨw baan tae mədaaŋ tee.

3-B. Transformation Drill

Repeat the above drill, substituting ponnoh for tee in the transform.

Model: Teacher	Student
nɨw nih miən bəy rədəw.	nɨw nih miən tae bəy rədəw ponnoh.

4. The Word pɨñ

The word pɨñ is basically a verb meaning 'to be full', as in kaew pɨñ haəy. 'The glass is full.'. However, it also frequently occurs with a prepositional function meaning 'filling, throughout, to the extent of', as in:

pii-msəl-məñ, pliəŋ pɨñ mə-tŋay.	Yesterday, it rained all day (throughout one day).
qəwpuk kñom baan twəə-srae pɨñ muəy ciwɨt.	My father was a farmer all his life (throughout one life).

4-A. Substitution Drill

Teacher	Student
kñom trəw twəə-kaa pɨñ muəy tŋay.	kñom trəw twəə-kaa pɨñ muəy tŋay.
bəy khae.	kñom trəw twəə-kaa pɨñ bəy khae.
pram cnam.	kñom trəw twəə-kaa pɨñ pram cnam.
prambəy maoŋ.	kñom trəw twəə-kaa pɨñ prambəy maoŋ.
muəy ciwɨt.	kñom trəw twəə-kaa pɨñ muəy ciwɨt.
pii tŋay.	kñom trəw twəə-kaa pɨñ pii tŋay.
muəy maoŋ.	kñom trəw twəə-kaa pɨñ muəy maoŋ.
muəy cnam.	kñom trəw twəə-kaa pɨñ muəy cnam.

5. taŋ-pii . . . rəhout dal

The construction pii . . . tɨw 'from . . . to' may be used in stating the limits of an interval of time or space, as in:

pii khae-minaa tɨw khae-quhsəphiə   from March to May
pii pnum-pɨñ tɨw qəŋkɔɔ-woŏt   from Phnom Penh to Angkor Wat

However, when one wishes to emphasize the inclusiveness or continuity of the interval involved, the expression taŋ-pii . . . rəhout dɑl 'starting from . . . all the way to' is used, as in:

rədəw-pliəŋ kɨɨ taŋ-pii khae-   The rainy season is (lasts) from
mithonaa rəhout dɑl khae-tolaa.   June all the way to October.

5-A. Multiple Substitution Drill

Teacher	Student
kñom twəə-kaa pii khae-mithonaa tɨw khae-tolaa.	kñom twəə-kaa pii khae-mithonaa tɨw khae-tolaa.
(khae-wɨccəkaa . . . khae-kumpheəq)	kñom twəə-kaa pii khae-wɨccəkaa tɨw khae-kumpheəq.
(maoŋ prambəy . . . maoŋ pram)	kñom twəə-kaa pii maoŋ prambəy tɨw maoŋ pram.
(tŋay-trɑŋ . . . yup)	kñom twəə-kaa pii tŋay-trɑŋ tɨw yup.
(tŋay-nih . . . sqaek)	kñom twəə-kaa pii tŋay-nih tɨw sqaek.
(khae-minaa . . . khae-quhsəphiə)	kñom twəə-kaa pii khae-minaa tɨw khae-quhsəphiə.

5-B. Substitution Drill

Repeat the above drill, using taŋ-pii . . . rəhout dɑl instead of pii . . . tɨw.

Model: Teacher	Student
kñom twəə-kaa taŋ-pii khae-mithonaa rəhout dɑl khae-tolaa.	kñom twəə-kaa taŋ-pii khae-mithonaa rəhout dɑl khae-tolaa.
(khae-wɨccəkaa . . . khae-kumpheəq)	kñom twəə-kaa taŋ-pii khae-wɨccəkaa rəhout dɑl khae-kumpheəq.
[Etc.]	

6. douc 'like, as'

In the construction mɨn + adjectival verb + douc, the word douc functions as a comparative preposition, and the construction means 'not as V as', e.g.:

mɨn rəŋiə douc srok-qaamerɨc tee.   [It's] not as cold as America.

6-A. Substitution Drill

Teacher	Student
tŋay-nih mɨn rəŋiə douc msəl-məñ tee.	tŋay-nih mɨn rəŋiə douc msəl-məñ tee.
kdaw	tŋay-nih mɨn kdaw douc msəl-məñ tee.
trəceəq	tŋay-nih mɨn trəceəq douc msəl-məñ tee.
lqɑɑ	tŋay-nih mɨn lqɑɑ douc msəl-məñ tee.
sruəl	tŋay-nih mɨn sruəl douc msəl-mɨñ tee.

Teacher	Student
krouc nih mɨn <u>thom</u> douc krouc nuh tee.	krouc nih mɨn <u>thom</u> douc krouc nuh tee.
<u>tlay</u>	krouc nih mɨn <u>tlay</u> douc krouc nuh tee.
<u>lɡɑɑ</u>	krouc nih mɨn <u>lɡɑɑ</u> douc krouc nuh tee.
srok-kmae mɨn <u>thom</u> douc srok-baraŋ tee.	srok-kmae mɨn <u>thom</u> douc srok-baraŋ tee.
<u>trəceə̆q</u>	srok-kmae mɨn <u>trəceə̆q</u> douc srok-baraŋ tee.

7. The Preverbal Auxiliary <u>kroə̆n-tae</u>

<u>kroə̆n-tae</u> is a preverbal auxiliary which belongs to the same word class as <u>kɑmpuŋ-tae</u> 'in the process of' (Lesson 6, B, 3). It means 'only, just, just enough to', and is frequently coupled with a final limiting element <u>tee</u> or <u>ponnoh</u> 'that's all'. It has been encountered in the following sentences:

kñom <u>kroə̆n-tae</u> mɔɔk daə-leeŋ tee.	I just came for the fun of it.
<u>kroə̆n-tae</u> trəceə̆q lmɔɔm <u>ponnoh</u>.	[It's] just pleasantly cool, that's all.

7-A. Transformation Drill

Teacher	Student
kñom daə-leeŋ.	kñom <u>kroə̆n-tae</u> daə-leeŋ <u>tee</u>.
kñom mɔɔk məəl.	kñom <u>kroə̆n-tae</u> mɔɔk məəl <u>tee</u>.
kñom mɔɔk rɔɔk puəq-maaq.	kñom <u>kroə̆n-tae</u> mɔɔk rɔɔk puəq-maaq <u>tee</u>.
kñom mɔɔk məəl kon.	kñom <u>kroə̆n-tae</u> mɔɔk məəl kon <u>tee</u>.
kñom yɔɔk kafei.	kñom <u>kroə̆n-tae</u> yɔɔk kafei <u>tee</u>.
kñom niyiəy ləəŋ.	kñom <u>kroə̆n-tae</u> niyiəy leeŋ <u>tee</u>.
kñom ñam baay.	kñom <u>kroə̆n-tae</u> ñam baay <u>tee</u>.

7-B. Transformation Drill

Repeat the above drill, substituting <u>ponnoh</u> for <u>tee</u> in the transform.

Model: Teacher	Student
kñom daə-leeŋ.	kñom <u>kroə̆n-tae</u> daə-leeŋ <u>ponnoh</u>.
kñom mɔɔk məəl.	kñom <u>kroə̆n-tae</u> mɔɔk məəl <u>ponnoh</u>.

8. The Meaning of <u>dae</u>

In Lesson 4, B, 7, it was pointed out that the final particle <u>dae</u> means 'also, as well', as opposed to <u>phɑɑŋ</u> 'too, in addition', as in:

kñom kɑɑ trəw tɨw twəə-kaa <u>dae</u>.	I have to go to work <u>too</u> (as well as you).

In many sentences, <u>dae</u> also has the meaning 'too, nevertheless, contrary to what has been suggested', as in:

mɨn rəŋiə douc srok-qaamerɨc tee, tae yup klah rəŋiə bəntɔc <u>dae</u>.	It's not as cold as America, but some nights <u>are</u> rather cold (nevertheless).
neə̆q-baək-taqsii kɑɑ rɔɔk praq krup-kroə̆n <u>dae</u>.	<u>Even</u> a taxi-driver can earn enough money (contrary to what one might think).

It would seem, from the standpoint of English, that dae must have "two meanings", but in fact it is probably a case of a Cambodian word which has no exact semantic equivalent in English, as is the case with haəy described in Lesson 2, B, 9.

9. Adverbials

In Cambodian, sentences are frequently preceded by adverbial elements which "set the stage" for the sentence with regard to mode, time, or place. These elements are typically set off from the rest of the sentence by a rising intonation (indicated by a comma in the transcription). Such elements may be single words, compounds, or phrases, and are collectively referred to as adverbials.

Examples:

qəñcəŋ, daə tɨw wɨñ ciə-muəy kniə.	Then [let's] walk back together.
nɨw nih, miən tae bəy rədəw tee.	Here there are only three seasons.
taam thoămmədaa, pliəŋ roăl-tŋay.	Usually it rains every day.

Alternatively, some adverbials may either follow the topic, as in:

qəwpuk kñom, kaal-mun twəə ciəŋ-chəə.	My father formerly was a carpenter.

or else come at the end of the sentence, as in:

baaŋ-proh kñom kəmpuŋ-tae riən wɨcciə-pɛɛt sap-tŋay-nih.	My older brother is studying medicine at present.

Adverbials typically occur in initial position; the effect of placing the adverbial at the end of the sentence is reduced emphasis of the adverbial element, e.g.:

tŋay-nih, kñom trəw tɨw psaa.	Today, I have to go to the market.
kñom trəw tɨw psaa tŋay-nih.	I have to go to the market today.

In the first example above, the primary emphasis is on 'Today'; in the second it is on 'going to the market'.

Some adverbials encountered so far are:

qəñcəŋ	then, therefore	cuən-kaal	sometimes
thoămmədaa	usually	nɨw nih	here
qae-nih	here	nɨw srok-qaamerɨc	in America
qae-nuh	there	tŋay-traŋ	at noon
tŋay-nih	today	bəntəc-tiət	soon
sqaek	tomorrow	kaal-mun	formerly
pii-msəl-məñ	yesterday	sap-tŋay-nih	at present
qəyləw-nih	now	taam-thoămmədaa	usually

9-A. Progressive Substitution Drill

Teacher	Student
tŋay-nih, tɨw naa mɔɔk naa pibaaq nah.	tŋay-nih, tɨw naa mɔɔk naa pibaaq nah.
thoămmədaa,	thoămmədaa, tɨw naa mɔɔk naa pibaaq nah.
nɨw srok-qaamerɨc,	nɨw srok-qaamerɨc, tɨw naa mɔɔk naa pibaaq nah.
tŋay-traŋ,	tŋay-traŋ, tɨw naa mɔɔk naa pibaaq nah.

Teacher	Student
nɨw psaa nih,	nɨw psaa nih, tɨw naa mɔɔk naa pibaaq nah.
cuən-kaal,	cuən-kaal, tɨw naa mɔɔk naa pibaaq nah.
pliəŋ tleə̆q klaŋ nah.	cuən-kaal, pliəŋ tleə̆q klaŋ nah.
bəntəc-tiət,	bəntəc-tiət, pliəŋ tleə̆q klaŋ nah.
tŋay-rəsiəl,	tŋay-rəsiəl, pliəŋ tleə̆q klaŋ nah.
qəyləw-nih,	qəyləw-nih, pliəŋ tleə̆q klaŋ nah.

9-B. Transformation Drill

Teacher	Student
kaal-mun, qəwpuk kñom twəə ciəŋ-chəə.	qəwpuk kñom, kaal-mun, twəə ciəŋ-chəə.
qəyləw-nih, qəwpuk kñom twəə ciəŋ-chəə.	qəwpuk kñom, qəyləw-nih, twəə ciəŋ-chəə.
thoə̆mmedaa, qəwpuk kñom twəə ciəŋ-chəə.	qəwpuk kñom, thoə̆mmedaa, twəə ciəŋ-chəə.
cuən-kaal, qəwpuk kñom twəə ciəŋ-chəə.	qəwpuk kñom, cuən-kaal, twəə ciəŋ-chəə.
tŋay-nih, qəwpuk kñom twəə ciəŋ-chəə.	qəwpuk kñom, tŋay-nih, twəə ciəŋ-chəə.
sɑp-tŋay-nih, qəwpuk kñom twəə ciəŋ-chəə.	qəwpuk kñom, sɑp-tŋay-nih, twəə ciəŋ-chəə.

9-C. Transformation Drill

Teacher	Student
thoə̆mmedaa, ceñcəm ciwɨt pibaaq nah.	cəñcəm ciwɨt pibaaq nah, thoə̆mmedaa.
sɑp-tŋay-nih, cəñcəm ciwɨt pibaaq nah.	cəñcəm ciwɨt pibaaq nah, sɑp-tŋay-nih.
qae-nih, cəñcəm ciwɨt pibaaq nah.	cəñcəm ciwɨt pibaaq nah, qae-nih.
nɨw srok-baraŋ, cəñcəm ciwɨt pibaaq nah.	cəñcəm ciwɨt pibaaq nah, nɨw srok-baraŋ.
qəñcəŋ, cəñcəm ciwɨt pibaaq nah.	cəñcəm ciwɨt pibaaq nah, qəñcəŋ.
kaal-mun, cəñcəm ciwɨt pibaaq nah.	cəñcəm ciwɨt pibaaq nah, kaal-mun.

10. mɔɔk as a Preverbal Auxiliary

The word mɔɔk 'to come' has occurred frequently as a primary verb in the preceding lessons, e.g.:

kñom mɔɔk pii-msəl-məñ.   I came yesterday.

mɔɔk has also occurred as a directional verb (Lesson 4, B, 10) with the meaning 'orientation of action toward the speaker', as in:

kñom som barəy muəy mɔɔk.   Could I have a cigarette?

mɔɔk also occurs as a member of the class of preverbal auxiliaries, to which soum 'please' belongs (see Lesson 3, B, 2), with the hortatory or mildly imperative meaning 'come on and . . . ', e.g.:

mɔɔk tɨw ñam baay nɨw haaŋ   Let's (come and) have something to
nuh sən.   eat in that shop.

10-A. Substitution Drill

Teacher	Student
mɔɔk tɨw ñam baay məplɛɛt sən.	mɔɔk tɨw ñam baay məplɛɛt sən.
daə-leeŋ	mɔɔk tɨw daə-leeŋ məplɛɛt sən.
tɨñ rəbah	mɔɔk tɨw tɨñ rəbah məplɛɛt sən.
məəl kon	mɔɔk tɨw məəl kon məplɛɛt sən.
twəə-kaa	mɔɔk tɨw twəə-kaa məplɛɛt sən.
qəŋkuy ləəŋ	mɔɔk tɨw qəŋkuy ləəŋ məplɛɛt sən.
ñam kafei	mɔɔk tɨw ñam kafei məplɛɛt sən.
məəl siəwphɨw	mɔɔk tɨw məəl siəwphɨw məplɛɛt sən.

11. taɑ tɨw tiət

The adverbial phrase taɑ tɨw tiət (or simply tɨw tiət) frequently occurs after active verbs, with the meaning 'continuing the action of the verb, on, further', as in:

mɔɔk daə taɑ tɨw tiət.	Let's walk on (let's continue walking).
ruəc kee twəə-kaa taɑ tɨw tiət.	Then they continued working.

11-A. Substitution Drill

Teacher	Student
ruəc kee daə taɑ tɨw tiət.	ruəc kee daə taɑ tɨw tiət.
niyiəy	ruəc kee niyiəy taɑ tɨw tiət.
ñam baay	ruəc kee ñam baay taɑ tɨw tiət.
twəə-kaa	ruəc kee twəə-kaa taɑ tɨw tiət.
daə-leeŋ	ruəc kee daə-leeŋ taɑ tɨw tiət.
riən	ruəc kee riən taɑ tɨw tiət.
məəl siəwphɨw	ruəc kee məəl siəwphɨw taɑ tɨw tiət.

12. Interrogative Adjectives

The words ponmaan 'how much, how many?', qwəy (sqəy, qəy) 'what?', and naa 'where?' have been met as interrogative pronouns, in which case they substitute for nouns, e.g.:

look trəw-kaa ponmaan?	How many (how much) do you want?
look trəw-kaa qwəy?	What do you want?
look tɨw naa?	Where are you going?

They also occur, however, as interrogative modifiers of nouns, in which case they function like interrogative adjectives, e.g.:

look trəw-kaa kawqəy ponmaan?	How many chairs do you need?
look bəŋriən wɨcciə qwəy?	What subject do you teach?
look mɔɔk pii srok naa?	Which (what) country do you come from?

ponmaan differs from qwəy and naa in that it precedes specifiers, such as tŋay, neəq, and daəm, while qwəy and naa always follow. In this respect it functions exactly like a numeral; thus we might call ponmaan a "pronumeral"; e.g.:

	look kɨt tɨw tŋay naa?	When (which day) do you plan to go?
	tŋay-nih kɨɨ tŋay qwəy?	What day is today?
But:	look mɔɔk ponmaan tŋay haəy?	How many days have you been here?

12-A. Substitution Drill

Teacher	Student
look kɨt tɨw <u>tŋay</u> naa?	look kɨt tɨw <u>tŋay</u> naa?
<u>khae</u>	look kɨt tɨw <u>khae</u> naa?
<u>cnam</u>	look kɨt tɨw <u>cnam</u> naa?
<u>kənlaəŋ</u>	look kɨt tɨw <u>kənlaeŋ</u> naa?
<u>srok</u>	look kɨt tɨw <u>srok</u> naa?

12-B. Substitution Drill

Teacher		Student
<u>tŋay</u> nih kɨɨ <u>tŋay</u> qəy?		<u>tŋay</u> nih kɨɨ <u>tŋay</u> qəy?
<u>khae</u>	<u>khae</u>	<u>khae</u> nih kɨɨ <u>khae</u> qəy?
<u>rədəw</u>	<u>rədəw</u>	<u>rədəw</u> nih kɨɨ <u>rədəw</u> qəy?
<u>srok</u>	<u>srok</u>	<u>srok</u> nih kɨɨ <u>srok</u> qəy?
<u>rooŋ</u>	<u>rooŋ</u>	<u>rooŋ</u> nih kɨɨ <u>rooŋ</u> qəy?

12-C. Substitution Drill

Teacher	Student
look trəw-kaa <u>barəy</u> ponmaan?	look trəw-kaa <u>barəy</u> ponmaan?
<u>kawqəy</u>	look trəw-kaa <u>kawqəy</u> ponmaan?
<u>siəwphɨw</u>	look trəw-kaa <u>siəwphɨw</u> ponmaan?
<u>ceik</u>	look trəw-kaa <u>ceik</u> ponmaan?
<u>krouc</u>	look trəw-kaa <u>krouc</u> ponmaan?
<u>kmaw-day</u>	look trəw-kaa <u>kmaw-day</u> ponmaan?

12-D. Substitution Drill

Teacher	Student
look trəw-kaa <u>kmaw-day</u> ponmaan daəm?	look trəw-kaa <u>kmaw-day</u> ponmaan daəm?
<u>dəy-saɑ</u>	look trəw-kaa <u>dəy-saɑ</u> ponmaan daəm?
<u>chəə-kuh</u>	look trəw-kaa <u>chəə-kuh</u> ponmaan daəm?
<u>barəy</u>	look trəw-kaa <u>barəy</u> ponmaan daəm?
look trəw-kaa <u>barəy</u> ponmaan <u>kəñcɑp</u>?	look trəw-kaa <u>barəy</u> ponmaan <u>kəñcɑp</u>?
<u>tae</u>	look trəw-kaa <u>tae</u> ponmaan kəñcɑp?
<u>skɑɑ</u>	look trəw-kaa <u>skɑɑ</u> ponmaan kəñcɑp?
<u>kafei</u>	look trəw-kaa <u>kafei</u> ponmaan kəñcɑp?

13. The Superlative <u>ciəŋ-kee</u>

In Lesson 8 the word <u>ciəŋ</u> occurred as a comparative adverb with the meaning 'more', e.g.:

kñom kɨt thaa twəə kruu-pɛɛt <u>lqɑɑ ciəŋ</u>.	I think it would be better to be a doctor.

<u>ciəŋ-kee</u> is the superlative adverb meaning 'most, most of all', as in:

kñom coul-cət rədəw-rəŋiə <u>ciəŋ-kee</u>.	I like the cold season <u>the most</u> (of all).
look coul-cət rədəw naa <u>ciəŋ-kee</u>?	What season do you like <u>best</u> (of all)?

13-A. Transformation Drill

Teacher	Student
kñom coul-cət rədəw-rəɲiə ciəɲ.	kñom coul-cət rədəw-rəɲiə ciəɲ-kee.
twəə kruu-pɛɛt lqɑɑ ciəɲ.	twəə kruu-pɛɛt lqɑɑ ciəɲ-kee.
kñom coul-cət ptĕəh nih ciəɲ.	kñom coul-cət ptĕəh nih ciəɲ-kee.
kñom coul-cət kon nih ciəɲ.	kñom coul-cət kon nih ciəɲ-kee.
krouc nih thom ciəɲ.	krouc nih thom ciəɲ-kee.
khae-meesaa kdaw ciəɲ.	khae-meesaa kdaw ciəɲ-kee.
srəy nuh lqɑɑ ciəɲ.	srəy nuh lqɑɑ ciəɲ-kee.
ceik muəy snət nih tum ciəɲ.	ceik muəy snət nih tum ciəɲ-kee.
qae-nuh miən mənuh craən ciəɲ.	qae-nuh miən mənuh craən ciəɲ-kee.
psaa nih thom ciəɲ.	psaa nih thom ciəɲ-kee.
laan nih tlay ciəɲ.	laan nih tlay ciəɲ-kee.
phiəsaa-cən pibaaq ciəɲ.	phiəsaa-cən pibaaq ciəɲ-kee.

[Tape 17]   C. COMPREHENSION

1. Going Out

sok: sɨm tɨw naa?

sɨm: baat, kñom tɨw məəl kon.

sok: yɔɔk chat tɨw; cɨt pliəɲ haəy.

sɨm: kñom kmiən chat tee; miən tae qaaw-pliəɲ.

sok: qəñcəɲ yɔɔk chat kñom tɨw.
          baə pliəɲ klaɲ, chat sruəl ciəɲ qaaw-pliəɲ.

sɨm: baat, nɨŋ haəy.

2. Discussing Seasons

sok: sɨm qaəɲ coul-cət rədəw naa ciəɲ-kee?

sɨm: kñom coul-cət rədəw-rəɲiə ciəɲ-kee.
          mɨn trəcĕəq, mɨn kdaw; sruəl lmɔɔm.
          coh, sok qaeɲ wɨñ?

sok: kñom coul-cət rədəw-pliəɲ.

sɨm: kñom mɨn coul-cət rədəw-pliəɲ tee; tɨw naa mɔɔk naa pibaaq nah.

sok: nɨŋ haəy, tae mɨn pliəɲ rŏəl-tɲay tee.
          thŏəmmedaa pliəɲ tae tɲay-rəsiəl tee.
          tae kñom mɨn coul-cət rədəw-kdaw sah.

sɨm: kñom kɑɑ mɨn coul-cət dae.
          yup klah kdaw peek; keeɲ mɨn luĕəq sah.

3. Discussing a Trip

          [srok-srae 'the country']
sok: baə sqaek mɨn pliəɲ, kñom tɨw leeɲ srok-srae.

sɨm: tɨw ciə-muəy nĕəq-naa?

sok: tɨw ciə-muəy bɑɑŋ-proh kñom.
        kñom miən puəq-maaq məneə̆q dael ciə neə̆q-twəə-srae.

        [tɨw taam 'to go by means of']
sɨm: sok kɨt tɨw taam qwəy?

sok: kñom nɨŋ baək laan kñom tɨw.
        sɨm qaeŋ cɑŋ tɨw ciə-muəy kñom tee?

sɨm: baə mɨn pliəŋ, kñom tɨw.
        qəyləw-nih khae-mithonaa haəy; bəntɑc-tiət muk-tae miən pliəŋ
        craən haəy.

4. The Weather in America

chɨn: look tɨw srok-qaamerɨc qəŋkal?

cuən: baat, kñom tɨw khae-kaññaa nih.

chɨn: look nɨŋ trəlɑp mɔɔk wɨñ qəŋkal?

suən: kñom nɨŋ trəlɑp mɔɔk wɨñ nɨw khae-meə̆qkəraa.

chɨn: nɨw srok-qaamerɨc, rədəw-rəŋiə trəceə̆q nah,
        haəy miən tɨk-kɑɑq phɑɑŋ.

suən: nɨŋ haəy, trəceə̆q nah.
        peel kñom tɨw dɑl, kñom nɨŋ tɨñ qaaw-rəŋiə.

D. CONVERSATION

1. Caught in the Rain

a) A exclaims that it is really raining hard.
b) B suggests that they take shelter under that tree, and says that it will
   probably quit soon.
c) A says that he forgot to bring an umbrella, and that he got all wet.
d) B says that he forgot to bring an umbrella too, then says that if he hadn't
   had a raincoat, he'd have gotten wet too.
e) A says he doesn't like the rainy season at all, [because] it's difficult to
   go anywhere.
f) B says he doesn't like the rainy season either.
g) A says that the rain has almost stopped, and suggests that they continue
   walking.

2. Discussing the Rainy Season

a) A asks B what month this is.
b) B replies that it is June, and says that soon there will likely be a lot of
   rain.
c) A asks B how many months there are in the rainy season.
d) B answers that there are five months, all the way from June to October.
e) A asks if it rains every day during the rainy season.
f) B replies that it usually rains every day.
g) A asks if it usually rains all day.
h) B answers that it sometimes rains every day, but that usually it rains
   only in the afternoon.

3. Discussing the Cold Season

   a) A asks B what season he likes best.
   b) B replies that he likes the cold season best.
   c) A asks B if the cold season is very cold.
   d) B replies that it isn't as cold as in America, but that some nights are rather cold, nevertheless.
   e) A asks if there is any snow during the cold season.
   f) B replies that there isn't; there is only a wind blowing from the north.
   g) A asks what month is the coldest.
   h) B replies that usually January is the coldest.

4. Seasons in General

   a) A asks B if it is right that there are only three seasons in Cambodia.
   b) B says that is right; there are only a rainy season, a cold season, and a hot season.
   c) A asks B how many months there are in the hot season.
   d) B replies that there are only three months in the hot season —from March to May.
   e) A asks B which month is the hottest.
   f) B replies that April is usually the hottest, and says that if you're not used to it, some nights you can't sleep.
   g) A asks B how many months there are in the cold season.
   h) B replies that there are four months in the cold season—from November to February.

LESSON 10. GETTING A ROOM AT A HOTEL

A. DIALOGUE

thɨm

1. som-tooh, look; miən pteə̆h-səmnaq nɨw cɨt nih tee?

Excuse me, sir; is there a hotel near here?

Stranger

pləw	street, way, road
preə̆h-baat	title for a king
mɔniiwuə̆ŋ	name of a former Cambodian king
preə̆h-baat mɔniiwuə̆ŋ	King Monivong
pləw preə̆h-baat mɔniiwuə̆ŋ	Preah-Bath Monivong Street

2. baat, look daə tɨw taam pləw preə̆h-baat mɔniiwuə̆ŋ nih.

Yes, walk along Preah-Bath Monivong Street here.

santhaakiə (santhəkiə)	hotel
mɔnoorum (mənoorum)	name of a hotel
santhəkiə-mənoorum	the Monorom Hotel

3. look nɨŋ khəəñ santhəkiə-mənoorum nɨw khaŋ-sdam-day.

You'll see the Monorom Hotel on the right-hand side.

claɑŋ	to cross; across
tnɑl	a paved road, street
sokkhaalay (sokkhəlay)	name of a hotel
santhəkiə-sokkhaalay	the Sukkhalay Hotel

4. baə look claɑŋ tnɑl, nɨŋ khəəñ santhəkiə muəy tiət, cmuə̆h santhəkiə-sokkhaalay.

If you cross the street, you'll see another hotel, the Sukkhalay Hotel.

cuən

thaok	cheap, inexpensive

5. santhəkiə teə̆ŋ-pii nuh, taə, santhəkiə naa tlay thaok ciəŋ?

Tell me, [of] those two hotels, which is the cheaper?

prɑhael (prəhael, pəhael)	to be similar
prəhael-prəhael kniə	similar, approximately the same

6. santhəkiə teə̆ŋ-pii nuh tlay prəhael-prəhael kniə.

Those two hotels are about equally expensive (cost about the same).

cuən

7. soum qɑɑ-kun.

Thank you.

[At the Hotel]

sqaat	to be clean, attractive, neat

8. santhəkiə nih sqaat lqɑɑ nah.

This hotel is quite clean.

132

thɨm
familiar response particle

qaə
9. qaə, sqaat mɛɛn.
Yes, it really is (clean).

[To the Clerk]

bəntup (bəntup, kətup)
room
10. miən bəntup tumnee tee?
Do [you] have any vacant rooms?

Clerk

11. baat, miən.
Yes, [we] have.

krɛɛ
bed
12. look trəw-kaa bəntup dael miən
krɛɛ muəy rɨɨ krɛɛ pii?
Do you want a single room or a double room?

bəntup-tɨk
cuən
bathroom
13. yəəŋ caŋ baan bəntup dael miən
krɛɛ pii haəy-nɨŋ bəntup-tɨk
phɑɑŋ.
We want a double room, and with a bathroom too.

Clerk

pisaa
to eat (polite)
14. look pisaa baay nɨw nih rɨɨ?
Will you take your meals here?

thɨm

prɨk
morning
baay prɨk
breakfast, morning meal
15. yɔɔk tae baay prɨk tee.
We'll need breakfast only.

Clerk

teˇəŋ
including
16. baat, mə-tŋay tlay mərɔɔy riəl
kɨt teˇəŋ baay prɨk phɑɑŋ.
It's one hundred riels a day, including breakfast (with breakfast figured in).

qaatɨt (qatɨt)
week; sun
coh
to lower; go down, descend
cuun
for [you], on your behalf (formal)
17. baə look nɨw muəy qatɨt, kñom
nɨŋ coh tlay cuun.
If you stay a week, I'll lower the price [for you].

mɨn-bac tee
[it's] not necessary
tŋay-prɑhoˇəh (prəhoˇəh,
pəhoˇəh)
Thursday
18. mɨn-bac tee; yəəŋ trəw cəñ
tŋay-prɑhoˇəh.
[That's] not necessary; we have to leave on Thursday.

Clerk

tŋay-can
Monday
19. tŋay-nih kɨɨ tŋay-can.
Today is Monday.

douccneh   thus, therefore
20. douccneh look nɨw bəy tŋay,   So you'll be here three days, right?
    mɛɛn tee?

suən

21. nɨŋ haəy.   That's right.

22. yəəŋ tɨw məəl bəntup sən baan tee?   Can we see the room first?

Clerk

23. soum qəñcəəñ.   Please go ahead.

baoy   boy, waiter
noə̆m   to lead, take, guide
leik   number, figure
24. baoy, noə̆m look tɨw məəl bəntup   Boy, take these gentlemen to see
    leik pii-rɔɔy dɑp-pii.   room number two hundred twelve.

Boy

khaaŋ-nih (khaŋ-nih)   this way
25. qəñcəəñ mɔɔk khaŋ-nih.   Please come this way.

tuliəy   to be spacious, roomy
baŋquəc (bəŋquəc, pəŋquəc)   window
26. bəntup nih tuliəy lqɑɑ, haəy miən   This room is quite spacious, and has
    bəŋquəc pii phɑɑŋ.   two windows too.

cruŋ   corner
27. bəntup-tɨk nɨw cruŋ nih.   The bathroom is in this corner.

thɨm

twiə   door
qaoy   for, on behalf of (familiar)
phɑɑŋ   please, will you
28. baək twiə qaoy kñom phɑɑŋ.   Open the door for me, will you?

məc   how?; how about it?
sok-cət   to agree (to), be willing (to)
29. məc, cuən; sok-cət yɔɔk bəntup   How about it, Chuen; shall we take
    nih tee?   this room?

cuən

miən qəy?   yes, of course, why not?
30. miən qəy?   Sure, why not?

khaaŋ-kraom (khaŋ-kraom)   below, downstairs
31. mɔɔk coh tɨw khaŋ-kraom sən.   Come on, let's go downstairs.

Boy

dɑq   to put, place, deposit
knoŋ   in, inside
32. kñom nɨŋ yɔɔk qəywan look tɨw dɑq   I'll take your things and put them
    knoŋ bəntup.   in the room.

cuən

pñeə̆q   to wake up (intr.)
prɔlɨm (prəlɨm, pəlɨm)   dawn
pii prəlɨm   at dawn, early
33. sqaek yəəŋ trəw pñeə̆q pii prəlɨm.   We have to wake up early tomorrow.

dah   to awaken (tr.)
34. dah yəəŋ maoŋ prampɨl phɑɑŋ   Could you call us at seven o'clock?
baan tee?

Boy

35. baat, miən qəy?   Yes, of course.

The Days of the Week

[Those days not yet introduced are preceded by an asterisk.]

tŋay-qaatɨt (-qatɨt)   Sunday
tŋay-can   Monday
*tŋay-qaŋkiə (-qəŋkiə, -ŋkiə)   Tuesday
*tŋay-put   Wednesday
tŋay-prɑhoə̆h (-prəhoə̆h, -pəhoə̆h)   Thursday
*tŋay-sok   Friday
*tŋay-saw   Saturday

B. GRAMMAR AND DRILLS

1. Seeking an Indefinite Place or Object

In Lesson 2 we met the pattern _____ nɨw qae-naa? 'Where is the _____?', in which the interrogator is seeking a definite place or object, as in:

psaa nɨw qae-naa?   'Where's the market?'

In the construction miən_____ nɨw qae-naa?, on the other hand, the place or object sought is indefinite: 'Where is there a _____?', as in:

miən pteə̆h-səmnaq nɨw cɨt nih tee?   Is there a hotel near here?

1-A. Substitution Drill

Teacher	Student
miən psaa nɨw cɨt nih tee?	miən psaa nɨw cɨt nih tee?
sɑnthəkiə	miən sɑnthəkiə nɨw cɨt nih tee?
salaa-riən	miən salaa-riən nɨw cɨt nih tee?
pteə̆h-səmnaq	miən pteə̆h-səmnaq nɨw cɨt nih tee?
siəwphɨw	miən siəwphɨw nɨw cɨt nih tee?
taqsii	miən taqsii nɨw cɨt nih tee?
phoocəniiyəthaan	miən phoocəniiyəthaan nɨw cɨt nih tee?
pteə̆h-luə̆q-kafei	miən pteə̆h-luə̆q-kafei nɨw cɨt nih tee?

2. prəhael-prəhael kniə

When the adverbial phrase prəhael-prəhael kniə follows an adjectival verb, such as lqɑɑ, thom, tlay, etc., it has the meaning 'about equally ___V___':

santhəkiə te͗əŋ-pii nuh tlay   Those two hotels are about equally
prəhael-prəhael kniə.   expensive.

2-A. Substitution Drill

Teacher	Student
bəntup te͗əŋ-pii nuh tlay prəhael-prəhael kniə.	bəntup te͗əŋ-pii nuh tlay prəhael-prəhael kniə.
thom	bəntup te͗əŋ-pii nuh thom prəhael-prəhael kniə.
lqɑɑ	bəntup te͗əŋ-pii nuh lqɑɑ prəhael-prəhael kniə.
thaok	bəntup te͗əŋ-pii nuh thaok prəhael-prəhael kniə.
touc	bəntup te͗əŋ-pii nuh touc prəhael-prəhael kniə.
sqaat	bəntup te͗əŋ-pii nuh sqaat prəhael-prəhael kniə.

2-B. Response Drill

Teacher	Student
santhəkiə te͗əŋ-pii nuh, taə, santhəkiə naa tlay ciəŋ?	santhəkiə te͗əŋ-pii nuh tlay prəhael-prəhael kniə.
pte͗əh te͗əŋ-pii nuh, taə, pte͗əh naa thom ciəŋ?	pte͗əh te͗əŋ-pii nuh thom prəhael-prəhael kniə.
ceik te͗əŋ-pii nuh, taə, ceik naa tum ciəŋ?	ceik te͗əŋ-pii nuh tum prəhael-prəhael kniə.
tok te͗əŋ-pii nuh, taə, tok naa touc ciəŋ?	tok te͗əŋ-pii nuh touc prəhael-prəhael kniə.
pte͗əh-səmnaq te͗əŋ-pii nuh, taə, pte͗əh-səmnaq naa sqaat ciəŋ?	pte͗əh-səmnaq te͗əŋ-pii nuh sqaat prəhael-prəhael kniə.
bəntup te͗əŋ-pii nuh, taə, bəntup naa thaok ciəŋ?	bəntup te͗əŋ-pii nuh thaok prəhael-prəhael kniə.
srəy te͗əŋ-pii ne͗əq nuh, taə, ne͗əq-naa lqɑɑ ciəŋ.	srəy te͗əŋ-pii ne͗əq nuh lqɑɑ prəhael-prəhael kniə.

3. The Final Particle sən

We have met the final particle sən as a polite imperative, as in:

mɔɔk tɨw ñam baay nɨw haaŋ nuh   Let's go get something to eat in
məplɛɛt sən.   that shop for a while, shall we?

sən also carries the implication 'first, now, before doing anything else', as in:

yəəŋ tɨw məəl bəntup <u>sən</u>, baan tee?   We'll go see the room <u>first</u>, O.K.?

This is not a "different meaning," but part of the total meaning of sen. In Drill A below, the primary function of sən is polite exhortation or persuasion, and is best translated something like 'come on and . . .', while in Drill B, the meaning 'first' is emphasized, although even here there is an element of solicitation of permission or approval.

3-A. Substitution Drill

Teacher	Student
mɔɔk tɨw <u>ñam baay</u> ciə-muəy kñom sən.	mɔɔk tɨw <u>ñam baay</u> ciə-muəy kñom sən.
<u>daə-leeŋ</u>	mɔɔk tɨw <u>daə-leeŋ</u> ciə-muəy kñom sən.
<u>məəl kon</u>	mɔɔk tɨw <u>məəl kon</u> ciə-muəy kñom sən.
<u>tɨñ qəywan</u>	mɔɔk tɨw <u>tɨñ qəywan</u> ciə-muəy kñom sən.
<u>twəə-kaa</u>	mɔɔk tɨw <u>twəə-kaa</u> ciə-muəy kñom sən.
<u>rɔɔk puəq-maaq kñom</u>	mɔɔk tɨw <u>rɔɔk puəq-maaq kñom</u> ciə-muəy kñom sən.

3-B. Substitution Drill

Teacher	Student
kñom tɨw <u>məəl bəntup</u> sən, baan tee?	kñom tɨw <u>məəl bəntup</u> sən, baan tee?
<u>tɨñ barəy</u>	kñom tɨw <u>tɨñ barəy</u> sən, baan tee?
<u>ñam baay</u>	kñom tɨw <u>ñam baay</u> sən, baan tee?
<u>daə-leeŋ</u>	kñom tɨw <u>daə-leeŋ</u> sən, baan tee?
<u>məəl kon</u>	kñom tɨw <u>məəl kon</u> sən, baan tee?
<u>twəə-kaa</u>	kñom tɨw <u>twəə-kaa</u> sən, baan tee?

4. The Response Particle qaə

qaə is a familiar response particle which belongs to the same class as <u>baat</u> and <u>caah</u> (see Lesson 2, B, 3), but is used only in conversation between intimate friends or by a superior to an inferior. Its typical function is to indicate agreement with a previous statement, as in:

sənthəkiə nih sqaat lqɑɑ nah.	This hotel is nice and clean.
qaə, sqaat mɛɛn.	Yes, it really is (clean)

Notice that in the Dialogue, cuən and thɨm use qaə in speaking with each other, but that the Clerk and the Boy use the more formal <u>baat</u> in speaking with them. Unlike <u>baat</u> and <u>caah</u>, qaə is used by both men and women. Its actual pronunciation may vary from qaə to qəə to qɨɨ in very colloquial speech, but will always be represented by qaə in this text; the student should always follow the pronunciation of the teacher.

4-A. Response Drill

Teacher	Student
sənthəkiə nih sqaat lqɑɑ nah.	qaə, sqaat mɛɛn.
bəntup nih thom lqɑɑ nah.	qaə, thom mɛɛn.
bəntup nuh tlay nah.	qaə, tlay mɛɛn.

Teacher	Student
srəy nuh lqɑɑ nah.	qaə, lqɑɑ mɛɛn.
tŋay-nih trəceəq nah.	qaə, trəceəq mɛɛn.
pɔɔŋ-moən nih touc nah.	qaə, touc mɛɛn.
phiəsaa-kmae sruəl nah.	qaə, sruəl mɛɛn.

5. Breakfast, Lunch, and Dinner

Cambodians do not usually use time-specific terms when referring to meals, preferring the general term ñam baay 'to have a meal, to eat'. When it is necessary to refer to a specific meal, baay is modified by the time of day, e.g.:

baay prɨk	morning meal, breakfast
baay tŋay-traŋ	noon meal, lunch
baay rəsiəl	afternoon meal, snack
[lŋiəc 'late afternoon, evening']	
baay lŋiəc	evening meal, dinner
baay yup	late evening meal, snack

5-A. Substitution Drill

Teacher	Student
kñom yɔɔk tae baay prɨk tee.	kñom yɔɔk tae baay prɨk tee.
baay lŋiəc	kñom yɔɔk tae baay lŋiəc tee.
baay tŋay-traŋ	kñom yɔɔk tae baay tŋay-traŋ tee.
baay rəsiəl	kñom yɔɔk tae baay rəsiəl tee.
baay yup	kñom yɔɔk tae baay yup tee.
baay prɨk	kñom yɔɔk tae baay prɨk tee.

6. Directional Verbs

Directional verbs occur after primary verbs which are non-specific as to direction or goal, and specify the direction or general orientation of the action initiated by the verb. Directional verbs occur both with and without a following object or goal. When followed by an object, such verbs are frequently best translated as prepositions in English, e.g.:

| baək twiə qaoy kñom phɑɑŋ. | Open the door for me, will you? |
| yɔɔk qəywan nih tɨw bəntup. | Take these things to the room. |

When not followed by an object, directional verbs function like adverbs:

| yɔɔk qəywan nih tɨw. | Take these things away. |
| yɔɔk qəywan nih mɔɔk taam. | Bring these things along. |

Notice that when the verb yɔɔk is followed by the directional verb tɨw, it is translated 'take', but when it is followed by mɔɔk, it is translated 'bring'.

Frequently two directional verbs occur in a sequence, as in the fourth example above, and in the example below:

| look daə tɨw taam pləw preəh-baat | Walk (away) along Preah-Bath |
| mɔniiwuəŋ nih. | Monivong Street here. |

Both cuun and qaoy as directional verbs have the meaning 'for, on behalf of, as a favor to'; cuun is the form used in formal or polite speech, while qaoy occurs in more familiar speech, e.g.:

kñom nɨŋ coh tlay <u>cuun</u> look.   I'll lower the price <u>for</u> you.
baək bəŋquəc <u>qaoy</u> kñom phaaŋ.   Open the window <u>for</u> me, will you?

Since the class of directional verbs is quite small, all its members are listed
here. Those verbs which have not yet been introduced (as directional verbs) are
preceded by an asterisk.

    1)   mɔɔk   orientation toward speaker in space
    2)   tɨw   orientation away from speaker in space
    3)   cuun   on behalf of, for (formal)
    4)   qaoy   on behalf of, for (familiar)
    5)   taam   along, following
    6)   nɨw   still, remaining at
    7) *coh   down, downward
    8) *laəŋ (ləə)   up (on), upward; (to ascend)
    9) *coul (knoŋ)   in, into; (to enter)
  10) *cəñ (pii)   out, out (of)

6-A. Substitution Drill

Teacher	Student
qaoy <u>siəwphɨw nuh</u> mɔɔk.	qaoy <u>siəwphɨw nuh</u> mɔɔk.
<u>barəy muəy</u>	qaoy <u>barəy muəy</u> mɔɔk.
<u>kawqəy nuh</u>	qaoy <u>kawqəy nuh</u> mɔɔk.
<u>kmaw-day nuh</u>	qaoy <u>kmaw-day nuh</u> mɔɔk.
<u>qəywan nuh</u>	qaoy <u>qəywan nuh</u> mɔɔk.
<u>chat nuh</u>	qaoy <u>chat nuh</u> mɔɔk.

6-B. Transformation Drill

Teacher	Student
qaoy siəwphɨw nuh mɔɔk.	qaoy siəwphɨw nuh mɔɔk kñom.
qaoy barəy muəy mɔɔk.	qaoy barəy muəy mɔɔk kñom.
qaoy kawqəy nuh mɔɔk.	qaoy kawqəy nuh mɔɔk kñom.
qaoy kmaw-day nuh mɔɔk.	qaoy kmaw-day nuh mɔɔk kñom.
qaoy qəywan nuh mɔɔk.	qaoy qəywan nuh mɔɔk kñom.

6-C. Substitution Drill

Teacher	Student
yɔɔk <u>qəywan nih</u> tɨw.	yɔɔk <u>qəywan nih</u> tɨw.
<u>siəwphɨw nih</u>	yɔɔk <u>siəwphɨw nih</u> tɨw.
<u>tok nih</u>	yɔɔk <u>tok nih</u> tɨw.
<u>kawqəy nih</u>	yɔɔk <u>kawqəy nih</u> tɨw.
<u>pɔɔŋ-moən nih</u>	yɔɔk <u>pɔɔŋ-moən nih</u> tɨw.
<u>plaə-chəə nih</u>	yɔɔk <u>plae-chəə nih</u> tɨw.

6-D. Transformation Drill

Teacher	Student
yɔɔk qəywan nih tɨw.	yɔɔk qəywan nih tɨw pteəh.
yɔɔk siəwphɨw nih tɨw.	yɔɔk siəwphɨw nih tɨw pteəh.

Teacher	Student
yɔɔk tok nih tɨw.	yɔɔk tok nih tɨw pteʼəh.
yɔɔk kawqəy nih tɨw.	yɔɔk kawqəy nih tɨw pteʼəh.
yɔɔk pɔɔŋ-moʼən nih tɨw.	yɔɔk pɔɔŋ-moʼən nih tɨw pteʼəh.

6-E. Substitution Drill

Teacher	Student
yɔɔk qəywan nuh tɨw pteʼəh.	yɔɔk qəywan nuh tɨw pteʼəh.
mɔɔk	yɔɔk qəywan nuh mɔɔk pteʼəh.
coul knoŋ	yɔɔk qəywan nuh coul knoŋ pteʼəh.
cəñ pii	yɔɔk qəywan nuh cəñ pii pteʼəh.
laəŋ ləə	yɔɔk qəywan nuh laəŋ ləə pteʼəh.
tɨw	yɔɔk qəywan nuh tɨw pteʼəh.

6-F. Substitution Drill

Teacher	Student
koʼət twəə-kaa nɨw pteʼəh.	koʼət twəə-kaa nɨw pteʼəh.
ñam baay	koʼət ñam baay nɨw pteʼəh.
keeŋ	koʼət keeŋ nɨw pteʼəh.
məəl siəwphɨw	koʼət məəl siəwphɨw nɨw pteʼəh.
cuəy mdaay	koʼət cuəy mdaay nɨw pteʼəh.

6-G. Substitution Drill

Teacher	Student
soum baək twiə qaoy kñom.	soum baək twiə qaoy kñom.
bət twiə	soum bət twiə qaoy kñom.
tɨñ barəy	soum tɨñ barəy qaoy kñom.
baək bəŋquəc	soum baək bəŋquəc qaoy kñom.
bət bəŋquəc	soum bət bəŋquəc qaoy kñom.
yɔɔk qəywan	soum yɔɔk qəywan qaoy kñom.

6-H. Transformation Drill

Teacher	Student
soum baək twiə qaoy kñom.	kñom nɨŋ baək twiə cuun look.
soum bət twiə qaoy kñom.	kñom nɨŋ bət twiə cuun look.
soum tɨñ barəy qaoy kñom.	kñom nɨŋ tɨñ barəy cuun look.
soum baək bəŋquəc qaoy kñom.	kñom nɨŋ baək bəŋquəc cuun look.
soum bət bəŋquəc qaoy kñom.	kñom nɨŋ bət bəŋquəc cuun look.
soum coh tlay qaoy kñom.	kñom nɨŋ coh tlay cuun look.

7. The Meaning of phɑɑŋ

The difference between phɑɑŋ 'too, in addition', and dae 'also, as well (but separately)', was pointed out in Lesson 4, B, 7. phɑɑŋ also frequently includes an element of mild supplication, as in:

baək twiə qaoy kñom phɑɑŋ.	Open the door for me, will you?

7-A. Substitution Drill

Teacher	Student
baək twiə qaoy kñom phaaŋ.	baək twiə qaoy kñom phaaŋ.
bət twiə	bət twiə qaoy kñom phaaŋ.
tɨñ barəy	tɨñ barəy qaoy kñom phaaŋ.
coh tlay	coh tlay qaoy kñom phaaŋ.
baək bəŋquəc	baək bəŋquəc qaoy kñom phaaŋ.
bət bəŋquəc	bət bəŋquəc qaoy kñom phaaŋ.

8. lqaa as an Adverb

It has been pointed out that when lqaa modifies an active verb, it means
'well', as in:

srəy nuh twəə-kaa lqaa.   That girl works well.

However, when lqaa modifies another adjectival verb, it has an intensifying effect,
somewhat like the English 'nice and _____, quite', as in:

santhəkiə nih sqaat lqaa nah.   This hotel is quite clean.

8-A. Progressive Substitution Drill

Teacher	Student
bəntup nih sqaat lqaa nah.	bəntup nih sqaat lqaa nah.
trəceəq	bəntup nih trəceəq lqaa nah.
tuliəy	bəntup nih tuliəy lqaa nah.
thom	bəntup nih thom lqaa nah.
psaa nih	psaa nih thom lqaa nah.
sqaat	psaa nih sqaat lqaa nah.
tuliəy	psaa nih tuliəy lqaa nah.

9. miən qəy?

miən qəy is a rather slangy expression which is used frequently in conversation between intimates and equals, or by a superior to an inferior. Its meaning is
'why not?, sure, of course'. It is a rhetorical question, and does not anticipate an
answer; it merely indicates agreement, as in:

məc cuən; sok-cət yɔɔk bəntup nih   How about it, Chuon; shall we take
    tee?   this room?
miən qəy?   Sure, why not?

9-A. Response Drill

Teacher	Student
yɔɔk bəntup nih tee?	baat, miən qəy?
kñom tɨw ciə-muəy phaaŋ baan tee?	baat, miən qəy?
mɔɔk tɨw daə-leeŋ tee?	baat, miən qəy?
mɔɔk tɨw ñam kafei tee?	baat, miən qəy?
mɔɔk tɨw məəl kon nih tee?	baat, miən qəy?
mɔɔk tɨw ñam baay nɨw haaŋ nuh tee?	baat, miən qəy?
mɔɔk tɨw rɔɔk puəq-maaq ciə-muəy knom tee?	baat, miən qəy?

10. <u>sok-cət</u>

When <u>sok-cət</u> precedes a primary verb, it functions as a modal verb (described in Lesson 5, B, 10), with the meaning 'to agree to, to be willing to, to be content to', as in:

cuən <u>sok-cət</u> yɔɔk bəntup nih tee?   Chuon, shall we take this room?
                                                 (Are you content to take this room?)

10-A. <u>Substitution Drill</u>

Teacher	Student
kñom sok-cət yɔɔk bəntup nuh.	kñom sok-cət <u>yɔɔk bəntup nuh</u>.
tɨw psaa.	kñom sok-cət <u>tɨw psaa</u>.
tɨw ciə-muəy phaaŋ.	kñom sok-cət <u>tɨw ciə-muəy dae</u>.
yɔɔk siəwphɨw nih.	kñom sok-cət <u>yɔɔk siəwphɨw nih</u>.
tɨw məəl kon.	kñom sok-cət <u>tɨw məəl kon</u>.
twəə-kaa tŋay-nih.	kñom sok-cət <u>twəə-kaa tŋay-nih</u>.

11. Days of the Week

The names of the days of the week are compounds composed of the head-word <u>tŋay</u> plus the appropriate specific proper name, as follows:

tŋay-qaatɨt (-qatɨt)	Sunday
tŋay-can	Monday
tŋay-qaŋkiə (-qəŋkiə, -ŋkiə)	Tuesday
tŋay-put	Wednesday
tŋay-prɑhŏəh (-prəhŏəh, -pəhŏəh)	Thursday
tŋay-sok	Friday
tŋay-saw	Saturday

11-A. <u>Response Drill</u>

Give the correct response, referring to the chart above.

Teacher	Student
tŋay-nih ciə tŋay-can.	douccneh sqaek ciə tŋay-qəŋkiə.
tŋay-nih ciə tŋay-qəŋkiə.	douccneh sqaek ciə tŋay-put.
tŋay-nih ciə tŋay-put.	douccneh sqaek ciə tŋay-prəhŏəh.
tŋay-nih ciə tŋay-prehŏəh.	douccneh sqaek ciə tŋay-sok.
tŋay-nih ciə tŋay-sok.	douccneh sqaek ciə tŋay-saw.
tŋay-nih ciə tŋay-saw.	douccneh sqaek ciə tŋay-qatɨt.
tŋay-nih ciə tŋay-qatɨt.	douccneh sqaek ciə tŋay-can.

11-B. <u>Response Drill</u>

Teacher	Student
baə tŋay-nih ciə tŋay-qatɨt, msəl-məñ ciə <u>tŋay qwəy</u>?	baə tŋay-nih ciə tŋay-qatɨt, msəl-məñ ciə <u>tŋay-saw</u>.
baə tŋay-nih ciə tŋay-sok, msəl-məñ ciə <u>tŋay qwəy</u>?	baə tŋay-nih ciə tŋay-sok, msəl-məñ ciə <u>tŋay-prəhŏəh</u>.

Teacher	Student
baə tŋay-nih ciə tŋay-qəŋkiə, msəl-məñ ciə <u>tŋay qwəy</u>?	baə tŋay-nih ciə tŋay-qəŋkiə, msəl-məñ ciə <u>tŋay-can</u>.
baə tŋay-nih ciə tŋay-prəhoə̆h, msəl-məñ ciə <u>tŋay qwəy</u>?	baə tŋay-nih ciə tŋay-prəhoə̆h, msəl-məñ ciə <u>tŋay-put</u>.
baə tŋay-nih ciə tŋay-can, msəl-məñ ciə <u>tŋay qwəy</u>?	baə tŋay-nih ciə tŋay-can, msəl-məñ ciə <u>tŋay-qatɨt</u>.
baə tŋay-nih ciə tŋay-put, msəl-məñ ciə <u>tŋay qwəy</u>?	baə tŋay-nih ciə tŋay-put, msəl-məñ ciə <u>tŋay-qəŋkiə</u>.
baə tŋay-nih ciə tŋay-saw, msəl-məñ ciə <u>tŋay qwəy</u>?	baə tŋay-nih ciə tŋay-saw, msəl-məñ ciə <u>tŋay-sok</u>.

11-C. **Response Drill**

Repeat Drill 11-A above, but with the chart covered.

11-D. **Response Drill**

Repeat Drill 11-B above, but with the chart covered.

[Tape 19] **C. COMPREHENSION**

1. **Going to Phnom Penh**

   mɔɔn: miən tɨw pnum-pɨñ, səmnaq nɨw qae-naa?

   [santhəkiə-haaway 'the Hawaii Hotel']
   miən: thoə̆mmədaa, kñom nɨw santhəkiə-haaway.

   mɔɔn: kənlaeŋ nuh sqaat tee?

   miən: qaə, sqaat lmɔɔm dae.
   haəy miən bəntup thom-tuliəy phɑɑŋ.

   mɔɔn: pteə̆h-səmnaq nuh miən haaŋ-baay tee?

   miən: qaə, miən.

   mɔɔn: kənlaeŋ nuh tlay tee?

   miən: mɨn tlay pənmaan tee.
   baə nɨw muəy qatɨt, kee coh tlay qaoy phɑɑŋ.

2. **Buying Furniture**

   sɨən: sɑɑn qaeŋ tɨw naa?

   sɑɑn: kñom tɨw haaŋ-luə̆q-tok-tuu.

   sɨən: tɨw tɨñ qəy?

   sɑɑn: kñom caŋ tɨñ tuu-daq-qəywan muəy, tok muəy, haəy-nɨŋ kawqəy buən.

   sɨən: trəw-kaa tɨñ krɛɛ tee?

   sɑɑn: tee, kñom miən krɛɛ haəy.

sɨən: pteə̆h sɑɑn qaeŋ miən bəntup ponmaan?

[bəntup-ñam-baay 'dining room']
[tɔtuəl (tətuəl) 'to receive']
[pñiəw 'guest(s)']
[bəntup-tətuəl-pñiəw 'receiving room, parlor']
[bəntup-keeŋ 'bedroom']

sɑɑn: miən bəntup teə̆ŋ-qɑh buən, kraw-pii bəntup-tɨk, kɨɨ bəntup-ñam-
baay, bəntup-tətuəl-pñiəw, haəy-nɨŋ bəntup-keeŋ pii.

3. Meeting in the Hotel

siəŋ: cumriəp-suə look Stan.

Stan: cumriəp-suə look siəŋ.
look nɨw santhəkiə nih dae rɨɨ?

siəŋ: baat, nɨŋ haəy.

Stan: look mɔɔk pnum-pɨñ twəə qwəy?

siəŋ: kñom mɔɔk leeŋ baaŋ-proh kñom məneə̆q dael ciə neə̆q-cumnuəñ.

Stan: look mɔɔk pii tŋay naa?

siəŋ: kñom mɔɔk pii tŋay-saw.

Stan: tŋay-nih kɨɨ tŋay-qəŋkiə.
douccneh look mɔɔk bəy tŋay haəy, mɛɛn tee?

siəŋ: nɨŋ haəy.
qəyləw-nih look qəñcəəñ tɨw naa?

Stan: kñom tɨw məəl kon.
look cɑŋ tɨw ciə-muəy kñom tee?

siəŋ: baat, qɑɑ-kun.

4. Getting a Room

chɑɑŋ: look miən bəntup tumnee tee?

Clerk: baat, miən.
look kɨt nɨw pənmaan tŋay?

chɑɑŋ: prəhael ciə pram tŋay.

Clerk: look trəw-kaa bəntup dael miən bəntup-tɨk tee?

chɑɑŋ: nɨŋ haəy.
bəntup nuh mə-tŋay tlay pənmaan?

Clerk: mə-tŋay tlay mərɔɔy.

chɑɑŋ: miən bəntup thaok ciəŋ nih tee?

Clerk: baat, miən bəntup muəy tiət tlay cətsəp-pram riəl.

chɑɑŋ: kñom tɨw məəl bəntup sən, baan tee?

Clerk: soum qəñcəəñ.

D. CONVERSATION

1. Looking for a Hotel

   a) A approaches B, and asks him if there is a hotel nearby.
   b) B replies that if he walks along this street, he'll see Monorom Hotel on the right.
   c) A asks B if that hotel is expensive.
   d) B replies that it isn't so expensive, then says that if he crosses the street, he'll see another hotel called the Sukkhalay Hotel.
   e) A asks which of these two hotels is the cheaper.
   f) B answers that they're both about equally expensive.
   g) A thanks B.
   h) B says he's welcome.

2. Getting a Room

   a) A asks the clerk if he has any vacant rooms.
   b) The clerk replies that he does, then asks A if he wants a room with one bed or two beds.
   c) A replies that he wants a room with one bed, and with a bathroom too.
   d) The clerk asks A if he'll take his meals (eat—formal) there.
   e) A replies that he'll take only dinner.
   f) The clerk says it's 120 riels per day, including dinner; then the clerk asks A when he plans to leave.
   g) A replies that he has to leave on Friday.
   h) The clerk says that today is Wednesday, and asks if it is right that A will be staying two nights.
   i) A says that's right.

3. Discussing the Hawaii Hotel

   a) A asks B if he has ever stayed at the Sukkhalay Hotel.
   b) B answers that he has stayed there, but usually he stays at the Hawaii Hotel because it's cheaper.
   c) A asks if the Hawaii Hotel is clean.
   d) B replies that it's clean enough, and that the rooms are quite spacious too.
   e) A asks if there is a dining room at the Hawaii.
   f) B replies that there is.
   g) A asks how much it costs per day at the Hawaii Hotel.
   h) B replies that it costs about 80 riels per day.

4. A Complaint

   a) A complains to the clerk that his room is too hot; he can't sleep.
   b) The clerk says he has another room which has two big windows, and that it is nice and cool.
   c) A asks how much that room costs.
   d) The clerk says that room is 125 riels per day.
   e) A says it's too expensive.
   f) The clerk says that, in that case, he'll lower the price for him.
   g) A asks if he can go see the room first.

h) The clerk tells him to go ahead, then instructs the Boy to take him to see room number 115.

i) Back at the desk, the clerk asks A if he is willing to take that room.

j) A says O.K.

k) The clerk tells the Boy to take A's things and put them in room number 115.

LESSON 11. GETTING DRESSED

[Tape 20]   A. DIALOGUE

nii

kraok	to rise, to get up
laəŋ	upward, up
naa (nah, nəh)	hortatory final particle
plɨɨ	to be bright, light, late (in the morning)

1. qei, kraok laəŋ nəh! plɨɨ haəy!   Hey, get up! It's late already.

nael

tmɨñ	tooth, teeth
pɛɛt-tmɨñ	dentist

2. nɨŋ haəy; tŋay-nih kñom trəw tɨw   Right; today I have to go to the dentist
   pɛɛt-tmɨñ maoŋ prambəy kənlah.   at eight-thirty.

nii

riəp-cam	to get ready
kluən	body; self, oneself
qaoy	to cause, make, let, allow
chap	to be fast, quick
qaoy chap	quickly
tɨw	imperative particle

3. qəñcəŋ riəp-cam kluən qaoy chap   Then hurry and get ready! (Then get
   tɨw!   ready quickly!)

nael

qwəy-klah	what (plural), what-all
tŋay-nɨŋ	colloquial variant of tŋay-nih

4. nii qaeŋ twəə qwəy-klah tŋay-nɨŋ?   What (pl.) do you plan to do today, Nii?

nii

cawwaay	boss, superior

5. kñom trəw tɨw ñam baay ciə-muəy   I have to have lunch (to eat) with my
   cawwaay kñom nɨw tŋay-trəŋ.   boss at noon.

nael

sliəq	to put on or wear below the waist
peəq	to put on or wear above the waist or on the feet
sliəq-peəq	to dress, to wear (in general)
sqaat-baat	neat, careful, proper

6. qəñcəŋ sliəq-peəq qaoy sqaat-baat   In that case, [you'd better] dress care-
   tɨw!   fully!

147

nii

khao	trousers, pants
khao-qaaw	suit; clothing
baok	to wash (by beating); to beat
qut	to iron
baok-qut	to launder
haaŋ-baok-qut	laundry

7. niŋ haəy, tae kñom mɨn-toăn yɔɔk khao-qaaw mɔɔk pii haaŋ-baok-qut phɑɑŋ.

Right, but I haven't yet gotten my clothes from the laundry.

miən-tae	there's only to, I'll have to
cah	old, worn, used

8. qəñcəŋ miən-tae sliəq khao cah.

So I'll have to wear some old pants (some pants which have been worn).

nael

kao	to shave
puk-moăt	beard (literally: mustache)

9. kñom tɨw kao puk-moăt sən.

I'll go shave (first).

nii

ŋuut	to bathe
ŋuut-tɨk	to bathe

10. prɨk nih nael qaeŋ ŋuut-tɨk tee?

Are you going to take a bath this morning?

nael

kcɨl	to be lazy; not feel like
lup	to wash (the face)
muk	face

11. kñom kcɨl ŋuut-tɨk nah tŋay-nih; kroăn-tae lup muk tee.

I don't feel like bathing today; [I'll] just wash [my] face.

nii

cam	to remember
craah (crah)	brush
doh	to brush
crah-doh-tmɨñ	toothbrush
qaa- (qa-)	pronominal prefix: the/a___one
qaanaa? (qanaa?)	which one?
qaanaa-muəy? (qanaa-muəy?)	which one?

12. nael cam tee, crah-doh-tmɨñ rəbɑh kñom qanaa-muəy?

Nael, do you remember which toothbrush is mine? (my toothbrush [is] which one?)

nael

rəbɑh nii qaeŋ	yours (of Nii yourself)
pɔə	color
khiəw	blue to green

pɔə-khiəw — the color blue; to be blue-colored

rəbah kñom — mine
krahaam (krəhaam, kəhaam) — red to orange
pɔə-krəhaam — the color red; to be red-colored

13. rəbah nii qaeŋ pɔə-khiəw; rəbah kñom pɔə-krəhaam. — Yours is blue; mine's red.

nii

tnam — medicine, preparation
tnam-doh-tmɨñ — toothpaste

14. tnam-doh-tmɨñ nih cɨt qah haəy. — This toothpaste is almost gone (used up).

tməy — to be new; some new, some more

15. trəw tɨñ tməy tiət. — [We'll] have to buy some more.

nael

cuəy — help by, please
hoc — to hand
saabuu (sabuu, səbuu) — soap
kansaeŋ (kənsaeŋ, kəsaeŋ) — handkerchief, cloth
cuut — to rub, wipe
kənsaeŋ-cuut-kluən — towel

16. cuəy hoc sabuu haey-nɨŋ kənsaeŋ-cuut-kluən qaoy kñom phaaŋ. — Please hand me the soap and a towel.

nii

neh — colloquial variant of <u>nih</u>
prəñap (prəñap, pəñap) — to hurry; to hurry and (do something)

twəə kluən (thəə kluən) — to prepare oneself, to get ready

17. neh; nael qaeŋ prəñap thəə kluən tɨw neh. — Here; you hurry and dress.

kaq — to wash (the hair), to shampoo

18. kñom caŋ ŋuut-tɨk haəy kaq saq phaaŋ. — I want to take a bath and wash [my] hair too.

nael

sraom — covering, envelope
cəəŋ — foot, leg
sraom-cəəŋ — socks, stockings
sot-tae (sət-tae) — inclusively, all without exception
krakwaq (krəkwaq, kəkwaq) — to be dirty

19. sraom-cəəŋ kñom sət-tae krəkwaq teᵊŋ-qah. — My socks are all (without exception) dirty.

20. nii qaeŋ peᵊq sraom-cəəŋ leik ponmaan? — What size socks to you wear?

nii

21. leik saamsəp. — Size (number) thirty.

nael

kcəy   to borrow
kuu   pair
22. kñom kcəy məkuu mɔɔk baan tee?   Could I borrow a pair?

nii

23. miən qəy; yɔɔk tɨw!   Of course; go ahead and take [some].

thaat-tuu   drawer
24. nɨw knoŋ thaat-tuu.   [They're] in the drawer.

nael

saa   white
caaŋ   to tie, to wear (a tie)
kraawat (krawat, krəwat)   necktie
baytaaŋ   green
kcəy   light, young, tender, inexperienced
baytaaŋ-kcəy   light green
25. qaa-kun. tŋay-nih kñom peˀəq qaaw   Thank you. Today I'm going to wear a
saa haəy-nɨŋ caaŋ krawat   white shirt and (wear) a light green
baytaaŋ-kcəy.   tie.

nii

sam   to be suitable, proper
cah   dark, deep, strong, concentrated
khiəw-cah   dark blue to green
26. qei, krawat pɔə qəy sam nɨŋ   Hey, what color tie goes with this dark
qaaw khiəw-cah nih?   blue shirt?

nael

chiəm   blood
cruuk   pig
chiəm-cruuk   pig's blood red, maroon
qaa-chiəm-cruuk   the maroon one
27. qaa-chiəm-cruuk nih sam haəy.   This maroon one [would be] fine.

nii

28. yii, nael qaeŋ sliəq-peˀəq yuu nah!   Boy, you really take a long time to
                                             dress, Nael!

nael

cam   to wait
sət   to comb
29. cam bəntəc; kñom sət saq sən.   Wait a little; I [have to] comb [my]
                                             hair first.

preiŋ   oil
liəp   to spread on, to paint
preiŋ-liəp-saq   hair-oil
30. qou, preiŋ-liəp-saq kñom qah haəy.   Oh, my hair-oil is all gone.

Color Terms

pɔə-krɑhɑɑm (cah/kcəy)	(dark/light) red to orange (non-khiəw)
pɔə-khiəw (cah/kcəy)	(dark/light) blue to green (non-krɑhɑɑm)
pɔə-baytaaŋ (cah/kcəy)	(dark/light) green
pɔə-lɨəŋ (cah/kcəy)	(dark/light) yellow
pɔə-sii-cəmpuu (cah/kcəy)	(dark/light) pink
pɔə-swaay (cah/kcəy)	(dark/light) purple
pɔə-kmaw	black
pɔə-sɑɑ	white
pɔə-prɑpheh (prəpheh, pəpheh)	grey
pɔə-sukkolaa	brown (chocolate)
pɔə-miəh	gold
pɔə-slaa-tum	orange (ripe areca-nut)
pɔə-chiəm-cruuk	maroon (pig's blood)
pɔə-ptɨy-meek	sky-blue (surface of the sky)

B. GRAMMAR AND DRILLS

1. tɨw as an Imperative Particle

tɨw 'to go', like mɔɔk 'to come', has a variety of duties in Cambodian. It occurs as a primary verb, as in

tŋay-nih kɲom trəw tɨw psaa.	Today I have to go to the market.

It is also an important member of the class of directional verbs (see Lesson 10, B, 6), as in

kɲom nɨŋ yɔɔk qəywan nih tɨw bəntup.	I'll take these things (go) to the room.

In this lesson, tɨw occurs for the first time as an imperative final phrase particle, with the meaning 'go on and . . . , go ahead and . . . ', as in

riəp-cam kluən qaoy chap tɨw!	(Go ahead and) hurry and get ready.
sliəq-peəq qaoy sqaat-baat tɨw!	(You'd better) dress carefully.
yɔɔk tɨw!	(Go ahead and) take [some].

1-A. Substitution Drill

Teacher	Student
riəp-cam kluən tɨw.	riəp-cam kluən tɨw.
sliəq-peəq	sliəq-peəq tɨw.
ñam baay	ñam baay tɨw.
twəə-kaa	twəə-kaa tɨw.
kraok laəŋ	kraok laəŋ tɨw.
məəl siəwphɨw	məəl siəwphɨw tɨw.
baək twiə	baək twiə tɨw.
doh tmɨñ	doh tmɨñ tɨw.
bət bəŋquəc	bət bəŋquəc tɨw.
sət sɑq	sət sɑq tɨw.

1-B. Transformation Drill

Teacher	Student
riəp-cɑm kluən qaoy chap.	riəp-cɑm kluən qaoy chap tɨw!
sliəq-peə̆q qaoy sqaat-baat.	sliəq-peə̆q qaoy sqaat-baat tɨw!
yɔɔk qəywan nih tɨw pteə̆h.	yɔɔk qəywan nih tɨw pteə̆h tɨw!
yɔɔk sraom-cəəŋ məkuu.	yɔɔk sraom-cəəŋ məkuu tɨw!
tɨw doh tmɨñ.	tɨw doh tmɨñ tɨw!
kraok laəŋ qaoy chap.	kraok laəŋ qaoy chap tɨw!
bət twiə qaoy kñom.	bət twiə qaoy kñom tɨw!
tɨw kao puk-moə̆t.	tɨw kao puk-moə̆t tɨw!

2. The Final Hortatory Particle naa (nah, nəh)

The particle naa (almost always reduced to nəh in colloquial speech) is used at the end of imperative sentences to soften the command or to solicit compliance, as in

kraok laəŋ nəh!   Get up (will you?)!

nəh thus frequently occurs after commands which include the imperative particle tɨw 'go ahead and . . . ', as in

prəñap sliəq-peə̆q tɨw nəh!   Hurry up and dress (will you?)!

In the speech of some individuals, the particle nəh tends to occur at the end of almost every sentence, as if to solicit agreement, or simply to maintain contact with a listener. In this function it is somewhat comparable to the rhetorical 'you know?' or 'you see?' which occurs in a narrative style in the speech of some English speakers.

2-A. Substitution Drill

Teacher	Student
kraok laəŋ nəh.	kraok laəŋ nəh!
sliəq-peə̆q	sliəq-peə̆q nəh!
ñam baay	ñam baay nəh!
twəə-kaa	twəə-kaa nəh!
məəl siəwphɨw	məəl siəwphɨw nəh!
doh tmɨñ	doh tmɨñ nəh!
sət sɑq	sət sɑq nəh!
baək siəwphɨw	baək siəwphɨw nəh!
yɔɔk məkuu	yɔɔk məkuu nəh!
bət twiə	bət twiə nəh!

2-B. Transformation Drill

Teacher	Student
riəp-cɑm kluən qaoy chap tɨw.	riəp-cɑm kluən qaoy chap tɨw nəh!
sliəq-peə̆q qaoy sqaat-baat tɨw.	sliəq-peə̆q qaoy sqaat-baat tɨw nəh!
yɔɔk qəywan nih tɨw psaa tɨw.	yɔɔk qəywan nih tɨw psaa tɨw nəh!
yɔɔk kafei məkaew tɨw.	yɔɔk kafei məkaew tɨw nəh!
tɨw doh tmɨñ tɨw.	tɨw doh tmɨñ tɨw nəh!
kraok laəŋ qaoy chap tɨw.	kraok laəŋ qaoy chap tɨw nəh!
baək laan qaoy chap tɨw.	baək laan qaoy chap tɨw nəh!
twəə kluən tɨw.	twəə kluən tɨw nəh!

3. qaoy as a Modal Verb

When qaoy precedes another verb, it functions as a modal verb with the meaning 'to cause, make, let, allow'. In the following examples qaoy precedes an adjectival verb with the meaning 'causing it to be ____, making it ____'. Such constructs can best be translated by adverbs in English.

riəp-cam kluən qaoy chap.	Get ready quickly (making it quick).
sliəq-peəq qaoy sqaat-baat.	Dress carefully (making it careful).
kñom niŋ pənyuəl qaoy cbah.	I'll explain it clearly (making it clear).

3-A. Substitution Drill

Teacher	Student
riəp-cam kluən qaoy chap tɨw.	riəp-cam kluən qaoy chap tɨw.
sliəq-peəq	sliəq-peəq qaoy chap tɨw.
ñam baay	ñam baay qaoy chap tɨw.
baok khao-qaaw	baok khao-qaaw qaoy chap tɨw.
lup muk	lup muk qaoy chap tɨw.
ŋuut-tɨk	ŋuut-tɨk qaoy chap tɨw.
sət saq	sət saq qaoy chap tɨw.
kao puk-moət	kao puk-moət qaoy chap tɨw.
kraok laəŋ	kraok laəŋ qaoy chap tɨw.

3-B. Substitution Drill

Teacher	Student
cou look niyiəy qaoy cbah.	cou look niyiəy qaoy cbah.
pənyuəl	cou look pənyuəl qaoy cbah.
claəy	cou look claəy qaoy cbah.
thaa	cou look thaa qaoy cbah.
təsei	cou look təsei qaoy cbah.
prae	cou look prae qaoy cbah.
məəl	cou look məəl qaoy cbah.

3-C. Substitution Drill

Teacher	Student
sliəq-peəq qaoy sqaat-baat tɨw.	sliəq-peəq qaoy sqaat-baat tɨw.
riəp-cam kluən	riəp-cam kluən qaoy sqaat-baat tɨw.
baok khao-qaaw	baok khao-qaaw qaoy sqaat-baat tɨw.
sət saq	sət saq qaoy sqaat-baat tɨw.
doh tmiñ	doh tmiñ qaoy sqaat-baat tɨw.
ŋuut-tɨk	ŋuut-tɨk qaoy sqaat-baat tɨw.
lup muk	lup muk qaoy sqaat-baat tɨw.
kao puk-moət	kao puk-moət qaoy sqaat-baat tɨw.
twəə kluən	twəə kluən qaoy sqaat-baat tɨw.

4. kluən as a Reflexive Pronoun

Certain verbs which express actions performed on the body may be followed by the word kluən 'body, self', which then functions as a kind of reflexive pronoun with the meaning 'oneself, yourself, himself, etc.', as in

riəp-cam kluən qaoy chap tɨw.	Get (yourself) ready quickly.

Other verbs which may be followed by kluən are top-taeŋ 'to decorate', cuut 'to wipe, rub' (cuut kluən 'to dry oneself'), and twəə 'to do' (twəə kluən 'to get ready').

4-A. Progressive Substitution Drill

Teacher	Student
riəp-cɑm kluən qaoy chap tɨw.	riəp-cɑm kluən qaoy chap tɨw.
top-taeŋ	top-taeŋ kluən qaoy chap tɨw.
cuut	cuut kluən qaoy chap tɨw.
twəə	twəə kluən qaoy chap tɨw.
sqaat	twəə kluən qaoy sqaat tɨw.
riəp-cɑm	riəp-cɑm kluən qaoy sqaat tɨw.
cuut	cuut kluən qaoy sqaat tɨw.
top-taeŋ	top-taeŋ kluən qaoy sqaat tɨw.

5. Interrogative Compounds with klah and muəy

The interrogative words qwəy 'what?' and naa 'where?, which?' are non-specific as to number. Number may be specified, however, by adding the words klah 'some, several' or muəy 'one', as in

| nii qaeŋ twəə qwəy-klah tŋay-nɨŋ? | What (plural) are you going to do today, Ni? |
| crah-doh-tmɨñ rəbɑh kñom qanaa-muəy? | Which toothbrush is mine? (My toothbrush [is] which one?) |

Like qwəy and naa, these compound interrogative words may function both as interrogative pronouns and as interrogative adjectives (see Lesson 9, B, 12):

As interrogative pronouns:

look kɨt tɨñ qwəy-muəy?	What (one thing) do you plan to buy?
look kɨt tɨñ qwəy-klah?	What (things) do you plan to buy?
look kɨt tɨñ (qa)naa-muəy?	Which (one) do you plan to buy?
look kɨt tɨw naa-klah?	Where (which places) do you plan to go?

As interrogative adjectives:

look nɨŋ tɨñ siəwphɨw qwəy-muəy?	What (one) book will you buy?
look nɨŋ tɨñ siəwphɨw qwəy-klah?	What (pl.) books will you buy?
look cɑŋ tɨw kənlaeŋ naa-muəy?	Where (which one place) do you want to go?
look cɑŋ tɨw kənlaeŋ naa-klah?	Where (which places) do you want to go?

naa-muəy does not occur as an interrogative pronoun except when preceded by the prefix qaa-, whose function is discussed below.

5-A. Substitution Drill

Teacher	Student
look cɑŋ twəə qwəy-klah?	look cɑŋ twəə qwəy-klah?
tɨñ	look cɑŋ tɨñ qwəy-klah?
məəl	look cɑŋ məəl qwəy-klah?
baan	look cɑŋ baan qwəy-klah?
ñam	look cɑŋ ñam qwəy-klah?
luəq	look cɑŋ luəq qwəy-klah?

5-B. Substitution Drill

Teacher	Student
look caŋ **məəl siəwphɨw** qwəy-muəy?	look caŋ **məəl siəwphɨw** qwəy-muəy?
məəl kon	look caŋ **məəl kon** qwəy-muəy?
ñam plae-chəə	look caŋ **ñam plae-chəə** qwəy-muəy?
riən phiəsaa	look caŋ **riən phiəsaa** qwəy-muəy?
bəŋriən tnaq	look caŋ **bəŋriən tnaq** qwəy-muəy?
tɨw salaa	look caŋ **tɨw salaa** qwəy-muəy?

5-C. Substitution Drill

Teacher	Student
look coul-cət **kon** qwəy-klah?	look coul-cət **kon** qwəy-klah?
siəwphɨw	look coul-cət **siəwphɨw** qwəy-klah?
plae-chəə	look coul-cət **plae-chəə** qwəy-klah?
rədəw	look coul-cət **rədəw** qwəy-klah?
pɔə	look coul-cət **pɔə** qwəy-klah?
phoocəniiyəthaan	look coul-cət **phoocəniiyəthaan** qwəy-klah?

5-D. Substitution Drill

Teacher	Student
look caŋ tɨñ **laan** naa-muəy?	look caŋ tɨñ **laan** naa-muəy?
qaaw	look caŋ tɨñ **qaaw** naa-muəy?
pɔə	look caŋ tɨñ **pɔə** naa-muəy?
krawat	look caŋ tɨñ **krawat** naa-muəy?
khao	look caŋ tɨñ **khao** naa-muəy?
crah-doh-tmɨñ	look caŋ tɨñ **crah-doh-tmɨñ** naa-muəy?

5-E. Substitution Drill

Teacher	Student
look coul-cət **siəwphɨw** naa-klah?	look coul-cət **siəwphɨw** naa-klah?
krawat	look coul-cət **krawat** naa-klah?
qaaw	look coul-cət **qaaw** naa-klah?
pɔə	look coul-cət **pɔə** naa-klah?
kənlaeŋ	look coul-cət **kənlaeŋ** naa-klah?
pteĕh	look coul-cət **pteĕh** naa-klah?

5-F. Transformation Drill

Teacher	Student
look caŋ tɨw **naa**?	look caŋ tɨw **naa-klah**?
look caŋ tɨñ **qwəy**?	look caŋ tɨñ **qwəy-klah**?
look coul-cət pɔə **naa**?	look coul-cət pɔə **naa-klah**?
look coul-cət plae-chəə **qwəy**?	look coul-cət plae-chəə **qwəy-klah**?
look caŋ tɨw kənlaeŋ **naa**?	look caŋ tɨw kənlaeŋ **naa-klah**?
look caŋ tɨñ pɔə **qwəy**?	look caŋ tɨñ pɔə **qwəy-klah**?

5-G. Transformation Drill

Teacher	Student
look kɨt tɨw salaa naa?	look kɨt tɨw salaa naa-muəy?
look caŋ tɨñ pɔə qwəy?	look caŋ tɨñ pɔə qwəy-muəy?
look bəŋriən tnaq qwəy?	look bəŋriən tnaq qwəy-muəy?
look kɨt tɨw tŋay naa?	look kɨt tɨw tŋay naa-muəy?
look chup twəə-kaa khae naa?	look chup twəə-kaa khae naa-muəy?
look kɨt tɨñ ptẽəh naa?	look kɨt tɨñ ptẽəh naa-muəy?

6. The Compound Auxiliary miən-tae

When miən-tae precedes a verb, it functions as an auxiliary of the same class as kampuŋ-tae 'in the process of' and krŏən-tae 'only, just', and has the meaning 'to have only to, the only thing to do is . . .', as in

qəñcəŋ miən-tae sliəq khao cah.   So [I'll] have to wear some old
                                       (worn) pants.

6-A. Substitution Drill

Teacher	Student
qəñcəŋ miən-tae sliəq khao cah.	qəñcəŋ miən-tae sliəq khao cah.
trəlɑp tɨw ptẽəh.	qəñcəŋ miən-tae trəlɑp tɨw ptẽəh.
tɨñ tməy tiət.	qəñcəŋ miən-tae tɨñ tməy tiət.
tɨw sqaek.	qəñcəŋ miən-tae tɨw sqaek.
kcəy məkuu mɔɔk.	qəñcəŋ miən-tae kcəy məkuu mɔɔk.
pẽəq qaaw khiəw.	qəñcəŋ miən-tae pẽəq qaaw khiəw.
cam nɨw qae-nih.	qəñcəŋ miən-tae cam nɨw qae-nih.
kcəy luy bəntəc.	qəñcəŋ miən-tae kcəy luy bəntəc.

7. kcɨl as a Modal Verb

As an adjectival verb, kcɨl means 'to be lazy'; as a modal verb, however, it means 'not to feel like (doing something), to be too lazy to (do something)', as in

kñom kcɨl ŋuut-tɨk nah;   I don't feel like taking a bath;
krŏən-tae lup muk tee.   [I'm] just [going to] wash [my] face.

7-A. Substitution Drill

Teacher	Student
kñom kcɨl ŋuut-tɨk nah tŋay-nih.	kñom kcɨl ŋuut-tɨk nah tŋay-nih.
riən	kñom kcɨl riən nah tŋay-nih.
tɨw twəə-kaa	kñom kcɨl tɨw twəə-kaa nah tŋay-nih.
məəl siəwphɨw	kñom kcɨl məəl siəwphɨw nah tŋay-nih.
sliəq-pẽəq	kñom kcɨl sliəq-pẽəq nah tŋay-nih.
kao puk-mŏət	kñom kcɨl kao puk-mŏət nah tŋay-nih.
doh tmɨñ	kñom kcɨl doh tmɨñ nah tŋay-nih.
sət saq	kñom kcɨl sət saq nah tŋay-nih.
cɑɑŋ krawat	kñom kcɨl cɑɑŋ krawat nah tŋay-nih.

8. The Pronominal Prefix qaa-

When qaa- (reduced to qa- when unstressed) is prefixed to any kind of modifying element, the resulting derivative is a pronominal compound with the meaning 'a___one, the ___one(s), (the) one which is ___, the ones which are ___', e.g.:

naa? 'which?'	>	qanaa? 'which one(s)?'
touc 'small'	>	qaa-touc 'a/the small one(s)'
chiəm-cruuk 'maroon'	>	qaa-chiəm-cruuk 'a/the maroon one(s)'
pɔə-krahaam 'red (color)'	>	qaa-pɔə-krahaam 'a/the red-colored one(s)'

Thus, in the sentence

crah-doh-tmɨñ rəbah kñom qanaa-muəy?   Which toothbrush is mine?

qa- is a pronominal substitute for crah-doh-tmɨñ, and the compound qanaa-muəy? substitutes for crah-doh-tmɨñ naa-muəy? 'which toothbrush?'.

The function of qaa- may be further clarified by the following examples:

siəwphɨw naa? 'which book(s)?'	>	qanaa? 'which one(s)?'
krouc thom 'large orange(s)'	>	qaa-thom 'a/the large one(s)'
sabuu thaok 'inexpensive soap'	>	qaa-thaok 'a/the inexpensive one(s)'
krawat krəhaam 'red tie(s)'	>	qaa-krəhaam 'a/the red one(s)'

8-A. Transformation Drill

Teacher	Student
look caŋ tɨñ crah-doh-tmɨñ naa-muəy?	look caŋ tɨñ qanaa-muəy?
kñom tɨñ krawat krəhaam nih.	kñom tɨñ qaa-krəhaam nih.
kñom nɨŋ tɨñ qaaw saa nih.	kñom nɨŋ tɨñ qaa-saa nih.
kñom yɔɔk prəqap thom nih.	kñom yɔɔk qaa-thom nih.
kñom caŋ baan khao pɔə-kmaw nih.	kñom caŋ baan qaa-pɔə-kmaw nih.
sraom-cəəŋ khiəw nih krəkwaq nah.	qaa-khiəw nih krəkwaq nah.
kñom som kcəy krawat krəhaam nih.	kñom som kcəy qaa-krəhaam nih.
krawat liəŋ nih sam haəy.	qaa-liəŋ nih sam haəy.
kñom mɨn coul-cət qaaw cah nih tee.	kñom mɨn coul-cət qaa-cah nih tee.

9. Truncated Possessive Phrases

When the antecedent of a possessive noun phrase has been established, the head noun may be omitted in second reference, as in the exchange:

crah-doh-tmɨñ rəbah kñom qanaa-muəy?   Which toothbrush is mine?

rəbah nii qaeŋ pɔə-khiəw;   Yours (of Ni) [is] blue;
rəbah kñom pɔə-krəhaam.   mine (of me) is red.

These truncated possessive phrases can be conveniently translated by the English possessive pronouns 'mine, yours, his, theirs, etc.', e.g.:

laan rəbah kñom 'my car'	>	rəbah kñom 'mine'
laan rəbah look 'your car'	>	rəbah look 'yours'
laan rəbah koət 'his car'	>	rəbah koət 'his, theirs'

9-A. Transformation Drill

Teacher	Student
laan rəbah kñom cah.	rəbah kñom cah.
laan rəbah look tməy.	rəbah look tməy.
qaaw rəbah kñom pɔə-krəhaam.	rəbah kñom pɔə-krəhaam.
qaaw rəbah look pɔə-kmaw.	rəbah look pɔə-kmaw.
crah-doh-tmɨñ rəbah look pɔə-lɨəŋ.	rəbah look pɔə-lɨəŋ.
pteʾəh rəbah kñom touc.	rəbah kñom touc.
pteʾəh rəbah kee thom.	rəbah kee thom.
laan rəbah nael tlay nah.	rəbah nael tlay nah.

10. cuəy as an Auxiliary of Request

The word cuəy 'to help' frequently precedes polite imperative sentences or requests for help. In this position it is similar in function to the auxiliaries soum 'please' and mɔɔk 'come on and', and can best be translated 'please', as in the sentence

| cuəy hoc sabuu haəy-nɨŋ | Please hand me the soap and |
| kənsaeŋ-cuut-kluən qaoy kñom phaaŋ. | a towel. |

10-A. Substitution Drill

Teacher	Student
cuəy hoc sabuu qaoy kñom phaaŋ.	cuəy hoc sabuu qaoy kñom phaaŋ.
kənsaeŋ-cuut-kluən	cuəy hoc kənsaeŋ-cuut-kluən qaoy kñom phaaŋ.
crah-doh-tmɨñ	cuəy hoc crah-doh-tmɨñ qaoy kñom phaaŋ.
siəwphɨw nuh	cuəy hoc siəwphɨw nuh qaoy kñom phaaŋ.
qaaw sɑɑ nuh	cuəy hoc qaaw sɑɑ nuh qaoy kñom phaaŋ.
tnam-doh-tmɨñ	cuəy hoc tnam-doh-tmɨñ qaoy kñom phaaŋ.
krawat krəhaam nuh	cuəy hoc krawat krəhaam nuh qaoy kñom phaaŋ.

10-B. Transformation Drill

Teacher	Student
hoc sabuu qaoy kñom phaaŋ.	cuəy hoc sabuu qaoy kñom phaaŋ.
bət twiə qaoy kñom phaaŋ.	cuəy bət twiə qaoy kñom phaaŋ.
baək bəŋquəc qaoy kñom phaaŋ.	cuəy baək bəŋquəc qaoy kñom phaaŋ.
haw taqsii qaoy kñom phaaŋ.	cuəy haw taqsii qaoy kñom phaaŋ.
daq qəywan nih nɨw knoŋ bəntup phaaŋ.	cuəy daq qəywan nih nɨw knoŋ bəntup phaaŋ.
tɨñ kmaw-day qaoy kñom phaaŋ.	cuəy tɨñ kmaw-day qaoy kñom phaaŋ.
dah yəəŋ maoŋ prammuəy phaaŋ.	cuəy dah yəəŋ maoŋ prammuəy phaaŋ.

11. The Modal Verb prəñap (prəñap, pəñap)

When prəñap precedes another verb, it is a modal verb with the meaning 'hurry and . . .', as in

| nael prəñap twəə kluən tɨw nəh! | Hurry and get dressed, Nael! |

11-A. Substitution Drill

Teacher	Student
prəñap sliəq-peə̆q tɨw nəh!	prəñap sliəq-peə̆q tɨw nəh!
kao puk-moə̆t	prəñap kao puk-moə̆t tɨw nəh!
riəp-cam kluən	prəñap riəp-cam kluən tɨw nəh!
sət saq	prəñap sət saq tɨw nəh!
ŋuut-tɨk	prəñap ŋuut-tɨk tɨw nəh!
doh-tmɨñ	prəñap doh tmɨñ tɨw nəh!
twəə kluən	prəñap twəə kluən tɨw nəh!

12. The Auxiliary sot-tae

sot-tae (sət-tae) is a compound preverbal auxiliary of the kampuŋ-tae class, and means 'inclusively, all without exception', as in

| sraom-cəəŋ kñom sət-tae krəkwaq teə̆ŋ-qah. | My socks are all (without exception) dirty (all). |

sət-tae before a verb is often reinforced at the end of the sentence by teə̆ŋ-qah 'all', which is redundant in the English translation.

12-A. Transformation Drill

Teacher	Student
sraom-cəəŋ kñom krəkwaq.	sraom-cəəŋ kñom sət-tae krəkwaq teə̆ŋ-qah.
khao-qaaw kñom cah.	khao-qaaw kñom sət-tae cah teə̆ŋ-qah.
mənuh nuh twəə tiəhiən.	mənuh nuh sət-tae twəə tiəhiən teə̆ŋ-qah.
laan nuh tməy.	laan nuh sət-tae tməy teə̆ŋ-qah.
kee niyiəy phiəsaa-baraŋ.	kee sət-tae niyiəy phiəsaa-baraŋ teə̆ŋ-qah.
santhəkiə nuh tlay.	santhəkiə nuh sət-tae tlay teə̆ŋ-qah.
krouc nuh touc.	krouc nuh sət-tae touc teə̆ŋ-qah.
qaaw kñom saa.	qaaw kñom sət-tae saa teə̆ŋ-qah.
koun-səh mɨn coul-cət riən.	koun-səh sət-tae mɨn coul-cət riən teə̆ŋ-qah.
koun-səh nuh pukae riən.	koun-səh nuh sət-tae pukae riən teə̆ŋ-qah.

13. sliəq, peə̆q, and caaŋ

The word sliəq means 'to put on' or 'to wear' with reference to any garment which is drawn over the legs and fixed around the waist, such as trousers, a skirt, or a sarong. peə̆q is used for putting on or wearing any other garment, such as a shirt, hat, or socks. Thus we might say that sliəq means 'to draw on' while peə̆q means 'to put on, to affix'. Both words are combined to form the compound sliəq-peə̆q 'to dress, to wear (clothes in general). The word caaŋ 'to tie' means 'to wear' in the sense of 'to tie on'.

13-A. Completion Drill

Teacher	Student
kñom nɨŋ ____ qaaw saa.	kñom nɨŋ peə̆q qaaw saa.
miən-tae ____ khao cah.	miən-tae sliəq khao cah.
look nɨŋ ____ krawat pɔə qəy?	look nɨŋ caaŋ krawat pɔə qəy?
kñom kmiən sraom-cəəŋ ____ sah.	kñom kmiən sraom-cəəŋ peə̆q sah.

Teacher	Student
look nɨŋ ____ khao pɔə qəy?	look nɨŋ sliəq khao pɔə qəy?
prəñap ____ qaaw khiəw nih.	prəñap peʼəq qaaw khiəw nih.
qəñcəŋ ____ qaoy sqaat-baat tɨw.	qəñcəŋ sliəq-peʼəq qaoy sqaat-baat tɨw.
cam bəntəc; kñom ____ krawat sən.	cam bəntəc; kñom cɑɑŋ krawat sən.
yii, nael ____ yuu nah!	yii, nael sliəq-peʼəq yuu nah!

14. Homophonous Pairs

This lesson contains three pairs of apparent homophones:

1) cah 'to be old, worn, used'; and cah 'to be dark (in color) or strong (in concentration)', as in the sentences

qəñcəŋ miən-tae sliəq khao cah.	So I'll have to wear some old pants.
krawat pɔə qəy sam nɨŋ qaaw khiəw-cah nih?	What color tie goes with this dark blue shirt?
kafei nih cah nah.	This coffee is very strong.

Here one can see a semantic connection between the two uses.

2) cam 'to remember'; cam 'to wait', as in

| nael cam tee, crah-doh-tmɨñ rəbɑh kñom qanaa-muəy? | Do you remember which toothbrush is mine, Nael? |
| cam bəntəc; kñom sət sɑq sən. | Wait a little; I [want to] comb [my] hair first. |

Here again, these two words seem to share a semantic bond of some kind of 'retention', mental in the first example and physical in the second.

3) kcəy 'to borrow', and kcəy 'to be light, young, tender, inexperienced', as in

| kñom kcəy məkuu mɔɔk baan tee? | Could I borrow a pair? |
| tŋay-nih kñom nɨŋ cɑɑŋ krawat baytaaŋ-kcəy. | Today I'm going to wear a light green tie. |

The first pair above is generally considered by Cambodians to be a single word; if we have difficulty accepting its semantic unity, it is because of preconceptions imposed by the semantic structure of our native language. The second pair, in spite of a semantic bond, is usually thought of by Cambodians as being two different words. The third pair are more clearly dichotomous, even from the standpoint of Cambodian structure, since they belong to different word classes, and have no logical semantic connection.

15. Cambodian Color Terminology

Cambodian color terms may be divided into two groups:

1) General, or cardinal, terms, which cover a broad range of the color spectrum, and may be modified by the terms cah 'dark' and kcəy 'light', or other appropriate words. The following color terms belong to this category:

pɔə-krɑhɑɑm (cah/kcəy)	(dark/light) red to orange (non-khiəw)
pɔə-khiəw (cah/kcəy)	(dark/light) blue to green (non-krɑhɑɑm)
pɔə-baytaaŋ (cah/kcəy)	(dark/light) green

poə-lɨəŋ (cah/kcəy)	(dark/light) yellow
poə-sii-cəmpuu (cah/kcəy)	(dark/light) pink
poə-swaay (cah/kcəy)	(dark/light) purple

2) Specific terms, which may not be modified for shade because they already refer to a specific shade. Such terms frequently include the name of an object which occurs in nature with a characteristic color, such as sky-blue, chocolate, gold, etc. Thus the inventory of such color terms is almost limitless; the following list includes only some of the more common terms:

poə-kmaw	black
poə-sɑɑ	white
poə-prɑpheh (prəpheh, pəpheh)	grey
poə-sukkolaa	brown (chocolate)
poə-miəh	gold
poə-slaa-tum	orange (ripe areca-nut)
poə-chiəm-cruuk	maroon (pig's blood)
poə-ptɨy-meek	sky-blue (surface of the sky)

15-A. Substitution Drill

Teacher	Student
kñom nɨŋ peəq qaaw poə-sɑɑ.	kñom nɨŋ peəq qaaw poə-sɑɑ.
poə-khiəw.	kñom nɨŋ peəq qaaw poə-khiəw.
poə-lɨəŋ.	kñom nɨŋ peəq qaaw poə-lɨəŋ.
poə-krəhaam.	kñom nɨŋ peəq qaaw poə-krəhaam.
poə-kmaw.	kñom nɨŋ peəq qaaw poə-kmaw.
poə-sii-cəmpuu.	kñom nɨŋ peəq qaaw poə-sii-cəmpuu.
poə-baytaaŋ.	kñom nɨŋ peəq qaaw poə-baytaaŋ.
kñom coul-cət krawat	kñom coul-cət krawat poə-baytaaŋ.
poə-swaay.	kñom coul-cət krawat poə-swaay.
poə-chiəm-cruuk.	kñom coul-cət krawat poə-chiəm-cruuk.
poə-ptɨy-meek.	kñom coul-cət krawat poə-ptɨy-meek.
poə-slaa-tum.	kñom coul-cət krawat poə-slaa-tum.

15-B. Transformation Drill

Teacher	Student
kñom caŋ baan poə-khiəw-cah.	kñom caŋ baan poə-khiəw-kcəy.
kñom caŋ baan poə-krəhaam-kcəy.	kñom caŋ baan poə-krəhaam-cah.
kñom caŋ baan poə-lɨəŋ-cah.	kñom caŋ baan poə-lɨəŋ-kcəy.
kñom caŋ baan poə-sii-cəmpuu-cah.	kñom caŋ baan poə-sii-cəmpuu-kcəy.
kñom caŋ baan poə-swaay-kcəy.	kñom caŋ baan poə-swaay-cah.
kñom caŋ baan poə-baytaaŋ-cah.	kñom caŋ baan poə-baytaaŋ-kcəy.
kñom caŋ baan poə-khiəw-kcəy.	kñom caŋ baan poə-khiəw-cah.
kñom caŋ baan poə-krəhaam-cah.	kñom caŋ baan poə-krəhaam-kcəy.

C. COMPREHENSION

1. <u>In a Variety Store</u>

    chɨən: sabuu nih tlay ponmaan?

              [dom 'specifier for pieces, nuggets']
    Clerk: mədom tlay pram riəl.
              sabuu nih thaok lmɔɔm; mədom tlay bəy riəl.

    chɨən: kñom yɔɔk qaa-thaok nih pii dom.

    Clerk: nih, look; look trəw-kaa qəy tiət?

    chɨən: kñom trəw-kaa tnam-doh-tmiñ.

    Clerk: qəñcəəñ mɔɔk khaŋ-neh.
              look trəw-kaa prəqap thom rɨɨ touc?

    chɨən: kñom yɔɔk qaa-thom nih.
              [krah-sət-saq 'comb']
              ruəc kñom trəw-kaa krah-sət-saq phaaŋ.
              kñom yɔɔk qaa-pɔə-kmaw nih.

    Clerk: look trəw-kaa preiŋ-liəp-saq tee?

    chɨən: mɨn-bac tee; kñom miən haəy.
              teəŋ-qah tlay ponmaan?

    Clerk: teəŋ-qah saamsəp-prambəy riəl.

2. <u>The Laundry</u>

    chaem: neəq-baok-qut mɔɔk maoŋ ponmaan?

    sam: roəl prɨk mɔɔk maoŋ prambəy-kənlah.

    chaem: kñom miən khao-qaaw krəkwaq craən nah.
             baok khao-qaaw nɨw kənlaeŋ nuh tlay tee?

    sam: mɨn tlay ponmaan tee; qaaw muəy bəy riəl, khao muəy bəy riəl.
             sraom-cəəŋ haəy-nɨŋ rəbah touc-touc mɨn tlay ponmaan tee.

    chaem: kee baok-qut sqaat tee?

    sam: miən qəy; kee baok-qut sqaat dae.

3. <u>Getting Up in the Morning</u>

    qɨən: peel prɨk qeim pñeəq maoŋ ponmaan?

    qeim: qou, kñom pñeəq prəhael maoŋ prampɨl.
             kñom trəw tɨw twəə-kaa maoŋ prambəy.

    qɨən: ŋuut-tɨk roəl prɨk tee?

    qeim: thoəmmədaa ŋuut roəl prɨk, tae cuən-kaal kroən-tae lup muk tee.
             qɨən qaeŋ kraok laəŋ maoŋ ponmaan?

    qɨən: kñom kraok laəŋ prəhael maoŋ prampɨl dae.
             tae kñom trəw tɨw riən maoŋ prambuən.

    qeim: qɨən qaeŋ sliəq-peəq yuu tee?

qɨən: mɨn yuu ponmaan tee, tae kñom trəw cam pqoun-srəy kñom dael
          tɨw riən ciə-muəy kñom.

          [srəy-srəy 'women (in general)']
qeim: nɨŋ haəy, srəy-srəy thŏəmmədaa sliəq-peəq yuu nah!

qɨən: nɨŋ haəy, coul-cət top-taeŋ kluən yuu nah!

4. Buying Clothes

Clerk: look trəw-kaa qəy?

          [sbaek 'skin, leather']
          [sbaek-cəəŋ 'shoe(s)']
sɑɑŋ: kñom cɑŋ tɨñ sbaek-cəəŋ məkuu nih.

Clerk: look peəq leik ponmaan?

sɑɑŋ: leik saamsəp-prambəy. ruəc kñom trəw-kaa krawat phɑɑŋ.

Clerk: nih krawat.

sɑɑŋ: kñom yɔɔk qaa-chiəm-cruuk nih.

Clerk: sqəy tiət tee, look?

sɑɑŋ: kñom trəw-kaa sraom-cəəŋ.

Clerk: look trəw-kaa ponmaan kuu?

sɑɑŋ: kñom yɔɔk pii kuu nih.
          teəŋ-qah tlay ponmaan?

Clerk: teəŋ-qah tlay buən-rɔɔy haasəp.

D. CONVERSATION

1. Time to Get Up!

a) A tells B to get up, [because] it's late already.
b) B asks A what time it is.
c) A replies that it is eight o'clock already.
d) B says he has to go to the doctor at nine o'clock.
e) A says that in that case he'd better get ready quickly.
f) B asks A what (pl.) he plans to do today.
g) A replies that he has to have lunch with his boss.
h) B says that in that case he'd better dress carefully.

2. Grooming

a) A asks B if he is going to take a bath this morning.
b) B replies that he doesn't feel like taking a bath today, and that he's only
   going to wash his face and shave.
c) A says that in that case he should hurry and shave, because he (A) wants
   to take a bath and wash his hair.
d) B asks A if he remembers which toothbrush is his (B's).
e) A replies that B's is red, and his (A's) is green.
f) B says that his toothpaste is nearly all gone, and that [he'll] have to buy
   some more.

g) A exclaims that B really takes a long time to shave.

h) B tells A to wait a minute, he has to comb his hair.

3. Getting Dressed

a) A says that he hasn't yet gotten his shirts from the laundry, so he'll have to wear an old one.

b) B says he's going to wear a white shirt and (tie) a dark blue tie.

c) A asks B what color tie would go with this light blue shirt.

d) B replies that this dark red one would do fine.
   B then remarks that his socks are all dirty, and asks A what size he wears.

e) A says size twenty-nine.

f) B asks if he could borrow a pair.

g) A says of course, and tells B to go ahead and put on these dark green ones.

4. The Laundry

a) A asks B if there is a laundry near here.

b) B replies that there is, and says that the laundryman comes every morning.

c) A asks if they launder clothes clean there.

d) B says of course, they wash them clean enough (dae).

e) A asks if it is expensive to have clothes done there.

f) B answers that it's not so expensive — it's five riels for a shirt, five riels for a [pair of] pants; for socks and little things it's about one riel.

g) A asks if the laundryman has come yet today.

h) B replies that he hasn't come yet, and that usually he comes about nine o'clock.

LESSON 12. EATING OUT

[Tape 22]   A. DIALOGUE

Bill

lŋiəc
late afternoon, evening
1. lŋiəc nih yəəŋ tɨw ñam baay niw kənlaeŋ naa?
Where are we going to eat this evening?

bein

naa
indefinite adjective: any, whichever
2. tɨw kənlaeŋ naa kɑ-baan dae.
[We] can go anywhere (whichever place) [you like].

srac-tae
[it] depends on, [it's] up to
3. srac-tae ləə look coh.
[It's] up to you. ([It] depends on you.)

mhoup
food
4. look coul-cət mhoup baraŋ, cən, rɨɨ mhoup kmae?
Would you like European, Chinese, or Cambodian food?

Bill

qwəy (qəy)
indefinite pronoun: anything, something, whatever
5. ñam qəy kɑ-baan dae.
[We] can eat whatever [you like].

lɔɔ-məəl
tentatively, as an experiment
6. tae kñom cɑŋ ñam mhoup kmae lɔɔ-məəl mədɑɑŋ.
But I'd like to try Cambodian food for once.

bein

baə qəñcəŋ
in that case
ləə-kok-dɔə
Le Coq d'Or (name of a restaurant in Phnom Penh)
7. baə qəñcəŋ, yəəŋ tɨw phoocəniiyəthaan ləə-kok-dɔə.
In that case, we'll go to Le Coq d'Or.

cŋañ
to be tasty, delicious
8. haaŋ nuh, kee twəə mhoup kmae cŋañ nah.
[At] that restaurant, they make delicious Cambodian food.

[At the Restaurant]

Bill

rəəh
to pick out, to choose
9. soum look cuəy rəəh mhoup qaoy kñom phɑɑŋ.
You go ahead and order (choose food) for me too.

bein

neəq-bɑmraə (-bəmraə)
waiter, servant
10. baat, cam kñom haw neəq-bəmraə sən.
Fine; just let me (wait until I) call a waiter.

165

[To the Waiter]

11. tŋay-nih miən qəy-klah?   What (pl.) do you have today?

                                   Waiter

    muk   kind, variety, dish
12. baat, miən mhoup craən muk.   [We] have a lot of things (many kinds
                                         of food).

                                   bein

    sŋao   to boil; boiled soup
    baŋkaaŋ (bəŋkaaŋ, pəkaaŋ)   prawns, river lobster
    sŋao-bəŋkaaŋ   prawn soup
    ñŏəm   meat salad
    mŏən   chicken
    ñŏəm-mŏən   chicken salad
    samlaa (səmlaa, səlaa)   stew (usually highly seasoned)
    mcuu   sour or pungent food
    səmlaa-mcuu   pungent stew
13. yɔɔk sŋao-bəŋkaaŋ, ñŏəm-mŏən,   [We'll] take prawn soup, chicken
    haəy-nɨŋ səmlaa-mcuu.   salad, and pungent stew.

                                   Waiter

    sac   meat, flesh, texture
    trəy   fish
    sac-trəy   fish (meat)
    sac-cruuk   pork
14. səmlaa-mcuu nuh, look yɔɔk   Do you want the pungent stew with
    sac-trəy rɨɨ sac-cruuk?   fish or pork?

                                   bein

    chaa   to fry; a fried meat and vegetable
                                             mixture
    koo   cow, ox
    sac-koo   beef
    caan   plate, dish
15. sac-trəy; haəy yɔɔk chaa-sac-koo   Fish; and [we'll] have a plate of
    məcaan phaaŋ.   fried beef too.

                                   Waiter

16. coh, baay?   What about rice?

                                   bein

    liiŋ   to fry, to braise
    baay-liiŋ   fried rice
    camhoy (cəmhoy)   to steam
    baay-cəmhoy   steamed rice, white rice
17. yɔɔk baay-liiŋ məcaan haəy-nɨŋ   [We'll] have a plate of fried rice and
    baay-cəmhoy məcaan.   a plate of steamed rice.

[To Bill]

    həl   to be hot, spicy
18. look ñam mhoup həl baan tee?   Can you eat spicy food?

Bill

      kom

19. kñom ñam baan, tae kom qaoy
    həl peek.

        negative imperative: don't

        I can eat [it], but don't make [it] too
        hot.

bein

[To Waiter]

      mteeh

20. kom daq mteeh craən peek nəh!

        hot (chili) peppers

        Don't put too many peppers [in it]
        now!

Waiter

      prap
      neə̆q-twəə-mhoup

21. baat, cam kñom prap neə̆q-twəə-
    mhoup.

        to tell, to inform
        cook

        Right, I'll tell the cook.

bein

      byeə

22. məc, ñam byeə tɔe?

        beer

        How about it, shall we have some
        beer?

Bill

23. miən qəy?

        Why not?

bein

[To Waiter]

      dɑɑp

24. qaoy byeə pii dɑɑp mɔɔk.

        bottle(s)

        Bring two bottles of beer.

Bill

      haet
      haet qwəy baan ciə
      kambət (kəmbət, kəbət)

25. haet qwəy baan ciə kmiən kəmbət
    nɨw ləə tok?

        reason, cause
        why?, why is it that . . .?
        knife
        Why aren't there any knives on the
        table?

bein

      praə
      sɑɑm
      slaap-priə

26. mhoup kmae, kee praə tae sɑɑm
    haəy-nɨŋ slaap-priə tee.

        to use
        fork
        spoon
        [With] Cambodian food, you use (one
        uses) only forks and spoons.

[Later]

Bill

      ciət

27. sŋao-bəŋkɑɑŋ nih miən ciət cŋañ
    nah; kee daq qwəy-klah?

        taste, flavor
        This prawn-soup has a very good taste;
        what do they put [in it]?

ktɨm   onions, garlic
tɨk-trəy   fish-sauce
krɨəŋ   thing, prerequisite (here: spices)
28. kraw-pii bəŋkaaŋ, kee daq qəŋkaa,   Besides prawns, they use (put) rice,
    ktɨm, tɨk-trəy, haəy-nɨŋ krɨəŋ   onions, fish-sauce, and various
    pseiŋ-pseiŋ.   spices.

[To Waiter]

bəŋqaem (bəŋqaem, pəŋqaem)   sweets, dessert
29. miən bəŋqaem qwəy-klah?   What desserts do you have?

Waiter

lhoŋ   papaya
mnŏəh   pineapple
swaay   mango(s)
30. baat, miən ceik, lhoŋ, mnŏəh,   Well, [we] have bananas, papaya,
    haəy-nɨŋ swaay.   pineapple, and mangos.

saŋkyaa (səŋkyaa)   custard, pudding
kareim   ice-cream
31. kraw-pii nuh, miən saŋkyaa   Besides that, [we] have custard and
    haəy-nɨŋ kareim phaaŋ.   ice-cream.

Bill

plae-swaay   mango
32. kñom caŋ ñam plae-swaay   I'd like to try mango once. (I want to
    lɔɔ-məəl mədaaŋ.   eat mango [and] try [it] once.)

bein

cqaet   to be (uncomfortably) full,
                                              stuffed
33. kñom mɨn yɔɔk qəy tee;   I'm not [going to] have anything;
    cqaet haəy.   [I'm] stuffed.

B. GRAMMAR AND DRILLS

1. qwəy and naa as Indefinite Pronouns and Adjectives

It was pointed out in Lesson 9, B, 12 that qwəy 'what?' and naa 'which?',
where?', as well as their compounds with muəy 'one' and klah 'some' (Lesson
11, B, 5), may occur both as interrogative pronouns and as interrogative adjectives, e.g.:

As interrogative pronouns:

look tɨw naa?   Where are you going?
look tɨñ qwəy?   What are you buying?

As interrogative adjectives:

look tɨw kənlaeŋ naa?   Which place are you going to?
look tɨñ siəwphɨw qwəy?   What book are you buying?

qwəy and naa also occur as indefinite pronouns and indefinite adjectives. These
indefinite words have a variety of translations in English, depending on the context.

qwəy as an indefinite pronoun may be translated either 'something', 'anything', or 'whatever'; the range of possibilities is shown in the following sentences:

koət tɨw tɨñ qəy nɨw psaa.	He went to buy something at the market.
kñom mɨn caŋ tɨñ qwəy tee.	I don't want to buy anything.
ñam qwəy ka-baan dae.	[We] can eat anything/whatever [you like].
baə look caŋ baan qwəy, kñom nɨŋ cuun.	If you want something/anything, I'll give it [to you].
	or: Whatever you want, I'll give it [to you].

Likewise, naa as an indefinite pronoun may be translated either 'somewhere', 'anywhere', or 'wherever', as in the following examples:

look tɨw naa tee?	Are you going somewhere/anywhere?
kñom mɨn tɨw naa tee.	I'm not going anywhere.
tɨw naa ka-baan dae.	[We] can go anywhere/wherever [you wish].
baə look caŋ tɨw naa, kñom nɨŋ cuun look tɨw.	If you want to go somewhere/anywhere, I'll take you.
	or: Wherever you want to go, I'll take you.

As an indefinite adjective, qwəy may be translated 'some/any/whatever', according to the context, e.g.:

look caŋ tɨñ siəwphɨw qwəy tee?	Do you want to buy some/any book?
kñom mɨn caŋ tɨñ siəwphɨw qwəy tee.	I don't want to buy any book.
tɨñ siəwphɨw qwəy ka-baan dae.	[You] can buy any/whatever book [you like].
baə look caŋ baan siəwphɨw qwəy, kñom nɨŋ tɨñ cuun.	If you want some/any book, I'll buy [it] for [you].
	or: I'll buy you whatever book you want.

Similarly, naa as an indefinite adjective can be translated 'some/any/whichever', as in:

look tɨw kənlaeŋ naa tee?	Are you going some/any place?
kñom mɨn tɨw kənlaeŋ naa tee.	I'm not going any place (anywhere).
tɨw kənlaeŋ naa ka-baan dae.	[We] can go anywhere/wherever [you wish].
baə look caŋ məəl woət naa, kñom nɨŋ cuun look tɨw.	If you want to see some/any temple, I'll take you.
	or: Whatever/whichever temple you want to see, I'll take you.

qwəy and naa also occur with the elements muəy and klah as compound indefinite pronouns and adjectives, as in the following examples:

As indefinite pronouns:

baə look caŋ ñam qwəy-muəy, prap knom mɔɔk.	If you want to eat something (sing.), just tell me.
baə look caŋ tɨñ qwəy-klah, tɨw psaa tɨw.	If you want to buy something (pl.), go ahead to the market.

baə look caŋ baan ɋanaa-muəy,   If you want any (one), just tell me.
prap kñom mɔɔk.

(naa-klah apparently does not occur as an indefinite pronoun.)

As indefinite adjectives (the second and fourth examples below would normally
occur without -klah, which is redundant here):

baə look caŋ baan siəwphɨw   If you would like to have any/some
qwəy-muəy, kñom nɨŋ tɨñ cuun.   (one) book, I'll buy it for you.
baə look caŋ tɨñ ɋəywan qwəy-klah,   If you want to buy some/any (pl.)
kñom nɨŋ cuəy tɨñ.   things, I'll help you buy them.
baə look caŋ tɨw kənlaeŋ naa-muəy,   If you want to go somewhere (some
kñom nɨŋ cuun look tɨw.   (one) place), I'll take you.
baə look caŋ məəl wŏət naa-klah,   Whatever temples you'd like to see,
kñom nɨŋ cuun look tɨw.   I'll take you.

1-A. Substitution Drill

Teacher	Student
ñam ɋəy kɑ-baan dae.	ñam ɋəy kɑ-baan dae.
twəə	twəə ɋəy kɑ-baan dae.
tɨñ	tɨñ ɋəy kɑ-baan dae.
məəl	məəl ɋəy kɑ-baan dae.
riən	riən ɋəy kɑ-baan dae.
yɔɔk	yɔɔk ɋəy kɑ-baan dae.
praə	praə ɋəy kɑ-baan dae.

1-B. Substitution Drill

Teacher	Student
tɨñ mhoup qwəy kɑ-baan dae.	tɨñ mhoup qwəy kɑ-baan dae.
siəwphɨw	tɨñ siəwphɨw qwəy kɑ-baan dae.
ɋaaw	tɨñ ɋaaw qwəy kɑ-baan dae.
pɔə	tɨñ pɔə qwəy kɑ-baan dae.
chaa	tɨñ chaa qwəy kɑ-baan dae.
sac	tɨñ sac qwəy kɑ-baan dae.
laan	tɨñ laan qwəy kɑ-baan dae.

1-C. Substitution Drill

Teacher	Student
kñom mɨn ñam ɋəy tee.	kñom mɨn ñam ɋəy tee.
twəə	kñom mɨn twəə ɋəy tee.
tɨñ	kñom mɨn tɨñ ɋəy tee.
məəl	kñom mɨn məəl ɋəy tee.
yɔɔk	kñom mɨn yɔɔk ɋəy tee.
praə	kñom mɨn praə ɋəy tee.
riən	kñom mɨn riən ɋəy tee.

1-D. Substitution Drill

Teacher	Student
kñom mɨn caŋ baan mhoup qwəy tee.	kñom mɨn caŋ baan mhoup qwəy tee.
siəwphɨw	kñom mɨn caŋ baan siəwphɨw qwəy tee.
plae-chəə	kñom mɨn caŋ baan plae-chəə qwəy tee.
pɔə	kñom mɨn caŋ baan pɔə qwəy tee.
bəŋqaem	kñom mɨn caŋ baan bəŋqaem qwəy tee.
laan	kñom mɨn caŋ baan laan qwəy tee.

1-E. Substitution Drill

Teacher	Student
tɨw kənlaeŋ naa kɑ-baan dae.	tɨw kənlaeŋ naa kɑ-baan dae.
pteəh	tɨw pteəh naa kɑ-baan dae.
santhəkiə	tɨw santhəkiə naa kɑ-baan dae.
phoocəniiyəthaan	tɨw phoocəniiyəthaan naa kɑ-baan dae.
psaa	tɨw psaa naa kɑ-baan dae.
woət	tɨw woət naa kɑ-baan dae.

1-F. Substitution Drill

Teacher	Student
tɨw tŋay naa kɑ-baan dae.	tɨw tŋay naa kɑ-baan dae.
khae	tɨw khae naa kɑ-baan dae.
cnam	tɨw cnam naa kɑ-baan dae.
qatɨt	tɨw qatɨt naa kɑ-baan dae.
peel	tɨw peel naa kɑ-baan dae.

1-G. Substitution Drill

Teacher	Student
kñom mɨn caŋ tɨw kənlaeŋ naa tee.	kñom mɨn caŋ tɨw kənlaeŋ naa tee.
pteəh	kñom mɨn caŋ tɨw pteəh naa tee.
psaa	kñom mɨn caŋ tɨw psaa naa tee.
woət	kñom mɨn caŋ tɨw woət naa tee.
santhəkiə	kñom mɨn caŋ tɨw santhəkiə naa tee.
phoocəniiyəthaan	kñom mɨn caŋ tɨw phoocəniiyəthaan naa tee.

2. The Verb srac-tae

srac-tae is a transitive verb which means '[it] depends on, [it's] up to' as in:

srac-tae ləə look coh.	(It's] up to you. (It depends on you.)
kñom tɨw rɨɨ mɨn tɨw	My going (or not going) depends on
srac-tae ləə qəwpuk kñom.	my father.

srac-tae also sometimes takes an entire clause (subject plus verb) as its object, as in:

srac-tae look kɨt coh.   [It] depends on [what] you decide (think).

2-A. Substitution Drill

Teacher	Student
tɨw naa kɑ-baan, srac tae ləə <u>look</u> coh.	tɨw naa kɑ-baan, srac-tae ləə <u>look</u> coh.
<u>bein qaeŋ</u>	tɨw naa kɑ-baan, srac-tae ləə <u>bein qaeŋ</u> coh.
<u>koun</u>	tɨw naa kɑ-baan, srac-tae ləə <u>koun</u> coh.
<u>Bill qaeŋ</u>	tɨw naa kɑ-baan, srac-tae ləə <u>Bill qaeŋ</u> coh.
<u>bɑɑŋ</u>	tɨw naa kɑ-baan, srac-tae ləə <u>bɑɑŋ</u> coh.
<u>pqoun</u>	tɨw naa kɑ-baan, srac-tae ləə <u>pqoun</u> coh.

2-B. Substitution Drill

Teacher	Student
<u>tɨw naa</u> kɑ-baan dae, srac-tae look kɨt coh.	<u>tɨw naa</u> kɑ-baan dae, srac-tae look kɨt coh.
<u>ñam qwəy</u>	<u>ñam qwəy</u> kɑ-baan dae, srac-tae look kɨt coh.
<u>twəə qwəy</u>	<u>twəə qwəy</u> kɑ-baan dae, srac-tae look kɨt coh.
<u>tɨw məəl qwəy</u>	<u>tɨw məəl qwəy</u> kɑ-baan dae, srac-tae look kɨt coh.
<u>tɨñ qwəy</u>	<u>tɨñ qwəy</u> kɑ-baan dae, srac-tae look kɨt coh.
<u>tɨw peel naa</u>	<u>tɨw peel naa</u> kɑ-baan dae, srac-tae look kɨt coh.
<u>peə̆q qwəy</u>	<u>peə̆q qwəy</u> kɑ-baan dae, srac-tae look kɨt coh.
<u>praə qwəy</u>	<u>praə qwəy</u> kɑ-baan dae, srac-tae look kɨt coh.

3. The Adverb <u>lɔɔ-məəl</u>

<u>lɔɔ-məəl</u> is a compound adverb composed of the verbs <u>lɔɔ</u> 'to try' and <u>məəl</u> 'to see, to watch'. It typically occurs after a primary verb (with or without an intervening object), with the adverbial meaning 'tentatively, as an experiment, as a trial', as in

tae kñom cɑŋ ñam mhoup kmae <u>lɔɔ-məəl</u> mədɑɑŋ.	But I'd like to <u>try</u> Cambodian food for once (<u>and see how I like it</u>).
kñom cɑŋ ñam plae-swaay <u>lɔɔ-məəl</u> mədɑɑŋ.	I'd like to <u>try</u> some mango once (<u>as an experiment</u>).

3-A. Substitution Drill

Teacher	Student
kñom caŋ ñam <u>mhoup kmae</u> lɔɔ-cci məl mədaaŋ.	kñom caŋ ñam <u>mhoup kmae</u> lɔɔ-məl mədaaŋ.
<u>plae-swaay</u>	kñom caŋ ñam <u>plae-swaay</u> lɔɔ-cci mədaaŋ.
<u>sŋao-mŏən</u>	kñom caŋ ñam <u>sŋao-mŏən</u> lɔɔ-cci mədaaŋ.
<u>sac-koo</u>	kñom caŋ ñam <u>sac-koo</u> lɔɔ-cci mədaaŋ.
<u>lhoŋ</u>	kñom caŋ ñam <u>lhoŋ</u> lɔɔ-cci mədaaŋ.
<u>saŋkyaa</u>	kñom caŋ ñam <u>saŋkyaa</u> lɔɔ-cci mədaaŋ.
<u>səmlaɑ-mcuu</u>	kñom caŋ ñam <u>səmlaɑ-mcuu</u> lɔɔ-cci mədaaŋ.
<u>mteeh</u>	kñom caŋ ñam <u>mteeh</u> lɔɔ-cci mədaaŋ.

3-B. Substitution Drill

Teacher	Student
kñom caŋ ñam mhoup kmae lɔɔ-məl mədaaŋ.	kñom caŋ <u>ñam</u> mhoup kmae lɔɔ-məl mədaaŋ.
<u>baək laan nuh</u>	kñom caŋ <u>baək laan nuh</u> lɔɔ-məl mədaaŋ.
<u>nɨw santhəkiə nih</u>	kñom caŋ <u>nɨw santhəkiə nih</u> lɔɔ-məl mədaaŋ.
<u>cih rəteh-pləəŋ</u>	kñom caŋ <u>cih rəteh-pləəŋ</u> lɔɔ-məl mədaaŋ.
<u>məl riəŋ nuh</u>	kñom caŋ <u>məl riəŋ nuh</u> lɔɔ-məl mədaaŋ.
<u>twəə kruu-bəŋriən</u>	kñom caŋ <u>twəə kruu-bəŋriən</u> lɔɔ-məl medaaŋ.
<u>twəə srae</u>	kñom caŋ <u>twəə srae</u> lɔɔ-məl mədaaŋ.
<u>riən wɨcciə-pɛɛt</u>	kñom caŋ <u>riən wɨcciə-pɛɛt</u> lɔɔ-məl mədaaŋ.
<u>twəə mhoup nuh</u>	kñom caŋ <u>twəə mhoup nuh</u> lɔɔ-məl mədaaŋ.

4. <u>cam</u> as an Initiating Auxiliary

   At the beginning of an imperative sentence, <u>cam</u> 'to wait' has the special meaning 'wait until . . . , wait and . . .', as in

<u>cam</u> kñom haw neəq-bəmraə sən.	Wait until I (just let me) call the waiter.

In this function, <u>cam</u> is parallel with the previously met auxiliaries <u>soum</u> 'please' (Lesson 3, B, 2), <u>mɔɔk</u> 'come on and' (Lesson 9, B, 10), and <u>cuəy</u> 'help by, please' (Lesson 11, B, 10).

4-A. Substitution Drill

Teacher	Student
cam kñom haw neəq-bəmraə sən.	càm kñom haw neəq-bəmraə sən.
<u>haw taqsii</u>	cam kñom <u>haw taqsii</u> sən.
<u>rəəh mhoup</u>	cam kñom <u>rəəh mhoup</u> sən.
<u>tɨw psaa</u>	cam kñom <u>tɨw psaa</u> sən.

Teacher	Student
sət sɑq	cam kñom sət sɑq sən.
baək twiə	cam kñom baək twiə sən.
twəə kluən	cam kñom twəə kluən sən.

4-B. Progressive Substitution Drill

Teacher	Student
cam tɨw psaa ciə-muəy kñom sən.	cam tɨw psaa ciə-muəy kñom sən.
soum	soum tɨw psaa ciə-muəy kñom sən.
mɔɔk	mɔɔk tɨw psaa ciə-muəy kñom sən.
baək twiə qaoy kñom sən.	mɔɔk baək twiə qaoy kñom sən.
soum	soum baək twiə qaoy kñom sən.
cuəy	cuəy baək twiə qaoy kñom sən.
cam	cam baək twiə qaoy kñom sən.

5. sac as a Compound-Former

sac 'meat, flesh, texture', like neəq 'person, the one who', khae 'month', pɔə 'color', etc., frequently occurs as the head of compounds. In such compounds sac is modified by the name of specific animals, fish, or fowl, and the resulting compounds refer to various kinds of meat; e.g.:

sac + koo 'cow'	>	sac-koo 'beef'
sac + cruuk 'pig'	>	sac-cruuk 'pork'
sac + moən 'chicken'	>	sac-moən 'chicken (flesh)'
sac + trəy 'fish'	>	sac-trəy 'fish (flesh)'
sac + bəŋkaaŋ 'prawn'	>	sac-bəŋkaaŋ 'prawn (flesh)'

5-A. Substitution Drill

Teacher	Student
qaoy chaa sac-koo məcaan mɔɔk phɑɑŋ.	qaoy chaa sac-koo məcaan mɔɔk phɑɑŋ.
sac-cruuk	qaoy chaa sac-cruuk məcaan mɔɔk phɑɑŋ.
sac-trəy	qaoy chaa sac-trəy məcaan mɔɔk phɑɑŋ.
sac-bəŋkaaŋ	qaoy chaa sac-bəŋkaaŋ məcaan mɔɔk phɑɑŋ.
sac-moən	qaoy chaa sac-moən məcaan mɔɔk phɑɑŋ.

6. The Negative Imperative Auxiliary kom

kom is the negative imperative auxiliary which means 'don't', as in

kom qaoy həl peek.	Don't make [it] too spicy.

kom never occurs with the final negative particle tee, but negative imperative sentences are frequently followed by the final hortatory particle nəh (Lesson 11, B, 2), as in

kom daq mteeh craən peek nəh!	Don't put too many hot peppers in [it]!

6-A. Substitution Drill

Teacher	Student
kom daq mteeh craən peek nəh!	kom daq mteeh craən peek nəh!
skɑɑ	kom daq skɑɑ craən peek nəh!

Teacher	Student
tɨk-dah-koo	kom daq tɨk-dah-koo craən peek nəh!
tɨk	kom daq tɨk craən peek nəh!
tɨk-trəy	kom daq tɨk-trəy craən peek nəh!
sac-koo	kom daq sac-koo craən peek nəh!
ktɨm	kom daq ktɨm craən peek nəh!

6-B. Transformation Drill

Teacher	Student
kñom praə kəmbət.	kom praə kəmbət nəh!
kñom tɨw kənlaeŋ nuh.	kom tɨw kənlaeŋ nuh nəh!
kñom məəl siəwphɨw nuh.	kom məəl siəwphɨw nuh nəh!
kñom daq mteeh craən peek.	kom daq mteeh craən peek nəh!
kñom peəq qaaw nih.	kom peəq qaaw nih nəh!
kñom niyiəy leeŋ.	kom niyiəy leeŋ nəh!
kñom ñam mhoup həl.	kom ñam mhoup həl nəh!
kñom qaoy həl peek.	kom qaoy həl peek nəh!

7. The Interrogative Phrase haet qwəy baan ciə

The interrogative phrase haet qwəy baan ciə occurs at the beginning of questions and can be conveniently translated 'why?' (literally: what reason results that . . . ?, why is it that . . . ?'), as in

haet qwəy baan ciə kmiən kəmbət nɨw ləə tok?	Why are there no knives on the table? (Why is it that there are no knives on the table?)

It is somewhat more formal than məc (kɑɑ) 'why?' (Lesson 3, B, 16), and would always replace məc in self-conscious speech.

7-A. Substitution Drill

Teacher	Student
haet qwəy baan ciə kmiən kəmbət nɨw ləə tok?	haet qwəy baan ciə kmiən kəmbət nɨw ləə tok?
caan	haet qwəy baan ciə kmiən caan nɨw ləə tok?
sɑɑm	haet qwəy baan ciə kmiən sɑɑm nɨw ləə tok?
slaap-priə	haet qwəy baan ciə kmiən slaap-priə nɨw ləə tok?
mhoup	haet qwəy baan ciə kmiən mhoup nɨw ləə tok?
skɑɑ	haet qwəy baan ciə kmiən skɑɑ nɨw ləə tok?
qwəy	haet qwəy baan ciə kmiən qwəy nɨw ləə tok?
siəwphɨw	haet qwəy baan ciə kmiən siəwphɨw nɨw ləə tok?

7-B. Transformation Drill

Teacher	Student
məc kɑɑ kmiən kəmbət nɨw ləə tok?	haet qwəy baan ciə kmiən kəmbət nɨw ləə tok?
məc kɑɑ look mɨn tɨw psaa?	haet qwəy baan ciə look mɨn tɨw psaa?
məc kɑɑ look luəq pteˇəh nih?	haet qwəy baan ciə look luəq pteˇəh nih?
məc kɑɑ look mɔɔk khaŋ-nih?	haet qwəy baan ciə look mɔɔk khaŋ-nih?
məc kɑɑ look riən phiəsaa-kmae?	haet qwəy baan ciə look riən phiəsaa-kmae?
məc kɑɑ look kraok laəŋ pii prəlɨm?	haet qwəy baan ciə look kraok laəŋ pii prəlɨm?
məc kɑɑ look trəlɑp tɨw pteˇəh?	haet qwəy baan ciə look trəlɑp tɨw pteˇəh?
məc kɑɑ look daə tɨw taam pləw nih?	haet qwəy baan ciə look daə tɨw taam pləw nih?
məc kɑɑ look mɔɔk pnum-pɨñ?	haet qwəy baan ciə look mɔɔk pnum-pɨñ?
məc kɑɑ look qəŋkuy kənlaeŋ nih?	haet qwəy baan ciə look qəŋkuy kənlaeŋ nih?

[Tape 23]   C. COMPREHENSION

1. Having Lunch

saran: yɨn, tɨw ñam qəy sən tee?

yɨn: tɨw kɑ-tɨw; saran cɑŋ tɨw kənlaeŋ naa?

        [kɑndaal (kəndaal, kədaal) 'middle, center; central']
        [psaa-kəndaal 'the Central Market']
saran: kñom cɑŋ tɨw psaa-kəndaal.

        [lɨən 'fast']
yɨn: tɨw qaoy lɨən; kñom klɨən nah!

saran: kñom kɑ-klɨən nah dae.
        mɔɔk qəŋkuy tok nih.

Waiter: look trəw-kaa qwəy?

saran: kñom yɔɔk baay-liiŋ.
        yɨn trəw-kaa qəy?

        [kuy-tiəw 'Chinese noodle dish']
yɨn: kñom yɔɔk kuy-tiəw.

        [phək 'to drink (familiar)']
saran: yɨn phək qəy tee?

yɨn: kñom yɔɔk byeə.

saran: yɔɔk byeə qaoy kñom pii dɑɑp.

[Waiter brings the food]

saran: yɨn, kuy-tiəw cŋañ tee?

yɨn: cŋañ nah. haəy baay-liiŋ cŋañ tee?

saran: cŋañ dae.
        yɨn trəw-kaa bəŋqaem tee?

yɨn: mɨn-bac tee; kñom cqaet haəy.

[To Waiter]

saran: teə̃ŋ-qɑh tlay ponmaan?

Waiter: baat, mhoup haəy-nɨŋ byeə tlay paetsəp-pram riəl.

2. Fruits

thuən: nɨw srok-qaamerɨc miən plae-chəə craən tee?

            [douc 'to be like, similar']
Paul: baat, tae mɨn douc plae-chəə nɨw srok-kmae tee.

thuən: look coul-cət plae-chəə kmae tee?

Paul: miən plae-chəə klah kñom coul-cət ñam, tae plae-chəə klah tiət kñom ñam mɨn baan tee.

thuən: look coul-cət plae-chəə qwəy ciəŋ-kee?

Paul: kñom coul-cət plae-swaay ciəŋ-kee; mətŋay kñom ñam məlou kɑ-qɑh dae.

thuən: srok-qaamerɨc miən plae-swaay tee?

            [pom 'apple(s)']
            [trɑɽeə̃ŋ-baay-cuu (trəpeə̃ŋ-, təpeə̃ŋ-) 'grape(s)']
Paul: miən klah dae, haəy-nɨŋ miən plae-chəə pseiŋ tiət, kɨɨ pom, trəpeə̃ŋ-baay-cuu, haəy-nɨŋ krouc.
            [thuureen (thureen) 'durian']
            [lmut 'sapodilla' (a sweet brown-skinned fruit with the texture of a
                ripe pear)]
            [muə̃ŋkhut (məŋkhut, məkhut) 'mangosteen']
            [yaaŋ 'kind, way, variety']
            [rɔɔk mɨn baan 'to be unable to find']
     srok-kmae miən plae-chəə craən yaaŋ dael rɔɔk mɨn baan nɨw srok-qaamerɨc, kɨɨ thureen, lmut, haəy-nɨŋ məŋkhut.

3. Discussing Food

kiən: look coul-cət mhoup kmae tee?

David: kñom kɑɑ coul-cət dae, tae mhoup klah həl peek; kñom ñam mɨn baan tee.

kiən: nɨw srok-qaamerɨc, miən phoocəniiyəthaan kmae tee?

David: kmiən tee, tae miən phoocəniiyəthaan cən craən nah.

kiən: look coul-cət mhoup cən tee?

David: baat, kñom coul-cət nah.

kiən: qəñcəŋ look cɑŋ tɨw pisaa baay nɨw phoocəniiyəthaan ciə-muəy kñom tee?

David: qɑɑ-kun nah.

D. CONVERSATION

1. <u>Discussing Restaurants</u>

   a) A asks B where he wants to eat this evening.
   b) B replies that they can go anywhere at all; it's up to A.
   c) A asks B if he would like European, Chinese, or Cambodian food.
   d) B replies that he can eat any kind of food at all, but that he'd like to try Cambodian food for once.
   e) A says that in that case, they'll go to Le Coq d'Or; then he asks B if he's ever been to that restaurant.
   f) B replies that he has never gone there.
   g) A says that they make very good Cambodian food there, and that they have many kinds of food there.

2. <u>Ordering Food</u>

   a) A asks B what he would like to eat.
   b) B asks A to go ahead and order for him too.
   c) A asks the Waiter what they have today.
   d) The Waiter replies that they have many kinds of food, and that it depends on what A decides.
   e) A orders chicken soup, fish salad, and sour soup.
   f) The Waiter asks A what meat he wants in the sour soup.
   g) A answers that he'll take pork, and orders a plate of fried beef too.
   h) The Waiter asks A if they want some fried rice.
   i) A answers that they'll take only steamed rice, and tells the waiter to bring two bottles of beer too.

3. <u>Ordering Dessert</u>

   a) The Waiter asks A if they want some dessert.
   b) A asks the Waiter what fruits they have today.
   c) The Waiter answers that they have bananas, pineapple, mango, and papaya.
   d) B asks the Waiter if they have any sweets besides fruits.
   e) The Waiter replies that they have custard, ice cream, and various kinds of cakes.
   f) B says he'll take some custard, and asks A what he wants.
   g) A replies that he'll try some papaya.

4. <u>Discussing Food</u>

   a) A asks B if he likes Cambodian food.
   b) B answers that he does like Cambodian food, but that he likes European food better.
   c) A asks B why he likes European food better than Cambodian food.
   d) B answers that Cambodian food is usually too hot, but that some dishes do have a very good flavor.
   e) A asks B if he likes Cambodian fruits.
   f) B answers that he does, and that he likes mango and papaya best of all.
   g) A asks B if they have papaya in America.
   h) B answers that there are some, and that there are other kinds of fruits which can't be found in Cambodia, such as apples and grapes.
   i) A asks B if he would like some mango now.
   j) B tells A not to joke (niyiəy leeŋ); he's already stuffed.

LESSON 13. REVIEW OF LESSONS 8-12

A. Review of Dialogues

In preparation for the review lesson, review the Dialogues of Lessons 8-12. To test yourself, cover the English column and supply the English equivalents of the Cambodian sentences; then cover the Cambodian column and supply the Cambodian equivalents of the English sentences. If you cannot produce the Cambodian equivalents quickly and smoothly, review the relevant sections of the Grammar and Drills.

B. Review of Comprehension

The teacher will read selected conversations from the Comprehension sections of Lessons 8-12, calling on individual students for English translations of the sentences.

C. Questions (Test for Comprehension and Fluency)

Provide an appropriate answer to each of the following oral questions. Make the answers factual when possible. Every response should be preceded by the appropriate response particle, baat or caah. "Yes" or "No" answers should be followed by an affirmation or negation of the content of the question, in either the full form or an appropriate abbreviated form, e.g.:

look tɨw psaa tee?	baat, mɨn tɨw tee.
Are you going to the market?	No, [I'm] not going.

Answers may be either written or oral; if oral, every student should have an opportunity to answer every question. If a test for grading purposes is desired, the answers may be written, but in either case the questions should be oral. The teacher will repeat each question twice. Listen to the question in its entirety the first time; an unfamiliar word may be cleared up by the context in which it occurs.

1. look (look-srəy) kliən baay tee?
2. miən bəntup tumnee tee?
3. look (look-srəy) ñam mhoup həl baan tee?
4. koət niyiəy phiəsaa-kmae baan tee?
5. som-tooh, qəwpuk look (look-srəy) twəə-kaa qwəy?
6. nɨw srok-kmae, miən ponmaan rədəw?
7. look (look-srəy) pisaa baay nɨw nih rɨɨ?
8. tŋay-nih kɨɨ tŋay qwəy?
9. pteəh look (look-srəy) miən bəntup ponmaan?
10. prɨk nih nael qaeŋ ŋuut-tɨk tee?
11. tŋay-nih yəəŋ tɨw ñam baay nɨw kənlaeŋ naa?
12. look (look-srəy) cəñ pii salaa, taə, kɨt twəə-kaa qwəy?
13. rədəw-kdaw miən ponmaan khae?
14. som-tooh, miən phoocəniiyəthaan nɨw cɨt nih tee?
15. look (look-srəy) coh tlay qaoy kñom baan tee?
16. (Student's name) peəq sraom-cəəŋ leik ponmaan?
17. tŋay-nih miən mhoup qwəy-klah?
18. look (look-srəy) caŋ bəŋriən tnaq qwəy?
19. taə, nɨw rədəw-pliəŋ miən pliəŋ roəl tŋay rɨɨ?
20. look (look-srəy) coul-cət mhoup baraŋ, kmae, rɨɨ mhoup cən?

179

21. kñom tɨw məəl bəntup sən baan tee?
22. douccneh look (look-srəy) nɨw muəy qatɨt, mɛɛn rɨɨ?
23. thoӗmmədaa, neĕq-baok-qut mɔɔk maoŋ ponmaan?
24. tŋay-nih look (look-srəy) peӗq qaaw pɔə qəy?
25. sŋao nuh, look (look-srəy) yɔɔk sac-moӗn rɨɨ sac-cruuk?
26. look (look-srəy) trəw-kaa bəntup dael miən krɛɛ muəy rɨɨ krɛɛ pii?
27. nɨw rədəw-pliəŋ miən pliəŋ pɨñ muəy tŋay rɨɨ?
28. look (look-srəy) cam tee, siəwphɨw rəbah kñom qanaa-muəy?
29. tŋay-nih look (look-srəy) kɨt twəə qwəy-klah?
30. krawat pɔə qəy sam nɨŋ qaaw khiəw-kcəy nih?
31. haaŋ nuh kee twəə mhoup kmae cŋañ tee?
32. look (look-srəy) twəə-kaa qae-nuh baan ponmaan khae haəy?
33. bɑɑŋ-proh look (look-srəy) trəw riən ponmaan cnam tiət?
34. look (look-srəy) coul-cət rədəw naa ciəŋ-kee?
35. look (look-srəy) trəw-kaa qwəy tiət tee?
36. pqoun-srəy look (look-srəy) miən pdəy haəy-rɨnɨw?
37. look (look-srəy) dael səmnaq nɨw santhəkiə-sokkhaalay tee?
38. look (look-srəy) coul-cət qaa-pɔə-krəhɑɑm nih tee?
39. look (look-srəy) tɨw srok-srae, taə tɨw taam qwəy?
40. baə tŋay-nih ciə tŋay-can, tŋay kraoy ciə tŋay qwəy?
41. peel-prɨk look (look-srəy) kraok laəŋ maoŋ ponmaan?
42. haet qwəy baan ciə kmiən siəwphɨw nɨw ləə tok?
43. baə khae nih ciə khae-meӗqkəraa, khae mun ciə khae qwəy?
44. laan teӗŋ-pii nuh, taə laan naa tlay thaok ciəŋ?
45. məc kɑɑ look (look-srəy) mɔɔk taam pləw nih?
46. baə tŋay-nih ciə tŋay-qatɨt, tŋay mun ciə tŋay qwəy?
47. look (look-srəy) tɨw naa tee?
48. haet qwəy baan ciə look (look-srəy) riən phiəsaa-kmae?
49. look (look-srəy) cɑŋ tɨñ laan naa-muəy tee?
50. look (look-srəy) cɑŋ baan plae-chəə qwəy-muəy tee?

D. Translation

1. My father is in government service.
2. I have to go to the barbershop (first).
3. Hey, [it's] really raining hard!
4. [We'll] take only dinner.
5. I have to go to the dentist today at nine o'clock.
6. Let me call a waiter (first).
7. I don't know yet for sure.
8. I think it would be better to be a teacher.
9. I forgot to bring an umbrella.
10. I don't feel like shaving today; [I'll] just wash my face.
11. I don't like the rainy season at all.
12. If you stay a week, I'll lower the price for you.
13. His is green; mine's red.
14. [We] can eat wherever [you like].
15. [We'll] take chicken soup, pork salad, and sour soup.
16. When I finish studying, I want to be a doctor.
17. I'm not so wet, because I'm wearing a raincoat.
18. The hot season is from March to May.
19. If you cross the street, you'll see another hotel, called the Monorom Hotel.

20. Get ready quickly! (Hurry and get ready!)
21. This toothpaste is almost gone.
22. Bring a plate of fried rice and two plates of steamed rice.
23. Don't put too many peppers in it now!
24. It takes a long time to study to be a doctor.
25. If you walk along this street, you'll see the Le Coq d'Or Restaurant on the right.
26. It's 125 riels per day, including breakfast.
27. If you want a lot of money, it would be better to go into business.
28. My younger uncle is the manager of a cigarette factory.
29. In the rainy season, it's difficult to go anywhere.
30. I don't want to go anywhere.
31. It's up to you.
32. There are about 100 workers, including clerks, salesmen, and laborers.
33. If this month is September, next month is October.
34. If today is Friday, yesterday was Thursday.
35. If you want to go anywhere (pl.), I'll take you (and go).
36. It's neither hot nor cold; it's just pleasant.
37. This red one would go with that dark blue shirt.
38. The rain has almost stopped now.
39. I don't want to eat anything more; I'm already full.
40. Take these gentlemen to see room number forty-eight.
41. I'd like to try some pineapple.
42. Cambodia isn't as cold as France; it's just comfortably cool, that's all.
43. Those two restaurants are about equally expensive.
44. If you'd like to buy something (pl.), go ahead to the market.
45. Come on, let's go downstairs.
46. If you'd like to eat some (one) fruit, just tell me.
47. We can go any place [you like].
48. [With] Cambodian food, they use only forks and spoons.
49. My house has a kitchen, a living room, and two bedrooms.
50. I'll take you to see whatever temples you want to see. (If you want to see any temples, I'll take you (and go).)

LESSON 14. STEAMBOAT TRAVEL

[Tape 24]   A. DIALOGUE

chəən

chap-chap	hurry!, quickly!
kraeŋ	to fear, be afraid (that)
tɨw mɨn toə̌n	to miss
kɑpal (kəpal)	ship, steamer

1. chap-chap laəŋ! kraeŋ tɨw mɨn toə̌n kəpal.
   Hurry up! [I'm] afraid [we'll] miss the boat.

sɨən

2. kəpal cəñ maoŋ ponmaan?
   When does the boat leave?

khɨn

3. thoə̌mmədaa cəñ maoŋ prampɨl prɨk.
   [It] usually leaves at seven o'clock in the morning.

yɨɨt	slow, late
məəl-tɨw (məə-tɨw)	perhaps, maybe

4. tae baə miən qəywan craən, prəhael-ciə cəñ yɨɨt haəy, məə-tɨw.
   But if there is a lot of baggage, [it] might leave late (perhaps).

sɨən

5. qei, kəpal yəəŋ mɔɔk dɑl haəy!
   Hey, our boat's here already!

sɑmbot (səmbot, səbot)	letter, ticket
sɑmbot-kɑpal	steamer-ticket

6. ɨɨ̃ səmbot-kəpal nɨw qae-naa?
   Where do [we] buy the tickets?

chəən

phae	pier, dock
kɑɑ-baan . . . kɑɑ-baan (kɑ-baan . . . kɑ-baan)	either . . . or . . . (is a possibility)

7. tɨɨ̃ nɨw ləə phae kɑ-baan, nɨw ləə kəpal kɑ-baan.
   [We] can buy [them] either on the pier or on the boat.

sɨən

həp	box, suitcase
həp-qəywan	things, luggage
yaaŋ-məc?	how?, in what way?

8. haəy həp-qəywan nih, kɨt twəə yaaŋ-məc?
   What are we going to do with this luggage? (And these things, [we] plan to do how?)

khɨn

kuulii (kulii)	coolie, porter

9. cam haw kulii qaoy yɔɔk qəywan tɨw daq ləə kəpal.
   [We'll] just get a porter to take the things and put [them] on the boat.

təəp(-tae)-nɨŋ (təəp-m)   just, just now
dək   to carry
dək-noə̆m   to carry, to transport, to haul

10. kəpal dael təəp-nɨŋ cəñ nuh dək-noə̆m qwəy?   What is that steamer that just left [there] hauling?

khɨn

siimaŋ (simaŋ)   cement
daek   iron, steel
sɑmpuə̆t (səmpuə̆t)   cloth; dhoti
khaet   province
taam khaet   in the province

11. kəpal nuh dək-noə̆m simaŋ, daek, haəy-nɨŋ səmpuə̆t tɨw luə̆q taam khaet.   That boat is carrying cement, steel, and cloth to sell in the provinces.

tuuk   boat
tnam   tobacco
kɑmpuə̆ŋ (kəmpuə̆ŋ, kəpuə̆ŋ)   port, riverine town
kɑmpuə̆ŋ-caam   Kampong Cham (name of a province)

12. haəy tuuk nuh dək tnam mɔɔk pii kəmpuə̆ŋ-caam.   And that boat is bringing tobacco from Kampong Cham.

chəən

13. qei, kəpal cəñ haəy! mɔɔk laəŋ chap-chap tɨw!   Hey, the boat's leaving! Get aboard quickly!

sɨən

14. nɨw khaŋ-kraom nih kdaw nah.   It's (very) hot down (below) here.

coə̆n   floor, level, stage, deck
khaaŋ-ləə (khaŋ-ləə)   above, upper (part)

15. mɔɔk tɨw coə̆n khaŋ-ləə wɨñ.   Let's go to the upper deck (instead).

khɨn

lhaəy   cool, refreshing

16. nɨŋ haəy; nɨw khaŋ-ləə trəceə̆q haəy lhaəy phɑɑŋ.   Yes, it's cool and refreshing above.

moə̆t   edge, side; mouth
tuə̆nlee (tənlee, təlee)   large river, long body of water
moə̆t-tuə̆nlee   river-bank

17. haəy sruəl məəl rəbɑh psein-psein nɨw taam moə̆t-tuə̆nlee phɑɑŋ.   And it's easy to see different things along the river-bank too.

sɨən

tuuk-kɑpal   boats in general, river traffic
prateə̆h (prəteə̆h, pəteə̆h)   to meet (by chance)
cuəp-prateə̆h   to happen to meet

18. nɨŋ haəy; kñom coul-cət məəl tuuk-kəpal dael yəəŋ cuəp-preteə̆h nɨw taam tuə̆nləə.   Right; I like to watch the boats we meet along the river.

khɨn

19. nɨw ləə kəpal miən kee luə̃q   Do they have food for sale on the boat?
    mhoup tee?   (Is there someone who sells food?)

chəən

      thəy mɨn (+verb)   of course (+verb)
        ~ həy mɨn (+ verb)
20. thəy mɨn miən!   Of course they have!

21. yəəŋ ñam baay tŋay-traŋ nɨw   We can eat lunch on the boat.
    ləə kəpal ka-baan.

22. ruəc yəəŋ caŋ ñam baay lŋiəc   Then we can eat dinner in Kampong
    nɨw kəmpuə̃ŋ-caam ka-baan dae,   Cham (if we wish), since they stop
    pruə̃h kee chup nɨw kənlaeŋ nuh   there about an hour.
    prəhael məmaoŋ.

sɨən

      kaal-naa?   when?
      krɑceh (krəceh, kəceh)   Kratie (seat of Kratie province)
23. kaal-naa baan yəəŋ tɨw dɑ!   When will we get to Kratie?
    krəceh?

chəən

24. məə-tɨw, prəhael sqaek maoŋ   Probably, we'll get there tomorrow
    pii lŋiəc baan yəəŋ tɨw dɑl.   at about two o'clock in the afternoon.

khɨn

      baə-douccnɑh   therefore, in that case
      damnaə (dəmnaə, ιʒmnaə)   trip; process
      neə̃q-damnaə   traveler, passenger
25. baə-douccnɑh, yup nɨŋ, neə̃q-   In that case, the passengers have to
    damnaə trəw keeŋ nɨw ləə   sleep on the boat tonight?
    kəpal, rɨɨ?

chəən

      qɑt (qət)   colloquial negative auxiliary
      kɑnteel (kənteel, kəteel)   a woven mat
26. nɨŋ haəy; khɨn qət yɔɔk kənteel   That's right; didn't you bring a mat
    mɔɔk tee rɨɨ?   [along]?

khɨn

27. qou, kñom qət yɔɔk mɔɔk tee!   Oh, I didn't bring [one]!

chəən

      cuəl   to rent, to hire
      qəŋrɨŋ (qəŋrɨŋ, ŋrɨŋ)   hammock
28. mɨn-qəy tee; cuəl qəŋrɨŋ muəy   Never mind; [you can] just rent a
    tɨw!   hammock.

sɨən

      biə   playing cards
29. chəən caŋ leeŋ biə tee?   Do you want to play cards, Choern?

chəən

30. sɨən haəy-nɨŋ khɨn qaeŋ leeŋ   You two (Soeun and Khin) go ahead
    coh.   and play.

    lbaeŋ   game
    mɨn-səw   hardly, not so very
31. lbaeŋ biə, kñom mɨn-səw pukae   I'm not very good [at] card games.
    tee.

    kaasaet (kasaet)   newspaper
32. kñom qəŋkuy məəl kasaet.   I'll [just] cit and read the paper.

The Provinces of Cambodia

 1. batdɑmbɑɑŋ (-dəmbɑɑŋ)   Battambang
 2. kɑmpuəŋ-caam (kəmpuəŋ-, kəpuəŋ-)   Kampong Cham
 3. kɑmpuəŋ-cnaŋ   Kampong Chhnang
 4. kɑmpuəŋ-spɨɨ   Kampong Speu
 5. kɑmpuəŋ-thom   Kampong Thom
 6. kampɔɔt (kəmpɔɔt, kəpɔɔt)   Kampot
 7. kɑndaal (kəndaal, kədaal)   Kandal
 8. kɑh-koŋ   Koh Kong
 9. krɑceh (krəceh, kəceh)   Kratie
10. muənduəlkirii   Mondulkiri
11. prɨy-wɛɛŋ   Prey Veng
12. poosat   Pursat
13. roəttənaqkirii   Ratanakiri
14. siəm-riəp   Siem Reap
15. stɨŋ-traeŋ   Stung Treng
16. swaay-riəŋ   Svay Rieng
17. taakaew (takaew, təkaew)   Takeo
18. preəh-wihiə   Preah Vihear

B. GRAMMAR AND DRILLS

1. Repetitive Compounds

One of the more productive derivational mechanisms of Cambodian is the reduplication of part or all of a base word to form a reduplicative compound with a slightly different meaning or function. When the entire base word is repeated, the resulting compound is called a repetitive compound. (Other kinds of reduplication will be discussed later.) The meaning of a repetitive compound depends on the class of the reduplicated word. When the base is a noun, the repetitive compound means 'plurality' or 'generality' in addition to the meaning of the base; e.g.:

srəy 'woman'   >   srəy-srəy 'several women, women in general'
proh 'man'   >   proh-proh 'several men, men in general'
kmein 'child'   >   kmein-kmein 'several children, children in
                         general'

Examples:

> srəy-srəy thoəmmədaa sliəq-peəq   <u>Women</u> (in general) usually take a
> yuu nah.   long time getting dressed.

> <u>kmeiŋ-kmeiŋ</u> sot-tae coul-cət   <u>Children</u> (in general) all like sweets.
> baŋqaem.

If the base is an adjectival verb, the resulting compound means 'intensification of
the meaning of the base', or 'plurality', or both; e.g.:

chap 'fast'	>	<u>chap-chap</u> 'very fast, quickly' (intensification)
<u>pseiŋ</u> 'different'	>	<u>pseiŋ-pseiŋ</u> 'various' (plurality)
<u>touc</u> 'small'	>	<u>touc-touc</u> 'quite small, small and numerous' (intensification and plurality)

Examples:

> <u>chap-chap</u> laəŋ!   Come quickly! (literally: More
>   quickly!)

> sruəl məəl rəbah <u>pseiŋ-pseiŋ</u>   [It's] easy to see the various things
> niw taam moət tuənlee phɑɑŋ.   along the river bank too.

> krouc nih <u>touc-touc</u> nah.   These oranges are extremely small.

We have met one example of an adverbial repetitive compound derived from a
numeral: <u>muəy</u> 'one' > <u>muəy-muəy</u> 'slowly', as in

> soum niyiəy <u>muəy-muəy</u>.   Please speak <u>slowly</u>.

Repetitive compounds are typically pronounced (especially in rapid speech) with
reduced stress on the first element and full stress on the second element.

1-A. Progressive Substitution Drill

Teacher	Student
srəy-srəy thoəmmədaa sliəq-peəq yuu nah.	srəy-srəy thoəmmədaa sliəq-peəq yuu nah.
proh-proh	proh-proh thoəmmədaa sliəq-peəq yuu nah.
kmeiŋ-kmeiŋ	kmeiŋ-kmeiŋ thoəmmədaa sliəq-peəq yuu nah.
sot-tae coul-cət baŋqaem.	kmeiŋ-kmeiŋ sot-tae coul-cət baŋqaem.
srəy-srəy	srəy-srəy sot-tae coul-cət baŋqaem.
proh-proh	proh-proh sot-tae coul-cət baŋqaem.
kmeiŋ-kmeiŋ	kmeiŋ-kmeiŋ sot-tae coul-cət baŋqaem.

1-B. Transformation Drill

In this drill the function of repetition is intensification of the meaning of the
base.

Teacher	Student
riəp-cam kluən qaoy <u>chap</u> tiw!	riəp-cam kluən qaoy <u>chap-chap</u> tiw!
baok khao-qaaw qaoy <u>sqaat</u> tiw!	baok khao-qaaw qaoy <u>sqaat-sqaat</u> tiw!
mɔɔk qaoy liən tiw!	mɔɔk qaoy <u>liən-liən</u> tiw!
mhoup nih <u>kdaw</u> nah.	mhoup nih <u>kdaw-kdaw</u> nah.
claəy qaoy <u>cbah</u> tiw!	claəy qaoy <u>cbah-cbah</u> tiw!
bəntup nih <u>sqaat</u> nah!	bəntup nih <u>sqaat-sqaat</u> nah!
kom daə liən peek!	kom daə <u>liən-liən</u> peek!

1-C. Transformation Drill

In this drill the function of repetition is both intensification and pluralization.

Teacher	Student
krouc nih <u>touc</u> nah.	krouc nih <u>touc-touc</u> nah.
kənlaeŋ nih miən daəm-chəə <u>thom</u> nah.	kənlaeŋ nih miən daəm-chəə <u>thom-thom</u> nah.
srəy tēəŋ-qah nuh <u>lqɑɑ</u> nah.	srəy tēəŋ-qah nuh <u>lqɑɑ-lqɑɑ</u> nah.
ptēəh tēəŋ-qah nuh <u>sqaat</u> nah.	ptēəh tēəŋ-qah nuh <u>sqaat-sqaat</u> nah.
miən mhoup craən muk <u>tlay</u> nah.	miən mhoup craən muk <u>tlay-tlay</u> nah.
rəbah <u>touc</u> mɨn tlay ponmaan tee.	rəbah <u>touc-touc</u> mɨn tlay ponmaan tee.

2. Completive Verbs

Completive verbs follow, and express the completion, expected result, or possibility of achievement, of primary verbs which initiate an action. When negated, the negative auxiliary precedes the completive verb rather than the primary verb; e.g.:

| kñom sdap <u>baan</u>. | I can understand. |
| kñom sdap <u>mɨn baan</u> tee. | I can't understand. |

When any other kind of verb phrase is negated, the negative auxiliary precedes the first verb of the sequence; e.g.:

kñom <u>mɨn</u> caŋ tɨw daə-leeŋ tee.   I don't want to go for a stroll.

There are two classes of completive verbs: 1) <u>specific completive verbs</u>, which have a resultative relationship with a specific primary verb (or with a specific semantic group of primary verbs), and 2) <u>general completive verbs</u>, which occur after a wide variety of verbs, and express the completion, or the possibility of achievement, of the initiated action. When an object occurs in a completive verb phrase, it typically follows specific completive verbs:

kraeŋ tɨw mɨn tōən <u>kəpal</u>.   [I'm] afraid [we'll] miss the <u>boat</u>.

but precedes general completive verbs:

kñom cih <u>kəpal</u> mɨn baan tee.   I can't ride the <u>boat</u>.

The negation of either class implies failure or inability to achieve the initiated action. The most important members of each class are listed below; those words which have not yet been introduced are preceded by an asterisk.

a) <u>Specific completive verbs</u>

1) khəəñ 'to see'
   kɨt 'to think' + khəəñ   >   kɨt khəəñ 'to solve, to figure out'
       kɨt mɨn khəəñ 'to be unable to figure out'
   məəl 'to look' + khəəñ   >   məəl khəəñ 'to see (to look and see)'
       məəl mɨn khəəñ 'to fail to see, to look but not see'
   rɔɔk 'to seek' + khəəñ   >   rɔɔk khəəñ 'to find'
       rɔɔk mɨn khəəñ 'to fail to find'
   *nɨk 'to reflect' + khəəñ   >   nɨk khəəñ 'to realize'
       nɨk mɨn khəəñ 'to fail to realize'

2) toə̆n 'to be on time (for)'
    tɨw 'to go' + toə̆n   >   tɨw toə̆n 'to catch, be on time (for)'
    tɨw mɨn toə̆n 'to miss, to fail to catch, to be too late (for)'
    (mɨn-toə̆n before a verb is a compound auxiliary meaning 'not yet'.)

3) luə̆q 'to fall asleep'
    *deik 'to lie down' + luə̆q   >   deik luə̆q 'to sleep, to lie down and sleep'
    deik mɨn luə̆q 'to be unable to sleep'
    keeŋ 'to sleep' + luə̆q   >   keeŋ luə̆q 'to sleep, to sleep successfully'
    keeŋ mɨn luə̆q 'to be unable to sleep'

4) *lɨɨ 'to hear'
    sdap 'to listen' + lɨɨ   >   sdap lɨɨ 'to hear (successfully)'
    sdap mɨn lɨɨ 'to fail to hear, to listen but not hear'
    (sdap baan, on the other hand, means 'to understand'.)

5) *thum 'to smell (to receive an aroma)'
    *hət 'to sniff' + thum   >   hət thum 'to smell'
    hət mɨn thum 'to be unable to smell, unable to catch an aroma'

E.g.:   kñom hət mɨn thum qwəy sɑh.   I can't smell anything at all.

6) *phot (pii) 'to be free of, clear of'
    *ciəh 'to avoid' + phot (pii) >   ciəh phot (pii) 'to escape (from)'
    ciəh mɨn phot (pii) 'to fail to avoid'

7) *mut 'to cut, go in'
    *caq 'to stab' + mut   >   caq mut 'to stab through, to pierce'
    caq mɨn mut 'to fail to pierce (to stab but fail to pierce)'

8) ceh 'to know'
    riən 'to study' + ceh   >   riən ceh 'to learn'
    riən mɨn ceh 'to fail to learn'

b) General completive verbs

The primary verbs used in the following completive verb phrases are only examples of the many verbs which may occur before general completive verbs.

1) baan 'to be able'
    tɨw 'to go' + baan   >   tɨw baan 'can go'
    tɨw mɨn baan 'can't go'

2) *kaət 'to be able' occurs less generally than baan, and usually only in negative expressions; e.g.:

    koə̆t tɨw mɨn kaət tee.   He can't go.

3) *ruəc 'to be able, to finish' occurs in two contexts:

    a) physical capability

        kñom *ləək tok nih   I can't lift this table.
        mɨn ruəc tee.

    b) completion in terms of time

        kñom məəl siəwphɨw   I haven't yet finished
        nih mɨn-toə̆n ruəc.   reading this book.

5) *c<u>a̱p</u> 'to complete, to get to the end'

kñom məəl kasaet nih m<u>ɨn ca̱p</u> tee.	I <u>didn't finish</u> reading this newspaper.

6) *<u>khaan</u> 'to lack, fail, miss'

look trəw tɨw <u>mɨn khaan</u>.	You must go <u>without fail</u>.
koət nɨŋ moɔk <u>mɨn khaan</u>.	He will <u>surely</u> come.

(<u>khaan</u> has also been met as a modal verb meaning 'to fail (to)', as in

<u>khaan</u> baan cuəp kniə yuu haəy.	[We] haven't seen each other for a long time. ([We've] <u>failed</u> to meet for a long time.)

2-A. Substitution Drill

Teacher	Student
kñom tɨw mɨn toən <u>kəpal</u>.	kñom tɨw mɨn toən <u>kəpal</u>.
<u>rəteh-pləəŋ</u>.	kñom tɨw mɨn toən <u>rəteh-pləəŋ</u>.
<u>laan</u>.	kñom tɨw mɨn toən <u>laan</u>.
<u>peel</u>.	kñom tɨw mɨn toən <u>peel</u>.
<u>kəpal-hɑh</u>.	kñom tɨw mɨn toən <u>kəpal-hɑh</u>.
<u>tuuk</u>.	kñom tɨw mɨn toən <u>tuuk</u>.

2-B. Transformation Drill

Teacher	Student
kñom sdap baan haəy.	kñom sdap mɨn baan tee.
kñom rɔɔk khəəñ haəy.	kñom rɔɔk mɨn khəəñ tee.
kñom məəl kasaet cɑp haəy.	kñom məəl kasaet mɨn cɑp tee.
kñom tɨw toən kəpal.	kñom tɨw mɨn toən kəpal tee.
kñom twəə kaa nuh ruəc haəy.	kñom twəə kaa nuh mɨn ruəc tee.
kñom claəy baan.	kñom claəy mɨn baan tee.
kñom kɨt khəəñ haəy.	kñom kɨt mɨn khəəñ tee.

2-C. Substitution Drill

Teacher	Student
kñom <u>sdap mɨn lɨɨ</u> qwəy sɑh.	kñom <u>sdap mɨn lɨɨ</u> qwəy sɑh.
<u>məəl mɨn khəəñ</u>	kñom <u>məəl mɨn khəəñ</u> qwəy sɑh.
<u>riən mɨn ceh</u>	kñom <u>riən mɨn ceh</u> qwəy sɑh.
<u>hət mɨn thum</u>	kñom <u>hət mɨn thum</u> qwəy sɑh.
<u>rɔɔk mɨn khəəñ</u>	kñom <u>rɔɔk mɨn khəəñ</u> qwəy sɑh.
<u>sdap mɨn lɨɨ</u>	kñom <u>sdap mɨn lɨɨ</u> qwəy sɑh.

2-D. Translation Drill

Teacher	Student
I can't hear.	kñom sdap mɨn lɨɨ tee.
He missed the train.	koət tɨw mɨn toən rəteh-pləəŋ.
I don't see anything.	kñom məəl mɨn khəəñ qwəy sɑh.
I don't understand.	kñom sdap mɨn baan tee.

Teacher	Student
He didn't realize [it].	koət nɨk mɨn khəəñ tee.
I didn't learn anything.	kñom riən mɨn ceh qwəy sɑh.
He will come without fail.	koət nɨŋ mɔɔk mɨn khaan.
I can't answer.	kñom claəy mɨn baan tee.
I haven't finished reading this book.	kñom məəl siəwphɨw nih mɨn cap.
I can't smell anything.	kñom hət mɨn thum qwəy sɑh.

3. The Adverbial məəl-tɨw

məəl-tɨw (məə-tɨw, mə-tɨw) is an adverbial which means 'perhaps, maybe, we'll see'. It may occur either at the beginning or at the end of the sentence:

məə-tɨw, prəhael sqaek maoŋ pii lŋiəc baan tɨw dɑl.	Perhaps we'll get there tomorrow at about two o'clock in the afternoon.
tae baə miən qəywan craən, prəhael- ciə cəñ yɨɨt haəy, məə-tɨw.	But if there is a lot of baggage, [it] might leave late (perhaps).

In both the foregoing examples, məəl-tɨw co-occurs with prəhael (ciə), which has approximately the same meaning, so that, at least in the English translation, məəl-tɨw is redundant; its occurrence seems to add an additional element of uncertainty or indefiniteness to the statement.

3-A. Expansion Drill

Teacher	Student
prəhael-ciə cəñ maoŋ pii.	prəhael-ciə cəñ maoŋ pii, məə-tɨw.
prəhael-ciə tɨw sqaek.	prəhael-ciə tɨw sqaek, məə-tɨw.
prəhael-ciə koət mɨn mɔɔk tee.	prəhael-ciə koət mɨn mɔɔk tee, məə-tɨw.
kraeŋ yəəŋ tɨw mɨn toən kəpal.	kraeŋ yəəŋ tɨw mɨn toən kəpal tee, məə-tɨw.
prəhael-ciə koət tɨw psaa.	prəhael-ciə koət tɨw psaa, məə-tɨw.
tuuk nuh prəhael-ciə dək tnam.	tuuk nuh, prəhael-ciə dək tnam, məə-tɨw.
prəhael-ciə kee tɨw coən khaŋ-ləə.	prəhael-ciə kee tɨw coən khaŋ-ləə, məə-tɨw.
prəhael-ciə kñom tɨw məəl kon.	prəhael-ciə kñom tɨw məəl kon, məə-tɨw.

3-B. Transformation Drill

Teacher	Student
prəhael-ciə cəñ maoŋ pii, məə-tɨw.	məə-tɨw, prəhael-ciə cəñ maoŋ pii.
prəhael-ciə tɨw sqaek, məə-tɨw.	məə-tɨw, prəhael-ciə tɨw sqaek.
prəhael-ciə koət mɨn mɔɔk tee, məə-tɨw.	məə-tɨw, prəhael-ciə koət mɨn mɔɔk tee.
kraeŋ yəəŋ tɨw mɨn toən kəpal, məə-tɨw.	məə-tɨw, kraeŋ yəəŋ tɨw mɨn toən kəpal tee.
prəhael-ciə koət tɨw psaa, məə-tɨw.	məə-tɨw, prəhael-ciə koət tɨw psaa.
tuuk nuh, prəhael-ciə dək tnam, məə-tɨw.	məə-tɨw, tuuk nuh prəhael-ciə dək tnam.

Teacher	Student
prəhael-ciə kee tɨw coăn khaŋ-ləə, **məə-tɨw**.	**məə-tɨw**, prəhael-ciə kee tɨw coăn khaŋ-ləə.
prəhael-ciə kñom tɨw məəl kon, **məə-tɨw**.	**məə-tɨw**, prəhael-ciə kñom tɨw məəl kon.

4. The Coordinate Construction kɑɑ-baan . . . kɑɑ-baan

It was pointed out in Lesson 8, B, 8 that <u>kɑɑ-baan</u> (kɑ-baan) is a completive verb which means 'to be a possibility, to be feasible', as in

yəəŋ tɨw məəl kon <u>kɑ-baan</u>.	We <u>can</u> go see a movie (<u>if you like</u>).

When <u>kɑɑ-baan</u> occurs in two successive coordinate phrases, the construction has the meaning 'either _____ or _____ is a possibility, both _____ and _____ are possibilities', as in:

tɨñ nɨw ləə phae <u>kɑ-baan</u>, nɨw ləə kəpal <u>kɑ-baan</u>.	[We] <u>can</u> buy [them] <u>either</u> on the pier <u>or</u> on the boat.

Notice that only as much of the sentence as is necessary to state the alternative is repeated; in the above example, the primary verb <u>tɨñ</u> serves as the antecedent for both alternatives. In the following example, the second alternative involves a second verb, while the subject <u>yəəŋ</u> serves both alternatives:

yəəŋ tɨw ñam baay <u>kɑ-baan</u>, tɨw məəl kon <u>kɑ-baan</u>.	We <u>can either</u> go eat <u>or</u> go to a movie.

Frequently only the two (or more) possibilities are repeated, coordinated by kɑ-baan, as in the following exchange:

look cɑŋ məəl kon nih rɨɨ kon nuh?	Do you want to see this movie or that movie?
kon nih <u>kɑ-baan</u>, kon nuh <u>kɑ-baan</u>.	Either one would be fine. (This film is fine, that film is fine.)

4-A. Transformation Drill

In the following sentences, form a coordinate construction with the use of the alternatives provided.

Teacher	Student
tɨñ nɨw ləə phae kɑ-baan. (nɨw ləə kəpal)	tɨñ nɨw ləə phae kɑ-baan, nɨw ləə kəpal kɑ-baan.
ñam mhoup kmae kɑ-baan. (mhoup cən)	ñam mhoup kmae kɑ-baan, mhoup cən kɑ-baan.
yəəŋ tɨw ñam baay kɑ-baan. (tɨw məəl kon)	yəəŋ tɨw ñam baay kɑ-baan, tɨw məəl kon kɑ-baan.
tɨñ pɔə-krəhɑɑm kɑ-baan. (pɔə-baytɑɑŋ)	tɨñ pɔə-krəhɑɑm kɑ-baan, pɔə-baytɑɑŋ kɑ-baan.
leeŋ biə kɑ-baan. (məəl siəwphɨw)	leeŋ biə kɑ-baan, məəl siəwphɨw kɑ-baan.

Teacher	Student
nɨw khaŋ-kraom kɑ-baan. (khaŋ-ləə)	nɨw khaŋ-kraom kɑ-baan, khaŋ-ləə kɑ-baan.
qɑŋkuy tok nih kɑ-baan. (tok nuh)	qɑŋkuy tok nih kɑ-baan, tok nuh kɑ-baan.
yɔɔk sac-cruuk kɑ-baan. (sac-mŏən)	yɔɔk sac-cruuk kɑ-baan, sac-mŏən kɑ-baan.
tɨw haaŋ nih kɑ-baan. (haaŋ nuh)	tɨw haaŋ nih kɑ-baan, haaŋ nuh kɑ-baan.
yəəŋ tɨw daə kɑ-baan. (cih taqsii)	yəəŋ tɨw daə kɑ-baan, cih taqsii kɑ-baan.

4-B. Response Drill

Answer the following questions, using the construction kɑ-baan . . . kɑ-baan.

Teacher	Student
look cɑŋ məəl kon nih rɨɨ kon nuh?	kon nih kɑ-baan, kon nuh kɑ-baan.
look cɑŋ ñam mhoup kmae rɨɨ mhoup cən?	mhoup kmae kɑ-baan, mhoup cən kɑ-baan.
look cɑŋ tɨw haaŋ nih rɨɨ haaŋ nuh?	haaŋ nih kɑ-baan, haaŋ nuh kɑ-baan.
yəəŋ tɨw ñam baay rɨɨ tɨw məəl kon?	tɨw ñam baay kɑ-baan, tɨw məəl kon kɑ-baan.
look cɑŋ ñam kafei rɨɨ byeə?	kafei kɑ-baan, byeə kɑ-baan.
look cɑŋ tɨñ siəwphɨw rɨɨ kasaet?	siəwphɨw kɑ-baan, kasaet kɑ-baan.
look cɑŋ tɨw khaŋ-ləə rɨɨ khaŋ-kraom?	khaŋ-ləə kɑ-baan, khaŋ-kraom kɑ-baan.
yəəŋ kɨt tɨw tŋay-nih rɨɨ sqaek?	tŋay-nih kɑ-baan, sqaek kɑ-baan.
look coul-cət pɔə-khiəw rɨɨ pɔə-lɨəŋ?	pɔə-khiəw kɑ-baan, pɔə-lɨəŋ kɑ-baan.
yəəŋ tɨw taam laan rɨɨ taam tuuk?	taam laan kɑ-baan, taam tuuk kɑ-baan.
look tɨw rɨɨ mɨn tɨw?	tɨw kɑ-baan, mɨn tɨw kɑ-baan.

5. The Interrogative yaaŋ-məc

yaaŋ-məc is a compound interrogative word which means 'how?, in what way?' as in

haəy həp-qəywan nih, kɨt twəə yaaŋ-məc?	What are we going to do with this luggage? (And these things, [we] plan to do how?)

5-A. Progressive Substitution Drill

Teacher	Student
qəywan nuh, kɨt twəə yaaŋ-məc?	qəywan nuh, kɨt twəə yaaŋ-məc?
praə	qəywan nuh, kɨt praə yaaŋ-məc?
lŭəq	qəywan nuh, kɨt lŭəq yaaŋ-məc?
yɔɔk tɨw	qəywan nuh, kɨt yɔɔk tɨw yaaŋ-məc?
tɨñ	qəywan nuh, kɨt tɨñ yaaŋ-məc?
mhoup nuh	mhoup nuh, kɨt tɨñ yaaŋ-məc?
ñam	mhoup nuh, kɨt ñam yaaŋ-məc?
yɔɔk	mhoup nuh, kɨt yɔɔk yaaŋ-məc?
twəə	mhoup nuh, kɨt twəə yaaŋ-məc?

6. The Compound Auxiliary təəp-(tae) (nɨŋ)

    təəp-(tae)(nɨŋ), like kampuŋ-tae 'in the process of', kroən-tae 'just, only', and muk-tae 'likely, probably', is a compound preverbal auxiliary; it's meaning is 'just now (+ verb), to have just (+ verb)', as in

kəpal dael təəp-nɨŋ cən nuh dək-noŏm qwəy?	What is that steamer that just now left carrying?

The full form təəp-tae-nɨŋ occurs only in a formal or literary style; təəp-tae sometimes occurs in normal speech, but the commonest form is teep-nɨŋ, reduced in rapid speech to təəp-m. The representation used here is təəp-nɨŋ; the student should imitate the form used by the teacher.

6-A. Substitution Drill

Teacher	Student
kñom təəp-nɨŋ cəñ pii pteə̆h.	kñom təəp-nɨŋ cəñ pii pteə̆h.
ñam baay.	kñom təəp-nɨŋ ñam baay.
chup twəə-kaa.	kñom təəp-nɨŋ chup twəə-kaa.
tɨñ laan tməy.	kñom təəp-nɨŋ tɨñ laan tməy.
mɔɔk pii pnum-pɨñ.	kñom təəp-nɨŋ mɔɔk pii pnum-pɨñ.
tɨw psaa.	kñom təəp-nɨŋ tɨw psaa.
məəl kon nuh.	kñom təəp-nɨŋ məəl kon nuh.
khəə̆ñ puəq-maaq kñom.	kñom təəp-nɨŋ khəə̆ñ puəq-maaq kñom.

6. Transformation Drill

Teacher	Student
koə̆t cəñ pii pteə̆h.	koə̆t təəp-nɨŋ cəñ pii pteə̆h.
kñom ñam baay.	kñom təəp-nɨŋ ñam baay.
kee chup twəə-kaa.	kee təəp-nɨŋ chup twəə-kaa.
qəwpuk kñom tɨñ pteə̆h tməy.	qəwpuk kñom təəp-nɨŋ tɨñ pteə̆h tməy.
baaŋ kñom mɔɔk pii qaŋkɔɔ-woə̆t.	baaŋ kñom təəp-nɨŋ mɔɔk pii qaŋkɔɔ-woə̆t.
kñom məəl kasaet nuh.	kñom təəp-nɨŋ məəl kasaet nuh.
wiə tɨw psaa.	wiə təəp-nɨŋ tɨw psaa.
yəəŋ tɨw məəl kon.	yəəŋ təəp-nɨŋ tɨw məəl kon.

7. kəpal cəñ haəy!

    Since Cambodian verbs are not marked for tense, the sentence kəpal cəñ haəy can mean either 'The boat has already left.' or 'The boat is leaving already.' In the following example, the ambiguity is resolved by the high sustained intonation (represented ! in the transcription), indicating urgency or emotional involvement, as well as by the general context:

qei, kəpal cəñ haəy! mɔɔk laəŋ chap-chap tɨw!	Hey, the boat's leaving! Get aboard quickly.

7-A. Progressive Substitution Drill

Teacher	Student
mɔɔk qaoy lɨən; kəpal cəñ haəy!	mɔɔk qaoy lɨən; kəpal cəñ haəy!
rəteh-pləəŋ	mɔɔk qaoy lɨən; rəteh-pləəŋ cəñ haəy!
laan	mɔɔk qaoy lɨən; laan cəñ haəy!
taqsii	mɔɔk qaoy lɨən; taqsii cəñ haəy!
mɔɔk	mɔɔk qaoy lɨən; taqsii mɔɔk haəy!
kəpal	mɔɔk qaoy lɨən; kəpal mɔɔk haəy!
rəteh-pləəŋ	mɔɔk qaoy lɨən; rəteh-pləəŋ mɔɔk haəy!
laan	mɔɔk qaoy lɨən; laan mɔɔk haəy!

8. theɨ mɨn + Verb

The phrase thəy mɨn + verb (həy mɨn + verb in some dialects) is an idiom meaning 'of course + verb', as in

thəy mɨn miən!	Of course [they] do!

The translation of the entire idiom depends on the context and the verb, as in the following examples:

look miən siəwphɨw tee?	Do you have a book?
thəy mɨn miən!	Of course [I] have!
koət tɨw psaa tee?	Is he going to the market?
thəy mɨn tɨw!	Of course [he's] going!

Notice that when the question includes a completive verb, it is the completive verb rather than the primary verb which occurs in the response:

look tɨw tŋay-nih baan tee?	Can you go today?
thəy mɨn baan!	Of course [I] can!

8-A. Response Drill

Teacher	Student
yəəŋ tɨw məəl kon tee?	thəy mɨn tɨw!
look ñam baay tee?	thəy mɨn ñam!
koət miən laan tee?	thəy mɨn miən!
kee ceh phiəsaa-baraŋ tee?	thəy mɨn ceh!
bɑɑŋ look mɔɔk tee?	thəy mɨn mɔɔk!
look ñam mhoup həl baan tee?	thəy mɨn baan!
look coul-cət mhoup kmae tee?	thəy mɨn coul-cət!
nɨw haaŋ nuh miən mhoup baraŋ tee?	thəy mɨn miən!

9. Another Use of baan

In some contexts, the word baan means 'results (in), is (that), is the reason (that)'. In such sentences baan always has a clause (consisting of a verb with or without a subject) as its complement, as in

kaal-naa baan yəəŋ tɨw dɑl krəceh?	When is it that we get to Kratie? (When do we get to Kratie?)
prəhael maoŋ pii lŋiəc baan yəəŋ tɨw dɑl.	It's about two o'clock in the afternoon that we get [there]. (We'll get there about two o'clock in the afternoon.)

In some sentences, <u>baan</u> in this function is followed by the relative conjunction
ciə 'that', as in

haet qwəy <u>baan ciə</u> kmiən kambət
niw ləə tok?

What reason <u>is it that</u> there are
no knives on the table? (Why are
there no knives on the table?)

kñom min-səw ciə tee, <u>baan ciə</u>
kñom min tiw.

'I'm not so well' <u>is the reason that</u>
I'm not going. (The reason that I'm
not going is that I'm not so well.)

9-A. Substitution Drill

Teacher	Student
kaal-naa baan yəəŋ <u>tiw dɑl krəceh?</u>	kaal-naa baan yəəŋ <u>tiw dɑl krəceh?</u>
<u>tiw srok-qaameric?</u>	kaal-naa baan yəəŋ <u>tiw srok-qaameric?</u>
<u>tiw ñam baay?</u>	kaal-naa baan yəəŋ <u>tiw ñam baay?</u>
<u>tiw məəl kon nuh?</u>	kaal-naa baan yəəŋ <u>tiw məəl kon nuh?</u>
<u>tiw kənlaeŋ nuh?</u>	kaal-naa baan yəəŋ <u>tiw kənlaeŋ nuh?</u>
<u>trəlɑp tiw pteəh?</u>	kaal-naa baan yəəŋ <u>trəlɑp tiw pteəh?</u>
<u>cəñ pii salaa?</u>	kaal-naa baan yəəŋ <u>cəñ pii salaa?</u>
<u>chup riən?</u>	kaal-naa baan yəəŋ <u>chup riən?</u>
<u>tiw daə-leeŋ?</u>	kaal-naa baan yəəŋ <u>tiw daə-leeŋ?</u>
<u>laŋ kəpal?</u>	kaal-naa baan yəəŋ <u>laŋ kəpal?</u>

9-B. Substitution Drill

Teacher	Student
prəhael maoŋ pii baan <u>yəəŋ tiw dɑl.</u>	prəhael maoŋ pii baan <u>yəəŋ tiw dɑl.</u>
<u>kñom tiw ñam baay.</u>	prəhael maoŋ pii baan <u>kñom tiw ñam baay.</u>
<u>kee chup twəə-kaa.</u>	prəhael maoŋ pii baan <u>kee chup twəə-kaa.</u>
<u>yəəŋ tiw məəl kon.</u>	prəhael maoŋ pii baan <u>yəəŋ tiw məəl kon.</u>
<u>kñom tiw riən.</u>	prəhael maoŋ pii baan <u>kñom tiw riən.</u>
<u>rəteh-pləəŋ mɔɔk dɑl.</u>	prəhael maoŋ pii baan <u>rəteh-pləəŋ mɔɔk dɑl.</u>
<u>yəəŋ cih kəpal.</u>	prəhael maoŋ pii baan <u>yəəŋ cih kəpal.</u>
<u>koət trəlɑp mɔɔk pteəh wiñ.</u>	prəhael maoŋ pii baan <u>koət trəlɑp mɔɔk pteəh wiñ.</u>
<u>kñom chup riən.</u>	prəhael maoŋ pii baan <u>kñom chup riən.</u>

10. The Negative Auxiliary qɑt (~ qət)

qɑt (~ qət) is a negative auxiliary which is used instead of mɨn in some
dialects, notably that of Phnom Penh, as in

qou, kñom qət yɔɔk mɔɔk tee!   Oh, I didn't bring [one]!

(The existence of two forms seems to be a matter of dialect difference (or free
variation) rather than of simple reduction; the form qɑt, which also occurs as a
verb meaning 'to lack, to do without', may have acquired the function of a gen-
eralized negative auxiliary because of its phonetic and semantic similarity to
qət 'not'. The representation qət is arbitrarily chosen here; the student should
imitate the teacher's pronunciation.)

10-A. Transformation Drill

Teacher	Student
kñom mɨn yɔɔk mɔɔk tee.	kñom qət yɔɔk mɔɔk tee.
kñom mɨn tɨw tee.	kñom qət tɨw tee.
mɨn qəy tee.	qət qəy tee.
kñom mɨn baan tɨñ qəy sɑh.	kñom qət baan tɨñ qəy sɑh.
kñom mɨn coul-cət mhoup cən tee.	kñom qət coul-cət mhoup cən tee.
knom mɨn miən luy sɑh.	knom qət miən luy sɑh.
kñom ñam mhoup həl mɨn baan tee.	kñom ñam mhoup həl qət baan tee.
koət mɨn baan tɨw psaa tee.	koət qət baan tɨw psaa tee.
yəəŋ mɨn-toən ñam baay tee.	yəəŋ qət-toən ñam baay tee.
kñom mɨn trəw-kaa kafei tee.	kñom qət trəw-kaa kafei tee.
kñom sdap mɨn baan tee.	kñom sdap qət baan tee.

11. Negative Questions

Negative questions are formed in Cambodian by simply adding the question
particle rɨɨ? to a negative statement, as in

look qət yɔɔk kənteel mɔɔk tee   Didn't you bring a mat [along]?
rɨɨ?

In such questions, the final negative particle tee frequently loses the falling intonation typical of statements, and is pronounced with reduced stress before
rɨɨ?, which has the rising intonation typical of questions.

11-A. Substitution Drill

Teacher	Student
look mɨn tɨw tee rɨɨ?	look mɨn tɨw tee rɨɨ?
mɔɔk	look mɨn mɔɔk tee rɨɨ?
coul-cət kon nih	look mɨn coul-cət kon nih tee rɨɨ?
leeŋ biə	look mɨn leeŋ biə tee rɨɨ?
praə kambət	look mɨn praə kambət tee rɨɨ?
trəw-kaa barəy	look mɨn trəw-kaa barəy tee rɨɨ?
dael tɨw	look mɨn dael tɨw tee rɨɨ?
sok-sapbaay ciə	look mɨn sok-sapbaay ciə tee rɨɨ?

11-B. Transformation Drill

Teacher	Student
look caŋ tɨw tee?	look mɨn caŋ tɨw tee rɨɨ?
look miən siəwphɨw tee?	look mɨn miən siəwphɨw tee rɨɨ?
look sdap baan tee?	look sdap mɨn baan tee rɨɨ?
look dael tɨw qəŋkɔɔ-wŏət tee?	look mɨn dael tɨw qəŋkɔɔ-wŏət tee rɨɨ?
look miən baaŋ-pqoun tee?	look mɨn miən baaŋ-pqoun tee rɨɨ?
look ñam mhoup həl baan tee?	look ñam mhoup həl mɨn baan tee rɨɨ?
look sok-sapbaay ciə tee?	look mɨn sok-sapbaay ciə tee rɨɨ?
kŏət coul-cət mhoup kmae tee?	kŏət mɨn coul-cət mhoup kmae tee rɨɨ?
kŏət baan tɨw srok-baraŋ tee?	kŏət mɨn baan tɨw srok-baraŋ tee rɨɨ?

12. The Auxiliary mɨn-səw

   mɨn-səw is a preverbal auxiliary which means 'hardly, not really, not
very much', as in

   lbaeŋ biə knom mɨn-səw pukae tee.   I'm not very good [at] card games.

(mɨn-səw is treated here as a compound preverbal auxiliary, parallel with mɨn-
tŏən 'not yet', since it typically occurs in negative form with the special meaning illustrated above; the non-negative form səw seems to occur only in a literary style, and then with a function which is not clearly related to mɨn-səw.)

12-A. Progressive Substitution Drill

Teacher	Student
mənuh nuh mɨn-səw pukae tee.	mənuh nuh mɨn-səw pukae tee.
sqaat	mənuh nuh mɨn-səw sqaat tee.
ciə	mənuh nuh mɨn-səw ciə tee.
ceh	menuh nuh mɨn-səw ceh tee.
kliən	mənuh nuh mɨn-səw kliən tee.
srəy nuh	srəy nuh mɨn-səw kliən tee.
lqaa	srəy nuh mɨn-səw lqaa tee.
pukae	srəy nuh mɨn-səw pukae tee.
sqaat	srəy nuh mɨn-səw sqaat tee.
ciə	srəy nuh mɨn-səw ciə tee.

12-B. Transformation Drill

Teacher	Student
lbaeŋ nuh, kñom mɨn pukae tee.	lbaeŋ nuh, kñom mɨn-səw pukae tee.
kñom mɨn kliən tee.	kñom mɨn-səw kliən tee.
kŏət mɨn coul-cət kaa nuh tee.	kŏət mɨn-səw coul-cət kaa nuh tee.
kñom mɨn miən praq craən tee.	kñom mɨn-səw miən praq craən tee.
bəntup nih mɨn sqaat tee.	bəntup nih mɨn-səw sqaat tee.
kənlaeŋ nuh mɨn sruəl tee.	kənlaeŋ nuh mɨn-səw sruəl tee.
krouc nih mɨn tlay tee.	krouc nih mɨn-səw tlay tee.
mhoup nih mɨn cŋañ tee.	mhoup nih mɨn-səw cŋañ tee.
tŋay-nih mɨn kdaw tee.	tŋay-nih mɨn-səw kdaw tee.

C. COMPREHENSION

1. <u>Discussing Boat Travel</u>

    sein: look dael cih kəpal tee?

    sɨm: baat, kñom dael cih kəpal craən dɑɑŋ dae.

    sein: look cih kəpal tɨw srok naa-klah?

    sɨm: kñom dael cih kəpal tɨw leeŋ krəceh mədɑɑŋ.

    sein: səmbot-kəpal tɨw krəceh tlay tee?

    sɨm: mɨn-səw tlay tee.
             səmbot muəy tlay tae haasəp-pram riəl ponnoh.

    sein: look dael tɨw leeŋ batdəmbɑɑŋ tee?

    sɨm: baat, kñom baan tɨw mədɑɑŋ dae.

             [prɨy-nəkɔɔ 'Saigon']
    sein: cih kəpal tɨw prɨy-nəkɔɔ baan tee?

             [tŭənlee-meekoŋ 'the Mekong River']
    sɨm: baat, baan; tɨw taam tŭənlee-meekoŋ.

2. <u>A Train Trip</u>

    krɨm: look qəñcəəñ tɨw naa?

    neet: baat, kñom tɨw batdəmbɑɑŋ.

    krɨm: look kɨt tɨw taam qəy?

    neet: kñom nɨŋ cih rəteh-pləəŋ.

             [kɑpal-hɑh 'airplane']
    krɨm: haet qwəy baan ciə look mɨn cih kəpal-hɑh tɨw?

             [hiən 'to dare; be brave']
             [klaac 'to fear, be afraid']
    neet: baat, kñom mɨn hiən cih kəpal-hɑh tee; kñom klaac nah.
             tɨw taam rəteh-pləəŋ thaok ciəŋ, haəy sruəl phɑɑŋ.

    krɨm: ponmaan maoŋ baan tɨw dɑl batdəmbɑɑŋ?

    neet: prəhael prampɨl maoŋ.

3. <u>On the Boat</u>

    chuən: cumriəp-suə look chiən.
             look cih kəpal dae, rɨɨ?

    chiən: nɨŋ haəy; kñom tɨw leeŋ puəq-maaq kñom məneəq nɨw kəmpuəŋ-
             caam.

    chuəh: puəq-maaq look twəə-kaa qəy nɨw kəmpuəŋ-caam?

    chiən: baat, kŏət twəə-kaa nɨw haaŋ-luəq-tnam.
             kŏət twəə-kaa nɨw kənlaeŋ nuh bəy cnam mɔɔk haəy.

    chuən: yɨi, look miən qəywan craən nah!

chɨən: baat, kñom tɨñ qaoy puəq-maaq kñom nɨw kəmpŭəŋ-caam.
       tɨw dɑl kəmpŭəŋ-caam, kñom nɨŋ cuəl kulii qaoy yɔɔk qəywan cəñ
       pii kəpal.

chuən: mɨn-bac haw kulii tee; cam kñom cuəy.

chɨən: qɑɑ-kun.

4. **Going to Battambang**

cuən: rəteh-pləəŋ tɨw batdəmbɑɑŋ cəñ maoŋ ponmaan?

neəq-lŭəq-səmbot: cəñ maoŋ dɑp-muəy prambəy niətii yup.

cuən: tɨw dɑl batdəmbɑɑŋ maoŋ ponmaan?

neəq-lŭəq-səmbot: dɑl batdəmbɑɑŋ maoŋ pram kənlah prɨk.

cuən: rəteh-pləəŋ peel prɨk cəñ maoŋ ponmaan?

neəq-lŭəq-səmbot: cəñ peel prɨk maoŋ prammuəy; tɨw dɑl batdəmbɑɑŋ
                  maoŋ mə-təndap prɨk.

cuən: səmbot tɨw batdəmbɑɑŋ tlay ponmaan?

neəq-lŭəq-səmbot: tnaq tii-muəy tlay mərɔɔy haasəp; tii-pii mərɔɔy riəl;
                  tii-bəy hoksəp.

cuən: kñom yɔɔk səmbot tnaq tii-pii.

D. CONVERSATION

1. **Catching the Boat**

    a) A asks B when the boat leaves.
    b) B answers that it usually leaves at 6 a.m., but adds that it might leave late today (perhaps).
    c) A asks B which boat goes to Kratie.
    d) B replies that the one which has three decks goes to Kratie.
    e) A asks B where the boat which has just left the dock is going.
    f) B replies that that boat is carrying cloth to Saigon.
    g) A asks B where one buys the steamer-tickets.
    h) B replies that they can buy them either on the pier or on the steamer.

2. **On the Boat**

    a) A asks B which deck he wants to go to.
    b) B suggests they go to the upper deck, because it's cool and refreshing there.
    c) A agrees, and says that he likes to watch the boats and steamers they meet along the river.
    d) B asks A if one can buy food on the steamer.
    e) A replies that of course one can, and adds that they can eat lunch either on the boat or in Kampong Cham, since they stop there about one hour.
    f) B asks A if the passengers sleep on the boat at night.
    g) A says that's right, and asks B if he didn't bring a mat.
    h) B replies that he forgot to bring one, and asks what (how) he will do tonight.

i) A replies that it doesn't matter; he can use a hammock.

j) B asks if someone rents hammocks on the boat.

k) A replies that of course they do.

l) B asks A what he wants to do now.

m) A replies that they can either sit and read or play cards, but adds that he isn't so good at card games.

3. Two Travelers Meet

a) A greets B, and asks him where he's going.

b) B replies that he's going to Stung Treng.

c) A asks B whether he's going by bus or by boat.

d) B replies that he's going to take a steamer as far as Kratie, then take a bus to Stung Treng.
B then asks A where he's coming from.

e) A replies that he has just come from Battambang.

f) B asks A how he went to Battambang.

g) A replies that he went by train.

h) B asks A if it isn't expensive to take the train to Battambang.

i) A replies that it isn't very expensive.

LESSON 15. A DAY IN THE COUNTRY

[Tape 26]   A. DIALOGUE

saɑŋ

mɨt	friend
1. tŋay-nih mɨt caŋ tɨw daə-leeŋ qae-naa?	Where would you (friends) like to go (for fun) today?

khɨn

pɨcnɨc	picnic
prɨy	forest
2. kñom caŋ tɨw twəə pɨcnɨc nɨw knoŋ prɨy.	I'd like to go for (do) a picnic in the forest.
miən	to happen to, have occasion to
3. miən skoël kənlaeŋ naa tee?	Do you (happen to) know of any place?

saɑŋ

tɨk-cruëh	spring, mountain stream, waterfall
4. miən kənlaeŋ tɨk-cruëh muəy nɨw cɨt nih.	There's a waterfall near here.
pnum	mountain, hill
laəŋ	to climb, ascend
5. haəy miən pnum muəy yəəŋ laəŋ tɨw leeŋ kɑ-baan.	And there's a mountain [which] we can climb (for fun).
suən	garden
suən-cbaa	flower-garden, park
dam	to plant
pkaa	flower
daəm-pkaa	flower plant, shrub
6. miən suən-cbaa nɨw kənlaeŋ nuh phɑɑŋ dael miən kee dam daəm-pkaa pseiŋ-pseiŋ.	There's a park there too, where they've planted various flowers and shrubs.
sɑmrap (səmrap)	to use; for, for the purpose of
7. haəy miən tok səmrap ñam baay phɑɑŋ.	And there are tables for eating too.

chəən

hael	to swim
hael-tɨk	to swim
8. nɨw kənlaeŋ nuh hael-tɨk baan tee?	Can [we] swim at that place?

saɑŋ

9. thəy mɨn baan!	Of course [we] can!

201

siən

10. qəñcəŋ tɨw kənlaeŋ nuh tɨw!   Then let's go there!

chəən

11. yəəŋ trəw tɨñ mhoup sən;   We should buy [some] food first;
    caŋ tɨñ qəy-klah?   what-all do [you] want to buy?

khɨn

cqaə   smoked, roasted
trəy-cqaə   smoked fish
prahok (prəhok, pəhok)   fermented fish paste
tiə   duck
pɔɔŋ-tiə   duck-egg
trasaq (trəsaq, təsaq)   cucumber

12. tɨñ trəy-cqaə, prəhok, pɔɔŋ-tiə,   [Let's] buy smoked fish, prahok,
    haəy-nɨŋ trəsaq.   duck-eggs, and cucumbers.

chəən

cnaŋ   pot, kettle
13. kom plɨc baay məcnaŋ phaaŋ!   Don't forget a pot of rice!

saaŋ

phuum ~ phum   village
14. yəəŋ tɨñ nɨw phuum cɨt tɨk-cruəh   We can buy [it] at the village near
    nuh ka-baan.   the waterfall.

[Later]

siən

15. dal haəy!   We're here! ([We've] arrived al-
                                                       ready.)

chəən

caat   to park, to moor
16. caat laan nɨw kraom daəm-chəə   Park the car under that tree.
    nuh tɨw.

mlup   shade
cŋaay   to be far, distant
17. miən mlup trəceəq, haəy mɨn-səw   There's cool shade, and [it's] not so
    cŋaay pii tɨk-cruəh phaaŋ.   far from the waterfall either.

siən

plah   to change
rɔhah (rəhah, ləhah)   fast, rapid
18. mɔɔk plah khao-qaaw qaoy rəhah   Hurry and change [your] clothes, and
    tɨw, haəy yəəŋ tɨw hael-tɨk.   we'll go swimming.

chəən

hou   to flow
lɨɨ   to hear; to sound
sou   sound, noise

19. qou, tɨk hou lɨɨ sou klaŋ nah!

    Hey, the water really makes a loud noise! (the water flows making a very loud noise)

saaŋ

20. thaa məc nɨŋ? kñom sdap mɨn lɨɨ tee.

    What did [you] say just now? I didn't hear [you].

khɨn

douc-ciə   seems (to be), appears (to be)
crɨw   to be deep

21. qou, tɨk nih douc-ciə crɨw nah!

    Oh, this water seems to be quite deep!

reəq   to be shallow

22. kñom nɨw tae kənlaeŋ reəq tee, pruəh kñom mɨn ceh hael-tɨk.

    I'm [going to] stay only in the shallow places, because I don't know how to swim.

chəən

luəŋ-tɨk   to sink (of a person); to drown
sraek   to shout

23. baə khɨn qaeŋ luəŋ-tɨk, sraek haw kñom tɨw; kñom nɨŋ cuəy.

    If you sink, Khin, just shout for me; I'll help you.

khɨn

prasap (prəsap, pəsap)   to be good (at), skillful (at)
wəəy!   interjection for attracting attention

24. yii, saaŋ prəsap hael-tɨk nah wəəy!

    Hey, [look] how well Sâng swims! (Sâng is really good at swimming!)

25. riən hael nɨw qae-naa nɨŋ?

    Where did you learn to swim like that?

saaŋ

tloəp   used to, be accustomed to

26. qou, kñom tloəp nɨw cɨt moət tuənlee.

    Oh, I used to live near the river-bank.

kaal nɨw pii touc   when I was still young, when I was a kid

27. kaal nɨw pii touc, kñom tloəp tɨw hael-tɨk roəl tŋay.

    When I was a kid, I used to go swimming every day.

chəən

twəə qaoy   makes, causes

28. yii, hael-tɨk twəə qaoy kñom kliən baay nah!

    Boy, swimming really makes me hungry!

noəm kniə   to do all together, to cooperate
ruət   to run
pranaŋ (prənaŋ, pənaŋ)   to compete, to race

29. mɔɔk noəm kniə ruət prənaŋ tɨw laan wɨñ.

    Let's all race back to the car.

snuət   to be dry
30. tɨw dɑl laan, muk-tae snuət   [When we] reach the car, [we'll]
kluən haəy.   probably be dry.

                        sɑɑn

kaal-naa   when, whenever
ruəc   to finish, to complete
31. kaal-naa ñam baay ruəc, yəən   When [we've] finished eating, we'll
tɨw laən pnum.   go climb the mountain.

                        khɨn

kamlaŋ (kəmlaŋ, kəlaŋ)   strength, power
qɑh-kamlaŋ   to be tired, exhausted
32. qou, kñom qɑh-kəmlaŋ nah!   Oh, I'm exhausted!

samraaq (səmraaq)   to rest
tmɑɑ   rock, stone
33. kñom səmraaq nɨw ləə tmɑɑ nih   I'm [going to] rest on this rock first.
sən.

B. GRAMMAR AND DRILLS

1. <u>miən</u> as a Modal Verb

   <u>miən</u> frequently occurs in the modal verb position with a meaning something
like 'to happen to, to have occasion to', as in

   miən skoəl kənlaeŋ naa tee?   Do [you] happen to know [of] some
                                            place?
                                    or: Do [you] have knowledge [of] some
                                            place?

In some dialects <u>miən</u> tends to replace the modal verb <u>baan</u> 'to have (done something), to have had occasion (to do something)', as in

   look <u>miən</u> tɨw qəŋkɔɔ-woət tee?   Have you <u>had occasion</u> to go to
                                            Angkor Wat?

1-A. Substitution Drill

Teacher	Student
kñom miən skoəl kənlaeŋ muəy.	kñom miən skoəl kənlaeŋ muəy.
tɨw pnum-pɨñ mədɑɑŋ.	kñom miən tɨw pnum-pɨñ mədɑɑŋ.
tɨñ laan tməy.	kñom miən tɨñ laan tməy.
luəq pteəh nuh haəy.	kñom miən luəq pteəh nuh haəy.
prəteəh puəq-maaq mənéəq.	kñom miən prəteəh puəq-maaq mənéəq.
riən kmae bəntəc-bəntuəc.	kñom miən riən kmae bəntəc-bəntuəc.
cih kəpal tɨw krəceh mədɑɑŋ.	kñom miən cih kəpal tɨw krəceh mədɑɑŋ.
tɨw dəə-leeŋ pii msəl-mɨñ.	kñom miən tɨw dəə-leeŋ pii msəl-mɨñ.
tɨw kənlaeŋ nuh mədɑɑŋ.	kñom miən tɨw kənlaeŋ nuh mədɑɑŋ.

2. The Modal Verb douc-ciə

When douc-ciə precedes a verb, it functions as a modal verb with the meaning 'seems (as if), appears (to be)', as in

qou, tɨk nih douc-ciə crɨw nah!	Oh, this water seems very deep!
mhoup nih douc-ciə həl nah!	This food seems to be very spicy!

2-A. Progressive Substitution Drill

Teacher	Student
tɨk nih douc-ciə crɨw nah.	tɨk nih douc-ciə crɨw nah.
reə̆q	tɨk nih douc-ciə reə̆q nah.
trəceə̆q	tɨk nih douc-ciə trəceə̆q nah.
kdaw	tɨk nih douc-ciə kdaw nah.
mhoup nih	mhoup nih douc-ciə kdaw nah.
cŋañ	mhoup nih douc-ciə cŋañ nah.
həl	mhoup nih douc-ciə həl nah.
tlay	mhoup nih douc-ciə tlay nah.
laan nuh	laan nuh douc-ciə tlay nah.
lɨən	laan nuh douc-ciə lɨən nah.
lqɑɑ	laan nuh douc-ciə lqɑɑ nah.
thaok	laan nuh douc-ciə thaok nah.

3. Omission of the Final Negative Particle tee

Up to this point in these lessons, every occurrence of mɨn (with the exception of one sentence in Lesson 14) has been followed by the final negative
particle tee, or by some other final negative particle such as sɑh '(not) at all'.
In certain circumstances, however, the occurrence of tee after mɨn is optional.
In an emphatic negative statement, tee (or some other final negative particle)
is compulsory, but in a complex sentence (consisting of more than one clause),
tee may be omitted in the less emphatic clause, as in

kñom nɨw tae kənlaeŋ reə̆q tee,	I'm [going to] stay only in the
pruəh kñom mɨn ceh hael-tɨk.	shallow places, because I don't
	know how to swim.
kñom mɨn-səw ciə tee,	I'm not so well, is the reason that
baan ciə kñom mɨn tɨw.	I'm not going.

The use of tee after completive verb phrases (see Lesson 14, B, 2) also seems
to be optional, as in

kraeŋ tɨw mɨn toən kəpal.	[I'm] afraid [we'll] miss the boat.
koət nɨŋ mɔɔk mɨn khaan.	He will come without fail.

3-A. Substitution Drill

Teacher	Student
kñom mɨn tɨw tee,	kñom mɨn tɨw tee,
pruəh kñom kmiən peel.	pruəh kñom kmiən peel.
mɨn-səw miən luy.	kñom mɨn tɨw tee,
	pruəh kñom mɨn-səw miən luy.

Teacher	Student
tɨw mɨn toə̆n kəpal.	kñom mɨn tɨw tee, pruə̆h kñom tɨw mɨn toə̆n kəpal.
mɨn coul-cət twəə dəmnaə.	kñom mɨn tɨw tee, pruə̆h kñom mɨn coul-cət twəə dəmnaə.
mɨn ceh hael-tɨk.	kñom mɨn tɨw tee, pruə̆h kñom mɨn ceh hael-tɨk.
mɨn-səw ciə.	kñom mɨn tɨw tee, pruə̆h kñom mɨn-səw ciə.
mɨn caŋ tɨw.	kñom mɨn tɨw tee, pruə̆h kñom mɨn caŋ tɨw.

3-B. Transformation Drill

Teacher	Student
kñom mɨn coul-cət cih tuuk tee.	kñom mɨn tɨw tee, pruə̆h kñom mɨn coul-cət cih tuuk.
kñom tɨñ səmbot mɨn baan tee.	kñom mɨn tɨw tee, pruə̆h kñom tɨñ səmbot mɨn baan.
kñom tɨw mɨn toə̆n laan tee.	kñom mɨn tɨw tee, pruə̆h kñom tɨw mɨn toə̆n laan.
kñom rɔɔk peel mɨn baan tee.	kñom mɨn tɨw tee, pruə̆h kñom rɔɔk peel mɨn baan.
kñom twəə-kaa mɨn cap tee.	kñom mɨn tɨw tee, pruə̆h kñom twəə-kaa mɨn cap.
kñom cuəl laan mɨn baan tee.	kñom mɨn tɨw tee, pruə̆h kñom cuəl laan mɨn baan.
kñom mɨn-toə̆n cəñ pii salaa tee.	kñom mɨn tɨw tee, pruə̆h kñom mɨn-toə̆n cəñ pii salaa.

4. The Modal Verb prɑsɑp

prɑsɑp (prəsɑp) as a modal verb means 'to be good at, skilled at', as in

| yii, saaŋ prəsɑp hael-tɨk nah wəəy! | Hey, look how well Sâng swims!
(Hey, Sâng is very good at swimming!) |

prəsɑp may also occur as a primary verb meaning 'clever, skilled', as in

| koun-səh nuh prəsɑp nah. | That student is very clever. |

4-A. Substitution Drill

Teacher	Student
koə̆t prəsɑp hael-tɨk nah.	koə̆t prəsɑp hael-tɨk nah.
baək laan	koə̆t prəsɑp baək laan nah.
məəl siəwphɨw	koə̆t prəsɑp məəl siəwphɨw nah.
twəə-kaa	koə̆t prəsɑp twəə-kaa nah.

Teacher	Student
twəə mhoup	kŏ̆ət prəsap twəə mhoup nah.
niyiəy phiəsaa-kmae	kŏ̆ət prəsap niyiəy phiəsaa-kmae nah.
səsei	kŏ̆ət prəsap səsei nah.
ruə̆t prənaŋ	kŏ̆ət prəsap ruə̆t prənaŋ nah.
laəŋ pnum	kŏ̆ət prəsap laəŋ pnum nah.

5. The Interjection wəəy!

wəəy! is a colloquial interjection which occurs in final position in exclamatory statements addressed to more than one person, or to a group of friends. Its function is to attract the attention of the group, or to reinforce an imperative statement made to a group of friends or workers, as in

| yii, sɑɑŋ prəsap hael-tɨk nah wəəy! | Hey, look how well Sâng swims! |
| mɔɔk qaoy chap-chap wəəy! | Hurry up, all of you! |

wəəy is typically accompanied by a high sustained intonation, represented by ! in the transcription.

5-A. Substitution Drill

Teacher	Student
yii, sɑɑŋ prəsap hael-tɨk nah wəəy!	yii, sɑɑŋ prəsap hael-tɨk nah wəəy!
laəŋ pnum	yii, sɑɑŋ prəsap laəŋ pnum nah wəəy!
baək laan	yii, sɑɑŋ prəsap baək laan nah wəəy!
məəl siəwphɨw	yii, sɑɑŋ prəsap məəl siəwphɨw nah wəəy!
twəə mhoup	yii, sɑɑŋ prəsap twəə mhoup nah wəəy!
ruə̆t prənaŋ	yii, sɑɑŋ prəsap ruə̆t prənaŋ nah wəəy!

5-B. Expansion Drill

Teacher	Student
tɨk nih trəceə̆q nah!	tɨk nih trəceə̆q nah wəəy!
mɔɔk laəŋ kəpal tɨw!	mɔɔk laəŋ kəpal tɨw wəəy!
sɑɑŋ prəsap hael-tɨk nah!	sɑɑŋ prəsap hael-tɨk nah wəəy!
srəy nuh lqɑɑ nah!	srəy nuh lqɑɑ nah wəəy!
sliəq-peə̆q qaoy sqaat-baat tɨw!	sliəq-peə̆q qaoy sqaat-baat tɨw wəəy!
twəə-kaa qaoy chap tɨw!	twəə-kaa qaoy chap tɨw wəəy!
prəñap twəə kluən tɨw!	prəñap twəə kluən tɨw wəəy!
pteə̆h nih thom nah!	pteə̆h nih thom nah wəəy!

6. The Modal Verb tloə̆p

We met tloə̆p in Lesson 9 as a primary verb with the meaning 'to be used to (something), accustomed (to something)', as in

| peel yup, baə mɨn tloə̆p, keeŋ mɨn luə̆q tee. | At night, if [you're] not used to [it], [you] can't sleep. |

As a modal verb tloə̆p means 'habitually (+ verb), used to (+ verb)', as in

| kñom tloə̆p nɨw cɨt moə̆t-tuə̆nlee. | I used to live near the river-bank. |
| kñom tloə̆p tɨw hael-tɨk roə̆l tŋay. | I used to go swimming every day. |

6-A. Substitution Drill

Teacher	Student
kñom tloŏp tɨw hael-tɨk roŏl tŋay.	kñom tloŏp tɨw hael-tɨk roŏl tŋay.
daə-leeŋ	kñom tloŏp tɨw daə-leeŋ roŏl tŋay.
twəə-kaa	kñom tloŏp tɨw twəə-kaa roŏl tŋay.
məəl kon	kñom tloŏp tɨw məəl kon roŏl tŋay.
riən	kñom tloŏp tɨw riən roŏl tŋay.
leeŋ biə	kñom tloŏp tɨw leeŋ biə roŏl tŋay.
laəŋ pnum	kñom tloŏp tɨw laəŋ pnum roŏl tŋay.
cih kəpal	kñom tloŏp tɨw cih kəpal roŏl tŋay.

7. kaal nɨw pii touc

kaal nɨw pii touc is an idiomatic adverbial phrase meaning 'when I was still young, when I was a kid', as in

kaal nɨw pii touc, knom tloŏp tɨw hael-tɨk roŏl tŋay.	When I was a kid, I used to go swimming every day.

7-A. Substitution Drill

Teacher	Student
kaal nɨw pii touc, kñom tloŏp tɨw hael-tɨk roŏl tŋay.	kaal nɨw pii touc, kñom tloŏp tɨw hael-tɨk roŏl tŋay.
cuəy qəwpuk-mdaay.	kaal nɨw pii touc, kñom tloŏp cuəy qəwpuk-mdaay.
tɨw salaa roŏl tŋay.	kaal nɨw pii touc, kñom tloŏp tɨw salaa roŏl tŋay.
twəə-kaa nɨw knoŋ prɨy.	kaal nɨw pii touc, kñom tloŏp twəə-kaa nɨw knoŋ prɨy.
leeŋ ciə-muəy baaŋ-pqoun kñom.	kaal nɨw pii touc, kñom tloŏp leeŋ ciə-muəy baaŋ-pqoun kñom.
nɨw cɨt moŏt-tuənlee.	kaal nɨw pii touc, kñom tloŏp nɨw cɨt moŏt-tuənlee.
cih kəpal tɨw krəceh.	kaal nɨw pii touc, kñom tloŏp cih kəpal tɨw krəceh.
tɨw twəə pɨcnɨc.	kaal nɨw pii touc, kñom tloŏp tɨw twəə pɨcnɨc.

8. Nominal Use of Verbs

Cambodian verbs frequently function as nouns; i.e. they may function as subjects and objects of other verbs. Such verbs can usually be translated 'verb + -ing' or 'to + verb' in English. In the following sentence, hael-tɨk 'to swim' is the subject of twəə qaoy 'causes, makes':

hael-tɨk twəə qaoy kñom kliən nah.	Swimming makes me very hungry.
	or: To swim makes me very hungry.

In the following example, luə̆q 'to sell' is the object of miən 'to have':

niw haaŋ nuh kee miən luə̆q   At that shop they sell (have
mhoup kmae.   the selling of) Cambodian food.

8-A. Multiple Substitution Drill

Teacher		Student
hael-tik twəə qaoy kñom klian.		hael-tik twəə qaoy kñom klian.
rian	ceh.	rian twəə qaoy kñom ceh.
twəə-kaa	qah-kəmlaŋ.	twəə-kaa twəə qaoy kñom qah-kəmlaŋ.
cih kəpal	klaac.	cih kəpal twəə qaoy kñom klaac.
tiw daə-leeŋ	qah praq.	tiw daə-leeŋ twəə qaoy kñom qah praq.
hael-tik	rəŋiə.	hael-tik twəə qaoy kñom rəŋiə.
laəŋ pnum	klian.	laəŋ pnum twəə qaoy kñom klian.
ñam numpaŋ	cqaet.	ñam numpaŋ twəə qaoy kñom cqaet.

8-B. Substitution Drill

Teacher	Student
kənlaeŋ nuh kee miən luə̆q plae-chəə.	kənlaeŋ nuh kee miən luə̆q plae-chəə.
twəə pteə̆h.	kənlaeŋ nuh kee miən twəə pteə̆h.
baok khao-qaaw.	kənlaeŋ nuh kee miən baok khao-qaaw.
cuəl laan.	kənlaeŋ nuh kee miən cuəl laan.
kcəy praq.	kənlaeŋ nuh kee miən kcəy praq.
bəŋriən phiəsaa.	kənlaeŋ nuh kee miən bəŋriən phiəsaa.
twəə laan.	kənlaeŋ nuh kee miən twəə laan.

9. noə̆m kniə

The phrase noə̆m kniə frequently precedes primary verbs with the meaning
'to do (something) all together, to cooperate (in doing something)', as in

mɔɔk noə̆m kniə ruə̆t prənaŋ tiw   Let's all race back to the car
laan wiñ.   together.

9-A. Substitution Drill

Teacher	Student
mɔɔk noə̆m kniə ruə̆t prənaŋ tiw wiñ.	mɔɔk noə̆m kniə ruə̆t prənaŋ tiw wiñ.
tiw məəl kon.	mɔɔk noə̆m kniə tiw məəl kon.
tiw daə-leeŋ.	mɔɔk noə̆m kniə tiw daə-leeŋ.
tiw rɔɔk puəq-maaq yəəŋ.	mɔɔk noə̆m kniə tiw rɔɔk puəq-maaq yəəŋ.
tiw twəə-kaa.	mɔɔk noə̆m kniə tiw twəə-kaa.
tiw ñam baay.	mɔɔk noə̆m kniə tiw ñam baay.
tiw laəŋ pnum.	mɔɔk noə̆m kniə tiw laəŋ pnum.
tiw twəə picnic.	mɔɔk noə̆m kniə tiw twəə picnic.

10. The Auxiliary muk-tae

The compound auxiliary muk-tae 'likely to, probably' has been met in the
following sentences:

bəntəc-tiət <u>muk-tae</u> rẻəŋ haəy.   [It] will <u>probably</u> quit soon.
tɨw dɑl laan, <u>muk-tae</u> sŋuət   [When we] reach the car, [we'll]
   kluən haəy.   <u>probably</u> be dry.

10-A. <u>Substitution Drill</u>

<u>Teacher</u>   <u>Student</u>

bəntəc-tiət muk-tae <u>sŋuət kluən haəy</u>.   bəntəc-tiət muk-tae <u>sŋuət kluən haəy</u>.
                    <u>rẻəŋ haəy</u>.   bəntəc-tiət muk-tae <u>rẻəŋ haəy</u>.
                    <u>tleẻq pliəŋ haəy</u>.   bəntəc-tiət muk-tae <u>tleẻq pliəŋ haəy</u>.
                    <u>tɨw dɑl krəceh haəy</u>. bəntəc-tiət muk-tae <u>tɨw dɑl krəceh
                                                     haəy</u>.

                    <u>twəə cɑp haəy</u>.   bəntəc-tiət muk-tae <u>twəə cɑp haəy</u>.
                    <u>ceh hael-tɨk haəy</u>.   bəntəc-tiət muk-tae <u>ceh hael-tɨk haəy</u>.
                    <u>luẻŋ-tɨk haəy</u>.   bəntəc-tiət muk-tae <u>luəŋ-tɨk haəy</u>.
                    <u>tɨw ñam baay</u>.   bəntəc-tiət muk-tae <u>tɨw ñam baay</u>.
                    <u>qɑh-kəmlaŋ haəy</u>.   bəntəc-tiət muk-tae <u>qɑh-kəmlaŋ haəy</u>.

11. <u>kaal-naa</u> as a Subordinating Conjunction

In Lesson 14, <u>kaal-naa</u> was met as an interrogative word meaning 'when?'
in the sentence:

<u>kaal-naa</u> baan yəəŋ tɨw dɑl krəceh?   <u>When</u> will we get to Kratie?

<u>kaal-naa</u> also occurs as a subordinating conjunction meaning 'when, whenever',
as in

<u>kaal-naa</u> ñam baay ruəc, yəəŋ nɨŋ   <u>When</u> [we've] finished eating, we'll
tɨw laəŋ pnum.   go climb the mountain.

<u>kaal-naa</u> tɨw dɑl krəceh haəy,   <u>When</u> [we] get to Kratie, we'll go
yəəŋ nɨŋ tɨw rɔɔk puəq-maaq.   visit our friends.

11-A. <u>Substitution Drill</u>

<u>Teacher</u>   <u>Student</u>

kaal-naa <u>ñam baay</u> ruəc,   kaal-naa <u>ñam baay</u> ruəc,
yəəŋ nɨŋ tɨw daə-leeŋ.   yəəŋ nɨŋ tɨw daə-leeŋ.

         <u>twəə-kaa</u>   kaal-naa <u>twəə-kaa</u> ruəc,
                                               yəəŋ nɨŋ tɨw daə-leeŋ.

         <u>məəl siəwphɨw</u>   kaal-naa <u>məəl siəwphɨw</u> ruəc,
                                               yəəŋ nɨŋ tɨw daə-leeŋ.

         <u>twəə mhoup</u>   kaal-naa <u>twəə mhoup</u> ruəc,
                                               yəəŋ nɨŋ tɨw daə-leeŋ.

         <u>ŋuut-tɨk</u>   kaal-naa <u>ŋuut-tɨk</u> ruəc,
                                               yəəŋ nɨŋ tɨw daə-leeŋ.

         <u>plah khao-qaaw</u>   kaal-naa <u>plah khao-qaaw</u> ruəc,
                                               yəəŋ nɨŋ tɨw daə-leeŋ.

         <u>məəl kasaet</u>   kaal-naa <u>məəl kasaet</u> ruəc,
                                               yəəŋ nɨŋ tɨw daə-leeŋ.

Teacher	Student
sət saq	kaal-naa sət saq ruəc, yəəŋ nɨŋ tɨw daə-leeŋ.
sliəq-peə̆q	kaal-naa sliəq-peə̆q ruəc, yəəŋ nɨŋ tɨw daə-leeŋ.

[Tape 27]   C. COMPREHENSION

1. Discussing the Merits of a Picnic

   cham: chum coul-cət tɨw pɨcnɨc tee?

   chum: tee, kñom mɨn coul-cət tee.
       [muuh 'mosquito']
       [srɑmaoc (srəmaoc, səmaoc) 'ant']
       thoə̆mmədaa nɨw prɨy miən muuh haəy-nɨŋ srəmaoc craən nah.

   cham: tae nɨw knoŋ prɨy trəceə̆q səpbaay nah.

   chum: ñam baay nɨw knoŋ prɨy pibaaq nah.

   cham: mɨn pibaaq ponmaan tee, baə yəəŋ yɔɔk kənteel tɨw.

       [ptoə̆l 'against, next to']
       [dəy 'ground, earth']
   chum: qəŋkuy ptoə̆l dəy mɨn sruəl tee.

   cham: baə mɨn caŋ qəŋkuy ptoə̆l dəy, qəŋkuy ləə tmɑɑ tɨw.

       [tuə̆h-yaaŋ-naa-kɑ-daoy 'however it may be, nevertheless']
   chum: tuə̆h-yaaŋ-naa-kɑ-daoy, kñom coul-cət ñam baay nɨw pteə̆h ciəŋ.

2. Discussing Swimming

   cuən: cɨm ceh hael-tɨk tee?

   cɨm: thəy mɨn ceh!

   cuən: riən hael pii-qəŋkal?

   cɨm: bɑɑŋ-proh kñom bəŋriən kñom pii cnam mun.
      cuən qaeŋ ceh hael-tɨk tee?

   cuən: kñom mɨn-səw prəsɑp hael-tɨk tee.
       [reə̆q-reə̆q 'quite shallow']
       kñom hael tae kənlaeŋ reə̆q-reə̆q tee.

   cɨm: baə hael roə̆l tŋay tɨw, ceh hael douc kñom haəy.

3. Going on a Picnic

   chum: kñom nɨŋ cɑɑn tɨw ñam baay nɨw knoŋ prɨy.
      sɨm cɑŋ tɨw ciə-muəy yəəŋ tee?

   sɨm: tɨw kɑ-tɨw, tae kñom kmiən mhoup tee.

   cɑɑn: mɨn qəy tee; yəəŋ miən mhoup craən dae.

   sɨm: yəəŋ daə tɨw rɨɨ cih laan?

chum: yəəŋ daə tɨw taam pləw nih.
       kənlaeŋ nuh mɨn cŋaay ponmaan tee.

[Later]

caan: yii, kñom qɑh-kəmlɑŋ nah!
      yəəŋ daə mɔɔk yuu haəy!
      kənlaeŋ nuh nɨw cŋaay tiət rɨɨ?

chum: cɨt dɑl haəy.

caan: tmɑɑ nuh sqaat nah; mɔɔk yəəŋ tɨw ñam baay nɨw kenlaeŋ nuh.

chum: ñam baay haəy, yəəŋ noə̆m kniə tɨw leeŋ ləə pnum.

4. At the River-side

siəŋ: pteə̆h laa qaeŋ nɨw qae-naa?

laa: pteə̆h kñom nɨw moə̆t tuə̆nlee.

siəŋ: qəñcəŋ laa qaeŋ hael tɨk leeŋ roə̆l tŋay rɨɨ?

laa: tee; kaal nɨw pii touc, kñom hael tae roə̆l tŋay.
    tae qəyləw-nih, kñom mɨn coul-cət ponmaan tee.
    [tlaa 'to be clear, transparent']
    tɨk mɨn-səw tlaa sɑh.
    qəyləw-nih kñom coul-cət qəŋkuy məəl kəpal taam moə̆t tuə̆nlee.

siəŋ: miən kəpal thom-thom baək taam moə̆t-tuə̆nlee nih tee?

laa: miən, tae mɨn-səw miən craən douc pii mun tee.
    sɑp tŋay nih neə̆q-dəmnaə coul-cət cih laan nɨŋ kəpal-hɑh ciəŋ kəpal.

D. CONVERSATION

1. Discussing A Picnic

   a) A asks B where he went yesterday (for fun).
   b) B replies that he and three friends went for a picnic in the forest.
   c) A asks B what he took to eat on the picnic.
   d) B says that they bought smoked fish, prahok, duck eggs, cucumbers, and
      a pot of rice.
   e) A asks B if they had to eat on the ground.
   f) B replies negatively, and says that at that place they have tables for
      picnicking, then adds that they also have a park where various flowers
      and shrubs have been planted.
   g) A asks B if one can swim at that place.
   h) B replies of course one can; there is a waterfall (place) there [where]
      one can swim.

2. Discussing Swimming

   a) A asks B if he likes to swim.
   b) B replies that he's not very good at swimming, and that he stays only in
      the shallow places.
      B then asks A how about himself, if he knows how to swim.

    c) A replies that he does, then explains that he lives near the river-bank, and that when he was a kid, he used to go swimming every day.

    d) B says that his village is near the forest, is the reason that he's not so good at swimming, but adds that he is good at mountain-climbing.

    e) A says that swimming makes him hungry, and adds that whenever he goes swimming, he takes a lot of food along.

    f) B says he prefers playing games to swimming.

3. <u>Three Friends on an Outing</u>

    a) A says this water seems very deep.

    b) B says that if he sinks, just call him (B) and he'll help.

    c) C says that swimming makes him cold; then suggests that they all (together) go change their clothes.

    d) A asks B where he parked the car.

    e) B replies that he parked the car under a tree where there's cool shade; then adds that it's not so far.

    f) A suggests that they race back to the car; and adds that by the time they get to the car, they'll likely be dry.

    g) C calls attention to how good A is at running.

    h) B says that when they've changed their clothes, they'll go climb the mountain.

    i) C says that mountain-climbing makes him very tired.

    j) B suggests that in that case they rest for awhile on that rock.

    k) C comments that this mountain appears to be quite large.

    l) B says that when they've climbed the mountain, they'll go back and eat.

LESSON 16. A TRIP BY CAR

[Tape 28]　　　　　　　A. DIALOGUE

khɨn

| coc | to punch, depress |
| suflei (~ suplei) | horn; to blow a horn |

1. hei, coc suflei tɨw! — Hey, blow the horn!

2. sɨən mɨn-toən coh mɔɔk pii pteəh tee. — Soeun hasn't come (down) out of the house yet.

chəən

| ciə-nɨc | always |

3. sɨən thəə qəy, kaa yɨɨt ciə-nɨc. — Whatever Soeun does, he's always late.

| naa | demonstrative interjection: look!, there! |

4. naa! sɨən mɔɔk haəy! — There he comes! (There! Soeun's coming.)

sɨən

| qat-tooh | Excuse me, I'm sorry |
| waen-taa | glasses |

5. qat-tooh, kñom rɔɔk waen-taa mɨn khəəñ tee, baan ciə knom yɨɨt bəntəc. — I'm sorry; I couldn't find my glasses, is why I'm a little late.

khɨn

| puəq-yəəŋ | we (exclusive) |
| caol | to leave, abandon, throw away |

6. baə yɨɨt bəntəc tiət, puəq-yəəŋ tɨw caol haəy! — If [you] had been a little later, we'd have gone without (leaving) [you].

| tŋay nah haəy | to be very late (in the morning) |

7. tŋay nah haəy; yəəŋ trəw tɨw tətuəl saaŋ tiət. — It's late already; we still have to go pick up Sâng.

sɨən

| kiloumaet | kilometer |

8. ponmaan kiloumaet baan tɨw dal siəm-riəp? — How many kilometers is it (to go) to Siem Reap?

chəən

| camŋaay (cəmŋaay) | distance |

9. pii pnum-pɨñ tɨw siəm-riəp cəmŋaay prəhael bəy-rɔɔy dap-buən kiloumaet. — From Phnom Penh to Siem Reap [is] a distance of about 314 kilometers.

10. haəy pii siəm-riəp tɨw qəŋkɔɔ-woət prammuəy kiloumaet tiət. — And from Siem Reap to Angkor Wat [is] six kilometers further.

khɨn

choɔ — to stand

11. nuh, saɑŋ choɔ cam yəəŋ nɨw muk ptëʾəh.
There, Sâng's (standing) waiting for us in front of the house.

ciə — relative conjunction: that

12. qei, qəywan saɑŋ craən nah; mɨn dəŋ ciə daq kənlaeŋ naa tee.
Hey, you (Sâng) have a lot of things; [I] don't know where [we'll] put [them].

saɑŋ

chap — to be quick to

13. rəbɑh tëəŋ-qɑh nih samrap puʾəq-yəəŋ ñam; bəə yəəŋ ñam taam pləw, muk-tae chap qɑh haəy.
All these things are for us to eat; if we eat [them] along the way, [they'll] likely be used up quickly.

sɨən

khouc — to be broken, damaged, or spoiled
prɑdap (prədap, pədap) — tool, instrument
cuəh-cul — to repair
prədap cuəh-cul — tools

14. bəə laan khouc taam pləw, taə miən prədap cuəh-cul tee?
If the car breaks down along the way, do you have tools?

chəən

kom . . . qəy — emphatic negative imperative
phɨy — to be afraid
krup — all, every
baep — kind, variety

15. kom phɨy qəy; kñom miən prədap krup baep.
Don't worry; I have all kinds of tools.

tuənəwih — screw-driver
dɑŋkap (dəŋkap, təkap) — pliers
ñɔñuə (ñəñuə, qañuə) — hammer
klei — wrench

16. miən tuənəwih, dəŋkap, ñəñuə, haəy-nɨŋ klei psein-psein.
[I] have a screw-driver, pliers, a hammer, and an assortment of wrenches.

khɨn

kɑŋ — wheel (including tire); bicycle
baek — to break (intr.)

17. bəə kɑŋ baek taam pləw, thəə məc tɨw?
If we have a blowout along the way, what'll we do?

chəən

səkuə — emergency, extra
kɑŋ səkuə — spare wheel

18. kñom yɔɔk kɑŋ səkuə mɔɔk dae.
I brought a spare wheel along too.

kriip ~ krɨp — a jack, lift
snɑp — an air pump
puʾəh-wiən — inner-tube

19. kraw-pii nuh, miən kriip, snɑp, haəy-nɨŋ puʾəh-wiən phɑɑŋ.
Besides that, there's a jack, a pump, and an inner-tube too.

saɑŋ

cnuəl   rent, hire (noun)
laan-cnuəl   hired car, bus
waa   to pass, to overtake

20. laan-cnuəl nuh douc-ciə cɑŋ   That bus seems to want to pass us.
waa yəəŋ haəy.

chəən

spiən   bridge
phot   to be free (of), clear (of)
qaac   to have the power or ability (to)

21. dɑl kɦom clɑɑŋ spiən nuh phot,   As soon as I've gotten across that
kee qaac tɨw mun baan.   bridge, they'll be able to go ahead.

[Later]

saŋ   gasoline
22. qou, saŋ cɨt qɑh haəy.   Oh, we're almost out of gas (the gas
                                          is almost gone).

khɨn

coul   to enter
23. nuh kənlaeŋ luəq saŋ;   There's a place [where they] sell gas;
coul chup kənlaeŋ nuh.   go in [and] stop there.

saɑŋ

maasiin (masɨn)   machine, motor
preiŋ-masɨn   motor-oil
24. trəw-kaa preiŋ-masɨn tee?   Do [we] need oil?

chəən

25. mɨn-bac tee.   It's not necessary.

caq   to insert, inject
boum   to pump
klañ   grease
caq preiŋ boum klañ   to lubricate

26. kɦom baan yɔɔk laan tɨw caq   I took the car [and had it] lubricated
preiŋ boum klañ mun cəñ dəmnaə.   before leaving [on the] trip.

sɨən

krɑŋeik-krɑŋɑq   to be crooked, to zigzag
   (krəŋeik-krəŋɑq,
   kəŋeik-kəŋɑq)

27. yii, pləw nih krəŋeik-krəŋɑq nah!   Boy, this road is really crooked!

prəyat (prəyat, pəyat)   to be careful (to), take care (in)
mɛɛn-tɛɛn   really, truly, extremely

28. prəyat baək laan qaoy mɛɛn-tɛɛn   Drive very carefully! (Be really care-
tɨw!   ful in driving the car!)

chəən

sŋiəm   to be quiet, silent
tuk-cət   to have confidence (in), rely (on)

khaaŋ

29. qəŋkuy qaoy sɲiəm tɨw! tuk-cət
    ləə kñom coh, khaaŋ baək laan.

in the area of, in the matter of
Just sit quietly! Have confidence in
me, in the matter of driving a car.

quhsaa

30. kñom quhsaa mɔɔk taam pləw nih
    nah.

frequently, often
I've driven (come along) this road
often.

B. GRAMMAR AND DRILLS

1. The Adverbial ciə-nɨc

ciə-nɨc is a final adverbial which means 'always, invariably', as in

sɨən thəə qəy, kɑɑ yɨɨt ciə-nɨc.

Whatever Soeun does, he's always
late.

1-A. Substitution Drill

Teacher	Student
sɨən thəə qəy, kɑɑ yɨɨt ciə-nɨc.	sɨən thəə qəy, kɑɑ yɨɨt ciə-nɨc.
chap	sɨən thəə qəy, kɑɑ chap ciə-nɨc.
pukae	sɨən thəə qəy, kɑɑ pukae ciə-nɨc.
coul-cət	sɨən thəə qəy, kɑɑ coul-cət ciə-nɨc.
rəhah	sɨən thəə qəy, kɑɑ rəhah ciə-nɨc.
pibaaq	sɨən thəə qəy, kɑɑ pibaaq ciə-nɨc.
sruəl	sɨən thəə qəy, kɑɑ sruəl ciə-nɨc.
səpbaay	sɨən thəə qəy, kɑɑ səpbaay ciə-nɨc.
prəsɑp	sɨən thəə qəy, kɑɑ prəsɑp ciə-nɨc.
kcɨl	sɨən thəə qəy, kɑɑ kcɨl ciə-nɨc.

2. rɔɔk mɨn baan vs. rɔɔk mɨn khəəñ

rɔɔk mɨn baan is a completive verb phrase which means 'to be unable to
find, to be unsuccessful at finding (because it wasn't there)', as in

kñom rɔɔk waen-taa mɨn baan tee.   I couldn't find my glasses.
kñom rɔɔk peel tɨw mɨn baan tee.   I couldn't find time to go.

rɔɔk mɨn khəəñ, on the other hand, means 'to be unable to find, or to come across,
something which is nevertheless there to be found (such as one's own possession)',
as in

kñom rɔɔk waen-taa mɨn khəəñ tee,   I couldn't find my glasses is why
baan ciə kñom yɨɨt bəntəc.   I'm a little late.

In this example, one assumes he found the glasses, but it was the necessity of looking for them that caused the delay.

2-A. Substitution Drill

Teacher	Student
kñom rɔɔk waen-taa mɨn khəəñ tee.	kñom rɔɔk waen-taa mɨn khəəñ tee.
khao-qaaw	kñom rɔɔk khao-qaaw mɨn khəəñ tee.
luy	kñom rɔɔk luy mɨn khəəñ tee.

Teacher	Student
laan kñom	kñom rɔɔk laan kñom mɨn khəəñ tee.
mɨt kñom	kñom rɔɔk mɨt kñom mɨn khəəñ tee.
krah-sət-saq	kñom rɔɔk krah-sət-saq mɨn khəəñ tee.
crah-doh-tmɨñ	kñom rɔɔk crah-doh-tmɨñ mɨn khəəñ tee.
sraom-cəəŋ	kñom rɔɔk sraom-cəəŋ mɨn khəəñ tee.
siəwphɨw kñom	kñom rɔɔk siəwphɨw kñom mɨn khəəñ tee.
kmaw-day	kñom rɔɔk kmaw-day mɨn khəəñ tee.

3. The Connective Verb Phrase baan ciə

It was pointed out in Lesson 14, B, 9 that baan ciə frequently connects a subject clause with a complement which is also a clause (consisting of a verb with or without a subject) with the meaning 'is the reason that, is why', as in

kñom mɨn-səw ciə tee	I'm not so well is the reason that
baan ciə kñom mɨn tɨw.	I'm not going.

In the translation of such sentences, it is convenient to transpose the two clauses and to translate baan ciə as 'because', but notice that, in the English translation, the subject of baan ciə becomes the complement of 'because', as in

kñom rɔɔk waen-taa mɨn khəəñ tee, baan ciə kñom yɨɨt bəntəc.	I'm a little late because I couldn't find my glasses. (I couldn't find my glasses is why I'm a little late.)
kñom qɑh barəy haəy, baan ciə kñom tɨw psaa.	I'm going to the market because I'm out of cigarettes. (I'm out of cigarettes is why I'm going to the market.)

3-A. Substitution Drill

Teacher	Student
kñom rɔɔk waen-taa mɨn khəəñ tee, baan ciə kñom yɨɨt bəntəc.	kñom rɔɔk waen-taa mɨn khəəñ tee, baan ciə kñom yɨɨt bəntəc.
kñom ñam baay mɨn-toən ruəc tee.	kñom ñam baay mɨn-toən ruəc tee, baan ciə kñom yɨɨt bəntəc.
kñom rɔɔk chat mɨn khəəñ tee,	kñom rɔɔk chat mɨn khəəñ tee, baan ciə kñom yɨɨt bəntəc.
kñom prətəəh mɨt məneəq,	kñom prətəəh mɨt məneəq, baan ciə kñom yɨɨt bəntəc.
kñom rɔɔk barəy mɨn baan tee,	kñom rɔɔk barəy mɨn baan tee, baan ciə kñom yɨɨt bəntəc.
kñom trəw tɨw psaa sən,	kñom trəw tɨw psaa sən, baan ciə kñom yɨɨt bəntəc.

Teacher	Student
kñom trəw sət saq sən,	kñom trəw sət saq sən, baan ciə kñom yɨɨt bəntəc.
kñom cuəl laan mɨn baan tee,	kñom cuəl laan mɨn baan tee, baan ciə kñom yɨɨt bəntəc.

3-B. Transformation Drill

Teacher	Student
kñom yɨɨt bəntəc, pruˇəh kñom rɔɔk waen-taa mɨn khəəñ.	kñom rɔɔk waen-taa mɨn khəəñ tee, baan ciə kñom yɨɨt bəntəc.
kñom mɨn tɨw tee, pruˇəh kñom mɨn caŋ tɨw.	kñom mɨn caŋ tɨw tee, baan ciə kñom mɨn tɨw.
kñom tɨw mɨn baan tee, pruˇəh kñom twəə-kaa mɨn-toˇən cap.	kñom twəə-kaa mɨn-toˇən cap tee, baan ciə kñom tɨw mɨn baan.
kñom mɨn caŋ tɨw tee, pruˇəh kñom rɔɔk peel mɨn baan.	kñom rɔɔk peel mɨn baan tee, baan ciə kñom mɨn caŋ tɨw.
kñom mɨn baan mɔɔk tee, pruˇəh kñom cuəl laan mɨn baan.	kñom cuəl laan mɨn baan tee, baan ciə kñom mɨn baan mɔɔk.
kñom mɨn-səw ciə tee, pruˇəh kñom ñam baay craən peek.	kñom ñam baay craən peek, baan ciə kñom mɨn-səw ciə.
kñom klaac tɨk crɨw, pruˇəh kñom mɨn ceh hael-tɨk.	kñom mɨn ceh hael-tɨk tee, baan ciə kñom klaac tɨk crɨw.
kñom chup kənlaeŋ nih pruˇəh saŋ cɨt qah haəy.	saŋ cɨt qah haəy, baan ciə kñom chup kənlaeŋ nih.
kñom səmraaq nɨw ləə tmaa nih pruˇəh kñom qah-kəmlaŋ nah.	kñom qah-kəmlaŋ nah, baan ciə kñom səmraaq nɨw ləə tmaa nih.

4. The Pronoun puəq-yəəŋ

The pronoun yəəŋ 'we' may be either singular or plural. The compound pronoun puəq-yəəŋ, on the other hand, usually means 'we, our group (as opposed to you)', and conveys a degree of solidarity or exclusiveness on the part of the group referred to, as in

baə yɨɨt bəntəc tiət, puəq-yəəŋ tɨw caol haəy!	If [you] had been a little later, we'd have gone without [you].

4-A. Substitution Drill

Teacher	Student
puəq-yəəŋ tɨw ñam baay; mɨt caŋ tɨw tee?	puəq-yəəŋ tɨw ñam baay; mɨt caŋ tɨw tee?
məəl kon	puəq-yəəŋ tɨw məəl kon; mɨt caŋ tɨw tee?

Teacher	Student
daə-leeŋ	puəq-yəəŋ tɨw daə-leeŋ; mɨt caŋ tɨw tee?
laəŋ pnum	puəq-yəəŋ tɨw laəŋ pnum; mɨt caŋ tɨw tee?
twəə pɨcnɨc	puəq-yəəŋ tɨw twəə pɨcnɨc; mɨt caŋ tɨw tee?
hael-tɨk	puəq-yəəŋ tɨw hael-tɨk; mɨt caŋ tɨw tee?
ruə̆t prənaŋ kniə	puəq-yəəŋ tɨw ruə̆t prənaŋ kniə; mɨt caŋ tɨw tee?
phək byeə	puəq-yəəŋ tɨw phək byeə; mɨt caŋ tɨw tee?

5. tɨw as a Preposition

In some contexts tɨw seems to have a purely prepositional function, as in

pii pnum-pɨñ tɨw siəm-riəp cəmŋaay prəhael pii-rɔɔy dap-buən kiloumaet.	From Phnom Penh to Siem Reap [is] a distance of about 314 kilometers.

pii pnum-pɨñ tɨw siəm-riəp 'from Phnom Penh to Siem Reap' is the topic of the sentence, and the sentence has no main verb. Its structure is parallel with the sentence (Lesson 6, B, 2):

mənuh nuh qayuq məphɨy-pram cnam.	That man [is] 25 years old.

5-A. Multiple Substitution Drill

Teacher	Student
pii pnum-pɨñ tɨw siəm-riəp, cəmŋaay prəhael bəy-rɔɔy dap-buən kiloumaet.	pii pnum-pɨñ tɨw siəm-riəp, cəmŋaay prəhael bəy-rɔɔy dap-buən kiloumaet.
qəŋkɔɔ-woə̆t bəy-rɔɔy məphɨy	pii pnum-pɨñ tɨw qəŋkɔɔ-woə̆t, cəmŋaay prəhael bəy-rɔɔy məphɨy kiloumaet.
batdəmbaaŋ pii-rɔɔy kawsəp	pii pnum-pɨñ tɨw batdəmbaaŋ, cəmŋaay prəhael pii-rɔɔy kawsəp kiloumaet.
kəmpuə̆ŋ-caam mərɔɔy məphɨy-pram	pii pnum-pɨñ tɨw kəmpuə̆ŋ-caam, cəmŋaay prəhael mərɔɔy məphɨy-pram kiloumaet.
prɨy-nəkɔɔ pii-rɔɔy saesəp	pii pnum-pɨñ tɨw prɨy-nəkɔɔ, cəmŋaay prəhael pii-rɔɔy saesəp kiloumaet.
krəceh bəy-rɔɔy saesəp	pii pnum-pɨñ tɨw krəceh, cəmŋaay prəhael bəy-rɔɔy saesəp kiloumaet.
kəmpɔɔt mərɔɔy haasəp	pii pnum-pɨñ tɨw kəmpɔɔt, cəmŋaay prəhael mərɔɔy haasəp kiloumaet.
baŋkaaq (Bangkok) prampɨl-rɔɔy saamsəp-pram	pii pnum-pɨñ tɨw baŋkaaq, cəmŋaay prəhael prampɨl-rɔɔy saamsəp-pram kiloumaet.

6. cia as a Relative Conjunction

cia occurs with three different functions, as follows:

1) As a copulative, or connecting verb, meaning 'be, is', as in

qəwpuk kñom cia neə̃q-twəə-srae.   My father is a farmer.
kñom mɨn dəŋ cia prakɑt tee.   I don't know for sure (being sure).

2) As an adjectival verb meaning 'to be well', as in

look sok-səpbaay cia tee?   How are you? (Are you well?)
kñom mɨn-səw cia tee.   I'm not so well.

3) As a relative conjunction meaning 'that', as in

kñom mɨn dəŋ cia daq kənlaeŋ   I don't know where [we'll] put
naa tee.   [them]. (I don't know that [we'll]
                                     put [them] what place.)

haet qwəy baan cia kmiən kambət   Why are there no knives on the
nɨw ləə tok?   table? (What reason is it that
                                     there are no knives on the table?)

6-A. Substitution Drill

   Teacher   Student

kñom mɨn dəŋ cia daq kənlaeŋ naa tee.   kñom mɨn dəŋ cia daq kənlaeŋ naa tee.
              tɨw kənlaeŋ naa   kñom mɨn dəŋ cia tɨw kənlaeŋ naa tee.
              twəə yaaŋ-məc   kñom mɨn dəŋ cia twəə yaaŋ-məc tee.
              tɨñ qwəy   kñom mɨn dəŋ cia tɨñ qwəy tee.
              ñam kənlaeŋ naa   kñom mɨn dəŋ cia ñam kənlaeŋ naa tee.
              twəə-kaa qwəy   kñom mɨn dəŋ cia twəə-kaa qwəy tee.
              kŏət nɨw qae-naa   kñom mɨn dəŋ cia kŏət nɨw qae-naa tee.
              tɨw kaal-naa   kñom mɨn dəŋ cia tɨw kaal-naa tee.

6-B. Response Drill

   Teacher   Student

kŏət twəə-kaa qwəy?   kñom mɨn dəŋ cia kŏət twəə-kaa qwəy tee.
kŏət nɨw qae-naa?   kñom mɨn dəŋ cia kŏət nɨw qae-naa tee.
kŏət tɨw kaal-naa?   kñom mɨn dəŋ cia kŏət tɨw kaal-naa tee.
kŏət tɨw naa?   kñom mɨn dəŋ cia kŏət tɨw naa tee.
kŏət tɨñ qwəy?   kñom mɨn dəŋ cia kŏət tɨñ qwəy tee.
kŏət daq kənlaeŋ naa?   kñom mɨn dəŋ cia kŏət daq kənlaeŋ naa tee.
kŏət ñam mhoup qwəy?   kñom mɨn dəŋ cia kŏət ñam mhoup qwəy tee.
kŏət twəə yaaŋ-məc?   kñom mɨn dəŋ cia kŏət twəə yaaŋ-məc tee.
kŏət thaa məc?   kñom mɨn dəŋ cia kŏət thaa məc tee.

7. General Specifiers

   General specifiers are words that occur in the specifier position (NX___) after
a wide variety of nouns. baep 'kind, variety', and *yaaŋ 'kind, variety, way, method'
are the commonest members of the class. kuu 'pair, couple' may follow any noun
whose referent typically occurs in pairs.

Examples:

kñom miən prədap krup <u>baep</u>.   I have all <u>kinds</u> of tools.
kee luăq siəwphɨw craən <u>yaaŋ</u>.   They sell many <u>kinds</u> of books.
kñom caŋ tɨñ sbaek-cəəŋ muəy <u>kuu</u>.   I want to buy a <u>pair</u> of shoes.

7-A. Substitution Drill

Teacher	Student
haaŋ nuh miən <u>siəwphɨw</u> craən yaaŋ.	haaŋ nuh miən <u>siəwphɨw</u> craən yaaŋ.
khao-qaaw	haaŋ nuh miən <u>khao-qaaw</u> craən yaaŋ.
qəywan	haaŋ nuh miən <u>qəywan</u> craən yaaŋ.
mhoup	haaŋ nuh miən <u>mhoup</u> craən yaaŋ.
laan	haaŋ nuh miən <u>laan</u> craən yaaŋ.
prədap	haaŋ nuh miən <u>prədap</u> craən yaaŋ.
krɨəŋ-tok-tuu	haaŋ nuh miən <u>krɨəŋ-tok-tuu</u> craən yaaŋ.

7-B. Substitution Drill

Teacher	Student
kənlaeŋ nuh kee luăq <u>prədap</u> krup baep.	kənlaeŋ nuh kee luăq <u>prədap</u> krup baep.
plae-chəə	kənlaeŋ nuh kee luăq <u>plae-chəə</u> krup baep.
siəwphɨw	kənlaeŋ nuh kee luăq <u>siəwphɨw</u> krup baep.
qəywan	kənlaeŋ nuh kee luăq <u>qəywan</u> krup baep.
mhoup	kənlaeŋ nuh kee luăq <u>mhoup</u> krup baep.
laan	kənlaeŋ nuh kee luăq <u>laan</u> krup baep.

7-C. Substitution Drill

Teacher	Student
kñom miən <u>sraom-cəəŋ</u> pii kuu.	kñom miən <u>sraom-cəəŋ</u> pii kuu.
sbaek-cəəŋ	kñom miən <u>sbaek-cəəŋ</u> pii kuu.
koo	kñom miən <u>koo</u> pii kuu.
moăn	kñom miən <u>moăn</u> pii kuu.
cruuk	kñom miən <u>cruuk</u> pii kuu.
tiə	kñom miən <u>tiə</u> pii kuu.

8. The Modal Verb qaac

qaac as a modal verb means 'to be able to, to have the power, ability, or authority, to'. It typically co-occurs with the completive verb <u>baan</u> 'to be able to', as in

dɑl kñom clɑɑŋ spiən nuh phot,   As soon as I've gotten across that
kee <u>qaac</u> tɨw mun <u>baan</u>.   bridge, they'll <u>be able to</u> go ahead.

8-A. Substitution Drill

Teacher	Student
kñom twəə-kaa ruəc, kñom qaac <u>tɨw ñam baay</u> baan.	kñom twəə-kaa ruəc, kñom qaac <u>tɨw ñam baay</u> baan.
<u>tɨw dəə-leeŋ</u>	kñom twəə-kaa ruəc, kñom qaac <u>tɨw dəə-leeŋ</u> baan.

Teacher	Student
tɨw məəl kon	kñom twəə-kaa ruəc, kñom qaac tɨw məəl kon baan.
tɨw hael-tɨk	kñom twəə-kaa ruəc, kñom qaac tɨw hael-tɨk baan.
cuəh-cul laan	kñom twəə-kaa ruəc, kñom qaac cuəh-cul laan baan.
plah khao-qaaw	kñom twəə-kaa ruəc, kñom qaac plah khao-qaaw baan.
tɨw pnum-pɨñ	kñom twəə-kaa ruəc, kñom qaac tɨw pnum-pɨñ baan.
tɨw twəə mhoup	kñom twəə-kaa ruəc, kñom qaac tɨw twəə mhoup baan.

9. The Adverbial mɛɛn-tɛɛn

mɛɛn-tɛɛn is a reduplicative adverbial compound derived from the verb mɛɛn 'to be true'. Its meaning is 'really, truly, seriously', as in

prəyat baək laan qaoy mɛɛn-tɛɛn tɨw!	Drive (the car) extremely carefully! (Be extremely careful in driving the car.)
koun-səh nuh pukae mɛɛn-tɛɛn.	That student is really clever.
tŋay-nih kdaw mɛɛn-tɛɛn.	It's really hot today.

9-A. Substitution Drill

Teacher	Student
prəyat baək laan qaoy mɛɛn-tɛɛn tɨw!	prəyat baək laan qaoy mɛɛn-tɛɛn tɨw!
məəl siəwphɨw	prəyat məəl siəwphɨw qaoy mɛɛn-tɛɛn tɨw!
səsei	prəyat səsei qaoy mɛɛn-tɛɛn tɨw!
riən	prəyat riən qaoy mɛɛn-tɛɛn tɨw!
hael-tɨk	prəyat hael-tɨk qaoy mɛɛn-tɛɛn tɨw!
sliəq-peəq	prəyat sliəq-peəq qaoy mɛɛn-tɛɛn tɨw!
baok khao-qaaw	prəyat baok khao-qaaw qaoy mɛɛn-tɛɛn tɨw!
twəə-kaa	prəyat twəə-kaa qaoy mɛɛn-tɛɛn tɨw!

10. The Function of khaaŋ

khaaŋ is one of a class of nouns which serve to introduce adverbial phrases which are best translated as prepositional phrases in English. khaaŋ has been met, usually with reduced vowel length, as the head of compounds which specify direction or location, as in

khaŋ-sdam	'right'	khaŋ-ləə	'above'
khaŋ-cweiŋ	'left'	khaŋ-kraom	'under'
khaŋ-muk	'ahead'	khaŋ-nih	'this way'
khaŋ-kraoy	'behind'	khaŋ-nuh	'that way'

At the head of adverbial phrases, khaaŋ means 'in the area of, in the field of, in the matter of', as in

tuk-cət ləə kñom coh, <u>khaaŋ</u>   Have confidence in me, <u>in the</u>
baək laan.   <u>matter of</u> driving a car.

Another member of the class which we have met is <u>camnaek</u> 'part, share', which,
at the head of an adverbial phrase, means 'on the part of, as for'; e.g.:

<u>cəmnaek</u> kñom wɨñ, kñom mɨn caŋ   <u>As for</u> me, I don't want to go.
tɨw tee.   (On my part, I don't want to go.)

10-A. <u>Substitution Drill</u>

<u>Teacher</u>   <u>Student</u>

tuk-cət ləə kñom coh, khaaŋ <u>baək laan.</u>   tuk-cət ləə kñom coh, khaaŋ <u>baək laan.</u>
    <u>leeŋ biə.</u>   tuk-cət ləə kñom coh, khaaŋ <u>leeŋ biə.</u>
    <u>hael-tɨk.</u>   tuk-cət ləə kñom coh, khaaŋ <u>hael-tɨk.</u>
    <u>cih tuuk.</u>   tuk-cət ləə kñom coh, khaaŋ <u>cih tuuk.</u>
    <u>cuəh-cul laan.</u>   tuk-cət ləə kñom coh, khaaŋ <u>cuəh-cul</u>
                                                                <u>laan.</u>
    <u>twəə mhoup.</u>   tuk-cət ləə kñom coh, khaaŋ <u>twəə mhoup.</u>
    <u>twəə dəmnaə.</u>   tuk-cət ləə kñom coh, khaaŋ <u>twəə dəmnaə.</u>
    <u>praə kambət.</u>   tuk-cət ləə kñom coh, khaaŋ <u>praə kambət.</u>
    <u>tɨñ pteəh.</u>   tuk-cət ləə kñom coh, khaaŋ <u>tɨñ pteəh.</u>
    <u>səsei səmbot.</u>   tuk-cət ləə kñom coh, khaaŋ <u>səsei səmbot.</u>

11. The Modal Verb quhsaa

As a primary verb <u>quhsaa</u> means 'to be diligent, industrious', as in

koun-səh nuh <u>quhsaa</u> nah.   That student is very <u>industrious.</u>

In the modal verb position, however, <u>quhsaa</u> means 'frequently, often', as in

kñom <u>quhsaa</u> mɔɔk taam pləw nih   I've <u>often</u> come along this road.
nah.

11-A. <u>Substitution Drill</u>

<u>Teacher</u>   <u>Student</u>

kñom quhsaa <u>mɔɔk taam pləw nih</u> nah.   kñom quhsaa <u>mɔɔk taam pləw nih</u> nah.
    <u>ñam baay baraŋ</u>   kñom quhsaa <u>ñam baay baraŋ</u> nah.
    <u>tɨw pnum-pɨñ</u>   kñom quhsaa <u>tɨw pnum-pɨñ</u> nah.
    <u>cih kəpal</u>   kñom quhsaa <u>cih kəpal</u> nah.
    <u>baək laan</u>   kñom quhsaa <u>baək laan</u> nah.
    <u>tɨw hael-tɨk</u>   kñom quhsaa <u>tɨw hael-tɨk</u> nah.
    <u>cih rəteh-pləəŋ</u>   kñom quhsaa <u>cih rəteh-pləəŋ</u> nah.
    <u>tɨw daə-leeŋ</u>   kñom quhsaa <u>tɨw daə-leeŋ</u> nah.
    <u>cuəh-cul laan</u>   kñom quhsaa <u>cuəh-cul laan</u> nah.
    <u>twəə mhoup</u>   kñom quhsaa <u>twəə mhoup</u> nah.

C. COMPREHENSION

1. **A Bus Trip**

    baan: haan dael tɨw siəm-riəp tee?

    haan: kñom baan tɨw mədaaŋ dae.

    baan: haan qaeŋ baək laan tɨw rɨɨ cih laan-cnuəl?

    haan: kñom cih laan-cnuəl.
             [tɨw mɔɔk 'to go and come']
             miən laan-cnuəl tɨw mɔɔk tae roəl tŋay.

    baan: cih laan-cnuəl, ponmaan maoŋ baan tɨw dɑl siəm-riəp?

    haan: prəhael prambəy maoŋ baan tɨw dɑl.
             kee chup taam pləw qaoy neəq-dəmnaə tɨñ mhoup.

    baan: cih laan-cnuəl tɨw, qɑh-kəmlaŋ tee?

    haan: mɨn qɑh-kəmlaŋ ponmaan tee.

2. **A Blowout**

    saem: sqəy nɨŋ; phɨm qaeŋ lɨɨ tee?
             [baek-kɑŋ 'to have a blowout']
             lɨɨ sou douc baek-kɑŋ.

    phɨm: qou, kɑŋ nuh cah haəy.

    saem: baek-kɑŋ mɛɛn; kɑŋ kraoy khaŋ-sdam baek haəy!

    phɨm: cuəy yɔɔk kriip mɔɔk qaoy kñom neh.
             ruəc yɔɔk kɑŋ səkuə mɔɔk qaoy kñom phɑɑŋ.

    saem: qou, kɑŋ nih kmiən kyɑl sɑh!

             [sɑp 'to inflate, pump air into']
    phɨm: qəñcəŋ yɔɔk snɑp tɨw sɑp tɨw.

    saem: puəh-wiən nih prəhael ciə baek phɑɑŋ, məə-tɨw.

             [pah 'to patch']
    phɨm: qəñcəŋ kñom nɨŋ pah puəh-wiən nih sən.
             cuəy hoc ñəñuə qaoy kñom bentəc.

3. **A Truck-driver**

    phɑɑŋ: sərii-qaeŋ twəə-kaa qəy?

             [tumnɨñ 'merchandise']
             [laan-dək-tumnɨñ 'truck, van']
    sərii: kñom baək laan-dək-tumnɨñ.

    phɑɑŋ: thoəmmədaa dək tumnɨñ qəy?

    sərii: thoəmmədaa kñom dək kriəŋ psein-psein tɨw luəq taam khaet.
             [srəw 'unhusked rice, paddy']
             ruəc dək srəw pii khaet mɔɔk luəq nɨw pnum-pɨñ.

phɑɑŋ: dael miən laan khouc taam pləw tee?

sərii: thəy mɨn miən; quhsaa baek-kaŋ nah.

[sii 'to eat (of animals); to use, consume']
phɑɑŋ: laan thom-thom qəñcəŋ sii saŋ craən nah, mɛɛn tee?

[liit 'liter']
sərii: nɨŋ haəy; mərɔɔy kiloumaet sii prəhael məphɨy liit.

4. Two Friends Discuss Driving

meeŋ: hiəŋ ceh baək laan tee?

[stoət 'to be good (at), skilled (at)']

hiəŋ: baat, kñom ceh, tae mɨn stoət ponmaan tee.

meeŋ: hiəŋ-qaeŋ baək laan ponmaan cnam mɔɔk haəy?

hiəŋ: qou, prəhael məcnam haəy.
       qəwpuk kñom bəŋriən kñom nɨw srok-srae.

məəŋ: baək laan nɨw knoŋ kroŋ pibaaq nah, pruəh miən laan tɨw mɔɔk craən
       peek.

hiəŋ: tae qəyləw-nih baək laan nɨw taam khaet kɑɑ mɨn-səw sruəl dae.
       miən laan-dək-tumnɨñ haəy-nɨŋ laan-cnuəl craən nah.

meeŋ: nɨŋ haəy; baək laan, trəw prəyat qaoy mɛɛn-tɛɛn.

D. CONVERSATION

1. Getting Ready to Leave on a Trip

a) Joe asks Bill if Fred has arrived yet.
b) Bill replies that he hasn't arrived yet, and says that he doesn't know
   where he is.
c) Joe comments that it's already late in the day, and they still have to go
   pick up John.
d) Bill says that wherever Fred goes, he's always late.
e) Joe says perhaps Fred went to have the car lubricated.
f) Bill says there he comes now.

2. Getting Started

a) Fred says he's sorry, and explains that the reason he's late is that he had
   a blowout on the way.
b) Joe asks Fred if he had a spare and a jack.
c) Fred answers that of course he had, but now he has to take the inner-tube
   and have it patched.
d) Joe asks Fred what they will do if the car breaks down along the road.
e) Fred replies that he has all kinds of tools, such as a screw-driver, pliers,
   a hammer, and various wrenches.
f) Joe asks Fred if he knows how to repair cars.
g) Fred tells Joe to rely on him when it comes to repairing cars.

3. <u>On the Way</u>

   a) Bill asks how far it is to Battambang.

   b) John replies that from Phnom Penh to Battambang is a distance of about 290 kilometers.

   c) Bill asks how long it will take to get to Battambang.

   d) John replies that if they drive fast, they will get there in about seven hours, but adds that the road to Battambang is very crooked; one must drive very carefully.

   e) Bill says that that truck seems to want to pass them.

   f) John says as soon as they get across that bridge, the truck will be able to go ahead.

4. <u>Getting Gas</u>

   a) Joe says that riding in a car makes him very tired, and asks how many more hours it will take (<u>baan</u>) to get to Battambang.

   b) Fred says that it's still a long way (still far further).

   c) Joe complains that he's hungry; the food that John brought is all gone.

   d) Fred tells him to sit quietly; then adds that pretty soon he'll have to stop and buy some gas; they can rest there.

   e) Joe asks Fred if his car uses much gas.

   f) Fred replies that it doesn't use so much; in 100 kilometers [it] uses about seven liters.

LESSON 17. SIGHTSEEING

[Tape 30]   A. DIALOGUE

chaan

1. tŋay-nih look caŋ twəə qwəy?   What do you want to do today?

George

tii-kroŋ   city
2. tŋay-nih kñom caŋ tɨw məəl   Today I'd like to go sightseeing
kənlaeŋ psein-psein knoŋ   (go see the various places) in
tii-kroŋ pnum-pɨñ.   Phnom Penh.

chaan

3. qou, kñom nɨŋ cuun look tɨw.   Oh, I'll take you around. (I'll accompany you [and] go.)

krasuəŋ (krəsuəŋ, kəsuəŋ)   department; function, duty
krasuəŋ-teehsəcaa   Department of Tourism
4. pruəh kñom tloŏp twəə-kaa nɨw   Because I used to work for (in) the
krəsuəŋ-teehsəcaa.   Department of Tourism.

George

5. tŋay-nih look qət rəwuəl tee rɨɨ?   You're not busy today?

chaan

6. baat, kñom tumnee pɨñ mə-tŋay.   No, I'm free all day.

baŋqah (bəŋqah, pəŋqah)   most, most of all
mun baŋqah   first of all
preəh- (prə-)   word prefixed to sacred objects
or to verbs performed by
sacred persons

preəh-wihiə   sacred temple
preəh-wihiə preəh-kaew   Wat Preah-Kaew (the Silver
Pagoda)
7. mun bəŋqah, kñom nɨŋ cuun look   First of all, I'll take you to see Wat
tɨw məəl preəh-wihiə preəh-kaew.   Preah-Kaew.

8. kɨɨ ciə preəh-wihiə muəy lqaa   [It's] the (one) most beautiful
ciəŋ-kee nɨw pnum-pɨñ.   temple in Phnom Penh.

[On the way]

George

9. sqəy nuh?   What's that?

chaan

sthaanii   station, place
qayeə̆qsmaayiən   train (elegant)
sthaanii-qayeə̆qsmaayiən   train station
10. nuh kɨɨ ciə sthaanii-qayeə̆qsmaayiən. That's the train station.

228

prum-daen   border, territorial limit
siəm   Thai; Thailand (Siam)
srok-siəm   Thailand

11. miən rəteh-pləəŋ tɨw dɑl   There are trains that go as far as
prum-daen srok-siəm.   the border of Thailand.

[At Wat Preah-Kaew]

George

12. qei, miən mənuh craən nah!   Hey, there are a lot of people [here]!
kee mɔɔk kənlaeŋ nih thəə qəy?   What have they come for (to do)?

chaɑn

twaay   to give, offer, present (elegant)
baŋkum (bəŋkum)   to greet with palms joined
twaay-baŋkum   to venerate, to greet respectfully
preəh   the Buddha

13. baat, kee mɔɔk twaay-baŋkum   Well, they've come to pay respects to
preəh.   the Buddha.

George

kuə   suitable, appropriate
kuə qaoy   worthy of, conducive to
kuə qaoy cɑŋ məəl   worth seeing, interesting

14. qou, preəh-wihiə nih lqɑɑ nah;   Oh, this temple is very beautiful;
kuə qaoy cɑŋ məəl.   [it's certainly] interesting (makes
         one want to see it).

tii-kɑnlaeŋ   place, establishment

15. tii-kɑnlaeŋ thom nuh kɨɨ qwəy?   What's that big place?

chaɑn

preəh-bɑromməriəccəweəŋ   the Royal Palace

16. nuh kɨɨ ciə preəh-   That's the Royal Palace.
bɑromməriəccəweəŋ.

George

17. yii, piəq nuh pibaaq thaa nah!   Gee, that word's hard to say!

chaɑn

weəŋ   palace

18. qəñcəŋ haw tae weəŋ tɨw   Then [you] can just call it <u>weəŋ</u>
kɑ-baan dae.   (palace).

George

19. teehsəcɑɑ coul məəl weəŋ baan   Can tourists go in and see the
tee?   palace?

chaɑn

ləək-lɛɛŋ-tae   except, except for

20. thəy mɨn baan; kee baək roəl   Of course; they're open every day
tŋay ləək-lɛɛŋ-tae tŋay-qatɨt.   except Sunday.

cbap   permission; single issue
qaqnuññaat   permission; to grant permission
cbap-qaqnuññaat   a permit

21. kñom nɨŋ tɨw som cbap-qaqnuññaat   I'll go ask for a permit to enter the
    coul weəŋ.   palace.

George

luəŋ   king
kuə̆ŋ   to sit, stay, reside (of royalty
                                              or clergy)

22. taə, luəŋ kuə̆ŋ nɨw kənlaeŋ nih rɨɨ?   Say, does the king reside here?

chɑɑn

dɑmnaq (dəmnaq, təmnaq)   royal residence
cɑmkaa-mɔɔn   Chamcar Mon (a district in
                                              Phnom Penh)

23. nɨŋ haəy, tae miən dəmnaq muəy   Right, but there's another royal
    tiət nɨw cəmkaa-mɔɔn.   residence at Chamcar Mon.

George

24. qəyləw tɨw kənlaeŋ naa tiət?   Now where else shall [we] go?

chɑɑn

woə̆t-qonaalaom (∼ woə̆t-   Wat Onalaom (seat of the
    prɑloom)   Patriarch of the Mahanikay
                                              Sect in Cambodia)

25. baat, tɨw məəl woə̆t-qonaalaom,   Well, [let's] go see Wat Onalaom,
    nɨw cɨt nih.   [which is] near here.

George

qaakiə (qakiə)   building, house
26. coh, qakiə teə̆ŋ-qɑh nih sqəy?   Tell me, what are all these buildings?

chɑɑn

kot   monastery, monk's quarters
look-sɑŋ   monk, priest

27. nuh kɨɨ ciə kot səmrap look-sɑŋ   Those are the quarters for the monks
    kuə̆ŋ nɨw.   to live in.

caetdəy (cədəy)   stupa, chedi, tapering monument
pacchaa (pəchaa)   crematorium

28. kraw-pii nuh, miən preə̆h-wihiə,   Besides that, there are the temple,
    caetdəy pseiŋ-pseiŋ, haəy-nɨŋ   various stupas, and a crematorium.
    pacchaa.

woə̆t-pnum   Wat Phnom (the foundation
                                             site of Phnom Penh)

29. qəyləw kñom cuun look tɨw məəl   Now I'll take you to see Wat Phnom.
    woə̆t-pnum.

kpuə̆h   to be high
bɑmphot (bəmphot)   most, most of all

30. woə̆t nuh kɨɨ ciə woə̆t kpuə̆h   That temple is the highest temple of
    ciəŋ-kee bəmphot nɨw pnum-pɨñ.   all in Phnom Penh.

[After visiting Wat Phnom]

raccənaa
salaa-raccənaa

fine arts, handicraft; to decorate
School of Fine Arts; also
commonly used to refer to
the National Museum

31. qəyləw look caŋ tɨw məəl
salaa-raccənaa tee?

Now would you like to go see the
National Museum?

George

32. baat, tɨw. nɨw kənlaeŋ nuh
miən qəy-klah?

Fine. What-all do they have there?

chaan

taŋ	to set up, display
woətthoq	articles, artifacts
bouraan (boraan)	ancient, former
woətthoq-bouraan	ancient artifacts
douc-ciə	such as
kbac	design
camlaq (cəmlaq)	carving, sculpture
kbac-camlaq	sculpture
miəh	gold
pɨc	diamond, precious stone
kriəŋ-miəh-pɨc	jewelry
kriəŋ preəh-riəccətroəp	royal treasures
ciə-daəm	as examples, and so forth, et cetera

33. nɨw tii-nuh, miən taŋ
woətthoq-bouraan, douc-ciə
kbac-cəmlaq, kriəŋ-miəh-pɨc,
haəy-nɨŋ kriəŋ preəh-riəccətroəp
ciə-daəm.

There they have displayed ancient
artifacts, such as sculpture, jewelry,
(and) royal treasures, and so forth.

bəntoəp pii nuh

after that

34. bəntoəp pii nuh, yəəŋ nɨŋ tɨw
psaa-kəndaal.

After that, we'll go to the Central
Market.

B. GRAMMAR AND DRILLS

1. baŋqah and bamphot

baŋqah and bamphot are both adverbs which add a superlative meaning, such
as 'most, last, most of all' to the words they modify, as in the following examples:

mun baŋqah, kñom nɨŋ cuun look
tɨw məəl preəh-wihiə preəh-kaew.

First of all, I'll take you to see
Wat Preah-Kaew.

kraoy baŋqah, yəəŋ nɨŋ tɨw
psaa-kandaal.

Last of all, we'll go to the
Central Market.

kraoy bamphot, yəəŋ nɨŋ tɨw məəl
woət-pnum.

Last of all, we'll go to see Wat
Phnom.

Notice that when <u>bamphot</u> modifies <u>ciəŋ-kee</u> 'most', it is redundant in the English translation:

wŏət nuh kɨɨ ciə wŏət kpuə̆h   That temple is <u>the highest temple of</u>
ciəŋ-kee bamphot nɨw pnum-pɨñ.   <u>all</u> in Phnom Penh.

1-A. Progressive Substitution Drill

Teacher	Student
mun baŋqah, kñom nɨŋ cuun look tɨw məəl <u>preə̆h-wihiə preə̆h-kaew.</u>	mun baŋqah, kñom nɨŋ cuun look tɨw məəl <u>preə̆h-wihiə preə̆h-kaew.</u>
<u>preə̆h-baromməriəccəweə̆ŋ.</u>	mun baŋqah, kñom nɨŋ cuun look tɨw məəl <u>preə̆h-baromməriəccəweə̆ŋ.</u>
<u>wŏət-qonaalaom.</u>	mun baŋqah, kñom nɨŋ cuun look tɨw məəl <u>wŏət-qonaalaom.</u>
<u>salaa-raccənaa.</u>	mun baŋqah, kñom nɨŋ cuun look tɨw məəl <u>salaa-raccənaa.</u>
<u>wŏət-pnum.</u>	mun baŋqah, kñom nɨŋ cuun look tɨw məəl <u>wŏət-pnum.</u>
<u>psaa-kandaal.</u>	mun baŋqah, kñom nɨŋ cuun look tɨw məəl <u>psaa-kandaal.</u>
<u>sthaanii-qayeə̆qsmaayiən.</u>	mun baŋqah, kñom nɨŋ cuun look tɨw məəl <u>sthaanii-qayeə̆qsmaayiən.</u>
<u>kraoy baŋqah,</u> kñom nɨŋ cuun look tɨw məəl sthaanii-qayeə̆qsmaayiən.	<u>kraoy baŋqah,</u> kñom nɨŋ cuun look tɨw məəl sthaanii-qayeə̆qsmaayiən.
<u>preə̆h-wihiə preə̆h-kaew.</u>	kraoy baŋqah, kñom nɨŋ cuun look tɨw məəl <u>preə̆h-wihiə preə̆h-kaew.</u>
<u>preə̆h-baromməriəccəweə̆ŋ.</u>	kraoy baŋqah, kñom nɨŋ cuun look tɨw məəl <u>preə̆h-baromməriəccəweə̆ŋ.</u>
<u>wŏət-qonaalaom.</u>	kraoy baŋqah, kñom nɨŋ cuun look tɨw məəl <u>wŏət-qonaalaom.</u>
<u>salaa-raccənaa.</u>	kraoy baŋqah, kñom nɨŋ cuun look tɨw məəl <u>salaa-raccənaa.</u>
<u>wŏət-pnum.</u>	kraoy baŋqah, kñom nɨŋ cuun look tɨw məəl <u>wŏət-pnum.</u>
<u>psaa-kandaal.</u>	kraoy baŋqah, kñom nɨŋ cuun look tɨw məəl <u>psaa-kandaal.</u>

1-B. Progressive Substitution Drill

Teacher	Student
wŏət nuh kɨɨ ciə wŏət kpuə̆h ciəŋ-kee bamphot nɨw pnum-pɨñ.	wŏət nuh kɨɨ ciə wŏət <u>kpuə̆h</u> ciəŋ-kee bamphot nɨw pnum-pɨñ.
<u>thom</u>	wŏət nuh kɨɨ ciə wŏət <u>thom</u> ciəŋ-kee bamphot nɨw pnum-pɨñ.

Teacher		Student
	cah	woət nuh kɨɨ ciə woət cah ciəŋ-kee bamphot nɨw pnum-pɨñ
	lqaa	woət nuh kɨɨ ciə woət lqaa ciəŋ-kee bamphot nɨw pnum-pɨñ.
psaa	psaa	psaa nuh kɨɨ ciə psaa lqaa ciəŋ-kee bamphot nɨw pnum-pɨñ.
	tlay	psaa nuh kɨɨ ciə psaa tlay ciəŋ-kee bamphot nɨw pnum-pɨñ.
	thom	psaa nuh kɨɨ ciə psaa thom ciəŋ-kee bamphot nɨw pnum-pɨñ.
	thaok	psaa nuh kɨɨ ciə psaa thaok ciəŋ-kee bamphot nɨw pnum-pɨñ.
	cah	psaa nuh kɨɨ ciə psaa cah ciəŋ-kee bamphot nɨw pnum-pɨñ.

1-C. Transformation Drill

Teacher	Student
woət nuh kɨɨ ciə woət kpuəh ciəŋ-kee bamphot nɨw pnum-pɨñ.	woət nuh kɨɨ ciə woət kpuəh ciəŋ-kee baŋqah nɨw pnum-pɨñ.
woət nuh kɨɨ ciə woət thom ciəŋ-kee bamphot nɨw pnum-pɨñ.	woət nuh kɨɨ ciə woət thom ciəŋ-kee baŋqah nɨw pnum-pɨñ.
woət nuh kɨɨ ciə woət cah ciəŋ-kee bamphot nɨw pnum-pɨñ.	woət nuh kɨɨ ciə woət cah ciəŋ-kee baŋqah nɨw pnum-pɨñ.
psaa nuh kɨɨ ciə psaa thom ciəŋ-kee bamphot nɨw pnum-pɨñ.	psaa nuh kɨɨ ciə psaa thom ciəŋ-kee baŋqah nɨw pnum-pɨñ.
qakiə nuh kɨɨ ciə qakiə kpuəh ciəŋ-kee bamphot nɨw pnum-pɨñ.	qakiə nuh kɨɨ ciə qakiə kpuəh ciəŋ-kee baŋqah nɨw pnum-pɨñ.
mun bamphot, kñom nɨŋ cuun look tɨw məəl salaa-raccənaa.	mun baŋqah, kñom nɨŋ cuun look tɨw məəl salaa-raccənaa.
kraoy bamphot, yəəŋ tɨw psaa-kandaal.	kraoy baŋqah, yəəŋ tɨw psaa-kandaal.
srəy nuh kɨɨ ciə srəy lqaa ciəŋ-kee bamphot.	srəy nuh kɨɨ ciə srəy lqaa ciəŋ-kee baŋqah.

2. kuə qaoy caŋ + Verb

The phrase kuə qaoy caŋ means 'is worth, is worthy of, inspires one to, makes one want to, is interesting to'. Its translation is determined by the nature of the subject and the stock of adjectives usually associated with it in English, as in the following sentences:

qou, preəh-wihie nih lqaa nah; kuə qaoy caŋ məəl.	Oh, this temple is very beautiful; [it's certainly] interesting (makes one want to see it).

mhoup nih cŋañ nah;	This food is very delicious;
kuə qaoy caŋ ñam.	[it's] tempting (to eat).
siəwphɨw nih lqaa nah;	This book is very good;
kuə qaoy caŋ məəl.	[it's] worth reading.
laan nih lqaa nah;	This car is very pretty;
kuə qaoy caŋ tɨñ.	[it] makes [one] want to buy [it].
phiəsaa nuh sruəl nah;	That language is very easy;
kuə qaoy caŋ niyiəy.	[it] makes [one] want to speak [it].

2-A. Multiple Substitution Drill

Teacher		Student
woət nuh kuə qaoy caŋ məəl.		woət nuh kuə qaoy caŋ məəl.
laan	baək.	laan nuh kuə qaoy caŋ baək.
phiəsaa	niyiəy.	phiəsaa nuh kuə qaoy caŋ niyiəy.
siəwphɨw	məəl.	siəwphɨw nuh kuə qaoy caŋ məəl.
mhoup	ñam.	mhoup nuh kuə qaoy caŋ ñam.
kaa	twəə.	kaa nuh kuə qaoy caŋ twəə.
tɨk	ɲuut.	tɨk nuh kuə qaoy caŋ ɲuut.
qaaw	tɨñ.	qaaw nuh kuə qaoy caŋ tɨñ.

2-B. Expansion Drill

Add the phrase kuə qaoy caŋ + an appropriate verb to the sentences provided by the teacher.

Teacher	Student
woət nuh lqaa nah.	woət nuh lqaa nah; kuə qaoy caŋ məəl.
laan nuh liən nah.	laan nuh liən nah; kuə qaoy caŋ baək.
siəwphɨw nuh lqaa nah.	siəwphɨw nuh lqaa nah; kuə qaoy caŋ məəl.
mhoup nuh cŋañ nah.	mhoup nuh cŋañ nah; kuə qaoy caŋ ñam.
qaaw nuh thaok nah.	qaaw nuh thaok nah; kuə qaoy caŋ tɨñ.
phiəsaa nuh sruəl nah.	phiəsaa nuh sruəl nah; kuə qaoy caŋ n yiəy.
tɨk nuh traceəq nah.	tɨk nuh traceəq nah; kuə qaoy caŋ ɲuut.
kaa nuh sruəl nah.	kaa nuh sruəl nah; kuə qaoy caŋ twəə.

3. Formal vs. Colloquial Vocabulary

In Cambodian, as in other languages, many formal, literary, or learned vocabulary items which occur in speeches, radio broadcasts, or in written Cambodian, are replaced in normal conversation by shorter terms having essentially the same meaning. Examples from English are such pairs as metropolis : city; convocation : meeting; conflagration : fire. A similar pair is illustrated in the following exchange:

preəh-baromməriəccəweəŋ pibaaq thaa nah.	preəh-baromməriəccəweəŋ (royal palace) is (very) hard to say.
qəñcəŋ haw tae weəŋ tɨw ka-baan dae.	Then [you] can just call [it] weəŋ (palace).

Other examples from Cambodian are the following:

Formal	Colloquial
sthaanii-qayeəqsmaayiən	gaa (Fr. gare) 'train station'
preəh-wihiə preəh-kaew	woət-prəkaew 'Wat Preah-Kaew'
woət-qonaalaom	woət-prəloom 'Wat Onalaom'
sɑnthaakiə, sɑnthəkiə	ptĕəh-sɑmnaq, hotael 'hotel'
phoocəniiyəthaan	haaŋ-baay 'restaurant'
cbap-qaqnuññaat	cbap 'permission'
sɑmliəq-bɑmpeə̆q	khao-qaaw 'clothing'
saareə̆qmuə̆ntii-ciət	salaa-raccənaa 'the National Museum'

3-A. Response Drill

Teacher	Student
preə̆h-bɑrommərɪəccəweə̆ŋ pibaaq thaa nah.	qəñcəŋ haw tae <u>weə̆ŋ</u> tɨw kɑ-baan dae.
<u>sthaanii-qayeə̆qsmaayiən</u> pibaaq thaa nah.	qəñcəŋ haw tae <u>gaa</u> tɨw kɑ-baan dae.
<u>cbap-qaqnuññaat</u> pibaaq thaa nah.	qəñcəŋ haw tae <u>cbap</u> tɨw kɑ-baan dae.
<u>phoocəniiyəthaan</u> pibaaq thaa nah.	qəñcəŋ haw tae <u>haaŋ-baay</u> tɨw kɑ-baan dae.
<u>sɑnthəkiə</u> pibaaq thaa nah.	qəñcəŋ haw tae <u>hotael</u> tɨw kɑ-baan dae.
<u>preə̆h-wihiə preə̆h-kaew</u> pibaaq thaa nah.	qəñcəŋ haw tae <u>woət-prəkaew</u> tɨw kɑ-baan dae.
<u>woət-qonaalaom</u> pibaaq thaa nah.	qəñcəŋ haw tae <u>woət-preloom</u> tɨw kɑ-baan dae.
<u>sɑmliəq-bɑmpeə̆q</u> pibaaq thaa nah.	qəñcəŋ haw tae <u>khao-qaaw</u> tɨw kɑ-baan dae.
<u>saareə̆qmuə̆ntii-ciət</u> pibaaq thaa nah.	qəñcəŋ haw tae <u>salaa-raccənaa</u> tɨw kɑ-baan dae.

4. ləək-lɛɛŋ-tae

ləək-lɛɛŋ-tae is a compound preposition with the meaning 'except for, with the exception of', as in

kee baək roə̆l tŋay ləək-lɛɛŋ-tae tŋay-qatɨt.	They open [it] every day <u>except</u> Sunday.

4-A. Substitution Drill

Teacher	Student
kee baək roə̆l tŋay ləək-lɛɛŋ-tae <u>tŋay-qatɨt</u>.	kee baək roə̆l tŋay ləək-lɛɛŋ-tae <u>tŋay-qatɨt</u>.
<u>tŋay-sok</u>.	kee baək roə̆l tŋay ləək-lɛɛŋ-tae <u>tŋay-sok</u>.
<u>tŋay-saw</u>.	kee baək roə̆l tŋay ləək-lɛɛŋ-tae <u>tŋay-saw</u>.
<u>tŋay-put</u>.	kee baək roə̆l tŋay ləək-lɛɛŋ-tae <u>tŋay-put</u>.
<u>tŋay-prɑhoə̆h</u>.	kee baək roə̆l tŋay ləək-lɛɛŋ-tae <u>tŋay-prɑhoə̆h</u>.

Teacher	Student
	kee baək roӗl tŋay ləək-lɛɛŋ-tae tŋay-can.
tŋay-can.	
	kee baək roӗl tŋay ləək-lɛɛŋ-tae tŋay-qɑŋkiə.
tŋay-qɑŋkiə.	

4-B. Substitution Drill

Teacher	Student
kee baək roӗl-tŋay ləək-lɛɛŋ-tae tŋay-qatɨt.	kee baək roӗl tŋay ləək-lɛɛŋ-tae tŋay-qatɨt.
twəə-kaa	kee twəə-kaa roӗl tŋay ləək-lɛɛŋ-tae tŋay-qatɨt.
ləəŋ kon	kee leeŋ kon roӗl tŋay ləək-lɛɛŋ-tae tŋay-qatɨt.
tɨw riən	kee tɨw riən roӗl tŋay ləək-lɛɛŋ-tae tŋay-qatɨt.
bət	kee bət roӗl tŋay ləək-lɛɛŋ-tae tŋay-qatɨt.
twəə mhoup	kee twəə mhoup roӗl tŋay ləək-lɛɛŋ-tae tŋay-qatɨt.
luӗq qəywan	kee luӗq qəywan roӗl tŋay ləək-lɛɛŋ-tae tŋay-qatɨt.
qaoy coul	kee qaoy coul roӗl tŋay ləək-lɛɛŋ-tae tŋay-qatɨt.
tɨw psaa	kee tɨw psaa roӗl tŋay ləək-lɛɛŋ-tae tŋay-qatɨt.

5. cbap-qaqnuññaat

qaqnuññaat occurs both as a noun meaning 'permission' and as a verb meaning 'to grant permission, to permit'. The compound cbap-qaqnuññaat means 'a sheet of paper granting permission, a permit'. When it precedes a verb or verb phrase, cbap-qaqnuññaat means 'a permit to ___', as in:

knom nɨŋ tɨw som cbap-qaqnunnaat coul weӗŋ.	I'll go ask for a permit to enter the palace.

5-A. Substitution Drill

Teacher	Student
kñom nɨŋ tɨw som cbap-qaqnuññaat coul weӗŋ.	kñom nɨŋ tɨw som sbap-qaqnuññaat coul weӗŋ.
baək laan.	kñom nɨŋ tɨw som cbap-qaqnuññaat baək laan.
luӗq mhoup.	kñom nɨŋ tɨw som cbap-qaqnuññaat luӗq mhoup.

Teacher	Student
luə̆q-dou.	kñom nɨŋ tɨw som cɓap-qaqnuññaat luə̆q-dou.
coul salaa.	kñom nɨŋ tɨw som cɓap-qaqnuññaat coul salaa.
baŋriən.	kñom nɨŋ tɨw som cɓap-qaqnuññaat baŋriən.
cən pii salaa.	kñom nɨŋ tɨw som sɓap-qaqnuññaat cəñ pii salaa.
twəə-kaa.	kñom nɨŋ tɨw som cɓap-qaqnuññaat twəə-kaa.

6. bantoə̆p pii nuh

bantoə̆p is a preposition which means 'next, after, following (in succession)'. In the prepositional phrase bantoə̆p pii nuh it means 'next, after that', as in

| bantoə̆p pii nuh, yəəŋ nɨŋ tɨw psaa-kandaal. | After that, we'll go to the Central Market. |

6-A. Substitution Drill

Teacher	Student
bantoə̆p pii nuh, yəəŋ nɨŋ tɨw psaa-kandaal.	bantoə̆p pii nuh, yəəŋ nɨŋ tɨw psaa-kandaal.
laəŋ pnum.	bantoə̆p pii nuh, yəəŋ nɨŋ tɨw laəŋ pnum.
twəə pɨcnɨc.	bantoə̆p pii nuh, yəəŋ nɨŋ tɨw twəə pɨcnɨc.
hael-tɨk.	bantoə̆p pii nuh, yəəŋ nɨŋ tɨw hael-tɨk.
məəl kon.	bantoə̆p pii nuh, yəəŋ nɨŋ tɨw məəl kon.
ñam baay.	bantoə̆p pii nuh, yəəŋ nɨŋ tɨw ñam baay.
cih kəpal.	bantoə̆p pii nuh, yəəŋ nɨŋ tɨw cih kəpal.
rɔɔk puə̆q-maaq.	bantoə̆p pii nuh, yəəŋ nɨŋ tɨw rɔɔk puə̆q-maaq.
məəl woə̆t-pnum.	bantoə̆p pii nuh, yəəŋ nɨŋ tɨw məəl woə̆t-pnum.
salaa-raccənaa.	bantoə̆p pii nuh, yəəŋ nɨŋ tɨw salaa-raccənaa.

7. <u>douc-ciə</u> . . . <u>ciə-daəm</u>

A list or sequence of items is frequently preceded by <u>douc-ciə</u> 'such as' (or by <u>kɨɨ</u> 'being'), and followed after the last item of the list by <u>ciə-daəm</u> 'as examples, and so forth, et cetera', as in

nɨw tii-nuh, miən taŋ   There they have ancient artifacts,
woʾɘtthoq-bouraan, douc-ciə   <u>such as</u> sculpture, jewelry, (and)
kbac-camlaq, krɨəŋ-miəh-pɨc,   royal treasures, <u>and so forth</u>.
haəy-nɨŋ krɨəŋ preʾəh-riəccətroʾəp
ciə-daəm.

Notice that <u>haəy-nɨŋ</u> 'and' before the last item of the list is redundant if one translates <u>ciə-daəm</u> as 'and so forth, et cetera', but is necessary if it is translated literally 'as examples'.

7-A. <u>Expansion Drill</u>

For each of the following sentences supplied by the teacher, provide a list of three likely items, preceded by <u>douc-ciə</u> and followed by <u>ciə-daəm</u>; the sentences on the right are merely models, and need not be followed by the student.

Teacher	Student
nɨw psaa nuh miən qəywan craən yaaŋ.	nɨw psaa nuh miən qəywan craən yaaŋ, douc-ciə mhoup, khao-qaaw, haəy-nɨŋ siəwphɨw ciə-daəm.
nɨw srok-kmae miən plae-chəə craən yaaŋ.	nɨw srok-kmae miən plae-chəə craən yaaŋ, douc-ciə krouc, ceik, haəy-nɨŋ mnoʾəh ciə-daəm.
miən mhoup craən muk.	miən mhoup craən muk, douc-ciə samlaɑ-mcuu, baay-chaa, haəy-nɨŋ noʾəm-moʾən ciə-daəm.
haaŋ nuh luʾəq khao-qaaw craən yaaŋ.	haaŋ nuh luʾəq khao-qaaw craən yaaŋ, douc-ciə qaaw, sampuʾət, haəy-nɨŋ sraom-cəəŋ ciə-daəm.
miən sac craən yaaŋ.	miən sac craən yaaŋ, douc-ciə sac-moʾən, sac-koo, haəy-nɨŋ sac-cruuk ciə-daəm.
kñom miən pradap cuəh-cul laan craən yaaŋ.	kñom miən pradap cuəh-cul laan craən yaaŋ, douc-ciə tuənəwih, daŋkap, haəy-nɨŋ ñɔñuə ciə-daəm.
koʾət niyiəy phiəsaa craən.	koʾət niyiəy phiəsaa craən, douc-ciə kmae, qaŋglee, haəy-nɨŋ cən ciə-daəm.
kee miən sampuʾət craən pɔə.	kee miən sampuʾət craən pɔə, douc-ciə pɔə-krahaam, pɔə-khiəw, haəy-nɨŋ pɔə-lɨəŋ ciə-daəm.
haaŋ nuh miən krɨəŋ-tok-tuu craən yaaŋ.	haaŋ nuh miən krɨəŋ-tok-tuu craən yaaŋ, douc-ciə tok, kawqəy, haəy-nɨŋ krɛɛ ciə-daəm.

1. <u>Sightseeing in Phnom Penh</u>

   mɨən: look nɨŋ nɨw pnum-pɨñ ponmaan tŋay?

   Robert: kñom nɨŋ nɨw tae bəy tŋay ponnoh.
            bəy tŋay məəl krup kənlaeŋ nɨw pnum-pɨñ baan tee?

   mɨən: baat, baan; tii-kroŋ pnum-pɨñ mɨn thom ponmaan tee.

   Robert: nɨw pnum-pɨñ mɨən kənlaeŋ naa-klah dael kuə tɨw məəl?

   mɨən: baat, kənlaeŋ dael teehsəcaa coul-cət tɨw məəl bəmphot kɨɨ
            preəh-bəromməriəccəweəŋ.
            tae kee coul-cət tɨw məəl woət-pnum dae.
            nɨw kənlaeŋ nuh mɨn-bac som cbap-qaqnuññaat tee.

   Robert: ruəc-pii nuh mɨən kənlaeŋ naa-klah tiət?

   mɨən: ruəc-pii nuh mɨən woət-qonaalaom, preəh-wihiə preəh-kaew,
            haəy-nɨŋ salaa-raccənaa.

   Robert: nɨw knoŋ salaa-raccənaa mɨən rəbah qwəy-klah?

   mɨən: mɨən krɨəŋ-miəh-pɨc, krɨəŋ-preəh-riəccətroəp, haəy-nɨŋ
            woətthoq-bouraan pseiŋ-pseiŋ.

   Robert: salaa-raccənaa kee baək qaoy coul məəl nɨw tŋay naa-klah?

   mɨən: kee baək qaoy coul məəl roəl tŋay ləək-lɛɛŋ-tae tŋay-qatɨt.
            bəntoəp pii pnum-pɨñ, look nɨŋ tɨw kənlaeŋ naa tiət?

   Robert: kñom caŋ tɨw məəl qəŋkɔɔ-woət.
            [piphup-look 'world']
            qəŋkɔɔ-woət kɨɨ ciə woət muəy thom ciəŋ-kee bəmphot knoŋ piphup-
            look.

2. <u>Working as a Tourist Guide</u>

   phɔɔn: qəyləw-nih phaen-qaeŋ twəə-kaa qəy?

   phaen: kñom cuun teehsəcaa tɨw məəl kənlaeŋ pseiŋ-pseiŋ.

   phɔɔn: qəñcəŋ thəə-kaa nɨw krəsuəŋ-teehsəcaa rɨɨ?

   phaen: nɨŋ haəy, nɨw krəsuəŋ-teehsəcaa.

   phɔɔn: noəm kee tɨw məəl qəy-klah?

   phaen: kñom noəm kee tɨw məəl kənlaeŋ pseiŋ-pseiŋ nɨw tii-kroŋ pnum-pɨñ.

   phɔɔn: taam-thoəmmədaa, teehsəcaa coul-cət tɨw məəl kənlaeŋ naa-klah?

   phaen: thoəmmədaa kee coul-cət tɨw məəl woət pseiŋ-pseiŋ.
            cuən-kaal kee coul-cət dəə tɨw tɨñ rəbah nɨw psaa.

   phɔɔn: thoəmmədaa teehsəcaa craən mɔɔk pii srok naa?

            [yipun (~ cipun) 'Japan; Japanese']
   phaen: kee craən mɔɔk pii srok-qaamerɨc, srok-baraŋ, haəy-nɨŋ srok-cipun.

phɔɔn: phaen-qaeŋ miən dael tɨw kənlaeŋ naa kraw-pii pnum-piñ tee?

[qotdoŋ ~ qutdoŋ 'Oudong (a historic site in Kampong Chhnang
  Province)']
[bokkoo 'Bokor (a mountain resort in Kampot Province)']
[kaep 'Kep (a seaside resort in Kampot Province)']

phaen: nɨŋ haǝy, kñom dael noǝm kee wɨt məǝl qəŋkɔɔ-woǝt, qotdoŋ, bokkoo,
        haǝy-nɨŋ kaep.

D. CONVERSATION

1. A Visit to the Royal Palace

a) A asks B if he has ever gone to see the Royal Palace.
b) B replies that he has been to see the Royal Palace many times.
c) A asks B if, in that case, he could take him to see the palace.
d) B replies that he can, because he's free all day today.
e) A asks B if the palace is open to tourists on Wednesdays.
f) B replies affirmatively, and adds that they open it every day except
Sunday.
g) A suggests that they go to see the palace right now.
h) B agrees, but adds that they'll have to ask for permission to enter the
palace.

2. Working for the Department of Tourism

a) A asks B what work he is doing now.
b) B replies that he works for the Department of Tourism.
c) A asks him what he does at the Department of Tourism.
d) B replies that he takes tourists to see various places in Phnom Penh.
e) A asks B what places tourists usually like to go to see.
f) B replies that they usually like to go to see the various temples, such as
the Silver Pagoda, Wat Phnom, and Wat Onalaom, as examples.
g) A asks B if he ever takes tourists anywhere outside of Phnom Penh.
h) B replies that of course he does, and adds that sometimes he takes them
to see Oudong, Bokor, Angkor Wat, and Kêp.

3. A Visit to the Silver Pagoda

a) A asks B if he's ever been to see the Silver Pagoda.
b) B replies that he's never been to see it.
c) A says that he's not busy today, and that he'll take B to see it.
d) B remarks that there are a lot of people there, and asks what they have
come for.
e) A replies that he doesn't know for sure, but he thinks that they have come
to pay respects to the Buddha.
f) B remarks that this temple is very beautiful, and that it's very worth seeing.
g) A agrees, and says that this temple is one of the most beautiful temples in
Phnom Penh.
h) B asks A what these yellow buildings are.
i) A replies that they are quarters for the monks to live in.
A then adds that, besides the temple, wats are likely to have monk's quarters,
various stupas, and a crematorium.

4. A Visit to the Museum

  a) A asks B where else they might go now.
  b) B replies that now he'll take B to see the National Museum.
  c) A asks what things they have there.
  d) B replies that they have many kinds of ancient artifacts, such as sculpture, jewelry, and royal treasures (and so forth).
  e) A says that last of all they'll go eat something at the Central Market.
  f) B asks A when he has to go to the train station.
  g) A replies that the train to Battambang leaves at 5:15.

LESSON 18. AT THE THEATER

[Tape 32]   A. DIALOGUE

chaem

lkhaon	drama, play
1. yup nih yəəŋ niŋ tɨw məəl lkhaon.	We're going to see a play this evening.
2. look caŋ tɨw tee?	Would you like to go?

Jack

3. baat, miən qəy.	Sure, why not?
rɨəŋ	story, subject, matter
4. yup nih lkhaon leeŋ rɨəŋ qəy?	What story is playing tonight?

phɨm

preəh-cɨnnəwuəŋ	a Cambodian drama
psaa-kap-koo	the ox-slaughter market; name of a market in Phnom Penh
rooŋ psaa-kap-koo	the psaa-kap-koo Theater
5. yup nih kee leeŋ rɨəŋ preəh-cɨnnəwuəŋ nɨw rooŋ psaa-kap-koo.	They're putting on the story of preəh-cɨnnəwuəŋ at the psaa-kap-koo Theater tonight.
lqɑɑ-məəl	to be interesting (to see or to watch)
snae-haa	love, romance
6. rɨəŋ nih lqɑɑ-məəl nah, piprŭəh ciə rɨəŋ snae-haa.	This story is very interesting, because it's a love story.
tuə-qaek	principal character
tuə-qaek-proh-srəy	the hero and heroine
srɑlañ (srəlañ, səlañ)	to love
srɑlañ kniə	to love each other
7. tuə-qaek-proh-srəy srəlañ kniə nah.	The hero and heroine love each other very much.

Jack

qae-tiət (qitiət)	other
8. coh, rooŋ qae-tiət kee leeŋ rɨəŋ qəy-klah?	What stories are they showing at the other theaters?

chaem

psaa-siləp	a market in Phnom Penh
srɑtɔɔp (srətɔɔp, sətɔɔp)	skin, bark
srɑtɔɔp-ceik	banana-tree bark; name of a Cambodian drama
9. nɨw rooŋ psaa-siləp kee leeŋ rɨəŋ srətɔɔp-ceik.	At the psaa-siləp theater they're putting on the story of srətɔɔp-ceik.

242

kɑmsɑt (kəmsɑt, kəsɑt)   sad, miserable, destitute; beggar, destitute person

qaanət (qanət)   to pity, take pity on

kuə qaoy qaanət   pitiable, deserving of sympathy

10. knoŋ rɨəŋ nuh miən tuə-qaek kəmsɑt nah; kuə qaoy qaanət.   In that story the main character is very sad; [he's] deserving of sympathy.

Jack

rɔbam (rəbam)   dance; dancing

roə̆m   to dance

roə̆m-kbac   stylized dancing

rɔbam-roə̆m-kbac   ballet

11. kñom baan lɨɨ thaa nɨw srok-kmae miən rəbam-roə̆m-kbac lqɑɑ nah.   I've heard that Cambodia has very beautiful ballet.

phɨm

riəm-kei   the Ream-Kerti (Cambodian version of the Ramayana)

craən(-tae)   usually, mostly

12. nɨŋ haəy; rəbam-roə̆m-kbac nuh kee craən roə̆m rɨəŋ riəm-kei.   That's right; the ballet usually performs stories from the Ream-Kerti.

13. tae yup nih kee kmiən roə̆m-kbac tee.   But there's no ballet tonight.

chaem

14. qəñcəŋ mɔɔk, yəəŋ noə̆m look Jack tɨw məəl rɨəŋ srətɔɔp-ceik.   Then let's take Jack to see srətɔɔp-ceik.

[At the Theater]

samleiŋ (səmleiŋ)   voice, sound

15. mɔɔk tɨw qəŋkuy khaŋ-muk, pruə̆h sruəl məəl haəy lɨɨ səmleiŋ cbah phɑɑŋ.   Let's go sit in front, because it's easy to see and [one can] hear (the voices) clearly too.

phɨm

16. nuh, miən kənlaeŋ tumnee bəy.   There are three vacant seats.

Jack

ñɨk-ñoə̆p   often, frequently

17. chaem tɨw məəl lkhaon ñɨk-ñoə̆p tee?   Do you go to the theater often, Chhem?

chaem

18. mɨn ñɨk-ñoə̆p ponmaan tee; kñom coul-cət məəl kon ciəŋ.   Not so often; I prefer movies.

Jack

19. look coul-cət məəl kon rɨəŋ qəy ciəŋ-kee?   What kind of film do you most like to see?

chaem

qaa-	diminutive or derogatory prefix
kɨñ	police
cao	thief
qaakɨñ-qaacao	cops and robbers
rɨəŋ qaakɨñ-qaacao	police story, crime story
cambaŋ (cəmbaŋ, cəbaŋ)	battle, war
rɨəŋ cambaŋ	war story

20. kñom coul-cət rɨəŋ qaakɨñ-qaacao   I like police stories and war stories
    haəy-nɨŋ rɨəŋ cəmbaŋ craən   best of all.
    ciəŋ-kee.

21. coh, look?   What about you?

Jack

kamplaeŋ (kəmplaeŋ, kəplaeŋ)	funny, humorous
rɨəŋ kamplaeŋ	comedy

22. kñom craən-tae tɨw məəl rɨəŋ   I usually go to see comedies.
    kəmplaeŋ.

roöŋ-kon   cinema, movie-theater
23. nɨw rooŋ-kon kmae kee miən leeŋ   Do they show only Cambodian films
    tae rɨəŋ kmae tee rɨɨ?   in Cambodian movie theaters?

chaem

bɑɑrəteeh	abroad, foreign countries
kləŋ	Indian
ruhsii	Russian; Russia

24. tee, miən rɨəŋ mɔɔk pii bɑɑrəteeh   No, [we] have films (stories) from
    dae, kɨɨ baraŋ, qaamerikaŋ, kləŋ,   abroad too, such as French, American,
    ruhsii, haəy-nɨŋ cən ciə-daəm.   Indian, Russian, and Chinese (and so
                                                   forth).

pdaəm   to begin (to)
25. qou, lkhaon cɨt pdaəm leeŋ haəy.   Oh, the play is about to start (playing).

Jack

26. kee kraok chɔɔ thəə qəy nɨŋ?   What are they standing up for?

chaem

daəmbəy(-nɨŋ)	in order to
koorup	to honor, pay respect to
bat	set, composition, verse, song
qaŋkɔɔ-riəc (qəŋkɔɔ-, ŋkɔɔ-)	kingdom, nation
bat qaŋkɔɔ-riəc	royal anthem

27. kee kraok chɔɔ daəmbəy koorup   They're standing up in order to pay
    bat qəŋkɔɔ-riəc.   respect to the royal anthem.

phɨm

chaaq	scene, set
pleeŋ	song, music (instrumental)

28. kee laeŋ pleeŋ baək chaaq haəy.   They're playing the overture now
                                                   (the curtain-opening song).

Jack

piruəh   to be pretty, sweet (to hear)
29. yii, pleeŋ nuh piruəh nah!   Hey, that music is very pretty.

samliəq (səmliəq)   clothing worn around the waist
bampeə̆q (bəmpeə̆q)   clothing other than samliəq
samliəq-bampeə̆q   clothing (elegant)
neə̆q-leeŋ-lkhaon   actor(s), player(s)
30. haəy-nɨŋ səmliəq-bəmpeə̆q   And the costumes of the players are
    neə̆q-leeŋ-lkhaon lqɑɑ nah.   very attractive.

[Later]

chaem

cɑp   to finish, come to a close
31. lkhaon cɑp haəy.   The play is over.

Jack

teə̆h   to slap, smack
teə̆h-day   to clap the hands
32. qei, kee teə̆h-day klaŋ nah!   Hey, they're really clapping loudly!

B. GRAMMAR AND DRILLS

1. The Adjectival Verb lqɑɑ-məəl

There is no single word in Cambodian which is semantically equivalent to the English word 'interesting'. We learned in Lesson 17 that kuə qaoy cɑŋ (+ verb) can in some instances be translated 'interesting to (+ verb)'. The compound lqɑɑ-məəl comes as close as any word to the meaning 'interesting', but its application is limited to such things as books, stories, films, pictures, etc. which may be mentally as well as visually interesting, as in

rɨəŋ nih lqɑɑ-məəl nah, pipruəh   This story is very interesting,
ciə rɨəŋ snae-haa.   because it's a love story.

1-A. Substitution Drill

Teacher	Student
rɨəŋ nih lqɑɑ-məəl nah.	rɨəŋ nih lqɑɑ-məəl nah.
siəwphɨw nuh	siəwphɨw nuh lqɑɑ-məəl nah.
lkhaon nih	lkhaon nih lqɑɑ-məəl nah.
kon nuh	kon nuh lqɑɑ-məəl nah.
rəbam-roə̆m-kbac	rəbam-roə̆m-kbac lqɑɑ-məəl nah.
rɨəŋ kamplaeŋ	rɨəŋ kamplaeŋ lqɑɑ-məəl nah.
kbac nih	kbac nih lqɑɑ-məəl nah.
lbaeŋ nuh	lbaeŋ nuh lqɑɑ-məəl nah.

2. qae-tiət

qae-tiət 'other' is one of the few words in Cambodian which occur only as modifiers, and can thus truly be called an adjective, as in the following sentences:

rooŋ qae-tiət kee ləeŋ rɨəŋ qəy-klah?	What stories are they showing at the <u>other</u> theaters?
kñom caŋ tɨw məəl kon <u>qae-tiət.</u>	I want to go see <u>another</u> (different) film.

Notice that kon qae-tiət in the second example above means 'another film' in the sense of 'a different film', and not 'an additional film', which would be <u>kon muəy tiət</u>, as in

kñom caŋ tɨw məəl <u>kon muəy tiət.</u>	I want to go see <u>another (additional) film.</u>

2-A. Substitution Drill

Teacher	Student
kñom caŋ tɨw <u>məəl kon</u> qae-tiət.	kñom caŋ tɨw <u>məəl kon</u> qae-tiət.
<u>rooŋ-kon</u>	kñom caŋ tɨw <u>rooŋ-kon</u> qae-tiət.
<u>rooŋ-lkhaon</u>	kñom caŋ tɨw <u>rooŋ-lkhaon</u> qae-tiət.
<u>kanlaeŋ</u>	kñom caŋ tɨw <u>kanlaeŋ</u> qae-tiət.
<u>phoocəniiyəthaan</u>	kñom caŋ tɨw <u>phoocəniiyəthaan</u> qae-tiət.
<u>pteə̆h-samnaq</u>	kñom caŋ tɨw <u>pteə̆h-samnaq</u> qae-tiət.
<u>woə̆t</u>	kñom caŋ tɨw <u>woə̆t</u> qae-tiət.
<u>salaa</u>	kñom caŋ tɨw <u>salaa</u> qae-tiət.
<u>srok</u>	kñom caŋ tɨw <u>srok</u> qae-tiət.

3. <u>kuə qaoy</u>

In Lesson 17 it was pointed out that kuə qaoy caŋ (+ verb) means 'worthy of, makes one want to', as in

preə̆h-wihiə nih lqaa nah; kuə qaoy caŋ məəl.	This temple is very beautiful; [it's] worth seeing (makes one want to see it).

<u>kuə qaoy</u> can frequently be translated by the English suffix '-able', as in

knoŋ rɨəŋ nuh miən tuə-qaek kamsat nah; <u>kuə qaoy qaanət.</u>	In that story the hero is very sad; [he's] <u>pitiable</u> (deserving of sympathy).

Other examples are the following; new vocabulary is starred:

kuə qaoy coul-cət	'likable'	kuə qaoy koorup	'honorable'
kuə qaoy sralañ	'lovable'	kuə qaoy tuk cət	'dependable'
kuə qaoy caŋ baan	'desirable'	kuə qaoy *sqap	'detestable'
kuə qaoy caŋ ñam	'delectable'	kuə qaoy *nɨk-rolɨk	'memorable'

3-A. <u>Expansion Drill</u>

Teacher	Student
tuə-qaek nuh kamsat nah. (qaanət)	tuə-qaek nuh kamsat nah; <u>kuə qaoy qaanət.</u>
tuə-qaek-srəy lqaa nah. (sralañ)	tuə-qaek-srəy lqaa nah; <u>kuə qaoy sralañ.</u>

Teacher	Student
mənuh nuh pukae nah. (tuk cət)	mənuh nuh pukae nah; kuə qaoy tuk cət.
rɨəŋ nuh kamplaeŋ nah. (coul-cət)	rɨəŋ nuh kamplaeŋ nah; kuə qaoy coul-cət.
pkaa nuh lqaa nah. (caŋ baan)	pkaa nuh lqaa nah; kuə qaoy caŋ baan.
taa nuh cah nah. (koorup)	taa nuh cah nah; kuə qaoy koorup.
pleeŋ nuh pirŭəh nah. (caŋ sdap)	pleeŋ nuh pirŭəh nah; kuə qaoy caŋ sdap.
mhoup nuh cŋañ nah. (caŋ ñam)	mhoup nuh cŋañ nah; kuə qaoy caŋ ñam.

4. <u>thaa</u> as a Quotative Conjunction

It was pointed out in Lesson 3 that <u>thaa</u> functions both as a <u>transitive verb</u>, as in

look <u>thaa</u> məc?	What did you <u>say</u>?

and as a <u>quotative conjunction</u> after certain verbs, with the meaning 'that, saying, as follows', as in

rəbah nih kee haw <u>thaa</u> qwəy?	What is this thing called? (This thing they call <u>saying</u> what?)

In addition to <u>haw</u> 'to call', six more verbs have been encountered which occur before <u>thaa</u>:

<u>niyiəy</u>:	kñom <u>niyiəy thaa</u> mɨn tɨw tee.	I <u>said</u> (<u>that</u>) I'm not going.
<u>məəl</u>:	piəq nih <u>məəl thaa</u> məc?	How is this word pronounced? (This word <u>reads saying</u> how?)
<u>prae</u>:	kliə nih <u>prae thaa</u> məc?	How is this sentence translated? (This sentence <u>translates as</u> how?)
<u>kɨt</u>:	kñom <u>kɨt thaa</u> look qayuq prəhael məphɨy-pram.	I <u>think that</u> you're about twenty-five.
<u>prap</u>:	kñom <u>prap thaa</u> tɨw mɨn baan tee.	I <u>told</u> [them] <u>that</u> I couldn't go.
<u>lɨɨ</u>:	kñom baan <u>lɨɨ thaa</u> nɨw srok-kmae miən rɔbam- roə̆m-kbac lqaa nah.	I've <u>heard that</u> Cambodia has beautiful ballet.

Thus it can be seen that <u>thaa</u> tends to occur after verbs which express the action of speaking or of mental processes and relates these verbs to their direct objects or complements.

4-A. Progressive Substitution Drill

Teacher	Student
mənuh nuh <u>niyiəy</u> thaa məc?	mənuh nuh <u>niyiəy</u> thaa məc?
<u>prap</u>	mənuh nuh <u>prap</u> thaa məc?
<u>kɨt</u>	mənuh nuh <u>kɨt</u> thaa məc?
<u>haw</u>	mənuh nuh <u>haw</u> thaa məc?
<u>piəq nuh</u>	<u>piəq nuh</u> haw thaa məc?
<u>məəl</u>	piəq nuh <u>məəl</u> thaa məc?
<u>prae</u>	piəq nuh <u>prae</u> thaa məc?

4-B. Progressive Substitution Drill

Teacher	Student
kñom <u>kɨt</u> thaa look qayuq məphɨy-pram.	kñom <u>kɨt</u> thaa look qayuq məphɨy-pram.
<u>lɨɨ</u>	kñom <u>lɨɨ</u> thaa look qayuq məphɨy-pram.
<u>niyiəy</u>	kñom <u>niyiəy</u> thaa look qayuq məphɨy-pram.
<u>koət mɔɔk pii-msəl-məñ.</u>	kñom niyiəy thaa <u>koət mɔɔk pii-msəl-məñ.</u>
<u>prap</u>	kñom <u>prap</u> thaa koət mɔɔk pii-msəl-məñ.
<u>kɨt</u>	kñom <u>kɨt</u> thaa koət mɔɔk pii-msəl-məñ.
<u>koət nɨŋ mɔɔk sqaek.</u>	kñom kɨt thaa <u>koət nɨŋ mɔɔk sqaek.</u>
<u>lɨɨ</u>	kñom <u>lɨɨ</u> thaa koət nɨŋ mɔɔk sqaek.
<u>prap</u>	kñom <u>prap</u> thaa koət nɨŋ mɔɔk sqaek.

5. The Adverb ñɨk-ñoəp

ñɨk-ñoəp is an adverb meaning 'often, frequently', as in

chaem tɨw məəl lkhaon ñɨk-ñoəp tee?	Do you (Chhem) go to the theater often?
mɨn ñɨk-ñoəp ponmaan tee.	Not so often.

5-A. Substitution Drill

Teacher	Student
look tɨw məəl lkhaon ñɨk-ñoəp tee?	look tɨw məəl lkhaon ñɨk-ñoəp tee?
<u>tɨw məəl kon</u>	look <u>tɨw məəl kon</u> ñɨk-ñoəp tee?
<u>tɨw hael-tɨk</u>	look <u>tɨw hael-tɨk</u> ñɨk-ñoəp tee?
<u>tɨw məəl rəbam-roəm-kbac</u>	look <u>tɨw məəl rəbam-roəm-kbac</u> ñɨk-ñoəp tee?
<u>mɔɔk kanlaeŋ nih</u>	look <u>mɔɔk kanlaeŋ nih</u> ñɨk-ñoəp tee?
<u>cih kəpal</u>	look <u>cih kəpal</u> ñɨk-ñoəp tee?
<u>tɨw pnum-pɨñ</u>	look <u>tɨw pnum-pɨñ</u> ñɨk-ñoəp tee?
<u>tɨw twəə picnɨc</u>	look <u>tɨw twəə picnɨc</u> ñɨk-ñoəp tee?
<u>tɨw qaŋkɔɔ-woət</u>	look <u>tɨw qaŋkɔɔ-woət</u> ñɨk-ñoəp tee?

5-B. Response Drill

Teacher	Student
look tɨw məəl lkhaon ñɨk-ñoəp tee?	mɨn ñɨk-ñoəp ponmaan tee.
look tɨw məəl kon ñɨk-ñoəp tee?	mɨn ñɨk-ñoəp ponmaan tee.
look tɨw hael-tɨk ñɨk-ñoəp tee?	mɨn ñɨk-ñoəp ponmaan tee.

Teacher	Student
look tɨw məəl rəbam-roə̆m-kbac ñɨk-ñoə̆p tee?	mɨn ñɨk-ñoə̆p ponmaan tee.
look mɔɔk kɑnlaeŋ nih ñɨk-ñoə̆p tee?	mɨn ñɨk-ñoə̆p ponmaan tee.
look cih kəpal ñɨk-ñoə̆p tee?	mɨn ñɨk-ñoə̆p ponmaan tee.
look tɨw pnum-pɨñ ñɨk-ñoə̆p tee?	mɨn ñɨk-ñoə̆p ponmaan tee.
look tɨw twəə pɨcnɨc ñɨk-ñoə̆p tee?	mɨn ñɨk-ñoə̆p ponmaan tee.
look tɨw qɑŋkɔɔ-woə̆t ñɨk-ñoə̆p tee?	mɨn ñɨk-ñoə̆p ponmaan tee.

6. The Preverbal Auxiliary craən(-tae)

When craən-tae (in rapid speech shortened to craən) precedes a primary or modal verb, it functions as a preverbal auxiliary with the meaning 'usually, mostly', as in

| rəbam-roə̆m-kbac nuh kee craən roə̆m rɨəŋ rɨəm-kei. | The ballet usually performs stories from the Ream-Kerti. |
| kñom craən-tae tɨw məəl rɨəŋ kɑmplaeŋ. | I mostly go to see comedies. |

6-A. Substitution Drill

Teacher	Student
kee craən-tae roə̆m rɨəŋ rɨəm-kei.	kee craən-tae roə̆m rɨəŋ rɨəm-kei.
məəl rɨəŋ kɑmplaeŋ.	kee craən-tae məəl rɨəŋ kɑmplaeŋ.
tɨw məəl woə̆t-pnum.	kee craən-tae tɨw məəl woə̆t-pnum.
mɔɔk twaay-bɑŋkum preə̆h.	kee craən-tae mɔɔk twaay-bɑŋkum preə̆h.
tɨw rɨən peel prɨk.	kee craən-tae tɨw rɨən peel prɨk.
qɑŋkuy khɑŋ-muk.	kee craən-tae qɑŋkuy khɑŋ-muk.
teə̆h-day klɑŋ nah.	kee craən-tae teə̆h-day klɑŋ nah.
leeŋ tae rɨəŋ kmae.	kee craən-tae leeŋ tae rɨəŋ kmae.
mɔɔk taam pləw nih.	kee craən-tae mɔɔk taam pləw nih.
tɨw taam rəteh-pləəŋ.	kee craən-tae tɨw taam rəteh-pləəŋ.

7. Review of Preverbal Auxiliaries

Preverbal auxiliaries are words which qualify a following modal verb or primary verb, but which never themselves occur as verbs, or whose meanings as auxiliaries differ from their meanings as verbs. Auxiliaries are defined by the following criteria:

1) In sentences involving both auxiliaries and modal verbs, auxiliaries precede modal verbs.

2) They never occur as verbs.

3) They are never negated (although some are inherently negative).

Many compound auxiliaries include the preposition tae 'but, only, just' or the future auxiliary nɨŋ, or both; e.g.:

koə̆t təəp-nɨŋ cəñ pii salaa.	He's just now gotten out of school.
koə̆t təəp-tae cəñ pii salaa.	(Same)
koə̆t təəp-tae-nɨŋ cəñ pii salaa.	(Same)

In other auxiliaries, <u>tae</u> is a derivational element which derives auxiliaries from verbs. In the following example, <u>ceh</u> is a modal verb which means 'to know how to':

> kee <u>ceh</u> niyiəy phiəsaa-kmae.   He <u>knows how to</u> speak Cambodian.

<u>ceh-tae</u>, however, is a compound auxiliary which means 'always', as in

> kee <u>ceh-tae</u> niyiəy phiəsaa-kmae.   He <u>always</u> speaks Cambodian.

The future auxiliary <u>niŋ</u> 'will, about to' precedes negative auxiliaries but follows all other auxiliaries, as in

> khom <u>cɨt niŋ mɨn</u> tɨw tee.   I almost didn't go.
>   or: I'm on the point of not going.

Following is a list of the commonest preverbal auxiliaries. Those which have not yet been introduced in the lessons are preceded by an asterisk.

mɨn	'not'	kampuŋ(-tae)(-nɨŋ)	'in the process of'
qat (qət)	'not (colloq.)'	təəp(-tae)(-nɨŋ)	'just now'
*pum	'not (literary)'	kroǒn-tae	'just, only'
kom	'don't'	muk-tae	'probably, likely to'
mɨn-səw	'hardly, not very'	*ceh-tae	'always'
mɨn-toǒn	'not yet'	*kuə-tae	'should'
nɨŋ	'will, about to'	*srap-tae	'suddenly'
cɨt	'nearly, almost'	*taeŋ-tae	'usually'
kaɑ	'so, then, accordingly'	*rɨt-tae	'increasingly'
craən(-tae)	'usually, mostly'	*kan-tae	'increasingly'
sot(-tae)	'all without exception'	*trəw-tae	'absolutely must'

7-A. Progressive Substitution Drill

Teacher	Student
khom <u>mɨn</u> coul-cət tɨw psaa tee.	khom <u>mɨn</u> coul-cət tɨw psaa tee.
qət	khom <u>qət</u> coul-cət tɨw psaa tee.
baan tɨw psaa tee.	khom qət <u>baan tɨw psaa tee.</u>
mɨn-toǒn	khom <u>mɨn-toǒn</u> baan tɨw psaa tee.
mɨn	khom <u>mɨn</u> baan tɨw psaa tee.

7-B. Progressive Substitution Drill

Teacher	Student
kee <u>nɨŋ</u> tɨw məəl lkhaon.	kee <u>nɨŋ</u> tɨw məəl lkhaon.
craən-tae	kee <u>craən-tae</u> tɨw məəl lkhaon.
təəp-nɨŋ	kee <u>təəp-nɨŋ</u> tɨw məəl lkhaon.
muk-tae	kee <u>muk-tae</u> tɨw məəl lkhaon.
sot-tae	kee <u>sot-tae</u> tɨw məəl lkhaon.
kroǒn-tae	kee <u>kroǒn-tae</u> tɨw məəl lkhaon.
kampuŋ-tae	kee <u>kampuŋ-tae</u> tɨw məəl lkhaon.
chup twəə-kaa.	kee kampuŋ-tae <u>chup twəə-kaa.</u>
nɨŋ	kee <u>nɨŋ</u> chup twəə-kaa.
craən-tae	kee <u>craən-tae</u> chup twəə-kaa.
təəp-nɨŋ	kee <u>təəp-nɨŋ</u> chup twəə-kaa.
muk-tae	kee <u>muk-tae</u> chup twəə-kaa.
sot-tae	kee <u>sot-tae</u> chup twəə-kaa.

7-C. Translation Drill

Teacher	Student
I haven't yet gone to the market.	kñom mɨn-toən tɨw psaa tee.
I usually go to the market on Saturday.	kñom craən-tae tɨw psaa tŋay-saw.
She's not very good at driving a car.	koət mɨn-səw pukae baək laan tee.
Don't forget to take an umbrella.	kom plɨc yɔɔk chat tɨw.
I will go to Battambang tomorrow.	kñom nɨŋ tɨw batdəmbaaŋ sqaek.
This toothpaste is almost all gone.	tnam-doh-tmiñ nih cɨt qah haəy.
We just now saw a funny movie.	yəəŋ təəp-nɨŋ məəl kon kamplaeŋ.
I just came to look, that's all.	kñom krɔən-tae mɔɔk məəl ponnoh.
I'm (in the process of) reading a book.	kñom kampuŋ-tae məəl siəwphɨw.
He's just left the house.	koət təəp-tae cəñ pii pteəh.
I don't like the rainy season either.	kñom kaa mɨn coul-cət rədəw-pliəŋ dae.
They'll probably go along this road.	kee muk-tae tɨw taam pləw nih.
Don't make it too spicy.	kom qaoy həl peek.
The students all went into the school.	koun-səh sot-tae coul salaa teəŋ-qah.
They usually come on Sunday.	kee craən-tae mɔɔk tŋay-qatɨt.
The play is about to begin (to play).	lkhaon cɨt pdaəm leeŋ haəy.

8. The Subordinating Conjunction daəmbəy(-nɨŋ)

The function of a subordinating conjunction is to introduce a subordinate clause in a complex sentence. The subordinating conjunction daəmbəy (sometimes followed by nɨŋ) means 'in order to, with the intention of', as in

kee kraok chɔɔ daəmbəy koorup   They're standing up in order to
bat qaŋkɔɔ-riəc.   pay respect to the national anthem.

8-A. Substitution Drill

Teacher	Student
kee kraok chɔɔ daəmbəy koorup bat qaŋkɔɔ-riəc.	kee kraok chɔɔ daəmbəy koorup bat qaŋkɔɔ-riəc.
məəl qaoy khəəñ.	kee kraok chɔɔ daəmbəy məəl qaoy khəəñ.
teəh-day.	kee kraok chɔɔ daəmbəy teəh-day.
plah kanlaeŋ qaŋkuy.	kee kraok chɔɔ daəmbəy plah kanlaeŋ qaŋkuy.
peəq qaaw.	kee kraok chɔɔ daəmbəy peəq qaaw.
cəñ pii rooŋ-lkhaon.	kee kraok chɔɔ daəmbəy cəñ pii rooŋ-lkhaon.
məəl neəq-leeŋ-lkhaon.	kee kraok chɔɔ daəmbəy məəl neəq-leeŋ-lkhaon.
rɔɔk puəq-maaq.	kee kraok chɔɔ daəmbəy rɔɔk puəq-maaq.
tɨw tɨñ mhoup.	kee kraok chɔɔ daəmbəy tɨw tɨñ mhoup.

8-B. Translation Drill

Teacher	Student
They're standing up in order to leave the theater.	kee kraok chɔɔ daəmbəy cəñ pii rooŋ lkhaon.
I'm going home in order to change clothes.	kñom tɨw pteəh daəmbəy plah khao-qaaw.

Teacher	Student

He came to Phnom Penh in order to buy things.

kŏət mɔɔk pnum-piñ daəmbəy tiñ qəywan.

They went to Siem Reap in order to see Angkor Wat.

kee tɨw siəm-riəp daəmbəy məəl qaŋkɔɔ-wŏət.

I'll ask for a permit in order to enter the palace.

kñom nɨŋ som cbap-qaqnuññaat daəmbəy coul wĕəŋ.

They went to that restaurant in order to have some Chinese food.

kee tɨw haaŋ-baay nuh daəmbəy ñam mhoup cən.

He rented a car in order to learn to drive.

kŏət cuəl laan daəmbəy riən baek.

Students go to school in order to learn.

koun-səh tɨw salaa daəmbəy riən.

We work in order to get a salary.

yəəŋ twəə-kaa daəmbəy baan praq-khae.

[Tape 33]   C. COMPREHENSION

1. Going to a Film

sɑmbat: yup nih yəəŋ tɨw daə-leeŋ kənlaeŋ naa?

phan: tɨw naa kɑ-baan, tae sɑmbat cɑŋ tɨw kənlaeŋ naa?

sɑmbat: cam tɨw tiñ kasaet mɔɔk məəl sən.

phan: qəñcəŋ tɨw; kñom kɑɑ mɨn baan məəl kasaet dae, tŋay-nih.

[pləw-baek 'intersection']
sɑmbat: kee miən luĕq kasaet nɨw pləw-baek.
[To neĕq-luĕq-kasaet]
         qaoy kasaet muəy mɔɔk.

phan: baək məəl tumpɔə khaŋ-kraoy məə.
         kee miən daq riəŋ kon knoŋ tumpɔə nuh.

[rooŋ-kaasinou 'the Casino Theater']
sɑmbat: qei, miən riəŋ qaakiñ-qaacao leeŋ nɨw rooŋ-kaasinou.
[rooŋ-qeidaen 'the Eden Theater']
         haəy-nɨŋ nɨw rooŋ-qeidaen miən leeŋ riəŋ cəmbaŋ.

phan: kñom mɨn-səw coul-cət riəŋ cəmbaŋ rɨɨ riəŋ qaakiñ-qaacao tee.
         coh, sɑmbat qaeŋ?

sɑmbat: kñom coul-cət məəl riəŋ kəmplaeŋ craən ciəŋ-kee.
         tae riəŋ qəy kɑɑ kñom məəl baan dae.

phan: coh, lkhaon kee leeŋ riəŋ qəy-klah?

sɑmbat: nɨw rooŋ psaa-kap-koo kee leeŋ riəŋ srətɔɔp-ceik.
         cɑŋ tɨw məəl riəŋ nuh tee?

phan: miən qəy.
         tae rooŋ psaa-kap-koo nɨw cŋaay nah; kñom klaac yəəŋ daə tɨw mɨn tŏən.

[rooŋ-siineluc 'the Cinelux Theater']

sambat: baə qəñcəŋ, yəəŋ tɨw məəl rɨəŋ kləŋ nɨw rooŋ-siineluc nəh!
[criəŋ 'to sing']
rɨəŋ nuh miən tuə-qaek-proh kee coul-cət məəl nah, haəy-nɨŋ
tuə-qaek-srəy criəŋ piruəh phaaŋ.

phan: qəñcəŋ tɨw!

2. An Evening Out

tun: cumriəp-suə suəŋ.

suəŋ: cumriəp-suə tun.
kñom cam yuu nah haəy; kɨt thaa tun-qaeŋ qat məək tee.

tun: qat-tooh, kñom yɨɨt bəntəc.
suəŋ cam kñom yuu rɨɨ?

suəŋ: qaə, kñom cam prəhael pram-dəndap niətii haəy.
mɨn-qəy tee; kñom nɨŋ qat-tooh qaoy mədaaŋ, pontae tŋay kraoy
kom yɨɨt tiət nəh!

tun: tŋay kraoy kñom nɨŋ məək qaoy toən maoŋ.

suəŋ: qəyləw tun-qaeŋ kɨt tɨw daə-leeŋ kənlaeŋ naa?

tun: srac-tae ləə suəŋ-qaeŋ coh.
[baa 'bar']
yəəŋ tɨw məəl kon ka-baan, lkhaon ka-baan, rɨɨ tɨw roəm nɨw baa
ka-baan.

suəŋ: kon leeŋ rɨəŋ qəy?

tun: miən kon lqaa-lqaa craən, tae nɨw rooŋ-kon haaway kee leeŋ rɨəŋ
kmae.

suəŋ: coh, lkhaon kee leeŋ rɨəŋ qəy?

tun: yup nih kee miən rəbam-roəm-kbac.

suəŋ: qou, kñom mɨn dael tɨw məəl roəm-kbac sah.

tun: qəñcəŋ tɨw məəl yup nih tɨw!

suəŋ: miən qəy; yəəŋ kɨt cih qəy tɨw?

tun: cih laan kñom tɨw!

D. CONVERSATION

1. At the Theater

a) A comments that a lot of people have come to see the play tonight.

b) B agrees, and says that the story of srat<ɔ>ɔp-ceik is a very popular story
(is a story which they like to see very much).

c) A asks B where he wants to sit.

d) B suggests they sit in front, because it's easy to see the actors.

e) A agrees, and says that in front one can hear the voices clearly too.

f) B points out two vacant seats, and suggests they sit there.

g) A remarks that the play is about to begin (playing), because they're playing the overture already.

h) B asks if they usually clap when the play is over.

i) A replies that they don't, but that they usually stand up in order to pay respect to the royal anthem.

2. Discussing the Ballet

a) A asks B if he has ever been to see the ballet.

b) B replies that he has never had the occasion to go.

c) A says he heard that they're having a ballet at the palace tonight, and asks B if he wants to go.

d) B says that it's fine with him, and asks A what story they're portraying (dancing) tonight.

e) A replies that he doesn't know for sure, but that they usually portray stories from the Ream-Kerti.

[At the Ballet]

f) B exclaims that the music is very pretty.

g) A agrees, and says that the players' costumes are very pretty too.

3. Discussing Films

a) A asks B if he'd like to go to the movies tonight.

b) B replies that it's fine with him, and asks what stories they're showing at the various theaters.

c) A replies he doesn't know, because he hasn't yet seen a newspaper.

d) B says he hears there's a police story playing at the Hawaii Theater.

e) A comments that he likes comedies best of all, but that sometimes he likes to go see a love story.

f) B says he likes police stories and war stories best.

g) A asks B what's playing at the Cinelux Theater.

h) B says he doesn't know, but that at the Cinelux they usually show foreign films (films from abroad).

i) A asks B if he likes foreign films.

j) B replies that he sometimes goes to see a French or Indian film, but that he usually goes to Cambodian films.

k) A asks B if he goes to the movies often.

l) B replies that he doesn't go so often; about once in two weeks.

A. Review of Dialogues

In preparation for the review lesson, review the Dialogues of Lessons 14-18. To test yourself, cover the English column and supply the English equivalents of the Cambodian sentences; then cover the Cambodian column and supply the Cambodian equivalents of the English sentences. If you cannot produce the Cambodian equivalents quickly and smoothly, review the relevant sections of the Grammar and Drills.

B. Review of Comprehension

The teacher will read selected conversations from the Comprehension sections of Lessons 14-18, calling on individual students for English translations of the sentences.

C. Test for Comprehension

Write the numbers 1-50 on a sheet of paper. The teacher will read 50 statements at normal speed. Write "true" or "false" beside the appropriate number. Most of the statements will be inherently true or false, although a few may be based on simple facts covered in the Dialogues. With true-or-false questions it is always possible to quibble by pointing out exceptions and extreme cases, but if the student considers each statement in general, the intent of the statement should be obvious. The teacher will repeat each statement twice. Listen to the statement in its entirety the first time; an unfamiliar word may be cleared up by the context in which it occurs.

1. nɨw srok-kmae miən prambəy-dəndɑp khaet.
2. baə yəəŋ daə yɨɨt, muk-tae tɨw mɨn tŏən kəpal.
3. tɨñ səmbot-kəpal nɨw ləə kəpal kɑ-baan.
4. neəq-dəmnaə tɨñ mhoup nɨw ləə kəpal mɨn baan tee.
5. kəmpuəŋ-caam nɨw cɨt mŏət-tuənlee.
6. kee craən-tae cih kəpal tɨw batdəmbɑɑŋ.
7. baə kmiən kənteel, miən kee cuəl qəŋrɨŋ nɨw ləə kəpal.
8. baə cɑŋ cih kəpal, trəw tɨñ səmbot-kəpal-hah.
9. kee craən-tae cuəl kulii qaoy yɔɔk qəywan cəñ pii kəpal.
10. nɨw knoŋ suən-cbaa muk-tae miən dam daəm-pkaa.
11. nɨw knoŋ prɨy miən pləw-tnɑl craən nah.
12. kee craən-tae coul-cət tɨw twəə pɨcnɨc nɨw cɨt tɨk-cruəh.
13. mənuh dael nɨw cɨt mŏət-tuənlee muk-tae prəsɑp hael-tɨk nah.
14. laəŋ pnum muk-tae twəə qaoy yəəŋ qɑh-kəmlaŋ nah.
15. baə mɨn stŏət hael-tɨk ponmaan tee, trəw nɨw tae kənlaeŋ tɨk crɨw.
16. nɨw kraom daəm-chəə, muk-tae miən mlup trəceəq.
17. mənuh dael prəsɑp hael-tɨk muk-tae luəŋ-tɨk ñɨk-ñoəp.
18. hael-tɨk twəə qaoy yəəŋ kliən baay nah.
19. ñam baay nɨw ptеəh pibaaq ciəŋ ñam baay nɨw knoŋ prɨy.
20. baə hael rŏəl tŋay tɨw, muk-tae pukae hael-tɨk nah.
21. baə yɨɨt haəy, trəw daə chap-chap laəŋ.
22. pii pnum-pɨñ tɨw siəm-riəp cəmŋaay prəhael bəy-rɔɔy dɑp-buən kiloumaet.
23. baə laan khouc taam pləw, trəw cuəh-cul laan tɨw.
24. kee praə snɑp səmrap sɑp puəh-wiən.

25. kee praə spiən səmrap claaŋ tŭənlee.
26. baə pləw krəŋeik-krəŋaq, trəw baək qaoy lɨən.
27. kee muk-tae yɔɔk laan tɨw caq preiŋ boum klañ mun cəñ dəmnaə.
28. baə kaŋ baek, trəw praa kaŋ-səkuə.
29. baə mɨn stŏət baək laan ponmaan tee, trəw prəyat qaoy mɛɛn-tɛɛn.
30. kee craən-tae baək laan-dək-tumnɨñ knoŋ tŭənlee.
31. wŏət preəh-kaew kɨɨ ciə wŏət muəy lqaa ciəŋ-kee nɨw pnum-pɨñ.
32. baə caŋ cih kəpal-hah, trəw tɨw sthaanii-qayeəqsmaayiən.
33. kee craən-tae tɨw wŏət daəmbəy twaay-bəŋkum preəh.
34. preəh-bɑrommərɪəccəweəŋ haw thaa salaa-raccənaa kɑ-baan dae.
35. look-sɑŋ craən-tae kŭəŋ nɨw kot.
36. qəŋkɔɔ-wŏət kɨɨ ciə wŏət muəy thom ciəŋ-kee knoŋ piphup-look.
37. luəŋ miən dəmnaq muəy tiət nɨw psaa-kəndaal.
38. nɨw salaa-raccənaa kee miən taŋ wŏətthoq-bɔraan pseiŋ-pseiŋ.
39. nɨw wŏət muk-tae miən preəh-wihiə, kot, haəy-nɨŋ caetdəy.
40. teehsəcɑɑ craən-tae tɨw tɨñ qəywan nɨw wŏət pseiŋ-pseiŋ.
41. baə caŋ məəl lkhaon, kee craən-tae tɨw rooŋ psaa-siləp.
42. nɨw rooŋ-kon kmae, kmiən rɨəŋ mɔɔk pii bɑɑrəteeh tee.
43. kee craən-tae kraok chɔɔ daəmbəy koorup bɑt qəŋkɔɔ-rɪəc.
44. lkhaon leeŋ cɑp haəy, kee craən-tae teəh-day.
45. rɨəŋ qaakɨñ-qaacao kɨɨ ciə rɨəŋ snae-haa.
46. rəbam-rŏəm-kbac kee craən-tae rŏəm rɨəŋ rɪəm-kei.
47. baə qəŋkuy khaŋ-muk, sdap mɨn lɨɨ qwəy sah.
48. thŏəmmədaa tuə-qaek kəmsɑt nah kuə qaoy qaanət.
49. neəq-rŏəm-kbac craən-tae miən səmliəq-bəmpeəq lqaa nah.
50. baə kñom coul-cət rɨəŋ-kəmplaeŋ, knom tɨw məəl rɨəŋ-cəmbaŋ.

D. Translation

1. When does the plane leave?
2. We can eat either on the boat or in Kampong Cham.
3. Our steamer has just arrived at the pier.
4. That boat carries cement to sell in the provinces.
5. Just call a coolie to take those things off the boat.
6. Hey, the train's leaving! Get aboard quickly!
7. There are a lot of people in third class.
8. Have you bought your steamer-ticket yet?
9. We can sleep either on a mat or on a hammock.
10. How much does it cost to rent a car to go to Kêp?
11. When will we get to Battambang?
12. If [one] wants to take a steamer to Saigon, [one] goes by the Mekong River.
13. There's a mountain near here which we can climb.
14. Eating in the forest is not so comfortable.
15. If there are tables for picnicking, it's not so difficult.
16. We can swim at the waterfall.
17. There's a village near the waterfall [where] we can buy food.
18. Where are you going to park the car?
19. Under that tree there's cool shade, and it's not very far from the house, either.
20. I swim only in the shallow places, because I'm afraid of drowning.

21. Săng's not afraid of deep water, because he's a good swimmer (he's good at swimming).
22. After I've changed my clothes, I'm going to the movies.
23. Swimming makes me very tired.
24. Let's go rest for awhile on that big rock.
25. Whatever John does, he's always clever [at it].
26. I ate too much, is the reason that I don't feel too well.
27. There he comes now! (There! [He's] coming already!)
28. It's late (in the morning) already; we still have to go pick up George.
29. From Phnom Penh to Battambang is a distance of 290 kilometers.
30. I don't know where he's gone. (I don't know that he's gone where.)
31. If you amuse yourself (tɨw daə-leeŋ) a lot, [your] money is likely to be used up quickly.
32. If the car breaks down along the way, I have tools of all kinds.
33. Don't worry about anything; I'm good at fixing a car.
34. I'm stopping here because we're about out of gas.
35. I'm going to drive carefully because this road is very crooked.
36. Have confidence in me in the matter of traveling.
37. I very frequently drive to Siem Reap.
38. Chăn used to work for the department of tourism.
39. First of all, I'll take you to see the royal palace.
40. Wat Phnom is the highest wat in Phnom Penh.
41. Last of all, we'll go to the train station.
42. This temple is very beautiful; it's worth seeing.
43. They're open every day except Saturday.
44. Besides a temple, wats usually have various stupas, and quarters for the monks to live in.
45. In the national museum they have on display various ancient artifacts, such as jewelry and sculpture.
46. This play is very interesting, because the hero is very sad.
47. In a love story the hero and heroine usually love each other very much.
48. I've heard that they're going to perform (dance) a story from the Ream-Kerti.
49. I like crime stories better than comedies.
50. In Phnom Penh they have films from abroad too, such as French, American, Indian, (and) Russian, and so forth.

LESSON 20. AROUND THE HOUSE

[Tape 34]   A. DIALOGUE

qɑɑn

cət	heart, mind; disposition
sapbaay-cət (səpbaay-, səbaay-)	to be happy, content, glad
daoy	with, with the fact that; because

baaŋ — husband; you (wife to husband)

1. kñom səpbaay-cət nah daoy baaŋ mɨn tɨw twəə-kaa tŋay-nih.
I'm (very) glad (that) you (Husband) are not going to work today.

but

2. kñom kaa səpbaay dae.
I'm glad too.

muəy-qaatɨt (maatɨt)	[in] a week, [in] the week
paa	Father; you (child to father)

3. maatɨt paa nɨw pteʾəh tae mə-tŋay tee.
You (Father) are home only one day a week.

qɑɑn

4. baaŋ tŋay-nih nɨw pteʾəh kɨt thəə qəy?
What do you plan to do [while] you're home today?

bun

baaŋ	I (husband to wife)
but	Bouth (personal name)
rɔbaaŋ (rəbaaŋ)	fence, hedge
kat rəbaaŋ	to trim the hedge

5. baaŋ kɨt noʾəm but tɨw kat rəbaaŋ nɨw muk pteʾəh.
I plan to take Bouth and go trim the hedge in front of the house.

ruəc pii nuh	after that
kolaap	rose
daəm-pkaa-kolaap	rose-bush
bəy-buən	three or four

6. ruəc pii nuh, baaŋ caŋ dam daəm-pkaa-kolaap bəy-buən daəm nɨw knoŋ suən phaaŋ.
After that, I want to plant three or four rose-bushes in the garden too.

qoun	Wife; you (husband to wife)
qoun-qaeŋ	you yourself (husband to wife)

7. coh, qoun-qaeŋ kɨt thəə qəy tŋay-nih?
Say, what do you (Wife) plan to do today?

qɑɑn

mhoup — various kinds of food

8. lŋiəc nih pñiəw maok leeŋ pteʾəh, haəy kñom trəw twəə mhoup-mhaa tətuəl pñiəw phaaŋ.
Guests are coming to visit this evening, and I must prepare the food for (receiving) them.

258

baoh
səmqaat (səmqaat)
baoh-səmqaat

to sweep
to clean, make clean
to clean

9. mun pñiəw mɔɔk, kñom trəw
baoh-səmqaat pteəh.

Before the guests come I have to
clean the house.

babaa (bəbaa, pəbaa)

soup, porridge (usually eaten
for breakfast)

qambaoh (qəmbaoh, mbaoh)

broom

10. ñam bəbaa ruəc, som baaŋ tɨw
tɨñ qəmbaoh tməy mɔɔk qaoy kñom
muəy.

[When] you've finished your breakfast (soup), would you please go buy
me a new broom.

rɨc-rɨl

decrepit, disintegrated, worn
out

11. qəmbaoh nih cah rɨc-rɨl nah.

This broom is completely worn out.

bopphaa

Boppha (common name for
girls)

12. kñom baoh pteəh ruəc, kñom
qaoy bopphaa cuut tok-tuu nɨw
knoŋ bəntup-tətuəl-pñiəw.

[When] I've finished sweeping the
house, I'll have Boppha dust the
furniture in the living room.

[In the Garden]

but

riik

to bloom, to flourish

13. paa, pkaa nih cɨt riik haəy.

Dad, these flowers are about to
bloom.

klən
kraqoup (krəqoup, kəqoup)

odor, smell
to be sweet-smelling

14. haəy miən klən krəqoup phaaŋ.

And they have a sweet smell too.

bun

thou

vase

15. but kom plɨc kat pkaa klah
yɔɔk tɨw daq thou.

(Bouth) don't forget to cut some
flowers and put them in a vase.

but

smaw
doh
daaq

grass, hay
to come up, to grow
to pull up, extract

16. yii, smaw doh craən nah; cam kñom
daaq caol.

Boy, a lot of grass has come up;
I'll (wait until I) pull [it] up and
throw [it] away.

bun

17. qaə, nɨŋ haəy.

That's a good idea. (Yes, right.)

but

sat

animal, creature (human or
otherwise)

yum

to cry, wail, howl

18. qei, sat qəy nuh yum?

Hey, what animal is that [that's]
crying?

bun

cmaa

cap

caap

cat

to catch

sparrow, rice bird

19. qou, cmaa wiə cap caap.

Oh, a cat's caught a bird.

but

20. cmaa kñom rɨɨ?

Is it my cat?

bun

koun

koun-qaeŋ

ceh-tae

deik

haal

Child; you (parent to child)

you yourself (parent to child)

always, typically, persist in

to lie down; to sleep

to spread out, to expose to

21. mɨn mɛɛn tee; cmaa koun-qaeŋ
kcɨl nah; ceh-tae deik haal
tŋay tee.

No it's not; your cat is very lazy;
[he's] always lying (spread out) in
the sun.

ckae

kɑkaay (kekaay)

ruuŋ

suən-pkaa

dog

to dig, to scratch about

hole

flower-garden

22. qou, ckae kəkaay ruuŋ nɨw knoŋ
suən-pkaa muəy tiət haəy!

Oh, the dog has dug another hole
in the flower-garden!

lup

to erase, to cover over

23. but tɨw yɔɔk dəy mɔɔk lup tɨw.

Bouth, go get some dirt and fill [it]
up (cover [it] over).

paa

cɑmkaa (cəmkaa, cəkaa)

beh

bənlae (bənlae, pəlae)

Father; I (father to child)

garden, plantation (other than
    wet rice)

to pick, gather

vegetable

24. qəyləw paa tɨw cəmkaa beh krouc
haəy-nɨŋ bənlae klah.

Now I'm going to the garden to gather
some oranges and some vegetables.

[In the House]

bopphaa

maq

Mother; you (child to mother)

25. qəyləw maq cɑŋ qaoy kñom thəə
qəy?

What would you (Mother) like to have
me do now?

qɑɑn

cuə̌ñcuun (cəñcuun)

liəŋ

to carry, move

to wash (the surface of)

26. qəyləw koun-qaeŋ cuə̌ñcuun caan
tɨw liəŋ tɨw nəh.

Now [would] you take the dishes and
wash [them].

sɑl

mhoup-sɑl

to remain, be left over

left-over food

27. haəy yɔɔk mhoup-sɑl nih tɨw
qaoy ckae sii tɨw.

Then take this left-over food [and]
give it to the dog to eat.

plǝǝŋ   fire, light
caŋkraan (cǝŋkraan,   stove
     cǝkraan)
rɔluǝt (rǝluǝt)   to go out, be extinguished

28. qou, plǝǝŋ nɨw knoŋ cǝŋkraan   Oh, the fire in the stove has com-
rǝluǝt qɑh haǝy.   pletely gone out.

tyuuŋ (kyuuŋ, kcuuŋ)   coal, charcoal
baŋkat (bǝŋkat, pǝkat)   to light, to ignite (trans.)

29. koun yɔɔk kcuuŋ mɔɔk bǝŋkat tiǝt   (You) bring some charcoal and
tɨw.   light it again.

bopphaa

cheh   to burn, to be on fire

30. plǝǝŋ cheh haǝy; maq kɨt thǝǝ qǝy?   The fire's burning; what are you
going to do?

qɑɑn

kɑmsiǝw (kǝmsiǝw, kǝsiǝw)   tea-kettle
dam   to cook, to boil

31. yɔɔk kǝmsiǝw daq tɨk dam sǝn tɨw.   First take the tea-kettle and put
[some] water in [it] to boil.

maq   I, me (mother to child)

32. ruǝc yɔɔk cnaŋ thom nuh mɔɔk   Then bring me that big pot, will
qaoy maq phɑɑŋ.   you?

rɨl   to be dull, worn

33. yii, kǝmbǝt nih rɨl nah.   Gee, this knife is really dull.

sɑmliǝŋ (sǝmliǝŋ)   to sharpen by whetting
mut   to cut; to be sharp (cutting)

34. yɔɔk tɨw qaoy paa sǝmliǝŋ qaoy   Take [it] and have [your] father
mut tɨw.   sharpen [it] (whet it making it sharp).

B. GRAMMAR AND DRILLS

1. Kinship Terms Used As Pronouns

It was pointed out in Lesson 4, B, 14 that among fairly close acquaintances, personal names are frequently used in place of a second-person (or third-person) pronoun, as in

sarɑɑn kliǝn baay tee?   Are you (Saran) hungry?

In Lesson 15, mɨt 'friend' is used instead of a pronoun in the sentence

tŋay-nih mɨt caŋ tɨw daǝ-leeŋ   Where would you (friends) like to
qae-naa?   go today (for amusement)?

In this lesson, we have seen that, within a family, kinship terms are frequently used instead of pronouns. Thus, in a given situation, the word which describes the speaker's relationship to the addressee is used for the first-person pronoun 'I', and the word which describes the addressee's relationship to the speaker is used for 'you', as in the following exchange:

Son

tŋay-nih <u>paa</u> kɨt twəə-kaa qwəy?   What do <u>you</u> (Father) plan to do today?

Father

tŋay-nih <u>paa</u> tɨw kat rəbaaŋ.   Today <u>I</u> (Father) am going to trim the hedge.

<u>koun</u> caŋ cuəy <u>paa</u> tee?   Would <u>you</u> (Child) like to help <u>me</u> (Father)?

Son

baat, <u>koun</u> cuəy.   Yes, <u>I</u> (Child) will help.

Between a husband and wife, baaŋ for the husband and qoun (a reduction of pqoun) for the wife may be used as terms of affection, as in the exchange:

Wife

<u>baaŋ</u> kɨt twəə qwəy tŋay-nih?   What do <u>you</u> (Husband) plan to do today?

Husband

<u>baaŋ</u> kɨt tɨw kat rəbaaŋ.   <u>I</u> (Husband) am going to trim the hedge.
coh, <u>qoun</u>(-qaeŋ) kɨt twəə qwəy dae?   Say, what do <u>you</u> (Wife) plan to do?

It should be pointed out, however, that these reciprocal kinships pronouns are used in place of the more impersonal kñom only when the speaker wishes to convey a certain amount of intimacy or affection. They are more commonly employed in place of second-person pronouns, especially when addressing an older friend or relative, such as <u>look-taa</u> 'Grandfather, old respected gentleman', <u>look-yiəy</u> 'Grandmother, old respected lady', <u>neə̀q-miiŋ</u> 'Auntie, older female friend of the family', etc.

The following chart shows the reciprocal kinship pronouns which might be used in specific situations. Those kinship terms which have not yet been introduced in the Lessons are preceded by an asterisk.

Kinship Terms Used As Pronouns

Situation	Sex	First Person	Second Person
Husband to wife		baaŋ	qoun
Wife to husband		qoun	baaŋ
Parent to child	m.	paa, *qəw, qəwpuk	koun
	f.	maq, *mae, mdaay	koun
Child to Parent	m.	koun	paa, qəw, qəwpuk, look-qəwpuk
	f.	koun	maq, mae, mdaay, *neə̀q-mdaay, *look-mae

Situation	Sex	First Person	Second Person
Older to younger friend or relative		baaŋ	pqoun
Younger to older friend or relative		pqoun	baaŋ
Grandparent to member of grandchild's generation	m. f.	taa yiəy	*caw, *koun-caw caw, koun-caw
Grandchild to member of grandparent's generation	m. f.	caw caw	taa, look-taa yiəy, look-yiəy
Older uncle or aunt to niece, nephew, or younger friend	m. f.	*qom qom	*kmuəy kmuəy
Niece or nephew to older uncle, aunt, or friend of the family	m. f.	kmuəy kmuəy	qom, *look-qom qom, look-qom
Younger uncle or aunt to niece, nephew, or younger friend	m. f.	*puu miiŋ	kmuəy kmuəy
Niece or nephew to younger uncle, aunt, or friend of the family	m. f.	kmuəy kmuəy	puu, *look-puu miiŋ, *neəq-miiŋ

1-A. Substitution Drill

Teacher	Student
maatɨt paa nɨw pteəh tae mə-tŋay tee.	maatɨt paa nɨw pteəh tae mə-tŋay tee.
maq	maatɨt maq nɨw pteəh tae mə-tŋay tee.
koun	maatɨt koun nɨw pteəh tae mə-tŋay tee.
qoun	maatɨt qoun nɨw pteəh tae mə-tŋay tee.
baaŋ	maatɨt baaŋ nɨw pteəh tae mə-tŋay tee.
look-taa	maatɨt look-taa nɨw pteəh tae mə-tŋay tee.
look-yiəy	maatɨt look-yiəy nɨw pteəh tae mə-tŋay tee.
pqoun	maatɨt pqoun nɨw pteəh tae mə-tŋay tee.
neəq-miiŋ	maatɨt neəq-miiŋ nɨw pteəh tae mə-tŋay tee.
look-puu	maatɨt look-puu nɨw pteəh tae mə-tŋay tee.
kmuəy	maatɨt kmuəy nɨw pteəh tae mə-tŋay tee.

1-B. Matching Drill

In the following drill, use an appropriate kinship pronoun in the question 'Do you want to go?', based on the kinship pronoun in the statement 'Today I'm thinking of going to the market.' supplied by the teacher. Refer to the preceding chart if necessary.

Teacher	Student
tŋay-nih paa kɨt tɨw psaa.	koun caŋ tɨw tee?
tŋay-nih qoun kɨt tɨw psaa.	baaŋ caŋ tɨw tee?
tŋay-nih baaŋ kɨt tɨw psaa.	(qoun) (pqoun) caŋ tɨw tee?
tŋay-nih miiŋ kɨt tɨw psaa.	kmuəy caŋ tɨw tee?
tŋay-nih maq kɨt tɨw psaa.	koun caŋ tɨw tee?
tŋay-nih koun kɨt tɨw psaa.	(paa) (maq) caŋ tɨw tee?
tŋay-nih kmuəy kɨt tɨw psaa.	(look-qom) (look-puu) (neˇəq-miiŋ) caŋ tɨw tee?
tŋay-nih taa kɨt tɨw psaa.	caw caŋ tɨw tee?
tŋay-nih caw kɨt tɨw psaa.	(look-taa) (look-yiəy) caŋ tɨw tee?
tŋay-nih pqoun kɨt tɨw psaa.	baaŋ caŋ tɨw tee?
tŋay-nih puu kɨt tɨw psaa.	kmuəy caŋ tɨw tee?
tŋay-nih yiəy kɨt tɨw psaa.	caw caŋ tɨw tee?

2. The Relative Conjunction daoy

We have met the relative conjunction ciə 'that' in the sentences

kñom mɨn dəy ciə daq kənlaeŋ naa tee.	I don't know where we'll put them. (I don't know that we'll put them where.)
kñom rɔɔk waen-taa mɨn khəəñ, baan ciə knom yɨɨt bəntəc.	I couldn't find my glasses, is the reason that I'm a little late.

daoy also occurs as a relative conjunction which introduces subordinate clauses in complex sentences, and which has a much wider range of occurrence than ciə. Its meaning is 'that, with the fact that, since, because', as in

kñom səpbaay-cət nah daoy baaŋ mɨn tɨw twəə-kaa tŋay-nih.	I'm very glad that you're (Husband) not going to work today.

daoy typically occurs after adjectival verbs describing emotions, such as sapbaay-cət 'happy, glad', *pruəy-cət 'sad', *treik-qaa 'happy', qaa-kun 'grateful', *pibaaq-cət 'unhappy', *khəŋ 'angry', etc.

2-A. Substitution Drill

Teacher	Student
kñom səpbaay-cət nah daoy baaŋ mɨn tɨw twəə-kaa tŋay-nih.	kñom səpbaay-cət nah daoy baaŋ mɨn tɨw twəə-kaa tŋay-nih.
baaŋ mɔɔk leeŋ pteˇəh kñom.	kñom səpbaay-cət nah daoy baaŋ mɔɔk leeŋ pteˇəh kñom.
yəəŋ tɨw daə-leeŋ tŋay-nih.	kñom səpbaay-cət nah daoy yəəŋ tɨw daə-leeŋ tŋay-nih.

Teacher	Student
	kñom səpbaay-cət nah daoy
baan skoəl look.	baan skoəl look.
	kñom səpbaay-cət nah daoy
koun mɨn tɨw riən tŋay-nih.	koun mɨn tɨw riən tŋay-nih.
	kñom səpbaay-cət nah daoy
look baan mɔɔk.	look baan mɔɔk.
	kñom səpbaay-cət nah daoy
yəəŋ twəə-kaa nih cap haəy.	yəəŋ twəə-kaa nih cap haəy.
	kñom səpbaay-cət nah daoy
yəəŋ tɨw məəl kon yup nih.	yəəŋ tɨw məəl kon yup nih.
	kñom səpbaay-cət nah daoy
look tɨw baan.	look tɨw baan.

2-B. **Progressive Substitution Drill**

Teacher	Student
kñom səpbaay-cət nah daoy	kñom səpbaay-cət nah daoy
look baan mɔɔk tŋay-nih.	look baan mɔɔk tŋay-nih.
qɑɑ-kun	kñom qɑɑ-kun nah daoy
	look baan mɔɔk tŋay-nih.
treik-qɑɑ	kñom treik-qɑɑ nah daoy
	look baan mɔɔk tŋay-nih.
	kñom treik-qɑɑ nah daoy
look mɨn mɔɔk tŋay-nih.	look mɨn mɔɔk tŋay-nih.
khəŋ	kñom khəŋ nah daoy
	look mɨn mɔɔk tŋay-nih.
pruəy-cət	kñom pruəy-cət nah daoy
	look mɨn mɔɔk tŋay-nih.
pibaaq-cət	kñom pibaaq-cət nah daoy
	look mɨn mɔɔk tŋay-nih.
səpbaay-cət	kñom səpbaay-cət nah daoy
	look mɨn mɔɔk tŋay-nih.

3. **bəy-buən**

Two alternatives, neither of which is crucial to the statement being made, are frequently expressed by means of a coordinate compound without an intervening 'or', as with bəy-buən 'three or four' in the sentence

kñom caŋ dam daəm-pkaa-kolaap   I want to plant three or four
bəy-buən daəm phɑɑŋ.   rose-bushes too.

When the alternatives are compound numerals larger than dap 'ten', the first numeral is usually truncated, e.g.:

pii-bəy-dəndɑp (but dɑp-pii-dɑp-bəy)   twelve or thirteen
haa-hoksəp   fifty or sixty
pii-bəy-rɔɔy   two or three hundred
prammuəy-prampɨl-poŏn   six or seven thousand

3-A. Progressive Substitution Drill

Teacher	Student
kñom nɨŋ tɨñ <u>daəm-pkaa-kolaap</u> bəy-buən daəm.	kñom nɨŋ tɨñ <u>daəm-pkaa-kolaap</u> bəy-buən daəm.
kmaw-day	kñom nɨŋ tɨñ <u>kmaw-day</u> bəy-buən daəm.
dəy-saɑ	kñom nɨŋ tɨñ <u>dəy-saɑ</u> bəy-buən daəm.
daəm-chəə	kñom nɨŋ tɨñ <u>daəm-chəə</u> bəy-buən daəm.
barəy	kñom nɨŋ tɨñ <u>barəy</u> bəy-buən daəm.
kəñcɑp.	kñom nɨŋ tɨñ barəy bəy-buən <u>kəñcɑp.</u>
tae	kñom nɨŋ tɨñ <u>tae</u> bəy-buən kəñcɑp.
<u>kafei</u>	kñom nɨŋ tɨñ <u>kafei</u> bəy-buən kəñcɑp.
<u>baay</u>	kñom nɨŋ tɨñ <u>baay</u> bəy-buən kəñcɑp.

3-B. Translation-Completion Drill

Teacher	Student
kñom trəw tɨñ barəy <u>two or three</u> daəm.	kñom trəw tɨñ barəy <u>pii-bəy</u> daəm.
knoŋ muəy liit baan tae <u>three or four</u> kiloumaet.	knoŋ muəy liit baan tae <u>bəy-buən</u> kiloumaet.
knoŋ mə-tŋay kñom tɨw psaa <u>four or five</u> daaŋ.	knoŋ mə-tŋay kñom tɨw psaa <u>buən-pram</u> daaŋ.
kənlaeŋ nuh miən kamməkaa <u>two or three hundred</u> neăq.	kənlaeŋ nuh miən kamməkaa <u>pii-bəy-rɔɔy</u> neăq.
bəntup nuh mə-tŋay tlay <u>fifty or sixty</u> riəl.	bəntup nuh mə-tŋay tlay <u>haa-hoksəp</u> riəl.
miən puəq-maaq mɔɔk prəhael <u>thirteen or fourteen</u> neăq.	miən puəq-maaq mɔɔk prəhael <u>bəy-buən-dəndɑp</u> neăq.
koŏt baan praq-khae prəhael <u>seven or eight thousand.</u>	koŏt baan praq-khae prəhael <u>prampɨl-prambəy-poŏn.</u>

4. ruəc as a Dependent Clause Marker

ruəc occurred in Lesson 15 as a completive verb with the meaning 'to finish, to complete' in the sentence

kaal-naa ñam baay <u>ruəc</u>, yəəŋ tɨw   When [we've] <u>finished</u> eating, we'll go
laəŋ pnum.   climb the mountain.

When <u>ruəc</u> occurs at the end of a dependent clause without an initial subordinating conjunction such as <u>kaal-naa</u> 'when', the clause may be translated '[when] (dependent clause) is finished, having (dependent clause) already', as in the following sentences in this lesson:

ñam bəbaɑ <u>ruəc</u>, som baaŋ tɨw tɨñ   [When you've] <u>finished</u> your breakfast,
qəmbaoh tməy mɔɔk qaoy kñom   would you please go buy me a new
muəy.   broom.

kñom baoh pteʾəh <u>ruəc</u>, kñom qaoy
bopphaa cuut tok-tuu nɨw knoŋ
bəntup-tətuəl-pñiəw.

[When] I've swept the house, I'll have
Boppha dust the furniture in the
living-room.

4-A. Substitution Drill

<u>Teacher</u>

ñam bəbɑɑ ruəc, som koun
<u>tɨw tɨñ</u> qəmbaoh tməy.

<u>tɨw psaa</u> qaoy kñom.

<u>tɨw cuəy paa</u> knoŋ suən-cbaa.

<u>tɨw liəŋ</u> caan.

<u>cuəy maq</u> bəntəc.

<u>prəñap tɨw riən</u>.

<u>yɔɔk mhoup-sɑl tɨw</u> qaoy ckae sii.

<u>yɔɔk kəmbət nih tɨw</u> qaoy paa.

<u>tɨw cuut</u> tok-tuu.

<u>tɨw baoh-səmqaat</u> pteʾəh.

<u>Student</u>

ñam bəbɑɑ ruəc, som koun
<u>tɨw tɨñ</u> qəmbaoh tməy.

ñam bəbɑɑ ruəc, som koun
<u>tɨw psaa</u> qaoy maq.

ñam bəbɑɑ ruəc, som koun
<u>tɨw cuəy paa</u> knoŋ suən-cbaa.

ñam bəbɑɑ ruəc, som koun
<u>tɨw liəŋ</u> caan.

ñam bəbɑɑ ruəc, som koun
<u>cuəy maq</u> bəntəc.

ñam bəbɑɑ ruəc, som koun
<u>prəñap tɨw riən</u>.

ñam bəbɑɑ ruəc, som koun
<u>yɔɔk mhoup-sɑl tɨw</u> qaoy ckae sii.

ñam bəbɑɑ ruəc, som koun
<u>yɔɔk kəmbət nih tɨw</u> qaoy paa.

ñam bəbɑɑ ruəc, som koun
<u>tɨw cuut</u> tok-tuu.

ñam bəbɑɑ ruəc, som koun
<u>tɨw baoh-səmqaat</u> pteʾəh.

4-B. Composition Drill

<u>Teacher</u>

kñom ñam bəbɑɑ.
kñom tɨw psaa.

kñom məəl kasaet.
kñom tɨw twəə-kaa

kñom baoh-səmqaat pteʾəh.
kñom cuut tok-tuu.

kñom kat rəbaaŋ.
kñom liəŋ laan.

kñom səmliəŋ kəmbət nih.
kñom tɨw kat smaw.

kñom ñam baay.
kñom tɨw liəŋ caan.

<u>Student</u>

kñom ñam bəbɑɑ ruəc,
kñom tɨw psaa.

kñom məəl kasaet ruəc,
kñom tɨw twəə-kaa.

kñom baoh-səmqaat pteʾəh ruəc,
kñom cuut tok-tuu.

kñom kat rəbaaŋ ruəc,
kñom liəŋ laan.

kñom səmliəŋ kəmbət nih ruəc,
kñom tɨw kat smaw.

kñom ñam baay ruəc,
kñom tɨw liəŋ caan.

Teacher	Student
kñom twəə-kaa.	kñom twəə-kaa ruəc,
kñom tɨw daə-leeŋ.	kñom tɨw daə-leeŋ.
kñom bəŋkat pləəŋ.	kñom bəŋkat pləəŋ ruəc,
kñom dam tɨk.	kñom dam tɨk.

5. Discontinuous Noun Phrases

It was pointed out in Lesson 3, B, 3 that, in a noun phrase, a numeral (with or without a following specifier) usually immediately follows an adjectival verb; e.g.:

qəmbaoh tməy muəy   'a new broom'

However, additional material may be inserted between the adjectival verb and the numeral (or numeral + specifier), as in the sentence

som baaŋ tɨw tɨñ <u>qəmbaoh tməy</u>   Would you (Husband) please go buy
mɔɔk qaoy kñom <u>muəy</u>.   me a new broom.

There seems to be little or no difference in meaning between the two alternative constructions, as shown in the following examples:

som look tɨw tɨñ <u>barəy mə-kəñcap</u>   Would you please go buy me a pack
mɔɔk qaoy kñom.   of cigarettes.

som look tɨw tɨñ <u>barəy</u> mɔɔk qaoy   (Same)
kñom <u>mə-kəñcap</u>.

5-A. Transformation Drill

Teacher	Student
som baaŋ tɨw tɨñ qəmbaoh tməy muəy mɔɔk qaoy kñom.	som baaŋ tɨw tɨñ qəmbaoh tməy mɔɔk qaoy kñom muəy.
kñom nɨŋ tɨñ barəy kmae mə-kəncap cuun look.	kñom nɨŋ tɨñ barəy kmae cuun look mə-kəncap.
qəwpuk kñom nɨŋ tɨñ laan tməy muəy qaoy kñom.	qəwpuk kñom nɨŋ tɨñ laan tməy qaoy kñom muəy.
kñom nɨŋ twəə mhoup cŋañ pii-bəy muk cuun look.	kñom nɨŋ twəə mhoup cŋañ cuun look pii-bəy muk.
kñom tɨñ qəŋkaa bəy kilou cuun maq.	kñom tɨñ qəŋkaa cuun maq bəy kilou.
kñom baan yɔɔk pkaa lqaa bəy tɨw salaa.	kñom baan yɔɔk pkaa lqaa tɨw salaa bəy.
kñom yɔɔk kawqəy thom bəy mɔɔk pteˇəh.	kñom yɔɔk kawqəy thom mɔɔk pteˇəh bəy.
miən baraŋ pii neˇəq cəñ pii pteˇəh.	miən baraŋ cəñ pii pteˇəh pii neˇəq.

6. Pronominal Reference to a Preceding Topic

In a colloquial style of speech, an announced topic is frequently followed by a pronoun which refers back to the topic and serves as the subject of a following verb, as in the following sentences:

qou, cmaa wiə cap caap.   Oh, the cat, it's catching a bird.
look-taa, ko͝ət tɨw psaa haəy.   Grandfather, he's gone to the market.
cmaa koun-qaeŋ, wiə kcɨl nah.   Your cat, it's very lazy.

The effect of such constructions seems to be to emphasize the topic announced, and is not unlike the effect achieved by the same kind of construction in colloquial English, as in 'Oh, Mother, she's always worrying.' or 'Cats, they're really a nuisance.'

6-A. Transformation Drill

Teacher	Student
cmaa koun-qaeŋ kcɨl nah. (wiə)	cmaa koun-qaeŋ wiə kcɨl nah.
look-puu tɨw psaa haəy. (ko͝ət)	look-puu ko͝ət tɨw psaa haəy.
ckae kñom ceh-tae kəkaay ruuŋ. (wiə)	ckae kñom wiə ceh-tae kəkaay ruuŋ.
look-taa coul-cət twəə-kaa nɨw knoŋ suən. (ko͝ət)	look-taa ko͝ət coul-cət twəə-kaa nɨw knoŋ suən.
qəwpuk kñom tɨw beh plae-chəə. (ko͝ət)	qəwpuk kñom ko͝ət tɨw beh plae-chəə.
cmaa coul-cət deik haal tŋay. (wiə)	cmaa wiə coul-cət deik haal tŋay.
mdaay kñom prəsɑp twəə mhoup nah. (ko͝ət)	mdaay kñom ko͝ət prəsɑp twəə mhoup nah.
koun kñom mɨn coul-cət tɨw riən sɑh. (wiə)	koun kñom wiə mɨn coul-cət tɨw riən sɑh.
miiŋ kñom coul-cət məəl siəwphɨw nah. (ko͝ət)	miiŋ kñom ko͝ət coul-cət məəl siəwphɨw nah.
puəq-maaq kñom ceh-tae tɨw daə-leeŋ. (kee)	puəq-maaq kñom kee coul-cət tɨw daə-leeŋ.

7. The Preverbal Auxiliary ceh-tae

ceh as a modal verb means 'to know how to', as in

ko͝ət ceh niyiəy phiəsaa-baraŋ.   They know how to speak French.

The compound preverbal auxiliary ceh-tae means 'always, typically, persist in', as in

ko͝ət ceh-tae niyiəy phiəsaa-baraŋ.   They always speak French.
cmaa kñom ceh-tae deik haal tŋay.   My cat always lies in the sun.

7-A. Progressive Substitution Drill

Teacher	Student
ckae kñom ceh-tae deik haal tŋay.	ckae kñom ceh-tae deik haal tŋay.
kəkaay ruuŋ.	ckae kñom ceh-tae kəkaay ruuŋ.
cap sat touc-touc sii.	ckae kñom ceh-tae cap sat touc-touc sii.
sii mhoup-sɑl.	ckae kñom ceh-tae sii mhoup-sɑl.
cmaa kñom	cmaa kñom ceh-tae sii mhoup-sɑl.
cap caap sii.	cmaa kñom ceh-tae cap caap sii.
deik haal tŋay.	cmaa kñom ceh-tae deik haal tŋay.
yum klaŋ nah.	cmaa kñom ceh-tae yum klaŋ nah.

7-B. Transformation Drill

Teacher	Student
cmaa kñom deik haal tŋay.	cmaa kñom ceh-tae deik haal tŋay.
kee mɔɔk taam pləw nih.	kee ceh-tae mɔɔk taam pləw nih.
mdaay kñom kraok laəŋ pii prəlɨm.	mdaay kñom ceh-tae kraok laəŋ pii prəlɨm.
kñom tɨw məəl kon tŋay-saw.	kñom ceh-tae tɨw məəl kon tŋay-saw.
qəwpuk nɨw pteəh tŋay-qatɨt.	qəwpuk ceh-tae nɨw pteəh tŋay-qatɨt.
puəq-maaq kñom tɨw daə-leeŋ.	puəq-maaq kñom ceh-tae tɨw daə-leeŋ.
look-taa coul-cət twəə-kaa nɨw knoŋ camkaa.	look-taa ceh-tae coul-cət twəə-kaa nɨw knoŋ camkaa.
ckae kñom kəkaay ruuŋ nɨw knoŋ suən-pkaa.	ckae kñom ceh-tae kəkaay ruuŋ nɨw knoŋ suən-pkaa.
bopphaa cuəy mdaay liəŋ caan.	bopphaa ceh-tae cuəy mdaay liəŋ caan.
kñom tɨw twəə-kaa maoŋ prambəy-kənlah.	kñom ceh-tae tɨw twəə-kaa maoŋ prambəy-kənlah.

8. qaoy with an Indirect Object

qaoy as a modal verb is frequently separated from a following primary verb by an indirect object, in which case the resulting verb phrase means 'have (someone) (do something)', as in

qəyləw maq caŋ qaoy kñom thəə qəy?   What would you (Mother) like to have me do now?

kñom baoh pteəh ruəc-haəy, kñom qaoy bopphaa cuut tok-tuu.   [When] I've finished sweeping the house, I'll have Boppha dust the furniture.

8-A. Substitution Drill

Teacher	Student
maq caŋ qaoy koun cuut tok-tuu.	maq caŋ qaoy koun cuut tok-tuu.
liəŋ caan.	maq caŋ qaoy koun liəŋ caan.
tɨw psaa qaoy maq.	maq caŋ qaoy koun tɨw psaa qaoy maq.
yɔɔk mhoup-sal tɨw qaoy ckae sii.	maq caŋ qaoy koun yɔɔk mhoup-sal tɨw qaoy ckae sii.
cuəy baoh-səmqaat pteəh.	maq caŋ qaoy koun cuəy baoh-səmqaat pteəh.
tɨw kat smaw nɨw muk pteəh.	maq caŋ qaoy koun tɨw kat smaw nɨw muk pteəh.
tɨw kat pkaa klah mɔɔk daq thou.	maq caŋ qaoy koun tɨw kat pkaa klah mɔɔk daq thou.
tɨw beh bənlae klah mɔɔk qaoy maq.	maq caŋ qaoy koun tɨw beh benlae klah mɔɔk qaoy maq.
tɨw tɨn qəmbaoh tməy mɔɔk qaoy maq muəy.	maq caŋ qaoy koun tɨw tɨn qəmbaoh tməy mɔɔk qaoy maq muəy.
prəñap tɨw riən.	maq caŋ qaoy koun prəñap tɨw riən.

9. Four Verbs Meaning 'to wash'

Cambodian verbs describing various ways of performing an action are
characterized by greater semantic specialization than are English verbs. The
multiplicity of verbs describing various ways of carrying was mentioned as an
example of this semantic specialization in Lesson 2, B, 1. So far we have met
four different verbs all of which can be translated 'to wash' in English:

lup   'to wash (the face); to erase (a blackboard, etc.); to cover over'
kaq   'to wash (the hair), to shampoo'
baok 'to wash (clothing), to wash by agitating'
liəŋ 'to wash (dishes, a car, the hands, etc.), to wash the surface of'

9-A. Completion Drill

Teacher	Student
koun yɔɔk caan nih tɨw ____ tɨw nəh.	koun yɔɔk caan nih tɨw liəŋ tɨw nəh.
tŋay-nih kñom caŋ ____ saq kñom.	tŋay-nih kñom caŋ kaq saq kñom.
kñom caŋ qaoy koun tɨw ____ laan.	kñom caŋ qaoy koun tɨw liəŋ laan.
kənlaeŋ nuh kee ____ khao-qaaw qaoy sqaat nah.	kənlaéŋ nuh kee baok khao-qaaw qaoy sqaat-ñah.
tŋay-nih kñom kroən-tae ____ muk tee.	tŋay-nih kñom kroən-tae lup muk tee.
kñom mɨn-toən ____ day tee.	kñom mɨn-toən liəŋ day tee.
yɔɔk plae-chəə nih tɨw ____ sən.	yɔɔk plae-chəə nih tɨw liəŋ sən.

[Tape 35]   C. COMPREHENSION

1. Two Neighbors

caaŋ: qei, phan twəə-kaa knoŋ suən-cbaa rɨɨ?

phan: baat, tee; kñom qət thəə qəy tee; kroən-tae daə məəl pkaa.
        kaal-naa kñom qət tɨw twəə-kaa, kñom coul-cət mɔɔk qəŋkuy ləəŋ
        nɨw kənlaeŋ nih.
        miən qakah trəceəq lqaa; qəŋkuy məəl daəm-chəə, haəy sdap caap
        yum; kuə qaoy səpbaay-cət.

caaŋ: pkaa-kolaap dael dam pii qatɨt mun, taə miən pkaa cəñ
        haəy-rɨnɨw?

phan: baat, mɨn-toən tee.
        tae miən pkaa qae-tiət riik haəy, haəy miən klən krəqoup phaaŋ.
        yii, bənlae caaŋ qaeŋ doh lqaa nah.

caaŋ: nɨŋ haəy; kñom kɨt beh yɔɔk tɨw pteəh klah.
        lŋiəc nih miən pñiəw mɔɔk craən nah, haəy prəpuən kñom trəw
        twəə mhoup-mhaa tətuəl pñiəw phaaŋ.

phan: ceik tum haəy-rɨnɨw?

caaŋ: baat, tum klah, mɨn-toən tum klah.
        tae krouc kñom tum qah haəy.
        baə phan qaeŋ trəw-kaa, kñom beh cuun klah.

phan: qaa-kun craən nah.
        cam kñom tɨw cuəy beh.

2. Discussing Pets

> [cəñcəm sat 'to keep pets, to raise animals']

qɨən: ptếəh kaem miən cəñcəm sat qəy-klah?

kaem: baat, ptếəh kñom miən cmaa muəy.

qɨən: wiə dael cap caap sii tee?

kaem: mɨn dael cap tee; cmaa kñom kcɨl nah; ceh-tae deik haal tɲay ponnoh.
coh, qɨən-qaeŋ miən cəñcəm qəy dae?

qɨən: baat, kñom miən ckae muəy.

kaem: ckae nuh thom tee?

qɨən: baat, thom nah; pɔə-kmaw.

kaem: wiə cap sat touc-touc sii tee?

qɨən: cuən-kaal kɑɑ cap dae, tae thoểmmədaa kñom qaoy wiə sii mhoup-sɑl.
tae sɑp-tɲay-nih wiə coul-cət kəkaay ruuŋ nɨw knoŋ suən-cbaa.
[khəŋ 'to be angry']
twəə qaoy paa kñom khəŋ nah.

3. Homework

khɨn: chəɨn miən dael cuəy qəwpuk-mdaay tee?

chəɨn: baat, kñom cuəy paa kñom twəə-kaa klah, haəy bɑɑŋ-srəy kñom cuəy
mdaay kñom twəə-kaa nɨw knoŋ ptếəh.
coh, khɨn-qaeŋ?

khɨn: kñom kɑɑ qəñcəŋ dae.
taə, chəɨn-qaeŋ thəə qəy-klah?

chəɨn: kñom cuəy paa dɑɑq smaw cəñ pii suən-cbaa, haəy-nɨŋ beh plae-chəə
pseiŋ-pseiŋ nɨw knoŋ cəmkaa.
coh, khɨn thəə qəy dae?

khɨn: thoểmmədaa paa kñom qaoy kñom liəŋ laan.
tae tɲay-nih kñom cuəy koểt kat smaw nɨw muk ptếəh.

chəɨn: kat smaw ruəc haəy-rɨnɨw?

khɨn: mɨn-toển ruəc tee.

chəɨn: qəñcəŋ kñom cuəy.

D. CONVERSATION

1. A Family Discusses Plans For The Day

Assign each student the role of a member of a family, such as Father, Mother, Son, Daughter, Auntie, Grandfather, etc. The teacher may also assume one of the roles. Then have them discuss plans for the day, using the reciprocal kinship pronouns illustrated in the Dialogues and in Grammar and Drills 1. The day's activities might include such things as doing housework, working in the yard, going on a picnic, taking a trip, going to the market, etc.

2. A Son Helps His Father

Have one student assume the role of the Father and another of the Son. Have the Father give the Son directions for helping him in various ways. The Son might respond to the Father's directions with objections, reservations, comments, or questions.

3. A Daughter Helps Her Mother

Have one student assume the role of the Mother and another of the Daughter. Have the Mother give the Daughter directions for helping her in various ways. The Daughter's responses might include such things as objections, reservations, comments, or questions.

4. Discussing Pets

Have two students assume roles as children (or adults) discussing their respective pets. Questions and answers might involve such things as what animals are raised, their descriptions, what their names are, what they typically do, and what they eat.

LESSON 21. RECEIVING GUESTS

A. DIALOGUE

bun

1. qoun kɨt thaa miən pñiəw mɔɔk   About how many guests do you (Wife)
   prəhael ponmaan nĕəq?   think will come?

saaŋ

    bɑɑŋ-tlay   older in-law of same generation
    bɑɑŋ-tlay-srəy   older sister-in-law
2. caah, miən tae bəy nĕəq tee, kɨɨ Well, there are only three—my older
   bɑɑŋ kñom, bɑɑŋ-tlay-srəy,   brother, [my] (older) sister-in-law,
   haəŋ-nɨŋ koun kŏət.   and their child.

but

    qom   older sibling of either parent
3. nuh, maq; kñom khəəñ qom daə   There, Mother; I see Uncle (and/or
   mɔɔk haəy.   Aunt) (walking) coming now.

    camlaek (cəmlaek)   strange, different
    mənuh-cəmlaek   stranger
4. miən mənuh-cəmlaek mɔɔk   There's a stranger (coming) with
   ciə-muəy qom phɑɑŋ.   them too.

saaŋ

5. koun-qaeŋ tɨw baək twiə qaoy qom Son, go open the gate for [your]
   coul phɑɑŋ.   Uncle (to come in).

but

    look-qom   older uncle or aunt
6. cumriəp-suə, look-qom;   Greetings, Uncle; how are you?
   sok-səpbaay ciə tee?

riəm

    kmuəy   niece or nephew
7. qaa-kun, kmuəy.   Thank you, Nephew.

    sampĕəh (səmpĕəh)   to greet with palms joined
    sampĕəh-suə   to greet
    puu   younger brother of either parent
    look-puu   younger uncle (polite)
8. sarɑan, mɔɔk səmpĕəh-suə   Saran, come greet [your] uncle.
   look-puu.

bun

9. yuu nah mɔɔk haəy bɑɑŋ mɨn dael   You haven't come to visit for a long
   mɔɔk leeŋ sɑh.   time, (Older) Brother.

riəm

10. qou, miən kaa craən nah; mɔɔk   Oh, I've been very busy; [I] can't
    leeŋ ñɨk-ñŏəp mɨn baan tee.   come visiting [very] often.

look smɨt   Mr. Smith

11. kñom nŏəm look smɨt mɔɔk leeŋ   I brought Mr. Smith to visit you; he
pqoun-qaeŋ; kŏət twəə-kaa   works with me.
ciə-muəy kñom.

                                    bun

12. soum qəñcəəñ laəŋ ləə ptĕəh.   Please come up into (onto) the house.

    mdaay-kmeik   mother-in-law
13. look smɨt, nih mdaay-kmeik   Mr. Smith, this [is] my mother-in-
kñom.   law.

                            look-yiəy

ləək   to raise, lift up
ləək day twaay prĕəh   a greeting used by some older
                                                people (lit.: lift your hands
                                                to God)

14. ləək day twaay prĕəh, koun.   Greetings, Son.

                                    but

mae   mother (respectful)
krom-hun   business, commercial company
riəm   eldest child (frequently used as a
                                                nickname for same)

15. mae, look smɨt nih twəə-kaa knoŋ   Mother, Mr. Smith here works in the
krom-hun bɑɑŋ-riəm.   [same] company with (Brother) Ream.

                            look-yiəy

caw   grandchild
caw-proh   grandson
16. koun, caw-proh mɨn mɔɔk tee rɨɨ?   Son, didn't [my] grandson come?

                                    riəm

kɑŋ   bicycle
qaa-   diminutive prefix
17. baat, mɔɔk; wiə tɨw cih kɑŋ leeŋ   Yes, [he] came; he's gone bicycle rid-
ciə-muəy qaa-bʉt haəy.   ing with little Bouth (already).

                            look-yiəy

kdaa   board, plank, flat surface
kdaa-ŋiə   a low platform or table used for
                                                sitting, sleeping, and eating
18. look qəŋkuy ləə kawqəy tɨw;   (You) have a chair; I'll sit on the
kñom qəŋkuy nɨw ləə kdaa-ŋiə.   kdaa-ŋiə.

                                    bun

19. soum qəñcəəñ pisaa barəy.   Please have (eat) a cigarette.

20. kñom miən tae barəy kmae tee;   I have only Cambodian cigarettes;
prəhael klaŋ bəntəc haəy.   [they] might be a little strong.

                                Smith

21. baat, barəy kmae mɨn-səw klaŋ   Oh, Cambodian cigarettes aren't so
ponmaan tee.   strong.

cŭəq — to inhale, to suck, to smoke
22. kñom tlŏəp cŭəq tae rŏəl tŋay. — I'm accustomed to smoking [them] (just) every day.

bun

sraa — alcohol, whisky
23. look caŋ ñam sraa tee? — Would you like to have [some] whisky?

Smith

qampii (qəmpii, mpii, pii) — of, from, consisting of
24. qɑɑ-kun; sraa nih twəə qəmpii srəw, mɛɛn rɨɨ? — Thank you; this whisky is made of rice, isn't it?

riəm

25. baat, mɛɛn haəy. — Yes, that's right.

srɑwəŋ (srəwəŋ, səwəŋ) — to be drunk, intoxicated, dizzy
26. kñom ñam sraa mɨn baan tee; kñom chap srəwəŋ nah. — I can't drink whisky; I get drunk very quickly.

bat — to disappear, to lose
27. srəy-srəy tɨw naa bat qɑh haəy? — Where did all the women disappear to?

bun

ptĕəh-baay — kitchen
28. kee nŏəm kniə tɨw niyiəy leeŋ nɨw knoŋ ptĕəh-baay. — They went off to the kitchen (together) to chat.

riəm

29. qaə, qɑɑn cəñ mɔɔk haəy. — Oh, there comes Sang now. (Sang has come out now.)

məñ (mɨñ) — last, past, preceding
qɑmbañ-məñ (qəmbañ-, mbañ-) — a moment ago, a while ago
30. qəmbañ-məñ nih yəəŋ kəmpuŋ-tae niyiəy qəmpii qɑɑn-qaeŋ. — We were just talking about you a moment ago.

bun

mhoup-cɑmnəy (-cəmnəy) — food, various kinds of food
haəy — to be ready, finished
31. mhoup-cəmnəy haəy-rɨnɨw? — Is the food ready yet?

saaŋ

32. caah, ruəc haəy. — Yes, [it's] finished already.

33. bɑɑŋ kliən baay tee? — Are you hungry, (Older) Brother?

riəm

səŋ(-tae) — almost, on the point of
dac — to be torn, burst, broken
pŭəh — stomach, intestines
dac pŭəh — to have a torn or burst stomach
slap — to die
dac pŭəh slap — to die of a torn stomach
34. qou, kliən səŋ-tae dac pŭəh slap haəy. — Oh, I'm nearly dying of hunger. (I'm hungry to the point of dying with a torn stomach.)

B. GRAMMAR AND DRILLS

1. Kinship Terminology and Related Pronouns

The basic Cambodian kinship terms were presented in Lesson 6, B, 1. There it was pointed out that Cambodian kinship terms are "classificatory" in the sense that they are based primarily on relative age rather than on sex or specific biological relationship. Thus baaŋ refers to any relative or friend who is older than the speaker but of the same generation. Sex can be specified by adding proh 'male' or sray' female' to non-sex-specific terms, e.g.: baaŋ-proh 'older male relative or friend', pqoun-sray 'younger female relative or friend'. While such terms as qəwpuk 'father' and mdaay 'mother' are unambiguous as to sex, they are classificatory as to generation, and are included in compounds referring to siblings of one's parents, e.g.: qəwpuk-thom 'older brother of either parent' and mdaay-miiŋ 'younger sister of either parent'.

The following chart attempts to provide a more or less complete picture of Cambodian kinship terminology. To do so it is necessary to distinguish between terms of reference on the one hand and terms of address (essentially the kinship pronouns described in Lesson 20, B, 1) on the other. For example, when referring to an uncle or aunt older than one's parents, one uses qəwpuk-thom and mdaay-thom respectively, but one uses look-qom in addressing either of them. Thus the terms of reference for older uncle or aunt are sex-specific, while the terms of address are not. Similarly one might say taa kñom 'my grandfather' and miiŋ kñom 'my aunt' in referring to them out of their presence, but in addressing them one would say look-taa and neəq-miiŋ respectively. Furthermore in terms of address the reflexive pronoun qaeŋ 'yourself, oneself' is frequently added to the kinship pronoun to soften a direct address, as in koun-qaeŋ 'you (Child) yourself' and baaŋ-qaeŋ 'you (Older Brother) yourself' or 'you (Husband) yourself'.

The following chart also includes the pronouns which would normally be associated with each term of reference (3rd person pronoun) and term of address (2nd person pronoun), since there is an overlapping of function between the two classes of words. It should be reemphasized, however, that the use of 2nd person pronouns in Cambodian is very rare, their function usually being assumed by a kinship term, a kinship term plus the addressee's personal name, or the addressee's personal name plus the reflexive pronoun qaeŋ. All terms which have not been previously introduced are preceded by an asterisk.

Relationship	Sex	Terms of Reference	Terms of Address
Father		(look)qəwpuk, *(look)qəw, (look)paa; koət	(look)qəwpuk, (look)qəw, (look)paa, *puk
Mother		(look)mdaay, (look)mae, maq, neəq-mdaay; koət	(look)mae, neəq-mdaay, maq; neəq
Son	m.	koun(proh); name; wiə, kee	koun(qaeŋ); name(qaeŋ); qaa-name
Daughter	f.	koun(sray); name; wiə, kee	koun(qaeŋ); name(qaeŋ); qaa-name; *niəŋ

Relationship	Sex	Terms of Reference	Terms of Address
Older sibling, relative, or friend of same generation	m.	bɑɑŋ(proh); name; kŏət, kee	bɑɑŋ(qaeŋ), look-bɑɑŋ; name(qaeŋ)
	f.	bɑɑŋ(srəy); name; kŏət, kee	bɑɑŋ(qaeŋ), neə̆q-bɑɑŋ; name(qaeŋ)
Younger sibling, friend, or relative of same generation	m.	pqoun(proh); name; wiə, kee	pqoun(qaeŋ); name(qaeŋ); qaa-name
	f.	pqoun(srəy); name; wiə, kee	pqoun(qaeŋ); name(qaeŋ); qaa-name
Grandfather; old man		(look)taa; kŏət	look-taa
Grandmother; old woman		(look)yiəy; kŏət	look-yiəy
Gt.-Grandfather		*taa-tuət, (look)taa; kŏət	look-taa
Gt.-Grandmother		*yiəy-tuət, (look)yiəy; kŏət	look-yiəy
Gt.-Gt.-Grandfather		*taa-luət, look-taa; kŏət	look-taa
Gt.-Gt.-Grandmother		*yiəy-luət, look-yiəy; kŏət	look-yiəy
Gt.-Gt.-Gt.-Grandfather		*taa-liə, look-taa kŏət	look-taa
Gt.-Gt.-Gt.-Grandmother		*yiəy-liə, look-yiəy; kŏət	look-yiəy
Grandson; or friend of grandson's generation		caw(proh); name; wiə, kee	caw(qaeŋ), koun-caw; name(qaeŋ); qaa-name
Granddaughter, or friend of granddaughter's generation		caw(srəy); name; wiə, kee	caw(qaeŋ), koun-caw; name(qaeŋ); qaa-name
Gt.-Grandson		*caw-tuət(proh); name; wiə, kee	caw(qaeŋ), koun-caw; name(qaeŋ); qaa-name
Gt.-Granddaughter		*caw-tuət(srəy); name; wiə, kee	caw(qaeŋ), koun-caw; name(qaeŋ); qaa-name

Relationship	Sex	Terms of Reference	Terms of Address
Gt.-Gt.-Grandson		*caw-luət(proh); name; wiə, kee	caw(qaeŋ), koun-caw; name(qaeŋ); qaa-name
Gt.-Gt.-Grand- daughter		*caw-luət(srəy); name; wiə, kee	caw(qaeŋ), koun-caw; name(qaeŋ); qaa-name
Gt.-Gt.-Gt.-Grand- son		*caw-liə(proh); name; wiə, kee	caw(qaeŋ), koun-caw; name(qaeŋ); qaa-name
Gt.-Gt.-Gt.- Granddaughter		*caw-liə(srəy); name; wiə, kee	caw(qaeŋ), koun-caw name(qaeŋ); qaa-name
Older sibling or friend of either parent	m.	qəwpuk-thom, qom(proh), look-qom; kŏət	look-qom; qom-name; look
	f.	mdaay-thom, qom(srəy), look-qom; kŏət	look-qom; qom-name; look
Younger sibling or friend of either parent	m.	(qəwpuk)miə, (look)puu; kŏət	look-puu; puu-name; look
	f.	(mdaay)miiŋ, nĕəq-miiŋ; kŏət	nĕəq-miiŋ; miiŋ-name; nĕəq
Nephew, or friend of nephew's generation		kmuəy(proh); name; wiə, kee	kmuəy(qaeŋ); name(qaeŋ)
Niece, or friend of niece's generation		kmuəy(srəy); name; wiə, kee	kmuəy(qaeŋ); name(qaeŋ); niəŋ
Older first cousin (having the same grandparents)	m.	baaŋ-cii-doun-muəy (proh); name; kŏət, kee	baaŋ(qaeŋ), look-baaŋ; name(qaeŋ)
	f.	baaŋ-cii-doun-muəy (srəy); name; kŏət, kee	baaŋ(qaeŋ), nĕəq-baaŋ; name(qaeŋ)
Younger first cousin (having the same grandparents)	m.	pqoun-cii-doun-muəy (proh); name; wiə, kee	pqoun(qaeŋ); name(qaeŋ); qaa-name
	f.	pqoun-cii-doun-muəy (srəy); name; wiə, kee	pqoun(qaeŋ); name(qaeŋ); qaa-name; nĕəq
Older second cousin (having the same gt.-grandparents)	m.	*baaŋ-cii-tuət-muəy (proh); name; kŏət, kee	baaŋ(qaeŋ), look-baaŋ; name(qaeŋ)
	f.	*baaŋ-cii-tuət-muəy (srəy); name; kŏət, kee	baaŋ(qaeŋ), nĕəq-baaŋ; name(qaeŋ)
Younger second cousin (having the same gt.-grandparents)	m.	*pqoun-cii-tuət-muəy (proh); name; wiə, kee	pqoun(qaeŋ); name(qaeŋ); qaa-name
	f.	*pqoun-cii-tuət-muəy (srəy); name; wiə, kee	pqoun(qaeŋ); name(qaeŋ); qaa-name; nĕəq

Relationship	Sex	Terms of Reference	Terms of Address
Older third cousin (having the same gt.-gt.-grand-parents	m.	*baaŋ-cii-luət-muəy (proh); name; kŏət, kee	baaŋ(qaeŋ), look-baaŋ; name(qaeŋ)
	f.	*baaŋ-cii-luət-muəy (srəy); name; kŏət, kee	baaŋ(qaeŋ), nĕəq-baaŋ; name(qaeŋ)
Younger third cousin (having the same gt.-gt.-grandparents)	m.	*pqoun-cii-luət-muəy (proh); name; wiə, kee	pqoun(qaeŋ); name(qaeŋ); qaa-name
	f.	*pqoun-cii-luət-muəy (srəy); name; wiə, kee	pqoun(qaeŋ); name(qaeŋ); qaa-name; nĕəq
Husband		pdəy, baaŋ, *qəwpuk-wiə, *swaaməy (lit.); kŏət, kee	baaŋ(qaeŋ), qəwpuk-wiə; name(qaeŋ); look
Wife		prapuən, *mdaay-wiə, *phĕəqriyiə (lit.); kŏət	qoun(qaeŋ), niəŋ(qaeŋ), mdaay-wiə; name(qaeŋ)
Older in-law of same generation	m.	baaŋ-tlay(proh); name; kŏət, kee	baaŋ(qaeŋ); look-baaŋ; name(qaeŋ)
	f.	baaŋ-tlay(srəy); name; kŏət, kee	baaŋ(qaeŋ), nĕəq-baaŋ; name(qaeŋ)
Younger in-law of same generation	m.	pqoun-tlay(proh); name; wiə, kee	pqoun(qaeŋ); name(qaeŋ); qaa-name
	f.	pqoun-tlay(srəy); name; wiə, kee	pqoun(qaeŋ); name(qaeŋ); qaa-name
Father-in-law		qəwpuk-kmeik; kŏət	look-qəwpuk, look-qom, look-puu
Mother-in-law		mdaay-kmeik; kŏət	nĕəq-mdaay, look-qom nĕəq-miiŋ; nĕəq
Son-in-law		*koun-prasaa(proh); name; wiə, kee	koun(qaeŋ); name(qaeŋ); qaa-name
Daughter-in-law		*koun-prasaa(srəy); name; wiə, kee	koun(qaeŋ); name(qaeŋ); qaa-name

In addition to the terms appearing in the chart, terms of reference and address may also consist of the appropriate kinship term plus a personal name, e.g.: baaŋ-riəm 'Older Brother Ream', qom-saaŋ '(Older) Uncle Sâng', koun-but 'Son Bouth', and caw-laa 'Grand(son) Laa'.

1-A. Substitution-Translation Drill

Teacher	Student
mənuh nuh kɨɨ ciə nephew kñom.	mənuh nuh kɨɨ ciə kmuəy-proh kñom.
grandfather	mənuh nuh kɨɨ ciə taa kñom.
younger uncle	mənuh nuh kɨɨ ciə (qəwpuk-miə, puu) kñom.

Teacher	Student
older brother-in-law	mənuh nuh kɨɨ ciə baaŋ-tlay-proh kñom.
older first cousin	mənuh nuh kɨɨ ciə baaŋ-cii-doun-muəy kñom.
mother-in-law	mənuh nuh kɨɨ ciə mdaay-kmeik kñom.
niece	mənuh nuh kɨɨ ciə kmuəy-srəy kñom.
older aunt	mənuh nuh kɨɨ ciə (mdaay-thom, qom) kñom.
younger female first cousin	mənuh nuh kɨɨ ciə pqoun-cii-doun-muəy-srəy kñom.
son-in-law	mənuh nuh kɨɨ ciə koun-prəsaa-proh kñom.
granddaughter	mənuh nuh kɨɨ ciə caw-srəy kñom.
son	mənuh nuh kɨɨ ciə koun-proh kñom.
father-in-law	mənuh nuh kɨɨ ciə qəwpuk-kmeik kñom.
younger sister-in-law	mənuh nuh kɨɨ ciə pqoun-tlay-srəy kñom.
older male first cousin	mənuh nuh kɨɨ ciə baaŋ-cii-doun-muəy-proh kñom.
older second cousin	mənuh nuh kɨɨ ciə baaŋ-cii-tuət-muəy kñom.
younger third cousin	mənuh nuh kɨɨ ciə pqoun-cii-luət-muəy kñom.
great-grandfather	mənuh nuh kɨɨ ciə taa-tuət kñom.
younger aunt	mənuh nuh kɨɨ ciə (mdaay-miiŋ, miiŋ) kñom.
great-great-grandmother	mənuh nuh kɨɨ ciə yiəy-luət kñom.
great-grandson	mənuh nuh kɨɨ ciə caw-tuət kñom.
great-great-granddaughter	mənuh nuh kɨɨ ciə caw-luət-srəy kñom.
older brother-in-law	mənuh nuh kɨɨ ciə baaŋ-tlay-proh kñom.
great-great-great-grandfather	mənuh nuh kɨɨ ciə taa-liə kñom.
older female third cousin	mənuh nuh kɨɨ ciə baaŋ-cii-luət-muəy-srəy kñom.

1-B. Completion Drill

It can be seen from the chart that koət may generally be used to refer to any older or respected person, such as grandparents, relatives of one's parents' generation, and older friends or relatives of one's own generation, while wiə may be used for persons who are younger and/or lower in status than the speaker, such as younger friends or relatives of one's own, one's children's, or one's grandchildren's generation. Use koət or wiə as appropriate in the completion of the following sentences.

Teacher	Student
look-taa kñom mɨn nɨw pteəh tee.	look-taa kñom mɨn nɨw pteəh tee; koət tɨw psaa haəy.
koun kñom mɨn nɨw pteəh tee.	koun kñom mɨn nɨw pteəh tee; wiə tɨw psaa haəy.

miiŋ kñom mɨn nɨw pteˇəh tee.

miiŋ kñom mɨn nɨw pteˇəh tee;
koˇət tɨw psaa haəy.

qəwpuk-kmeik kñom mɨn nɨw pteˇəh tee.

qəwpuk-kmeik kñom mɨn nɨw pteˇəh tee;
koˇət tɨw psaa haəy.

baaŋ-tlay kñom mɨn nɨw pteˇəh tee.

baaŋ-tlay kñom mɨn nɨw pteˇəh tee;
koˇət tɨw psaa haəy.

pdəy kñom mɨn nɨw pteˇəh tee.

pdəy kñom mɨn nɨw pteˇəh tee;
koˇət tɨw psaa haəy.

mdaay-thom kñom mɨn nɨw pteˇəh tee.

mdaay-thom kñom mɨn nɨw pteˇəh tee;
koˇət tɨw psaa haəy.

kmuəy kñom mɨn nɨw pteˇəh tee.

kmuəy kñom mɨn nɨw pteˇəh tee;
wiə tɨw psaa haəy.

koun-caw kñom mɨn nɨw pteˇəh tee.

koun-caw kñom mɨn nɨw pteˇəh tee;
wiə tɨw psaa haəy.

puu kñom mɨn nɨw pteˇəh tee.

puu kñom mɨn nɨw pteˇəh tee;
koˇət tɨw psaa haəy.

koun-prəsaa kñom mɨn nɨw pteˇəh tee.

koun-prəsaa kñom mɨn nɨw pteˇəh tee;
wiə tɨw psaa haəy.

pqoun-tlay kñom mɨn nɨw pteˇəh tee.

pqoun-tlay kñom mɨn nɨw pteˇəh tee;
wiə tɨw psaa haəy.

2. The Adverbial Phrase yuu nah mɔɔk haəy

In Lesson 5, B, 8 we met the adverbial phrase yuu nah mɔɔk haəy 'for a long time now (up to the present)' in final position and introduced by ciə, as in

kñom caŋ məəl qəŋkɔɔ-woˇət
ciə yuu nah mɔɔk haəy.

I've wanted to see Angkor Wat
for a long time now.

In this lesson, yuu nah mɔɔk haəy occurs as a preposed adverbial phrase without the copulative ciə, as in

yuu nah mɔɔk haəy baaŋ mɨn dael
mɔɔk leeŋ sah.

You (baaŋ) haven't come to visit
for a long time now.

2-A. Transformation Drill

Teacher	Student
baaŋ mɨn dael mɔɔk leeŋ ciə yuu nah mɔɔk haəy.	yuu nah mɔɔk haəy baaŋ mɨn dael mɔɔk leeŋ sah.
mdaay-miiŋ mɨn dael tɨw psaa ciə yuu nah mɔɔk haəy.	yuu nah mɔɔk haəy mdaay-miiŋ mɨn dael tɨw psaa sah.
kñom mɨn baan tɨw riən ciə yuu nah mɔɔk haəy.	yuu nah mɔɔk haəy kñom mɨn baan tɨw riən sah.
kñom keeŋ mɨn luˇəq ciə yuu nah mɔɔk haəy.	yuu nah mɔɔk haəy kñom keeŋ mɨn luˇəq sah.

Teacher	Student
kñom mɨn baan tətuəl-tiən mhoup ciə yuu nah mɔɔk haəy.	yuu nah mɔɔk haəy kñom mɨn baan tətuəl-tiən mhoup sah.
kñom mɨn dael tɨw qəŋkɔɔ-woət ciə yuu nah mɔɔk haəy.	yuu nah mɔɔk haəy kñom mɨn dael tɨw qəŋkɔɔ-woət sah.
look-taa mɨn dael məəl kasaet ciə yuu nah mɔɔk haəy.	yuu nah mɔɔk haəy look-taa mɨn dael məəl kasaet sah.
qəwpuk mɨn dael liəŋ laan ciə yuu nah mɔɔk haəy.	yuu nah mɔɔk haəy qəwpuk mɨn dael liəŋ laan sah.
yəəŋ mɨn dael tətuəl pñiəw ciə yuu nah mɔɔk haəy.	yuu nah mɔɔk haəy yəəŋ mɨn dael tətuəl pñiəw sah.

3. The Meaning of leeŋ

The word leeŋ has a wide semantic range, as illustrated by the following sentences:

kñom coul-cət tɨw daə-leeŋ.	I like to go around for fun.
yəəŋ kəmpuŋ-tae niyiəy kniə leeŋ.	We're just chatting (talking for fun).
kon nih cap leeŋ haəy.	This film has started playing already.
kee leeŋ pleeŋ baək chaaq haəy.	They're playing the overture already.
look coul-cət leeŋ biə tee?	Do you like to play cards?
wiə tɨw leeŋ ciə-muəy but haəy.	He's gone to play with Bouth.

In all of the above occurrences, leeŋ always includes an element of amusement or enjoyment. Thus it is not inconsistent that it should also occur with the meaning 'to visit, to enjoy oneself by visiting', as in

yuu nah mɔɔk haəy baaŋ mɨn dael mɔɔk leeŋ sah.	You haven't come to visit for a long time now.
kñom noəm look smɨt mɔɔk leeŋ nɨŋ pqoun-qaeŋ.	I brought Mr. Smith along to visit with you.
knom tɨw leeŋ pteəh puəq-maaq məneəq.	I went to visit the home of a friend.

3-A. Substitution Drill

Teacher	Student
kñom mɨn dael tɨw leeŋ pteəh look sah.	kñom mɨn dael tɨw leeŋ pteəh look sah.
qəŋkɔɔ-woət	kñom mɨn dael tɨw leeŋ qəŋkɔɔ-woət sah.
pnum-pɨñ	kñom mɨn dael tɨw leeŋ pnum-pɨñ sah.
pteəh baaŋ	kñom mɨn dael tɨw leeŋ pteəh baaŋ sah.
kaep	kñom mɨn dael tɨw leeŋ kaep sah.
pteəh kee	kñom mɨn dael tɨw leeŋ pteəh kee sah.
suən-cbaa nuh	kñom mɨn dael tɨw leeŋ suən-cbaa nuh sah.
woət-pnum	kñom mɨn dael tɨw leeŋ woət-pnum sah.

4. Context-Oriented Vocabulary

In many areas of vocabulary, such as pronouns, response particles, and common content-words such as 'to eat,' 'to sleep,' and parts of the body, Cambodian has specialized vocabulary for royalty, the clergy, and commoners, although basic function-words (such as conjunctions and auxiliaries) are shared by all three levels. Even within the level of common vocabulary, the choice of a word tends to be context-oriented, much like kinship terms and pronouns. One of the fullest illustrations of context-oriented vocabulary can be found in the various terms for 'to eat', as shown in the following list. Those terms not yet introduced are preceded by an asterisk.

pisaa	formal, polite, with reference to guests or superiors
tɔtuəl-tiən	formal, polite, with reference to oneself (literally: to receive a gift)
ñam	familiar, between equals
sii	(to consume) with reference to animals, machines, inferiors
*baariphook	elegant, literary
*phook-kdaa	literary
*houp	dialectal, rural
*chan	with reference to clergy
*saoy	with reference to royalty
*chəy	literary

4-A. Completion Drill

Complete the following sentences with one of the first four terms in the list above, all of which have been introduced in the lessons. It may be possible to use more than one of the four terms in some of the slots, since it is difficult to convey total context in a single sentence. The student should therefore accept the usage of the teacher.

Teacher	Student
qəñcəəñ look mɔɔk ____ baay nɨw pteəh kñom.	qəñcəəñ look mɔɔk pisaa baay nɨw pteəh kñom.
qaa-kun look nəh, kñom ____ baay ruəc-haəy.	qaa-kun look nəh, kñom tɔtuəl-tiən baac ruəc-haəy.
mɔɔk tɨw ____ baay nɨw haaŋ nuh sən.	mɔɔk tɨw ñam baay nɨw haaŋ nuh sən.
yɔɔk mhoup-sɑl nih tɨw qaoy ckae ____.	yɔɔk mhoup-sɑl nih tɨw qaoy ckae sii.
look qəñcəəñ ____ barəy tee?	look qəñcəəñ pisaa barəy tee?
qəwpuk-kmeik kñom haw kñom tɨw ____ baay.	qəwpuk-kmeik kñom haw kñom tɨw tɔtuəl-tiən baay.
neəq-dəmnaə craən-tae ____ baay nɨw ləə kəpal.	neəq-dəmnaə craən-tae ñam baay nɨw ləə kəpal.
laan kñom ____ saŋ craən nah.	laan kñom sii saŋ craən nah.

5. The Meaning of tae

tae has been met with the meanings 'only' and 'but', as in

kñom trəw-kaa tae kənlah lou tee.	I need only a half-dozen.
phiəsaa cən sruəl niyiəy, tae pibaaq səsei.	Chinese is easy to speak, but difficult to write.

But the semantic range of tae is broader than that of the two English words 'but' and 'only'; in many occurrences it seems to have the meaning 'just, precisely, exactly, specifically', as in

kñom tloŏp cuŏq tae roŏl tŋay.   I'm used to smoking [them] (precisely) every day.

tae seems to have a similar meaning in compound auxiliaries:

koŏt tŏŏp-tae cŏñ pii pteŏh.   He has just now left the house.
yŏŏŋ kŏmpuŋ-tae niyiŏy leeŋ.   We're just chatting.

5-A. Substitution Drill

Teacher	Student
kñom tloŏp cuŏq tae roŏl tŋay.	kñom tloŏp cuŏq tae roŏl tŋay.
ñam sraa	kñom tloŏp ñam sraa tae roŏl tŋay.
daŏ-leeŋ	kñom tloŏp daŏ-leeŋ tae roŏl tŋay.
tɨw mŏŏl kon	kñom tloŏp tɨw mŏŏl kon tae roŏl tŋay.
leeŋ biŏ	kñom tloŏp leeŋ biŏ tae roŏl tŋay.
ñam mhoup hŏl	kñom tloŏp ñam mhoup hŏl tae roŏl tŋay.
phŏk byiŏ	kñom tloŏp phŏk byeŏ tae roŏl tŋay.
tɨw pnum-pɨñ	kñom tloŏp tɨw pnum-pɨñ tae roŏl tŋay.

5-B. Expansion Drill

Teacher	Student
kñom tɨw twŏŏ-kaa roŏl tŋay.	kñom tɨw twŏŏ-kaa tae roŏl tŋay.
kñom tɨw daŏ-leeŋ roŏl yup.	kñom tɨw daŏ-leeŋ tae roŏl yup.
kñom tɨw pnum-pɨñ roŏl qatɨt.	kñom tɨw pnum-pɨñ tae roŏl qatɨt.
qŏwpuk kñom tɨw srok-baraŋ roŏl cnam.	qŏwpuk kñom tɨw srok-baraŋ tae roŏl cnam.
kñom tŏtuŏl praq-khae roŏl khae.	kñom tŏtuŏl praq-khae tae roŏl khae.
kñom ŋuut-tɨk roŏl prɨk.	kñom ŋuut-tɨk tae roŏl tŋay.
miŏn rŏteh-plŏŏŋ cŏñ roŏl maoŋ.	miŏn rŏteh-plŏŏŋ cŏñ tae roŏl maoŋ.
koŏt tɨñ laan tmŏy roŏl cnam.	koŏt tɨñ laan tmŏy tae roŏl cnam.

6. chap as a Modal Verb

chap as a modal verb means 'to be quick to, to be inclined to, as in

kñom ñam sraa mɨn baan tee;   I can't drink whisky; I get drunk very
kñom chap srŏwŏŋ nah.   quickly. (I'm very quick to get drunk.)

baŏ yŏŏŋ ñam taam plŏw, muk-tae   If we eat [it] along the way, [it'll]
chap qɑh haŏy.   likely be used up quickly. (It'll likely
                                     be quick to be consumed.)

6-A. Substitution Drill

Teacher	Student
qŏwpuk kñom chap srŏwŏŋ nah.	qŏwpuk kñom chap srŏwŏŋ nah.
khŏŋ	qŏwpuk kñom chap khŏŋ nah.
qɑh-kŏmlaŋ	qŏwpuk kñom chap qɑh-kŏmlaŋ nah.

Teacher	Student
cqaet	qəwpuk kñom chap <u>cqaet</u> nah.
keeŋ luəq	qəwpuk kñom chap <u>keeŋ luəq</u> nah.
pñeəq	qəwpuk kñom chap <u>pñeəq</u> nah.
səpbaay	qəwpuk kñom chap <u>səpbaay</u> nah.

7. bat qah haəy

The phrase <u>bat qah haəy</u> frequently occurs in an adverbial function with the meaning 'all disappeared, every last one of them', as in

| srəy-srəy tɨw naa <u>bat qah haəy</u>? | Where did all the women disappear to? (Where did the women go <u>disappearing completely</u>?) |
| kee tɨw pnum-pɨñ <u>bat qah haəy</u>. | They've all gone to Phnom Penh. (They've gone to Phnom Penh, <u>every last one of them</u>.) |

7-A. Substitution Drill

Teacher	Student
kee <u>tɨw pnum-pɨñ</u> bat qah haəy.	kee <u>tɨw pnum-pɨñ</u> bat qah haəy.
tɨw məəl kon	kee <u>tɨw məəl kon</u> bat qah haəy.
tɨw twəə-kaa	kee <u>tɨw twəə-kaa</u> bat qah haəy.
tɨw ñam sraa	kee <u>tɨw ñam sraa</u> bat qah haəy.
kaa prəpuən	kee <u>kaa prəpuən</u> bat qah haəy.
tɨw srok-baraŋ	kee <u>tɨw srok-baraŋ</u> bat qah haəy.
tɨw baarəteeh	kee <u>tɨw baarəteeh</u> bat qah haəy.
tɨw daə-leeŋ	kee <u>tɨw daə-leeŋ</u> bat qah haəy.

8. The Adverbial qambañ-məñ

We have met the element <u>məñ</u> 'last, just past, just preceding' in <u>pii msəl-məñ</u> 'yesterday'. It also occurs in <u>yup məñ</u> 'last night'. In this lesson it occurs in the compound adverbial <u>qambañ-məñ</u> 'a moment ago, a while ago, just now', as in

| <u>qambañ-məñ</u> nih yəəŋ kəmpuŋ-tae niyiəy qəmpii qoun-qaeŋ. | We were just now (just a moment ago) talking about you (qoun). |

Frequently <u>qambañ-məñ</u> co-occurs with the preverbal auxiliary <u>teep-nɨŋ</u> 'just, just now', as in

| kee <u>təəp-nɨŋ</u> cəñ tɨw <u>qambañ-məñ</u>. | They <u>just</u> left <u>a moment ago</u>. |

8-A. Substitution Drill

Teacher	Student
kee təəp-nɨŋ <u>cəñ tɨw</u> qambañ-məñ.	kee təəp-nɨŋ <u>cəñ tɨw</u> qambañ-məñ.
coul mɔɔk	kee təəp-nɨŋ <u>coul mɔɔk</u> qambañ-məñ.
baək chaaq	kee təəp-nɨŋ <u>baək chaaq</u> qambañ-məñ.
niyiəy qəmpii look	kee təəp-nɨŋ <u>niyiəy qəmpii look</u> qəmbañ-məñ.

Teacher	Student
ñam sraa	kee təəp-nɨŋ ñam sraa qəmbañ-məñ.
mɔɔk dɑl	kee təəp-nɨŋ mɔɔk dɑl qəmbañ-məñ.
baək twiə	kee təəp-nɨŋ baək twiə qəmbañ-məñ.
chup twəə-kaa	kee təəp-nɨŋ chup twəə-kaa qəmbañ-məñ.
pdaəm leeŋ	kee təəp-nɨŋ pdaəm leeŋ qəmbañ-məñ.

9. The Auxiliary səŋ(-tae)

səŋ-tae is a preverbal auxiliary which means 'almost, to the extent of, on the point of'. It frequently occurs without the element -tae with no apparent change of meaning.

qou, kliən səŋ-tae dac puˇəh slap haəy.	Oh, I'm nearly dying of hunger! (I'm hungry to the point of dying of a torn stomach.)

9-A. Substitution Drill

Teacher	Student
kñom kliən səŋ-tae slap haəy.	kñom kliən səŋ-tae slap haəy.
rəŋiə	kñom rəŋiə səŋ-tae slap haəy.
srəlañ srəy nuh	kñom srəlañ srəy nuh səŋ-tae slap haəy.
riən	kñom riən səŋ-tae slap haəy.
kcɨl	kñom kcɨl səŋ-tae slap haəy.
qɑh-kəmlaŋ	kñom qɑh-kəmlaŋ səŋ-tae slap haəy.
hael-tɨk	kñom hael-tɨk səŋ-tae slap haəy.
ñam sraa	kñom ñam sraa səŋ-tae slap haəy.
ruˇət prənaŋ	kñom ruˇət prənaŋ səŋ-tae slap haəy.
khəŋ	kñom khəŋ səŋ-tae slap haəy.

[Tape 37]   C. COMPREHENSION

1. An Invitation

suən: cumriəp-suə, neˇəq-miiŋ.

miiŋ: ləək day twaay preˇəh, kmuəy.
kmuəy mɔɔk qəŋkuy ləə kawqəy nih.
yuu nah mɔɔk haəy kmuəy mɨn dael mɔɔk leeŋ miiŋ sɑh.

suən: baat, kñom miən kaa craən nah.
sɑp-tŋay-nih, kñom rəwuəl luˇəq siəwphɨw.

miiŋ: kmuəy cap luˇəq pii tŋay naa?

suən: baat, pii qatɨt mun.

miiŋ: qəwpuk-mdaay kmuəy sok-səpbaay ciə tee?

suən: baat, koˇət sok-səpbaay ciə tee.
maq qaoy kñom mɔɔk qəñcəəñ neˇəq-miiŋ haəy-nɨŋ look-puu tɨw pisaa baay pteˇəh kñom nɨw tŋay-put kraoy.

miiŋ: cumriəp maq thaa miiŋ qɑɑ-kun craən nah.
       qaoy miiŋ tɨw maoŋ ponmaan?

suən: baat, maoŋ prammuəy lŋiəc.
       baaŋ kñom dael twəə tiəhiən nuh koət kɑɑ mɔɔk leeŋ pteəh dae nɨw
       tŋay nuh.

       [cuəp-cum 'to meet together']
miiŋ: qəñcəŋ cuəp-cum kniə craən nah.
       taa haəy-nɨŋ yiəy sok-səpbaay ciə tee?

suən: baat, koət sok-səpbaay ciə tee.

miiŋ: kmuəy ñam qəy bəntəc-bəntuəc sən rɨɨ?

suən: baat, mɨn-qəy tee.

2. Discussing a Wedding

       [sambot-kaa 'wedding invitation']
miəq: qou, kñom təəp-nɨŋ tətuəl səmbot-kaa muəy.
       baaŋ-cii-doun-muəy kñom koət riəp-kaa.

phɔɔn: baaŋ-cii-doun-muəy look riəp-kaa nɨw qae-naa?

suən: koət riəp-kaa nɨw khaet prɨy-wɛɛŋ.
       kñom khaan cuəp koət pram cnam mɔɔk haəy.

       [thom-dom 'big, important, impressive']
       [qɨkkəthɨk 'loud and boistrous, festive, gay']
phɔɔn: kaa thom-dom qɨkkəthɨk nah, məəl-tɨw.

suən: baat, nɨŋ haəy.
       [wuĕŋ-dantrəy 'orchestra, circle of musicians']
       [kamdɑɑ (kəmdɑɑ, kədɑɑ) 'to accompany, attend, assist at']
       miən haw pñiəw craən nah, haəy miən wuĕŋ-dantrəy mɔɔk leeŋ
       kəmdɑɑ phɑɑŋ.

       [cɑɑŋ-day 'to make a presentation to newlyweds (literally: to tie
         the hands)']
phɔɔn: look baan qəy yɔɔk tɨw cɑɑŋ-day baaŋ look?

suən: kñom kɨt tɨñ prəqɑp barəy praq yɔɔk tɨw cɑɑŋ-day koət.

       [thɑɑt ruup 'to take a picture, to photograph']
       [masɨn-thɑɑt-ruup 'camera']
phɔɔn: look miən yɔɔk masɨn-thɑɑt-ruup tɨw ciə-muəy phɑɑŋ tee?

suən: baat, thəy mɨn yɔɔk.

3. Making a Date by Telephone

Operator: look cɑŋ haw leik ponmaan?

kaaŋ: baat, leik pram-rɔɔy hoksəp-buən.

               [qaloo 'hello']
neəq-bamraə: qaloo, look cɑŋ niyiəy ciə-muəy neəq-naa?

kaaŋ: baat, kñom cɑŋ niyiəy ciə-muəy look-sɑɑŋ; koət nɨw pteəh
               tee?

neəq-bɑmraə: caah, nɨw; soum look cam məplɛɛt.

saɑŋ: qaloo, neəq-naa nɨŋ?

kaɑŋ: kɲom kaɑŋ.
               saɑŋ qaeŋ kəmpuŋ thəə qəy nɨŋ?

saɑŋ: qou, kəmpuŋ məəl siəwphɨw.
               bɑɑŋ qaeŋ miən kaa qəy tee?

kaɑŋ: tee, kmiən kaa qəy tee; kɲom cɑŋ haw tɨw məəl kon.

saɑŋ: kee leeŋ rɨəŋ qəy?

kaɑŋ: miən rɨəŋ kəmplaeŋ muəy leeŋ nɨw qaa-Hawaii.

saɑŋ: qou, kɲom cɑŋ məəl rɨəŋ nuh yuu nah mɔɔk haəy.

kaɑŋ: qəɲcəŋ maoŋ prampɨl kɲom mɔɔk tətuəl nəh.

saɑŋ: nɨŋ haəy; qɑɑ-kun craən; liə haəy.

kaɑŋ: liə haəy.

D. CONVERSATION

1. Discussing Relatives

Have the students address questions to each other concerning various
relatives. Questions and answers might involve such things as how many older
and younger uncles and aunts one has, what work they do, how old they are, and
where they live.

2. Conversations between Relatives

Have each two students assume the roles of two relatives of differing
generations, such as a father and son, a grandmother and granddaughter, an
uncle and nephew, an aunt and niece, etc. Topics might include such things as
what activities each is engaged in at present, questions about common relatives,
etc.

3. Receiving Guests

Assign the role of host or hostess to one student and the role of guest to another. Topics for discussion might include invitations on the part of the host to
sit down, to have some food, cigarettes, or whisky, and questions about common
friends or relatives.

4. A Telephone Conversation

Have each student simulate a telephone call to another. If so desired, a
third and fourth student may assume the roles of the operator and the servant.
Topics of conversation might include an invitation to go to a movie, to go out to
eat, to come to the caller's house for a meal, an invitation to go to a wedding,
etc.

LESSON 22. AT THE HOSPITAL

[Tape 38]   A. DIALOGUE

manii

kaət   to be born, to give birth; to
                              happen, arise, develop; (here:
                              to catch a disease, etc.)
sruəl kluən   to feel well, to be well
1. kñom mɨn dəŋ ciə kaət qəy tee;   I don't know what [I've] got; I never
   ceh-tae mɨn sruəl kluən.   feel good (I'm always feeling unwell).

sarɨn

chɨɨ   to be ill, to hurt
2. chɨɨ yaaŋ məc?   What hurts? (How are you sick?)

manii

kdaw kluən   to feel hot
kbaal   head
chɨɨ kbaal   to have a headache
3. kñom kdaw kluən haəy-nɨŋ chɨɨ   I feel hot and I have a headache.
   kbaal.

sarɨn

krun   to have a fever
4. prəhael ciə krun haəy, qəñcəŋ.   Maybe you have a fever, then.

leep   to swallow
kroəp   specifier for grains, pills
5. leep tnam pii kroəp nih, haəy   Take (swallow) these two pills, and
   keeŋ tɨw.   lie down.

kroən-baə   to be better, improved
6. məc, kroən-baə haəy-rɨnɨw? How about it, do you feel better yet?

manii

7. mɨn kroən-baə ponmaan tee.   I'm not much better.

yuu-yuu-mədaaŋ   once in a while, from time to
                            time, intermittently
ñɔə   to tremble, to shake
ñɔə kluən   to tremble, to shake
kdaw-rɔŋiə   to be intermittently hot and cold,
                            to have chills
8. yuu-yuu-mədaaŋ kñom ñɔə kluən   From time to time I tremble, and
   haəy kdaw-rəŋiə.   I've got chills.

sarɨn

9. qəñcəŋ kñom tɨw rɔɔk haw   In that case, I'm going to call a doctor.
   kruu-pɛɛt sən.

[Later]

kruu-pɛɛt

biəm   to hold in the mouth
teəmoumaet   thermometer

10.   som biəm teəmoumaet nih məəl.   Please hold this thermometer in your mouth [and we'll] see.

kamdaw (kəmdaw, kədaw)   heat, temperature
qaŋsaa   degree (of temperature)

11.   yii, look krun klaŋ nah! miən kəmdaw dɑl tɨw saesəp qaŋsaa.   Say, you have a high (strong) fever! [Your] temperature's up to forty degrees.

tnam-krun   fever-medicine

12.   kñom nɨŋ caq tnam-krun cuun look.   I'll give you an injection of fever-medicine.

bañcuun (bəñcuun, pəcuun)   to send
keeŋ pɛɛt   to be hospitalized, to sleep in the hospital

13.   ruəc kñom trəw bəñcuun look qaoy tɨw keeŋ pɛɛt.   Then I'll have to send you to stay in the hospital.

pradap-pradaa (prədap-prədaa)   instruments, equipment

krup-sɑp   every, all, complete
pyiəbaal   to treat, care for
cumŋɨɨ   illness, disease
neəq-cumŋɨɨ   patient, sick person

14.   nɨw nuh miən prədap-prədaa krup-sɑp teəŋ-qɑh səmrap pyiəbaal neəq-cumŋɨɨ.   There [they] have all kinds of facilities for taking care of patients.

[sarɨn visits manii in the hospital]

sarɨn

piinɨt (pinɨt)   to observe, oversee
piinɨt-məəl   to examine, investigate

15.   məc, miən kruu-pɛɛt mɔɔk pinɨt-məəl haəy-rɨnɨw?   Say, has the doctor examined you yet?

manii

krun-cañ   malaria; to have malaria
cumŋɨɨ-krun-cañ   malaria

16.   baat, kee prap kñom thaa kñom chɨɨ cumŋɨɨ-krun-cañ.   Yes, they told me I have malaria (I'm sick [with] malaria).

sarɨn

tŋuǎn   to be heavy, serious

17.   qou, cumŋɨɨ nuh mɨn tŋuǎn ponmaan tee.   Oh, that disease isn't so serious.

manii

srɑlah (srəlah, səlah)	to be clear, completely cleared up
ciə srɑlah	to be completely well
bɑndaal (bəndaal, pədaal)	to cause, lead to
qaac bəndaal qaoy	can lead to, can cause
kɑɑ miən (kɑ-miən)	does happen, is possible

18. nɨŋ haəy, tae baə mɨn məəl qaoy ciə srəlah, qaac bəndaal qaoy slap kɑ-miən.

Right, but if one doesn't watch [it] until (making it) completely cleared up, [it] can even cause death. (can lead to causing to die, it does happen.)

sarɨn	a personal name

19. sarɨn-qaeŋ miən dael keeŋ pɛɛt tee?

Have you ever been hospitalized, Sarin?

sarɨn

qapaŋdisiit	appendicitis

20. mədɑɑŋ dae, kaal dael kñom miən qapaŋdisiit.

Yes, once, the time I had appendicitis.

dambouŋ (dəmbouŋ, təbouŋ)	first, original, in the beginning
mun-dambouŋ	at first, in the beginning
cok	to have a pain
cok puəh	to have stomach pains, cramps

21. mun-dəmbouŋ, krŏən-tae cok puəh bəntəc.

At first, [I] had only a little pain in the stomach.

laəŋ	increasingly
klaŋ laəŋ	increasingly strong, worse
sɑmrac (səmrac)	to decide (to)
weəh	to cut open
weəh-kat	to operate
pliəm	immediately

22. haəy bəntŏəp mɔɔk, kɑɑ cok puəh klaŋ laəŋ, haəy kruu-pɛɛt səmrac weəh-kat pliəm.

Then later, the pain in my stomach got worse (increasingly strong), and the doctor decided to operate immediately.

manii ·

trəw	to be subjected to, to meet with
kruəh-tnaq	accident; danger
bok	to collide with, run into
kruəh-tnaq bok laan	an automobile(-hitting-)accident

23. pii msəl-məñ miən mənuh mənĕəq trəw kruəh-tnaq bok laan.

Yesterday there was a man who had (met with) an automobile accident.

baq	to break (intrans.), to be broken
baq cəəŋ	to have a broken leg
baek kbaal	to have a fractured skull
paŋsəmaŋ	to bandage; bandages
pɨñ teəŋ kluən	the whole body, all over the body

24. baq cəəŋ haəy-niŋ baek kbaal, haəy kee paŋsəmaŋ piñ teəŋ kluən.

[He] had a broken leg and a fractured skull, and they bandaged him from head to foot.

sarɨn

puthaw	ax, hatchet
kap	to cut, hack, chop
crɔluəh (crəluəh, cəluəh)	to slip, do by accident
trəw	to hit, coincide with
cuəŋkuəŋ (cəŋkuəŋ, cəkuəŋ)	knee

25. kaal nɨw pii touc, kñom yɔɔk puthaw tɨw kap daəm-chəə, pontae wiə crəluəh mɔɔk trəw cəŋkuəŋ wɨn.

When I was a kid, I took an ax out to cut wood, but it slipped and hit my knee.

dei	to sew
rɔbuəh (rəbuəh)	a wound; to be wounded
muk-rɔbuəh	a cut, a wound

26. kñom trəw tɨw pɛɛt qaoy kee dei muk-rəbuəh qaoy kñom phaaŋ.

I had to go to the doctor and have him sew up the cut for me.

27. mənuh deik ləə krɛɛ nuh chɨɨ qəy?

What's wrong with the person (sleeping) on that bed?

manii

muəl	dysentery
cumŋɨɨ-muəl	dysentery
deik pɛɛt	to stay in the hospital, be hospitalized

28. baat, miən cumŋɨɨ-muəl; deik pɛɛt pii qatɨt haəy.

Oh, [he] has dysentery; [he's] been in the hospital for two weeks.

sarɨn

neəq-naa	someone, anyone, whoever
qaasɑnnərook (qasɑntərook)	cholera

29. nɨw kənlaeŋ nih miən neəq-naa kaət cumŋɨɨ qasɑnnərook tee?

Is there anyone here [who] has cholera?

manii

rook	disease
rook-claaŋ	contagious disease
tae məneəq qaeŋ	alone, by oneself

30. baat, miən, tae neəq-naa miən rook-claaŋ kee qaoy tɨw deik tae məneəq qaeŋ.

Yes, there are, but whoever has a contagious disease they put in isolation (have him go sleep by himself).

kqaaq — to cough, to have a cough

31. sarɨn, mɨn sruəl kluən rɨɨ, baan ciə kqaaq?

Sarin, aren't you well, that you're coughing?

sarɨn

pdahsaay — to have a cold

32. baat, kñom krɔ́ən-tae pdahsaay bəntɔc-bəntuəc tee.

Oh, I just have a little cold.

B. GRAMMAR AND DRILLS

1. The Meaning of kaət

The verb kaət has a wide semantic range. As a transitive verb, it means 'to give birth (to), to create, to develop, catch (a disease)', as in the following examples:

prəpuĕn kñom kaət koun-proh.	My wife gave birth to a son.
qəwpuk kñom kaət rook.	My father has caught (developed) a disease.
kñom mɨn dəŋ ciə kaət qəy tee.	I don't know what I've caught.

As an intransitive verb, kaət (usually followed by laəŋ) means 'to arise, develop, happen', as in

qasɑnnərook kaət laəŋ nɨw srok-cən.	Cholera has developed in China.
miən cɑmbaŋ kaət laəŋ nɨw khaet nuh.	Fighting has broken out in that province.
pii msəl-məñ miən kruĕh-tnaq kaət laəŋ.	An accident happened yesterday.

We have also met kaət as a completive verb in Lesson 14, B, 2 with the meaning 'to be (physically) able', as in

kñom tɨw twəə-kaa tŋay-nih mɨn kaət tee.	I can't go to work today.

1-A. Substitution Drill

Teacher	Student
kñom mɨn dəŋ ciə kaət qəy tee; ceh-tae mɨn sruəl kluən.	kñom mɨn dəŋ ciə kaət qəy tee; ceh-tae mɨn sruəl kluən.
chɨɨ kbaal.	kñom mɨn dəŋ ciə kaət qəy tee; ceh-tae chɨɨ kbaal.
kdaw kluən.	kñom mɨn dəŋ ciə kaət qəy tee; ceh-tae kdaw kluən.
chɨɨ puĕh.	kñom mɨn dəŋ ciə kaət qəy tee; ceh-tae chɨɨ puĕh.
kdaw-rəŋiə.	kñom mɨn dəŋ ciə kaət qəy tee; ceh-tae kdaw-rəŋiə.
krun.	kñom mɨn dəŋ ciə kaət qəy tee; ceh-tae krun.
ñɔə kluən.	kñom mɨn dəŋ ciə kaət qəy tee; ceh-tae ñɔə kluən.
pdahsaay.	kñom mɨn dəŋ ciə kaət qəy tee; ceh-tae pdahsaay.
qɑh kəmlaŋ.	kñom mɨn cəŋ ciə kaət qəy tee; ceh-tae qɑh kəmlaŋ.
kqaɑq.	kñom mɨn dəŋ ciə kaət qəy tee; ceh-tae kqaɑq.

2. Nominal Modifiers

In Cambodian, ailments of the body and emotional states are typically expressed by means of a verb descriptive of the ailment or emotional state, modified by a noun referring to that part of the body to which the ailment or condition applies, as in

kñom <u>kdaw kluən</u> haəy-nɨŋ <u>chɨɨ kbaal</u>.	I'm <u>hot (in the body)</u> and I have a <u>headache (sick with regard to the head)</u>.

It is tempting to analyze such sequences as compounds composed of a verb plus noun, since they are limited primarily to physical or mental conditions, and since verbs are not normally modified by nouns, but the pattern seems to be sufficiently widespread in the language to say that a verb followed by a nominal modifier is a perfectly acceptable pattern of Cambodian syntax. Consider the following examples:

kñom mɨn dael tɨw <u>leeŋ kaep</u> sɑh.	I've never been to visit (<u>play</u> [in] Kep.
yəəŋ mɨn dael <u>ñam baay haaŋ</u> nuh tee.	We've never <u>eaten</u> [in] <u>that restaurant</u>.
kñom <u>qɑh barəy</u> haəy.	I'm <u>out of cigarettes</u>.
koət mɨn dael tɨw <u>keeŋ pɛɛt</u> tee.	He's never gone to <u>stay</u> [in] <u>the hospital</u>.
kee prap kñom thaa kñom <u>chɨɨ cumŋɨɨ-krun-cañ</u>.	They told me that I'm <u>ill</u> [with] <u>malaria</u>.

Following is a list of verbs followed by nominal modifiers. Those words not yet introduced in the Dialogues are preceded by an asterisk.

chɨɨ kbaal	to have a headache (sick with regard to the head)
chɨɨ puəh	to have an upset stomach (sick in the stomach)
sruəl kluən	to be well (comfortable in the body)
kdaw kluən	to be hot (hot with regard to the body)
ñɔə kluən	to tremble (tremble in the body)
cok day	to have a pain (in the) hand
cok puəh	to have a pain (in the) stomach
mut day	to have a cut hand (to be cut in the hand)
baq cəəŋ	to have a broken leg (broken with regard to the leg)
baek kbaal	to have a fractured skull (broken in the head)
*kwən day	to have a paralyzed hand
*kwən cəəŋ	to have a paralyzed leg or foot
*wɨl muk	to be dizzy (revolve with regard to the face)
qɑh kəmlaŋ	to be exhausted (out of strength)
sapbaay cət	to be happy (to be happy in the mind or heart)
*pruəy cət	to be sad (sad in the heart)
*pibaaq cət	to be unhappy (to have difficulty in the mind)
keeŋ pɛɛt	to be hospitalized (sleep in the hospital)

2-A. Substitution Drill

Teacher	Student
tŋay-nih kñom <u>chɨɨ kbaal</u> nah.	tŋay-nih kñom <u>chɨɨ kbaal</u> nah.
<u>cok puəh</u>	tŋay-nih kñom <u>cok puəh</u> nah.
<u>kdaw kluən</u>	tŋay-nih kñom <u>kdaw kluən</u> nah.
<u>cok day</u>	tŋay-nih kñom <u>cok day</u> nah.
<u>sruəl kluən</u>	tŋay-nih kñom <u>sruəl kluən</u> nah.
<u>chɨɨ puəh</u>	tŋay-nih kñom <u>chɨɨ puəh</u> nah.
<u>ñɔə kluən</u>	tŋay-nih kñom <u>ñɔə kluən</u> nah.
<u>wɨl muk</u>	tŋay-nih kñom <u>wɨl muk</u> nah.
<u>səpbaay cət</u>	tŋay-nih kñom <u>səpbaay cət</u> nah.
<u>pruəy cət</u>	tŋay-nih kñom <u>pruəy cət</u> nah.

3. <u>yuu-yuu-mədaaŋ</u>

<u>yuu-yuu-mədaaŋ</u> is an adverbial phrase which may occur either initially or finally in the sentence, and which means 'once in a while, from time to time, intermittently', as in

yuu-yuu-mədaaŋ kñom ñɔə kluən   From time to time I tremble and
haəy kdaw-rəŋiə.   [I've] got chills.

3-A. Substitution Drill

Teacher	Student
yuu-yuu-mədaaŋ kñom <u>ñɔə kluən</u>.	yuu-yuu-mədaaŋ kñom <u>ñɔə kluən</u>.
<u>kdaw kluən</u>.	yuu-yuu-mədaaŋ kñom <u>kdaw kluən</u>.
<u>chɨɨ kbaal</u>.	yuu-yuu-mədaaŋ kñom <u>chɨɨ kbaal</u>.
<u>pdahsaay</u>.	yuu-yuu-mədaaŋ kñom <u>psahsaay</u>.
<u>chɨɨ puəh</u>.	yuu-yuu-mədaaŋ kñom <u>chɨɨ puəh</u>.
<u>krun</u>.	yuu-yuu-mədaaŋ kñom <u>krun</u>.
<u>qah kəmlaŋ</u>.	yuu-yuu-mədaaŋ kñom <u>qah kəmlaŋ</u>.
<u>wɨl muk</u>.	yuu-yuu-mədaaŋ kñom <u>wɨl muk</u>.
<u>mɨn sruəl kluən</u>.	yuu-yuu-mədaaŋ kñom <u>mɨn sruəl kluən</u>.

4. Coordinate Compounds

A very common derivational technique in Cambodian is the joining of two words of the same or similar meaning to form a coordinate compound whose meaning is more general than that of either constituent, or is the sum of the meanings of the two constituents. Following are some of the many examples which have been met so far.

Nouns:

qəwpuk-mdaay	(father/mother) parents
tuuk-kəpal	(boat/steamer) river craft
həp-qəywan	(box/things) things, baggage
khao-qaaw	(trousers/shirt, coat) clothing
pləw-tnal	(road, way/hard-top road, street) streets and roads
peel-weliə	(time, occasion/time) time
mhoup-camnəy	(food/sweets) various kinds of food
kbac-camlaq	(design/sculpture, carving) sculpture

Verbs:

sliəq-peăq	(to wear around the waist/to wear above the waist or on the feet) to dress, wear
dək-noăm	(to carry/to lead) to transport
baoh-samqaat	(to sweep/to clean) to clean
luăq-dou	(to sell/to trade) to do trade
piinɨt-məəl	(to observe/to look at) to examine, oversee
sok-sapbaay	(to be healthy/to be happy) to be well and happy
cumriəp-suə	(to inform/to inquire) to greet
thae-reăqsaa	(to take care of/to take care of) to take care of

4-A. Expansion Drill

In the following sentences, form a coordinate compound at the appropriate place in the sentences provided by the teacher.

Teacher	Student
nɨw phae miən tuuk craən yaaŋ.	nɨw phae miən tuuk-kəpal craən yaaŋ.
kñom twəə-kaa nɨw haaŋ-kat-khao.	kñom twəə-kaa nɨw haaŋ-kat-khao-qaaw.
nɨw pnum-pɨñ miən plɤw craən nah.	nɨw pnum-pɨñ miən plɤw-tnal craən nah.
mdaay kñom trɤw twəə mhoup craən nah tŋay-nih.	mdaay kñom trɤw twəə mhoup-camnəy craən nah tŋay-nih.
qəwpuk-miə kñom miən haaŋ-luăq-tok.	qəwpuk-miə kñom miən haaŋ-luăq-tok-tuu.
kñom coul-cət məəl riəŋ qaakɨñ.	kñom coul-cət məəl riəŋ qaakɨñ-qaacao.
kñom miən baaŋ bəy neăq.	kñom miən baaŋ-pqoun bəy neăq.
kñom trɤw yɔɔk həp nih tɨw daq ləə kəpal.	kñom trɤw yɔɔk həp-qəywan nih tɨw daq ləə kəpal.
samliəq neăq-leeŋ-lkhaon lqaa nah.	samliəq-bampeăq neăq-leeŋ-lkhaon lqaa nah.

4-B. Expansion Drill

Teacher	Student
tŋay-nih maq qaoy koun baoh pteăh.	tŋay-nih maq qaoy koun baoh-samqaat pteăh.
kruu-pɛɛt mɔɔk piinɨt haəy-rɨnɨw?	kruu-pɛɛt mɔɔk piinɨt-məəl haəy-rɨnɨw?
tŋay-nih trɤw sliəq qaoy sqaat-baat.	tŋay-nih trɤw sliəq-peăq qaoy sqaat-baat.
tuuk nuh dək tnam mɔɔk pii kəmpuăŋ-caam.	tuuk nuh dək-noăm tnam mɔɔk pii kəmpuăŋ-caam.
pqoun-tlay-srəy kñom cuəy thae koun.	pqoun-tlay-srəy kñom cuəy thae-reăqsaa koun.
kñom mɨn tɨw məəl lkhaon ñoăp tee.	kñom mɨn tɨw məəl lkhaon ñɨk-ñoăp tee.
but tɨw sampeăh look-puu tɨw.	but tɨw sampeăh-suə look-puu tɨw.
kñom trɤw tɨw haaŋ-baok-khao-qaaw.	kñom trɤw tɨw haaŋ-baok-qut-khao-qaaw.
pii-msəl-məñ kñom cuəp puəq-maaq məneăq.	pii-msəl-məñ kñom cuəp-prəteăh puəq-maaq məneăq.

5. Reduplication

Another common derivational mechanism in Cambodian is __reduplication__, in which part or all of a base is reduplicated to form a __reduplicative__ whose meaning

differs in some way from that of either of its constituents. Sometimes both constituents of a reduplicative are bound (i.e. have no independent meaning), and
sometimes only one constituent is bound; if neither constituent is bound, the
form is both a coordinate compound (as in 4 above) and a reduplicative, and we
can call it a <u>reduplicative compound</u>. Reduplicatives are of the following types:

1) <u>Ablauted reduplicatives</u> (reduplication of the base with vowel change)

bəntəc-bəntuəc	(a little/ -)	some, somewhat, a little
*teeŋ-taaŋ	(- / -)	incoherent, confused
*krɑweem-krɑwaam	(- / -)	marked up, disfigured

2) <u>Rhyming reduplicatives</u>

thom-dom	(big/ -)	grand, important
mɛɛn-tɛɛn	(to be true/ -)	really, seriously
sqaat-baat	(to be clean/ -)	neat, attractive

3) <u>Alliterative reduplicatives</u>

mhoup-mhaa	(food/ -)	various kinds of food
prɑdap-prɑdaa	(instrument/ -)	tools, equipment, instruments
krɑŋeik-krɑŋɑq	(- /crooked)	extremely crooked, tortuous

4) <u>Repetitive reduplicatives</u> (discussed in Lesson 14, B, 1)

srəy-srəy	(woman/woman)	women in general
touc-touc	(small/small)	small and numerous
pseiŋ-pseiŋ	(different/different)	various

5-A. <u>Expansion Drill</u>

Use a reduplicative where possible in the following sentences.

Teacher	Student
mun-dəmbouŋ kñom chɨɨ puəh <u>bəntəc</u>.	mun-dəmbouŋ kñom chɨɨ puəh <u>bəntəc-bəntuəc</u>.
<u>srəy</u> twəə qəy kɑɑ yɨɨt ciə-nɨc.	<u>srəy-srəy</u> twəə qəy kɑɑ yɨɨt ciə-nɨc.
look chɨɨ kbaal <u>mɛɛn</u> tee?	look chɨɨ kbaal <u>mɛɛn-tɛɛn</u> tee?
kñom miən <u>prədap</u> krup baep səmrap cuəh-cul laan.	kñom miən <u>prədap-prədaa</u> krup baep səmrap cuəh-cul laan.
krouc nih <u>touc</u> nah.	krouc nih <u>touc-touc</u> nah.
look miən kaa <u>thom</u> nɨw pnum-pɨñ tee?	look miən kaa <u>thom-dom</u> nɨw pnum-pɨñ tee?
pləw nih <u>krəŋɑq</u> nah.	pləw nih <u>krəŋeik-krəŋɑq</u> nah.
miən mənuh craən neǎq mɔɔk <u>cuəp</u> kniə.	miən mənuh craən neǎq mɔɔk <u>cuəp-cum</u> kniə.
haaŋ nuh miən <u>mhoup</u> craən muk.	haaŋ nuh miən <u>mhoup-mhaa</u> craən muk.

6. <u>bɑndaal qaoy</u> + Verb

<u>bɑndaal qaoy</u> + verb is a causative verb phrase which means 'leads to, causes'
the action or condition described by the following verb. When preceded by the
modal verb <u>qaac</u> 'can, has the power to', the entire phrase means 'can lead to, can
cause (+ verb)', as in

baə mɨn məəl qaoy ciə srəlah,
qaac bəndaal qaoy slap.

If one doesn't watch it until it's
completely cleared up, it <u>can cause</u>
<u>death</u> (can lead to causing to die).

6-A. Substitution Drill

Teacher	Student
<u>cumŋɨɨ-krun-cañ</u> qaac bəndaal qaoy slap.	<u>cumŋɨɨ-krun-cañ</u> qaac bəndaal qaoy slap.
<u>qasannərook</u>	<u>qasannərook</u> qaac bəndaal qaoy slap.
<u>cumŋɨɨ-muəl</u>	<u>cumŋɨɨ-muəl</u> qaac bəndaal qaoy slap.
<u>qapaŋdisiit</u>	<u>qapaŋdisiit</u> qaac bəndaal qaoy slap.
<u>krŭəh-tnaq</u>	<u>krŭəh-tnaq</u> qaac bəndaal qaoy slap.
<u>bok laan</u>	<u>bok laan</u> qaac bəndaal qaoy slap.
<u>weə̆h-kat</u>	<u>weə̆h-kat</u> qaac bəndaal qaoy slap.

6-B. Multiple Substitution Drill

Teacher	Student
<u>cumŋɨɨ-krun-cañ</u> qaac bəndaal qaoy <u>slap.</u>	<u>cumŋɨɨ-krun-cañ</u> qaac bəndaal qaoy <u>slap.</u>
<u>baək lɨən</u>, <u>mɨən krŭəh-tnaq.</u>	<u>baək lɨən</u> qaac bəndaal qaoy <u>mɨən krŭəh-tnaq.</u>
<u>twəə-kaa</u>, <u>qah kəmlaŋ.</u>	<u>twəə-kaa</u> qaac bəndaal qaoy <u>qah kəmlaŋ.</u>
<u>cuə̆q barəy</u>, <u>kqaaq.</u>	<u>cuə̆q barəy</u> qaac bəndaal qaoy <u>kqaaq.</u>
<u>ñam sraa</u>, <u>srəwəŋ.</u>	<u>ñam sraa</u> qaac bəndaal qaoy <u>srəwəŋ.</u>
<u>cumŋɨɨ-muəl</u>, <u>tɨw keeŋ pɛɛt.</u>	<u>cumŋɨɨ-muəl</u> qaac bəndaal qaoy <u>tɨw keeŋ pɛɛt.</u>
<u>praə kambət</u>, <u>mut day.</u>	<u>praə kambət</u> qaac bəndaal qaoy <u>mut day.</u>

7. The Completive Verb <u>kaɑ-mɨən</u>

<u>kaɑ-mɨən</u> is a completive verb which is very similar in form, function, and
meaning to the completive verb <u>kaɑ-baan</u> 'is a possibility, is feasible' (Lesson 8,
B, 8). Its meaning is something like 'it happens that, it <u>does</u> happen that, it even
happens that, there is even, there <u>are</u> cases of', as in

cuən-kaal kee ñam baay baraŋ   Sometimes they <u>do</u> eat French food.
kɑ-mɨən.   <u>or</u>: They <u>also</u> sometimes eat French food.

In the sentence

cumŋɨɨ-krun-cañ qaac bəndaal qaoy   Malaria can <u>even</u> lead to death.
slap <u>kɑ-mɨən.</u>

the sense of <u>kɑ-baan</u> can best be rendered 'even'. Its function could also be
approximated if one were to translate the above sentence 'Malaria <u>can</u> lead to
death.' with emphasis on the word <u>can</u>. It can thus be seen that the general meaning of <u>kaɑ-mɨən</u> is that 'it doesn't usually happen, but it is a possibility; it <u>does</u>
happen; it <u>can</u> happen'.

7-A. <u>Substitution Drill</u>

<u>Teacher</u>	<u>Student</u>
<u>cumŋɨɨ-krun-cañ</u> qaac bəndaal qaoy slap kɑ-miən.	<u>cumŋɨɨ-krun-cañ</u> qaac bəndaal qaoy slap kɑ-miən.
<u>qasɑnnərook</u>	<u>qasɑnnərook</u> qaac bəndaal qaoy slap kɑ-miən.
<u>cumŋɨɨ-muəl</u>	<u>cumŋɨɨ-muəl</u> qaac bəndaal qaoy slap kɑ-miən.
<u>qapɑŋdisiit</u>	<u>qapɑŋdisiit</u> qaac bəndaal qaoy slap kɑ-miən.
<u>krŭəh-tnɑq</u>	<u>krŭəh-tnɑq</u> qaac bəndaal qaoy slap kɑ-miən.
<u>bok laan</u>	<u>bok laan</u> qaac bəndaal qaoy slap kɑ-miən.
<u>weə̆h-kat</u>	<u>weə̆h-kat</u> qaac bəndaal qaoy slap kɑ-miən.

7-B. <u>Substitution Drill</u>

<u>Teacher</u>	<u>Student</u>
cuən-kaal kee <u>trəw tɨw keeŋ pɛɛt</u> kɑ-miən.	cuən-kaal kee <u>trəw tɨw keeŋ pɛɛt</u> kɑ-miən.
<u>tɨw twaay-bɑŋkum</u>	cuən-kaal kee <u>tɨw twaay-bɑŋkum preə̆h</u> kɑ-miən.
<u>tɨw leeŋ kaep</u>	cuən-kaal kee <u>tɨw leeŋ kaep</u> kɑ-miən.
<u>luə̆q laan</u>	cuən-kaal kee <u>luə̆q laan</u> kɑ-miən.
<u>tɨñ prəpuə̆n</u>	cuən-kaal kee <u>tɨñ prəpuə̆n</u> kɑ-miən.
<u>roə̆m-kbac</u>	cuən-kaal kee <u>roə̆m-kbac</u> kɑ-miən.
<u>leeŋ rɨən cɑmbɑŋ</u>	cuən-kaal kee <u>leeŋ rɨən cɑmbɑŋ</u> kɑ-miən.
<u>cəñ maoŋ prampɨl</u>	cuən-kaal kee <u>cəñ maəŋ prampɨl</u> kɑ-miən.
<u>ñam baay barɑŋ</u>	cuən-kaal kee <u>ñam baay barɑŋ</u> kɑ-miən.
<u>bok laan</u>	cuən-kaal kee <u>bok laan</u> kɑ-miən.

8. <u>laəŋ</u> as an Aspectual Particle

When <u>laəŋ</u> modifies a preceding adjectival verb, it functions as an aspectual particle meaning 'increasingly, more', as in the following sequence:

mun-dəmbouŋ, kñom kroə̆n-tae cok puə̆h bəntəc.	At first, I only had a little pain in the stomach.
haəy bəntoə̆p mɔɔk, kɑɑ cok puə̆h <u>klaŋ laəŋ</u>.	Then later, the pain in my stomach got worse (increasingly strong).

<u>laəŋ</u> in this function was also met in the sentence

chap-chap <u>laəŋ</u>!	Hurry up! (<u>Increasingly</u> fast!)

8-A. Response Drill

Teacher	Student
mun-dəmbouŋ, kñom kroĕn-tae cok puǝh bəntəc.	haǝy bəntoĕp mɔɔk, kaa cok puǝh klaŋ laəŋ.
mun-dəmbouŋ, kñom kroĕn-tae chɨɨ bəntəc.	haǝy bəntoĕp mɔɔk, kaa chɨɨ klaŋ laəŋ.
mun-dəmbouŋ, kñom kroĕn-tae krun bəntəc.	haǝy bəntoĕp mɔɔk, kaa krun klaŋ laəŋ.
mun-dəmbouŋ, kñom kroĕn-tae kdaw kluǝn bəntəc.	haǝy bəntoĕp mɔɔk, kaa kdaw kluǝn klaŋ laəŋ.
mun-dəmbouŋ, kñom kroĕn-tae cok day bəntəc.	haǝy bəntoĕp mɔɔk, kaa cok day klaŋ laəŋ.
mun-dəmbouŋ, kñom kroĕn-tae chɨɨ kbaal bəntəc.	haǝy bəntoĕp mɔɔk, kaa chɨɨ kbaal klaŋ laəŋ.
bun-dəmbouŋ, kñom kroĕn-tae chɨɨ puǝh bəntəc.	haǝy bəntoĕp mɔɔk, kaa chɨɨ puǝh klaŋ laəŋ.
mun-dəmbouŋ, kñom kroĕn-tae ñɔǝ kluǝn bəntəc.	haǝy bəntoĕp mɔɔk, kaa ñɔǝ kluǝn klaŋ laəŋ.
mun-dəmbouŋ, kñom kroĕn-tae wɨl muk bəntəc.	haǝy bəntoĕp mɔɔk, kaa wɨl muk klaŋ laəŋ.

9. The Adverbial Phrase pɨñ teĕŋ kluǝn

The adverbial phrase pɨñ teĕŋ kluǝn means literally 'fully all of the body', and can best be translated 'all over the body, throughout the body, from head to toe', as in

kee paŋsəmaŋ pɨñ teĕŋ kluǝn.	They bandaged [him] from head to toe.

9-A. Substitution Drill

Teacher	Student
kñom paŋsəmaŋ pɨñ teĕŋ kluǝn.	kñom paŋsəmaŋ pɨñ teĕŋ kluǝn.
chɨɨ	kñom chɨɨ pɨñ teĕŋ kluǝn.
kdaw	kñom kdaw pɨñ teĕŋ kluǝn.
rəŋiǝ	kñom rəŋiǝ pɨñ teĕŋ kluǝn.
krun	kñom krun pɨñ teĕŋ kluǝn.
ñɔǝ	kñom ñɔǝ pɨñ teĕŋ kluǝn.
trəceĕq	kñom trəceĕq pɨñ teĕŋ kluǝn.

10. The Meaning of trəw

The verb trəw occurs with a number of seemingly unrelated functions and meanings. It has been met as an adjectival verb meaning 'to be right, correct', as in

trəw haǝy.	That's right, that's it, that's correct.
camlaəy look mɨn trəw tee.	Your answer isn't correct.

It also occurs frequently as a <u>modal verb</u> meaning 'to have to, to fall to one's lot to, must', as in

kñom <u>trəw</u> tɨw psaa tŋay-nih.	I <u>have to</u> go to the market today.
koun <u>trəw</u> sliəq-peăq qaoy sqaat-baat.	You <u>must</u> dress neatly, Child.

In this lesson, <u>trəw</u> occurs as a <u>transitive verb</u> meaning 'to hit, to come in contact with', as in

wiə crəluəh mɔɔk <u>trəw</u> cəŋkuăŋ wɨñ.	It slipped and (came and) <u>hit</u> [my] knee.

In some contexts, <u>trəw</u> is best translated in the <u>passive voice</u> in English, with the meaning 'to be subjected to, to meet with', as in

pii-msəl-məñ miən mənuh məneăq trəw kruăh-tnaq bok laan.	Yesterday there was a man who had (<u>met with</u>) an automobile accident.
pii-msəl-məñ kñom trəw ckae kham.	Yesterday I was bitten by a dog. (I was <u>subjected to</u> a dog biting.)

At first glance, the various meanings of <u>trəw</u> appear to be too divergent to be related. On closer inspection, however, it can be seen that all the uses of <u>trəw</u> cited above share a common semantic bond which can be defined something like 'to come in contact with, to coincide with'. It is instructive that <u>trəw</u> is considered by Cambodians to be 'the same word' in all its uses above. Here is yet another example of a Cambodian word whose semantic boundaries are not "<u>trəw</u>" with those of any single word in English.

10-A. <u>Substitution Drill</u>

Teacher	Student
pii-msəl-məñ kñom trəw <u>baek kbaal.</u>	pii-msəl-məñ kñom trəw <u>baek kbaal.</u>
<u>rəbuəh baq cəəŋ.</u>	pii-msəl-məñ kñom trəw <u>rəbuəh baq cəəŋ.</u>
<u>laan bok kñom.</u>	pii-msəl-məñ kñom trəw <u>laan bok kñom.</u>
<u>kee bəñcuun tɨw pɛɛt.</u>	pii-msəl-məñ kñom trəw <u>kee bəñcuun tɨw pɛɛt.</u>
<u>pɛɛt caq tnam.</u>	pii-msəl-məñ kñom trəw <u>pɛɛt caq tnam.</u>
<u>ckae kham.</u>	pii-msəl-məñ kñom trəw <u>ckae kham.</u>
<u>kee cuun tɨw weăŋ.</u>	pii-msəl-məñ kñom trəw <u>kee cuun tɨw weăŋ.</u>
<u>pliəŋ tətɨk qɑh.</u>	pii-msəl-məñ kñom trəw <u>pliəŋ tətɨk qɑh.</u>

10-B. <u>Substitution Drill</u>

New vocabulary necessary for this drill:

mriəm-day	'finger'	kɑɑ-day	'wrist'
kɑɑ	'neck, throat'	kɑɑ-cəəŋ	'ankle'

Teacher	Student
puthaw crəluəh mɔɔk trəw <u>cəŋkuăŋ</u> kñom.	puthaw crəluəh mɔɔk trəw <u>cəŋkuăŋ</u> kñom.
<u>day</u>	puthaw crəluəh mɔɔk trəw <u>day</u> kñom.
<u>kbaal</u>	puthaw crəluəh mɔɔk trəw <u>kbaal</u> kñom.
<u>cəəŋ</u>	puthaw crəluəh mɔɔk trəw <u>cəəŋ</u> kñom.

Teacher	Student
mriəm-day	puthaw crəluəh mɔɔk trəw mriəm-day kñom.
puə̆h	puthaw crəluəh mɔɔk trəw puə̆h kñom.
kɑɑ	puthaw crəluəh mɔɔk trəw kɑɑ kñom.
kɑɑ-day	puthaw crəluəh mɔɔk trəw kɑɑ-day kñom.
kɑɑ-cəəŋ	puthaw crəluəh mɔɔk trəw kɑɑ-cəəŋ kñom.

11. The Pronoun neə̆q-naa

neə̆q-naa 'who', like qwəy and naa (Lesson 12, B, 1) occurs both as an interrogative pronoun and as an indefinite pronoun. neə̆q-naa differs from qwəy and naa, however, in that it may occur either initially or finally in the sentence.

As an interrogative pronoun:

| neə̆q-naa cɑŋ tɨw məəl kon? | Who wants to go to the movies? |
| koə̆t kaa ciə-muəy neə̆q-naa? | Whom is he marrying? |

As an indefinite pronoun:

| neə̆q-naa miən rook clɑɑŋ, kee qaoy tɨw deik tae məneə̆q qaen. | Whoever has a contagious disease they have go sleep by himself. |
| kñom min tɨw ciə-muəy neə̆q-naa tee. | I'm not going with anyone. |

11-A. Substitution Drill

Teacher	Student
neə̆q-naa cɑŋ tɨw məəl kon?	neə̆q-naa cɑŋ tɨw məəl kon?
tɨw daə-leeŋ?	neə̆q-naa cɑŋ tɨw daə-leeŋ?
ñam baay kmae?	neə̆q-naa cɑŋ ñam baay kmae?
tɨw kaep?	neə̆q-naa cɑŋ tɨw kaep?
tɨw twəə-kaa?	neə̆q-naa cɑŋ tɨw twəə-kaa?
məəl siəwphɨw?	neə̆q-naa cɑŋ məəl siəwphɨw?
tɨñ kasaet?	neə̆q-naa cɑŋ tɨñ kasaet?

11-B. Response Drill

Teacher	Student
look tɨw ciə-muəy neə̆q-naa?	kñom min tɨw ciə-muəy neə̆q-naa tee.
look twəə-kaa ciə-muəy neə̆q-naa?	kñom min twəə-kaa ciə-muəy neə̆q-naa tee.
look ñam baay ciə-muəy neə̆q-naa?	kñom min ñam baay ciə-muəy neə̆q-naa tee.
look tɨw daə-leeŋ ciə-muəy neə̆q-naa?	kñom min tɨw daə-leeŋ ciə-muəy neə̆q-naa tee.
look tɨw riən ciə-muəy neə̆q-naa?	kñom min tɨw riən ciə-muəy neə̆q-naa tee.
look tɨw psaa ciə-muəy neə̆q-naa?	kñom min tɨw psaa ciə-muəy neə̆q-naa tee.
look kaa ciə-muəy neə̆q-naa?	kñom min kaa ciə-muəy neə̆q-naa tee.
look tɨw kaep ciə-muəy neə̆q-naa?	kñom min tɨw kaep ciə-muəy neə̆q-naa tee.

11-C. Substitution Drill

Teacher	Student
baə look caŋ <u>tɨw</u> ciə-muəy neə̆q-naa, prap kñom tɨw.	baə look caŋ <u>tɨw</u> ciə-muəy neə̆q-naa, prap kñom tɨw.
<u>twəə-kaa</u>	baə look caŋ <u>twəə-kaa</u> ciə-muəy neə̆q-naa prap kñom tɨw.
<u>riən</u>	baə look caŋ <u>riən</u> ciə-muəy neə̆q-naa, prap kñom tɨw.
<u>kaa</u>	baə look caŋ <u>kaa</u> ciə-muəy neə̆q-naa, prap kñom tɨw.
<u>ñam baay</u>	baə look caŋ <u>ñam baay</u> ciə-muəy neə̆q-naa, prap kñom tɨw.
<u>tɨw daə-leeŋ</u>	baə look caŋ <u>tɨw daə-leeŋ</u> ciə-muəy neə̆q-naa, prap kñom tɨw.
<u>tɨw kaep</u>	baə look caŋ <u>tɨw kaep</u> ciə-muəy neə̆q-naa, prap kñom tɨw.
<u>tɨw psaa</u>	baə look caŋ <u>tɨw psaa</u> ciə-muəy neə̆q-naa, prap kñom tɨw.

11-D. Substitution Drill

Teacher	Student
neə̆q-naa miən <u>rook-claaŋ</u>, kee qaoy tɨw keeŋ pɛɛt.	neə̆q-naa miən <u>rook-claaŋ</u>, kee qaoy tɨw keeŋ pɛɛt.
<u>qasɑnnərook</u>,	neə̆q-naa miən <u>qasɑnnərook</u>, kee qaoy tɨw keeŋ pɛɛt.
<u>qapɑɲdisiit</u>,	neə̆q-naa miən <u>qapɑɲdisiit</u>, kee qaoy tɨw keeŋ pɛɛt.
<u>cumŋɨɨ-muəl</u>,	neə̆q-naa miən <u>cumŋɨɨ-muəl</u>, kee qaoy tɨw keeŋ pɛɛt.
<u>krun-cañ</u>,	neə̆q-naa miən <u>krun-cañ</u>, kee qaoy tɨw keeŋ pɛɛt.
<u>baek kbaal</u>,	neə̆q-naa miən <u>baek kbaal</u>, kee qaoy tɨw keeŋ pɛɛt.
<u>baq cəəŋ</u>,	neə̆q-naa miən <u>baq cəəŋ</u>, kee qaoy tɨw keeŋ pɛɛt.
<u>cumŋɨɨ tɲuə̆n</u>,	neə̆q-naa miən <u>cumŋɨɨ tɲuə̆n</u>, kee qaoy tɨw keeŋ pɛɛt.

12. The Adverbial Phrase <u>tae mɔneə̆q qaeŋ</u>

<u>tae mɔneə̆q qaeŋ</u> is an adverbial phrase which means 'by oneself, alone, only oneself', as in

neə̆q-naa miən rook-claaŋ, kee qaoy tɨw deik <u>tae mɔneə̆q qaeŋ</u>.	Whoever has a contagious disease, they have go sleep <u>by himself</u>.

12-A. Substitution Drill

Teacher	Student

knom coul-cət t\i{}w hael-t\i{}k
tae məneə̈q qaeŋ.

     t\i{}w daə-leeŋ

     t\i{}w psaa

     t\i{}w məəl kon

     twəə dəmnaə

     baək kəpal-hɑh

     twəə mhoup

     twəə-kaa

kñom coul-cət t\i{}w hael-t\i{}k
tae məneə̈q qaeŋ.

kñom coul-cət t\i{}w daə-leeŋ
tae məneə̈q qaeŋ.

kñom coul-cət t\i{}w psaa
tae məneə̈q qaeŋ.

kñom coul-cət t\i{}w məəl kon
tae məneə̈q qaeŋ.

kñom coul-cət twəə dəmnae
tae məneə̈q qaeŋ.

kñom coul-cət baək kəpal-hɑh
tae məneə̈q qaeŋ.

kñom coul-cət twəə mhoup
tae məneə̈q qaeŋ.

kñom coul-cət twəə-kaa
tae məneə̈q qaeŋ.

[Tape 39]   C. COMPREHENSION

1. First Aid

chiən: qei, kaət qəy?

s\i{}m: qou, kñom mut day.

chiən: thəə qəy baan ciə mut day?

s\i{}m: kñom kap sac-cruuk ruəc crəluəh kap day.

chiən: [chiəm 'blood']
yii, miən chiəm cəñ craən nah.
qaoy kñom t\i{}w haw kruu-pɛɛt r\i{}\i{}?

s\i{}m: m\i{}n-bac tee; mut m\i{}n cr\i{}w tee.
kñom paŋsəmaŋ kluən-qaeŋ kɑ-baan dae.

chiən: [liəp 'to rub on, smear on, paint']
liəp tnam t\i{}w, mun paŋsəmaŋ.

s\i{}m: qou, kñom kmiən tnam qəy sɑh.

chiən: [faaməsii 'pharmacy']
qəñcəŋ kñom t\i{}w t\i{}ñ n\i{}w faamasii.

s\i{}m: qɑɑ-kun craən nah.

2. Discussing the Hospital

siim: laa qaeŋ dael t\i{}w keeŋ pɛɛt tee?

laa: kñom m\i{}n dael keeŋ pɛɛt tee; kñom klaac pɛɛt nah.

siim: baə chɨɨ klaŋ yəəŋ trəw tɨw keeŋ pɛɛt.
     [muə̆ntii-pɛɛt 'hospital']
     nɨw muə̆ntii-pɛɛt kee miən tnam haəy-nɨŋ prədap-prədaa sap-krup
     teə̆ŋ-qɑh səmrap pyiəbaal neə̆q-cumŋɨɨ.

laa: coh, siim qaeŋ dael tɨw keeŋ pɛɛt tee?

siim: baat, kñom tɨw keeŋ pɛɛt mədaaŋ, kaal kñom chɨɨ muəl.

laa: keeŋ pɛɛt ponmaan tŋay?

siim: baat, kñom keeŋ tae pram tŋay tee.

laa: coh, kee qaoy tnam qəy-klah?

siim: kee qaoy kñom leep tnam, haəy caq tnam qaoy kñom phaaŋ.
     bəntoə̆p mɔɔk miən kruu-pɛɛt pinɨt-məəl kñom rŏə̆l tŋay.

laa: peel nuh miən krun tee?

siim: baat, miən; kee daq teəmomaet məəl rŏə̆l tŋay.

laa: siim qaeŋ tɨw keeŋ pɛɛt naa?

     [muə̆ntii-pɛɛt preə̆h-keit-miəliə 'Preah-Ket Mealea Hospital'
     (legendary name of King Jayavarman II)]
siim: baat, kñom tɨw muə̆ntii-pɛɛt preə̆h-keit miəliə.

3. **A Visit to the Doctor**

kruu-pɛɛt: look chɨɨ qəy?

neə̆q-cumŋɨɨ: kñom ceh-tae pdahsaay.

kruu-pɛɛt: look dael krun tee?

neə̆q-cumŋɨɨ: baat, kñom krun yuu-yuu-mədaaŋ.

kruu-pɛɛt: som biəm teəmomaet nih məəl.
         look dael kqaaq tee?

neə̆q-cumŋɨɨ: baat, kqaaq, pontae craən-tae nɨw peel yup.

         [haa 'to open (the mouth)']

kruu-pɛɛt: som haa moə̆t.
         look dael chɨɨ kbaal tee?

neə̆q-cumŋɨɨ: baat, haəy mɨn kliən baay sɑh.

kruu-pɛɛt: kñom cuun tnam look pii muk.
         tnam krŏə̆p nih səmrap chɨɨ kbaal; buən maoŋ look leep
         pii krŏə̆p.
         tnam nih səmrap kqaaq; mə-tŋay pisaa bəy slaap-priə.

neə̆q-cumŋɨɨ: kñom tɨw twəə-kaa baan tee?

kruu-pɛɛt: mɨn baan tee; look trəw tɨw pteə̆h səmraaq.
         cumŋɨɨ nih claaŋ nah.

neə̆q-cumŋɨɨ: soum qɑɑ-kun.

D. CONVERSATION

1. Discussing Symptoms

Have one student assume that he isn't feeling well. Have a second student question him with regard to just how he feels. The discussion might include the symptoms, whether or not the doctor should be called, and whether or not he should go to the hospital.

2. Experiences in the Hospital

Have two students question each other with regard to their respective experiences in the hospital. Questions might involve such things as whether or not one has ever been hospitalized, for what reasons, how long he had to stay there, and what treatment was administered.

3. A Visit to the Doctor

Assign one student the role of a patient, and the other the role of the doctor. The doctor questions the patient as to his symptoms, gives instructions pertinent to the examination, and prescribes treatment for him.

4. The Medical Profession

Have the students engage in free conversation about various aspects of the medical profession, doctors, hospitals, specific diseases, etc.

LESSON 23. POST OFFICE AND BANK

[Tape 40]   A. DIALOGUE

ŋɔɔn

krɑdaah (krədaah, kədaah)   paper
krədaah-səsei-səmbot   letter paper, stationery
sraom-səmbot   envelope
1. kñom trəw tɨw psaa tɨñ   I have to go to the market and buy
   krədaah-səsei-səmbot haəy-nɨŋ   some writing paper and some en-
   sraom-səmbot phɑɑŋ.   velopes too.

hii

sɑŋsaa (səŋsaa)   sweetheart
2. ŋɔɔn-qaeŋ səsei səmbot tɨw   You're writing to your sweetheart,
   sɑŋsaa mɛɛn tee?   right?

ŋɔɔn

pñaə   to send
3. mɨn mɛɛn tee; kñom səsei tɨw   No, I'm writing to my parents to
   maq-paa qaoy koət pñaə   have them send me some money.
   praq mɔɔk qaoy kñom.

slaap-paqkaa (-pəkaa)   fountain pen
tɨk-kmaw   ink (of any color)
4. yii, slaap-pəkaa nih qɑh   Oh, this pen's out of ink!
   tɨk-kmaw haəy!

5. hii-qaeŋ miən tɨk-kmaw tee?;   Do you have some ink, Hee?; let
   kñom som boum bəntəc.   me have (pump) some.

hii

way   to hit, strike, type
teelekraam   telegram; to telegraph
way teelekraam   to send a telegram
6. kñom kmiən tee; məc kɑɑ mɨn   I don't have any; why don't you
   way teelekraam tɨw?   send a telegram?

ŋɔɔn

7. tɨw teelekraam nɨw qae-naa?   Where [does one] go to telegraph?

hii

prehsəniiyəthaan   post office
8. kee way teelekraam nɨw   They send telegrams at the post
   prehsəniiyəthaan.   office.

ŋɔɔn

9. qəñcəŋ tɨw.   Let's go then.

[At the Post Office]

10. kñom cɑŋ pñaə səmbot nih tɨw   I want to send this letter to
    srok-baraŋ.   France.

308

Clerk

taam kəpal-hɑh
taam kəpal-tɨk
11. look pñaə taam kəpal-hɑh rɨɨ
taam kəpal-tɨk?

by air (by airplane)
by sea (by ship)
Are you sending it by air or by sea?

ŋɔɔn

12. baat, taam kəpal-hɑh.

By air.

Clerk

bət
taem
13. look trəw bət taem
prammuəy-dəndɑp riəl.

to attach, affix
stamp
You'll have to put on a sixteen-riel
stamp.

rɨkkəmɑndei
14. look pñaə rɨkkəmɑndei tee?

to register; registered
Do you want it registered? (Are you
sending it registered?)

ŋɔɔn

sɑmkhan (səmkhan)
15. mɨn bac tee; səmbot nih pñaə tɨw
puəq-maaq kñom; mɨn səmkhan
ponmaan tee.

to be important
It's not necessary; this letter's going
to my friend; it's not very important.

hii

16. pñaə kəñcap nih tɨw srok-
qaamerɨc tlay ponmaan?

How much is it to send this package
to America?

Clerk

tləŋ
17. cam kñom tləŋ məəl sən.

to weigh (trans.)
Let me weigh it first (and see).

tumŋuˇən (təmŋuˇən)
kraam
18. tumŋuˇən pii kilou pii-rɔɔy kraam.

weight
gram(s)
It weighs (its weight is) two kilos
two hundred grams.

hii

bɑh

traa
bɑh traa
kom qaoy
bɑh-baok (baok-bɑh)
19. soum look bɑh traa prap kee
kom qaoy bɑh-baok klaŋ peek.

to throw, drive (a nail or stake),
    stamp, print
a seal, stamp, mark
to stamp (with a seal)
don't allow (here: not to)
to throw about, to handle roughly
Would you please stamp it "Handle with
Care"? (Would you please stamp it
telling them not to throw it around too
hard?)

20. haəy kñom trəw-kaa taem-pram-
riəl dɑp nɨŋ taem-dɑp-riəl pram.

And I need ten five-riel stamps and
five ten-riel stamps.

Clerk

21. tlay te̊əŋ-qɑh bəy-rɔɔy   Altogether it's three hundred fifty-
    haasəp-prambəy riəl.   eight riels.

hii

    bɑŋ (~ baŋ)   bank
22. qəyləw kñom trəw yɔɔk praq tɨw   Now I have to go deposit some money
    daq bɑŋ sən.   in the bank.

ŋɔɔn

    koŋ   account
23. hii-qaeŋ miən koŋ nɨw bɑŋ naa?   In what bank do you have your account?

hii

    thəniəkiə   bank
    ciət   nation; national
    thəniəkiə-ciət   the National Bank
24. nɨw thəniəkiə-ciət.   In the National Bank.

ŋɔɔn

    sɑnsɑm (sənsɑm)   to save up, collect
25. qou, qəñcəŋ sənsɑm luy baan craən Oh, then you've saved up a lot of
    haəy, mɛɛn tee?   money, right?

hii

    stəə-tae   almost, on the point of
    caay   to pay out, to spend
26. sənsɑm qae-naa? stəə-tae rɔɔk   How would I save? I just barely
    luy caay mɨn kroə̆n phɑɑŋ.   make enough to spend.

ŋɔɔn

    niyiəy qañcəŋ   speaking of that, now that you
                         mention it, by the way
    šaek (~ saek)   check
    baək   to cash (a check)
27. qou, niyiəy qəñcəŋ, kñom miən šaek Oh, now that you mention it, I have
    muəy kñom cɑŋ yɔɔk tɨw baək dae. a check I want to take and cash too.

[At the Bank]

hii

    təc   to be few, little (in quantity)
28. tɨw kənlaeŋ nuh wɨñ; mənuh təc [Let's] go over there; there aren't too
    bəntəc.   many people. (the people are rather few.)

[To Clerk]

    poə̆n   thousand
    məpoə̆n   one thousand
29. kñom cɑŋ daq praq məpoə̆n nih   I want to deposit this one thousand
    knoŋ koŋ kñom.   [riels] in my account.

Clerk

prɑkan (prəkan, pəkan)   to maintain, guarantee
prɑkan-day   receipt
30. nih prəkan-day.   Here's [your] receipt.

ŋɔɔn

31. kñom caŋ baək šaek nih.   I want to cash this check.

Clerk

siññei   to sign
32. soum look siññei cmuəh sən.   Please sign [your] name first.

ŋɔɔn

kbaal   specifier for books, volumes,
                                      tablets, and certain animals
33. haəy kñom trəw-kaa šaek muəy   And I need another check-book.
    kbaal tiət.

[They leave the bank]

hii

prɑqap-sɑmbot   letter-box
34. qou, kñom plɨc daq səmbot nih nɨw   Oh, I forgot to put this letter in the
    knoŋ prəqap-səmbot haəy.   letter-box.

ŋɔɔn

poh   post office
35. qəñcəŋ tɨw poh wɨñ.   Then [let's] go back to the post office.

B. GRAMMAR AND DRILLS

1. Word Study: Affixation

It is one of the clichés about Cambodian that it has a complex system of
prefixes and infixes. This statement is misleading if it leads to the conclusion
that Cambodian speakers "use" affixation as a derivational process in speaking.
It is a fact that the Cambodian lexicon contains a large number of words (derivatives) which are related to other words (bases) by various prefixes and infixes,
but these affixes are not productive in the modern language. An example of a
productive affix is the English prefix re- 'to repeat an action', which can be freely applied to any English verb: redo, remake, replay, rewrite, etc. This is not
true of any Cambodian affix. Thus Cambodian affixes are "frozen" or "crystal-
lized" in the words in which they occur; they are roughly analogous to such prefixes as in- in English, which in a great many words functions as a negative prefix, as in inaccurate, incorrect, incapable, etc., but which in other words has a
different function, e.g. incite, indicate, induce, etc., and which cannot be freely
applied to any word, e.g. unable, not *inable; undo, not *indo; unhappy, not *in-
happy. It would be misleading to tell a foreign student of English that he can use
in- whenever he wants to negate a verb or adjective; all that we could usefully
tell him is that in many words in- has a negative meaning; this might help him

to infer the meaning of some (but not all) words with initial in- which he hears
or reads. This, aside from its intrinsic interest as a feature of the lexicon, is
our sole justification for investigating Cambodian prefixes and infixes in a course
in spoken Cambodian.

While Cambodian affixes may historically have had clearly defined functions
(and were perhaps productive), a given affix may now have a variety of functions,
while a given function, e.g. nominalization, is represented by several different
affixes. We will attempt here to present only the commonest affixes with their
commonest, or typical, functions. Affixes will be cited only in their full or unreduced forms; reduction in unstressed syllables is discussed in Lesson 8, B, 9.
Bases or derivatives not previously introduced are preceded by an asterisk.

A. Prefixes

1) Prefixes of Shape C (Consonant)

/p t c k s/ all occur as prefixes. (These same consonants also commonly occur as the first member of initial consonant sequences in words which
are not derivatives; e.g. pteəh 'house', tməy 'new', ckae 'dog', kbaal 'head', and
sdap 'listen'.) /p/ is by far the most common prefix of this shape, and its typical
function is 'causation', e.g.:

dac 'to tear (intrans.)'	*pdac 'to tear (trans.), to cut off'
kaət 'to be born'	*pkaət 'to create, cause'
*saŋ 'to be tame'	*psaŋ 'to tame'

Other functions of /p/:

tuk 'to put'	*ptuk 'to load (a boat, etc.)'
daəm 'origin'	pdaəm 'to begin, to originate (trans.)'
kuu 'pair'	*pkuu 'to pair off'
leeŋ 'to play'	pleeŋ 'song (instrumental)'

Other single-consonant prefixes have mixed functions:

*biət(-biən) 'to oppress'	*tbiət 'to pinch'
*muul 'round'	*cmoul 'to make into a ball' (with vowel change)
*bɑt 'to turn, to fold'	*kbat 'to deceive, betray
miən 'to have'	kmiən 'not have, not exist'
*dɑh 'to take off, loose'	*sdɑh 'to expectorate'

2) Prefixes of Shape CV- (Consonant + Vowel)

When C of a CV- prefix is the same consonant as the first C of the base,
it is a reduplicative prefix; the function of such prefixes is usually 'repetitive
action' or 'intensification', or both:

*kaay 'to dig (with the hands)'	kɑkaay 'to dig around, scratch about'
teəh 'to slap'	*tɔteəh 'to flap (the wings)'
baoh 'to sweep'	*bɑbaoh 'to sweep energetically back and forth, raise a dust'

Some words seem to have a reduplicative prefix but no underlying base; e.g.

*bɑbuəl 'to agree, to persuade'
*bɑbou 'the lips'

Another common CV- prefix is rɔ-; in some words it derives adjectival verbs from transitive verbs or from intransitive verbs:

daɑq 'to pull up'   *rɔdaɑq 'uprooted'
*luət 'to extinguish'   rɔluət 'extinguished'
*wɔuəl 'to revolve'   rɔwuəl 'to be busy'

In other words it derives intransitive verbs from transitive verbs:

*bout 'to pull off'   *rɔbout 'to come off, slip off'

In still other words its function is nominalization:

*baŋ 'to hide'   *rɔbaŋ 'a screen, shade'

The prefix mə- is a reduction of muəy 'one':

daɑŋ 'time, occasion'   mədaɑŋ 'once'
neĕq 'person'   məneĕq 'alone, one person'
*-phɨy 'twenty'   məphɨy 'twenty'

3) Prefixes of Shape CrV-

Prefixes of shape CrV- are prV-, trV-, crV-, krV-, or srV-, with prV- by far the most frequent. (CrV- is also a common unstressed syllable shape in unanalyzable words: pradap 'instrument', *traciəq 'ear', *cramoh 'nose', *krabəy 'water buffalo', and sramaoc 'ant'.) The function of CrV- prefixes is vague and inconsistent. Perhaps the typical function of prV- is 'reciprocity':

*kham 'to bite'   *prakham 'to bite each other'
*cluəh 'to argue'   *pracluəh 'to argue back and forth'

Other CrV- prefixes and their functions are shown below:

kaət 'to be born'   *prakaət 'to originate, set up'
douc 'to be similar'   *pradouc 'to compare'
*kan 'to hold, believe'   prakan 'to maintain, be conservative'
*baac 'to scatter'   *trabaac 'to crumble in the fingers'
*muc 'to dive, go under'   *cramuc 'to put under, submerge'
*wiəc 'crooked'   *krawiəc 'twisted and deformed'
*qap 'to be dim'   *sraqap 'to be obscure, foggy'

4) Prefixes of Shape CVN- (Consonant-Vowel-Nasal)

In most prefixes of shape CVN-, N is a nasal which assimilates to a following consonant according to the following pattern:

N becomes /m/ before / b p m n ŋ/
         /n/ before / d t l y s/
         /ñ/ before / c ñ/
         /ŋ/ before / k r h w q f/

(CVN- also occurs as an unstressed syllable in many unanalyzable disyllables: baŋquəc 'window', *damlouŋ 'potato', kanlaeŋ 'place', tuənlee 'river', cuəñceə̆ŋ 'wall'.) By far the most common prefix of shape CVN- is baN- whose principal function is 'causation':

baek 'to break (intrans.)'   *bambaek 'to cause to break'
daə ' to walk'   *bandaə 'to walk (a dog, etc.)'
cəñ 'to exit'   *bañcəñ 'to expel, send out'
riən 'to study, learn'   baŋriən 'to teach, cause to learn'

In some words the function of bɑN- is nominalization:

peə̆q 'to wear above the waist, or on the feet'	bɑmpeə̆q	1. 'clothing worn above the waist'
		2. 'to decorate, attach (a medal, etc.)'
tuk 'to place, put'	*bɑntuk 'cargo, load'	

Other CVN- prefixes have mixed and inconsistent functions:

kat 'to cut'	bɑŋkat 'to ignite; to create a half-breed'
kat 'to cut'	*sɑŋkat 'division, sector'
*sɑm 'to match, go together'	sɑnsɑm 'to save, amass'
*trɑɑŋ 'to strain, filter'	*kɑntrɑɑŋ 'a strainer, filter'
dəŋ 'to know'	*dɑndəŋ 'to ask in marriage'
dɑp 'ten	dɑndɑp '-teen'
leep 'to swallow'	*rumleep 'to cause to swallow'
baoh 'to sweep'	qɑmbaoh 'a broom'
*teə̆q 'to trap, snare'	*qɑnteə̆q 'a trap, snare'
nɨw 'to stay, live, reside'	*lumnɨw 'address, residence'
daə 'to walk'	*cuə̆ndaə 'stairs'

5) The Prefix qaa-

The pronominal prefix qaa-, unlike the prefixes discussed above, is productive, which explains the fact that it has already been introduced in Lesson 11, B, 8. It has a pronominalizing function before adjectival verbs or adjectives:

naa? 'which'	qaa-naa? 'which one?'
touc 'small'	qaa-touc 'the small one(s)'
pɔə-kmaw 'black'	qaa-pɔə-kmaw 'the black one(s)'

Before nouns, pronouns, or proper names, it has a diminutive or derogatory meaning (which is probably not entirely absent from its apparently purely pronominal use above):

cao 'thief'	*qaa-cao 'you thief!'
*qaeŋ 'you (familiar)'	*qaa-qaeŋ 'you (derogatory)'
but 'Bouth (a personal name)'	qaa-but 'little Bouth'

6) The Negative Prefix qaq-

The negative prefix qaq- (qa-) occurs in many words of Pali or Sanskrit origin, and is not generally productive:

phɨy 'to be afraid'	*qaqphɨy 'without fear, fearless'
mənuh 'human being'	*qaqmənuh 'supernatural being'
*yuttəthɔə 'justice'	*qaqyuttəthɔə 'injustice'

B. Infixes

1) Infixes of Shape -C-

Single-consonant infixes are one of the consonants /n b m ŋ/, with /n/ by far the most common. (These same consonants also commonly occur as C_2 in unanalyzable words, or perhaps in derivatives whose underlying forms have been lost.) The function of almost all single-consonant infixes is 'nominalization':

cuəl 'to rent'	cnuəl 'rent (n.)'
*siət 'to insert'	*sniət 'an insert, a wedge'
cam 'to wait'	cnam 'a year'
lɨən 'fast'	*lbɨən 'speed'
leeŋ 'to play'	lbaeŋ 'game' (with vowel change)
soum 'to beg'	*smoum 'beggar'
*saoy 'to eat (royal)'	*sŋaoy 'royal food'

Initial /b/ and /d/ in the base change to /p/ and /t/ before an infix:

baek 'to break'	*pnaek 'section, fragment'
dam 'to plant'	tnam 'a plant, herb, medicine'

Initial /r/ in the bases changes to /rɔ-/ before an infix:

*roə̆h 'to rake'	*rɔnoə̆h 'a rake'
roə̆m 'to dance'	rɔbam 'a dance' (with vowel change)

2) Infixes of Shape -Vm-

In infixes of shape -Vm-, -V- is /ɑ/ or /u/, and /m/ is invariable. The typical function of the infix -Vm- is 'causation'. Since it occurs only in derivatives whose bases have an initial consonant sequence, it is probably to be related to the causative prefix bɑN-, which occurs only in derivatives whose bases have a single initial consonant.

sqaat 'to be clean'	sɑmqaat 'to clean, to make clean'
sruəl 'to be easy'	*sɑmruəl 'to facilitate, make easy'
slap 'to die'	*sɑmlap 'to kill'
*criəp 'to learn'	cumriəp 'to inform'
tleə̆q 'to fall'	*tumleə̆q 'to fell, overthrow'

The following examples illustrate some marginal functions of -Vm-:

*skɔɔm 'to be slender'	*sɑmkɔɔm 'ridiculously slender'
claaŋ 'to cross'	*cɑmlaaŋ 'to copy'
*krət 'law'	*kɑmrət 'to decree; a decree'
*kraa 'to be poor'	*kɑmraa 'to be poor at'

3) Infixes of Shape -VN(n)-

The commonest infix in Cambodian is the infix -VN(n)-, whose primary function is 'nominalization'. The shape -VN- occurs in bases with an initial consonant sequence, and the shape -Vmn- in bases with a single initial consonant, with -n- providing the initial of the second syllable of the derivative. In the shape -VN-, -V- is /ɑ/, /u/, or /uə̆/, and -N- is a nasal which in some words assimilates to a following consonant according to the pattern described in A, 4 above, but which in most words remains invariably /m/. The shape -Vmn- is either /ɑmn/ or /umn/.

a) Derivatives of bases with initial consonant sequences:

Shape -Vm- (where /-m-/ is invariable):

kdaw 'hot'	kɑmdaw 'heat'
klaŋ 'strong'	kɑmlaŋ 'strength'
khəŋ 'angry'	*kɑmhəŋ 'anger'
cŋaay 'distant'	cɑmŋaay 'distance'
*criəŋ 'to sing'	cɑmriəŋ 'song'

craən 'much, many'   *camraən 'success, increase; to
                                        increase'
*claq 'to carve'   camlaq 'carving, sculpture'
*slɑɑ 'to make a stew'   samlɑɑ 'stew'
claəy 'to answer'   *camlaəy 'an answer'
tloə̆p 'accustomed to'   *tumloə̆p 'custom'
tŋuə̆n 'to be heavy'   tumŋuə̆n 'weight'
lqɑɑ 'to be pretty'   *lumqɑɑ 'beauty, embellishment'
crɨw 'to be deep'   *cumrɨw 'depth'

Shape -VN- (where -N- assimilates to a following consonant):

sdap 'to listen, understand'   *sandap 'understanding, convention'
klah 'some'   kanlah 'half'
*kcap 'to wrap'   kañcap 'parcel, bundle'
*chan 'to eat (of clergy)'   *caŋhan 'priest's food'
tloə̆p 'accustomed to'   *tuə̆nloə̆p 'custom' (a doublet)
plɨɨ 'to be bright'   *puə̆nlɨɨ 'light'

Initial /p/ and /t/ change to /b/ and /d/ before -ɑN-:

praə 'to use'   bamraə 'servant'
pqaem 'to be sweet'   baŋqaem 'sweets, dessert'
tlay 'expensive'   *damlay 'value'
*tbaañ 'to weave'   dambaañ 'weaving'
tləŋ 'to weigh'   *damləŋ 'an ounce'

b) Derivatives of bases with single consonant initial:

dəŋ 'to know'   *damnəŋ 'information'
dam 'to plant'   *damnam 'a plant'
kat 'to cut'   *kamnat 'a cut piece, a slice'
daə 'to walk'   damnaə 'trip, process'
suə 'to ask'   samnuə 'a question'
qaoy 'to give'   *qamnaoy 'a gift'
kaət 'to give birth'   *kamnaət 'birth'
tɨñ 'to buy'   tumnɨñ 'merchandise'
kɨt 'to think'   *kumnɨt 'thought'
cɨə 'to believe'   *cumnɨə 'belief'

Initial /p/ and /t/ change to /b/ and /d/ before /-amn-/:

*paɑŋ 'to hope, intend'   *bamnaɑŋ 'hope, aim, intention'
taɑ 'to continue'   *damnaɑ 'extension'

4) Infixes of Shape -rV(n)-

In a few words the infix -rV(n)- (-rV- in bases with an initial consonant sequence, and -rVn- in bases with a single initial consonant) occurs with the function of 'nominalization':

*saok 'to pity'   *srɑnaok 'pity'
*tum 'to perch'   *trɔnum 'a perch'
*stɔɔp 'to cover, envelop'   sratɔɔp 'covering, bark (of the
                                        banana tree)'

C. Résumé

Of all the affixes discussed above, only the causative affixes bɑN-/-Vm- and the nominalizing infix -VN(n)- occur with significant frequency in the language. The only productive affixes discussed above are the pronominalizing prefix qɑɑ-, and to a lesser degree, the reduplicative prefixes of shape CV-.

2. məc kɑɑ mɨn + Verb

In Lesson 3, B, 16 it was pointed out that məc (kɑɑ) at the beginning of a sentence means 'why?'. məc kɑɑ mɨn . . . at the beginning of a question, then, means 'Why don't you . . . ?, why isn't it . . . ?, etc.' as in

məc kɑɑ mɨn way teelekraam tɨw?   Why don't you send a telegram?

2-A. Response Drill

Teacher	Student
kñom səsei səmbot. (way teelekraam)	məc kɑɑ mɨn way teelekraam?
kñom praə kmaw-day. (praə slaap-pəkaa)	məc kɑɑ mɨn praə slaap-pəkaa?
kñom tɨw twəə-kaa. (tɨw daə-leeŋ)	məc kɑɑ mɨn tɨw daə-leeŋ?
kñom tɨw məəl kon. (tɨw məəl lkhaon)	məc kɑɑ mɨn tɨw məəl lkhaon?
kñom kcəy luy. (baək šaek)	məc kɑɑ mɨn baək šaek?
kñom məəl kasaet. (məəl siəwphɨw)	məc kɑɑ mɨn məəl siəwphɨw?
kñom tɨw taam rəteh-pləəŋ.	məc kɑɑ mɨn tɨw taam kəpal-hah?
(tɨw taam kəpal-hah)	
kñom pñaə taam kəpal-tɨk.	məc kɑɑ mɨn pñaə taam kəpal-hah?
(pñaə taam kəpal-hah)	
kñom cih taqsii. (tɨw daə)	məc kɑɑ mɨn tɨw daə?
kñom tɨñ pɔə-krəhaam. (tɨñ pɔə-khiəw)	məc kɑɑ mɨn tɨñ pɔə-khiəw?

3. Idiomatic Use of qae-naa

The interrogative word qae-naa 'where?' sometimes occurs with the idiomatic meaning 'where would I . . ., how could I . . .'. qae-naa in this function typically occurs after an assertion, implication, or suggestion which the speaker wishes to ridicule, as in the following exchange:

qəñcəŋ sənsam luy baan craən haəy, mɛɛn tee?	Then you've saved a lot of money, right?
sənsam qae-naa! stəə-tae rɔɔk luy caay mɨn krɔən phɑɑŋ.	How would I save? I just barely make enough to spend.

3-A. Response Drill

Teacher	Student
məc kɑɑ mɨn sənsam luy?	sənsam qae-naa!
məc kɑɑ mɨn ñam baay?	ñam qae-naa!
məc kɑɑ mɨn tɨw məəl kon?	tɨw məəl qae-naa!
məc kɑɑ mɨn kcəy luy?	kcəy qae-naa!
məc kɑɑ mɨn tɨñ laan?	tɨñ qae-naa!
məc kɑɑ mɨn rɔɔk kaa twəə?	rɔɔk qae-naa!
məc kɑɑ mɨn məəl kasaet?	məəl qae-naa!
məc kɑɑ mɨn səsei səmbot?	səsei qae-naa!
məc kɑɑ mɨn baək laan?	baək qae-naa!

4. The Compound Auxiliary stəə-tae

stəə-tae belongs to the class of preverbal auxiliaries discussed in Lesson 18, B, 7. Its meaning is 'almost, on the point of, just about to', as in

kñom kliən stəə-tae slap haəy.   I'm almost dying of hunger. (I'm hungry almost to the point of dying.)

When stəə-tae is followed by the negative auxiliary mɨn at any point in the predicate, the two auxiliaries, taken together, mean 'almost not, barely, hardly, scarcely', as in

stəə-tae rɔɔk luy caay mɨn krŏən.   I hardly make enough money to spend. (I almost make money to spend not enough.)

4-A. Substitution Drill

Teacher	Student
kñom kliən stəə-tae slap haəy.	kñom kliən stəə-tae slap haəy.
qah-kəmlaŋ	kñom qah-kəmlaŋ stəə-tae slap haəy.
kcɨl	kñom kcɨl stəə-tae slap haəy.
rəŋiə	kñom rəŋiə stəə-tae slap haəy.
kdaw	kñom kdaw stəə-tae slap haəy.
khəŋ	kñom khəŋ stəə-tae slap haəy.
ñam sraa	kñom ñam sraa stəə-tae slap haəy.
riən	kñom riən stəə-tae slap haəy.

4-B. Substitution Drill

Teacher	Student
kñom stəə-tae rɔɔk luy caay mɨn krŏən.	kñom stəə-tae rɔɔk luy caay mɨn krŏən.
tɨw kənlaeŋ nuh mɨn baan.	kñom stəə-tae tɨw kənlaeŋ nuh mɨn baan.
keeŋ mɨn luŏq.	kñom stəə-tae keeŋ mɨn luŏq.
twəə mhoup mɨn krŏən.	kñom stəə-tae twəə mhoup mɨn krŏən.
riən mɨn cap.	kñom stəə-tae riən mɨn cap.
tɨw rəteh-pləəŋ mɨn tŏən.	kñom stəə-tae tɨw rəteh-pləəŋ mɨn tŏən.
rɔɔk waen-taa mɨn khəən.	kñom stəə-tae rɔɔk waen-taa mɨn khəən.
cəñcəm ciiwɨt mɨn baan.	kñom stəə-tae cəñcəm ciiwɨt mɨn baan.
twəə kaa nuh mɨn ruəc.	kñom stəə-tae twəə kaa nuh mɨn ruəc.
məəl kasaet mɨn cap.	kñom stəə-tae məəl kasaet mɨn cap.

5. The Adverbial Phrase niyiəy qəñcəŋ

When the adverbial phrase niyiəy qəñcəŋ precedes a proposition, it means 'by the way, speaking of that, now that you mention it', as in

qou, niyiəy qəñcəŋ, kñom miən šaek muəy kñom caŋ yɔɔk tɨw baək dae.   Oh, now that you mention it, I have a check I want to cash too.

In a more literary style of Cambodian, niyiəy qəñcəŋ as a preposed adverbial may also mean 'having said that, having spoken in this manner'.

5-A. Substitution Drill

Teacher	Student
niyiəy qəñcəŋ, kñom cɑŋ <u>baək šaek muəy</u> dae.	niyiəy qəñcəŋ, kñom cɑŋ <u>baək šaek muəy</u> dae.
<u>yɔɔk səmbot nih tɨw poh</u>	niyiəy qəñcəŋ, kñom cɑŋ <u>yɔɔk səmbot nih tɨw poh</u> dae.
<u>tɨw psaa</u>	niyiəy qəñcəŋ, kñom cɑŋ <u>tɨw psaa</u> dae.
<u>tɨw baŋ</u>	niyiəy qəñcəŋ, kñom cɑŋ <u>tɨw baŋ</u> dae.
<u>way teelekraam</u>	niyiəy qəñcəŋ, kñom cɑŋ <u>way teelekraam</u> dae.
<u>səsei səmbot</u>	niyiəy qəñcəŋ, kñom cɑŋ <u>səsei səmbot</u> dae.
<u>tɨñ taem-bət-səmbot</u>	niyiəy qəñcəŋ, kñom cɑŋ <u>tɨñ taem-bət-səmbot</u> dae.
<u>tɨw haaŋ nuh</u>	niyiəy qəñcəŋ, kñom cɑŋ <u>tɨw haaŋ nuh</u> dae.
<u>tɨñ kasaet</u>	niyiəy qəñcəŋ, kñom cɑŋ <u>tɨñ kasaet</u> dae.

6. The Adjectival Verb <u>təc</u>

<u>təc</u> is an adjectival verb meaning 'to be little (in quantity), few', as in

tɨw kənlaeŋ nuh wɨn; mənuh <u>təc</u> bəntəc.	[Let's] go over there; there aren't too many people. (the people are rather <u>few</u>.)

<u>təc</u> is thus the antonym of <u>craən</u> 'much, many'. It is also the base from which are derived the adverb <u>bəntəc</u> 'a little, somewhat', and the reduplicative <u>bəntəc-bəntuəc</u> 'just a little bit'.

6-A. Transformation Drill

Teacher	Student
kñom miən luy <u>craən</u> nah.	kñom miən luy <u>təc</u> nah.
nɨw knoŋ wŏət miən mənuh <u>craən</u> nah.	nɨw knoŋ wŏət miən mənuh <u>təc</u> nah.
kŏət baan praq-khae <u>craən</u> nah.	kŏət baan praq-khae <u>təc</u> nah.
wiə ñam baay <u>craən</u> nah.	wiə ñam baay <u>təc</u> nah.
tŋay-nih kñom twəə-kaa <u>craən</u> nah.	tŋay-nih kñom twəə-kaa <u>təc</u> nah.
psaa nuh miən luəq qəywan <u>craən</u> nah.	psaa nuh miən luəq qəywan <u>təc</u> nah.
phuum nuh miən ptĕəh <u>craən</u> nah.	phuum nuh miən ptĕəh <u>təc</u> nah.
mənuh nuh miən ñiət-səndaan <u>craən</u> nah.	mənuh nuh miən ñiət-səndaan <u>təc</u> nah.
ptĕəh nuh miən siəwphɨw <u>craən</u> nah.	ptĕəh nuh miən siəwphɨw <u>təc</u> nah.

7. <u>kbaal</u> as a Specifier

In Lesson 22 we met <u>kbaal</u> as a noun meaning 'head' in

baq cəəŋ haəy-nɨŋ baek <u>kbaal</u>.	[He] had a broken leg and a fractured skull. (broken <u>head</u>)

<u>kbaal</u> also occurs as a specifier meaning 'books, volumes, tablets', as in

kñom trəw-kaa šaek muəy <u>kbaal</u> tiət.	I need another <u>book</u> of checks.
kñom miən siəwphɨw pram <u>kbaal</u>.	I have five (<u>volumes of</u>) books.

kbaal also occurs as a specifier after the names of certain animals, such as koo 'ox' and krabəy 'water-buffalo', with the meaning 'head', very much as in English.

qəwpuk kñom miən koo-krabəy dap   My father has ten <u>head</u> of livestock.
kbaal.

7-A. <u>Substitution Drill</u>

Teacher	Student
kñom t<u>i</u>ñ siəwph<u>i</u>w bəy kbaal.	kñom t<u>i</u>ñ <u>siəwph<u>i</u>w</u> bəy kbaal.
šaek	kñom t<u>i</u>ñ <u>šaek</u> bəy kbaal.
krədaah-səsei	kñom t<u>i</u>ñ <u>krədaah-səsei</u> bəy kbaal.
səmbot-kəpal	kñom t<u>i</u>ñ <u>səmbot-kəpal</u> bəy kbaal.
kasaet	kñom t<u>i</u>ñ <u>kasaet</u> bəy kbaal.
koo	kñom t<u>i</u>ñ <u>koo</u> bəy kbaal.
krabəy	kñom t<u>i</u>ñ <u>krabəy</u> bəy kbaal.
koo-krabəy	kñom t<u>i</u>ñ <u>koo-krabəy</u> bəy kbaal.

[Tape 41]   C. COMPREHENSION

1. <u>Writing a Letter</u>

daeŋ: yii, kñom baq kmaw-day haəy!
        ñaem-qaeŋ miən kmaw-day tee, qaoy kñom som kcəy muəy mɔɔk?

ñaem: kmiən tee. kñom miən tae slaap-pəkaa; yɔɔk tee?

daeŋ: baat, qɑɑ-kun.

ñaem: səsei səmbot t<u>i</u>w neᵊq-naa?

daeŋ: kñom səsei t<u>i</u>w sɑŋsaa kñom n<u>i</u>w khaet kampuᵊŋ-caam.
        kñom khaan səsei t<u>i</u>w pii qat<u>i</u>t mɔɔk haəy.

        [daqtilou 'typewriter']
        [way daqtilou 'to type']
ñaem: məc kɑɑ m<u>i</u>n way daqtilou?

        [qaŋkulileik (another word for 'typewriter')]
daeŋ: kñom m<u>i</u>n-səw prəsɑp way qaŋkulileik tee.
        coh, ñaem-qaeŋ riən way qaŋkulileik n<u>i</u>w qae-naa?

ñaem: kñom cuəl qaoy kee bəŋriən way.

        [khoh 'to be wrong, different']
daeŋ: yii, səsei khoh bəntəc!

ñaem: cɑŋ lup tee? kñom miən cɔə-lup.

daeŋ: qɑɑ-kun.

2. <u>Two Friends Discuss Correspondence</u>

chum: pñaə səmbot t<u>i</u>w srok-yipun taam kəpal-hɑh tlay ponmaan?

cheiŋ: srac-tae tumŋuᵊn tee.

[sraal 'to be light (in weight)']
[sɑnlək (sənlək, sələk) 'specifier for sheets or leaves']
[sdaəŋ 'to be thin']
[sdaəŋ-sdaəŋ 'to be very light and thin']

chum: qou, səmbot kñom sraal tee.
        kñom səsei tae pii sənlək ponnoh, haəy krədaah sdaəŋ-sdaəŋ nah.

chein: prəhael ciə mɨn tlay ponmaan tee.
        chum-qaeŋ tɨw poh rɨɨ?

chum: baat, kñom trəw səsei səmbot muəy tiət yɔɔk tɨw daq poh.

chein: qəñcəŋ tɨñ krədaah-səsei-səmbot haəy-nɨŋ sraom-səmbot qaoy
        kñom phɑɑŋ baan tee?

chum: chein-qaeŋ trəw-kaa tɨk-kmaw tee?

chein: tee, tae som tɨñ taem-pram-riəl qaoy kñom dɑp phɑɑŋ.

        [neə̆q-ruə̆t-səmbot 'postman']
chum: neə̆q-ruə̆t-səmbot craən-tae mɔɔk maoŋ ponmaan?

chein: baat, thoə̆mmədaa maoŋ dɑp prɨk.

chum: prɨk nih kñom miən səmbot tee?

chein: kmiən tee; miən tae kasaet.

3. Working at the Post Office

sɨən: sein-qaeŋ twəə-kaa qəy?

sein: kñom twəə-kaa nɨw prehsəniiyəthaan.

sɨən: thəə qəy-klah?

sein: kñom luə̆q taem haəy-nɨŋ tətuəl kəñcɑp dael kee pñaə tɨw bɑɑrəteeh.

sɨən: sein-qaeŋ baan praq-khae craən tee?

sein: mɨn craən ponmaan tee; lmɔɔm tae cəñcəm kruəsaa.

sɨən: sein sənsɑm luy baan klah tee?

sein: sənsɑm qae-naa baan? lmɔɔm tae caay ponnoh.

4. Cashing a Check

chum: kñom təəp-nɨŋ tətuəl šaek muəy pii qəwpuk kñom.
        dəŋ tee, kñom tɨw baək qae-naa baan?

chein: chum miən koŋ nɨw bɑŋ naa tee?

chum: kmiən tee; kñom mɨn dael miən praq sɑl tee.

chein: qəñcəŋ tɨw baək nɨw bɑŋ kñom tɨw; kñom miən koŋ muəy nɨw
        thəniəkiə-kmae.

chum: kee baək qaoy tee?

chein: thəy mɨn baək qaoy? tae kñom trəw siññei nɨw ləə šaek nuh dae.

D. CONVERSATION

1. Writing Letters

Have two students discuss the letters they are writing. The discussion might include such things as asking to borrow various writing materials, the merits of typing as opposed to writing with a pen, inquiring as to the destination or intention of the respective letters.

2. At the Post Office

Have one student assume the role of the clerk and another of a customer needing his services. The conversation might include the cost of sending a letter or a parcel to various countries, whether it is to be sent by air or by surface, its weight, registration, the purchase of various denominations of stamps, sending a telegram, etc.

3. In a Stationary Store

Have one student assume the role of a customer and another of the clerk. Items to be purchased might include writing paper, envelopes, fountain pens, ink, pencils, erasers, etc.; the color of the ink, the weight of the paper, etc.

4. At the Bank

Have one student assume the role of a customer and another of the clerk. Topics might include depositing money, getting a receipt, cashing a check, whether or not one has an account in that bank, signing one's name, etc.

LESSON 24. EDUCATION

[Tape 42]   A. DIALOGUE

Bill

kmeiŋ	to be young; child(ren)
koun-kmeiŋ	children
coul riən	to begin studying, to start to school

1. nɨw srok-kmae qayuq ponmaan koun-kmeiŋ coul riən?

At what age do children start to school in Cambodia?

bun

2. baat, thŏəmmədaa qayuq prammuəy cnam.

Usually at age six.

kaal pii daəm	originally, formerly
kmeiŋ-proh-proh	boys
salaa-wŏət	pagoda school

3. kaal pii daəm, kmeiŋ-proh-proh tloəp tɨw riən nɨw salaa-wŏət.

Formerly, boys used to study in the pagoda schools.

kmeiŋ-proh-srəy	boys and girls
salaa-riəcckaa	government school

4. tae sap-tŋay-nih kmeiŋ-proh-srəy craən-tae tɨw riən nɨw salaa-riəcckaa.

But these days boys and girls mostly study in the government schools.

Bill

səksaa	to study, learn; education
pathɑm	first, primary
pathɑm-səksaa (pathɑmməsəksaa)	primary education

5. pathɑmməsəksaa kee riən ponmaan cnam təəp cap?

In primary school, how many years do they study (before finishing)?

bun

tnaq tii-dɑp-pii	12th grade (1st year)
tnaq tii-prampɨl	

*6. baat, prammuəy cnam, kɨɨ taŋ-pii tnaq tii-dɑp-pii tɨw tnaq tii-prampɨl.

Six years, from the 12th grade to the 7th grade.

---

*At the teacher's discretion, the sentences preceded by an asterisk in this lesson need not be memorized by the student, since they involve no new patterns. However, the student should master the vocabulary involved, and be able to translate the sentences into English and vice versa, precisely because they involve no new patterns.

Bill

salaa-pathɑmməsəksaa	primary school
7. nɨw salaa-pathɑmməsəksaa kee bəŋriən qwəy-klah?	What (plural) do they teach in primary school?

bun

muk-wɨcciə	subject, study
hat	to practice, to drill
qaan	to pronounce, to read aloud
hat-qaan	reading practice, pronunciation
taeŋ	to write, compose
səc-kdəy	composition, matter, story
taeŋ-səc-kdəy	composition, writing
twəə-leik	arithmetic
phuumisaah	geography
*8. qou, kee bəŋriən muk-wɨcciə craən nah, douc-ciə hat-qaan, twəə-leik, taeŋ-səc-kdəy, haəy-nɨŋ phuumisaah ciə-daəm.	Oh, they teach many subjects, such as reading, arithmetic, writing, and geography (as examples).

qɑp-rum	to train, to discipline
withii	way, method
bɑŋkaa (bəŋkaa)	to prevent
withii-bɑŋkaa-rook	disease prevention, hygiene
dɑmboun-miən (dəmboun-miən)	deportment, good manners
*9. kraw-pii nuh kee qɑp-rum kmeiŋ khaaŋ withii-bəŋkaa-rook haəy-nɨŋ dəmboun-miən.	Besides that, they train the children in hygiene and good manners.

Bill

mattyum	middle, medium
mattyum-səksaa (mattyumməsəksaa)	secondary education
*10. nɨw mattyumməsəksaa riən ponmaan cnam?	How many years do they study in secondary school?

bun

caek	to divide
pnaek	section, part, fragment
mattyumməsəksaa tii-muəy	1st cycle of secondary school
mattyumməsəksaa tii-pii	2nd cycle of secondary school
11. baat, mattyumməsəksaa caek ciə pii pnaek, kɨɨ mattyumməsəksaa tii-muəy haəy-nɨŋ tii-pii.	Secondary education is divided into two parts—the first cycle and the second cycle (of secondary education).

qanuq-wɨttyiəlay (∼-wɨcciəlay)	junior high school (French <u>collège</u>)
tumnəəp	modern, recent (here: secondary)
tnaq tii-prammuəy tumnəəp	6th grade, secondary (7th year)
tnaq tii-bəy tumnəəp	3rd grade, secondary (10th year)
*12. mattyumməsəksaa tii-muəy, rɨɨ qanuq-wɨttyiəlay, cap pii tnaq tii-prammuəy tumnəəp tɨw tnaq tii-bəy tumnəəp.	The first cycle of secondary education, or junior high school, lasts (begins) from the 6th to the 3rd grade.

coŋ | end, point
pralaaŋ (prəlaaŋ) | to compete, to take an examination
saññaabat | certificate
diiploum (diploum) | secondary diploma (French <u>diplôme</u>)

13. coŋ cnam tnaq tii-bəy tumnəəp, koun-səh trəw prəlaaŋ yɔɔk saññaabat diploum. | At the end of the 3rd grade, students have to take an examination for the diploma.

pisaeh (piseh) | to be special; precious
wɨcciə piseh | special subjects
təcnɨc | technical; technique
salaa-təcnɨc | technical school

*14. koun-səh klah coul riən wɨcciə piseh, douc-ciə salaa-təcnɨc rɨɨ salaa-raccənaa ciə-daəm. | Some students study special subjects, such as [in a] technical school, or the School of Fine Arts (as examples).

kuruq-wɨcciə | pedagogy
salaa-kuruq-wɨcciə | School of Pedagogy, Teachers' College

15. douc-ciə kñom ciə-daəm, kñom tɨw riən nɨw salaa-kuruq-wɨcciə. | Such as myself, for example; I entered the School of Pedagogy.

bantaa (bəntaa, pətaa) | to continue, to extend
wɨttyiəlay (~ wɨcciəlay) | senior high school (French <u>lycée</u>)
wɨttyiəlay sisowat | Lycée Sisowath

*16. koun-səh qae-tiət bəntaa wɨcciə nɨw wɨttyiəlay, douc-ciə wɨttyiəlay sisowath nɨw pnum-pɨñ. | Other students continue their studies at a senior high school, such as Lycée Sisowath in Phnom Penh.

Bill

*17. nɨw wɨttyiəlay kee riən qəy-klah? | What do they study in secondary school?

bun

qaqsaa | letters, writing
qaqsaasaah | letters, literature
prawoə̆ttəsaah (prəwoə̆ttəsaah) | history
mat | math
wɨttyiəsaah (~ wɨcciəsaah) | science

*18. kee riən qaqsaasaah, prəwoə̆ttəsaah, mat, haəy-nɨŋ wɨttyiəsaah ciə-daəm. | They study literature, history, math, and science (as examples).

məhaa-wɨttyiəlay (~ -wɨcciəlay) | university
bañcap (bəñcap, pəcap) | to finish, complete

19. baə koun-səh caŋ coul riən məhaa-wɨttyiəlay, kee trəw bəñcap mattyummasəksaa tii-pii. | If the student wants to enter the university, he must complete the second cycle of secondary school.

Bill

20. kee trəw riən ponmaan cnam nɨw   How many years do they have to study
    mattyumməsəksaa tii-pii?   in the 2nd cycle of secondary school?

bun

    tnaq tii-pii tumnəəp   2nd grade, secondary (11th year)
    tnaq tii-muəy tumnəəp   1st grade, secondary (12th year)
    tnaq cɔŋ bamphot   final grade (13th year)

*21. thoə̆mmədaa bəy cnam, kɨɨ tnaq   Usually three years—the 2nd grade,
    tii-pii tumnəəp, tnaq tii-muəy   the 1st grade, and the final grade.
    tumnəəp, haəy-nɨŋ tnaq cɔŋ
    bamphot.

    baasou   baccalaureate degree (Fr. bachot)
    baasou tii-muəy   1st baccalaureate degree

22. nɨw cɔŋ cnam tnaq tii-muəy   At the end of the 1st grade, they must
    tumnəəp, kee trəw prəlaaŋ yɔɔk   take an examination for the 1st bac-
    baasou tii-muəy.   calaureate degree.

    coə̆p   to stick, be attached; to pass
    prəlaaŋ coə̆p   to succeed, pass an examination
    laəŋ tnaq   to advance a grade, be promoted
    baasou tii-pii   2nd baccalaureate degree

23. baə kee prəlaaŋ coə̆p, kee qaac   If they pass the exam, they can advance
    laəŋ tnaq cɔŋ bamphot haəy prəlaaŋ   to the final grade and take the exam for
    yɔɔk baasou tii-pii.   the 2nd baccalaureate degree.

Bill

    prəlaaŋ tleə̆q   to fail in an examination

24. coh, baə prəlaaŋ tleə̆q, kee   Say, if one fails, can he take the
    prəlaaŋ mədaaŋ tiət baan tee?   examination again?

bun

    ponmaan   however many

25. baat, prəlaaŋ ponmaan daaŋ   Yes, [he] can take the exam as many
    ka-baan dae.   times [as he wishes].

Bill

    wɨcciə coə̆n kpuə̆h   higher education

*26. koun-səh kmae tɨw riən wɨcciə   Where do Cambodian students go for
    coə̆n kpuə̆h nɨw qae-naa?   their higher education?

bun

*27. riən nɨw srok-kmae ka-baan,   They can study in Cambodia or
    nɨw baarəteeh ka-baan.   abroad.

Bill

    kəylaa (kelaa)   sports, games

28. koun-səh kmae leeŋ kəylaa   What sports do Cambodian students
    qwəy-klah?   play?

bun

bal	ball
toət	to kick
bal-toət	soccer
wɑllay-bal	volleyball
səy	a feathered projectile
toət-səy	kicking a feathered projectile

29. kee leeŋ bal-toət, wɑllay-bal, haəy-niŋ toət-səy ciə-daəm.

They play soccer, volleyball, and toət-səy (as examples).

Bill

30. kee leeŋ toət-səy yaaŋ-məc?

How do they play toət-səy?

bun

poət	to surround, encircle
wuəŋ	circle
pii muəy tɨw muəy	from one to another

31. kee chɔɔ poət wuəŋ toət səy pii muəy tɨw muəy mɨn qaoy tleəq dɑl dəy.

They stand around in a circle [and] kick the səy from one to another without letting [it] fall to the ground.

Bill

32. kee praə kbaal baan tee?

Can they use their heads?

bun

kom-qaoy-tae

so long as [one, it] doesn't, provided that [you, they] don't

33. baat, praə qwəy kɑ-baan, kom-qaoy-tae trəw dəy.

Yes, [they] can use whatever [they like], so long as [it] doesn't hit the hands.

B. GRAMMAR AND DRILLS

1. The Cambodian System of Education

The following chart provides a summary of the organization of the Cambodian education system up to the university level, as revealed in the Dialogue:

pathɑmməsəksaa	Elementary education
tnaq tii-dɑp-pii	12th grade (1st year)
tnaq tii-dɑp-muəy	11th grade (2nd year)
tnaq tii-dɑp	10th grade (3rd year)
tnaq tii-prambuən	9th grade (4th year)
tnaq tii-prambəy	8th grade (5th year)
tnaq tii-prampɨl	7th grade (6th year)

mattyumməsəksaa tii-muəy (qanuq-wɨcciəlay)	First cycle of secondary education (junior high school)
tnaq tii-prammuəy tumnəəp	6th grade, secondary (7th year)
tnaq tii-pram tumnəəp	5th grade, secondary (8th year)
tnaq tii-buən tumnəəp	4th grade, secondary (9th year)
tnaq tii-bəy tumnəəp	3rd grade, secondary (10th year)
diiploum	secondary diploma

mattyumməsəksaa tii-pii (wɨcciəlay)	Second cycle of secondary school (senior high school, lycée)
tnaq tii-pii tumnəəp	2nd grade, secondary (11th year)
tnaq tii-muəy tumnəəp	1st grade, secondary (12th year)
baasou tii-muəy	First baccalaureate degree
tnaq coŋ bamphot	Final grade (13th year)
baasou tii-pii	Second baccalaureate degree
səksaa cöən kpuɜh (məhaa-wɨttyiəlay)	Higher education (university)

As can be seen from the chart, the Cambodian system numbers grades in descending order, starting with grade 12, after the French system. An qanuq-wɨttyiəlay (junior high school, French collège) includes the first four grades of secondary school, with the diiploum (French diplôme) as its culmination. A wɨttyiəlay (French lycée) includes all seven grades of secondary school, with the baasou tii-pii (French bachot deux) as its culmination. The term tumnəəp is the Cambodian translation of the French 'moderne', as in tnaq tii-bəy tumnəəp 'classe de troisième moderne', and occurs in the names of all the secondary grades except the tnaq coŋ bamphot 'final grade'.

1-A. Translation-Substitution Drill

Provide the Cambodian equivalents in the following sentences; in each case the correct equivalent can be obtained by subtracting the grade given from 13.

Teacher	Student
cnam nih kñom coul riən the third grade.	cnam nih kñom coul riən tnaq tii-dap.
the first grade.	cnam nih kñom coul riən tnaq tii-dap-pii.
the fifth grade.	cnam nih kñom coul riən tnaq tii-prambəy.
the twelfth grade.	cnam nih kñom coul riən tnaq tii-muəy tumnəəp.
the final grade.	cnam nih kñom coul riən tnaq coŋ bamphot.
the seventh grade.	cnam nih kñom coul riən tnaq tii-prammuəy tumnəəp.
the tenth grade.	cnam nih kñom coul riən tnaq tii-bəy tumnəəp.
the fourth grade.	cnam nih kñom coul riən tnaq tii-prambuən.
the ninth grade.	cnam nih kñom coul riən tnaq tii-buən tumnəəp.
the eighth grade.	cnam nih kñom coul riən tnaq tii-pram tumnəəp.

Teacher	Student
the second grade.	cnam nih kñom coul riən tnaq tii-dɑp-muəy.
the eleventh grade.	cnam nih kñom coul riən tnaq tii-pii tumnəəp.
the sixth grade.	cnam nih kñom coul riən tnaq tii-prampɨl.

2. Word Study: Pseudo-compounds

Many Cambodian words contain meaningful elements (morphemes) which recur with the same meaning in a number of complex words, but which do not occur as independent words (free forms). Since true compounds consist of two or more free forms used together with a unitary meaning, we can call complex words containing one or more bound elements pseudo-compounds. The constituents of pseudo-compounds are usually of Pali or Sanskrit origin, and are not generally productive in the language. Pseudo-compounds are further distinguished by the fact that the modifier constituent precedes the modified constituent, contrary to the modified-modifier pattern of Cambodian syntax. Some constituents which occur as free forms have special combining forms in pseudo-compounds. Following are some of the pseudo-compounds which have been met so far:

qanuq- 'second, following' + wɨttyiəlay 'high school'
> qanuq-wɨttyiəlay 'junior high school'
məhaa- 'big, great' + wɨttyiəlay 'high school'
> məhaa-wɨttyiəlay 'university'
pathɑm(mə-) + səksaa 'study, education' > pathɑmməsəksaa 'primary education'
mattyum(mə-) + səksaa 'study' > mattyumməsəkaa 'secondary education'
prəwoăt(tə-) 'history' + -saah 'study, science' > prəwoăttəsaah 'history'
phuum(i-) 'village, land' + -saah 'study' > phuumisaah 'geography'
qaqsɑɑ 'letters, writing' + -saah 'study' > qaqsɑɑsaah 'literature'
wɨttyiə 'science' + -saah 'study' > wɨttyiəsaah 'the study of science'
kam(mə-) 'action, conduct' + -kɑɑ 'personnel' > kamməkɑɑ 'workers, laborers'
phoocənii(yə-) 'food' + thaan 'place' > phoocəniiyəthaan 'restaurant'
prehsənii(yə-) 'mail' + thaan 'place' > prehsəniiyəthaan 'post-office'

2-A. Substitution Drill

Teacher	Student
kñom coul-cət riən phuumisaah ciəŋ-kee.	kñom coul-cət riən phuumisaah ciəŋ-kee.
qaqsɑɑsaah	kñom coul-cət riən qaqsɑɑsaah ciəŋ-kee.
prəwoăttəsaah	kñom coul-cət riən prəwoăttəsaah ciəŋ-kee.
wɨttyiəsaah	kñom coul-cət riən wɨttyiəsaah ciəŋ-kee.

Teacher	Student
mat	kñom coul-cət riən <u>mat</u> ciəŋ-kee.
taeŋ-səc-kdəy	kñom coul-cət riən <u>taeŋ-səc-kdəy</u> ciəŋ-kee.
twəə-leik	kñom coul-cət riən <u>twəə-leik</u> ciəŋ-kee.
hat-qaan	kñom coul-cət riən <u>hat-qaan</u> ciəŋ-kee.
kuruq-wɨcciə	kñom coul-cət riən <u>kuruq-wɨcciə</u> ciəŋ-kee.

3. caek ciə pii pnaek

In some contexts the verb ciə 'to be' is best translated 'into, making' as in the sentence:

mattyumməsəksaa caek <u>ciə</u> pii pnaek.	Secondary education is divided <u>into</u> two parts.

Other examples of this use of <u>ciə</u>:

praq nuh kee caek <u>ciə</u> pii *camnaek.	That money they divide <u>into</u> two parts (shares).
chəə nuh kee kat <u>ciə</u> pii *kamnat.	That (piece of) wood they cut <u>into</u> two pieces.
rɨəŋ nih kee prae <u>ciə</u> phiəsaa-kmae.	That story they translated <u>into</u> Cambodian.

3-A. Substitution Drill

Teacher	Student
mattyumməsəksaa caek ciə pii pnaek.	mattyumməsəksaa caek ciə pii pnaek.
pathamməsəksaa	pathamməsəksaa caek ciə pii pnaek.
baasou	baasou caek ciə pii pnaek.
rɨəŋ nuh	rɨəŋ nuh caek ciə pii pnaek.
kaa nuh	kaa nuh caek ciə pii pnaek.
siəwphɨw nuh	siəwphɨw nuh caek ciə pii pnaek.
krəsuəŋ nuh	krəsuəŋ nuh caek ciə pii pnaek.
dəmnəə nuh	dəmnəə nuh caek ciə pii pnaek.

4. Two More Specific Completive Verbs: coŏp and tleŏq

In Lesson 14, B, 2 we discussed the class of <u>specific completive verbs</u> which occur with a resultative meaning after specific primary verbs. The verbs <u>coŏp</u> 'to stick, be attached' and <u>tleŏq</u> 'to fall' occur as completive verbs after the primary verb <u>pralaaŋ</u> 'to compete, to take an examination':

<u>pralaaŋ coŏp</u> (to compete + to stick) 'to pass an examination'
<u>pralaaŋ tleŏq</u> (to compete + to fall) 'to fail an examination'

Examples:

bae kee prɑlɑɑŋ cŏəp, kee qaac laəŋ tnaq coŋ bamphot.

If they pass the examination, they can advance to the final grade.

bae prɑlɑɑŋ tleə̆q, kee prəlɑɑŋ mədɑɑŋ tiət baan tee?

If they fail the examination, can they try again?

4-A. Substitution Drill

Teacher	Student
baə kñom prəlɑɑŋ cŏəp, kñom nɨŋ laəŋ tnaq tii-pram tumnəəp.	baə kñom prəlɑɑŋ cŏəp, kñom nɨŋ laəŋ tnaq tii-pram tumnəəp.
tnaq tii-prampɨl.	baə kñom prəlɑɑŋ cŏəp, kñom nɨŋ laəŋ tnaq tii-prampɨl.
tnaq tii-pii tumnəəp.	baə kñom prəlɑɑŋ cŏəp, kñom nɨŋ laəŋ tnaq tii-pii tumnəəp.
tnaq coŋ bamphot.	baə kñom prəlɑɑŋ cŏəp, kñom nɨŋ laəŋ tnaq coŋ bamphot.
tnaq tii-dɑp-muəy.	baə kñom prəlɑɑŋ cŏəp, kñom nɨŋ laəŋ tnaq tii-dɑp-muəy.
tnaq tii-prammuəy tumnəəp.	baə kñom prəlɑɑŋ cŏəp, kñom nɨŋ laəŋ tnaq tii-prammuəy tumnəəp.

4-B. Substitution Drill

Teacher	Student
baə kñom prəlɑɑŋ tleə̆q, kñom riən tnaq tii-prampɨl mədɑɑŋ tiət.	baə kñom prəlɑɑŋ tleə̆q, kñom riən tnaq tii-prampɨl mədɑɑŋ tiət.
tnaq tii-muəy tumnəəp	baə kñom prəlɑɑŋ tleə̆q, kñom riən tnaq tii-muəy tumnəəp mədɑɑŋ tiət.
tnaq coŋ bamphot	baə kñom prəlɑɑŋ tleə̆q, kñom riən tnaq coŋ bamphot mədɑɑŋ tiət.
tnaq tii-bəy tumnəəp	baə kñom prəlɑɑŋ tleə̆q, kñom riən tnaq tii-bəy tumnəəp mədɑɑŋ tiət.
tnaq tii-prambəy	baə kñom prəlɑɑŋ tleə̆q, kñom riən tnaq tii-prambəy mədɑɑŋ tiət.
tnaq tii-dɑp	baə kñom prəlɑɑŋ tleə̆q, kñom riən tnaq tii-dɑp mədɑɑŋ tiət.

5. The Functions of ponmaan

The word ponmaan occurs in a set of functions which are not quite parallel with those of any other word in the language. Like qwəy and naa, it occurs both as a pronoun and as an adjective, but in addition it occurs in the role of a numeral before specifiers, and as an adverb after adjectival verbs. In interrogative sentences, ponmaan means 'how much?, how many?, to what extent?'; e.g.:

Pronoun:	look trəw-kaa <u>ponmaan</u>?	<u>How many</u> (<u>how much</u>) do you want?
Adjective:	look miən praq <u>ponmaan</u>?	<u>How much</u> money do you have?
Numeral:	look tɨñ qəŋkaa <u>ponmaan</u> kilou?	<u>How many</u> kilos of rice did you buy?

In <u>affirmative sentences</u>, <u>ponmaan</u> means 'however much, however many, to whatever extent'; e.g.:

Pronoun:	tɨñ <u>ponmaan</u> ka-baan dae.	[You] can buy <u>as much</u> (<u>as many</u>) [as you like]. (You can buy <u>however many</u> (<u>much</u>).)
Adjective:	tɨñ siəwphɨw <u>ponmaan</u> ka-baan dae.	[You] can buy <u>as many</u> books [as you like].
Adverb (usually with <u>ka-daoy</u> 'although'):	tlay <u>ponmaan</u> ka-daoy, kñom kaa tɨñ dae.	<u>However</u> expensive [they] are, I'll buy [them].
Numeral:	prəlaaŋ <u>ponmaan</u> daaŋ ka-baan dae.	[They] can take the examination <u>as many</u> times [as they wish].

In <u>negative sentences</u>, <u>ponmaan</u> means 'not so much, not so many, not so very, not to any extent'; e.g.:

Pronoun:	kñom mɨn trəw-kaa <u>ponmaan</u> tee.	I don't need <u>so very many</u>.
Adjective:	kñom mɨn trəw-kaa praq <u>ponmaan</u> tee.	I don't need <u>so much</u> money.
Adverb:	kñom mɨn kliən <u>ponmaan</u> tee.	I'm <u>not so very</u> hungry.
Numeral:	mɨn miən neăq-cumŋɨɨ <u>ponmaan</u> neăq tee.	There aren't <u>so many</u> patients.

5-A. Substitution Drill

Teacher	Student
<u>prəlaaŋ</u> ponmaan daaŋ ka-baan dae.	<u>prəlaaŋ</u> ponmaan daaŋ ka-baan dae.
<u>tɨw</u>	<u>tɨw</u> ponmaan daaŋ ka-baan dae.
<u>tɨw məəl</u>	<u>tɨw məəl</u> ponmaan daaŋ ka-baan dae.
<u>toăt</u>	<u>toăt</u> ponmaan daaŋ ka-baan dae.
<u>teăh</u>	<u>teăh</u> ponmaan daaŋ ka-baan dae.
<u>praə</u>	<u>praə</u> ponmaan daaŋ ka-baan dae.
<u>niyiəy</u>	<u>niyiəy</u> ponmaan daaŋ ka-baan dae.
<u>chup səmraaq</u>	<u>chup səmraaq</u> ponmaan daaŋ ka-baan dae.
<u>leeŋ</u>	<u>leeŋ</u> ponmaan daaŋ ka-baan dae.

5-B. Response Drill

Teacher	Student
prəlaaŋ mədaaŋ tiət baan tee?	prəlaaŋ ponmaan daaŋ ka-baan dae.
kñom tɨñ barəy pii kəñcap baan tee?	tɨñ ponmaan kəñcap ka-baan dae.
kñom tɨñ məyaaŋ tiət baan tee?	tɨñ ponmaan yaaŋ ka-baan dae.
kñom ñam kafei məpɛɛŋ tiət baan tee?	ñam ponmaan pɛɛŋ ka-baan dae.

Teacher	Student
kñom məəl siəwphɨw mə-kbaal tiət baan tee?	məəl ponmaan kbaal kɑ-baan dae.
kñom kcəy sraom-cəəŋ məkuu tiət baan tee?	kcəy ponmaan kuu kɑ-baan dae.
kee coul riən mədɑɑŋ tiət baan tee?	coul riən ponmaan dɑɑŋ kɑ-baan dae.
kee nɨw bəy tŋay baan tee?	nɨw ponmaan tŋay kɑ-baan dae.
kñom kcəy krədaah-səsei mə-sənlək tiət baan tee?	kcəy ponmaan sənlək kɑ-baan dae.
kñom twəə-kaa pii khae tiət baan tee?	twəə-kaa ponmaan khae kɑ-baan dae.

6. pii muəy tɨw muəy

The adverbial phrase <u>pii muəy tɨw muəy</u> means 'from one to another, from one to the other', as in

kee cɔɔ poət wuən toət səy pii muəy tɨw muəy.	They stand around in a circle [and] kick the caneball <u>from one to another.</u>

6-A. Substitution Drill

Teacher	Student
kee <u>toət səy</u> pii muəy tɨw muəy.	kee <u>toət səy</u> pii muəy tɨw muəy.
<u>toət bal</u>	kee <u>toət bal</u> pii muəy tɨw muəy.
<u>teəh bal</u>	kee <u>teəh bal</u> pii muəy tɨw muəy.
<u>niyiəy kniə</u>	kee <u>niyiəy kniə</u> pii muəy tɨw muəy.
<u>way kniə</u>	kee <u>way kniə</u> pii muəy tɨw muəy.
<u>prap kniə</u>	kee <u>prap kniə</u> pii muəy tɨw muəy.
<u>bɑh həp</u>	kee <u>bɑh həp</u> pii muəy tɨw muəy.
<u>bɑh bal</u>	kee <u>bɑh bal</u> pii muəy tɨw muəy.

7. The Compound Conjunction <u>kom-qaoy-tae</u>

<u>kom-qaoy-tae</u> is a compound conjunction which means 'so long as not', so long as [one, it] doesn't, provided that [you, they] don't', as in

kee praə qwəy kɑ-baan, <u>kom-qaoy-tae</u> trəw day.	They can use anything at all, <u>so long as</u> [it] doesn't come in contact with the hands.

7-A. Completion Drill

Teacher	Student
kee praə qwəy kɑ-baan. (trəw day)	kee praə qwəy kɑ-baan, kom-qaoy-tae <u>trəw day.</u>
koun twəə qwəy kɑ-baan. (tɨw ləə pləw)	koun twəə qwəy kɑ-baan, kom-qaoy-tae <u>tɨw ləə pləw.</u>
ñam qwəy kɑ-baan. (həl peek)	ñam qwəy kɑ-baan, kom-qaoy-tae <u>həl peek.</u>
tɨw naa kɑ-baan. (cŋaay peek)	tɨw naa kɑ-baan, kom-qaoy-tae <u>cŋaay peek.</u>

Teacher	Student
tɨñ qwəy kɑ-baan. (tlay peek)	tɨñ qwəy kɑ-baan, kom-qaoy-tae <u>tlay peek</u>.
baək lɨən ponmaan kɑ-baan. (miən kruˇəh-tnaq)	baək lɨən ponmaan kɑ-baan, kom-qaoy-tae <u>miən kruˇəh-tnaq</u>.
riən wɨcciə qwəy kɑ-baan. (prəlaɑŋ tleˇəq)	riən wɨcciə qwəy kɑ-baan, kom-qaoy-tae <u>prəlaɑŋ tleˇəq</u>.
sliəq-peˇəq qwəy kɑ-baan. (pɔə kmaw)	sliəq-peˇəq qwəy kɑ-baan, kom-qaoy-tae <u>pɔə kmaw</u>.
laəŋ qae-naa kɑ-baan. (tleˇəq)	laəŋ qae-naa kɑ-baan, kom-qaoy-tae <u>tleˇəq</u>.

[Tape 43]   C. COMPREHENSION

1. **Two Friends Discuss School**

   lɨm: qei, hol tɨw naa?

   hol: kñom tɨw haaŋ-luˇəq-siəwphɨw tɨñ siəwphɨw wɨttyiəsaah.

   lɨm: kñom kɑɑ tɨw dae; trəw tɨñ siəwphɨw-səsei haəy-nɨŋ slaap-pəkaa.

   [kɑɑŋ 'term, cycle, year']
   hol: coul kɑɑŋ, lɨm-qaeŋ riən qwəy-klah?

   [kiimii 'chemistry']
   lɨm: kñom riən kiimii, mat, haəy-nɨŋ phiəsaa-qaŋglee.
         coh, hol-qaeŋ riən qwəy dae?

   hol: kñom riən phiəsaa-qaŋglee dae.
         kraw-pii nuh, knom riən qaqsɑɑ-baraŋ, phuumisaah, haəy-nɨŋ
         prəwoˇəttəsaah.

   lɨm: pii-məsl-məñ hol tɨw prəlaɑŋ phiəsaa-qaŋglee tee?

   hol: nɨŋ haəy; pibaaq nah.
         kñom mɨn dəŋ ciə coˇəp rɨɨ tleˇəq tee.
         coh, lɨm wɨñ?

   lɨm: kñom kɨt thaa prəhael ciə tleˇəq haəy.
         miən səmnuə craən nah dael kñom qət yuˇəl.

2. **Discussing the Soccer Game**

   lɨm: tŋay-nih hol kɨt tɨw məəl bal-toˇət tee?

   hol: kñom tɨw mɨn baan tee; kñom trəw tɨw leeŋ wallay-bal.
         puəq naa leeŋ nɨŋ puəq naa?

   [lihsei dekaat 'Lycée Descartes']
   lɨm: puəq lihsei dekaat haəy-nɨŋ puəq salaa-kuruq-wɨcciə.

   hol: puəq naa pukae ciəŋ?

[cneə̈h 'to win, to defeat']
lɨm: puəq lihsei dekaat cneə̈h pii cnam haəy,
tae cnam nih salaa-kuruq-wɨcciə prəhael ciə cneə̈h haey.

[bɑn 'to hope, to pray']
[cañ 'to lose to, be defeated (by)]
hol: kñom bɑn qaoy salaa-dekaat cañ.

3. **Going to the Library**

hol: tɨw naa, lɨm?

[pannaalay 'library']
lɨm: kñom tɨw pannaalay; kñom trəw taeŋ səc-kdəy muəy.

hol: taeŋ qəmpii qwəy?

[sdac 'king']
[cɨyyeə̈qwɑɑrəman 'Jayavarman']
[sdac cɨyyeə̈qwɑɑrəman tii-prampɨl 'King Jayavarman VII']
lɨm: kñom səsei qəmpii sdac cɨyyeə̈qwɑɑrəman tii-prampɨl.

hol: qəñcəŋ kñom tɨw ciə-muəy dae.
[sŋat 'quiet, peaceful']
kñom coul-cət səsei səmbot nɨw pannaalay, pruə̈h sŋat.

lɨm: pii-msəl-məñ hol miən coul riən prəwoə̈ttəsaah tee?

hol: thəy mɨn tɨw; məc kɑɑ lɨm-qaeŋ mɨn tɨw?

[peeŋ-poŋ 'ping-pong']
lɨm: pii-msəl-məñ kñom plɨc; rəwuə̈l leeŋ peeŋ-poŋ.
[sahstraacaa 'teacher, professor']
sahstraacaa koə̈t niyiəy qəmpii qwəy?

[sourəyaawɑɑrəman 'Suryavarman']
[sdac sourəyaawɑɑrəman tii-pii 'King Suryavarman II']
hol: koə̈t niyiəy qəmpii sdac sourəyaawɑɑrəman tii-pii.

[kɑɑ-saaŋ 'to build, construct']
lɨm: sdac nuh kɑɑ-saaŋ qəŋkɔɔ-woə̈t, mɛɛn rɨɨ?

[mee-riən 'lesson']
[camlɑɑŋ (cəmlɑɑŋ) 'to copy']
hol: nɨŋ haəy; baə trəw-kaa mee-riən nuh, cəmlɑɑŋ taam siəwphɨw kñom tɨw.

lɨm: qɑɑ-kun.

D. CONVERSATION

1. The Cambodian System of Education

Have one student assume the role of a Cambodian student and another that of an American student. The American asks various questions about the Cambodian school system. Topics might include such things as when children start to school, how many divisions there are in the system, how many years there are in each division, what is taught in each division, etc.

2. <u>Discussing School</u>

Have two students assume the roles of two Cambodian students who discuss their respective programs. Topics might include what grade they are in this year, what subjects they are studying, what schools they attend, what subjects they like best, what their future educational plans are, etc.

3. <u>Discussing a Game</u>

Have two students discuss a game, whether <u>toət-səy</u>, soccer, ping-pong, or volleyball. Topics for discussion might include who is playing, which side is stronger, how the game is played, who won, who lost, etc.

4. <u>Writing a Composition</u>

Have two students discuss their respective compositions. Topics might include what class the paper is intended for, what the topic of the paper is, where each is going to write it, how many pages he intends to write, etc.

LESSON 25. REVIEW OF LESSONS 20-24

A. Review of Dialogues

In preparation for the review lesson, review the Dialogues of Lessons 20–24. To test yourself, cover the English column and supply the English equivalents of the Cambodian sentences; then cover the Cambodian column and supply the Cambodian equivalents of the English sentences. If you cannot supply an appropriate translation quickly and smoothly, review the relevant sections of the Grammar and Drills.

B. Review of Comprehension

The teacher will read selected conversations from the Comprehension sections of Lessons 20–24, calling on individual students for English translations of the sentences.

C. Test for Comprehension

Write the numbers 1–50 on a sheet of paper. The teacher will read 50 statements at normal speed. Write "true" or "false" beside the appropriate number. Most of the statements will be inherently true or false, although a few may be based on simple facts covered in the Dialogues. With true-or-false questions it is always possible to quibble by pointing out exceptions and extreme cases, but if the student considers each statement in general, the intent of the statement should be obvious. The teacher will repeat each statement twice. Listen to the statement in its entirety the first time; an unfamiliar word may be cleared up by the context in which it occurs.

1. kee praə qambaoh samrap baoh pteə̆h.
2. baə miən pñiəw mɔɔk, trəw twəə mhoup craən.
3. mun pñiəw mɔɔk, kee craən-tae baoh-samqaat pteə̆h.
4. kee craən-tae dam daəm-pkaa-kolaap nɨw knoŋ bantup-tɔtuəl-pñiəw.
5. ckae coul-cət kakaay ruuŋ.
6. ñam baay ruəc-haəy, kee craən-tae cuə̆ñcuun caan tɨw caol.
7. baə pləəŋ knoŋ caŋkraan rɔluət haəy, trəw baŋkat mədaaŋ tiət.
8. baə kambət mut haəy, trəw yɔɔk tɨw samliəŋ tiət.
9. baə krouc mɨn-toə̆n tum tee, muk-tae pqaem nah.
10. kaal-naa ceik tum haəy, yəəŋ tɨw beh baan.
11. thoə̆mmədaa ckae haəy-nɨŋ cmaa sralañ kniə nah.
12. baaŋ qəwpuk kñom haw thaa look-qom.
13. pqoun-proh mdaay kñom haw thaa neə̆q-miiŋ.
14. koun rəbah baaŋ-pqoun kñom haw thaa kmuəy.
15. pqoun rəbah prapuə̆n kñom haw thaa baaŋ-tlay.
16. ñam sraa twəə qaoy yəəŋ srawəŋ.
17. mdaay rəbah pdəy kñom haw thaa qəwpuk-kmeik.
18. baə miən pñiəw mɔɔk craən, muk-tae miən kaa qɨkkəthɨk nah.
19. koun rəbah koun kñom haw thaa caw-tuət.
20. taa rəbah qəwpuk kñom haw thaa taa-tuət.
21. baə yəəŋ kdaw kluən haəy-nɨŋ chɨɨ kbaal, prəhael ciə krun haəy.
22. baə mɨn sruəl kluən, trəw tɨw haw meethiəwii.
23. teə̆moumaet samrap məəl kamdaw kluən.
24. qasannərook qaac bandaal qaoy slap ka-miən.

337

25. neə̆q-naa miən rook-claaŋ kee qaoy tɨw keeŋ tae mənĕə̆q-qaeŋ.
26. neə̆q-naa miən cumŋɨɨ tŋuə̆n kee qaoy tɨw daə-leeŋ.
27. neə̆q-naa pdahsaay kee qaoy tɨw keeŋ-pɛɛt.
28. baək lɨən qaac bandaal qaoy miən kruə̆h-tnaq.
29. nɨw muə̆ntii-pɛɛt miən pradap-pradaa krup-sap teə̆ŋ-qah samrap cuəh-cul laan.
30. neə̆q-naa miən cumŋɨɨ krun-cañ trəw paŋsəmaŋ pɨñ teə̆ŋ kluən.
31. kee way teelekraam nɨw prehsəniiyəthaan.
32. pñaə sambot taam kəpal-tɨk chap ciəŋ taam kəpal-hah.
33. baə sambot mɨn samkhan ponmaan tee, kee craən-tae pñaə taam kəpal-tɨk.
34. baə pñaə kañcap tɨw srok-baraŋ, kee qaac pñaə taam rəteh-pləəŋ.
35. pii poə̆n kraam tŋuə̆n ciəŋ pii kɨlou.
36. baə pñaə kañcap tɨw naa, kee trəw tləŋ məəl sən.
37. baə caŋ baək šaek, trəw siññei cmuəh sən.
38. miən praq-khae təc peek, stəə-tae cəñcəm ciiwɨt mɨn baan.
39. mənuh dael miən luy təc muk-tae kmiən koŋ nɨw baŋ naa tee.
40. nɨw srok-kmae koun-kmeiŋ coul riən qaayuq prammuəy cnam.
41. kaal pii daəm kmeiŋ-proh-srəy tɨw riən nɨw salaa-woə̆t.
42. pathamməsəksaa kee riən prammuəy cnam.
43. pathamməsəksaa kpuə̆h ciəŋ mattyumməsəksaa.
44. nɨw salaa-pathamməsəksaa kee qap-rum kmeiŋ khaaŋ damboun-miən.
45. tnaq tii-prambəy kpuə̆h ciəŋ tnaq tii-prambuən.
46. wɨttyiəlay kpuə̆h ciəŋ qanuq-wɨttyiəlay.
47. coŋ cnam tii-bəy tumnəəp, koun-səh pralaaŋ yɔɔk saññaabat diploum.
48. baasou kee caek ciə pii pnaek.
49. baə pralaaŋ tleə̆q, kee pralaaŋ mədaaŋ tiət mɨn baan tee.
50. toə̆t-səy nuh kee praə day way səy pii muəy tɨw muəy.

D. Translation

1. I'm very glad that you've come to visit today.
2. I go to school only one day a week.
3. Say, what do you (Father) plan to do today?
4. [When] I've finished eating, I'm going to take these dishes and wash them.
5. [When you've] finished your breakfast (porridge), please (Husband) take this knife and sharpen it.
6. These flowers have a sweet smell.
7. [When] I've finished pulling this grass, I'll cut some flowers [and] take [them and] put [them in a] vase.
8. My dog always digs holes in the flower garden.
9. [When you've] finished dusting the furniture, I want to have you [Child] go [and] pick some vegetables.
10. Bring that big pot to me [Mother], will you?
11. My younger sister and my younger brother-in-law are coming to visit today.
12. You haven't come to visit for a long time, (Younger) Uncle.
13. I'm accustomed to smoking Cambodian cigarettes every day.
14. I have only Cambodian whiskey; perhaps it's a little strong.
15. That man is my older male second cousin.
16. My great-grandmother has just died.
17. My father-in-law is a doctor at Preah-Ket Mealea Hospital.
18. Where did all the children disappear to?

19. They just opened the door a moment ago.
20. I'm nearly dying of anger. (I'm angry almost to the point of dying.)
21. I don't know what's wrong; I always have a headache.
22. Take (swallow) two of these pills, and call the doctor.
23. From time to time I feel a little better.
24. If you have a high fever, I'll have to send you to the hospital.
25. The doctor came and examined me every day.
26. They told me I have cholera.
27. If you don't watch it until it's completely cleared up, malaria can even lead to death.
28. At first, I had only a little fever; then later on the fever got worse.
29. The doctor decided to operate immediately.
30. The knife slipped and hit my knee.
31. Yesterday I met with an automobile accident.
32. I'm writing to my older uncle to have him send me some money.
33. Do you have any writing paper?; let me borrow a little bit.
34. Why don't you type [it]?
35. I want to send this package to Japan by sea.
36. Let me weigh it first (and see).
37. Please stamp it "Handle with Care" (stamp it telling them not to throw it around).
38. I have an account at the National Bank.
39. How could I save?; I can barely make a living.
40. Now that you mention it, I have to go to the bank to cash a check too.
41. At what age do children start to school in France?
42. Elementary education lasts (has) six years—from the 1st to the 6th grade (12th to 7th).
43. In elementary school they study reading, writing, arithmetic, and geography.
44. The baccalaureate [degree] they divide into two parts—the first baccalaureate and the second baccalaureate.
45. At the end of the first cycle of secondary school, the student must take an examination for the diploma.
46. I'm studying history and French literature at Lycée Descartes.
47. Some students begin studying special subjects, such as myself, for example: I entered a technical school.
48. If I pass, I'll advance to the final year and sit for the second baccalaureate degree.
49. They can take the exam as many times [as they wish].
50. [You] can study any subject at all, so long as [you] don't fail.

LESSON 26. AGRICULTURE

[Tape 44] A. DIALOGUE

saphein

kaal	when, at the time of (in the past)
peel-chup-riən	vacation (from school)
sarun	Sarun (a personal name)

1. kaal peel-chup-riən, sarun-qaeŋ tɨw naa? — Where did you go at vacation-time, Sarun?

sarun

2. qou, kɦom tɨw leeŋ qəwpuk kɦom nɨw srok-srae; koət twəə-srae nɨw kəmpuə̆ŋ-thom. — Oh, I went to visit my father in the country; he's a farmer (makes rice-fields) in Kampong Thom.

saphein

3. nɨw kəmpuə̆ŋ-thom kee twəə-srae yaaŋ-məc klah? — How do they do rice-farming in Kampong Thom?

sarun

srae-wuə̆hsaa	wet (season) rice-field
praŋ	dry (season)
srae-praŋ	dry (season) rice-field

4. kee twəə srae pii yaaŋ, kɨɨ srae-wuə̆hsaa haəy-nɨŋ srae-praŋ. — They do two kinds of rice-fields: wet (season) rice-fields and dry (season) rice-fields.

saphein

rɔbiəp (rəbiəp, ləbiəp)	method, way, order
khoh kniə	to be different from each other

5. rəbiəp teə̆ŋ-pii nuh khoh kniə yaaŋ-məc? — How do those two methods differ?

sarun

srəw-wuə̆hsaa	wet (season) rice
cumnuə̆n	flood
qae	at; as for, with regard to, with
srəw-praŋ	dry (season) rice
baŋhou (bəŋhou, pəŋhou)	to cause to flow, direct the flow of
bəŋhou tɨk coul srae	to irrigate the rice-field

6. srəw-wuə̆hsaa doh daoy tɨk cumnuə̆n; qae srəw-praŋ wɨñ, kee trəw bəŋhou tɨk coul srae. — Wet (season) rice grows by means of flood water; as for dry (season) rice, they have to irrigate the rice-field.

bəŋ	lake, pond
moə̆t-bəŋ	the banks of a lake

7. srəw-wuə̆hsaa kee craən dam nɨw taam moə̆t-bəŋ rɨɨ moə̆t-tuə̆nlee. — Wet (season) rice they usually plant along the banks of lakes and rivers.

340

haet nih haəy baan ciə   this is the reason that,
                                             this is why

srəw-laəŋ-tɨk   floating rice (rice which rises
                                             on the water)

8. srəw klah doh knoŋ tɨk crɨw baan;   Some rice can grow in deep water;
     haet nih haəy baan ciə kee haw   that's why they call [it] floating rice.
     thaa srəw-laəŋ-tɨk.

saphein

9. kee dam srəw yaaŋ-məc?   How do they plant rice?

sarun

cap-pdaəm   to begin
tuăn   to be soft, pliable

10. kee craən cap-pdaəm nɨw   They usually begin in April, because
     khae-meesaa, pruăh miən pliəŋ   there's [some] rain and the ground
     tleăq haəy dəy tuăn phɑɑŋ.   is soft (too).

tiəñ   to pull, to draw
nuăŋkoăl ~ qaŋkoăl   a plow
   (qəŋkoăl, ŋkoăl)
pcuə ~ pyuə   to plow
roăh   to rake, harrow
lqət   fine, powdered

11. kee praə koo rɨɨ krəbəy tiəñ   They use oxen or water-buffalo to pull
     qəŋkoăl pcuə srae, nɨŋ roăh dəy   the plow to plow the rice-field, and
     qaoy lqət.   rake the ground to make it fine.

puuc   seed, stock
srəw-puuc   seed-rice
saap   to sow, scatter
tnaal   nursery-plot, seedbed

12. mun-dəmbouŋ kee yɔɔk   First of all they take seed-rice and
     srəw-puuc mɔɔk saap knoŋ tnaal.   sow it in the nursery-plot.

sɑmnaap (səmnaap)   seedling, plant
hat   cubit (about 18 inches)
muəy hat (məhat)   one cubit
puəq-srəy-srəy   women, the women
stuuŋ   to plant by pushing into the
                          ground, to transplant

13. kaal-naa səmnaap doh baan   When the seedlings have reached [a
     prəhael məhat haəy,   height of] about one cubit, the women
     puəq-srəy-srəy dɑɑq səmnaap   pull up the seedlings (and take them)
     nuh yɔɔk tɨw stuuŋ nɨw knoŋ   and transplant [them] in the other
     srae qae-tiət.   rice-fields.

saphein

14. haet qwəy baan ciə kee qaoy tae   Why do they have only the women do
     puəq-srəy stuuŋ?   the transplanting?

sarun

qat	to do without, to resist
thu̎ən	to endure, to withstand
qat-thu̎ən	to withstand, resist, endure
ceh qat-thu̎ən	to be persistent, patient

15. pru̎əh srəy-srəy ceh qat-thu̎ən cieŋ proh-proh.

Because women are more patient than men.

saphein

pru̎əh	to sow, scatter, broadcast
tae-mədaaŋ	directly, at once, in one operation

16. haet qwəy baan ciə kee mɨn pru̎əh srəw tɨw knoŋ srae tae-mədaaŋ?

Why don't they sow the rice directly in the rice-field (in one operation)?

sarun

srəw-stuuŋ	transplanted rice
phal	yield, result, harvest
srəw-pru̎əh	broadcast rice

17. nɨw kənlaeŋ klah kee pru̎əh dae, tae srəw-stuuŋ qaoy phal craən cieŋ srəw-pru̎əh.

In some places they do broadcast [it], but transplanted rice gives a higher yield than broadcast rice.

saphein

crout	to reap, to harvest

18. kee crout srəw nɨw khae naa?

In what month do they harvest the rice?

sarun

19. tho̎əmmədaa kee crout nɨw khae-tnuu rɨɨ khae-me̎əqkəraa.

Usually they harvest [it] in December or January.

kandiəw (kəndiəw, kədiəw)	sickle, scythe
kandap (kəndap, kədap)	grasp, handful, sheaf, bundle
kɔɔ	to pile up
kumnɔɔ (kəmnɔɔ)	a pile, stack

20. kee yɔɔk kəndiəw tɨw crout srəw, ruəc caaŋ ciə kəndap yɔɔk mɔɔk kɔɔ ciə kumnɔɔ.

They take a sickle and harvest the rice, then tie it into bundles [and] (bring it and) pile it into piles.

rəteh-koo	ox-cart

21. ruəc kee yɔɔk rəteh-koo dək srəw pii srae mɔɔk pte̎əh haəy baok yɔɔk kro̎əp srəw.

Then they use ox-carts to haul the paddy from the rice-fields to the house, and beat it to get the grains of rice.

bañco̎ən (bəñco̎ən)	to trample, stomp
cruh	to shed, drop off, loosen

22. cuən-kaal kee yɔɔk koo-krəbəy tɨw bəñco̎ən srəw qaoy cruh kro̎əp.

Sometimes they use oxen and buffalo to trample the paddy to (making it) loosen the grains.

saphein

23. twəə yaaŋ-məc tɨw, baan tɨw ciə qəŋkaa?

What do they do to convert [it] into (husked) rice?

sarun

kən   to thresh, to mill
rooŋ-kən-srəw   rice-mill

24. qəyləw-nih kee craən yɔɔk srəw   These days they usually take the paddy
tɨw kən nɨw roog-kən-srəw.   and [have it] milled in a rice-mill.

neəq-srae   farmers, peasants
bok   to pound (in a pestle), to mill by
                                   pounding
tbal   a mill, millstone
tbal-bok   family rice-mill, mortar and
                                   pestle

25. pontae neəq-srae klah bok srəw   But some farmers pound the paddy
kluən-qaeŋ daoy praə tbal-bok.   themselves by means of a mortar and
                                   pestle.

saphein

26. kraw-pii srəw, kee miən dam qwəy   Besides rice, what else do they plant?
tiət?

sarun

damnam (dəmnam, təmnam)   a plant, crop
poot   corn (maize)
kapbaah ~ krɑbaah (krəbaah,   cotton
   kəbaah)
sɑndaek (səndaek)   bean(s)
sɑndaek-dəy   peanut(s)
mrɨc   black pepper
tnam-cuəq   smoking tobacco

27. kee miən dam dəmnam craən tiət,   They plant many other crops, such as
douc-ciə poot, kəbaah, sɑndaek-   corn, cotton, peanuts, black pepper,
dəy, mrɨc, haəy-nɨŋ tnam-cuəq.   and smoking tobacco.

douŋ   coconut(s)
daəm-douŋ   coconut palm
tnaot   sugar-palm

28. kraw-pii nuh, neəq-srae craən dam   Besides that, farmers usually plant
daəm-douŋ, krouc, tnaot, swaay,   coconut palms, orange (trees), sugar-
ceik ciə-daəm.   palm (trees), mango (trees), [and]
                                   banana (trees), for example.

slək   leaf, leaves
slək-tnaot   sugar-palm leaves
praq   to thatch, to roof
rɔliə (rəliə, ləliə)   shell, frame, skull
rɔliə-douŋ   coconut-shell
trɑlaok (trəlaok, təlaok)   dipper, ladle
dɑɑŋ   to dip up, draw up
trɑlaok-dɑɑŋ-tɨk   water-dipper

29. kee yɔɔk slək-tnaot tɨw praq ptɛəh,   They use sugar-palm leaves to thatch
haəy yɔɔk rəliə-douŋ twəə trəlaok-   their houses, and use coconut-shells
dɑɑŋ-tɨk rɨɨ krɨəŋ psein-psein.   to make water-dippers or various
                                   [other] utensils.

sarun

kaa	work, activity (forms abstract noun compounds with verbs and verb phrases)
rɔɔk-sii	to earn a living
kaa-rɔɔk-sii	earning a living

30. qəñcəŋ kaa-rɔɔk-sii twəə-srae   Then earning a living [by] farming is
    sapbaay nah.   very pleasant.

B. GRAMMAR AND DRILLS

1. <u>kaal</u> vs. <u>dɑl</u>

We have met <u>kaal</u> 'time, occasion' in the following contexts:

qəwpuk kñom, <u>kaal-mun</u> twəə   My father was <u>formerly</u> a
    ciəŋ-chəə.   carpenter.
<u>cuən-kaal</u> pliəŋ pɨñ mə-tŋay.   <u>Sometimes</u> it rains all day.
<u>kaal</u> nɨw pii touc, kñom tlŏəp   <u>When I was still a kid</u>, I used to
    tɨw hael-tɨk rŏəl tŋay.   go swimming every day.
<u>kaal-naa</u> baan yəəŋ tɨw dɑl   <u>When</u> will we get to Kratie?
    krɑceh?
<u>kaal-naa</u> ñam baay ruəc, yəəŋ   <u>When</u> [we've] finished eating, we'll
    laəŋ pnum.   go climb the mountain.

When <u>kaal</u> occurs as a conjunction or preposition, its meaning is 'when (in the
past), at the (past) time of', as in

<u>kaal</u> peel-chup-riən, sarun-qaeŋ   Where <u>did</u> you go <u>at</u> vacation-time,
    tɨw naa?   Sarun?
kñom tɨw srok-baraŋ mədaaŋ, <u>kaal</u>   I went to France once, <u>when I was</u>
    kñom twəə tiəhiən.   a soldier.

<u>dɑl</u> as a conjunction, on the other hand, means 'when (in the future), at the
(future) time of', as in

<u>dɑl</u> peel-chup-riən, sarun-qaeŋ   Where are you going <u>during</u> (at the
    tɨw naa?   time of) vacation, Sarun?
<u>dɑl</u> look chup riən, taə, kɨt   <u>When</u> you finish school, say, what
    twəə-kaa qwəy?   do you plan to do?

1-A. Transformation Drill

Convert the following future-time sentences to past-time, and vice versa.

Teacher	Student
<u>kaal</u> peel-chup-riən, kñom tɨw srok-srae.	<u>dɑl</u> peel-chup-riən, kñom tɨw srok-srae.
<u>dɑl</u> kñom chup riən, kñom twəə tiəhiən.	<u>kaal</u> kñom chup riən, kñom twəə tiəhiən.
<u>dɑl</u> kñom kaa haəy, kñom twəə-srae.	<u>kaal</u> kñom kaa haəy, kñom twəə-srae.
<u>kaal</u> kñom ñam baay ruəc, kñom tɨw twəə-kaa.	<u>dɑl</u> kñom ñam baay ruəc, kñom tɨw twəə-kaa.
<u>dɑl</u> kñom twəə-kaa ruəc, kñom tɨw ñam baay.	<u>kaal</u> kñom twəə-kaa ruəc, kñom tɨw ñam baay.

Teacher	Student
<u>kaal</u> kñom prəlaaŋ cŏəp, kñom laəŋ tnaq.	<u>dɑl</u> kñom prəlaaŋ cŏəp, kñom laəŋ tnaq.
<u>dɑl</u> kñom məəl kasaet cɑp, kñom tɨw deik.	<u>kaal</u> kñom məəl kasaet cɑp, kñom tɨw deik.
<u>kaal</u> kñom tɨw dɑl siəm-riəp, kñom tɨw məəl qəŋkɔɔ-wŏət.	<u>dɑl</u> kñom tɨw dɑl siəm-riəp, kñom tɨw məəl qəŋkɔɔ-wŏət.

2. <u>khoh kniə</u> vs. <u>douc kniə</u>

    In Lesson 23-C we met the word <u>khoh</u> 'to be wrong', in:

yii, səsei <u>khoh</u> bəntəc!	Darn, I've <u>made a mistake</u> (in writing)!

<u>khoh kniə</u> means 'to differ, to be different from each other', as in

rəbiəp tĕəŋ-pii nuh <u>khoh kniə</u> yaaŋ-məc?	How do those two methods <u>differ</u>? (How are those two methods different from each other?)

2-A. <u>Substitution Drill</u>

Teacher	Student
rəbiəp tĕəŋ-pii nuh khoh kniə yaaŋ-məc?	rəbiəp tĕəŋ-pii nuh khoh kniə yaaŋ-məc?
<u>ptĕəh</u>	<u>ptĕəh</u> tĕəŋ-pii nuh khoh kniə yaaŋ-məc?
<u>siəwphɨw</u>	<u>siəwphɨw</u> tĕəŋ-pii nuh khoh kniə yaaŋ-məc?
<u>plae-chəə</u>	<u>plae-chəə</u> tĕəŋ-pii nuh khoh kniə yaaŋ-məc?
<u>sat</u>	<u>sat</u> tĕəŋ-pii nuh khoh kniə yaaŋ-məc?
<u>rɨəŋ</u>	<u>rɨəŋ</u> tĕəŋ-pii nuh khoh kniə yaaŋ-məc?
<u>laan</u>	<u>laan</u> tĕəŋ-pii nuh khoh kniə yaaŋ-məc?
<u>phiəsaa</u>	<u>phiəsaa</u> tĕəŋ-pii nuh khoh kniə yaaŋ-məc?

    The opposite of <u>khoh kniə</u> is <u>douc kniə</u> 'to be similar, alike', as in

rəbiəp tĕəŋ-pii nuh <u>douc kniə</u>.	Those two methods <u>are alike</u>.

2-B. <u>Transformation Drill</u>

    In the following sentences replace <u>khoh kniə</u> 'different' with <u>douc kniə</u> 'alike', and vice versa.

Teacher	Student
rəbiəp tĕəŋ-pii nuh mɨn <u>khoh kniə</u> ponmaan tee.	rəbiəp tĕəŋ-pii nuh mɨn <u>douc kniə</u> ponmaan tee.
rɨəŋ tĕəŋ-pii nuh <u>douc kniə</u> nah.	rɨəŋ tĕəŋ-pii nuh <u>khoh kniə</u> nah.
siəwphɨw tĕəŋ-pii nuh <u>douc kniə</u> yaaŋ-məc?	siəwphɨw tĕəŋ-pii nuh <u>khoh kniə</u> yaaŋ-məc?
phiəsaa tĕəŋ-pii nuh niyiəy <u>khoh kniə</u> nah.	phiəsaa tĕəŋ-pii nuh niyiəy <u>douc kniə</u> nah.
srəw pii yaaŋ nuh <u>douc kniə</u> nah.	srəw pii yaaŋ nuh <u>khoh kniə</u> nah.
mənuh tĕəŋ-pii nuh sliəq-pĕəq <u>douc kniə</u> nah.	mənuh tĕəŋ-pii nuh sliəq-pĕəq <u>khoh kniə</u> nah.
srae-wŭəhsaa haəy-nɨŋ srəw-praŋ dam <u>douc kniə</u>.	srae-wŭəhsaa haəy-nɨŋ srae-praŋ dam <u>khoh kniə</u>.
mhoup-kmae haəy-nɨŋ mhoup-baraŋ <u>khoh kniə</u> nah.	mhoup-kmae haəy-nɨŋ mhoup-baraŋ <u>douc kniə</u> nah.

3. The Preposition qae

qae has been met in the compound interrogative word qae-naa?'where?', as in

kee dam srəw-wŭəhsaa nɨw qae-naa? Where do they plant wet (season) rice?

qae as a preposition frequently occurs after the verb nɨw 'to be located, reside', with the meaning 'at', as in

qəwpuk kñom nɨw qae pteˇəh.   My father is at the house.

When qae occurs in a preposed adverbial phrase, it means 'as for, with regard to, with', as in

qae srəw-praŋ wɨñ, kee trəw   As for dry (season) paddy, on the
bəŋhou tɨk tɨw srae.   other hand, they have to irrigate
                                     the rice-field.

3-A. Transformation Drill

Teacher	Student
srəw-praŋ kee trəw bəŋhou tɨk coul srae.	qae srəw-praŋ wɨñ, kee trəw bəŋhou tɨk coul srae.
rɨəŋ nuh kñom mɨn coul-cət sah.	qae rɨəŋ nuh wɨñ, kñom mɨn coul-cət sah.
kon nuh mɨn-səw lqɑɑ-məəl tee.	qae kon nuh wɨñ, mɨn-səw lqɑɑ-məəl tee.
laan nuh tlay peek.	qae laan nuh wɨñ, tlay peek.
srəw-stuuŋ qaoy phɑl craən nah.	qae srəw-stuuŋ wɨñ, qaoy phɑl craən nah.
mənuh nuh koˇət twəə meethiəwii.	qae mənuh nuh wɨñ, koˇət twəə meethiəwii.
proh nuh wiə ciə neˇəq-srae.	qae proh nuh wɨñ, wiə ciə neˇəq-srae.
srəw-pruˇəh qaoy phɑl təc nah.	qae srəw-pruˇəh wɨñ, qaoy phɑl təc nah.

4. haet nih haəy baan ciə

In Lesson 12, B, 7 we discussed the interrogative phrase haet qwəy baan ciə . . . 'Why is it that . . . ?'. The idiomatic phrase haet nih haəy baan ciə . . . means 'this is the reason that, this is why', as in

haet nih haəy baan ciə kee haw   This is why they call it floating rice.
thaa srəw-laəŋ-tɨk.

4-A. Response Drill

Teacher	Student
kee dam nɨw moˇət-tuˇənlee; kee haw thaa srəw-laəŋ-tɨk.	haet nih haəy baan ciə kee haw thaa srəw-laəŋ-tɨk.
kee dam nɨw rədəw-wuˇəhsaa; kee haw thaa srəw-wuˇəhsaa.	haet nih haəy baan ciə kee haw thaa srəw-wuˇəhsaa.
kee dam nɨw rədəw-praŋ; kee haw thaa srəw-praŋ.	haet nih haəy baan ciə kee haw thaa srəw-praŋ.
kee stuuŋ srəw nɨw knoŋ srae; kee haw thaa srəw-stuuŋ.	haet nih haəy baan ciə kee haw thaa srəw-stuuŋ.

Teacher	Student
kee pruəh nɨw knoŋ srae tae-mədaaŋ; kee haw thaa srəw-pruəh.	<u>haet nih haəy baan ciə</u> kee haw thaa srəw-pruəh.
srəw nuh doh daoy tɨk cumnuən; kee haw thaa srəw-wuəhsaa.	<u>haet nih haəy baan ciə</u> kee haw thaa srəw-wuəhsaa.
kee yɔɔk srəw mɔɔk saap nɨw kənlaeŋ nuh; kee haw thaa səmnaap.	<u>haet nih haəy baan ciə</u> kee haw thaa səmnaap.
koət rɔɔk-sii twəə-srae; kee haw thaa neəq-twəə-srae.	<u>haet nih haəy baan ciə</u> kee haw thaa neəq-twəə-srae.

5. The Adverbial tae-mədaaŋ

The adverbial <u>tae-mədaaŋ</u>, depending on the context, can be translated 'all at once, directly (without doing anything else), in one operation, once and for all', as in

haet qwəy baan ciə kee mɨn pruəh srəw tɨw knoŋ srae <u>tae-mədaaŋ</u>?	Why don't they sow the paddy <u>directly</u> into the rice-field (in one operation; i.e. without first making a nursery plot and then transplanting)?
nɨw rooŋ-kən-srəw kee kən srəw tɨw ciə qəŋkaa <u>tae-mədaaŋ</u>.	At a rice-mill they convert the paddy into (husked) rice <u>in one operation</u>.
pii srok-yipun kñom tɨw srok-qaamerɨc <u>tae-mədaaŋ</u>.	From Japan I went <u>directly</u> to America (without stopping over).
haet qwəy baan ciə kee mɨn way teelekraam <u>tae-mədaaŋ</u>?	Why don't they send a telegram <u>and be done with it</u>?

5-A. Substitution Drill

Teacher	Student
haet qwəy baan ciə kee mɨn <u>pruəh srəw</u> tae-mədaaŋ?	haet qwəy baan ciə kee mɨn <u>pruəh srəw</u> tae-mədaaŋ?
<u>tɨw srok-baraŋ</u>	haet qwəy baan ciə kee mɨn <u>tɨw srok-baraŋ</u> tae-mədaaŋ?
<u>riəp-kaa</u>	haet qwəy baan ciə kee mɨn <u>riəp-kaa</u> tae-mədaaŋ?
<u>tɨñ teəŋ-qah</u>	haet qwəy baan ciə kee mɨn <u>tɨñ teəŋ-qah</u> tae-mədaaŋ.
<u>tɨw psaa</u>	haet qwəy baan ciə kee mɨn <u>tɨw psaa</u> tae-mədaaŋ?
<u>bok srəw</u>	haet qwəy baan ciə kee mɨn <u>bok srəw</u> tae-mədaaŋ?
<u>way teelekraam</u>	haet qwəy baan ciə kee mɨn <u>way teelekraam</u> tae-mədaaŋ?
<u>cih kəpal-hɑh tɨw</u>	haet qwəy baan ciə kee mɨn <u>cih kəpal-hɑh tɨw</u> tae-mədaaŋ?

6. **tɨw ciə**

In Lesson 24, B, 3 it was pointed out that **ciə** in some contexts is best translated 'into', as in

mattyumməsəksaa caek **ciə** pii pnaek.	Secondary education is divided **into** two parts.

tɨw ciə means 'to change into, to be converted into', as in

twəə yaaŋ-məc tɨw, baan tɨw ciə qəŋkaa?	What do they do to **convert [it] into** (husked) rice? (How do they proceed, so that it **changes into** husked rice?)

6-A. **Substitution Drill**

Teacher	Student
twəə yaaŋ-məc tɨw, baan tɨw ciə **qəŋkaa?**	twəə yaaŋ-məc tɨw, baan tɨw ciə **qəŋkaa?**
skaa	twəə yaaŋ-məc tɨw, baan tɨw ciə **skaa?**
trəlaok	twəə yaaŋ-məc tɨw, baan tɨw ciə **trəlaok?**
prəhok	twəə yaaŋ-məc tɨw, baan tɨw ciə **prəhok?**
səmpuət	twəə yaaŋ-məc tɨw, baan tɨw ciə **səmpuət?**
kroəp srəw	twəə yaaŋ-məc tɨw, baan tɨw ciə **kroəp srəw?**
numpaŋ	twəə yaaŋ-məc tɨw, baan tɨw ciə **numpaŋ?**
tnaal	twəə yaaŋ-məc tɨw, baan tɨw ciə **tnaal?**
cnaŋ	twəə yaaŋ-məc tɨw, baan tɨw ciə **cnaŋ?**
tɨk-kmaw	twəə yaaŋ-məc tɨw, baan tɨw ciə **tɨk-kmaw?**

7. Word Study: The Compound-Formers **tii**, **kaa**, and **səc-kdəy**

The words **tii** 'place', **kaa** 'work', and **səc-kdəy** 'matter, topic' occur frequently as heads of compounds with a function very similar to that of derivational affixes (Lesson 23, B, 1). Such compounds occur much more frequently in formal speech or written Cambodian than in colloquial speech.

1) tii 'place, of the order of, that which is'

Derives adverbs from demonstratives:

nih 'this'	tii-nih 'here'
nuh 'that'	tii-nuh 'there'

Occurs as an ordinalizing prefix before numerals and **ponmaan**:

pii 'two'	tii-pii 'second'
saamsəp-pram 'thirty-five'	tii-saamsəp-pram 'thirty-fifth'
ponmaan 'how many?'	tii-ponmaan 'the how-many'th?'

Derives nouns from verbs and adverbs:

snae-haa 'love; to love'	tii-snae-haa 'loved one'
koorup 'to respect'	tii-koorup 'respected one'
bamphot 'most, last'	tii-bamphot 'the most, the last (one)'

Occurs as first constituent of noun compounds:

kroŋ 'city'   tii-kroŋ 'city, metropolis (elegant)'
kɑnlaeŋ 'place'   tii-kɑnlaeŋ 'place, site (elegant)'

2) <u>kaa</u> 'work, the act of, affairs of'

Derives abstract nouns from verbs and verb phrases, and from nouns:

niyiəy 'to speak'   kaa-niyiəy 'speaking'
twəə-srae 'to rice-farm'   kaa-twəə-srae 'rice-farming'
tətuəl pñiəw 'to receive guests'   kaa-tətuəl-pñiəw 'receiving guests'
riəcckaa 'civil service (as a   kaa-riəcckaa 'civil service (as a
   branch of government)'   profession)'
bɑɑrəteeh 'foreign countries'   kaa-bɑɑrəteeh 'foreign affairs'

3) <u>səc-kdəy</u> 'situation, case, matter, quality of'

Derives abstract nouns from verbs:

lqɑɑ 'to be good, pretty'   səc-kdəy-lqɑɑ 'goodness, beauty'
sapbaay 'to be happy'   səc-kdəy-sapbaay 'happiness'
dəŋ-kun 'to be grateful'   səc-kdəy-dəŋ-kun 'gratitude'

The distinction between the functions of <u>kaa</u> and <u>səc-kdəy</u> can be illustrated with the verb <u>slap</u> 'to die':

kaa-slap '(the act of) dying'   səc-kdəy-slap 'death'

Since in colloquial speech verbs may function as nouns (see 15, B, 8), these specifically nominal constructions tend to occur only in a more formal style of speech and in written Cambodian, e.g.:

Colloquial

<u>twəə-srae</u> pibaaq nah.   <u>Farming</u> is very difficult.

Formal

<u>kaa-twəə-srae</u> ciə muk-rəbɑɑ   <u>Farming</u> is a very important
səmkhan nah nɨw srok-kmae.   occupation in Cambodia.

[Tape 45]   C. COMPREHENSION

1. <u>Discussing Vacations</u>

    miəc: cnam nih dɑl peel-chup-riən, phɔɔn-qaeŋ cɑŋ tɨw leeŋ qae-naa?

             [srɑmot (srəmot, səmot) 'sea, ocean')
             [mŏət-səmot 'seaside')
    phɔɔn: kñom kɨt tɨw leeŋ mŏət-səmot.
             qəwpuk kñom miən ptĕəh nɨw qae-nuh, haəy kruəsaa kñom tɨw tae
             rŏəl cnam.
             coh, miəc wɨñ, tɨw leeŋ kɑnlaeŋ naa?

    miəc: kñom tɨw leeŋ srok-srae.
             qəwpuk-thom kñom ciə neăq-twəə-srae.

[wiqswaakɑɑ 'engineering']
[ciik 'to dig']
[prɑlaay (prəlaay, pəlaay) 'ditch, small canal']
kñom riən khaaŋ wiqswaakɑɑ, haəy koᵊt caŋ qaoy kñom cuəy ciik
prəlaay muəy tməy.

phɔɔn: ciik prəlaay twəə qwəy?

miəc: koᵊt caŋ ciik prəlaay bəŋhou tɨk coul srae.
       baə miən prəlaay, koᵊt qaac twəə-srae muəy cnam baan pii dɑɑŋ.

2. Life in the Country

phɔɔn: nɨw srok-srae sapbaay tee?

miəc: baat, kñom coul-cət nah, haəy miən kyal-qakaah lqɑɑ phɑɑŋ.
       kñom coul-cət məəl kee twəə-srae nah.
       [neᵊq-cɨt-khaaŋ 'neighbor(s)']
       dɑl peel crout srəw neᵊq-cɨt-khaaŋ mɔɔk cuəy crout yaaŋ sapbaay.

phɔɔn: dɑl coŋ cnam kee tuk srəw klah rɨɨ luᵊq teᵊŋ-qah?

miəc: kee tuk klah, luᵊq klah.
       [samraŋ (səmraŋ) 'to select, choose, extract']
       tae kee səmraŋ srəw lqɑɑ klah tuk twəə puuc cnam kraoy.

phɔɔn: qəwpuk-thom look miən dam dəmnam qwəy tiət tee?

miəc: koᵊt miən dam səndaek-dəy, mrɨc, poot, haəy-nɨŋ bənlae pseiŋ-
       pseiŋ.

       [chəə-plae 'fruit tree(s)']
phɔɔn: koᵊt miən dam chəə-plae tee?

miən: baat, koᵊt miən dam daəm-tnaot, douŋ, ceik, haəy-nɨŋ daəm-swaay.
       slək-tnaot kee yɔɔk mɔɔk praq pteᵊh.
       kee yɔɔk rəliə-douŋ mɔɔk twəə trəlaok-dɑɑŋ-tɨk kɑ-ḅaan dae.

3. Two Farmers Discuss Rice-Planting

sɑɑy: sɨm-qaeŋ cap-pdaəm pcuə srae haəy-rɨnɨw?

       [rɨŋ 'to be hard']
sɨm: mɨn-toᵊn pcuə tee; dəy nɨw rɨŋ nah.
       pii-msəl-məñ kñom tɨw pcuə lɔɔ-məəl; tae qəŋkoᵊl mɨn mut sah.

sɑɑy: qaə, cnam nih pliəŋ tleᵊq mɨn craən douc roᵊl cnam tee.
       kñom trəw bəŋhou tɨk coul tnaal sən.

sɨm: cnam nih sɑɑy-qaeŋ miən səmnaap krup-kroᵊn tee?

sɑɑy: prəhael mɨn krup-kroᵊn tee.

sɨm: baə trəw-kaa, kñom qaoy klah baan.

sɑɑy: qɑɑ-kun craən nah.

sɨm: qəyləw-nih krəbəy kñom muəy chɨɨ haəy.
       kñom som kcəy krəbəy muəy mɔɔk pcuə srae sən baan tee?

sɑɑy: miən qəy.
       [rɔnoᵊh (rənoᵊh) 'a rake, harrow']
       qəyləw kñom trəw tɨw twəə rənoᵊh tməy.

D. CONVERSATION

1. Discussing Vacations

Have two students discuss what they plan to do during the coming vacation
from school. Possibilities might include going to the seaside, working on a farm,
studying, traveling, etc.

2. Discussing Rice-Planting

Have one student assume the role of a city-dweller and another that of a
rice-farmer. The city-dweller asks the rice-farmer various questions about
rice-farming, such as what kinds of rice are planted, when the planting takes
place, how the plowing is done, how the planting is done, etc.

3. Discussing Rice-Harvest

A city-dweller questions a rice-farmer about the methods used in harvest-
ing rice. Questions might include such things as when the harvest is begun, how
the rice is cut, how it is brought from the fields, how the grain is separated from
the stalks, and how it is milled.

4. Urban vs. Country Living

Have two students discuss the merits of country living versus the merits
of urban living. Points might include the availability of the theatre, restaurants,
schools, friends, etc. in the city, versus the fresh air, gardening, the satisfaction
of work, etc. of country life.

5. Agricultural Products

Have one student question another about agricultural products raised on
Cambodian farms in addition to rice. The discussion might include such things
as vegetable crops, fruit trees, utensils, animals, etc.

LESSON 27. GEOGRAPHY

A. DIALOGUE

kruu

qathaathibaay — explanation, lecture
prɑteeh (prəteeh, pəteeh) — country, state
kampucciə — Cambodia
prɑteeh-kampucciə — Cambodia

1. tŋay-nih kñom trəw twəə qathaathibaay qəmpii phuumisaah prəteeh-kampucciə. — Today I'm going to give a lecture (make an explanation) about the geography of Cambodia.

neə̆q — you (familiar)
prɑteeh-kmae — Cambodia
qaekkəriəc — to be independent, sovereign
qaazii (~ qaasii) — Asia
paek — part, region
qaqknee — southeast
qaazii-paek-qaqknee — Southeast Asia

2. neə̆q teəŋ-qɑh kniə trəw dəŋ thaa prɑteeh-kampucciə ciə prɑteeh qaekkəriəc muəy nɨw qaazii-paek-qaqknee. — You should all know that Cambodia is an independent country in Southeast Asia.

tumhum — size
tumhum-dəy — area (of land)
saen — hundred-thousand
muəy-saen (məsaen) — one hundred-thousand
məɨn — ten-thousand
prambəy-məɨn — eight ten-thousands
muəy-saen prambəy-məɨn muəy-poə̆n — one hundred eighty-one thousand
krɑlaa (krəlaa, kəlaa) — square

3. prɑteeh-kampucciə miən tumhum-dəy muəy-saen prambəy-məɨn muəy-poə̆n kiloumaet krəlaa. — Cambodia has an area of one hundred eighty-one thousand square kilometers.

phiəq — part, share
phiəq-rɔɔy — percent
haasəp phiəq-rɔɔy — fifty percent
lɨc — to sink, be submerged
lɨc tɨk — to sink in the water, be under water

4. dəy nɨw knoŋ prɨy miən haasəp phiəq-rɔɔy; dəy dael lɨc tɨk miən prəhael dɑp phiəq-rɔɔy. — Fifty percent of the land is in forests; about ten percent of the land is under water.

srae-cɑmkaa (-cəmkaa) — arable land, cultivated land
twəə-srae-cəmkaa — to cultivate, farm (the land)

5. dəy dael kee twəə-srae-cəmkaa miən prəhael dɑp phiəq-rɔɔy. — About ten percent of the land is under cultivation.

cəəŋ	north
khaaŋ-cəəŋ (khaŋ-cəəŋ)	northern direction; the north
ləc	west
khaaŋ-ləc (khaŋ-ləc)	western direction; the west
khaaŋ-cəəŋ-cruŋ-khaaŋ-ləc	northwest; the northwest
prɑteeh-thay-lɑŋ (∼ srok-siəm)	Thailand, Siam

6. khaŋ-cəəŋ-cruŋ-khaŋ-ləc coǎp niŋ prɑteeh-thay-lɑŋ.

The northwestern [region] borders on (is attached to) Thailand.

liəw	Lao; Laos
prɑteeh-liəw (∼ srok-liəw)	Laos

7. khaŋ-cəəŋ coǎp niŋ prɑteeh-liəw.

The northern [region] borders on Laos.

kaət	east
khaaŋ-kaət (khaŋ-kaət)	eastern direction; the east
tɨh	direction
tɨh-qaqknee	southeastern direction; the southeast

yuən	Vietnamese; Vietnam
prɑteeh-wiət-naam (-yiət-naam) (∼ srok-yuən)	Vietnam

8. khaŋ-kaət haəy-niŋ tɨh-qaqknee coǎp niŋ prɑteeh-wiət-naam.

The eastern and southeastern [regions] border on Vietnam.

tbouŋ	south
khaaŋ-tbouŋ (khaŋ-tbouŋ)	southern direction; the south
khaaŋ-tbouŋ-cruŋ-khaaŋ-ləc	southwestern direction; the southwest

chuuŋ	bay, gulf
səmot-siəm	the Sea of Thailand
chuuŋ səmot-siəm	The Gulf of Thailand

9. khaŋ-tbouŋ-cruŋ-khaŋ-ləc coǎp niŋ chuuŋ səmot-siəm.

The southwestern [region] borders on the Gulf of Thailand.

wiəl	plain, field
tuǎnlee-saap (tənlee-, təlee-)	the Tonle Sap (the Sap River)
bəŋ tuǎnlee-saap	the Tonle Sap Lake

10. niw kəndaal srok-kmae miən wiəl thom dael kee twəə-srae, haəy miən bəŋ thom muəy cmuǎh bəŋ tuǎnlee-saap.

In the center of Cambodia there is a large plain where (which) they grow rice, and there's a large lake named the Tonle Sap Lake.

11. niw rədəw-pliəŋ bəŋ tuǎnlee-saap miən tumhum thom ciəŋ thoǎmmədaa prampil dɑɑŋ.

In the rainy season the Tonle Sap Lake has an area seven times larger than normal.

dɑɑŋ	handle
rɛɛk	to carry suspended from both ends of a pole across the shoulder

dɑɑŋ-rɛɛk	a carrying-pole
pnum-dɑɑŋ-rɛɛk	the Dang Raek Mountains (the carrying-pole mountains)

tuǎl	to prop up, support
tuǎl niŋ	supporting, against, next to

12. wiəl kəndaal miən pnum poət
    cumwɨñ, kɨɨ pnum-daaŋ-rɛɛk
    khaŋ-cəəŋ tuəl nɨŋ prum-daen
    srok-siəm.

      niərədəy
      tɨh-niərədəy

      cuə
      krɑwaañ (krəwaañ, kəwaañ)
      pnum-krəwaañ

13. nɨw tɨh-niərədəy miən pnum muəy
    cuə tiət, haw thaa pnum-krəwaañ.

      qəysaan
      tɨh-qəysaan

      dəy-kpuəh

14. tɨh-qəysaan miən dəy-kpuəh,
    kɨɨ khaet-roəttənaqkirii,
    muənduəlkirii, stɨŋ-traəŋ, haəy-
    nɨŋ khaet-krəceh.

      kmae-ləə
      pnɔɔŋ

      kuəy
      rɔdae (rədae)
      cɔɔŋ

15. nɨw khaet nuh miən puəq kmae-ləə
    pseiŋ-pseiŋ, douc-ciə pnɔɔŋ, kuəy,
    rədae, cɔɔŋ, ciə-daəm.

      pləw-tɨk
      prɑwaeŋ (prəwaeŋ, pəwaeŋ)

16. pləw-tɨk nɨw srok-kmae miən
    prəwaeŋ ciəŋ muəy-poən kiloumaet.

17. tuənlee dael səmkhan ciəŋ-kee
    knoŋ srok-kmae kɨɨ tuənlee-
    meekoŋ, dael hou kat pii khaŋ-
    cəəŋ tɨw tbouŋ.

      nimuəy
      nimuəy-nimuəy

18. kraw-pii tuənlee, miən pləw-tnɑl
    cəñ pii pnum-pɨñ tɨw khaet
    nimuəy-nimuəy.

      pləw-rəteh-pləəŋ

19. qae pləw-rəteh-pləəŋ wɨñ, miən
    pii pnum-pɨñ tɨw dɑl prum-daen
    siəm, haəy-nɨŋ pii pnum-pɨñ
    tɨw kampɔɔt.

The central plain is surrounded by
mountains, such as the Dang Raek
Mountains to the north, next to the
border of Thailand.

      southwest
      southwestern direction; the south-
         west
      row, range, chain
      cardamom
      the Cardamom Mountains

In the southwest there is another
chain of mountains, called the
Cardamom Mountains.

      northeast
      northeastern direction; the north-
         east
      high ground, plateau

[In] the northeastern [region] there is
a plateau consisting of Ratanakiri
Province, Mondolkirii, Stung Treng,
and Kratie Province.

      Upper Khmer, hill tribes
      Pnong (a hill tribe) or mountain
         tribes in general
      Kuy, Kuoy (a hill tribe)
      Rade, Rhade (a hill tribe)
      Chong (a hill tribe)

In those provinces there are various
hill tribes, such as the Pnong, the
Kuoy, the Rade, [and] the Chong (as
examples).

      waterway(s)
      length; to have a length of

There are more than one thousand
kilometers of waterways in Cambodia.

The most important river in Cambodia
is the Mekong River, which flows
(cutting) from north to south.

      each
      each, one by one, the various

Besides rivers, there are roads going
out from Phnom Penh to the various
provinces.

      railway(s)

As for railways, there is [one] from
Phnom Penh to the Thai border, and
[one] from Phnom Penh to Kampot.

20. baə ne̊əq-naa mɨn yŭəl rɨəŋ qwəy,   If anyone doesn't understand some
     suə kñom mɔɔk.   point, [just] ask me.

koun-səh

praciəcŭən (prəciəcŭən)   people, population
liən   million

21. nɨw knoŋ srok-kmae miən   How many millions of people are
     prəciəcŭən ponmaan liən ne̊əq?   there in Cambodia?

kruu

prammuəy-liən   six million

22. baat, sɑp-tŋay-nih miən prəhael   Well, at the present time there are
     prammuəy-liən haəy.   about six million.

riəccəthiənii   royal capital, capital city
cumnuən (cəmnuən)   number, quantity, total

23. miən ne̊əq-naa dəŋ tee, nɨw   Does anyone know how many people
     riəccəthiənii miən mənuh   there are in the capital? (Does any-
     cəmnuən ponmaan ne̊əq?   one know, in the capital there a total
                                        of how many people?)

koun-səh

24. nɨw riəccəthiənii miən prəhael   There are approximately five
     pram-saen ne̊əq.   hundred thousand people in the
                                        capital.

kruu

25. trəw haəy; sqaek kñom niyiəy   Right; tomorrow I'll talk about the
     qəmpii khaet nimuəy-nimuəy   various provinces in Cambodia.
     knoŋ prəteeh-kampuc̦ciə.

B. GRAMMAR AND DRILLS

1. Personal Pronouns

One of the most difficult problems in Cambodian for a foreign student (and indeed for Cambodians themselves) is the choice of appropriate pronouns. This stems from the fact that personal pronouns in Cambodian are context-oriented; i.e. they are determined by the status of the speaker vis-à-vis the addressee. Thus there are no general pronouns such as "you" which are appropriate for all situations. For example, the 2nd person pronoun ne̊əq occurs for the first time in this lesson, in the sentence

ne̊əq teəŋ-qɑh kniə trəw dəŋ thaa   You all should know that Cambodia
prəteeh-kampuc̦ciə ciə prəteeh   is an independent country.
qaekkəriəc muəy.

The contexts in which ne̊əq may occur as a 2nd person pronoun are quite limited; it usually implies that the speaker is older or of otherwise higher status than the addressee, such as a teacher to student (as in the above example), a government official to a farmer, a businessman to a cyclo-driver, or a master to a servant (if the relationship between the master and servant is rather formal; otherwise he would use either the servant's name or a classificatory kinship term which would reflect the age-relationship between them). neəq may also occur as a 2nd person pronoun between equals of relatively low status, such as between two farmers or two cyclo-drivers, especially if the relationship between them is too formal to permit the use of a personal name. neəq is also used in some families when addressing one's mother, and between children of roughly equivalent age.

Although the 2nd person pronoun look has traditionally been reserved for conversation between an inferior and a superior, or between equals of relatively high status, its use is apparently gaining ground at the expense of neəq among equals of relatively low status.

Personal pronouns are non-specific as to gender and number, although plurality can be specified by adding teəŋ-qah or *teəŋ-laay 'all, inclusive' to the personal pronoun, as in the example above.

As pointed out in Lesson 21, B, 1, the use of 2nd person pronouns is normally avoided in Cambodian because of the semantic implications of the choice of a given pronoun; their function is usually assumed by a kinship term, a title, a personal name, or a personal name plus the reflexive pronoun qaeŋ 'yourself'. Thus the class of personal pronouns per se is quite limited. For example, the forms look and neəq also occur as titles, as in look sim 'Mr. Sim', look-srəy 'Madam', and neəq-mdaay 'Mother'. The commonest Cambodian pronouns, or titles serving as pronouns, are listed below with the contexts in which they characteristically occur.

a) 1st Person Pronouns

   1) kñom (general, polite; literal meaning 'slave')
   2) *qañ (between intimate friends, superior to inferior, or adult to child; otherwise insulting)
   3) yəəŋ (singular between equals in some dialects; otherwise plural)
   4) kniə (singular, among intimates)
   5) *kñom-preəh-baat ~ kñom-prəbaat ~ kñom-baat (inferior to superior, respectful or extremely formal)
   6) *kñom-preəh-kaqrunaa ~ kñom-kənaa (layman to priest; inferior to superior of exalted rank; commoner to king)
   7) *qaatmaaphiəp ~ qaatmaa (priest to layman)

b) 2nd Person Pronouns

   1) look (masculine; formal, polite; inferior to superior; between equals of relatively high status)
   2) look-srəy (feminine; formal, polite; inferior to superior; between married women of relatively high status)
   3) neəq (superior to inferior; older to younger; between equals of relatively low status; to one's mother)
   4) neəq-srəy (feminine; polite; superior to inferior; between equals)
   5) *qaeŋ (reflexive connotation; between intimates; superior to inferior; otherwise insulting; usually paired reciprocally with qañ 'I')
   6) *qaa-qaeŋ (derogatory; good-natured insult between friends; adult to child)
   7) *preəh-daccéəh-preəh-kun ~ preəh-dac-preəh-kun (inferior to superior of exalted rank; layman to priest)

c) 3rd Person Pronouns

3rd person pronouns are context-oriented only if the referent is present. Otherwise the choice of pronoun depends on the absolute status of the referent outside the face-to-face context.

1) koət (respectful; younger of older; inferior of superior)
2) kee (informal; other; indefinite, as in

    <u>kee</u> thaa lqɑɑ nah.   <u>They</u> say [it's] very pretty.

3) wiə (superior of inferior; adult of child; otherwise insulting)

<u>wiə</u> also occurs as a neuter pronoun, as in

    ckae kñom <u>wiə</u> kcɨl nah.   My dog, <u>he</u>'s very lazy.

A further use of <u>wiə</u> is as an expletive pronoun, as in

    <u>wiə</u> kdaw nah tnaŋ-nih.   <u>It's</u> very hot today.

2. Numeral Constructions

The structure of the Cambodian numeral system up to one hundred was discussed in Lesson 2, B, 11. The structure of Cambodian numbers larger than 100 differs from English in that each successively larger unit is identified by a specific denominational term. These terms occur as multiplicands in multiplicative compounds after the numerals 'one' to 'nine'; e.g.:

muəy-poən (məpoən)	one thousand
pii-məɨn	two ten-thousands
bəy-saen	three hundred-thousands
buən-liən	four millions
pram-*kaot	five ten-millions

Multiplicative compounds in numeral constructions containing more than one compound are in additive construction, and may be separated in deliberate speech by a rising intonation (indicated by a comma), as in the following example:

muəy-kaot, prambəy-liən, prambuən-saen, buən-məɨn, bəy-poən, pii-rɔɔy, haasəp-prampɨl

(one ten-million, eight million, nine hundred-thousands, four ten-thousands, three thousand, two hundred, fifty-seven)

'18,943,257'

2-A. Translation Drill

Say the following numbers in Cambodian:

Teacher	Student
5,643	pram-poən prammuəy-rɔɔy saesəp-bəy
17,570	muəy-məɨn prampɨl-poən pram-rɔɔy cətsəp
29,792	pii-məɨn prambuən-poən prampɨl-rɔɔy kawsəp-pii
453,913	buən-saen pram-məɨn bəy-poən prambuən-rɔɔy dap-bəy
836,481	prambəy-saen bəy-məɨn prammuəy-poən buən-rɔɔy paetsəp-muəy
5,142,365	pram-liən muəy-saen buən-məɨn pii-poən bəy-rɔɔy hoksəp-pram
7,987,475	prampɨl-liən prambuən-saen prambəy-məɨn prampɨl-poən buən-rɔɔy cətsəp-pram
36,490,150	bəy-kaot prammuəy-liən buən-saen prambuən-məɨn muəy-rɔɔy haasəp
92,632,412	prambuən-kaot pii-liən prammuəy-saen bəy-məɨn pii-poən buən-rɔɔy dap-pii

3. Cardinal and Intermediate Directions

The cardinal directions in Cambodian are normally expressed by compounds composed of the element khaaŋ (khaŋ-) 'side, direction' plus a term identifying the direction. In sentences involving more than one direction, the element khaaŋ may occur only in the name of the first direction, e.g.:

tŭənlee dael səmkhan ciəŋ-kee knoŋ srok-kmae kɨɨ tŭənlee-meekoŋ, dael hou kat pii khaŋ-cəəŋ tɨw tbouŋ.	The most important river in Cambodia is the Mekong River, which flows (cutting) from north to south.

The intermediate directions are normally expressed by compounds in which the two cardinal directions concerned are connected by the word cruŋ 'corner, angle', as in

khaŋ-cəəŋ-cruŋ-khaŋ-ləc cŏəp niŋ prəteeh-thay-laŋ.	The northwestern region borders on (is attached to) Thailand.

Both the cardinal and intermediate directions have corresponding sets of terms borrowed from Sanskrit. Except for qaqknee 'southeast' in the stylized compound qaazii-paek-qaqknee 'Southeast Asia', these alternate forms are limited to formal spoken or literary Cambodian. The names of the cardinal and intermediate directions, along with their formal alternates, are shown in the chart below.

Common Term	Literary Term	
khaaŋ-cəəŋ	*tɨh-qotdɑɑ	'north'
khaaŋ-kaət	*tɨh-bou	'east'
khaaŋ-tbouŋ	*tɨh-teəqsən	'south'
khaaŋ-ləc	*tɨh-baccəm	'west'
khaaŋ-cəəŋ-cruŋ-khaaŋ-kaət	tɨh-qəysaan	'northeast'
khaaŋ-tbouŋ-cruŋ-khaaŋ-kaət	tɨh-qaqknee	'southeast'
khaaŋ-tbouŋ-cruŋ-khaaŋ-ləc	tɨh-niərədəy	'southwest'
khaaŋ-cəəŋ-cruŋ-khaaŋ-ləc	*tɨh-piəyŏəp	'northwest'

3-A. Substitution-Translation Drill

Use the common term for the directions in the following sentences:

Teacher	Student
phuum kñom nɨw north pnum-pɨñ.	phuum kñom nɨw khaŋ-cəəŋ pnum-pɨñ.
south	phuum kñom nɨw khaŋ-tbouŋ pnum-pɨñ.
southeast	phuum kñom nɨw khaŋ-tbouŋ-cruŋ-khaŋ-kaət pnum-pɨñ.
west	phuum kñom nɨw khaŋ-ləc pnum-pɨñ.
northwest	phuum kñom nɨw khaŋ-cəəŋ-cruŋ-khaŋ-ləc pnum-pɨñ.
east	phuum kñom nɨw khaŋ-kaət pnum-pɨñ.
southwest	phuum kñom nɨw khaŋ-tbouŋ-cruŋ-khaŋ-ləc pnum-pɨñ.
northeast	phuum kñom nɨw khaŋ-cəəŋ-cruŋ-khaŋ-kaət pnum-pɨñ.

4. **Multiplicative Comparison**

The phrase <u>thom ciəŋ thŏəmmədaa prampɨl daaŋ</u> means 'seven times as large as normal' or 'seven time larger than normal', as in

nɨw rədəw-pliəŋ, bəŋ tuənlee-saap miən tumhum <u>thom ciəŋ thŏəmmədaa prampɨl daaŋ</u>.

In the rainy season, the Tonle Sap Lake has a size [which is] <u>seven times larger than normal</u>.

A substantive object may also be substituted in the thŏəmmədaa slot, as in

pteəh nih thom ciəŋ <u>pteəh nuh</u> pii daaŋ.

This house is twice (two times) as large as <u>that house</u>.

4-A. **Multiple Substitution Drill**

Teacher		Student
pteəh nih thom ciəŋ pteəh nuh pii daaŋ.		pteəh nih thom ciəŋ pteəh nuh pii daaŋ.
tuənlee	tuənlee	tuənlee nih thom ciəŋ tuənlee nuh pii daaŋ.
prəteeh	prəteeh	prəteeh nih thom ciəŋ prəteeh nuh pii daaŋ.
pnum	pnum	pnum nih thom ciəŋ pnum nuh pii daaŋ.
wiəl	wiəl	wiəl nih thom ciəŋ wiəl nuh pii daaŋ.
daəm-chəə	daəm-chəə	daəm-chəə nih thom ciəŋ daəm-chəə nuh pii daaŋ.
khaet	khaet	khaet nih thom ciəŋ khaet nuh pii daaŋ.
bəŋ	bəŋ	bəŋ nih thom ciəŋ bəŋ nuh pii daaŋ.

4-B. **Transformation Drill**

Teacher	Student
pteəh nih thom ciəŋ pteəh nuh.	pteəh nih thom ciəŋ pteəh nih <u>pii daaŋ</u>.
laan nih lɨən ciəŋ laan nuh.	laan nih lɨən ciəŋ laan nuh <u>pii daaŋ</u>.
bəŋ nih crɨw ciəŋ bəŋ nuh.	bəŋ nih crɨw ciəŋ bəŋ nuh <u>pii daaŋ</u>.
mhoup nih cŋañ ciəŋ mhoup nuh.	mhoup nih cŋañ ciəŋ mhoup nuh <u>pii daaŋ</u>.
cumnuən nih craən ciəŋ cumnuən nuh.	cumnuən nih craən ciəŋ cumnuən nuh <u>pii daaŋ</u>.
pɨc nih tlay ciəŋ pɨc nuh.	pɨc nih tlay ciəŋ pɨc nuh <u>pii daaŋ</u>.
srok-baraŋ cŋaay ciəŋ srok-yipun.	srok-baraŋ cŋaay ciəŋ srok-yipun <u>pii-daaŋ</u>.
tuənlee-meekoŋ wɛɛŋ ciəŋ tuənlee-saap.	tuənlee-meekoŋ wɛɛŋ ciəŋ tuənlee-saap <u>pii daaŋ</u>.
pnum-krəwaañ kpuəh ciəŋ pnum-daaŋ-rɛɛk.	pnum-krəwaañ kpuəh ciəŋ pnum-daaŋ-rɛɛk <u>pii daaŋ</u>.

5. **suə kñom mɔɔk**

In Lesson 4, B, 10 it was pointed out that <u>mɔɔk</u> as a directional verb means 'orientation toward the speaker', as in

kñom som barəy muəy <u>mɔɔk</u>.

Could I have a cigarette?
(I ask for cigarette one <u>come</u>)

Similarly, mɔɔk occurs in the phrase suə kñom mɔɔk 'ask me' because the question is to be directed toward the teacher, who is the speaker, as in

| baə neə̆q-naa mɨn yuə̆l rɨəŋ qwəy, suə kñom mɔɔk. | If anybody doesn't understand some point, [just] ask me (come). |

5-A. Substitution Drill

Teacher	Student
baə neə̆q-naa mɨn yuə̆l rɨəŋ qwəy, suə kñom mɔɔk.	baə neə̆q-naa mɨn yuə̆l rɨəŋ qwəy, suə kñom mɔɔk.
pɨəq	baə neə̆q-naa mɨn yuə̆l pɨəq qwəy, suə kñom mɔɔk.
kliə	baə neə̆q-naa mɨn yuə̆l kliə qwəy, suə kñom mɔɔk.
səmnuə	baə neə̆q-naa mɨn yuə̆l səmnuə qwəy, suə kñom mɔɔk.
səc-kdəy	baə neə̆q-naa mɨn yuə̆l səc-kdəy qwəy, suə kñom mɔɔk.
cəmlaəy	baə neə̆q-naa mɨn yuə̆l cəmlaəy qwəy, suə kñom mɔɔk.
kaa	baə neə̆q-naa mɨn yuə̆l kaa qwəy, suə kñom mɔɔk.
mee-rɨən	baə neə̆q-naa mɨn yuə̆l mee-rɨən qwəy, suə kñom mɔɔk.

6. mɨən neə̆q-naa dəŋ tee . . .

The verb dəŋ 'to know' in affirmative sentences is connected with an object clause by means of one of the conjunctions thaa or ciə, as in the following sentences:

| neə̆q teəŋ-qɑh trəw dəŋ thaa prəteeh-kampucciə ciə prəteeh qaekkəriəc muəy. | You all should know that Cambodia is an independent country. |
| kñom mɨn dəŋ ciə daq kənlaeŋ naa tee. | I don't know where [we'll] put [them]. (I don't know that [we'll] put [them] where.) |

In interrogative sentences, however, ciə and thaa are replaced by the question particle tee before a clause object, as in

| mɨən neə̆q-naa dəŋ tee, nɨw riəccəthiənii mɨən mənuh cumnuən ponmaan neə̆q? | Does anyone know how many people there are in the capital? |

6-A. Substitution Drill

Teacher	Student
mɨən neə̆q-naa dəŋ tee, nɨw riəccəthiənii mɨən mənuh cumnuən ponmaan neə̆q?	mɨən neə̆q-naa dəŋ tee, nɨw riəccəthiənii mɨən mənuh cumnuən ponmaan neə̆q?

Teacher	Student
pnum-pɨñ	miən neə̆q-naa dəŋ tee, nɨw pnum-pɨñ miən mənuh cumnuən ponmaan neə̆q?
srok-kmae	miən neə̆q-naa dəŋ tee, nɨw srok-kmae miən mənuh cumnuən ponmaan neə̆q?
srok-baraŋ	miən neə̆q-naa dəŋ tee, nɨw srok-baraŋ miən mənuh cumnuən ponmaan neə̆q?
paarii	miən neə̆q-naa dəŋ tee, nɨw paarii miən mənuh cumnuən ponmaan neə̆q?
khaet-takaew	miən neə̆q-naa dəŋ tee, nɨw khaet-takaew miən mənuh cumnuən ponmaan neə̆q?
batdəmbaaŋ	miən neə̆q-naa dəŋ tee, nɨw batdəmbaaŋ miən mənuh cumnuən ponmaan neə̆q?
niw-yɔɔk	miən neə̆q-naa dəŋ tee, nɨw niw-yɔɔk miən mənuh cumnuən ponmaan neə̆q?
səhaqroə̆t-qaamerɨc	miən neə̆q-naa dəŋ tee, nɨw səhaqroə̆t-qaamerɨc miən mənuh cumnuən ponmaan neə̆q?

6-B. Transformation Drill

Teacher	Student
nɨw srok-kmae miən khaet ponmaan?	miən neə̆q-naa dəŋ tee, nɨw srok-kmae miən khaet ponmaan?
khaet sɨəm-rɨəp nɨw khaaŋ-naa?	miən neə̆q-naa dəŋ tee, khaet-sɨəm-rɨəp nɨw khaaŋ-naa?
rɨəccəthɨənii rəbah səhaqroə̆t-qaamerɨc cmuə̆h qwəy?	miən neə̆q-naa dəŋ tee, rɨəccəthɨənii rəbah səhaqroə̆t-qaamerɨc cmuə̆h qwəy?
nɨw tii-kroŋ paarii miən prəcɨəcuə̆n cumnuən ponmaan neə̆q?	miən neə̆q-naa dəŋ tee, nɨw tii-kroŋ paarii miən prəcɨəcuə̆n cumnuən ponmaan neə̆q?
baaŋ kñom tɨw naa?	miən neə̆q-naa dəŋ tee, baaŋ kñom tɨw naa?
rəteh-pləəŋ cəñ maoŋ ponmaan?	miən neə̆q-naa dəŋ tee, rəteh-pləəŋ cəñ maoŋ ponmaan?
laan nuh tlay ponmaan?	miən neə̆q-naa dəŋ tee, laan nuh tlay ponmaan?
kee nɨŋ cəñ tŋay-naa?	miən neə̆q-naa dəŋ tee, kee nɨŋ cəñ tŋay-naa?
koə̆t tɨw srok-baraŋ twəə qwəy?	miən neə̆q-naa dəŋ tee, koə̆t tɨw srok-baraŋ twəə qwəy?
kee trəlap mɔɔk qəŋkal?	miən neə̆q-naa dəŋ tee, kee trəlap mɔɔk qəŋkal?

7. Truncation of Compounds in a Sequence

In sentences which contain a sequence of nouns which would in isolation be expressed by compounds with a common head, the common head typically occurs only in the first noun and is omitted in succeeding nouns, e.g.:

kraw-pii nuh, ne̊əq-srae craən dam daəm-douŋ, krouc, tnaot, swaay, ceik ciə-daəm.	Besides that, farmers usually plant coconut <u>trees</u>, orange (trees), sugar-palm (trees), mango (trees), [and] banana (trees) for example.
douc-ciə nɨw twiip-qəɨrop miən prəteeh-baraŋsaeh, qaaləman, qiitalii, qaŋglee ciə-daəm.	For example on the continent of Europe, there's <u>(the country of)</u> France, Germany, Italy, [and] England (among others).

However, when the conjunction <u>haəy-nɨŋ</u> 'and' is inserted before the last item of the sequence, the headword usually reoccurs in the final item, as in:

tɨh-qəysaan miən dəy-kpůəh, kɨɨ <u>khaet</u>-ro̊əttənaqkirii, můəndůəlkirii, stɨŋ-traeŋ, haəy-nɨŋ <u>khaet</u>-krəceh.	[In] the northeastern region there is a plateau consisting of Ratanakiri <u>Province</u>, Mondolkiri, Stung Treng, and Kratie <u>Province</u>.
tho̊əmmədaa kee dɑm <u>daəm</u>-tnaot, ceik, krouc, douŋ, haəy-nɨŋ <u>daəm</u>-swaay.	Usually they plant sugar-palm <u>trees</u>, banana (trees), orange (trees), and mango <u>trees</u>.

It is as if the headword of the first item applies also to succeeding items in the sequence, unless or until that sequence is broken by haəy-nɨŋ, at which point the headword must be reintroduced.

7-A. <u>Transformation Drill</u>

Omit the headword in the appropriate places in the following sentences without <u>haəy-nɨŋ</u>:

Teacher	Student
ne̊əq-srae craən dam daəm-ceik, daəm-swaay, daəm-tnaot, daəm-douŋ ciə-daəm.	ne̊əq-srae craən dam daəm-ceik, swaay, tnaot, douŋ ciə-daəm.
miən pliəŋ nɨw khae-mithonaa, khae-kaqkədaa, khae-səyhaa, khae-kaññaa ciə-daəm.	miən pliəŋ nɨw khae-mithonaa, kaqkədaa, səyhaa, kaññaa ciə-daəm.
kee tɨw riən tŋay-can, tŋay-qəŋkiə, tŋay-put, tŋay-sok ciə-daəm.	kee tɨw riən tŋay-can, qəŋkiə, put, sok ciə-daəm.
nɨw qəɨrop miən prəteeh-qaŋglee, prəteeh-qiitalii, prəteeh-qaaləman, prəteeh-baraŋsaeh ciə-daəm.	nɨw qəɨrop miən prəteeh-qaŋglee, qiitalii, qaaləmɑn, baraŋsaeh ciə-daəm.
nɨw haaŋ nuh kee miən lůəq mhoup-cən, mhoup-baraŋ, mhoup-kmae ciə-daəm.	nɨw haaŋ nuh kee miən lůəq mhoup-cən, baraŋ, kmae ciə-daəm.

Teacher	Student
sɨm ceh niyiəy phiəsaa-qaŋglee, phiəsaa-baraŋ, phiəsaa-cən, phiəsaa-yuən ciə-daəm.	sɨm ceh niyiəy phiəsaa-qaŋglee, baraŋ, cən, yuən ciə-daəm.
kee dam srəw nɨw krup khaet, douc-ciə khaet-kəndaal, khaet-kəmpuʷəŋ-caam, khaet-kəmpuʷəŋ-thom, khaet-batdəmbɑɑŋ ciə-daəm.	kee dam srəw nɨw krup khaet, douc-ciə khaet-kəndaal, kəmpuʷəŋ-caam, kəmpuʷəŋ-thom, batdəmbɑɑŋ ciə-daəm.

7-B. <u>Transformation Drill</u>

Omit the headword in the appropriate places in the following sentences with haəy-nɨŋ:

Teacher	Student
neə̆q-srae craən dam daəm-ceik, daəm-swaay, daəm-tnaot, haəy-nɨŋ daəm-douŋ ciə-daəm.	neə̆q-srae craən dam daəm-ceik, swaay, tnaot, haəy-nɨŋ daəm-douŋ ciə-daəm.
miən pliəŋ nɨw khae-mithonaa, khae-kaqkədaa, khae-səyhaa, haəy-nɨŋ khae-kaññaa ciə-daəm.	miən pliəŋ nɨw khae-mithonaa, kaqkədaa, səyhaa, haəy-nɨŋ khae-kaññaa ciə-daəm.
kee tɨw riən tŋay-can, tŋay-qəŋkiə, tŋay-put, haəy-nɨŋ tŋay-sok ciə-daəm.	kee tɨw riən tŋay-can, qəŋkiə, put, haəy-nɨŋ tŋay-sok ciə-daəm.
nɨw qəɨrop miən prəteeh-qaŋglee, prəteeh-qiitalii, prəteeh-qaaləmɑn, haəy-nɨŋ prəteeh-baraŋsaeh ciə-daəm.	nɨw qəɨrop miən prəteeh-qaŋglee, qiitalii, qaaləmɑn, haəy-nɨŋ prəteeh-baraŋsaeh ciə-daem.
sɨm ceh niyiəy phiəsaa-qaŋglee, phiəsaa-baraŋ, phiəsaa-cən, haəy-nɨŋ phiəsaa-yuən ciə-daəm.	sɨm ceh niyiəy phiəsaa-qaŋglee, baraŋ, cən, haəy-nɨŋ phiəsaa-yuən ciə-daəm.
nɨw haaŋ nuh kee miən luʷəq mhoup-cən, mhoup-baraŋ, haəy-nɨŋ mhoup-kmae ciə-daəm.	nɨw haaŋ nuh kee miən luʷəq mhoup-cən, baraŋ, haəy-nɨŋ mhoup-kmae ciə-daəm.
kee dam srəw nɨw krup khaet, douc-ciə khaet-kəndaal, khaet-kəmpuʷəŋ-caam, khaet-kəmpuʷəŋ-thom, haəy-nɨŋ khaet-batdəmbɑɑŋ ciə-daəm.	kee dam srəw nɨw krup khaet, douc-ciə khaet-kəndaal, kəmpuʷəŋ-caam, kəmpuʷəŋ-thom, haəy-nɨŋ khaet-batdəmbɑɑŋ ciə-daəm.

[Tape 47]   C. COMPREHENSION

1. <u>A Geography Lesson</u>

[ptɨy 'surface']
[ptɨy-dəy 'surface of the earth, topography']
knoŋ phuumisaah yəəŋ riən qəmpii ptɨy-dəy knoŋ piphup-look.

ptɨy-dəy nuh caek ciə pii phiəq, kɨɨ dəy haəy-nɨŋ tɨk.

niw ləə dəy miən pnum, priy, haəy-niŋ wiəl.

[mɔhaa-səmot (məhaa-səmot) 'ocean']
cəmnaek tik wiñ miən bəŋ, tuənlee, səmot, haəy-niŋ məhaa-səmot.

[twiip 'continent, body of land']
piphup-look caek ciə twiip psein-psein, haəy twiip nimuəy-nimuəy caek ciə
prəteeh psein-psein.

[qəirop 'Europe']
[twiip-qəirop 'the continent of Europe']
[prəteeh-baraŋsaeh, (-baraŋseh) 'France']
[qaaləmaŋ 'Germany']
[qiitalii 'Italy']
douc-ciə niw twiip-qeirop miən prəteeh-baraŋseh, qaaləmaŋ, qiitalii, qaŋglee
ciə-daəm.

[phɑl-dɑmnam (phɑl-dəmnam) 'crops, agricultural products']
niw prəteeh nimuəy-nimuəy yəəŋ riən qəmpii prum-daen, tumhum-dəy, cəmnuən
prəciəcuən, haəy-niŋ phɑl-dəmnam psein-psein.

[thiət-qakaah 'atmosphere, weather']
kraw-pii nuh yəəŋ riən qəmpii thiət-qakaah phɑɑŋ, kii pliəŋ, kyɑl, haəy-niŋ
rədəw psein-psein.

[phaen-tii 'map']
knoŋ phuumisaah kee trəw-kaa phaen-tii craən daəmbəy-niŋ riən qəmpii ptiy-
dəy psein-psein.

[caŋqol (cəŋqol) 'to point out, indicate']
[caŋqol-prap 'to indicate, point out, show']
[kɑh 'island']
thoəmmədaa phaen-tii cəŋqol-prap pnum, wiəl, tuənlee, bəŋ, səmbot, haəy-niŋ
kɑh psein-psein.

haəy qaac qaoy yəəŋ dəŋ thaa prəteeh naa coəp niŋ prəteeh naa.

2. Questions and Answers

kruu: baə neəq-naa cɑŋ suə qəmpii phuumisaah kmae, ləək day laəŋ.

sim: niw srok-kmae miən prəciəcuən cəmnuən ponmaan neəq?

kruu: miən prəciəcuən teəŋ-qɑh prammuəy-liən neəq.

kim: thoəmmədaa prəciəcuən kmae rɔɔk-sii twəə-kaa qwəy?

[kaqseqkam (kaqsəkam) 'agriculture']
kruu: kee craən-tae twəə-kaa khaaŋ kaqsəkam, kii twəə-srae-cəmkaa.

sim: niw pnum-piñ miən mənuh cəmnuən ponmaan neəq?

kruu: niw pnum-piñ miən prəciəcuən prəhael pram-saen neəq.
        pnum-piñ ciə riəccəthiənii, haəy ciə tii-kroŋ thom ciəŋ-kee bəmphot
        knoŋ srok-kmae.
        bəntoəp pii pnum-pin, tii-kroŋ thom qae-tiət kii kəmpuəŋ-caam
        haəy-niŋ batdəmbɑɑŋ.

kim: kəmpuəŋ-caam haəy-niŋ batdəmbɑɑŋ niw qae-naa?

kruu: kəmpuˇəŋ-caam nɨw taam tuˇənlee-meekoŋ khaŋ-cəəŋ khaet-kəndaal,
        haəy-nɨŋ batdəmbaaŋ nɨw khaŋ-ləc cɨt srok-siəm.

        [dɑmbɑn (dəmbɑn, təmbɑn) 'region, area, sector, zone']
sɨm: dəmbɑn naa-klah dael miən prəciəcuˇən craən ciəŋ-kee?

kruu: miən prəciəcuˇən craən nɨw taam tuˇənlee-meekoŋ haəy-nɨŋ tuˇənlee-
        saap, pruˇəh nɨw taam moˇət-tɨk kee qaac rɔɔk-sii cəñcəm-ciwɨt sruəl
        nah.

D. CONVERSATION

1. Cambodian Geography

Have one student assume the role of the teacher, who asks the other students
in the class various questions about the geography of Cambodia. Questions might
include such things as the size and population of the country, the number, names,
and locations of the various provinces and major cities, the location of various
rivers, plateaux, and mountain chains, the location and names of some of the hill
tribes, which countries border Cambodia and at what points, the principal products
of the country, etc.

2. Geography in general

Have one student question another about the subject matter of geography.
Topics might include the various aspects of geography, such as topography,
demography, principal products, etc; the use of maps; examples of the makeup of
specific continents, etc.

3. Describing one's own country

Have each student describe the geography of his own country or state. Other
students might question the speaker about various points he neglects to mention.
Topics should be limited to the kinds of information covered in the lesson, and as
outlined in Conversation 1 above.

LESSON 28. INDUSTRY

A. DIALOGUE

Jones

quhsaahaqkam	industry
yaaŋ-məc-klah	what kinds, in what ways

1. nɨw srok-kmae miən quhsaahaqkam yaaŋ-məc-klah?

What kinds of industry are there in Cambodia?

saphan

teəq-tɔɔŋ	to be related to, concerned with
phallɨttəphal	products, resources
phallɨttəphal kaqsəkam	agricultural products

2. quhsaahaqkam səmkhan bəmphot nɨw srok-kmae teəq-tɔɔŋ nɨŋ phallɨttəphal kaqsəkam.

The most important industry in Cambodia is related to agricultural products.

3. kaqsəkam dael qaoy phal craən ciəŋ-kee bəmphot nɨw srok-kmae kɨɨ srəw.

The most profitable agricultural [product] in Cambodia is rice.

4. nɨw pnum-pɨñ miən rooŋ-kən-srəw craən kənlaeŋ.

In Phnom Penh there are many rice-mills (in many places).

Jones

rooŋ-caq	factory, industrial plant

5. kraw-pii rooŋ-kən-srəw, taə, miən rooŋ-caq qwəy-klah tiət?

Tell me, besides rice-mills, what [kinds of] factories are there?

saphan

qaa	to saw
rooŋ-qaa-chəə	saw-mill
rooŋ-twəə-skaa	sugar refinery
rooŋ-twəə-sraa	distillery

6. kraw-pii rooŋ-kən-srəw, miən rooŋ-qaa-chəə, rooŋ-twəə-barəy, rooŋ-twəə-skaa, rooŋ-twəə-sraa, haəy-nɨŋ rooŋ-dəmbaañ.

Besides rice-mills, there are saw-mills, cigarette factories, sugar refineries, distilleries, and weaving mills.

Jones

7. chəə nuh kee yɔɔk mɔɔk pii naa?

Where do they get the wood you mentioned?

saphan

damrəy (dəmrəy, təmrəy)	elephant(s)
bandaet (bəndaet, pədaet)	to float (trans.)

8. chəə nuh kee tɨw kap taam khaet, haəy kee yɔɔk dəmrəy tiəñ coul tuənlee, ruəc bəndaet taam tɨk tɨw rooŋ-qaa-chəə.

They cut the wood in the provinces, and they use elephants to pull [it] into the river, then float it (by water) to the saw-mills.

Jones

krɑnat (krənat, kənat)   cloth; a cloth
9. nɨw rooŋ-dəmbaañ kee twəə krənat   What [kinds of] cloth are made in the
qəy-klah?   weaving mills?

saphan

sout   silk
qɑmbɑh (qəmbɑh, mbɑh)   cotton cloth; thread
10. nɨw rooŋ-dəmbaañ nuh kee tbaan   In the weaving mills they weave silk
krənat sout həy-nɨŋ qɑmbɑh.   and cotton cloth.

sɑmləy (səmləy)   raw fiber
rɔwɨy (rəwɨy, ləwɨy)   to rotate, spin
11. kruəsaa klah yɔɔk səmləy kəbaah   Some families take cotton or silk
rɨɨ sout tɨw rəwɨy daəmbəy-nɨŋ   fiber [and] spin [it] in order to
tbaañ kluən-qaeŋ.   weave [it] themselves.

Jones

12. haəy miən phɑl-dəmnam   Then what other agricultural products
qwəy-klah tiət?   are there?

saphan

kawsuu   rubber
kɔɔ   kapok
lŋɔɔ   sesame
13. phɑl-dəmnam qae-tiət kɨɨ kawsuu,   Other products are rubber, corn, beans,
poot, səndaek, mrɨc, kɔɔ, haəy-nɨŋ   pepper, kapok, and sesame.
lŋɔɔ.

Jones

14. kawsuu kee dam nɨw khaet naa?   In what province do they raise (plant)
rubber?

saphan

cɑmkaa-kawsuu   rubber plantation
rooŋ-twəə-kawsuu   rubber factory
15. miən cɑmkaa-kawsuu haəy-nɨŋ   There are rubber plantations and rub-
rooŋ-twəə-kawsuu nɨw khaet   ber factories in Kampong Cham Pro-
kəmpuəŋ-caam.   vince.

Jones

16. kraw-pii phɑl-dəmnam, miən   Besides agricultural crops, what
phɑllɨttəphɑl səmkhan qwəy tiət?   other important products are there?

saphan

neesaat (nesaat)   to fish
kaa-nesaat-trəy   fishing, the fishing industry
17. kraw-pii nuh, miən kaa-nesaat-   Besides that, there's the fishing in-
trəy.   dustry.

pray   to be salty, seasoned
trəy-tɨk-pray   salt-water fish
saap   to bland, unseasoned
trəy-tɨk-saap   fresh-water fish
18. trəy miən pii yaaŋ, kɨɨ trəy-tɨk-   There are two kinds of fish—salt-
    pray haəy-nɨŋ trəy-tɨk-saap.   water fish and fresh-water fish.

ŋiət   to be dried and salted
trəy-ŋiət   dried salted fish
19. kee yɔɔk trəy tɨw twəə trəy-ŋiət,   They use the fish to make dried fish,
    trəy-cqaə, tɨk-trəy, haəy-nɨŋ   smoked fish, fish-sauce, and prahok
    prəhok ciə daəm.   (as examples).

Jones

qandouŋ (qəndouŋ, ndouŋ)   well, mine
rae   mineral ore
qandouŋ-rae   (ore) mine
20. nɨw srok-kmae miən qəndouŋ-   Are there [any] mines in Cambodia?
    rae tee?

saphan

daek   iron, steel
spoĕn   copper
21. baat, miən; nɨw kəmpuĕŋ-thom   Yes, there are; in Kampong Thom
    miən qəndouŋ-rae yɔɔk daek,   there are mines [from which they]
    spoĕn, miəh, haəy-nɨŋ kyuuŋ.   get iron, copper, gold, and coal.

fosfat   phosphate
cii   fertilizer
22. nɨw batdəmbaaŋ haəy-nɨŋ khaet   In Battambang and Kampot Province
    kəmpɔɔt miən fosfat dael   there is phosphate which they (take
    kee yɔɔk tɨw praə ciə cii.   and) use for fertilizer.

tbouŋ   (precious) stone
tbouŋ-pɨc   jewels, precious stones
tbouŋ-kandiəŋ (-kəndiəŋ,   sapphire
   -kədiəŋ)
tɔtɨm (tətɨm) ~ kratɨm   pomegranate
   (krətɨm, kətɨm)   ruby
tbouŋ-tɔtɨm ~ tbouŋ-kratɨm
23. haəy miən tbouŋ-pɨc pseiŋ-pseiŋ,   And there are various [kinds of]
    kɨɨ tbouŋ-kəndiəŋ haəy-nɨŋ   precious stones, such as sapphires
    tbouŋ-krətɨm ciə-daəm.   and rubies.

Jones

bañcuun (bəñcuun, pəcuun)   to send out, send away
bañcuun tɨw luĕq nɨw   to export
baarəteeh
24. phallɨttəphal qwəy-klah dael kee   What products do they export (send
    bəñcuun tɨw luĕq nɨw baarəteeh?   away to sell abroad)?

saphan

25. rəbah səmkhan bəmphot kɨɨ srəw,   The most important things are rice,
    kawsuu, poot, trəy, haəy-nɨŋ mrɨc.   rubber, corn, fish, and pepper.

Jones

krɨəŋ laan	automobile parts
maasiin ~ maasɨn (masɨn)	machines, motor(s), machinery
tɨñ pii bɑɑrəteeh	to import

26. cəmnaek krɨəŋ laan haəy-nɨŋ masɨn psein-psein, trəw tɨñ pii bɑɑrəteeh, mɛɛn tee?

As for automobile parts and various [kinds of] machinery, [they] have to import [them] (buy from abroad), right?

saphan

dɑmlaəŋ (dəmlaəŋ)	to set up, assemble
rooŋ-dəmlaəŋ-laan	automobile assembly plant
siitroqaen	Citroën (a make of automobile

27. baat, haəy nɨw tii-krɔŋ pnum-pɨñ miən rooŋ-dəmlaəŋ-laan siitroqaen muəy.

Yes, and in Phnom Penh there's a Citroën automobile assembly plant.

B. GRAMMAR AND DRILLS

1. <u>klah</u> in Interrogative Words

The pluralizing function of <u>klah</u> after interrogative and indefinite pronouns and adjectives was discussed in Lesson 11, B, 5; e.g.:

look cɑŋ tɨñ qwəy?	<u>What</u> would you like to buy?
look cɑŋ tɨñ qwəy-klah?	<u>What-all</u> would you like to buy?
look cɑŋ tɨw naa?	<u>Where</u> would you like to go?
look cɑŋ tɨw naa-klah?	<u>Where-all</u> would you like to go?

<u>klah</u> occurs with a pluralizing and generalizing function in several interrogative compounds in this lesson:

nɨw srok-kmae miən quhsaahaqkam <u>yaaŋ-məc-klah</u>?	<u>What kinds</u> of industry are there in Cambodia?
kraw-pii rooŋ-kən-srəw, taə, miən rooŋ-caq <u>qwəy-klah</u> tiət?	Besides rice-mills, tell me, <u>what (pl.)</u> other factories are there?
nɨw rooŋ-dəmbaañ kee twəə krənat <u>qwəy-klah</u>?	<u>What (pl.)</u> [kinds of] cloth are made in the weaving mills?
haəy miən phɑl-dəmnam <u>qwəy-klah</u> tiət?	And <u>what (pl.)</u> other agricultural products are there?

1-A. <u>Substitution Drill</u>

<u>Teacher</u>	<u>Student</u>
nɨw srok-kmae miən <u>quhsaahaqkam</u> yaaŋ-məc-klah?	nɨw srok-kmae miən <u>quhsaahaqkam</u> yaaŋ-məc-klah?
<u>phɑl-dəmnam</u>	nɨw srok-kmae miən <u>phɑl-dəmnam</u> yaaŋ-məc-klah?
<u>rəbiəp səksaa</u>	nɨw srok-kmae miən <u>rəbiəp səksaa</u> yaaŋ-məc-klah?

kaqsəkam   nɨw srok-kmae miən kaqsəkam
                    yaaŋ-məc-klah?

kaa-rɔɔk-sii   nɨw srok-kmae miən kaa-rɔɔk-sii
                    yaaŋ-məc-klah?

rooŋ-caq   nɨw srok-kmae miən rooŋ-caq
                    yaaŋ-məc-klah?

kaa-nesaat-trəy   nɨw srok-kmae miən kaa-nesaat-trəy
                    yaaŋ-məc-klah?

kaa-twəə-dəmnaə   nɨw srok-kmae miən kaa-twəə-
                    dəmnaə yaaŋ-məc-klah?

ptɨy-dəy   nɨw srok-kmae miən ptɨy-dəy
                    yaaŋ-məc-klah?

kəylaa   nɨw srok-kmae miən kəylaa
                    yaaŋ-məc-klah?

1-B. Transformation Drill

Teacher	Student
nɨw srok-kmae miən quhsaahaqkam yaaŋ-məc?	nɨw srok-kmae miən quhsaahaqkam yaaŋ-məc-klah?
haəy miən phɑl-dəmnam qwəy tiət?	haəy miən phɑl-dəmnam qwəy-klah tiət?
kee tɨw riən tŋay naa?	kee tɨw riən tŋay naa-klah?
kee dam kawsuu nɨw khaet naa?	kee dam kawsuu nɨw khaet naa-klah?
prəciəcuən rɔɔk-sii yaaŋ naa?	prəciəcuən rɔɔk-sii yaaŋ naa-klah?
look teəq-tɔɔŋ nɨŋ neəq-naa?	look teəq-tɔɔŋ nɨŋ neəq-naa-klah?
nɨw pnum-pɨñ miən rooŋ-caq qwəy?	nɨw pnum-pɨñ miən rooŋ-caq qwəy-klah?
kee tɨñ masɨn pii srok naa?	kee tɨñ masɨn pii srok naa-klah?

2. teəq-tɔɔŋ nɨŋ

teəq-tɔɔŋ nɨŋ means 'to be related to, involved with, attached to, concerned with', as in:

quhsaahaqkam səmkan bəmphot   Industry in Cambodia is primarily
nɨw srok-kmae teəq-tɔɔŋ nɨŋ   related to agricultural products.
phɑllɨttəphɑl kaqsəkam.

Following are some further examples of the use of teəq-tɔɔŋ nɨŋ:

krəsuəŋ-kaqsəkam teəq-tɔɔŋ nɨŋ   The Department of Agriculture
neəq-srae.   is concerned with farmers.

mənuh nuh miən kaa teəq-tɔɔŋ nɨŋ   That man is (has work) affiliated with
krəsuəŋ-teehsəcaɑ.   the Department of Tourism.

krəsuəŋ-baarəteeh teəq-tɔɔŋ nɨŋ   The Department of Foreign Affairs
prəteeh-kraw.   is involved with foreign countries.

2-A. Substitution Drill

Teacher	Student
mənuh nuh teə̆q-tɔɔŋ nɨŋ krəsuəŋ-teehsəcɑɑ.	mənuh nuh teə̆q-tɔɔŋ nɨŋ krəsuəŋ-teehsəcɑɑ.
krəsuəŋ-quhsaahaqkam.	mənuh nuh teə̆q-tɔɔŋ nɨŋ krəsuəŋ-quhsaahaqkam.
krəsuəŋ-kaqsəkam.	mənuh nuh teə̆q-tɔɔŋ nɨŋ krəsuəŋ-kaqsəkam.
krəsuəŋ-kaa-bɑɑrəteeh.	mənuh nuh teə̆q-tɔɔŋ nɨŋ krəsuəŋ-kaa-bɑɑrəteeh.
krəsuəŋ-kaqsəkam teə̆q-tɔɔŋ nɨŋ neə̆q-srae.	krəsuəŋ-kaqsəkam teə̆q-tɔɔŋ nɨŋ neə̆q-srae.
kaa-twəə-srae-cəmkaa.	krəsuəŋ-kaqsəkam teə̆q-tɔɔŋ nɨŋ kaa-twəə-srae-cəmkaa.
phallɨttəphɑl kaqsəkam.	krəsuəŋ-kaqsəkam teə̆q-tɔɔŋ nɨŋ phallɨttəphɑl kaqsəkam.
rəbiəp twəə-srae.	krəsuəŋ-kaqsəkam teə̆q-tɔɔŋ nɨŋ rəbiəp twəə-srae.

3. **rooŋ** vs. **rooŋ-caq**

The word **rooŋ-caq** refers specifically to an industrial plant involving machinery of some kind, as in

kraw-pii rooŋ-kən-srəw, taə,	Besides rice-mills, tell me,
miən **rooŋ-caq** qwəy-klah teət?	what other **factories** are there?

rooŋ, on the other hand, has a much more general meaning, and refers to any hall, building, or establishment which has some practical use, whether industrial or otherwise. **rooŋ** occurs as the headword in compounds referring both to industrial and non-industrial establishments, since its nature is specified in such compounds by the accompanying modifier; e.g.:

rooŋ-kon	'cinema'	rooŋ-twəə-barəy	'cigarette factory'
rooŋ-dəmbaañ	'weaving mill'	rooŋ-dəmlaəŋ-laan	'automobile
rooŋ-lkhaon	'theater'		assembly plant'
rooŋ-kən-srəw	'rice-mill'	rooŋ-twəə-skɑɑ	'sugar refinery'
rooŋ-qaa-chəə	'saw-mill'	rooŋ-twəə-sraa	'distillery'

3-A. Substitution Drill

Teacher	Student
nɨw pnum-pɨñ miən rooŋ-kən-srəw craən kənlaeŋ.	nɨw pnum-pɨñ miən rooŋ-kən-srəw craən kənlaeŋ.
rooŋ-dəmbaañ	nɨw pnum-pɨñ miən rooŋ-dəmbaañ craən kənlaeŋ.
rooŋ-twəə-barəy	nɨw pnum-pɨñ miən rooŋ-twəə-barəy craən kənlaeŋ.

Teacher	Student
roon-kon	nɨw pnum-pɨñ miən roon-kon craən kənlaen.
roon-twəə-sraa	nɨw pnum-pɨñ miən roon-twəə-sraa craən kənlaen.
roon-twəə-skɑɑ	nɨw pnum-pɨñ miən roon-twəə-skɑɑ craən kənlaen.
roon-lkhaon	nɨw pnum-pɨñ miən roon-lkhaon craən kənlaen.
roon-dəmlaən-laan	nɨw pnum-pɨñ miən roon-dəmlaən-laan craən kənlaen.
roon-qaa-chəə	nɨw pnum-pɨñ miən roon-qaa-chəə craən kənlaen.
roon-twəə-kawsuu	nɨw pnum-pɨñ miən roon-twəə-kawsuu craən kənlaen.

4. Preposed Objects before Certain Verb Phrases

In Lesson 3, B, 8 it was suggested that a substantive object occurs as a pre-posed topic when the object rather than the subject is the paramount topic, or the topic to be emphasized in the sentence, e.g.:

piəq nuh, kñom mɨn yuəl tee.	That word, I don't understand.

Preposed objects also seem to occur in sentences in which the occurrence of an object in the normal position after the primary verb would tend to interrupt or break up a rather cohesive verb phrase, as in the following sentences:

phallɨttəphal qwəy-klah dael kee bəñcuun tɨw luəq nɨw baarəteeh?	What products do they export (send away to sell abroad)?
cəmnaek kriən-laan haəy-nɨŋ masɨn psein-psein, trəw tɨñ pii baarəteeh, mɛɛn tee?	As for automobile parts and various [kinds of] machinery, [they] have to import [them] (buy from abroad), right?

The objects in the above examples, however, may occur in the normal object position, as in the following examples:

kee bəñcuun phallɨttəphal qwəy-klah tɨw luəq nɨw baarəteeh?	What products do they export?
kee trəw tɨñ kriən-laan haəy-nɨŋ masɨn psein-psein pii baarəteeh.	They have to import automobile parts and various machinery.

4-A. Transformation Drill

Teacher	Student
kee bəñcuun phallɨttəphal kaqsəkam tɨw luəq nɨw baarəteeh.	phallɨttəphal kaqsəkam kee bəñcuun tɨw luəq nɨw baarəteeh.
kee bəñcuun srəw tɨw luəq nɨw baarəteeh.	srəw kee bəñcuun tɨw luəq nɨw baarəteeh.

Teacher	Student
kee bəñcuun <u>kawsuu</u> tɨw luə̆q nɨw baarəteeh.	<u>kawsuu</u> kee bəñcuun tɨw luə̆q nɨw baarəteeh.
kee bəñcuun <u>mrɨc</u> tɨw luə̆q nɨw baarəteeh.	<u>mrɨc</u> kee bəñcuun tɨw luə̆q nɨw baarəteeh.
kee bəñcuun <u>poot</u> tɨw luə̆q nɨw baarəteeh.	<u>poot</u> kee bəñcuun tɨw luə̆q nɨw baarəteeh.
kee bəñcuun <u>trəy-ŋiət</u> tɨw luə̆q nɨw baarəteeh.	<u>trəy-ŋiət</u> kee bəñcuun tɨw luə̆q nɨw baarəteeh.
kee bəñcuun <u>tbouŋ-krətɨm</u> tɨw luə̆q nɨw baarəteeh.	<u>tbouŋ-krətɨm</u> kee bəñcuun tɨw luə̆q nɨw baarəteeh.
kee bəñcuun <u>chəə</u> tɨw luə̆q nɨw baarəteeh.	<u>chəə</u> kee bəñcuun tɨw luə̆q nɨw baarəteeh.

4-B. Transformation Drill

Teacher	Student
kee tɨñ <u>kriəŋ-laan</u> pii baarəteeh.	<u>kriəŋ-laan</u> kee tɨñ pii baarəteeh.
kee tɨñ <u>masɨn pseiŋ-pseiŋ</u> pii baarəteeh.	<u>masɨn pseiŋ-pseiŋ</u> kee tɨñ pii baarəteeh.
kee tɨñ <u>laan</u> pii baarəteeh.	<u>laan</u> kee tɨñ pii baarəteeh.
kee tɨñ <u>tuu-tɨk-kaaq</u> pii baarəteeh.	<u>tuu-tɨk-kaaq</u> kee tɨñ pii baarəteeh.
kee tɨñ <u>preiŋ-saŋ</u> pii baarəteeh.	<u>preiŋ-saŋ</u> kee tɨñ pii baarəteeh.
kee tɨñ <u>prədap-thaat-ruup</u> pii baarəteeh.	<u>prədap-thaat-ruup</u> kee tɨñ pii baarəteeh.
kee tɨñ <u>daek</u> pii baarəteeh.	<u>daek</u> kee tɨñ pii baarəteeh.
kee tɨñ <u>masɨn-qaŋkulileik</u> pii baarəteeh.	<u>masɨn-qaŋkulileik</u> kee tɨñ pii baarəteeh.
kee tɨñ <u>tnam-pɛɛt</u> pii baarəteeh.	<u>tnam-pɛɛt</u> kee tɨñ pii baarəteeh.

[Tape 49]   C. COMPREHENSION

1. <u>Making a Living in Cambodia</u>

     [rɔbaa (rəbaa) 'trade, profession']
     [rɔbaa-rɔɔk-sii 'trade, method of earning a living']

Bill: prəciəcuən kmae miən rəbaa-rɔɔk-sii qwəy-klah?

saen: prəciəcuən kmae craən rɔɔk-sii twəə-srae haəy-nɨŋ nesaat-trəy.

Bill: kraw-pii nuh, miən rəbaa qwəy tiət?

saen: miən neə̆q klah tiət rɔɔk-sii kap chəə.
     cuən-kaal kee qaa chəə kluən-qaeŋ, rɨɨ kee yɔɔk chəə bəndaet taam
     tɨk tɨw rooŋ-qaa-chəə nɨw pnum-pɨñ.
     [prayaoc (prəyaoc, pəyaoc) 'purpose, usefulness; to be useful']
     [saŋ 'to build']
     chəə nɨw srok-kmae miən prəyaoc nah, kɨɨ səmrap saŋ pteə̆h
     haəy-nɨŋ twəə tok-tuu pseiŋ-pseiŋ.

     [daəm-kawsuu 'rubber trees']

Bill: kñom baan lɨɨ thaa nɨw srok-kmae miən dam daəm-kawsuu,
     mɛɛn tee?

saen: baat, miən dam kawsuu craən nah nɨw khaet-kəmpuʼəŋ-caam.

Bill: rəbaɑ teʼəŋ-qah nih teʼəq-tɔɔŋ nɨŋ srok-srae-cəmkaa.
       taə, prəciəcuʼən nɨw tii-kroŋ twəə-kaa qwəy?

saen: nɨw tii-kroŋ kee craən twəə-kaa nɨw rooŋ-caq pseiŋ-pseiŋ, kɨɨ
       rooŋ-twəə-barəy, rooŋ-dəmbaañ, rooŋ-twəə-skaɑ, rooŋ-twəə-cʼəə-
       kuh, haəy-nɨŋ rooŋ-twəə-siimɑŋ.
       [qaqkiisənii 'electricity']
       [rooŋ-qaqkiisənii 'generating plant']
       kraw-pii nuh, miən haaŋ-cuəh-cul-laan, rooŋ-qaqkhiisənii, haəy-nɨŋ
       kaaŋ-twəə-krɨəŋ-miəh-pɨc.

Bill: nɨw srok-kmae kee twəə krɨəŋ-miəh-pɨc qəmpii qwəy?

saen: qou, twəə pii miəh, praq, haəy-nɨŋ tbouŋ pseiŋ-pseiŋ.
       [hotael 'hotel']
       kraw-pii nuh kee twəə kamməkaɑ nɨw kənlaeŋ pseiŋ-pseiŋ, douc-ciə
       nɨw hotael, haaŋ-luʼəq-baay, rooŋ-kon ciə-daəm.

2. Working in a Weaving Mill

sein: saɑŋ-qaeŋ twəə-kaa nɨw qae-naa?

saaŋ: kñom twəə-kaa nɨw rooŋ-dəmbaañ.

sein: kee tbaañ krənat qwəy-klah?

saaŋ: kee tbaañ krənat-sout haəy-nɨŋ krənat-qəmbah.

sein: kee tɨñ kəbaah mɔɔk pii naa?

saaŋ: kee tɨñ kəbaah pii khaet pseiŋ-pseiŋ haəy rəwɨy ciə qəmbah.

sein: kee tɨñ sout mɔɔk pii naa?

       [prɑteeh-kraw 'foreign countries, abroad']
       [koun-niəŋ 'silk-worms']
saaŋ: kee tɨñ sout klah mɔɔk pii prɑteeh-kraw, haəy klah tiət pii neʼəq-
       cəmkaa pseiŋ-pseiŋ dael cəñcəm koun-niəŋ.

sein: nɨw rooŋ-dəmbaañ nuh kee miən kamməkaɑ ponmaan neʼəq?

saaŋ: qou, prəhael mərɔɔy neʼəq.

sein: coul-cət twəə-kaa nɨw kənlaeŋ nuh tee?

saaŋ: tee, mɨn coul-cət ponmaan tee.
       kñom kɨt tɨw twəə-kaa nɨw haaŋ-cuəh-cul-laan rəbah baɑŋ kñom wɨñ.

C. CONVERSATION

1. Discussing Industry in Cambodia

       Have one student assume the role of a foreigner and another the role of a
native Cambodian. The foreigner questions the Cambodian about industry in
Cambodia. Questions might include such things as the most important agricultural products in Cambodia, what kinds of factories there are in Cambodia,
what products are exported, and what products are imported.

2. Discussing the Fishing Industry

Have one student question another about the fishing industry in Cambodia. Questions might include such things as what kinds of fishing are carried on, where the fish are caught, the various forms in which the fish are marketed, and the various kinds of fish products.

3. Discussing the Lumber Industry

Have one student question another about the lumber industry in Cambodia. Questions might include such things as where the wood is cut, how it is transported to the saw-mills, what the uses of wood are in Cambodia, and whether wood and wood products are exported.

4. Working in a Weaving Mill

Have one student question another about his work in a weaving mill. Questions might include such things as what kinds of cloth are produced in the mill, where the raw materials come from, how the raw materials are made into cloth, which materials are exported and imported, etc.

5. Discussing Various Kinds of Work

Have each student discuss the various kinds of work he has done in his lifetime. The student should try to use the vocabulary and structures already introduced so far as possible; when unfamiliar vocabulary is necessary, it may be supplied by the teacher.

LESSON 29. GOVERNMENT

[Tape 50]

A. DIALOGUE

John

krɔɔŋ	to regulate, govern
krup-krɔɔŋ	to oversee, administer, govern
rəbiəp-krup-krɔɔŋ	system of government

1. nɨw prəteeh-kampucciə miən rəbiəp-krup-krɔɔŋ yaaŋ-məc? — What system of government do you have in Cambodia?

bopphaa

qaanaacaq (qanaacaq)	realm, domain, country
riəc	royal; reign, dynasty
riəc-qanaacaq	royal domain, kingdom
preəh-riəc-qanaacaq (prəriəc-qanaacaq, priəc-qanaacaq)	kingdom
ksat	ruler, royalty
preəh-məhaa-ksat	king, monarch
neəq-dək-noəm	leader

2. caah, prəteeh-kampucciə kɨɨ ciə preəh-riəc-qanaacaq miən preəh-məhaa-ksat ciə neəq-dək-noəm. — Cambodia is a kingdom having a monarch as leader.

John

3. prəteeh-kampucciə baan qaekkəriəc pii cnam naa? — When (from what year) did Cambodia achieve [her] independence?

bopphaa

nɔrootdɑm siihanuq	Norodom Sihanouk
preəh-baat nərootdɑm siihanuq	King Norodom Sihanouk
tiəm-tiə	to wrest away, obtain by bargaining
qaekkəriəc ciət	national independence
krɨhsaqkəraac	Christian Era, A.D.
krɨhsaqkəraac muəy-poən prambuən-rɔɔy haasəp-bəy	1953 A.D.

4. preəh-baat nərootdɑm siihanuq baan tiəm-tiə qaekkəriəc ciət pii prəteeh-baraŋ nɨw krɨhsaqkəraac muəy-poən prambuən-rɔɔy haasəp-bəy. — King Norodom Sihanouk succeeded in obtaining national independence from France in 1953 A.D.

kan	to hold, believe, maintain
latthiq (lətthiq)	concept, belief, faith, principle
prɑciəthɨppətay (prəciəthɨpptay)	democracy
roətthaqthoəmmənuñ	constitution

5. prəteeh-kampucciə kan lətthiq prɑciəthɨppətay daoy miən roətthaqthoəmmənuñ. — Cambodia maintains the principle of democracy by having a constitution.

John

6. baə douccnah, rŏə̆tthaqthŏə̆mmənuñ   In that case, when (from what year)
   nuh kaət laəŋ pii cnam naa?   did the constitution originate?

bopphaa

saoy-riəc   to rule, to reign
prĕə̆h-qaŋ   3rd person pronoun for royal
                                      persons; specifier for royal
                                      persons

taŋ   to establish, set up, appoint

7. kaal prĕə̆h-baat siihanuq nɨw   When King Sihanouk was still reign-
   saoy-riəc, prĕə̆h-qaŋ baan taŋ   ing, he established the constitution
   rŏə̆tthaqthŏə̆mmənuñ nɨw knoŋ   in 1947 A.D.
   krɨhsaqkəraac məpŏə̆n prambuən-
   rɔɔy saesəp-prampɨl.

John

nɔyoobaay (nəyoobaay)   policy
8. prəteeh-kampucciə miən nəyoobaay   What kind of policy does Cambodia
   yaaŋ-məc-klah?   have?

bopphaa

qaqpyiəkrət (qapyiəkrət)   neutralism; neutralist
9. cap taŋ-pii baan qaekkəriəc mɔɔk   Ever since gaining [her] independence,
   prəteeh-kampucciə baan kan   Cambodia has maintained a policy of
   nəyoobaay qapyiəkrət.   neutralism.

John

niqteqpaññat   legislative (branch)
10. qae niqteqpaññat wɨñ, miən rəbiəp How is the legislative (branch)
    yaaŋ-naa-klah?   organized? (As for the legislative
                                       (branch), what's the system like?)

bopphaa

saphiə (səphiə)   house, chamber, assembly
rŏə̆t   state, political entity
rŏə̆t-səphiə   the National Assembly
krom   group, council
prɨksaa   to advise, counsel
krom-prɨksaa-prĕə̆h-riəc-   Council of the Kingdom
qanaacaq
11. caah, prəteeh-kampucciə miən   Well, Cambodia has two houses—the
    səphiə pii, kɨɨ rŏə̆t-səphiə nɨŋ   National Assembly and the Council
    krom-prɨksaa-prĕə̆h-riəc-   of the Kingdom.
    qanaacaq.

praciə (prəciə)   people, populace
riəh   people, populace
praciəriəh (prəciəriəh)   people, populace
cnaot   ticket, vote
bɑh cnaot   to cast one's ballot, to vote
crəəh   to choose
rəəh   to pick out, select

crəəh-rəəh
bɑh cnaot crəəh-rəəh
samaaciq (səmaacɨk)
nɨy

to choose, select
to elect
member
of, belonging to

12. prəciərieh bɑh cnaot crəəh-rəəh
səmaacɨk nɨy roŏt-səphiə.

The people elect the members of the National Assembly.

phiəreŏq
cbap
kaa-twəə-cbap-tməy
kae

duty, responsibility
law, custom
making new laws, legislation
to change, correct, revise, repair

13. roŏt-səphiə miən phiəreŏq khaaŋ
kaa-twəə-cbap-tməy haəy-nɨŋ
kae roŏtthaqthoŏmmənuñ.

The National Assembly has the responsibility for (in the area of) making new laws and revising the constitution.

prɔɔm
yuŏl-prɔɔm
twaay
preŏh-kaqrunaa

to agree (to)
to approve, consent (to)
to offer, present
term of reference for the king

14. qae krom-prɨksaa-preŏh-riəc-
qanaacaq wɨñ, trəw piinɨt nɨŋ
yuŏl-prɔɔm cbap nuh mun nɨŋ
bəñcuun tɨw twaay preŏh-
kaqrunaa.

As for the Council of the Kingdom, [it] must examine and approve these laws before sending (and presenting) [them] to the king.

John

nɔnaa (nənaa)
roŏtthaaphibaal
(~ roŏtthaqphibaal)

who, anyone, someone, whoever
the government, the administration

15. nənaa taŋ roŏtthaaphibaal?

Who appoints the government?

bopphaa

muŏntrəy
roŏt-muŏntrəy
niəyuŏq-roŏt-muŏntrəy
pramuk (prəmuk)

minister
government minister
prime minister
head, chief

16. caah, preŏh-kaqrunaa crəəh-rəəh
niəyuŏq-roŏt-muŏntrəy ciə
prəmuk roŏtthaaphibaal.

Well, the king chooses the prime minister to be head of the government.

kənaq
kənaq-roŏt-muŏntrəy

party, group
group of ministers, the cabinet

17. ruəc pii nuh tɨw, niəyuŏq-roŏt-
muŏntrəy qaac crəəh-rəəh
səmaacɨk nɨy kənaq-roŏt-
muŏntrəy baan.

From that point on, the prime minister can select the members of his cabinet.

kaa-yuŏl-prɔɔm
səc-kdəy-tuk-cət

approval, consent
confidence

18. niəyuŏq-roŏt-muŏntrəy haəy-nɨŋ
səmaacɨk nɨy kənaq-roŏt-muŏntrəy
trəw tətuəl kaa-yuŏl-prɔɔm haəy-
nɨŋ səc-kdəy-tuk-cət pii roŏt-səphiə.

The prime minister and the members of the cabinet must receive the approval and the confidence of the National Assembly.

John

qɑmnaac (qəmnaac)	power, authority
19. qəñcəŋ roə̆t-səphiə miən qəmnaac nah!	Then the National Assembly has a lot of power!

bopphaa

dɑmnaaŋ (dəmnaaŋ, təmnaaŋ)	representative
tuə-tɨw (tuu-tɨw)	all, all over, in general
20. caah, trəw haəy; pruə̆h səmaacɨk roə̆t-səphiə ciə dəmnaaŋ rəbɑh prəciəcuə̆n tuu-tɨw.	Yes, that's right; because the members of the National Assembly are the representatives of the general population.

ŋiə	duty, function
21. səmaacɨk kənaq-roə̆t-muə̆ntrəy miən ŋiə ciə roə̆t-muə̆ntrəy nɨy krəsuəŋ psein-psein.	The members of the cabinet function as ministers of the various departments.

John

22. miən krəsuəŋ qwəy-klah tɨw?	What are some of the departments?

bopphaa

yutteqthɔə (yuttəthɔə)	justice
krɑsuəŋ-yuttəthɔə	Department of Justice
kaa-piə	to protect, defend
kaa-piə-prəteeh	defense; to defend the country
khoosnaakaa	information, publicity
mɔhaa-ptɨy (məhaa-ptɨy)	interior
krɑsuəŋ-mɔhaa-ptɨy	Department of Interior
23. caah, miən krɑsuəŋ-yuttəthɔə, kaa-piə-prəteeh, kaa-bɑɑrəteeh, khoosnaakaa, haəy-nɨŋ krəsuəŋ-məhaa-ptɨy ciə-daəm.	Well, there are the Departments of Justice, Defense, Foreign Affairs, Information, and (the Department of) Interior, for example.

B. GRAMMAR AND DRILLS

1. Another Translation for ciə

In Lessons 24, B, 3 and 26, B, 6 we saw that ci̲ə̲ as a copulative or connective verb is sometimes best translated 'into', as in

mattyumməsəksaa caek ci̲ə̲ pii pnaek.	Secondary education is divided i̲n̲t̲o̲ (making, being) two parts.

In this lesson ci̲ə̲ occurs in several sentences in which it can be translated by the preposition 'as'; e.g.:

prəteeh-kampucciə kɨɨ ciə preə̆h-riəc-qɑnaacaq miən preə̆h-məhaa-ksat ci̲ə̲ neə̆q-dək-noə̆m.	Cambodia is a kingdom having a monarch a̲s̲ (being) leader.

preǝh-kaqrunaa crǝǝh-rǝǝh niǝyuǝq-   The king selects the prime minister
roǔt-muǔntrǝy cia prǝmuk   as (to be) head of the government.
roǔtthaaphibaal.

sǝmaacɨk kanaq-roǔt-muǔntrǝy   The members of the cabinet function
miǝn ŋiǝ cia roǔt-muǔntrǝy nɨy   as (have the duty to be) ministers
krǝsuǝŋ psein-psein.   of the different departments.

Note that the function of cia in these sentences is structurally identical with that
of cia in the first example above; the difference lies only in the English translation.

1-A. Substitution Drill

Teacher	Student
mǝnuh nuh miǝn ŋiǝ cia roǔt-muǔntrǝy nɨy krǝsuǝŋ-kaa-bɑɑrǝteeh.	mǝnuh nuh miǝn ŋiǝ cia roǔt-muǔntrǝy nɨy krǝsuǝŋ-kaa-bɑɑrǝteeh.
krǝsuǝŋ-teehsǝcɑɑ.	mǝnuh nuh miǝn ŋiǝ cia roǔt-muǔntrǝy nɨy krǝsuǝŋ-teehsǝcɑɑ.
krǝsuǝŋ-kaqsǝkam.	mǝnuh nuh miǝn ŋiǝ cia roǔt-moǔntrǝy nɨy krǝsuǝŋ-kaqsǝkam.
krǝsuǝŋ-kaa-piǝ-prǝteeh.	mǝnuh nuh miǝn ŋiǝ cia roǔt-muǔntrǝy nɨy krǝsuǝŋ-kaa-piǝ-prǝteeh.
krǝsuǝŋ-khoosnaakaa.	mǝnuh nuh miǝn ŋiǝ cia roǔt-muǔntrǝy nɨy krǝsuǝŋ-khoosnaakaa.
krǝsuǝŋ-yuttǝthǝǝ.	mǝnuh nuh miǝn ŋiǝ cia roǔt-muǔntrǝy nɨy krǝsuǝŋ-yuttǝthǝǝ.
krǝsuǝŋ-mǝhaa-ptɨy.	mǝnuh nuh miǝn ŋiǝ cia roǔt-muǔntrǝy nɨy krǝsuǝŋ-mǝhaa-ptɨy.
krǝsuǝŋ-quhsaahaqkam.	mǝnuh nuh miǝn ŋiǝ cia roǔt-muǔntrǝy nɨy krǝsuǝŋ-quhsaahaqkam.

1-B. Transformation Drill

Teacher	Student
mǝnuh nuh cia prǝmuk roǔtthaaphibaal.	mǝnuh nuh kee crǝǝh-rǝǝh cia prǝmuk roǔtthaaphibaal.
mǝnuh nuh cia sǝmaacɨk.	mǝnuh nuh kee crǝǝh-rǝǝh cia sǝmaacɨk.
mǝnuh nuh cia roǔt-muǔntrǝy.	mǝnuh nuh kee crǝǝh-rǝǝh cia roǔt-muǔntrǝy.
mǝnuh nuh cia niǝyuǝq-roǔt-muǔntrǝy.	mǝnuh nuh kee crǝǝh-rǝǝh cia niǝyuǝq-roǔt-muǔntrǝy.
mǝnuh nuh cia smiǝn.	mǝnuh nuh kee crǝǝh-rǝǝh cia smiǝn.
mǝnuh nuh cia neǝq-dǝk-noǔm.	mǝnuh nuh kee crǝǝh-rǝǝh cia neǝq-dǝk-noǔm.

Teacher	Student
mənuh nuh ciə dəmnaaŋ.	mənuh nuh kee crəəh-rəəh ciə dəmnaaŋ.
mənuh nuh ciə preə̆h-məhaa-ksat.	mənuh nuh kee crəəh-rəəh ciə preə̆h-məhaa-ksat.

2. <u>pii</u> in Expressions of Time

<u>pii</u> in expressions of time usually indicates past time, and means 'from (the time of), since, at (a given time in the past)', as in

prəteeh-kampucciə baan qaekkeriəc <u>pii</u> cnam naa?	When (from what year) did Cambodia get her independence?
roə̆tthaqthoə̆mmənuñ nuh kaət laəŋ <u>pii</u> cnam naa?	When (from what year) did the constitution come into existence?
look mɔɔk pnum-pɨñ <u>pii</u> tŋay naa?	When (on what day in the past) did you come to Phnom Penh?

2-A. <u>Progressive Substitution Drill</u>

Teacher	Student
roə̆tthaqthoə̆mmənuñ nuh kaət laəŋ pii <u>cnam</u> naa?	roə̆tthaqthoə̆mmənuñ nuh kaət laəŋ pii <u>cnam</u> naa?
<u>tŋay</u>	roə̆tthaqthoə̆mmənuñ nuh kaət laəŋ pii <u>tŋay</u> naa?
<u>kaal</u>	roə̆tthaqthoə̆mmənuñ nuh kaət laəŋ pii <u>kaal</u> naa?
<u>qatɨt</u>	roə̆tthaqthoə̆mmənuñ nuh kaət laəŋ pii <u>qatɨt</u> naa?
<u>khae</u>	roə̆tthaqthoə̆mmənuñ nuh kaət laəŋ pii <u>khae</u> naa?
<u>roə̆tthaaphibaal</u>	<u>roə̆tthaaphibaal</u> nuh kaət laəŋ pii <u>khae</u> naa?
<u>cnam</u>	roə̆tthaaphibaal nuh kaət laəŋ pii <u>cnam</u> naa?
<u>tŋay</u>	roə̆tthaaphibaal nuh kaət laəŋ pii <u>tŋay</u> naa?
<u>qatɨt</u>	roə̆tthaaphibaal nuh kaət laəŋ pii <u>qatɨt</u> naa?
<u>kaal</u>	roə̆tthaaphibaal nuh kaət laəŋ pii <u>kaal</u> naa?

3. <u>tɨw</u> and <u>mɔɔk</u> as Aspectual Particles

The words <u>tɨw</u> 'to go' and <u>mɔɔk</u> 'to come' are two of the most important words in Cambodian grammar because of the many roles they play, as shown in the following sentences:

As primary verbs:

> kñom tɨw pteʼəh.   I'm going home.
> koʼət mɔɔk haəy.   He's come already.

As directional verbs (see Lesson 10, B, 6):

> yɔɔk qəywan nih tɨw.   Take these things away.
> kñom som barəy muəy mɔɔk.   Could I have a cigarette (come)?

mɔɔk also occurs as an auxiliary (see Lesson 9, B, 10), as in

> mɔɔk tɨw ñam baay nɨw haaŋ nuh   Come have something to eat in that
> sən.   shop first.

tɨw also occurs as an imperative particle (see Lesson 11, B, 1), as in

> riəp-cam kluən qaoy chap tɨw!   (Go ahead and) get ready quickly!

In addition to the above functions, tɨw and mɔɔk also occur as aspectual particles
which show time relationships. mɔɔk as an aspectual particle means 'continuing
from a point in the past up to the present', as in the following examples:

> kñom caŋ məəl qəŋkɔɔ-woʼət   I've wanted to see Angkor Wat for a
> ciə yuu nah mɔɔk haəy.   long time now (since a long time
>   come already).

> kñom baan nɨw srok-kmae   I've lived in Cambodia for a year
> muəy cnam mɔɔk haəy.   (a year come already).

> haəy bəntoʼəp mɔɔk, kɑɑ cok puʼəh   Then later on, [my] stomach-ache
> klaŋ laəŋ.   got worse.

> cap taŋ pii baan qaekkəriəc mɔɔk,   Ever since gaining independence (come),
> prəteeh-kampucciə baan kan   Cambodia has maintained a policy of
> nəyoobaay qapyiəkrət.   neutrality.

tɨw as an aspectual particle means 'continuing onward from the present; onward
from a point in the past to an indefinite point in the future; on, onward, further',
as in the following examples:

> mɔɔk daə tɑɑ tɨw tiət.   Let's walk on.

> ruəc pii nuh tɨw, niəyuʼəq-roʼət-   From that point on, the prime minister
> muʼəntrəy qaac crəəh-rəəh səmaacɨk   can select the members of the cabinet.
> nɨy kənaq-roʼət-muʼəntrəy baan.

In the following examples, the meaning of tɨw as an aspectual particle is rather
more subtle, but its function is structurally equivalent to that of tɨw in the above
examples; its meaning in these examples appears to be 'indefiniteness; continuing
to an indefinite point; further':

> prəhael ciə tɨw sqaek haəy,   Perhaps [I'll] go tomorrow, [we'll]
> məəl-tɨw.   see (indefinite).

> twəə yaaŋ-məc tɨw, baan tɨw   What do they do (further, indefinite)
> ciə qəŋkɑɑ?   to make it into husked rice?

> miən krəsuəŋ qwəy-klah tɨw?   What are the various (further, indefi-
>   nite) departments?

Contrast the last example above with the sentence

miən krəsuəŋ qwəy-klah?   What are the various (specific)
                                          departments?

3-A. Substitution Drill

Teacher	Student

cap taŋ pii tŋay nuh mɔɔk, prəteeh-
kampucciə miən roə̆tthaqthoə̆mmənuñ.

cia prəteeh qaekkəriəc.

kan nəyoobaay qapyiəkrət.

miən səphiə pii.

kan lətthiq prəciəthɨppətay.

miən quhsaahaqkam craən nah.

bəñcuun srəw tɨw luə̆q nɨw
bɑɑrəteeh.

cap taŋ pii tŋay nuh mɔɔk, prəteeh-
kampucciə miən roə̆tthaqthoə̆mmənuñ.

cap taŋ pii tŋay nuh mɔɔk, prəteeh-
kampucciə kan nəyoobaay qapyiəkrət.

cap taŋ pii tŋay nuh mɔɔk, prəteeh-
kampucciə ciə prəteeh qaekkəriəc.

cap taŋ pii tŋay nuh mɔɔk, prəteeh-
kampucciə miən səphiə pii.

cap taŋ pii tŋay nuh mɔɔk, prəteeh-
kampucciə kan lətthiq prəciəthɨppətay.

cap taŋ pii tŋay nuh mɔɔk, prəteeh-
kampucciə miən quhsaahaqkam craən
nah.

cap taŋ pii tŋay nuh mɔɔk, prəteeh-
kampucciə bəñcuun srəw tɨw luə̆q
nɨw bɑɑrəteeh.

3-B. Substitution Drill

Teacher	Student

cap taŋ pii tŋay nih tɨw, kñom nɨŋ
chup cuə̆q barəy.

kham twəə-kaa.

tɨw daə-leeŋ roə̆l tŋay.

riən khaaŋ prəwoə̆ttəsaah.

twəə-kaa nɨw rooŋ-qaa-chəə.

twəə-srae.

twəə kruu-bəŋriən.

cap taŋ pii tŋay-nih tɨw, kñom nɨŋ
chup cuə̆q barəy.

cap taŋ pii tŋay-nih tɨw, kñom nɨŋ
kham twəə-kaa.

cap taŋ pii tŋay-nih tɨw, kñom nɨŋ
tɨw daə-leeŋ roə̆l tŋay.

cap taŋ pii tŋay-nih tɨw, kñom nɨŋ
riən khaaŋ prəwoə̆ttəsaah.

cap taŋ pii tŋay-nih tɨw, kñom nɨŋ
twəə-kaa nɨw rooŋ-qaa-chəə.

cap taŋ pii tŋay-nih tɨw, kñom nɨŋ
twəə-srae.

cap taŋ pii tŋay-nih tɨw, kñom nɨŋ
twəə kruu-bəŋriən.

3-C. Transformation Drill

Teacher	Student
ruəc pii nuh t<u>ɨ</u>w, kñom twəə-kaa nɨw haaŋ-lŭəq-baay.	ruəc pii nuh <u>mɔɔk</u>, kñom twəə-kaa nɨw haaŋ-lŭəq-baay.
ruəc pii nuh t<u>ɨ</u>w, kñom riən khaaŋ wiqswaakɑɑ.	ruəc pii nuh <u>mɔɔk</u>, kñom riən khaaŋ wiqswaakɑɑ.
ruəc pii nuh t<u>ɨ</u>w, kñom ceh baək laan.	ruəc pii nuh <u>mɔɔk</u>, kñom ceh baək laan.
ruəc pii nuh t<u>ɨ</u>w, kñom twəə kaa-riəcckaa.	ruəc pii nuh <u>mɔɔk</u>, kñom twəə kaa-riəcckaa.
ruəc pii nuh t<u>ɨ</u>w, kñom nɨw srok-baraŋ.	ruəc pii nuh <u>mɔɔk</u>, kñom nɨw srok-baraŋ.
ruəc pii nuh t<u>ɨ</u>w, kñom riən twəə mhoup baraŋ.	ruəc pii nuh <u>mɔɔk</u>, kñom riən twəə mhoup baraŋ.
ruəc pii nuh t<u>ɨ</u>w, kñom tɨw daə-leeŋ.	ruəc pii nuh <u>mɔɔk</u>, kñom tɨw daə-leeŋ.

3-D. Transformation Drill

Teacher	Student
miən krəsuəŋ qwəy-klah?	miən krəsuəŋ qwəy-klah t<u>ɨ</u>w?
miən ŋiə qwəy-klah?	miən ŋiə qwəy-klah t<u>ɨ</u>w?
miən phiəreə̆q qwəy-klah?	miən phiəreə̆q qwəy-klah t<u>ɨ</u>w?
miən khaet qwəy-klah?	miən khaet qwəy-klah t<u>ɨ</u>w?
miən səmaacɨk qwəy-klah?	miən səmaacɨk qwəy-klah t<u>ɨ</u>w?
miən rɨəŋ qwəy-klah?	miən rɨəŋ qwəy-klah t<u>ɨ</u>w?
miən mhoup qwəy-klah?	miən mhoup qwəy-klah t<u>ɨ</u>w?

4. <u>mun nɨŋ</u>

When the conjunction <u>mun</u> 'before' introduces a dependent clause, it is frequently followed by the future auxiliary <u>nɨ</u>ŋ, since the action of the dependent clause is necessarily posterior to that of the main clause; e.g.:

kee trəw piinɨt nɨŋ yŭəl-prɔɔm cbap nuh <u>mun nɨŋ</u> bəñcuun tɨw twaay preə̆h-kaqrunaa.	They must examine and agree to these laws <u>before</u> sending (and presenting) [them] to the king.

4-A. Transformation Drill

Teacher	Student
kee trəw piinɨt nɨŋ yŭəl-prɔɔm cbap nuh. [kee] bəñcuun tɨw twaay preə̆h-kaqrunaa.	kee trəw piinɨt nɨŋ yŭəl-prɔɔm cbap nuh mun nɨŋ bəñcuun tɨw twaay preə̆h-kaqrunaa.
kee trəw rəwɨy səmləy ciə qəmbɑh. [kee] tbaañ ciə krənat.	kee trəw rəwɨy səmləy ciə qəmbɑh mun nɨŋ tbaañ ciə krənat.
kee trəw pcuə srae. [kee] prŭə̆h srəw.	kee trəw pcuə srae mun nɨŋ prŭə̆h srəw.

Teacher	Student
kee trəw dɑɑq səmnaap.	kee trəw dɑɑq səmnaap
[kee] stuuŋ nɨw knoŋ srae.	mun nɨŋ stuuŋ nɨw knoŋ srae.
kee trəw baoh pteə̆h.	kee trəw baoh pteə̆h
[kee] cuut tok-tuu.	mun nɨŋ cuut tok-tuu.
kee trəw twəə mhoup-mhaa.	kee trəw twəə mhoup-mhaa
[kee] tətuəl pñiəw.	mun nɨŋ tətuəl pñiəw.
kee trəw cuəh-cul laan.	kee trəw cuəh-cul laan
[kee] twəə dəmnaə tɨw siəm-riəp.	mun nɨŋ twəə dəmnaə tɨw siəm-riəp.
kee trəw tɨñ səmbot.	kee trəw tɨñ səmbot
[kee] coul məəl kon.	mun nɨŋ coul məəl kon.

5. nɔnaa

nɔnaa is an alternative form of the pronoun neə̆q-naa 'who, someone, anyone, whoever' (see Lesson 22, B, 11), as in

nɔnaa taŋ roə̆tthaaphibaal?	Who appoints the government?
suə nɔnaa kɑ-baan.	Ask anyone at all.

5-A. Transformation Drill

Teacher	Student
neə̆q-naa taŋ roə̆tthaaphibaal?	nɔnaa taŋ roə̆tthaaphibaal?
tɨw ciə-muəy neə̆q-naa kɑ-baan.	tɨw ciə-muəy nɔnaa kɑ-baan.
neə̆q-naa cɑŋ tɨw məəl kon?	nɔnaa cɑŋ tɨw məəl kon?
look kɨt tɨw ciə-muəy neə̆q-naa?	look kɨt tɨw ciə-muəy nɔnaa?
baə neə̆q-naa mɨn yuə̆l riəŋ qwəy, suə kñom mɔɔk.	baə nɔnaa mɨn yuə̆l riəŋ qwəy, suə kñom mɔɔk.
look mɔɔk rɔɔk neə̆q-naa?	look mɔɔk rɔɔk nɔnaa?
baə look cɑŋ tɨw ciə-muəy neə̆q-naa, prap kñom tɨw.	baə look cɑŋ tɨw ciə-muəy nɔnaa, prap kñom tɨw.
neə̆q-naa miən rook claɑŋ kee qaoy tɨw deik tae-məneə̆q-qaeŋ.	nɔnaa miən rook claɑŋ kee qaoy tɨw deik tae-məneə̆q-qaeŋ.

6. The Preposition nɨy

nɨy is a preposition meaning 'of, belonging to' which normally replaces rɔbɑh in formal spoken or literary Cambodian, as in:

niəyuə̆q-roə̆t-muə̆ntrəy qaac crəəh-rəəh səmaacɨk nɨy kənaq-roə̆t-muə̆ntrəy baan.	The prime minister can select the members of the cabinet.
səmaacɨk nimuəy-nimuəy miən ŋiə ciə roə̆t-muə̆ntrəy nɨy krəsuəŋ psein-psein.	The various members function as ministers of the different departments.

6-A. Transformation Drill

Teacher	Student

kee trəw crəəh-rəəh səmaacɨk <u>rəbah</u>
kənaq-roət-muə̆ntrəy.

kee trəw crəəh-rəəh səmaacɨk <u>nɨy</u>
kənaq-roət-muə̆ntrəy.

mənuh nuh ciə səmaacɨk <u>rəbah</u>
roət-səphiə.

mənuh nuh ciə səmaacɨk <u>nɨy</u>
roət-səphiə.

səmaacɨk roət-səphiə ciə dəmnaaŋ
<u>rəbah</u> prəciəcuə̆n.

səmaacɨk roət-səphiə ciə dəmnaaŋ
<u>nɨy</u> prəciəcuə̆n.

koə̆t miən ŋiə ciə roət-muə̆ntrəy
<u>rəbah</u> krəsuəŋ-kaa-baarəteeh.

koə̆t miən ŋiə ciə roət-muə̆ntrəy
<u>nɨy</u> krəsuəŋ-kaa-baarəteeh.

preə̆h-məhaa-ksat ciə prəmuk <u>rəbah</u>
prəteeh-kampucciə.

preə̆h-məhaa-ksat ciə prəmuk <u>nɨy</u>
prəteeh-kampucciə.

niəyuə̆q-roət-muə̆ntrəy ciə prəmuk
<u>rəbah</u> roə̆tthaaphibaal.

niəyuə̆q-roət-muə̆ntrəy ciə prəmuk
<u>nɨy</u> roə̆tthaaphibaal.

mənuh nuh ciə smiən <u>rəbah</u> roə̆t-
səphiə.

mənuh nuh ciə smiən <u>nɨy</u> roə̆t-
səphiə.

nəyoobaay <u>rəbah</u> prəteeh-kampucciə.
yaaŋ-məc-klah?

nəyoobaay <u>nɨy</u> prəteeh-kampucciə.
yaaŋ-məc-klah?

krom-preə̆h-riəc-qanaacaq ciə səphiə
muəy <u>rəbah</u> roə̆tthaaphibaal-kampucciə.

krom-preə̆h-riəc-qanaacaq ciə səphiə
muəy <u>nɨy</u> roə̆tthaaphibaal-kampucciə.

preə̆h-qaŋ baan taŋ roə̆tthaqthoə̆mmənuñ
<u>rəbah</u> prəteeh-kampucciə.

preə̆h-qaŋ baan taŋ roə̆tthaqthoə̆mmənuñ
<u>nɨy</u> prəteeh-kampucciə.

[Tape 51]   C. COMPREHENSION

1. Discussing Elections

John: tŋay-nih mɨt qət tɨw twəə-kaa tee rɨɨ?

saphan: baat, tee; tŋay-nih kmiən nɔnaa tɨw twəə-kaa tee, pruə̆h ciə
          tŋay-bah-cnaot.

John: kee bah cnaot crəəh-rəəh qwəy?

          [dəmnaaŋ-riəh 'representative of the people, assemblyman']
saphan: baat, kee bah cnaot crəəh-rəəh dəmnaaŋ-riəh.

          [coə̆p cnaot 'to win an election']
John: baə baan coə̆p cnaot, dəmnaaŋ-riəh nuh tɨw twəə-kaa nɨw qae-naa?

saphan: baat, kee nɨŋ tɨw twəə ciə səmaacɨk roət-səphiə nɨw pnum-piñ.

John: thoə̆mmədaa kee twəə dəmnaaŋ-riəh baan ponmaan cnam?

saphan: tae buən cnam tee; baə kee caŋ twəə taa tɨw tiət, kee trəw coh
          cmuə̆h qaoy kee bah cnaot qaoy mədaaŋ tiət.

John: qəñcəŋ kee bah cnaot rəəh dəmnaaŋ-riəh cəmnuən buən cnam
          mədaaŋ rɨɨ?

saphan: baat, nɨŋ haəy.

2. Discussing Government

John: nɨw prəteeh-kampucciə miən nəyoobaay yaaŋ-məc?

bopphaa: caah, miən nəyoobaay qapyiəkrət.

John: haəy miən kaa-krup-krɔɔŋ yaaŋ-məc-klah?

bopphaa: caah, miən preə̆h-məhaa-ksat ciə prəmuk roə̆t.
            miən kənaq-roə̆t-muə̆ntrəy haəy-nɨŋ səphiə pii.

John: prəteeh-kampucciə miən roə̆tthaqthoə̆mmənuñ tee?

bopphaa: caah, prəteeh-kampucciə ciə preə̆h-riəc-qanaacaq kan lətthiq
            prəciəthɨppətay daoy miən roə̆tthaqthoə̆mmənuñ phaaŋ.

John: qəñcəŋ prəteeh-kampucciə miən sdac krup-krɔɔŋ douc prəteeh-
            qaŋglee, yipun, siəm?

            [ksattrəyaanii 'queen']
            [mɔhaa-ksattrəyaanii 'royal queen; Her Majesty the Queen']
bopphaa: caah, nɨŋ haəy; tae qəyləw-nih prəteeh-kmae miən tae məhaa-
            ksattrəyaanii tee.

            [samdac (səmdac) 'title for high-ranking royalty; prince, princess']
            [samdac siihanuq 'Prince Sihanouk']
John: coh, səmdac siihanuq ciə qwəy?

bopphaa: caah, səmdac siihanuq ciə prəmuk-roə̆t nɨy prəteeh-kampucciə,
            mɨn mɛɛn ciə preə̆h-məhaa-ksat tee.

3. Local Government

John: nɨw taam khaet miən rəbiəp-krup-krɔɔŋ yaaŋ-məc tɨw?

            [srok 'district, administrative division of a khaet']
            [khum 'commune, administrative division of a srok']
bopphaa: caah, khaet nimuəy-nimuəy caek ciə srok;
            srok nimuəy-nimuəy caek ciə khum;
            khum nimuəy-nimuəy caek ciə phuum.

John: miən neə̆q-riəcckaa qwəy-klah?

            [cawwaay-khaet 'provincial governor']
            [cawwaay-srok 'administrative head of a srok, district-chief']
            [mee-khum (mekhum) 'administrative head of a khum, commune-
            chief, mayor']
bopphaa: nɨw khaet nimuəy-nimuəy miən cawwaay-khaet ciə prəmuk.
            qae knoŋ srok wɨñ, miən cawwaay-srok, haəy nɨw khum
            nimuəy-nimuəy miən mekhum.

            [thom 'to be important']
John: neə̆q-riəcckaa teə̆ŋ-qah nih, taə, neə̆q-naa thom ciəŋ-kee?

            [truət-traa 'to oversee, supervise, administer']
bopphaa: cawwaay-khaet miən phiəreə̆q truət-traa cawwaay-srok haəy-nɨŋ
            mekhum teə̆ŋ-qah nɨw knoŋ khaet kluən.

John: yii, twəə cawwaay-khaet miən phiəreə̆q thom nah!

            [saq 'rank, grade']
bopphaa: caah, nɨŋ haəy; phiəreə̆q kɑɑ thom, saq kɑɑ thom.

D. CONVERSATION

1. Discussing the Cambodian National Government

Have one student assume the role of a westerner and another of a native Cambodian. The westerner questions the Cambodian about Cambodian government. Questions might include such things as what form of government Cambodia has, when Cambodia got her independence, whether Cambodia has a constitution, when it came into existence, what kind of foreign policy Cambodia follows, and how laws are made.

2. The Formation of a Government

Have one student question another about the formation of an executive government in Cambodia. Questions might include such things as how the prime minister is appointed, who appoints the members of the cabinet, how they are approved, and what the various departments of the government are.

3. Discussing Elections

One student questions another about elections in Cambodia. Questions might include who can vote, what officials are elected, for how long, how many legislative houses there are, and what they are.

4. Discussing Local Government

One student questions another about the organization of local government in Cambodia. Questions could include what the administrative units of government are below the national level, who is in charge of each, who has authority over whom, etc.

5. The Form of Government in One's Own Country

Ask a student to volunteer to describe the form of government in his own country. He should rely on the constructions of the preceding lesson as much as possible; where additional vocabulary is needed, he may consult the teacher.

LESSON 30. THE COUNTRY AND ITS PEOPLE

[Tape 52]   A. DIALOGUE

thət — to be placed, situated
canlah (cənlah, cəlah) — intervening space; between

1. prəteeh-kampuccia cia prəteeh
qaekkəriəc muəy niw qaazii-
paek-qaqknee thət niw cənlah
prəteeh-thay-laŋ haəy-niŋ
prəteeh-wiət-naam.

Cambodia is an independent country
in Southeast Asia situated between
(in the intervening space between)
Thailand and Vietnam.

prɛɛk — stream, large canal
bəŋ-prɛɛk-stiŋ-tuɐnlee — (lakes-streams-tributaries-
rivers) lakes, rivers, and
streams, sources of water
cia craən — in abundance (being many)

2. niw prəteeh-kampuccia kaqsəkam
qaoy phal craən nah pruɐh miən
bəŋ-prɛɛk-stiŋ-tuɐnlee cia
craən.

Farming in Cambodia yields plentiful
crops because there are lakes, rivers,
and streams in abundance.

3. phaliittəphal səmkhan ciəŋ kee
niw prəteeh-kampuccia kii sraw,
trəy, kawsuu, poot, mric, səndaek,
haəy-niŋ plae-chəə psein-psein.

The most important products in Cambodia are rice, fish, rubber, corn, pepper, beans, and various [kinds of]
fruits.

phal knoŋ dəy — underground products, mineral
resources

4. kraw pii phaliittəphal kaqsəkam,
miən phal knoŋ dəy cia craən, kii
spoɐn, daek, miəh, haəy-niŋ tbouŋ-
pic psein-psein.

Besides agricultural products, there
are mineral resources in abundance,
such as copper, iron, gold, and various
precious stones.

riəciəthippətay — monarchy
riəciəthippətay dael miən
roɐtthaqthoɐmmənuñ — constitutional monarchy

5. qae rəbiəp-krup-krɔɔŋ wiñ, prəteeh-
kampuccia cia riəcciəthippətay
dael miən roɐtthaqthoɐmmənuñ.

As for [its] system of government,
Cambodia is a constitutional monarchy.

rɔwiəŋ (rəwiəŋ) — interval, duration; during
knoŋ rəwiəŋ pii-poɐn cnam
mɔɔk haəy — for the past two thousand years
daaraap (daraap) — always; since
cia daraap — always, continuously

6. knoŋ rəwiəŋ pii-poɐn cnam mɔɔk
haəy, prəteeh-kampuccia miən
preɐh-məhaa-ksat saoy-riəc cia
daraap.

For the past two thousand years, Cambodia has been continuously ruled by
monarchs.

saqmay (samay)   time, era, period
paccopban (paccobɑn)   the present, modern times
samay paccobɑn   the present era, modern times
baek-caek   to divide, be divided

7. prəwŏəttəsaah prəteeh-kampucciə The history of Cambodia prior to
mun samay paccobɑn kee craən   modern times is usually divided into
caek ciə pram cəmnaek.   five parts.

fuunɑɑn (funɑɑn)   Funan
samay funɑɑn   the Funan Period
sattəwŏət   century, era
sattəwŏət tii-muəy   the first century
sattəwŏət tii-prammuəy the sixth century

8. cəmnaek tii-muəy kɨɨ samay funɑɑn, The first part is the Funan Period,
pii sattəwŏət tii-muəy tɨw   from the first century to the sixth
sattəwŏət tii-prammuəy.   century.

prapɨynii (prəpɨynii)   custom(s); culture
qəndiə   India; Indian
prəteeh-qəndiə   India
saasnaa (sahsnaa)   religion
latthiq sahsnaa   religious belief

9. knɔŋ samay nuh kee yɔɔk prəpɨynii In that period they borrowed many
mɔɔk pii prəteeh-qəndiə craən   aspects of their culture from India,
yaaŋ, douc ciə rəbiəp-krup-krɔɔŋ, such as [their] system of government,
lətthiq sahsnaa, haəy-nɨŋ   religious beliefs, and literature (as
qaqsɑɑsaah ciə-daəm.   examples).

cənlaa   Chenla
samay cənlaa   the Chenla Period

10. cəmnaek tii-pii kɨɨ samay cənlaa, The second part is the Chenla Period,
pii sattəwŏət tii-prammuəy tɨw   from the sixth century to the ninth
sattəwŏət tii-prambuən.   century.

samay qaŋkɔɔ (qəŋkɔɔ)   the Angkor Period

11. bəntŏəp pii sattəwŏət tii-prambuən (Following) from the ninth century to
tɨw sattəwŏət tii-dɑp-pram kɨɨ   the fifteenth century was the Angkor
ciə samay qəŋkɔɔ.   Period.

praasaat (prasaat)   palace; sacred monument, temple
qəŋkɔɔ-thom (qəŋkɔɔ-)   Angkor Thom
lbəy-cmuəh   fame, renown, reputation

12. knɔŋ samay nuh kee kɑɑ-saaŋ   In that period they built the monuments
prasaat qəŋkɔɔ-thom haəy-nɨŋ   of Angkor Thom and Angkor Wat, which
qəŋkɔɔ-wŏət dael miən lbəy-cmuəh are famous (have fame) all over the
tuu-tɨw knɔŋ piphup-look.   world.

tuˇəhsəniə   to observe, inspect, sight-see
teˇəŋ nih   all these

13. sɑp-tŋay-nih miən teehsəcɑɑ   These days a great many foreign
baarəteeh ciə craən mɔɔk   tourists come to observe all these
tuˇəhsəniə prasaat boraan teˇəŋ nih. ancient monuments.

samay kɑndaal (kəndaal) the Middle Period

14. pii sattəwŏət tii-dɑp-pram tɨw   From the fifteenth to the nineteenth
sattəwŏət tii-dɑp-prambuən kee   centuries they call the Middle Period.
haw thaa samay kəndaal.

qaanaapyiəbaal (qanaapyiəbaal)
15. bəntoəp pii samay kəndaal dɑl
krɨhsaqkəraac muəy-poən
prambuən-rɔɔy haasəp-bəy, preəh-
riəc-qanaacaq kampuccia nɨw kraom
qanaapyiəbaal prəteeh-baraŋ.

protectorate, protectorship
Following the Middle Period up to 1953 A.D., Cambodia was under the protectorship of France.

ruəp-ruəm
qənduucən ~ qəndoucən
(qəndocən)
qəndocən baraŋsaeh
16. knoŋ rəwiəŋ peel nuh, prəteeh-
kampuccia, prəteeh-liəw, haəy-nɨŋ
prəteeh-wiət-naam ruəp-ruəm
kniə ciə qəndocən baraŋsaeh.

to combine, assemble, collect
Indochina

French Indochina
During that time, Cambodia, Laos, and Vietnam were combined as French Indochina.

17. prəteeh-kampuccia baan tətuəl
qaekkəriəc-ciət nɨw cnam muəy-
poən prambuən-rɔɔy haasəp-bəy.

Cambodia received her national independence in 1953.

puttəsahsnaa
preəh-puttəsahsnaa
18. prəciəcuən kmae kan preəh-
puttəsahsnaa kawsəp phiəq-rɔɔy.

Buddhism
(sacred-) Buddhism
Ninety percent of the Cambodian population believe in Buddhism.

qihslaam (~ qehslaam)
krɨhsahsnaa
19. prəciəcuən klah tiət kan sahsnaa
qihslaam rɨɨ krɨhsahsnaa.

Islam
Christianity
Others (of the population) believe in Islam or Christianity.

neəq-kan-preəh-puttəsahsnaa

a Buddhist, a follower of Buddhism

prɑprɨt (prəprɨt, pəprɨt)
thɔə
thɔə pram
sɑmlap (səmlap)
luəc
luəc prəpuən kee

to act, follow, practice
moral law, dharma
five rules, five laws
to kill
to steal
to steal another's wife, to commit adultery

kohɑq (kəhɑq) ~ krɑhɑq
(krɑhɑq, kəhɑq)
20. neəq-kan-preəh-puttəsahsnaa craən
prəprɨt thɔə pram, kɨɨ kom səmlap,
kom luəc, kom luəc prəpuən kee,
kom kəhɑq, haəy kom phək sraa.

to lie, to prevaricate

Buddhists usually follow five rules, (being) don't kill, don't steal, don't commit adultery, don't lie, and don't drink alcoholic beverages.

preəh-saŋ
mɔhaanikaay (məhaanikaay)

thoəmməyut
21. nɨw prəteeh-kampuccia preəh-saŋ
caek ciə pii puəq rɨɨ kənaq, kɨɨ
məhaanikaay haəy-nɨŋ thoəmməyut.

[Buddhist] priest, monk
the liberal sect (literally: large body)
the orthodox sect
Buddhist priests in Cambodia are divided into two groups or sects—the liberal [sect] and the orthodox [sect].

buəh
buəh ciə look-saŋ
yaaŋ təc nah

to enter the monkhood
to become a monk
at least, at the very least

22. thŏə̆mmədaa proh-proh craən   Usually the men (mostly) enter the
    buəh ciə look-saŋ yaaŋ təc nah   monkhood [for] at least one Lenten
    muəy wŭə̆hsaa, rɨɨ buəh qah   season, or sometimes all their lives
    muəy ciwɨt ka-miən.   (or become monks all their lives, it
                                          does happen).

        bon   merit, good deeds, merit-
                                                making
        twəə-bon   to make merit, do good deeds,
                                                hold a merit-making ceremony
        tiən   gift
        daq-tiən   to make a contribution, to give
                                                alms
        twəə-bon-daq-tiən   to make merit by giving alms,
                                                to perform generous deeds
        phɑl-bon   rewards, accumulated merit,
                                                karma
        ciət   life, existence, rebirth,
                                                reincarnation
        tɨw ciət kraoy   in later reincarnations
23. taam lətthiq preə̆h-puttəsahsnaa   According to Buddhist belief, we
    yəəŋ trəw twəə-bon-daq-tiən   should perform generous deeds in
    daəmbəy nɨŋ qaoy baan phɑl-bon   order that we might accumulate merit
    tɨw ciət kraoy.   in later reincarnations.

        sophiəp   to be polite, kind
        riəpsaa   to be proper, well-mannered,
                                                gentle
        sophiəp-riəpsaa   to be polite, well-mannered
        thureə̆q   problem, trouble, preoccupation
        cuəy thureə̆q   to help out in time of trouble
        tɨw wɨñ tɨw mɔɔk   back and forth, reciprocally
24. haet nih haəy baan ciə prəciəcuə̆n   That is why the Cambodian people
    kmae sophiəp-riəpsaa haəy cuəy   are polite and always help each other
    thurĕə̆q kniə tɨw wɨñ tɨw mɔɔk   [in times of] trouble.
    ciə-dɑraap.

B. GRAMMAR AND DRILLS

1. Nouns Which Are Translated as Prepositions

Some words which are most conveniently translated as prepositions are
nouns from the standpoint of Cambodian structure. The following are examples
from this lesson:

prəteeh-kampucciə thət nɨw cənlɑh   Cambodia is situated between (in the
prəteeh-thay-lɑŋ haəy-nɨŋ prəteeh-   intervening space [between]) Thailand
wiət-naam.   and Vietnam.

knoŋ rəwiəŋ pii-poə̆n cnam mɔɔk   During (in the interval [of]) the past
haəy, prəteeh-kampucciə miən-   two thousand years, Cambodia has
preə̆h-məhaa-ksat saoy-riəc   been continuously ruled by monarchs.
ciə-dɑraap.

knoŋ rəwiəŋ peel nuh, prəteeh-kampucciə, prəteeh-liəw, haəy-nɨŋ prəteeh-wiət-naam ruəp-ruəm kniə ćiə qəndocən baraŋsaeh.

During (for the duration [of]) that time, Cambodia, Laos, and Vietnam were combined as French Indochina.

Other examples of nouns we have met in this function are the following:

cəmnaek kñom wɨñ, kñom caŋ twəə kaa-riəcckaa.

As for (on the part of) me, I want to go into the civil service.

salaa kñom saŋ nɨw kəndaal phuum.

My school is built in the center [of] the village.

tuk-cət ləə kñom coh, khaaŋ baək laan.

Have confidence in me, [in the] matter [of] driving a car.

laan rəbah kñom khouc haəy.

My car (car-thing-mine) is broken down.

1-A. Multiple Substitution Drill

Teacher	Student
phuum kñom thət nɨw cənlah pnum-pɨñ haəy-nɨŋ prɨy-wɛɛŋ.	phuum kñom thət nɨw cənlah pnum-pɨñ haəy-nɨŋ prɨy-wɛɛŋ.
tuənlee-saap tuənlee-meekoŋ.	phuum kñom thət nɨw cənlah tuənlee-saap haəy-nɨŋ tuənlee-meekoŋ.
pnum-krəwaañ pnum-daaŋ-rɛɛk.	phuum kñom thət nɨw cənlah pnum-krəwaañ haəy-nɨŋ pnum-daaŋ-rɛɛk.
pləw nih pləw nuh.	phuum kñom thət nɨw cənlah pləw nih haəy-nɨŋ pləw nuh.
phuum nih phuum nuh.	phuum kñom thət nɨw cənlah phuum nih haəy-nɨŋ phuum nuh.
batdəmbaaŋ poosat.	phuum kñom thət nɨw cənlah batdəmbaaŋ haəy-nɨŋ poosat.
srae-cəmkaa prɨy.	phuum kñom thət nɨw cənlah srae-cəmkaa haəy-nɨŋ prɨy.

1-B. Substitution Drill

Teacher	Student
knoŋ rəwiəŋ pii cnam mɔɔk haəy, kñom twəə kaa-riəcckaa.	knoŋ rəwiəŋ pii cnam mɔɔk haəy, kñom twəə kaa-riəcckaa.
bəy tŋay	knoŋ rəwiəŋ bəy tŋay mɔɔk haəy, kñom twəə kaa-riəcckaa.
pram khae	knoŋ rəwiəŋ pram khae mɔɔk haəy, kñom twəə kaa-riəcckaa.
muəy qatɨt	knoŋ rəwiəŋ muəy qatɨt mɔɔk haəy, kñom twəə kaa-riəcckaa.
dap cnam	knoŋ rəwiəŋ dap cnam mɔɔk haəy, kñom twəə kaa-riəcckaa.

Teacher	Student
prambəy maoŋ	knoŋ rəwiəŋ <u>prambəy maoŋ</u> mɔɔk haəy kñom twəə kaa-riəcckaa.
craən cnam	knoŋ rəwiəŋ <u>craən cnam</u> mɔɔk haəy, kñom twəə kaa-riəcckaa.

2. cIə in Adverbial Phrases

The connective verb <u>ciə</u> frequently occurs as the first element of adverbial phrases, as in

kñom caŋ khəəñ qəŋkɔɔ-woŏt <u>ciə yuu nah mɔɔk haəy</u>.	I've wanted to see Angkor Wat <u>for (being) a long time now</u>.
sŧən thəə qəy, kaa yŧŧt <u>ciə-nŧc</u>.	Whatever Soeun does, [he's] <u>always</u> (being forever) late.
kee twəə-srae <u>ciə kaa thoŏmmədaa</u>.	They do rice-farming <u>as a matter of course</u> (as the usual thing).
kñom srəlañ srəy nuh <u>ciə tii-bəmphot</u>.	I love that girl (being) <u>the most of all</u>.
prəteeh-kampucciə miən preŏh-məhaa-ksat saoy-riəc <u>ciə daraap</u>.	Cambodia has been ruled by a monarch <u>continuously</u> (being always).
kee tŧw twəə-kaa <u>ciə-muəy kniə</u>.	They go to work <u>together</u> (being one together).

The difference in meaning between an adjectival verb such as <u>craən</u> 'to be much, many' and <u>ciə craən</u> 'abundantly, in abundance, in great quantity' is slight; the primary distinction appears to be that <u>craən</u> directly modifies a preceding noun or verb, while <u>ciə craən</u> generally modifies an entire clause or sentence adverbially, as shown in the following examples:

kraw pii phalliŧtəphal kaqsəkam, miən phal knoŋ dəy <u>craən</u>.	Besides agricultural products, there are <u>many</u> mineral resources.
kraw pii phalliŧtəphal kaqsəkam, miən phal knoŋ dəy <u>ciə craən</u>.	Besides agricultural products, there are mineral resources <u>in abundance</u>.

2-A. Substitution Drill

Teacher	Student
nŧw srok-kmae, kee twəə-srae <u>ciə craən</u>.	nŧw srok-kmae, kee twəə-srae <u>ciə craən</u>.
<u>ciə-nŧc</u>.	nŧw srok-kmae, kee twəə-srae <u>ciə-nŧc</u>.
<u>ciə kaa-thoŏmmədaa</u>.	nŧw srok-kmae, kee twəə-srae <u>ciə kaa thoŏmmədaa</u>.
<u>ciə daraap</u>.	nŧw srok-kmae, kee twəə-srae <u>ciə daraap</u>.

Teacher

cɨə yuu nah mɔɔk haəy.

Student

nɨw srok-kmae, kee twəə-srae
cɨə yuu nah mɔɔk haəy.

cɨə-muəy kniə.

nɨw srok-kmae, kee twəə-srae
cɨə-muəy kniə.

2-B. Transformation Drill

Teacher

nɨw srok-kmae miən phɑl-dəmnam
craən.

Student

nɨw srok-kmae miən phɑl-dəmnam
cɨə craən.

kee baan cap trəy craən nah.

kee baan cap trəy cɨə craən nah.

miən teehsəcɑɑ craən
mɔɔk tuə̆hsəniə prəsaat teə̆ŋ nih.

miən teehsəcɑɑ cɨə craən
mɔɔk tuə̆hsəniə prəsaat teə̆ŋ nih.

nɨw srok-kmae kee dam srəw
craən nah.

nɨw srok-kmae kee dam srəw
cɨə craən nah.

miən kaa-nesaat-trəy craən nah.

miən kaa-nəsaat-trəy cɨə craən nah.

nɨw kəmpuə̆ŋ-caam kee dam daəm-
kawsuu craən.

nɨw kəmpuə̆ŋ-caam kee dam kaəm-
kawsuu cɨə craən.

knoŋ samay nuh kee yɔɔk prəpɨynii
mɔɔk pii prəteeh-qəndiə craən yaaŋ.

knoŋ samay nuh kee yɔɔk prəpɨynii
mɔɔk pii prəteeh-qəndiə cɨə craən yaaŋ.

knoŋ samay nuh kee kɑɑ-saaŋ prəsaat
craən.

knoŋ samay nuh kee kɑɑ-saaŋ prəsaat
cɨə craən.

3. cɨə-nɨc vs. cɨə dɑraap

The distinction between cɨə-nɨc and cɨə dɑraap is roughly analogous to the difference between 'continually' and 'continuously' in English; cɨə-nɨc means 'always, invariably, habitually, characteristically, continually', while cɨə dɑraap means 'always, consistently, without stopping, continuously', as in the following examples:

mənuh nuh twəə-bon-daq-tiən
cɨə-nɨc.

That man continually (invariably)
performs generous deeds.

mənuh nuh twəə-bon-daq-tiən
cɨə dɑraap.

That man continuously (incessantly)
performs generous deeds.

3-A. Transformation Drill

Teacher

mənuh nuh twəə-bon-daq-tiən cɨə-nɨc.

Student

mənuh nuh twəə-bon-daq-tiən cɨə-
dɑraap.

prəciəcuə̆n kmae sophiəp-riəpsaa
cɨə-nɨc.

prəciəcuə̆n kmae sophiəp-riəpsaa
cɨə dɑraap.

prəteeh-kampucciə miən
preə̆h-məhaa-ksat saoy-riəc cɨə-nɨc.

prəteeh-kampucciə miən
preə̆h-məhaa-ksat saoy-riəc cɨə dɑraap.

Teacher	Student
mənuh nuh ceh-tae kəhɑq <u>ciə-nɨc</u>.	mənuh nuh ceh-tae kəhɑq <u>ciə dɑrɑɑp</u>.
mənuh nuh prəprɨt thɔə pram <u>ciə-nɨc</u>.	mənuh nuh prəprɨt thɔə pram <u>ciə dɑrɑɑp</u>.
neə̆q-srae kmae twəə-srae <u>ciə-nɨc</u>.	neə̆q-srae kmae twəə-srae <u>ciə dɑrɑɑp</u>.
srəy nuh ceh-tae niyiəy <u>ciə-nɨc</u>.	srəy nuh ceh-tae niyiəy <u>ciə dɑrɑɑp</u>.

4. The Preposition <u>teə̆ŋ</u>

<u>teə̆ŋ</u> perhaps characteristically occurs in the compound <u>teə̆ŋ-qɑh</u> 'all, everything', as in:

<u>teə̆ŋ-qɑh</u> tlay ponmaan?	How much is <u>everything</u>?
kee tɨw <u>teə̆ŋ-qɑh</u> kniə.	They went <u>all</u> together.

<u>teə̆ŋ</u> does occur by itself as a preposition, however, meaning 'all of, including, the whole', as in:

sɑp-tŋay-nih miən teehsəcɑɑ ciə craən mɔɔk məəl prəsaat <u>teə̆ŋ</u> nih.	These days a great many tourists come to see <u>all of</u> these monuments.
rəbɑɑ <u>teə̆ŋ</u> nuh teə̆q-tɔɔŋ nɨŋ srok-srae-cəmkaa.	<u>All of</u> those trades have to do with the rural areas.

When <u>teə̆ŋ</u> is repeated before two consecutive objects, the resulting discontinuous construction <u>teə̆ŋ</u> . . . <u>teə̆ŋ</u> means 'both . . . and', as in

kee twəə-kaa <u>teə̆ŋ</u> tŋay <u>teə̆ŋ</u> yup.	They work <u>both</u> day <u>and</u> night.

4-A. Expansion Drill

Teacher	Student
miən teehsəcɑɑ ciə craən mɔɔk məəl prəsaat nih.	miən teehsəcɑɑ ciə craən mɔɔk məəl prəsaat <u>teə̆ŋ</u> nih.
rəbɑɑ nuh teə̆q-tɔɔŋ nɨŋ srok-srae-cəmkaa.	rəbɑɑ <u>teə̆ŋ</u> nuh teə̆q-tɔɔŋ nɨŋ srok-srae-cəmkaa.
mənuh nuh twəə-kaa ciə kammə̆kɑɑ.	mənuh <u>teə̆ŋ</u> nuh twəə-kaa ciə kammə̆kɑɑ.
proh nih nɨŋ buəh ciə look-sɑŋ.	proh <u>teə̆ŋ</u> nih nɨŋ buəh ciə look-sɑŋ.
kee twəə-kaa tŋay, yup.	kee twəə-kaa <u>teə̆ŋ</u> tŋay <u>teə̆ŋ</u> yup.
haaŋ cən baək prɨk, lŋiəc.	haaŋ cən baək <u>teə̆ŋ</u> prɨk <u>teə̆ŋ</u> lŋiəc.
pteə̆h nih səmrap neə̆q-riəcckaa nɨw.	pteə̆h <u>teə̆ŋ</u> nih səmrap neə̆q-riəcckaa nɨw.
prəciəcuə̆n nuh kan lətthiq preə̆h-puttəsahsnaa.	prəciəcuə̆n <u>teə̆ŋ</u> nuh kan lətthiq preə̆h-puttəsahsnaa.

5. <u>yaaŋ təc nah</u>

<u>yaaŋ təc nah</u> is an adverbial phrase which means 'at least, at the very least'. It is typically preposed to the numeral or numeral plus specifier to which it applies, as in

thŏə̆mmədaa proh-proh buəh
<u>yaaŋ təc nah</u> muəy wŭə̆hsaa.

kee chup riən <u>yaaŋ təc nah</u>
bəy khae.

kŏə̆t baan praq-khae <u>yaaŋ təc nah</u>
pii-pŏə̆n.

Usually men enter the monkhood
[for] <u>at least</u> one Lenten season.

They're out of school (stop studying)
[for] <u>at least</u> three months.

He gets a salary [of] <u>at least</u>
two thousand.

5-A. <u>Substitution Drill</u>

<u>Teacher</u>	<u>Student</u>
kñom trəw twəə-kaa yaaŋ təc nah <u>muəy wŭə̆hsaa.</u>	kñom trəw twəə-kaa yaaŋ təc nah <u>muəy wŭə̆hsaa.</u>
<u>bəy khae.</u>	kñom trəw twəə-kaa yaaŋ təc nah <u>bəy khae.</u>
<u>pram tŋay.</u>	kñom trəw twəə-kaa yaaŋ təc nah <u>pram tŋay.</u>
<u>prambəy maoŋ.</u>	kñom trəw twəə-kaa yaaŋ təc nah <u>prambəy maoŋ.</u>
<u>pii qatɨt.</u>	kñom trəw twəə-kaa yaaŋ təc nah <u>pii qatɨt.</u>
<u>buən cnam.</u>	kñom trəw twəə-kaa yaaŋ təc nah <u>buən cnam.</u>
<u>bəy lŋiəc.</u>	kñom trəw twəə-kaa yaaŋ təc nah <u>bəy lŋiəc.</u>
<u>məphɨy cnam.</u>	kñom trəw twəə-kaa yaaŋ təc nah <u>məphɨy cnam.</u>

5-B. <u>Expansion Drill</u>

<u>Teacher</u>	<u>Student</u>
kñom trəw twəə-kaa buən cnam.	kñom trəw twəə-kaa <u>yaaŋ təc nah</u> buən cnam.
kee chup riən bəy khae.	kee chup riən <u>yaaŋ təc nah</u> bəy khae.
kŏə̆t baan praq-khae pram-pŏə̆n.	kŏə̆t baan praq-khae <u>yaaŋ təc nah</u> pram-pŏə̆n.
kŏə̆t phək sraa bəy kaew.	kŏə̆t phək sraa <u>yaaŋ təc nah</u> bəy kaew.
kee trəw pcuə srae pii daɑŋ.	kee trəw pcuə srae <u>yaaŋ təc nah</u> pii daɑŋ.
kñom trəw riən bəy cnam tiət.	kñom trəw riən <u>yaaŋ təc nah</u> bəy cnam tiət.
knoŋ muəy ciwɨt kee kaa prəpuə̆n bəy neə̆q.	knoŋ muəy ciwɨt kee kaa prəpuə̆n <u>yaaŋ təc nah</u> bəy neə̆q.
kñom trəw tɨñ krəbəy pii.	kñom trəw tɨñ krəbəy <u>yaaŋ təc nah</u> pii.

6. <u>tɨw wɨñ tɨw mɔɔk</u>

The adverbial phrase <u>tɨw wɨñ tɨw mɔɔk</u> means 'reciprocally, back and forth';
the entire adverbial phrase <u>(nɨŋ) kniə tɨw wɨñ tɨw mɔɔk</u> is partially redundant.

Literally it means 'together back and forth', and can usually be translated 'to/
with one another, to/with each other, among themselves', as in

prəciəcuən kmae sophiəp-riəpsaa haəy cuəy thureəq kniə tɨw wɨñ tɨw mɔɔk ciə-dɑraap.	The Cambodian people are polite and always help each other [in times of] trouble.

6-A. Substitution Drill

Teacher	Student
prəciəcuən kmae cuəy thureəq kniə tɨw wɨñ tɨw mɔɔk.	prəciəcuən kmae cuəy thureəq kniə tɨw wɨñ tɨw mɔɔk.
cuəy	prəciəcuən kmae cuəy kniə tɨw wɨñ tɨw mɔɔk.
cuəy twəə pteəh	prəciəcuən kmae cuəy twəə pteəh kniə tɨw wɨñ tɨw mɔɔk.
cuəy twəə-kaa	prəciəcuən kmae cuəy twəə-kaa kniə tɨw wɨñ tɨw mɔɔk.
cuəy twəə-srae	prəciəcuən kmae cuəy twəə-srae kniə tɨw wɨñ tɨw mɔɔk.
niyiəy	prəciəcuən kmae niyiəy kniə tɨw wɨñ tɨw mɔɔk.
teəq-tɔɔŋ	prəciəcuən kmae teəq-tɔɔŋ kniə tɨw wɨñ tɨw mɔɔk.

6-B. Expansion Drill

Teacher	Student
prəciəcuən kmae cuəy thureəq kniə.	prəciəcuən kmae cuəy thureəq kniə tɨw wɨñ tɨw mɔɔk.
puəq cao nuh way kniə.	puəq cao nuh way kniə tɨw wɨñ tɨw mɔɔk.
koun-səh nuh bəŋriən kniə.	koun-səh nuh bəŋriən kniə tɨw wɨñ tɨw mɔɔk.
puəq-kamməkɑɑ nuh cuəy twəə-kaa kniə.	puəq-kamməkɑɑ nuh cuəy twəə-kaa kniə tɨw wɨñ tɨw mɔɔk.
neəq-kan preəh-puttəsahsnaa craən-tae cuəy kniə.	neəq-kan-preəh-puttəsahsnaa craən-tae cuəy kniə tɨw wɨñ tɨw mɔɔk.
prəteeh teəŋ pii nuh tɨñ qəywan kniə.	prəteeh teəŋ pii nuh tɨñ qəywan kniə tɨw wɨñ tɨw mɔɔk.

[Tape 53]   C. COMPREHENSION

1. <u>A Letter from Cambodia</u>

   [New Vocabulary]

   suəsdəy   Greetings!, Hello! (formal, literary,
                                             or urban)
   suəsdəy mɨt   Dear Friend; Greetings, Friend
                                             (salutation used in friendly letters)
   qaŋ   specifier for priests and Buddhist images
   saaŋ   to repay, pay back, compensate
   kun   quality, merit, goodness
   thaan-suə   heaven, Nirvana
   kuə-sam   reasonable, proper, moderate; slang:
                                             not bad, pretty good
   cap cət   to be interested in, attracted by
   ruĕh   to live, be alive
   kaa-ruĕh-nɨw   life, living, existence
   trəm   proper; at, coincident with, as far as
   trəm nih   right here, at this point
   səc-kdəy-kuə-pum-kuə   mistakes (literally: both good and
                                             bad points)
   qaqphɨy (qaphɨy)   to be fearless, without fear
   qaqhɨy-tooh   to forgive, excuse
   daoy   with, by
   meetrəy-phiəp   friendship, affection
   daoy meetrəy-phiəp   With affection, Affectionately (close
                                             used in friendly letters)

   pnum-pɨñ, tŋay tii-pram maqkəraa, cnam muəy-pŏən
prambuən-rɔɔy cətsəp

   suəsdəy mɨt

   kñom baan mɔɔk dɑl srok-kmae pram tŋay mɔɔk haəy. srok-kmae sqaat lqɑɑ
nah haəy səpbaay phaaŋ. prəciəcuĕn kmae səphiəp-riəpsaa nah. kee kan preăh-
puttəsahsnaa kawsəp phiəq-rɔɔy. thŏĕmmədaa prəciəcuĕn kmae tuə-tɨw craən
prəprɨt thŏə pram, kɨɨ kom səmlap, kom luəc, kom kəhaq, kom luəc prəpuĕn kee,
haəy-nɨŋ kom phək sraa. preăh-saŋ nɨw srok-kmae caek ciə pii pnaek, kɨɨ kənaq
məhaanikaay haəy-nɨŋ thŏĕmməyut. nɨw taam phuum psein-psein miən wŏət ciə
craən; knoŋ wŏət nimuəy-nimuəy miən preăh-saŋ craən qaŋ. kee baan prap kñom
thaa taam thŏĕmmədaa proh-proh kmae buəh twəə look-saŋ yaaŋ tɑc nah muəy
wuĕhsaa. kee buəh ciə look-saŋ daəmbəy yɔɔk phal-bon saaŋ kun qəwpuk-mdaay,
pruĕh kee ciə thaa baə miən koun buəh ciə look-saŋ, qəwpuk-mdaay nɨŋ miən bon
haəy qaac laəŋ thaan-suə baan.

   mɨt dəŋ tee, srok-kmae ciə riəciəthɨppətay muəy dael baan tətuəl qaekkəriəc
ciət pii prəteeh-baraŋ taŋ pii krɨhsaqkəraac muəy-pŏən prambuən-rɔɔy haasəp-
bəy? nɨw srok-kmae kaqsəkam qaoy phal lqɑɑ nah. kee dam dəmnam psein-psein
ciə craən, douc ciə srəw, poot, kawsuu, səndaek ciə-daəm. kraw pii phal-dəmnam,
srəy-srəy nɨw srok-kmae kɑɑ lqɑɑ kuə-sam dae. kñom mɨn dəŋ ciə tɨw srok wɨñ
tŋay naa tee, pruĕh kñom cap cət srəlañ prəciəcuĕn haəy-nɨŋ kaa-ruĕh-nɨw nɨw
srok-kmae nah.

   kñom soum liə mɨt trəm nih sən haəy. səc-kdəy-kuə-pum-kuə soum mɨt
qaphɨy-tooh.

   daoy meetrəy-phiəp,

D. CONVERSATION

1. Discussing Cambodian History

Have one student question another about the history of Cambodia. Questions
might include such things as what the various periods of Cambodian history are,
how long each lasted, what happened during the Funan period, what monuments
were built during the Angkor Period, what were the countries of French Indochina, when did Cambodia get her independence, etc.

2. Discussing Religions in Cambodia

Have one student question another about religions in Cambodia. Questions
might include what religions are practiced in Cambodia, what percent of the
people believe in Buddhism, what rules Buddhists generally follow, what are the
Buddhist sects in Cambodia, who enters the monkhood, for how long and why, and
what characterizes Cambodian social relations.

3. Questions and Answers About Cambodia

Invite the students to question the teacher about aspects of Cambodia in
which they are interested. Students should confine themselves as much as possible to the vocabulary and structures which they have already met; necessary
new vocabulary may be provided by the teacher. In his answers, the teacher
should confine himself as far as possible to familiar vocabulary and structures;
he should explain any new vocabulary or structure, unless it can be ascertained
from the context.

LESSON 31. REVIEW OF LESSONS 26-30

A. Review of Dialogues

In preparation for the review lesson, review the Dialogues of Lessons 26–30. To test yourself, cover the English column and supply the English equivalents of the Cambodian sentences; then cover the Cambodian column and supply the Cambodian equivalents of the English sentences. If you cannot supply an appropriate translation quickly and smoothly, review the relevant sections of the Grammar and Drills.

B. Review of Comprehension

The teacher will read selected conversations from the Comprehension sections of Lessons 26–30, calling on individual students for English translations of the sentences.

C. Test for Comprehension

Write the numbers 1–50 on a sheet of paper. The teacher will read 50 statements at normal speed. Write "true" or "false" beside the appropriate number. Since Lessons 26–30 contain much specific information about Cambodia, a higher proportion of the true-or-false questions deal with facts covered in the lessons than in previous Review lessons. With true-or-false questions it is always possible to quibble by pointing out exceptions and extreme cases, but if the student considers each question in general, the intent of the question should be obvious. The teacher will repeat each statement twice. Listen to the statement in its entirety the first time; an unfamiliar word may be cleared up by the context in which it occurs.

1. nɨw srok-kmae miən prəciəcuən craən neəq twəə srae.
2. srae-wuəhsaa haəy-nɨŋ srae-praŋ kee twəə douc kniə.
3. srəw-wuəhsaa doh daoy tɨk cumnuən.
4. srəw-praŋ kee mɨn trəw bəŋhou tɨk coul srae tee.
5. kee cap-pdaəm pcuə srae nɨw khae-tnuu, mun miən pliəŋ tleəq.
6. kee praə dəmrəy tiəñ qəŋkoəl pcuə srae.
7. puəq-proh-proh daaq səmnaap yɔɔk tɨw stuuŋ nɨw knoŋ srae.
8. srəw-pruəh qaoy phal craən ciəŋ srəw-stuuŋ.
9. cuən-kaal kee yɔɔk koo-krəbəy tɨw bəñcoən srəw qaoy cruh kroəp.
10. nɨw srok-kmae kee dam chəə-plae craən yaaŋ, douc ciə daəm-douŋ, krouc, swaay, ceik ciə-daəm.
11. prəteeh-kampucciə ciə prəteeh qaekkəriəc muəy nɨw twiip-qeɨrop.
12. dəy dael kee twəə-srae-cəmkaa miən prəhael kawsəp phiəq-rɔɔy.
13. khaŋ-cəəŋ-cruŋ-khaŋ-ləc coəp nɨŋ srok-siəm.
14. nɨw rədəw-pliəŋ bəŋ tuənlee-saap miən tumhum thom ciəŋ thoəmmədaa prampɨl daaŋ.
15. khaŋ-ləc coəp nɨŋ prəteeh-wiət-naam.
16. nɨw khaŋ-tbouŋ miən pnum muəy cuə haw thaa pnum-daaŋ-rɛɛk.
17. tuənlee touc ciəŋ-kee nɨw srok-kmae kɨɨ tuənlee-meekoŋ.
18. prəciəcuən kmae sap-tŋay-nih miən prəhael prammuəy liən neəq.
19. batdəmbaaŋ kɨɨ ciə riəccəthiənii nɨy prəteeh-kampucciə.
20. nɨw riəccəthiənii miən prəciəcuən prəhael pram-saen neəq.
21. quhsaahaqkam nɨw srok-kmae craən-tae teəq-tɔɔŋ nɨŋ phallɨttəphal kaqsəkam.

401

22. phɑl-dəmnam səmkhan bəmphot nɨw srok-kmae kɨɨ səndaek.
23. kee tbaañ krənat nɨw rooŋ-kən-srəw.
24. kee dam kawsuu craən nɨw khaet-batdəmbaaŋ.
25. kee craən cap trəy-tɨk-saap nɨw moŏt səmot-siəm.
26. nɨw srok-kmae miən qəndouŋ-rae yɔɔk daek, spoŏn, miəh, haəy-nɨŋ tbouŋ-pɨc pseiŋ-pseiŋ.
27. nɨw srok-kmae kmiən phɑl knoŋ dəy sɑh.
28. srok-kmae bəñcuun masɨn pseiŋ-pseiŋ tɨw luŏq nɨw baarəteeh.
29. srəw, kawsuu, haəy-nɨŋ mrɨc kee trəw tɨñ pii baarəteeh.
30. nɨw rooŋ-dəmbaañ kee twəə krənat sout haəy-nɨŋ qəmbɑh.
31. nɨw rooŋ-qaa-chəə kee twəə kriəŋ-laan pseiŋ-pseiŋ.
32. prəteeh-qaamerɨc kɨɨ ciə preŏh-riəc-qanaacaq miən preŏh-məhaa-ksat ciə neŏq-dək-noŏm.
33. prəteeh-kampucciə baan qaekkəriəc pii prəteeh-baraŋ nɨw krɨhsaqkəraac muəy-poŏn prambuən-rɔɔy haasəp-bəy.
34. roŏtthaqthoŏmmənuñ kmae kaət laəŋ kaal preŏh-baat siihanuq nɨw saoy-riəc.
35. knoŋ samay paccobɑn, prəteeh-kampucciə kan nəyoobaay qapyiəkrət.
36. prəciəriəh bɑh cnaot crəəh-rəəh roŏt-səphiə haəy-nɨŋ kənaq-roŏt-muŏntrəy.
37. niəyuŏq-roŏt-muŏntrəy miən phiəreŏq khaaŋ kaa-twəə-cbap-tməy.
38. samaacɨk kənaq-roŏt-muŏntrəy miən ŋiə ciə roŏt-muŏntrəy niy krəsuəŋ pseiŋ-pseiŋ.
39. niəyuŏq-roŏt-muŏntrəy haəy-nɨŋ samaacɨk kənaq-roŏt-muŏntrəy trəw tətuəl kaa-yuŏl-prɔɔm haəy-nɨŋ səc-kdəy-tuk-cət pii cawwaay-khaet pseiŋ-pseiŋ.
40. baə coŏp cnaot, dəmnaaŋ-riəh tɨw twəə ciə səmaacɨk niy roŏt-səphiə nɨw pnum-pɨñ.
41. krəsuəŋ-yuttəthɔə teŏq-tɔɔŋ nɨŋ kaa-baarəteeh.
42. prəteeh-kampucciə ciə riəciəthɨppətay dael miən roŏtthaqthoŏmmənuñ.
43. knoŋ rəwiəŋ pii poŏn cnam mɔɔk haəy, prəteeh-kampucciə miən məhaa-ksattrəyaanii saoy-riəc ciə dɑraap.
44. samay funɑɑn cap taŋ-pii sattəwoŏt tii-muəy tɨw sattəwoŏt tii-prammuəy.
45. knoŋ samay cənlaa kee kɑɑ-saaŋ prasaat qəŋkɔɔ-thom haəy-nɨŋ qəŋkɔɔ-woŏt.
46. pii sattəwoŏt tii-dɑp-pram tɨw sattəwoŏt tii-dɑp-prambuən kee haw thaa samay qəŋkɔɔ.
47. knoŋ rəwiəŋ samay kəndaal, preŏh-riəc-qanaacaq kampucciə nɨw kraom qanaapyiəbaal prəteeh-baraŋ.
48. prəciəcuŏn kmae kan lətthiq krɨhsahsnaa haasəp phiəq-rɔɔy.
49. nɨw srok-kmae kənaq məhaanikaay miən look-saŋ craən ciəŋ kənaq thoŏmməyut.
50. taam lətthiq preŏh-puttəsahsnaa, yəəŋ trəw twəə-bon-daq-tiən daəmbəy nɨŋ qaoy baan phɑl-bon tɨw ciət kraoy.

D. Translation

1. Where did you go at vacation-time?
2. Where will you go at vacation-time?
3. How do both these languages differ?
4. As for dry [season] rice, they have to irrigate the rice-fields.
5. This is the reason that they call it floating rice.
6. Why do they have only the women transplant [it]?

7. Why don't they sow the rice in the rice-field in one operation?
8. They use oxen or buffalo to pull the plow to plow the field, and rake the ground to make [it] soft.
9. What (how) do they do, to convert it into husked rice?
10. Besides that, Cambodian farmers usually plant coconut trees, orange [trees], mango [trees], and banana trees, for example.
11. Today the teacher is going to give a lecture about the geography of Cambodia.
12. Cambodia has an area of 181,000 square kilometers.
13. The land which they cultivate amounts to (has) about ten percent.
14. The northern region borders on (is attached to) Laos.
15. The eastern and southeastern regions border on Vietnam.
16. In the rainy season the Tonle Sap Lake has an area (size) seven times larger than normal (larger than normal seven times).
17. The most important river in Cambodia is the Mekong River, which flows (across) from north to south.
18. If anyone doesn't understand some question, [just] ask me.
19. The central plain is surrounded by mountains, (being) the Dang Raek Mountains [in] the north and the Cardamom Mountains [in] the southwest.
20. Phnom Penh is the capital, and is the largest city in Cambodia.
21. The most important industry in Cambodia has to do with agricultural products.
22. Besides rice-mills, there are saw-mills, cigarette factories, weaving mills, and cement factories.
23. They use (take) elephants to drag the wood into the river, then float [it] by water to the saw-mills.
24. Some families take cotton fiber [and] spin [it] in order to weave [it] themselves.
25. There are two kinds of fish, (being) salt-water fish and fresh-water fish.
26. In Kampong Thom there are mines [from which they] take copper, iron, gold, and coal.
27. They export rice, rubber, corn, fish, and pepper.
28. They import automobile parts and various [kinds of] machinery.
29. The Cambodian people mostly earn a living by rice-farming and fishing.
30. They buy some silk from abroad, and some (more) from various farmers (nèəq-cəmkaa) who raise silk-worms.
31. Cambodia is an independent kingdom having a monarch as leader.
32. When did Cambodia get her independence?
33. King Norodom Sihanouk succeeded in obtaining (baan + wrested) national independence from France in A.D. 1953.
34. When did the Cambodian constitution come into existence?
35. While King Sihanouk was still reigning, he established the constitution in A.D. 1947.
36. Cambodia has two houses, (being) the National Assembly and the Council of the Kingdom.
37. The National Assembly has the responsibility for (in the matter of) making new laws and revising the constitution.
38. The king selects the prime minister as head of the government.
39. From that point on, the prime minister can choose the members of [his] cabinet.
40. Cambodia maintains the principle of democracy by electing representatives of the people.

41. Cambodia is an independent country in Southeast Asia situated between (in the intervening space [between]) Thailand and Vietnam.
42. As for [its] system of government, Cambodia is a constitutional monarchy.
43. For the past two thousand years, Cambodia has been ruled by monarchs continuously.
44. In the Funan Period, they borrowed (took) many aspects (ways) of culture from India, such as [their] system of government, religious beliefs, and literature, as examples.
45. The monuments of Angkor Wat and Angkor Thom are famous (have fame) all over (in) the world.
46. These days there are foreign tourists in great numbers (being many) [who] come to see (observe) these ancient monuments.
47. During that time (in the interval of that time), Cambodia, Laos, and Vietnam were under the protectorship of France.
48. Ninety percent of the Cambodian people believe in (hold to) Buddhism.
49. Men usually enter the monkhood [for] at least one Lenten season.
50. This is why the Cambodian people are polite and always help each other [in times of] trouble.

CAMBODIAN-ENGLISH GLOSSARY

Since all Cambodian words begin with a consonant, the words in the following Glossary are listed primarily by initial consonant in the normal alphabetical order (with the insertion of ñ and ŋ after n), and secondarily by vowel, in the following order: a, aa, ae, aə, ao, ɑ, ɑɑ, e, eə̆, ee, ei, εε, i, ii, iə, ɨ, ɨɨ, ɨə, ə, əə, əɨ, o, ŏə, oo, ou, ɔɔ, ɔə, u, uə̆, uu, uə; all words beginning with a given initial consonant are followed by all words having the same initial consonant as the first member of a cluster; e.g.: kat, kaa, kae, kaət, kao, kaŋ, kɑɑ, kee, kei, kilou, kɨt, kɨɨ, kən, kon, kŏət, koo, koun, kɔɔ, kun, kŭəŋ, kuu, kuə; kbac, kcəy, kdaw, kham, khaaŋ, khae, klaŋ, kmae, kniə, kñŏm, kpŭəh, kqɑɑq, kraw, kraom, krahɑɑm, krεε, krɨəŋ, krup, kruu, ksat, ktɨm, kwən, kyɑl.

Each entry is followed by its grammatical designation(s) in parentheses, its translation(s), and the number of the lesson in which it first occurs; if a word first occurs in a lesson section other than A (Dialogue), it is indicated by B (Grammar and Drills) or C (Comprehension). Since many Cambodian words have no single equivalent in English, all translations separated by commas are to be taken as the composite meaning of an entry; different meanings or functions of a single entry are separated by semicolons.

The following abbreviations of grammatical designations are used, both in the Cambodian-English Glossary and the English-Cambodian Glossary:

Interjection	I	Completive Verb	cV
Response Particle	R	Copulative Verb	copV
Noun	N	Verb Phrase	VPh
Noun Phrase	NPh	Adverb; Adverbial Phrase	Adv
Numeral	X	Interrogative Adverb	intAdv
Specifier	S	Adjective	A
Pronoun	Pr	Interrogative Adjective	intA
Interrogative Pronoun	intPr	Indefinite Adjective	indA
Indefinite Pronoun	indPr	Auxiliary	Aux
Demonstrative Pronoun	Dp	Preposition	Prep
Demonstrative Adjective	Da	Conjunction	Conj
Transitive Verb	tV	Copulative Particle	cP
Intransitive Verb	iV	Aspectual Particle	aP
Adjectival Verb	aV	Final Particle	fP
Modal Verb	mV	Literary	lit
Directional Verb	dV		

b

bal (N) ball 24

bal-tŏət (N) soccer 24

baŋ (tV) to hide 23-B

baq (iV) to break, be broken 22

baq cəəŋ (VPh) to have a broken leg 22

bat (tV) to disappear, to lose 21

batdɑmbaaŋ (N) Battambang 14

baytaaŋ (aV) green 11

baytaaŋ-kcəy (aV) light green 11

baa (N) bar, nightclub 18-C

baac (tV) to scatter 23-B

baan (tV) to have, to get, to obtain 2;
  (cV) to be able to 3;
  (mV) to have (done sthg.), to have had the opportunity to 5

baaraŋ (A) French 5;
  (N) France

baarəy (N) cigarette 2

baasou (N) baccalaureate degree (French bachot) 24

baasou tii-muəy (N) first baccalaureate degree 24

baasou tii-pii (N) second baccalaureate degree 24

baat (R) polite response word used by men; in isolation: yes 2

baay (N) cooked rice; food 2

baay-cɑmhoy (N) steamed rice, white rice 12

baay-liiŋ (N) fried rice 12

baay prɨk (NPh) breakfast, morning meal 10

baek (iV) to break, shatter 16

baek-caek (iV) to divide, be divided

baek-kaŋ (VPh) to have a blowout 16-C

baek kbaal (VPh) to have a fractured skull 22

baep (S) kind, variety 16

baə (Conj) if 4

baə douccnah (Adv) there, in that case 14

baə qəñcəŋ (Adv) in that case 12

baək (tV) to open 3; to drive 8; to cash (a check, etc.) 23

baoh (tV) to sweep 20

baoh-samqaat (tV) to clean 20

baok (tV) to beat; to wash by beating 11

baok-qut (tV) to launder 11

baoy (N) boy, waiter 10

babaɑ (N) soup, porridge 20

bɑh (tV) to throw; drive (a nail), stamp, print 23

bɑh-baok (tV) to throw about, handle roughly 23

bɑh cnaot (VPh) to cast one's ballot, to vote 29

bɑh cnaot crəəh-rəəh (VPh) to elect 29

bɑh traa (VPh) to stamp with a seal 23

bambaek (tV) to break, cause to break 23-B

bamnaaŋ (N) hope, aim, intention 23-B

bampeəq (N) clothing worn above the waist or on the feet 18

bamphot (Adv) most, last, most of all 17

ban (iV, mV) to hope, to pray (that) 24-C

bandaal (tV) to cause, lead to 22

bandaet (tV) to float 28

bandaə (tV) to walk (a dog, etc.); (Adv) simultaneously 23-B

bandoh (tV) to grow, cause to grow, sprout

banlae (N) vegetable 20

bantaɑ (tV) to continue, extend 24

bantəc (Adv) some, a little 5

bantəc-bantuəc (Adv) a little bit, somewhat 5

bantəc-tiət (Adv) soon, in a little while 9

bantoʾəp (Adv) next, following in succession 3

bantoʾəp pii nuh (Adv) after that 17

bantuk (N) cargo, load 23-B

bantup (N) room 10

bantup-keeŋ (N) bedroom 10-C

bantup-ñam-baay (N) dining room 10

bantup-tɨk (N) bathroom 10

bantup-tɔtuəl-pñiəw (N) receiving room, parlor 10-C

bañcap (tV) to finish, complete 24

bañcəñ (tV) to expel, send out 23-B

bañcoʾən (tV) to trample, stomp 26

bañcuun (tV) to send out, send away 22

bañcuun tɨw luʾəq nɨw baarəteeh (VPh) to export 28

baŋ ~ baŋ (N) bank 23

baŋhou (tV) to cause to flow, direct the flow of 26

baŋhou tɨk coul srae (VPh) to irrigate the rice-field 26

baŋkat (tV) to light, ignite 20

baŋkaa (tV) to prevent 24

baŋkaət (tV) to create, give birth to 6

baŋkaaŋ (N) prawn, river lobster 12

baŋkum (tV) to greet with palms joined 17

baŋkuʾən (N) toilet 2

baŋqaem (N) sweets, dessert 12

baŋqah (Adv) most, most of all 17

baŋquəc (N) window 10

baŋriən (tV) to teach, cause to learn 6

baq (tV) to blow 9

bat (N) set, composition, verse, song 18

bat (tV) to turn, to fold 23-B

bat qaŋkɔɔ-riəc (NPh) royal anthem 18

baaŋ (N) older sibling 6; husband; (Pr) you (wife to husband); I (husband to wife) 20

baaŋ-pqoun (N) brothers and sisters (older and younger siblings) 6

baaŋ-pqoun-baŋkaət (N) full siblings 6

baaŋ-proh (N) older brother 6

baaŋ-srəy (N) older sister 6

baaŋ-tlay (N) older sibling-in-law 21

baaŋ-tlay-srəy (N) older sister-in-law 21

baariphook (tV) to eat (elegant, lit) 21-B

baarəteeh (N) abroad, foreign countries 18

beh (tV) to pick, gather 20

biə (N) playing cards 14

biəm (tV) to hold in the mouth 22

biət-biən (tV) to oppress 23-B

bəŋ (N) lake, pond 26

bəŋ-prɛɛk-stɨŋ-tuʾənlee (N) lakes, rivers, and streams 30

bət (tV) to close 3; to attach, affix 23

bəy (X) three 2

bəy-buən (X-X) three or four 20

bok (tV) to pound, to mill 26

bokkoo (N) Bokor (a mountain resort in Kampot Province) 17-C

bopphaa (N) Boppha (common name for girls; literally: flower) 20

bok (tV) to collide with, run into 22

bon (N) merit, good deeds 30

boum (tV) to pump 16

bouraan (A) ancient, former 17

bout (tV) to pull off 23-B

but (N) Bouth (personal name); son (elegant) 20

buəh (iV) to enter the monkhood 30

buəh ciə look-saŋ (VPh) to become a monk 30

buən (X) four 2

byeə (N) beer 12

c̲

cam (tV) to wait (for) 11; to remember
    11
cañ (tV) to lose (to), be defeated (by)
    24-C
cah (aV) old, worn, used 11;
    (aV) deep in color, strong, concen-
    trated 11
cap (tV) to catch 20;
    (mV) to begin (to) 2
cap cət (tV) interested (in), attracted
    (by) 30-C
cap-pdaəm (tV, mV) to begin (to) 26
caq (tV) to insert, inject 16
caq preiŋ boum klañ (VPh) to lubricate
    16
caw (N) grandchild 21
caw-liə (N) gt-gt-gt-grandchild 21-B
caw-luət (N) great-great-grandchild
    21-B
caw-proh (N) grandson 21
caw-tuət (N) great-grandchild 21-B
cawwaay (N) boss, supervisor 11
cawwaay-khaet (N) provincial governor
    29-C
cawwaay-srok (N) district chief 29-C
caah (R) polite response word used by
    women; in isolation: yes 2
caan (N, S) plate, dish 12
caaŋ-waaŋ (N) director, manager 8
caap (N) sparrow, ricebird 20
caay (tV) to pay out, spend 23
caek (tV) to divide 24
caetdəy (N) stupa, chedi, tapering monu-
    ment 17
cao (N) thief 18
caol (tV) to leave, abandon, throw away
    16
cambaŋ (N) battle, war 18
camhoy (tV) to steam 12
camkaa (N) garden, plantation (other than
    wet rice) 20
camkaa-kawsuu (N) rubber plantation 28
camkaa-mɔɔn (N) Chamcar Mon (a
    district in Phnom Penh) 17
camlaq (N) carving, sculpture 17
camlaek (aV) strange, different 21
camlaəy (N) answer 23-B
camlaaŋ (tV) to copy 24-B;
    (N) a copy
camnaek (N) part, share;
    (Prep) as for, on the part of 6
camnuən (N) number, total, quantity 8
camŋaay (N) distance 16
camraən (N) success, increase;
    (tV) to increase, prosper 23-B
canlah (N) intervening space;
    (Prep) between 30

caŋ (mV) to want to 2
caŋhan (N) priest's food 23-B
caŋkraan (N) stove 20
caŋqol (tV) to point out, indicate 27-C
caŋqol-prap (tV) indicate, tell, show
    27-C
cap (cV) to complete, get to the end
    14-B;
    (iV) to finish, come to a close 18
caaŋ (tV) to tie, to wear (a tie) 11
caaŋ-day (tV) to make a presentation to
    newly-weds (literally: to tie the
    hands) 21-C
caat (tV) to park, to moor 15
ceh (tV) to know, be educated;
    (mV) to know how to 5
ceh qat-thüən (VPh) to be persistent,
    patient 26
ceh-tae (Aux) always, typically, persist
    in 20
ceik (N) banana 4
cih (tV) to mount, to ride 8
cii (N) fertilizer 28
cii-doun-muəy (N) first cousin 6
cii-luət-muəy (N) third cousin 21-B
cii-tuət-muəy (N) second cousin 21-B
ciik (tV) to dig 26-C
ciiwɨt (N) life 8
ciə (aV) to be well 2;
    (copV) to be 3;
    (Conj) relative conjunction: that 16
ciə craən (Adv) in abundance 30
ciə-daəm (Adv) as examples, and so forth,
    et cetera 17
ciə-dɑraap (Adv) always, continuously 30
ciə-muəy (Prep) with, along with 4
ciə-muəy kniə (Adv) together 4
ciə-nɨc (Adv) always, continually 16
ciə praakɑt (Adv) for sure, surely 8
ciə srɑlah (aV) completely well 22
ciə yuu nah mɔɔk haəy (Adv) for a long
    time now 5
ciəh (tV) to avoid 14-B
ciəŋ (Prep) more - than 6;
    (Adv) more; -er 8
ciəŋ (N) skilled laborer, artisan 8
ciəŋ-chəə (N) carpenter 8
ciəŋ-kee (Adv) most, most of all 9
ciət (N) nation; national 23
ciət (N) taste, flavor 12
ciət (N) life, existence, reincarnation 30
cɨt (aV) near 8;
    (mV) nearly, almost 9
cɨyyeəqwɑɑrəman (N) Jayavarman 24-C
cən (A) Chinese;
    (N) China 5
cənlaa (N) Chenla 30
cəñ (iV) to exit, leave 2
cəñcəm (tV) to support, maintain, raise 8

cəñcəm ciiwɨt (VPh) to support oneself,
   to make a living 8
cəñcəm sat (VPh) to raise animals,
   keep pets 20-C
cət (N) heart, mind, disposition 20
cətsəp (X) seventy 2
cəəŋ (N) foot, leg 11
cəəŋ (N) north 9
coc (tV) to punch, depress 16
coh (I) and what about . . . ?, and how
   about . . . ? 2
coh (tV) to lower; go down, descend 10
cok (tV) to stopper, plug;
   (aV) to have a pain 22
cok puəh (VPh) to have stomach pains,
   cramps 22
coŋ (N) end, point 24
coən (N, S) floor, level, stage, deck 14
coəp (iV) to stick, be attached;
   (cV) to pass (an examination) 24
coəp cnaot (VPh) to win an election 29-C
cou (Aux) let's; go ahead and, please 3
coul (tV) to enter 16
coul-cət (tV, mV) to like (to) 4
coul riən (VPh) to begin studying, to
   start to school 24
cɔɔŋ (N) Chong (a hill tribe) 27
cɔə-lup (N) eraser 3
cumniə (N) belief 23-B
cumnuən (N) flood 26
cummuəñ (N) commerce 5
cumŋɨɨ (N) illness, disease 22
cumŋɨɨ-muəl (N) dysentery 22
cumŋɨɨ-krun-cañ (N) malaria 22
cumriəp (tV) to inform 2
cumriəp-suə (tV) to greet; in isolation:
   Greetings! 2
cumrɨw (N) depth 23-B
cuəndaə (N) stairs 23-B
cuəñcuun (tV) to carry, move 20
cuəŋkuəŋ (N) knee 22
cuəq (tV) to inhale, suck, smoke 21
cuun (tV) to accompany 6-C;
   (dV) for, on behalf of (formal) 10
cuut (tV) to rub, wipe 11
cuə (N) row, range, chain 27
cuəh-cul (tV) to repair 16
cuəl (tV) to rent, to hire 14
cuən-kaal (Adv) sometimes 9
cuəp-cum (tV) to meet together, convene
   21-C
cuəp-prəteəh (tV) to happen to meet 14
cuəy (tV, mV) to help (to) 6;
   (Aux) Help by . . . , Please . . . 11
cuəy thureəq (Idiomatic VPh) to help out
   in time of trouble 30
cbah (aV) to be clear 3
cbap (N) single issue; permission;
   custom; law 17
cbap-qaqmuññaat (N) a permit 17

chan (tV) to eat (of clergy) 23-B
chap (aV) fast, quick 11;
   (mV) to be quick to, prone to 16
chap-chap (aV, Adv) quickly, hurriedly
   14
chat (N) umbrella 9
chaa (tV) to fry, to braise;
   (N) a fried meat and vegetable mixture
   12
chaaq (N) scene, set 18
cheh (iV) to burn, be on fire 20
chiəm (N) blood 11
chiəm-cruuk (N) pig's blood;
   (aV) maroon 11
chɨɨ (aV) to be ill, to hurt 22
chɨɨ kbaal (VPh) to have a headache 22
chəə (N) wood 8
chəə-kuh (N) match 2
chəə-plae (N) fruit tree 26-C
chɔɔ (iV) to stand 16
chup (tV, mV) to stop, cease 8
chup riən (VPh) to stop studying, finish
   school, have a vacation from school 8
chuuŋ (N) bay, gulf 27
chuuŋ-səmot-siəm (N) Gulf of Thailand
   27
ckae (N) dog 20
claq (tV) to carve 23-B
claəy (tV) to answer 3
claɑŋ (tV) to cross 10;
   (dV) across
cluəh (iV) to argue 23-B
cmaa (N) cat 20
cmoul (tV) to make into a ball 23-B
cmuəh (N) name; to be named . . . 5
cnam (N, S) year 5
cnaŋ (N, S) pot, kettle 15
cnaot (N) ticket, vote 29
cneəh (tV) to win, to defeat 24-C
cnuəl (N) rent, hire 16
cnañ (aV) tasty, delicious 12
cnaay (aV) far, distant 15
cqaet (aV) full, satisfied 12
cqaə (aV) smoked, roasted 15
craah (N) brush 11
craah-doh-tmɨñ (N) toothbrush 11
craən (aV) to be much, many 2
craən(-tae) (Aux) usually, mostly 18
craluəh (iV) to slip, do by accident 22
cramoh (N) nose 23-B
cramuc (tV) to put under, submerge 23-B
criəŋ (tV) to sing 18-C
criəp (iV) to learn, discover 23-B
crɨw (aV) deep 15
crəəh (tV) to choose 29
crəəh-rəəh (tV) to choose, select, appoint
   29
crout (tV) to reap, harvest 26
crɔɔk (iV) to take shelter 9
cruh (iV) to shed, drip off, loosen 26

cruŋ (N) corner 10
cruuk (N) pig 11
cweiŋ (aV) left (side) 2
cweiŋ-day (aV) on the left 2

d̲

dac (iV) to tear, burst, break; be torn, burst, broken 21
dac pu̇əh slap (VPh) to die of a torn stomach 21
dah (tV) to awaken 10
dam (tV) to plant 15
dam (tV) to cook, boil 20
daq (tV) to put, place, deposit 10
daq-tiən (iV) to give alms 30
daqtilou (N) typewriter 23-C
day (N) hand 2
dae (Adv) also, as well; nevertheless 4
daek (N) iron, steel 14
dael (mV) to have ever 5
dael (Pr) relative pronoun: that, which, who 6
daə (iV) to walk 4
daə-leeŋ (iV) to stroll, amuse oneself, go around for fun 4
daəm (S) specifier for long slender objects, such as trees, pencils, cigarettes 4
daəm-chəə (N) tree 9
daəm-douŋ (N) coconut palm tree 26
daəm-kawsuu (N) rubber tree 28
daəm-pkaa (N) flower plant, shrub 15
daəm-pkaa-kolaap (N) rose-bush 20
daəmbəy(-nɨŋ) (Conj) in order to 18
daoy (Conj) with the fact that, because, since 20;
  (Prep) with, by 30-C
daoy meetrəy-phiəp (Adv) with affection, affectionately 30-C
dadael (A) the same 3
dah (tV) take off, loose 23-B
dal (tV) to reach, arrive at 2;
  (Conj) when (in the future) 8;
  (Prep) to, until, reaching to 9
dambaañ (N) weaving; woven 8
damban (N) area, region, sector, zone 27-C
damboun-miən (N) deportment, good manners 24
dambouŋ (A) first, original; in the beginning 22
damlay (N) value 23-B
damlaəŋ (tV) to set up, assemble 28
damləŋ (S) an ounce 23-B
damlouŋ (N) potato 23-B
damnam (N) plant, crop 26
damnaq (N) royal residence 17
damnaaŋ-riəh (N) representative of the people, assembly man 29-C

damnaə (N) trip, process 14
damnaa (N) extension 23-B
damnəŋ (N) information 23-B
damrəy (N) elephant 28
dandəŋ (tV) to ask in marriage 23-B
daŋkap (N) pliers, pincers 16
dap (X) ten 2
dap-muəy (X) eleven 2
dap-pii (X) twelve 2
dap-prammuəy (X) sixteen 2
daaŋ (S) time, occasion, occurrence 5
daaŋ (tV) to dip up, draw up 26
daaŋ (N) handle 27
daaŋ-rɛɛk (N) a carrying-pole 27
daap (N, S) bottle 12
daaq (tV) to pull up, extract 20
daaraap (Adv) always, since 30
dei (tV) to sew 22
deik (iV) to sleep 20
deik pɛɛt (VPh) to stay in the hospital, be hospitalized 22
diiploum (N) secondary diploma (French diplôme) 24
dək (tV) to carry 14
dək-nȯəm (tV) to carry, haul, transport 14
dəŋ (tV) to know, know about, be informed 8
dəŋ-kun (aV) grateful 26-B
dəy (N) ground, earth 15-C
dəy-kpu̇əh (N) plateau 27
dəy-saa (N) chalk 3
doh (tV) to brush 11
doh (iV) to come up, grow 20
dom (S) specifier for pieces, lumps, nuggets 11-C
dou (tV) to trade, exchange 8
douc (aV) similar to, like; as 5
douc-ciə (Prep) such as 17
douc-ciə (VPh) seems to be, appears to be 15
douccneh (Adv) thus, therefore 10
douŋ (N) coconut 26

f̲

faaməsii (N) pharmacy 22-C
fosfat (N) phosphate 28
fuunaan (N) Funan 30

h̲

hat (mV) to practice, drill 24
hat (S) cubit 26
hat-qaan (VPh) to practice reading;
  (N) reading practice, pronunciation 24
haw (tV) to call 3
haa (tV) to open (the mouth) 22-C
haal (tV) to spread out, expose to 20

haaŋ (N) shop, store 4
haaŋ-baok-qut (N) laundry 11
haaŋ-kat-saq (N) barbershop 8
haasəp (X) fifty 2
haasəp phiəq-rɔɔy (X-S) fifty percent 27
hael (iV) to swim 15
hael-tɨk (iV) to swim 15
haet (N) reason, cause 12
haet nih haəy baan ciə (NPh-VPh) this is
    the reason that, this is why 26
haet qwəy baan ciə (NPh-VPh) why?, why
    is it that . . . ? 12
haəy (Adv) already; indeed 2;
    (Conj) then, and then 4;
    (cV) to be ready, finished 21
haəy-nɨŋ (Conj) and 4
haəy-rɨɨ-nɨw? (Adv) yet? (already or not
    yet?) 4
hiən (aV) to be brave;
    (mV) to dare to 14-C
həl (aV) hot, spicy, pungent 12
həp (N) box, trunk, suitcase 14
həp-qəywan (N) things, luggage 14
hoc (tV) to hand 11
hoksəp (X) sixty 2
hotael (N) hotel 28
hou (iV) to flow 15
houp (tV) to eat (rural) 21-B

k

kambət (N) knife 12
kamməkaa (N) workers, laborers 8
kampucciə (N) Cambodia 27
kan (tV) to hold, believe, maintain 29
kan-tae (Aux) increasingly, persistently
    18-B
kaññaa (N) September 9
kap (tV) to cut, hack, chop 22
kapbaah ~ krabaah (N) cotton 26
kaqkədaa (N) July 9
kaqseqkam (N) agriculture 27-C
kareim (N) ice-cream 12
kawqəy (N) chair 3
kat (tV) to cut, snip 8
kawsəp (X) ninety 2
kawsuu (N) rubber 28
kaa (N) work, affairs 4
kaa (tV) to get married 6
kaa-baarəteeh (N) foreign affairs 26-B
kaa-neesaat-trəy (N) fishing, the fishing
    industry 28
kaa-niyiəy (N) speaking 26-B
kaa-piə (tV) to protect, defend 29
kaa-piə-prateeh (N) national defense 29
kaa-riəcckaa (N) government service,
    administration (as a profession) 8
kaa-rɔɔk-sii (N) earning a living 26
kaa-ruəh-nɨw (N) life, living, existence 30-C

kaa-slap (N) dying 26-B
kaa-tɔtuəl-pñiəw (N) receiving guests
    26-B
kaa-twəə-cbap-tməy (N) making new laws,
    legislation 27
kaa-twəə-srae (N) farming 26-B
kaa-yuəl-prɔɔm (N) approval, consent 29
kaafei (N) coffee 2
kaal (N) time, occasion 8
    (Conj) when (in the past) 26
kaal-mun (Adv) before, at first, in former
    times 8
kaal-naa (intAdv) when? 14;
    (Conj) when, whenever 15
kaal nɨw pii touc (Clause) when still young,
    when I was a kid 15
kaal pii daəm (Adv) originally, formerly
    24
kaasaet (N) newspaper 14
kaay (tV) to dig 23-B
kae (tV) to change, correct, revise, repair
    29
kaep (N) Kêp (a seaside resort in Kampot
    province) 17-C
kaew (N, S) glass; a glass (of) 2
kaət (cV) to be able 14-B;
    (tV) to give birth to, be born; to happen,
    arise, develop, catch (a disease, etc.)
    22
kaət (N) east 27
kao (tV) to shave 11
kaot (X) ten-million 27-B
kɑh (N) island 27-C
kɑh-koŋ (N) Koh Kong (Island, Province)
    14
kɑkaay (tV) to dig, scratch about 20
kɑmdaw (N) heat, temperature 22
kɑmdaa (tV) to accompany, attend 21-C
kɑmhəŋ (N) anger 23-B
kɑmlɑh (N) a bachelor;
    (aV) to be single (of a man) 6
kɑmlaŋ (N) strength, power 15
kɑmnat (N) cut piece, slice 23-B
kɑmnaət (N) birth 23-B
kɑmnat (N) agreement, fixed period,
    duration
kɑmpɔɔt (N) Kampot (Town, Province) 14
kɑmpuŋ(-tae) (Aux) in the process of 6
kɑmpuəŋ (N) port, riverine town 14
kɑmpuəŋ-caam (N) Kampong Cham (Town,
    Province) 14
kɑmpuəŋ-cnaŋ (N) Kampong Chhnang
    (Town, Province) 14
kɑmpuəŋ-spɨɨ (N) Kampong Speu (Town,
    Province) 14
kɑmpuəŋ-thom (N) Kampong Thom (Town,
    Province) 14
kɑmplaeŋ (aV) funny, humorous 18
kɑmraa (mV) to be poor at 23-B

kamrət (N) a decree;
  (tV) to decree 23-B

kamsat (aV) sad, miserable, destitute;
  (N) beggar, destitute person 18

kamsiəw (N) tea-kettle 20

kandap (N, S) grasp, handful, sheaf,
  bundle 26

kandaal (N) middle, center; central 12-C

kandaal (N) Kandal (Province) 14

kandiəw (N) sickle, scythe 26

kanlah (N, X) half 4

kanlaeŋ (N) place 4

kansaeŋ (N) handkerchief, cloth 11

kansaeŋ-cuut-kluən (N) towel 11

kanteel (N) a woven mat 14

kantraaŋ (N) strainer, filter 23-B

kañcap (N, S) small package 4

kaŋ (N) wheel 16; bicycle 21

kaŋ səkuə (NPh) spare wheel 16

kapal ~ kopal (N) ship, steamer 14

kapal-hah (N) airplane 14-C

kaq (tV) to wash (the hair) to shampoo
  11

kaa (Aux) so, then, accordingly 4

kaa (N) neck, throat 22-B

kaa-baan (cV) to be a possibility 8

kaa-baan . . . kaa-baan (cV . . . cV)
  either . . . or . . . is a possibility
  14

kaa-cəəŋ (N) ankle 22-B

kaa-day (N) wrist 22-B

kaa-miən (cV) does happen, is possible
  22

kaa-saaŋ (tV) to build, construct 24-C

kaaŋ (N) term, cycle, year 24-C

kaaq (aV) frozen, congealed 9

kee (Pr) 3rd person: he, she, they,
  one 3

keeŋ (iV) to recline, to sleep 9

keeŋ luəq (VPh) to get to sleep 9

keeŋ mɨn luəq (VPh) to be unable to
  sleep 9

keeŋ pɛɛt (VPh) to sleep in the hospital,
  be hospitalized 22

kei (N) heritage

kilou (S) kilogram 4

kiloumaet (S) kilometer 16

kiimii (N) chemistry 24-C

kɨñ (N) police 18

kɨt (tV) to think;
  (mV) to plan, intend to 8

kɨɨ (cP) is, being, equals, as follows 3

kən (tV) to thresh, to mill 16

kənaq (!) party, group 29

kənaq-rŏət-muĕntrəy (N) cabinet, group
  of ministers 29

kəylaa (N) sports, games 24

kohaq ~ krahaq (iV) to lie, prevaricate
  30

kolaap (N) rose 20

kom (Aux) negative imperative: don't 12

kom qaoy (Aux-mV) don't allow, not to
  23

kom-qaoy-tae (Conj) so long as not,
  provided one doesn't 24

kon (N) film, movie 2

koŋ (N) account 23

kot (N) monastery, monk's quarters 17

kŏət (Pr) respectful 3rd person pronoun:
  he, she, they 6

koo (N) cow, ox 12

koorup (tV) to honor, pay respect to 18

koun (N) offspring, child(ren) 6;
  (Pr) you (parent to child): I (child to
  parent) 20

koun-kmeiŋ (N) child (new) 24

koun-niən (N) silkworm 28

koun-prasaa (N) son- or daughter-in-law
  21-B

koun-proh (N) son 6

koun-qaeŋ (Pr) you yourself (parent to
  child) 20

koun-səh (N) student 6

koun-srəy (N) daughter 6

kɔɔ (tV) to pile up 26

kɔɔ (N) kapok 28

kumnɨt (N) thought 23-B

kumnɔɔ (N) pile, stack 26

kumpheəq (N) February 9

kun (N) quality, merit 30-C

kuruq-wɨcciə (N) pedagogy 24

kuy-tiəw (N) chinese noodles 12-C

kuĕŋ (iV) sit, stay, reside (of royalty or
  clergy) 17

kuu (S) pair 11

kuulii (N) coolie, porter 14

kuə (aV) suitable, appropriate 17

kuə qaoy (aV-mV) worthy of, conducive
  to 17

kuə qaoy caŋ məəl (VPh) worth seeing,
  interesting 17

kuə qaoy qaanət (VPh) pitiable, deserving
  of sympathy 18

kuə-sam (aV) reasonable, moderate;
  slang; not bad 30-C

kuəy (N) Kuy, Kuoy (a hill tribe) 27

kbac (N) design 17

kbac-camlaq (N) sculpture, frieze 17

kbaal (N) head 22

kbaal (S) specifier for books, volumes,
  tablets, and certain animals 23

kbat (tV) to deceive, betray 23-B

kcap (tV) to wrap 23-B

kcɨl (aV) to be lazy 20;
  (mV) to be too lazy to, disinclined to,
  not feel like 11

kcəy (tV) to borrow; to lend 11

kcəy (aV) light (in color), young, tender,
   inexperienced 11

kdaw (aV) hot 2

kdaw kluən (VPh) to feel hot 22

kdaw-rəɲiə (aV) intermittently hot and
   cold, to have chills 22

kdaa (N) board, plank, flat surface 21

kdaa-khiən (N) blackboard 3

kdaa-ɲiə (N) a low platform or table
   used for sitting, sleeping, and
   eating 21

kham (tV) to bite 23-B

khaan (mV) to fail to, miss, lack 6;
   (cV) (not) fail, miss 14-B

khaaŋ (N) side, direction 2;
   (Prep) in the area of, in the matter
   of 16

khaaŋ-cəəŋ (N) the north 9

khaaŋ-cəəŋ-cruŋ-khaaŋ-kaət (N)
   northeast 27-B

khaaŋ-cəəŋ-cruŋ-khaaŋ-ləc (N)
   the northwest 27

khaaŋ-cweiŋ-day (N) the left-hand side 2

khaaŋ-kaət (N) the east 27

khaaŋ-kraom (N) below, downstairs 10

khaaŋ-kraoy (N) the back, in back 2

khaaŋ-ləc (N) the west 27

khaaŋ-ləə (N) above, upper (part) 14

khaaŋ-muk (N) the front; in front 2

khaaŋ-nih (Adv) this way 10

khaaŋ-sdam-day (N) the right-hand side
   2

khaaŋ-tbouŋ (N) the south 27

khaaŋ-tbouŋ-cruŋ-khaaŋ-kaət (N)
   southeast 27-B

khaaŋ-tbouŋ-cruŋ-khaaŋ-ləc (N) the
   southwest 27

khae (N, S) month; moon 5

khae-kumpheəq (N) the month of
   February 9

khae-minaa (N) the month of March 9

khae-mithonaa (N) the month of June 9

khae-quhsəphiə (N) the month of May 9

khae-tolaa (N) the month of October 9

khae-wiccəkaa (N) the month of
   November 9

khaet (N) province 14

khao (N) trousers, pants 11

khao-qaaw (N) suit; clothing 11

khiəw (aV) blue to green 11

khiəw-cah (aV) dark blue to green 11

khəŋ (aV) angry 20-C

khəəñ (tV) to see, to perceive 5

khoh (aV) wrong, different 23-C

khoh kniə (VPh) different from each
   other 26

khoosnaakaa (N) information, publicity
   29

khouc (aV) broken, damaged, spoiled 16

khum (N) commerce, administrative
   division of a srok 29-C

klah (Adv) some 3

klañ (N) grease 16

klaŋ (aV) strong, hard, extreme 9

klaŋ laəŋ (VPh) increasingly strong, worse
   22

klaac (tV) to fear, be afraid (of) 14-C

klei (N) wrench 16

kliə (N) sentence, phrase; space 3

kliən (tV) to be hungry (for) 4

klən (N) odor, smell 20

kləŋ (N, A) Indian 18

kluən (N, Pr) body; self, oneself 11

kmaw-day (N) pencil 3

kmae (aV) Cambodian;
   (N) Cambodian 5

kmae-ləə (N) Upper Khmer, hill tribes
   27

kmeiŋ (aV) to be young;
   (N) child(ren) 24

kmeiŋ-proh-proh (N) boys 24

kmeiŋ-proh-srəy (N) boys and girls 24

kmiən (tV) not have, not exist 4

kmuəy (N) niece or nephew 21

kniə (Adv) together 3

knoŋ (Prep) in, inside 10

knoŋ rəwiəŋ pii-pɔən cnam mɔɔk haəy (Adv)
   for the past two thousand years 30

kñom (Pr) I, me, my 2

kñom-preəh-baat (Pr) I (inferior to superior)
   27-B

kñom-preəh-kaqrunaa (Pr) I (layman to
   priest; inferior to superior) 27-B

kpuəh (aV) high 17

kqaaq (iV) to cough, to have a cough 22

krah-sət-saq (N) comb 11-C

kraw (Prep) outside (of) 5

kraw pii (Prep) outside of, besides 5

kraam (S) gram 23

kraawat (N) necktie 11

kraeŋ (tV, mV) to fear, be afraid (that) 14

kraok (iV) to rise, get up 11

kraom (Prep) under, below 9

kraoy (Prep) after, behind 2

krabaah ~ kapbaah (N) cotton 26

kraceh (N) Kratie (Town, Province) 14

kradaah (N) paper 23

kradaah-sasei-sambot (N) letter-paper,
   stationery 23

krahaq ~ kohaq (iV) to lie, prevaricate
   30

krahaam (aV) red to orange 11

krakwaq (aV) dirty 11

kralaa (aV) square 27

kranat (N) cloth 28

kraŋeik-kraŋaq (aV) crooked, zig-zagging
   16

kraqoup (aV) sweet-smelling, fragrant 20

krɑsuəŋ (N) department; function, duty 17

krɑsuəŋ-mɔhaa-ptɨy (N) Department of Interior 29

krɑsuəŋ-teehsəcɑɑ (N) Department of Tourism 17

krɑsuəŋ-yuttəthɔə (N) Department of Justice 29

krɑwaañ (N) cardamom 27

krɑweem-krɑwaam (aV) marked up, disfigured 22-B

krɑwiəc (aV) twisted 23-B

krɑɑ (aV) to be poor 23-B

krɛɛ (N) bed 10

kriip ~ krɨp (N) jack, lift 6

krət (N) law, regulation 23-B

krɨhsahsnaa (N) Christianity 30

krɨhsaqkəraac (N) Christian Era, A.D. 29

krɨsaqkəraac muəy-poə̆n prambuən-rɔɔy haasəp-bəy (N-X) A.D. 1953 29

krɨəŋ (N) thing, accessory, instrument 8; ingredients, spices 12

krɨəŋ laan (N) automobile parts 28

krɨəŋ-preə̆h-riəccətroə̆p (N) royal treasures 17

krɨəŋ-tok-tuu (N) furniture 8

krom (N) group, council 29

krom-hun (N) business, commercial firm 21

krom-prɨksaa-preə̆h-riəc-qanaacaq (N) Council of the Kingdom 29

kroŋ (N) city 5

kroə̆n-baə (aV) better, improved 22

kroə̆n-tae (Aux) only, just 4

kroə̆p (S) specifier for grams, pills 22

krouc (N) orange, citrus fruit 4

krɔɔŋ (tV) to regulate, govern 29

krun (aV) to have a fever 22

krun-cañ (N, aV) malaria; to have malaria 22

krup (Prep) every, every last one of 16

krup-kroə̆n (aV) adequate, complete, full 8

krup-krɔɔŋ (tV) to oversee, administer, govern 29

krup-sɑp (A) every, all, complete 22

kruə̆h-tnaq (N) accident; danger 22

kruə̆h-tnaq bok laan (NPh) automobile accident 22

kruu (N) teacher, master 6

kruu-bɑŋriən (N) teacher 6

kruu-pɛɛt (N) doctor 8

kruəsaa (N) family 6

ksat (N) ruler, monarch 29

ksattrəyaanii (N) queen 29-C

ktɨm (N) onion, garlic 12

kwən cəəŋ (VPh) to have a paralyzed foot or leg 22-B

kwən day (VPh) to have a paralyzed hand 22-B

kyɑl (N) wind 9

kyuuŋ ~ tyuuŋ (N) coal, charcoal 20

l

latthiq (N) concept, faith, principle 29

latthiq sahsnaa (N) religious belief 30

laan (N) car, automobile 8

laan-cnuəl (N) hired car, bus 16

laan-dək-tumnɨn (N) truck, van 16-C

laəŋ (dV) upward, up 11; (tV) to climb, ascend 15; (aP) increasingly, more 22

laəŋ tnaq (VPh) to advance in rank, be promoted 24

leep (tV) to swallow 22

leik (N) number, figure 10

lihsei dekaat (N) Lycée Descartes 24-C

liiŋ (tV) to fry, to braise 12

liit (S) liter 16-C

liə (tV) to take leave, to say good-by 2

liən (X) million 27

liəŋ (tV) to wash (the surface of) 20

liəp (tV) to spread on, to paint 11

liəw (A) Lao 27; (N) Laos

lɨc (iV) to sink, be submerged 27

lɨc tɨk (VPh) sink in the water, under water 27

lɨɨ (tV) to hear, to sound 15

lɨən (aV) fast 12-C

ləc (N) west 27

ləə (Prep) on, above 3

ləə-kok-dɔə (N) Le Coq d'Or (name of a restaurant in Phnom Penh) 12

ləək (tV) to raise, lift up 21

ləək day twaay preə̆h (tV-N-dV-N) a greeting used by some older people (literally: lift your hands to God) 21

ləək-lɛɛŋ-tae (Prep) except, except for 17

look (N) Mr., Sir; (Pr) you (masc.) 2

look-puu (N) younger uncle (polite) 21

look-qom (N) older uncle or aunt (polite) 21

look-sɑŋ (N) monk, priest 17

look-smɨt (N) Mr. Smith 21

look-srəy (N) Mrs., Madam; (Pr) you (fem.) 2

look-taa (N) Grandfather (polite) 6

look-yiəy (N) Grandmother (polite) 6

lou (S) specifier for dozen 4

lɔɔ-məəl (Adv) tentatively, as an experiment 12

lumnɨw (N) address, residence 23-B

lumqɑɑ (N) beauty, embellishment 23-B

lup (tV) to rub, erase, wash (the face) 11

luy (N) money 8

luəŋ-tɨk (cV) to sink; to drown 15

luəq (tV) to sell 4

luəq (cV) to fall asleep 9

luəq-dou (tV) to do trade, carry on commerce 8

luət (tV) to extinguish 23-B

luəc (tV) to steal 30

luəc prɑpuən kee (VPh) to steal another's wife, to commit adultry 30

luəŋ (N) king (informal) 17

lbaeŋ (N) game 14

lbiən (N) speed 23-B

lbəy-cmuəh (N) fame, renown, reputation 30

lhaəy (aV) cool, refreshing 14

lhoŋ (N) papaya 12

lkhaon (N) drama, play 18

lmɔɔm (mV) enough (to), adequate (to) 8; (aV) enough, reasonable, rather

lmut (N) sapodilla (a sweet, brown-skinned fruit with the texture of a ripe pear) 12-C

lŋiəc (N) late afternoon; evening 12

lŋɔɔ (N) sesame 28

lqɑɑ (aV) good, pretty 4

lqɑɑ-məəl (aV) interesting (to see or watch) 18

lqət (aV) fine, powdered 26

m

maq (N) mother; (Pr) you (child to mother), I (mother to child) 20

mat (N) math 24

mattyum (A) middle, medium, average 24

mattyum-səksaa (N) secondary education 24

mattyum-səksaa tii-muəy (NPh) 1st cycle of secondary school 24

mattyum-səksaa tii-pii (NPh) 2nd cycle of secondary school 24

maasiin ∼ masɨn (N) motor, machine 16

maasɨn-thɑɑt-ruup (N) camera 21-C

maatɨt (< muəy qaatɨt) (Adv) in a week, per week 20

mae (N) Mother (respectful) 21

maoŋ (N, S) hour, time 2

meəqkəraa (N) January 9

mee-khum (N) commune chief 29-C

mee-riən (N) lesson 24-C

meesaa (N) April 9

meethiəwii (N) lawyer 8

meetrəy-phiəp (N) friendship, affection 30-C

meiŋ (N) Meng (a personal name) 4

meiŋ (N) Meng (a personal name) 4

mɛɛn (aV) to be right, true 2

mɛɛn-tɛɛn (Adv) really, truly, extremely 16

minaa (N) March 9

miqthonaa (N) June 9

miiŋ (N) younger sister of either parent 6

miəh (N) gold 17

miən (tV) to have, to exist 3; (mV) to happen to, have occasion to 15

miən qəy (Idiom) yes, of course, why not? 10

miən-tae (Aux) there's only to, [I'll] have to 11

mɨn (Aux) negative auxiliary 2

mɨn-bac-tee (VPh) it's not necessary 10

mɨn-dael (Aux-Vm) never to have (done sthg) 5

mɨn . . . ponmaan (Aux-Adv) not so very, not to any extent 5

mɨn-qəy tee (Idiom) Don't mention it; it's nothing; you're welcome 2

mɨn-səw (Aux) hardly, not so very 14

mɨn-tɔən (Aux) not yet 4

mɨt (N) friend 30-C; (Pr) you 15

məc (intAdv) how?, what? 3; (I) how?, how about it? 10

məc kɑɑ (Adv-Aux) why?, why is it that? 3

mədɑɑŋ (< muəy dɑɑŋ) (XS) once, one time 3; (Adv) once, once and for all

məlou (< muəy lou) (XS) a dozen, per dozen 4

məneəq (< muəy neəq) (XS) one person; alone 6

məñ (A) last, past, preceding 21

məpɔən (X) one thousand 23

məphɨy (X) twenty 2

məphɨy-muəy (X) twenty-one 2

məplɛɛt (Adv) awhile, for awhile, one moment 4

məsnət (XS) per hand, one bunch (of bananas) 4

məəl (tV) to read, to pronounce 3; to look at, to see 4

məəl-tɨw (Adv) perhaps, maybe 14

məɨn (X) ten-thousand 27

moən (N) chicken 12

moət (N) edge, rim; mouth 14

moət-bəŋ (N) banks of a lake 26

moət-səmot (N) seaside 26-C

moət-tuənlee (N) river-bank 14

mɔhaa-ksattrəyaanii (N) royal queen 29-C

mɔhaanikaay (N) liberal sect (literally: large body) 30

mɔhaa-ptɨy (N) interior (department) 29

mɔhaa-səmot (N) ocean 27-C

mɔhaa-wɨttyiəlay (N) university 24

mɔniiwŭəŋ (N) Monivong (a former king of Cambodia) 10

mɔnoorum (N) Monorom (name of a hotel) 10

mɔnuh (N) person, human being 4

mɔnuh-camlaek (N) stranger 21

mɔɔk (tV) to come (to) 2;
(dV) orientation of action toward speaker 4;
(Aux) come on and, do 4;
(aP) orientation toward speaker in time 5

muc (iV) to dive, go under 23-B

muk (Prep) in front of 2;
(N) face, front 11;
(S) kind, variety, dish (of food) 12

muk-rəbuəh (N) a cut, wound 22

muk-tae (Aux) probably, likely to 9

muk-wɨcciə (N) subject, field of study 24

mun (Prep) before (in time) 8

mun baŋqah (Adv) first of all 17

mun-dambouŋ (Adv) at first, in the beginning 22

mut (iV) to cut; to be sharp (cutting) 20

mŭəndŭəlkirii (N) Mondulkiri (Province) 14

mŭəntii-pɛɛt (N) hospital 22-C

mŭəntii-pɛɛt prĕəh-keit-miəliə (NPh) Preah-Ket Mealea Hospital 22-C

mŭəntrəy (N) minister 29

mŭəŋkhut (N) mangosteen 12-C

muuh (N) mosquito 15-C

muul (aV) round 23-B

muəl (N) dysentery 22

muəy (X) one 2

muəy-muəy (Adv) slowly, deliberately 3

muəy-rɔɔy (X) one-hundred 2

muəy-saen (X) one hundred-thousand 27

muəy-saen prambəy-məɨn muəy-pŏən (X) one hundred eighty-one thousand 27

mcuu (N) sour or pungent food 12

mdaay (N) mother 6

mdaay-kmeik (N) mother-in-law 21

mdaay-miiŋ (N) younger sister of either parent 6

mdaay-thom (N) older sister of either parent 6

mhoup (N) food 12

mhoup-camnəy (N) food, various kinds of food 21

mhoup-mhaa (N) various kinds of food, food in general 20

mhoup-sal (N) left-over food 20

mlup (N) shade 15

nmŏəh (N) pineapple 12

mriəm-day (N) finger 22-B

mrɨc (N) black pepper 26

msəl-məñ (Adv) yesterday 2

mteeh (N) hot (chili) peppers 12

n

nah (Adv) very, very much 2

naa (intPr) where? 2;
(intA) which? 3;
(indPr) anywhere, somewhere 9;
(indA) any, some, whichever 12

naa, nəh (fP) hortatory final particle 11

naa (I) demonstrative interjection: look!, there! 16

nĕəq (S) specifier for ordinary persons 4

nĕəq (Pr) you (familiar) 27

nĕəq-baək-taqsii (N) taxi-driver 8

nĕəq-bamraə (N) waiter, servant 12

nĕəq-cumnuəñ (N) businessman, merchant 5

nĕəq-cɨt-khaaŋ (N) neighbor 26-C

nĕəq-cumŋɨɨ (N) patient, sick person 22

nĕəq-damnaə (N) traveler, passenger 14

nĕəq-dək-nŏəm (N) leader 29

nĕəq-kan-prĕəh-puttəsahsnaa (N) Buddhist, follower of Buddhism 30

nĕəq-leeŋ-lkhaon (N) actor, player 18

nĕəq-lŭəq-kriəŋ-tok-tuu (N) furniture salesman 8

nĕəq-naa (intPr) who? 6-C;
(indPr) someone, anyone, whoever 22

nĕəq-rŭət-sambot (N) postman 23-C

nĕəq-srae (N) farmer, peasant 26

nĕəq-twəə-kaa (N) worker 8

nĕəq-twəə-mhoup (N) cook 12

nĕəq-twəə-srae (N) rice-farmer 8

neh (Dp) colloq. variant of nih: this, here 11

neesaat (tV) to fish 28

nih (Dp) this, these; here 3;
(Da) this, these

nimuəy (A) each 27

nimuəy-nimuəy (A) each, one by one, the various 27

niqsət (N) university student 5

niqteqpaññat (A, N) legislative 29

niyiəy (tV) to speak, talk 3

niyiəy qañcəŋ (Adv) by the way, speaking of that 23

niərədəy (N) southwest 27

niətii (S) minute (of time) 2

niəyŭəq-rŏət-mŭəntrəy (N) prime minister 29

nɨk (tV) to think (about); to miss 14-B

nɨŋ (Conj) and, with 2

nɨŋ (Aux) future auxiliary: will, about to 3

nɨŋ (Dp, Da) this, these, that, those 9

nɨŋ haəy (Dp-Adv) that's it, you've got it 9

nɨŋ kniə (Adv) together, to one another
     30
nɨw (tV) to be situated, reside, remain 2;
     (mV) to be still . . . , to remain 6;
     (Adv) yet, still 4
nɨw-laəy (Adv) still, up to the present 6
nɨy (Prep) of, belonging to 29
noəm (tV) to take, lead 10
noəm kniə (tV-Adv) to do all together,
     to cooperate (at) 15
nɔnaa (intPr) who?;
     (indPr) anyone, someone, whoever 29
nɔrootdɑm siihanuq (N) Norodom
     Sihanouk 29
nɔyoobaay (N) policy 29
nuh (Dp) that, those, there 3;
     (Da) that, those
numpaŋ (N) bread 2
nuəŋkoəl ~ qaŋkoəl (N) plow 26
ñam (tV) to eat or drink (informal) 2
ñam baay (VPh) to have a meal 2
ñiət-sɑndaan (N) relatives, family 6
ñɨk-ñoəp (aV) often, frequent(ly) 18
ñoəm (N) meat salad 12
ñoəm-moən (N) chicken salad 12
ñoəp (aV) fast, quick 5
ñɔñuə (N) hammer 16
ñɔə (iV) to tremble, shake 22
ñɔə kluən (VPh) tremble, shake 22
ŋiə (N) duty, function 2ʃ
ŋiət (aV) dried and salted 28
ŋuut (tV) to bathe 11
ŋuut-tɨk (iV) to bathe 11

p

pacchaa (N) crematorium 17
paccopbɑn (N) the present, modern
     times 30
pah (tV) to patch 16-C
pannaalay (N) library 24-C
pathɑm (A) first, primary 24
pathɑm-səksaa (N) primary education 24
paa (N) father
     (Pr) you (child to father); I (father
     to child) 20
paek (N) part, region 27
paetsəp (X) eighty 2
paŋsəmaŋ (N) bandages;
     (tV) to bandage 22
paaŋ (mV) to intend (to) 23-B
peəq (tV) to put on or wear above the
     waist or on the feet; to attach,
     affix 11
peek (Adv) too much, excessively 5
peeŋ-poŋ (N) ping-pong 24-C
peel (N) time, occasion 2
peel-chup-riən (N) vacation (from
     school) 26

peel-weeliə (N) time 8
peel-yup (Adv) at night 9
pɛɛt (N) medicine (as a science); doctor
     8
pɛɛt-tmɨñ (N) dentist 11
pibaaq (aV) difficult 5
pibaaq-cət (aV) unhappy 20-B
piphup-look (N) world 17-C
pipruəh (Conj) because 8
pipruəh (aV) pretty, sweet (to hear)
     18
pisaa (tV) to eat (polite, formal) 10
piseh (aV) special; precious 24
pii (Prep) from, since 2
pii (X) two 2
pii muəy tɨw muəy (Adv) from one to
     another 24
pii-msəl-məñ (Adv) yesterday 2
pii prɔlɨm (Adv) at dawn, early in the
     morning 10
pii-qaŋkal (intAdv) when (in the past)? 2
piinɨt (tV) to observe, oversee 22
piinɨt-məəl (tV) to examine, investigate
     22
piəq (N) work; speech 3
pɨc (N) diamond, precious stone 17
pɨcnɨc (N) picnic 15
pɨñ (aV) to be full;
     (Prep) fully, throughout 9
pɨñ muəy tŋay (Adv) all day 9
pɨñ teəŋ kluən (Adv) the whole body, all
     over the body 22
poh (N) post office 23
pom (N) apple 12
ponmaan (intAdv) how much?, how many?
     2;
     (intPr) how much?, how many? 4;
     (Adv) much, to any extent 5;
     (X) how many? 6;
     (indA, indPr) however many 24
ponnoh (Adv) only, only to that extent 5
pontae (Conj) but 8
poən (X) thousand 23
poət (tV) to surround, encircle 24
poosat (N) Pursat (Town, Province) 14
poot (N) corn (maize) 26
pɔɔŋ-moən (N) chicken-egg 2
pɔɔŋ-tiə (N) duck-egg 15
pɔə (N) color 11
pɔə-baytɑɑŋ (N, aV) green 11
pɔə-chiəm-cruuk (N, aV) maroon (pig's
     blood) 11
pɔə-khiəw (N, aV) the color blue; blue-
     colored 11
pɔə-kmaw (N, aV) black 11
pɔə-krɑhɑɑm (N, aV) the color red; red-
     colored 11
pɔə-lɨəŋ (N, aV) yellow 11

pɔə-miəh (N, aV) gold (color); to be gold-
   colored 11
pɔə-prɑpheh (N, aV) grey 11
pɔə-ptɨy-meek (N, aV) sky-blue (color of
   the surface of the sky) 11
pɔə-sɑɑ (N, aV) white 11
pɔə-sii-cumpuu (N, aV) pink 11
pɔə-sukkolaa (N, aV) brown (chocolate)
   11
pɔə-slaa-tum (N, aV) orange (ripe
   areca-nut)
pɔə-swaay (N, aV) purple 11
puk-moət (N) beard, mustache 11
pukae (aV, mV) clever, skillful (at) 5
pum (Aux) not (literary) 18-B
puthaw (N) ax, hatchet 22
puttəsahsnaa (N) Buddhism 30
puəh (N) stomach, intestines 21
puəh-wiən (N) innertube 16
puənlɨɨ (N) light 23-B
puənyuəl (tV) to explain 3
puu (N) younger brother of either parent
   21
puuc (N) seed, stock, background 26
puəq-maaq (N) friend 5
puəq-yəəŋ (Pr) we (exclusive) 16
puəq-srəy-srəy (N) women, the women
   26
pcuə ~ pyuə (N) to plow 26
pdac (tV) to tear, to cut off 23-B
pdahsaay (N) a cold
   (aV) to have a cold 22
pdaəm (tV, mV) to begin (to) 18
pdəy (N) husband 6
phae (N) pier, dock 14
phaen-tii (N) map 27-C
phal (N) yield, result, harvest, product
   26
phal-bon (N) reward, accumulated merit,
   karma 30
phal-damnam (N) crops, agricultural
   products 27-C
phal knoŋ dəy (N) underground products,
   mineral resources 30
phallɨttəphal (N) products, produce 28
phallɨttəphal kaqsəkam (N) agricultural
   products 28
phaan (N) Phân (a personal name) 6
phaaŋ (Adv) too, in addition 4;
   (fP) please, will you 10
pheəqriyiə (N) wife (elegant) 21-B
phiəq (N) part, share 27
phiəq-rɔɔy (S) percent 27
phiəreəq (N) duty, responsibility 29
phiəsaa (N, S) language 5
phiəsaa-kmae (N) the Cambodian language
   5
phiəsaa-qaŋglee (N) the English language 5
phɨy (tV) to fear, be afraid of 16

phək (tV) to drink (familiar) 12-C
phot (cV) to be free (of), clear (of) 16
phoocəniiyəthaan (N) restaurant 2
phuum (N) village, land 15
phuumisaah (N) geography 24
pkaa (N) flower 15
pkaət (tV) to create, to cause 23-B
pkuu (tV) to pair off 23-B
plah (tV) to change, replace 15
plae-chəə (N) fruit 4
plae-swaay (N) mango fruit 12
pleeŋ (N) song, music (instrumental) 18
pliəm (Adv) immediately 22
pliəŋ (N) rain 9;
   (iV) to rain 9
plɨc (tV) to forget 9
plɨɨ (aV) to be bright, light, late (in the
   morning) 11
pləw (N) street, way, road 10
pləw-baek (N) intersection 18-C
pləw preəh-baat mɔniiwuəŋ (N) Preah-
   Bath Monivong Street 10
pləw-rɔteh-pləəŋ (N) railway 27
pləw-tɨk (N) waterway 27
pləəŋ (N) fire, light 2
pnaek (N) section, part, fragment 24
pnɔɔŋ (N) Pnong; mountain tribes in
   general 27
pnum (N) mountain, hill 15
pnum-dɑɑŋ-rɛɛk (N) the Dong Raek
   Mountains 27
pnum-krɑwaañ (N) the Cardamom
   Mountains 27
pnum-pɨñ (N) Phnom Penh 5
pñaə (tV) to send 23
pñeəq (iV) to wake up 10
pñiəw (N) guest 10-C
pqoun (N) younger sibling 6
pqoun-cii-doun-muəy (N) younger first
   child 6
pqoun-cii-doun-muəy-srəy (N) younger
   female first cousin 6
pqoun-proh (N) younger brother 6
pqoun-srəy (N) younger sister 6
pram (X) five 2
pram-dɑndɑp (X) fifteen 6
prambəy (X) eight 2
prambəy-məin (X) eight ten-thousands
   27
prambuən (X) nine 2
prammuəy (X) six 2
prammuəy-liən (X) six million 27
prampɨl (X) seven 2
praŋ (aV) dry 26
prap (tV) to tell, to inform (familiar) 12
praq (N) money; silver 8
pray (aV) salty, seasoned 28
praakɑt (aV) to be sure, exact 8
praasaat (N) palace; sacred monument,
   temple 30

prae (tV) to translate 3

praə (tV) to use 12

praciə (N) people 29

praciəcuən (N) people, population 27

praciəriəh (N) people, populace, citizenry 29

praciəthippətay (N) democracy 29

pracluəh (iV) to argue back and forth 23-B

pradap (N) tool, instrument 16

pradap-cuəh-cul (N) tools 16

pradap-pradaa (N) instruments, equipment 22

pradouc (tV) to compare 23-B

prahael (Prep) about, approximately 5;
    (Conj) perhaps;
    (aV) to be similar 10

prahael ciə (Prep) about, approximately 5;
    (Conj) perhaps

prahael-prahael kniə (VPh) similar, approximately the same 10

prahok (N) fermented fish paste 15

prakan (tV) to maintain, guarantee 23

prakan-day (N) receipt 23

prakaət (tV) to originate, set up 23-B

prakham (tV) to bite each other 23-B

pralaay (N) ditch, small canal 26-C

pralaaŋ (iV) to take an examination, to compete 24

pralaaŋ coəp (VPh) to succeed at an examination 24

pralaaŋ tleəq (VPh) to fail in an examination 24

pramuk (N) head, chief 29

pranaŋ (iV) to race, to compete 15

prañap (aV) to hurry;
    (mV) to hurry to (do something) 11

prapiynii (N) custom, culture 30

prapuən (N) wife 6

paprit (N) to act, follow, practice 30

praq (tV) to thatch, roof 26

praqap (N, S) small box 4

praqap-sambot (N) letter-box 23

prasap (aV, mV) to be good (at), skillful (at) 15

prateəh (tV) to meet (by chance), come across 14

prateeh (N) country, state 27

prateeh-baraŋsaeh (N) France 27-C

prateeh-kampucciə (N) Cambodia 27

prateeh-kraw (N) foreign countries, abroad 28

prateeh-liəw (N) Laos 27

prateeh-qəndiə (N) India 30

prateeh-thay-laŋ (N) Thailand, Siam 27

prateeh-wiət-naam (-yiət-naam) (N) Vietnam 27

prawaeŋ (N) length; to have a length of 27

prawoəttəsaah (N) history 24

prayat (aV, mV) be careful (to), take care (in) 16

prayaoc (N) purpose, usefulness;
    (aV) useful 28-C

prehsəniiyəthaan (N) post-office 23

preəh (N) God, The Buddha 17

preəh (word prefixed to sacred object or to actions performed by sacred persons) 17

preəh-baat (N) title for a king 10

preəh-baat məniiwuəŋ (N) King Monivong 10

preəh-baat nərootdam siihanuq (N) King Norodom Sihanouk 29

preəh-baromməriəccəweəŋ (N) the Royal Palace 17

preəh-cinnəwuəŋ (N) a Cambodian drama 18

preəh-dacceəh-preəh-kun (Pr) you (inferior to superior of exalted rank; layman to priest) 27-B

preəh-kaqrunaa (N) king, his majesty 29

preəh-məkaa-ksat (N) king, monarch 29

preəh-puttəsahsnaa (N) Buddhism 30

preəh-qaŋ (Pr) 3rd person pronoun for royal persons 29;
    (S) specifier for royal persons

preəh-riəc-qanaacaq (N) royal kingdom 28

preəh-saŋ (N) priest, monk 30

preəh-wihiə (N) Preah Vihear (Temple, Province) 14; sacred temple 14

preəh-wihiə preəh-kaew (N) Wat Preah-Kaew (The Silver Pagoda) 17

preiŋ (N) oil 11

preiŋ-liəp-saq (N) hair-oil 11

preiŋ-masin (N) motor-oil 16

prɛɛk (N) stream, large canal 30

prik (N) morning 10

priksaa (tV) to advise, counsel 29

priy (N) forest 15

priy-nɔkɔɔ (N) Saigon 14-C

priy-wɛɛŋ (N) Prey Veng (Town, Province) 14

proh (N) man, male 6

prolim (N) dawn 10

prɔɔm (mV) to agree (to) 29

prum-daen (N) border, territorial limit 17

pruəh (Conj) because, since 9

pruəh (tV) to sow, scatter, broadcast 26

pruəy-cət (aV) sad 20-B

psaŋ (tV) to tame 23-B

psaa (N) market 4

psaa-kap-koo (N) the ox-slaughter market; name of a market in Phnom Penh 18

psaa-kandaal (N) the Central Market 12-C

psaa-siləp (N) a market in Phnom Penh 18

pseiŋ (aV) to be different 4

psein-psein (aV) various, different 4
pteǝh (N) house, shop, building 2
pteǝh-baay (N) kitchen 21
pteǝh-samnaq (N) hotel 2
ptɨy (N) surface 27-C
ptɨy-dǝy (N) surface of the earth,
   topography 27-C
ptoǝl (Prep) against, next to 15-C
ptuk (tV) to load (a boat, etc.) 23-B
pyiǝbaal (N) to treat, care for 22
pyuǝ ~ pcuǝ (tV) to plow 26

q

qaloo (I) Hello (telephone) 21-C
qanuq-wɨttyiǝlay (N) junior high school
   24
qañ (Pr) I (familiar, superior to
   inferior) 27-B
qap (aV) dim, dark 23-B
qapɑŋdisiit (N) appendicitis 22
qaqkiisǝnii (N) electricity 28-C
qaqknee (N) southeast 27
qaqmɔnuh (N) supernatural being 23-B
qaqnuññaat (N) permission;
   (iV) to grant permission 16
qaqphɨy (aV) fearless, without fear
   30-C
qaqphɨy-tooh (tV) to forgive, excuse
   30-C
qaqpyiǝkrǝt (N) neutralism;
   (A) neutralist 29
qaqsɑɑ (N) letters, writing 24
qaqsɑɑsaah (N) letters, literature 24
qaqyuttǝthɔǝ (N) injustice 23-B
qathaathibaay (N) explanation, lecture 27
qayeǝqsmaayiǝn (N) train (elegant) 17
qaa (Pr) pronominal prefix: a/the . . .
   one/s 11
qaa (diminutive or derogatory prefix) 18
qaa (tV) to saw (wood, etc) 28
qaa-but (N) little Bouth 21
qaa-cao (N) you thief! 23-B
qaa-chiǝm-cruuk (Pr-N) the maroon one
   11
qaanaa?(intPr) which one? 11
qaanaa-muǝy? (intPr) which one? 11
qaa-qaeŋ (Pr) you (derogatory) 23-B
qaac (mV) to have the power or ability
   to 16
qaac bɑndaal qaoy (mV-tV-mV) can lead
   to 22
qaakaah (N) air, weather 9
qaakiǝ (N) building, house 17
qaakɨñ-qaacao (N) cops and robbers 18
qaalǝmɑŋ (N) Germany 27-C;
   (A) German
qaamerikaŋ (N, A) American 5

qaamerɨc (N) America 5;
   (A) American
qaan (tV) to pronounce, to read aloud 24
qaanaacaq (N) realm, domain, country 27
qaanaakhaet (N) region, area, territory
qaanaapyiǝbaal (N) protectorate, protectorship 30
qaanǝt (tV) to pity, take pity on 18
qaasɑnnǝrook (N) cholera 22
qaazii (N) Asia 27
qaazii-paek-qaqknee (N) Southeast Asia
   27
qaatɨt (N, S) week; sun 10
qaatmaaphiǝp ~ qaatmaa (Pr) I (priest
   to layman) 27-B
qaaw (N) shirt, coat 9
qaaw-pliǝŋ (N) raincoat 9
qaayuq (N) age; to be of the age . . . 6
qae (Prep) at, as for, with regard to 26
qae-naa? (intAdv) where? 2
qae-nih (Adv) here 2
qae-nuh (Adv) there 2
qaekkǝriǝc (A) independent, sovereign 27;
   (N) independence, sovereignty 29
qaekkǝriǝe ciǝt (N) national independence
   29
qaeŋ (Pr) you, yourself 4
qaǝ (R) familiar response particle 10
qaoy (tV) to give 4;
   (dV) for, on behalf of (familiar) 10;
   (mV) to cause, make, let, allow 11
qah (tV) to use up, consume 8;
   (Adv) completely, entirely 9
qah-kamlaŋ (aV) to be tired, exhausted 15
qah peel-weeliǝ (VPh) to be time-consum-
   ing 8
qɑmbɑh (N) cotton cloth; thread 28
qɑmbañ-mǝñ (Adv) a moment ago, a while
   ago 21
qɑmbaoh (N) broom 20
qɑmnaac (N) power, authority 2ǝ
qɑmnaoy (N) gift 23-B
qɑmpii (Prep) of, from, consisting of 21
qɑndouŋ (N) well, mine 28
qɑndouŋ-rae (N) (ore) mine 28
qɑnteǝq (N) a trap, snare 23-B
qɑñcǝŋ (Adv) then, in that case 3
qɑñcǝǝñ (mV) word of polite invitation; in
   isolation: Please go ahead 2
qɑŋ (S) specifier for priests and Buddhist
   images 30-C
qɑŋglee (A) English 5;
   (N) England
qɑŋkal? (intAdv) when (in the future)? 2
qɑŋkɑɑ (N) uncooked (husked) rice 4
qɑŋkoǝl ~ nuǝŋkoǝl (N) plow 26
qɑŋkɔɔ (N) Angkor 5
qɑŋkɔɔ-riǝc (N) kingdom, nation 18

qaŋkɔɔ-thom (N) Angkor Thom 30

qaŋkɔɔ-woət (N) Angkor Wat 5

qaŋkulileik (N) typewriter 23-C

qaŋkuy (iV) to sit (down) 6

qaŋriŋ (N) hammock 14

qaŋsaa (S) degree (of temperature) 22

qap-rum (tV) to train, discipline 24

qat ~ qət (Aux) colloquial negative
    auxiliary 14

qat (tV) to do without, to resist 26

qat-tooh (I) Excuse me, I'm sorry 16

qat-thuən (tV) to withstand, resist,
    endure 26

qaa-kun (tV) to thank; in isolation: Thank
    you 2

qei! (I) Hey! (to attract attention) 4

qihslaam ~ qehslaam (N) Islam 30

qiitalii (N) Italy 27-C

qɨkkəthɨk (aV) loud, festive, gay 21-C

qəndiə (N) India 30;
    (A) Indian

qəndoucən (N) Indochina 30

qəndoucən baraŋsaeh (N) French
    Indochina 30

qəwpuk (N) father 6

qəwpuk-kmeik (N) father-in-law 21-B

qəwpuk-miə (N) younger brother of either
    parent 6

qəwpuk-mdaay (N) father and mother,
    parents 6

qəwpuk-thom (N) older brother of either
    parent 6

qəy (fP) emphatic particle after negative
    imperative: kom . . . qəy 16

qəyləw (Adv) now, right now 9

qəyləw-nih (Adv) now, at this time 8

qəysaan (N) northeast 27

qəywan (N) things, provisions, luggage
    6-C

qəɨrop (N) Europe 27-C

qom (N) older sibling of either parent 21

qotdoŋ ~ qutdoŋ (N) Oudong (a historic
    site in Kg. Chhnang Province) 17-C

qou (I) Oh 6

qoun (N) wife;
    (Pr) you (husband to wife); I (wife to
    husband) 20

qoun-qaen (Pr) you yourself (husband
    to wife) 20

quhsaa (aV) industrious, diligent;
    (mV) frequently, often 16

quhsaahaqkam (N) industry 28

quhsəphiə (N) May 9

qut (tV) to iron (clothes) 11

qwəy? (intPr) what? 2;
    (intA) what? 8;
    (indPr) anything, something, whatever
    12;
    (indA) whatever 12-B

qwəy-klah (intPr) what (plural)? what-all?
    11

r

raccənaa (N) fine arts, handicraft;
    (tV) to decorate 17

rae (N) mineral ore 28

reəŋ (iV) to dry up, to quit (of rain) 9

reəq (aV) shallow 15

reəq-reəq (aV) quite shallow 15-C

rɛɛk (tV) to carry suspended from both
    ends of a pole across the shoulder
    27

riik (iV) to bloom 20

riəc (A) royal;
    (N) reign, dynasty 29

riəc-qanaacaq (N) royal domain, kingdom
    29

riəciəthɨppətay (N) monarchy 30

riəciəthɨppətay dael miən roəthaq-
    thoəmmənuñ (NPh) constitutional
    monarchy 30

riəcckaa (N) government service 8

riəccəthiənii (N) royal capital 27

riəh (N) people, populace 29

riəl (S) riel (Cambodian monetary unit) 2

riəm (N) eldest child (frequently used as
    a nickname for same) 21

riəm-kei (N) Ream-Kerti (Cambodian
    version of the Ramayana) 18

riən (tV) to study, to learn 5

riəp-cam (tV) to get ready, prepare 11

riəp-kaa (iV) to have a wedding, to get
    married 6-C

riəpsaa (aV) proper, gentle, well-man-
    nered 30

rɨc-rɨl (aV) decrepit, disintegrated,
    worn out 20

rɨkkəmandei (tV) to register; registerd
    23

rɨl (aV) dull, worn 20

rɨŋ (aV) hard, tough 26-C

rɨt-tae (Aux) increasingly 18-B

rɨɨ (Conj) or 4;
    (fP) final question particle in either-or
    questions 5

rɨəŋ (N) story, subject, matter 18

rɨəŋ cambaŋ (N) war story 18

rɨəŋ kamplaeŋ (N) a comedy 18

rɨəŋ qaakɨñ-qaacao (N) police story,
    crime story 18

rəəh (tV) to pick out, to choose 12

roəh (tV) to rake, harrow 26

roəl (Prep) every (in succession) 9

roəl-tŋay (Adv) every day 9

roəm (tV) to dance 18

roəm-kbac (N) stylized dancing 18

roət (N) state, political entity 29

roət-muəntrəy (N) government minister 29

rŏə́t-saphiə (N) national assembly 29

rŏə́ttənaqkirii (N) Ratanakiri (Province) 14

rŏə́tthaqthŏə́mmənuñ (N) constitution 29

rŏə́tthaaphibaal (N) government, administration 29

rook (N) disease 22

rook-claaŋ (N) contagious disease 22

rooŋ (N) hall, building, factory 8

rooŋ-caq (N) factory, industrial plant 28

rooŋ-dambaañ (N) weaving mill 8

rooŋ-damlaəŋ-laan (N) automobile assembly plant 28

rooŋ-kaasinou (N) the Casino Theater 18-C

rooŋ-kən-srəw (N) rice-mill 26

rooŋ-kon (N) cinema, movie theater 18

rooŋ-qaqkiisənii (N) generating plant 28

rooŋ-qaa-chəə (N) sawmill 28

rooŋ-qeidaen (N) the Eden Theater 18-C

rooŋ-siineluc (N) the Cinelux Theater 18-C

rooŋ-twəə-barəy (N) cigarette factory 8

rooŋ-twəə-kawsuw (N) rubber factory 28

rooŋ-twəə-skaa (N) sugar refinery 28

rooŋ-twəə-sraa (N) distillery 28

rɔbam (N) dance; dancing 18

rɔbam-rŏə́m-kbac (N) ballet 18

rɔbaŋ (N) screen, shade 23-B

rɔbah (N) thing 3;
   (Conj) of, belonging to 8

rɔbah kñom (Prep-Pr) mine 11

rɔbaa (N) trade, profession 28-C

rɔbaa-rɔɔk-sii (N) trade, method of earning a living 28

rɔbaaŋ (N) fence, hedge 20

rɔbiəp (N) method, way, order 26

rɔbiəp-krup-krɔɔŋ (N) system of government 29

rɔbout (iV) to come off, slip off 23-B

rɔbuəh (N) wound;
   (aV) wounded 22

rɔdae (N) Radé, Rhadé (a hill tribe) 27

rɔdaaq (aV) uprooted 23-B

rɔdəw (N, S) season 9

rɔdəw-kdaw (N) the hot season 9

rɔdəw-pliəŋ (N) the rainy season 9

rɔdəw-rəŋiə (N) the cold season 9

rɔhah (aV) fast, rapid 15

rɔhout (Adv) throughout, all the way 9

rɔliə (N) shell, skull 26

rɔliə-douŋ (N) coconut-shell 26

rɔluət (iV) to go out, be extinguished 20

rɔnŏə́h (N) rake, harrow 26-C

rəŋiə (aV) cold, chilly 9

rɔsiəl (N) early afternoon 9

rɔteh (N) car, cart 2

rɔteh-pləəŋ (N) train 2

rɔteh-koo (N) ox-cart 26

rɔwiəŋ (N) interval, duration;
   (Prep) during 30

rɔwɨy (tV) to rotate, spin 28

rɔwuəl (aV) busy, preoccupied 6

rɔɔk (tV) to seek, to earn 8

rɔɔk mɨn baan (VPh) to be unable to find 12-C

rɔɔk-sii (tV) to earn a living (by) 26

ruhsii (N, A) Russia, Russian 18

rumleep (tV) to cause to swallow 23-B

ruə̌h (iV) to live, be alive 30-C

ruə́t (tV) to run 15

ruuŋ (N) hole 20

ruəc (Conj) then, besides 6;
   (cV) after negative: to be able 14-B;
   to finish, complete 15

ruəc-haəy (Adv) already 6

ruəc pii nuh (Adv) after that 20

ruəp-ruəm (tV) to combine, assemble, collect 30

S

sabuu (N) soap 11

sac (N) meat, flesh; texture 12

sac-koo (N) beef 12

sac-cruuk (N) pork 12

sac-trəy (N) fish (meat) 12

sahaqrŏə́t (N) union, confederation 5

sahaqrŏə́t-qaamerɨc (N) the United States 5

sahsnaa (N) religion 30

sahstraacaa (N) teacher, professor 24-C

salaa (N) hall; pavilion; school 2

salaa-kuruq-wɨcciə (N) School of Pedagogy, Teacher's College 24

salaa-pathammǝsǝksaa (N) primary school 24

salaa-raccǝnaa (N) School of Fine Arts; also commonly used to refer to the National Museum 17

salaa-riǝcckaa (N) government school 24

salaa-riǝn (N) school (building) 2

salaa-tǝcnɨc (N) technical school 24

salaa-wŏə́t (N) pagoda school 24

samay (N) time, era, period 30

samay cǝnlaa (N) the Chenla Period 30

samay fuunaan (N) the Funan Period 30

samay kandaal (N) the Middle Period 30

samay paccoban (N) the present era, modern times 30

samay qaŋkɔɔ (N) the Angkor Period 30

samaaciq ~ samaacɨk (N) member 29

sañ ñaabat (N) certificate 24

saŋ (N) gasoline 16

saŋ (aV) tame 23-B

sapbaay (aV) to be happy, pleasant 2

sapbaay-cət (aV) happy, content, glad 20

saphiə (N) house, chamber, assembly
   29

saq (N) rank, grade 29-C

saraan (N) Saran (a personal name) 4

saraan (N) you (personal name used as a
   pronoun) 4

sarɨn (N) Sarin (a personal name) 22

sarun (N) Sarun (a personal name) 26

sat (N) animal, creature (human or
   otherwise) 20

sattəwŏət (N) century, era 30

sattəwŏət tii-muəy (N) the first century

sattəwŏət tii-prammuəy (N) the sixth
   century 30

saah (N) race, religion, nationality

saamsəp (X) thirty 2

saap (tV) to sow, scatter 26

saap (aV) bland, unseasoned 28

saareəqmuəntii-ciət (N) national
   museum 17-B

saen (X) hundred-thousand 27

saesəp (X) forty 2

saok (tV) to pity 23-B

saoy (tV) to eat (royal) 23-B

saoy-riəc (tV) to rule, to reign 29

sah (fP) (not) at all 9

sal (aV) to remain, be left over 20

sam (aV) suitable, proper 11

sambot (N) letter, ticket 14

sambot-kapal (N) steamer ticket 14

sambou (aV) full, abundant, plentiful

samdac (N) prince, princess 29-C;
   title for high-ranking royalty

samdac siihanuq (N) Prince Sihanouk
   29-C

samkɔɔm (aV) ridiculously slender,
   skinny;
   (N) slender person 23-B

samkhan (aV) important 23

samlap (tV) to kill 30

samlaa (N) stew (usually highly
   seasoned) 12

samlaa-mcuu (N) pungent stew 12

samleiŋ (N) voice, sound 18

samliəŋ (tV) to sharpen by whetting 20

samliəq (N) clothing worn around the
   waist 18

samliəq-bampeəq (N) clothing, costume
   (elegant) 18

samləy (N) raw fiber (cotton, etc.) 28

samnaq (iV) to rest, stay 2

samnaap (N) seedling, plant 26

samnuə (N) question 3

sampeəh (tV) to greet with palms joined
   21

sampeəh-suə (tV) to greet 21

sampuət (N) cloth; dhoti 14

samq̀ʿat (tV) to clean, make clean 20

samrac (mV) to decide (to) 22

samraŋ (tV) to select, choose, extract
   26-C

samrap (tV, mV) to use for 15;
   (S) a set, suite

samraaq (iV) to rest, to stop work 15

samruəl (tV) to facilitate, make easy
   23-B

sandap (N) understanding, convention
   23-B

sandaek (N) bean 26

sandaek-dəy (N) peanut 26

sanlək (N, S) sheet, leaf 23-C

sansam (tV) to save, collect 23

santhaakiə (N) hotel 10

santhaakiə-haaway (N) the Hawaii Hotel
   10-C

santhaakiə-mɔnoorum (N) the Monorom
   Hotel 10

santhaakiə-sukkhaalay (N) the Sukkhalay
   Hotel 10

saŋ (tV) to build 28

saŋkat (N) division, sector 23-B

saŋkyaa (N) custard, pudding 12

saŋsaa (N) sweetheart, fiancé(e) 23

sap (Prep) every 8

sap (tV) to inflate, pump air into 16-C

sap-tŋay-nih (Adv) these days, at the
   present time 8

saq (N) hair 8

sasei (tV) to write 3

saa (aV) white 11

saam (N) fork 12

saaŋ (tV) to repay, compensate 30-C

siññei (tV) to sign 23

sii (tV) to eat (disrespectful, of animals);
   to use, consume 16-C

siimaŋ (N) cement 14

siitroqaen (N) Citroën (a make of automobile) 28

siəm (A) Thai; 17
   (N) Thailand, Siam

siəm-riəp (N) Siem Reap (Town, Province)
   14

siət (tV) to insert 23-B

siəwphɨw (N) book 3

səc-kdəy (N) composition; matter, story
   24

səc-kdəy-dəŋ-kun (N) gratitude 26-B

səc-kdəy-kuə-pum-kuə (N) mistakes 30-C

səc-kdəy-lqaa (N) goodness, beauty
   26-B

səc-kdəy-sapbaay (N) happiness 26-B

səc-kdəy-slap (N) death 26-B

səc-kdəy-tuk-cət (N) confidence 29

səkuə (A) emergency, extra 16

səksaa (tV) to study, learn, research;
(N) education 24

səmot ~ srɑmot (N) sea, ocean 26-C

səmot-siəm (N) Sea of Thailand 27

sən (fP) polite imperative: first; do 4

səŋ(-tae) (Aux) almost, on the point of 21

sət (tV) to comb 11

səy (N) a feathered projectile 24

səyhaa (N) August 9

sok (aV) to be happy, well 2

sok-cət (mV) to agree (to), be willing (to)
10

sok-sapbaay (aV) to be well and happy 2

sokkhaalay (N) Sukkhalay (name of a
hotel) 10

som (tV) to request, ask for 4

sophiəp (aV) polite, kind 30

sophiəp-riəpsaa (aV) polite and kind 30

sot-tae (Aux) inclusively, all without
exception 11

sou (N) sound, noise 15

soum (Aux) please 2

soum-tooh (I) Excuse me, I'm sorry 2

sourəyaawɑɑrəman (N) Suryavarman
24-C

suflei (N) horn;
(tV) to blow (a horn) 16

suən (N) garden 15

suən-cbaa (N) flower garden, park 15

suən-pkaa (N) flower garden 20

suə (tV) to question, to ask 2

suəsdəy (I) Greetings! Hello! (formal;
urban) 30-C

suəsdəy mɨt (I-Pr) Dear Friend;
Greetings, Friend 30-C

sbaek (N) skin, leather 11-C

sbaek-cəəŋ (N) shoes 11-C

sdac (N) king 24-C

sdac cɨyyeəqwɑɑrəman tii-prampɨl (N)
King Jayavarman VII 24-C

sdac sourəyaawɑɑrəman tii-pii (N)
King Suryavarman II 24-C

sdam (aV) right (side) 2

sdam-day (aV) on the right 2

sdap (tV) to listen (to) hear, obey 3

sdap baan (VPh) to be able to hear, to
understand 3

sdaəŋ (aV) thin 23-C

sdaəŋ-sdaəŋ (aV) very light and thin
23-C

skɑɑ (N) sugar 2

skoəl (tV) to know, be acquainted with,
know of 5

skɔɔm (aV) slender 23-B

slap (iV) to die 21

slaap-pɑqkaa (tV) fountain pen 23

slaap-priə (N) spoon 12

sliəq (tV) to put on or wear below the
waist 11

sliəq-peəq (tV) to dress, to wear 11

slək (N) leaf 26

slək-tnaot (N) sugar-palm leaf 26

smaw (N) grass, hay 20

smiən (N) clerk 8

smoum (N) beggar 23-B

snae-haa (N) love, romance 18

snɑp (N) air pump 16

sniət (N) insert, wedge 23-B

snət (S) specifier for hands of bananas 4

sŋat (aV) quiet, peaceful 24-C

sŋao (tV) to boil;
(N) boiled soup 12

sŋao-bɑŋkɑɑŋ (N) prawn soup 12

sŋaoy (N) royal food 23-B

sŋiəm (aV) quiet, silent 15

sŋuət (aV) to be dry 15

spiən (N) bridge 16

spoən (N) copper 28

sqaat (aV) clean, neat, attractive 10

sqaat-baat (aV) neat, careful, proper 11

sqaek (Adv) tomorrow 2

sqəy (intPr) what? 3

srɑc (cV) to decide on, dispose of,
finalize 14-B

srɑc-tae (tV) [it] depends on, [it's] up to
12

srɑp-tae (Aux) suddenly, unexpectedly
18-B

sraa (N) alcoholic beverage 21

sraal (aV) light (in weight) 23-C

srae (N) rice-field 8

srae-cɑmkaa (N) land under cultivation
27

srae-prɑŋ (N) dry (season) rice-field 26

srae-wuəhsaa (N) wet (season) rice-field
26

sraek (tV) to shout 15

sraom (N) covering, envelope 11

sraom-cəəŋ (N) socks, stockings 11

sraom-sɑmbot (N) envelope 23

srɑlah (aV) clear, cleared up 22

srɑlañ (tV) to love 18

srɑlañ kniə (VPh) to love each other 18

srɑmaoc (N) out 15-C

srɑmot ~ səmot (N) sea, ocean 26-C

srɑnaok (N) pity 23-B

srɑqap (aV) obscure, foggy 23-B

srɑtɔɔp (N) skin, bark 18

srɑtɔɔp-ceik (N) banana-tree bark; name
of a Cambodian drama 18

srɑwəŋ (aV) drunk, intoxicated, dizzy
21

srəw (N) unhusked rice, paddy 16-C

srəw-puuc (N) seed-rice 26

srəw-laəŋ-tɨk (N) floating rice 26

srəw-prɑŋ (N) dry (season) rice 26

srəw-pruəh (N) broadcast rice 26

srəw-stuuŋ (N) transplated rice 26

srəw-wuə̆hsaa (N) wet (season) rice 26
srəy (N) woman, female 6
srəy-srəy (N) women (in general) 11-C
srok (N) country, district 5; administra-
    tive division of a khaet 29-C
srok-baraŋ (N) France 5
srok-cən (N) China 5
srok-kmae (N) Cambodia 5
srok-qaamerɨc (N) America 5
srok-siəm (N) Thailand 17
srok-srae (N) the country, rural areas 9
sruəl (aV) comfortable, easy, pleasant 5
sruəl kluən (VPh) to feel well 22
stɨŋ-traeŋ (N) Stung Treng (Town,
    Province) 14
stəə-tae (Aux) almost, on the point of 23
stoə̆t (aV, mV) to be good (at), skilled
    (at) 16-C
stɔɔp (tV) to envelop 23-B
stuuŋ (tV) to insert into the ground, to
    transplant 26
sthaanii (N) station, place 17
sthaanii-qayeə̆qsmaayiən (N) train station
    17
swaaməy (N) husband (elegant) 21-B
swaay (N) mango 12
swaay-riəŋ (N) Svay Rieng (Town,
    Province) 14
šaek (N) check 23

t

taŋ (tV) to set up, display, establish 17;
    to appoint 29
taŋ-pii (Prep) from, starting from 9;
    ever since
taqsii (N) taxi 8
taa (N) grandfather, old man 6
taa-liə (N) gt-gt-gt-grandfather 21-B
taa-luət (N) great-great grandfather
    21-B
taa-tuət (N) great grandfather 21-B
taakaew (N) Takeo (Town, Province) 14
taam (tV) to follow;
    (dV) according to, after 3
taam kapal-hɑh (Adv) by air (by airplane)
    23
taam kapal-tɨk (Adv) by sea (by ship) 23
taam khaet (Adv) in the provinces 14
taam-thoə̆mmədaa (Adv) usually 9
tae (N) tea (leaves) 2
tae (Conj) but 4;
    (Prep) only 4
tae-mədɑɑŋ (Adv) directly, at once, in
    one operation 26
tae məneə̆q qaeŋ (Adv) alone, by oneself
    22
taem (N) stamp 23

taeŋ (tV) to write, compose 24
taeŋ səc-kdəy (VPh) to write a composi-
    tion;
    (N) composition, writing 24
taeŋ-tae (Aux) usually 18-B
taə (I) say, tell me 8
tɑɑ (iV) to continue 9
tɑɑ tɨw tiət (Adv) on, further, continuing
    on 9
teə̆h (tV) to slap, smack 18
teə̆h-day (iV) to clap the hands, applaud
    18
teə̆ŋ (Prep) including, all of 10
teə̆ŋ nih (Prep-Da) all these 30
teə̆ŋ-pii (Prep-X) both 6
teə̆ŋ-qɑh (Adv) all 3
teə̆ŋ-qɑh kniə (Adv) all together 3
teə̆q (tV) to trap, to snare 23-B
teə̆q-tɔɔŋ (iV) to be related (to) 28;
    concerned (with)
tee (fP) final question particle 2;
    emphatic final particle 2; final
    negative particle 2
teehsəcɑɑ (N) tourist, tourism 5
teelekraam (N) telegram;
    (tV) to telegraph 23
teeŋ-taaŋ (aV) incoherent, confused 22-B
teəmoumaet (N) thermometer 22
tii (N) ordinalizing prefix 3
tii-bɑmphot (N, Adv) to most, the last
    26-B
tii-kɑnlaeŋ (N) place, establishment 17
tii-koorup (N) respected one 26-B
tii-krɔŋ (N) city 17
tii-ponmaan? (A) the how-many'th? 3
tii-pram (A) fifth 3
tii-snaehaa (N) loved one 26-B
tiə (N) duck 15
tiəhiən (N) soldier 5
tiəm-tiə (tV) to wrest away, obtain by
    bargaining 29
tiən (N) gift 30
tiə̆ñ (tV) to pull, to draw along 26
tiət (Adv) again further 3
tɨh (N) direction 27
tɨh-baccəm (N) western direction; the
    west (lit.) 27-B
tɨh-bou (N) eastern direction; the east
    (lit.) 27-B
tɨh-niərədəy (N) southwestern direction;
    the southwest (lit.) 27
tɨh-piəyoə̆p (N) northwestern direction,
    the northwest (lit.) 27-B
tɨh-qaqknee (N) southeastern direction;
    the southeast (lit.) 27
tɨh-qəysaan (N) northeastern direction;
    the northeast (lit.) 27
tɨh-qotdɑɑ (N) northern direction; the
    north (lit.) 27-B

tɨh-teə̆qsən (N) southern direction; the south (lit.) 27-B

tɨk (N) water; liquid 2

tɨk-cruə̆h (N) spring, mountain stream, waterfall 15

tɨk-dah-koo (N) milk 2

tɨk-kaɑq (N) ice; ice-water; snow 9

tɨk-kmaw (N) ink 23

tɨk-tae (N) tea (liquid) 2

tɨk-trəy (N) fish-sauce 12

tɨñ pii baɑrəteeh (VPh) to import 28

tɨw (tV) to go 2;
  (dV) orientation of action away from speaker: to, up to 9;
  (aP) orientation away from speaker in time 9;
  (fP) imperative final particle: go ahead 11

tɨw ciət kraoy (Adv) in later reincarnations 30

tɨw mɨn toə̆n (VPh) to miss 14

tɨw mɔɔk (VPh) to go and come 16-C

tɨw naa mɔɔk naa (VPh) to go anywhere, to go and come 9

tɨw wɨñ tɨw mɔɔk (Adv) back and forth, reciprocally 30

təc (aV) few, little (in quantity) 23

təcnɨc (N) technique;
  (A) technical 24

təəp (Conj) then, after which 8

təəp(-tae)-nɨŋ (Aux) just, just now 14

tok (N) table 3

toqlaa (N) October 9

toə̆t (tV) to kick 24

toə̆t-səy (N) a game involving kicking a feathered projectile 24

touc (aV) to be small 4

touc-touc (aV) to be quite small (pl.) 4

tɔteə̆h (tV) to flap (the wings) 23-B

tɔtɨk (aV) to be wet 9

tɔtɨm ~ krɑtɨm (N) pomegranate 28

tɔtuəl (tV) to receive, accept 10-C

tɔtuəl-tiən (tV) to eat (polite; with reference to oneself) 2

tuk-cət (iV) to have confidence (in), rely (on) 16

tuliəy (aV) spacious, roomy 10

tum (aV) ripe 4

tum (iV) to perch 23-B

tumhum (N) size 27

tumhum-dəy (N) area (of land) 27

tumleə̆q (tV) to fell, overthrow 23-B

tumloə̆p (N) custom 23-B

tumnee (aV) free, vacant, at leisure 8

tumnɨñ (N) merchandise 16-C

tumnəəp (A) modern, recent 24

tumŋuə̆n (N) weight 23

tumpɔə (N) page, leaf 3

tuə̆h-yaaŋ-naa-kɑ-daoy (Adv) however it may be, nevertheless 15

tuə̆hsəniə (tV) to observe, inspect, sightsee 30

tuə̆l (tV) to prop up, support, touch 27

tuə̆l nɨŋ (tV-Prep) supporting, against, next to 27

tuə̆n (aV) soft, pliable 26

tuə̆nlee (N) large river; long body of water 14

tuə̆nlee-meekoŋ (N) the Mekong River 14-C

tuə̆nlee-saap (N) the Tonle Sap (the Sap River) 27

tuə̆nloə̆p (N) custom 23-B

tuu (N) cabinet, cupboard, chest 8

tuuk (N) boat 14

tuuk-kɑpal (N) boats, rivercraft 14

tuə-qaek (N) principal character 18

tuə-qaek-proh-srəy (N) the hero and heroine 18

tuə-tɨw (Adv) all over, in general 29

tuənəwih (N) screwdriver 16

tbal (N) mill, millstone 26

tbal-bok (N) rice-mill, mortar and pestle 26

tbiət (tV) to pinch 23-B

tbouŋ (N) south 27

tbouŋ (N) precious stone 28

tbouŋ-kɑndiəŋ (N) sapphire 28

tbouŋ-pɨc (N) jewels, precious stones 28

tbouŋ-tɔtɨm ~ -krɑtɨm (N) ruby 28

thaa (tV) to say 3;
  (Conj) that, saying, as follows 3

thaan-suə (N) heaven, Nirvana 30-C

thae-reə̆qsaa (tV) to care for, take care of 6

thaok (aV) cheap, inexpensive 10

thaat ruup (VPh) to take a picture, to photograph 21-C

thaat-tuu (N) drawer 8

thiət-qaakaah (N) atmosphere, weather 27-C

thəniəkiə (N) bank 23

thəniəkiə-ciət (N) the National Bank 23

thət (tV) to put, place; situated 30

thəy mɨn miən! ~ həy mɨn miən! (Idiom) of course they have!, of course there is/are! 14

thom (aV) large 4; important 29-C

thom-dom (aV) big, important, impressive 21-C

thoə̆mmədaa (Adv) usual, usually 9

thoə̆mməyut (N) the orthodox sect 30

thou (N) vase 20

thɔə (N) moral law, dharma 30

thum (tV) to smell, sniff 14-B

thureə̆q (N) problem, trouble, preoccupation 30

thuən (tV) to endure, withstand 26

thuureen (N) durian 12

tlay (aV) to be expensive; to cost 2;
  (N) price, cost 4

tlaa (aV) clear, transparent 15-C

tleəq (iV) to fall 9

tləŋ (tV) to weigh 23

tloəp (aV) to be accustomed 9;
  (mV) used to, customarily 15

tmaa (N) rock, stone 15

tmɨñ (N) tooth, teeth 11

tməy (aV) new; again, some more 11

tnam (N) medicine preparation 11;
  tobacco 14

tnam-cuəq (N) smoking tobacco 26

tnam-doh-tmɨñ (N) toothpaste 11

tnam-krun (N) fever medicine 22

tnaq (N) close, level 8

tnaq coŋ bamphot (N) final grade (13th
  year) 24

tnaq tii-bəy tumnəəp (N) 3rd grade,
  secondary (10th year) 24

tnaq tii-dap-pii (N) 12th grade (1st year)
  24

tnaq tii-muəy tumnəəp (N) 1st grade,
  secondary (12th year) 24

tnaq tii-pii tumnəəp (N) 2nd grade,
  secondary (11th year) 24

tnaq tii-prammuəy tumnəəp (N) 6th grade,
  secondary (7th year) 24

tnaq tii-prampɨl (N) 7th grade (6th year)
  24

tnaal (N) nursery plot, seedbed 26

tnaot (N) sugar-palm 26

tnal (N) paved road, street 10

tnuu (N) December 9

tŋay (N, S) day, sun 2

tŋay-can (N) Monday 10

tŋay nah haəy (VPh) it's late (in the
  morning) already 16

tŋay-nih (Adv) today 2

tŋay-nɨŋ (Adv) colloq. variant of
  tŋay-nih 11

tŋay-put (N) Wednesday 10

tŋay-prahoəh (N) Thursday 10

tŋay-qaatɨt (N) Sunday 10

tŋay-qaŋkiə (N) Tuesday 10

tŋay-rɔsiəl (Adv) in the early afternoon
  9

tŋay-saw (N) Saturday 10

tŋay-sok (N) Friday 10

tŋay-traŋ (Adv) at midday, noon 9

tŋuən (aV) heavy, serious 22

traa (N) seal, stamp, mark 23

trabaac (tV) to crumble in the fingers
  23-B

traceəq (aV) to be cool, fresh 9

traciəq (N) ear 23-B

tralaok (N) dipper, ladle 26

tralaok-daaŋ-tɨk (N) water-dipper 26

tralap (iV) to reverse, to turn around 4

traŋ (aV) straight, honest 9

trapeəŋ-baay-cuu (N) grape 12-C

trasaq (N) cucumber 15

traaŋ (tV) to strain, filter 23-B

treik-qaa (aV) happy 20-B

trəw (aV) to be right, correct 3;
  (mV) to have to, must 4;
  (tV) to hit, come in contact with; be
    subjected to, meet with 22

trəw-kaa (tV) to need, to want 2

trəw-tae (Aux) absolutely must 18-B

trəy (N) fish 12

trəy-cqaə (N) smoked fish 15

trəy-ŋiət (N) dried salted fish 28

trəy-tɨk-pray (N) salt-water fish 28

trəy-tɨk-saap (N) fresh-water fish 28

trəm (aV) proper;
  (Prep) at, coincident with 30-C

trəm nih (Prep-Da) right here, at this
  point 30-C

trɔnum (N) a perch 23-B

truət-traa (tV) oversee, supervise,
  administer 29-C

twaay (tV) to give, offer, present
  (elegant) 17

twaay-baŋkum (tV) to venerate, greet
  respectfully 17

twiip (N) continent 27-C

twiip-qəɨrop (N) the continent of Europe
  27-C

twiə (N) door, opening 10

twəə (tV) to make, to do 3; to work as,
  follow the profession of 5

twəə-bon (iV) to make merit, do good
  deeds 30

twəə-bon-daq-tiən (iV) to make merit by
  giving alms, to perform generous
  deeds 30

twəə-kaa (iV) to work 4

twəə kluən (VPh) to prepare oneself, get
  ready 11

twəə-leik (VPh) to do numbers;
  (N) arithmetic 24

twəə qaoy (VPh) makes, causes 15

twəə srae (VPh) to farm (raise rice) 8

twəə srae-camkaa (VPh) to cultivate,
  farm 27

tyuuŋ ~ kyuuŋ (N) coal, charcoal 20

w

way (tV) to hit, strike, type 23

way daqtilou (VPh) to type 23-C

waa (tV) to pass, overtake 16

waen-taa (N) eye-glasses 16

wallay-bal (N) volleyball 24

weə̆ŋ (N) palace 17

weə̆h (tV) to cut open 22

weə̆h-kat (iV) to operate 22

weeliə (N) time 8

wiqswaakɑɑ (N) engineering 26-C

withii (N) way, method 24

withii-baŋkaa-rook (N) disease prevention 24

wiə (Pr) familiar or derogatory 3rd person pronoun 6

wiəc (aV) crooked 23-B

wiəl (N) plain, field 27

wi̇cciə (N) science, field of study 8

wi̇cciə co̊ən kpu̇əh (NPh) higher education 24

wi̇cciə-pɛɛt (N) medicine (as a science) 8

wi̇cciə piseh (NPh) special subject 24

wi̇cciəlay (N) secondary school, lycée 8

wi̇ccəkaa (N) November 9

wi̇l muk (VPh) to be dizzy 22-B

wi̇ñ (Adv) contrastive adverb: back, again, on the other hand 4

wi̇ttyiəlay (N) secondary school, lycée 8

wi̇ttyiəlay siisowat (N) Lycée Sisonath 24

wi̇ttyiəsaah (N) science 24

wəəy! (I) interjection for attracting attention 15

wo̊ət (N) wat, temple compound 5

wo̊ət-pnum (N) Wat Phnom (site of the foundation of Phnom Penh) 17

wo̊ət-qonaalaom (N) Wat Onalaom (seat of the Mahanikay Sect) 17

wo̊ətthoq (N) article, artifact 17

wo̊ətthoq-bouraan (N) ancient artifacts 17

wu̇əl (iV) to revolve 23-B

wu̇əŋ (N) circle 24

wu̇əŋ-dantrəy (N) orchestra 21-C

y

yaaŋ (N, S) kind, way, variety 12-C

yaaŋ-məc (intAdv) how? in what way? 14

yaaŋ-məc-klah (intAdv) what kinds?; in what ways? 28

yaaŋ təc nah (Adv) at the very least, at least 30

yipun ~ cipun (A) Japanese; (N) Japan 17-C

yii! (I) interjection of surprise or mild annoyance 6

yiəy (N) grandmother, old woman 6

yiəy-liə (N) gt-gt-gt-grandmother 21-B

yiəy-luət (N) great-great-grandmother 21-B

yiəy-tuət (N) great-grandmother 21-B

yi̇it (aV) slow, late 14

yəəŋ (Pr) we (familiar) 6

yɔɔk (tV) to take, take in hand 4

yum (iV) to cry, wail, howl 20

yup (N) night, evening 9

yutteqthɔə (N) justice 29

yu̇əl (tV) to understand, to perceive 3

yu̇əl-prɔɔm (tV) to approve, consent (to) 29

yuu (aV) to be long (in time) 5

yuu-yuu-mədɑɑŋ (Adv) once in a while, from time to time, intermittently 22

yuən (A) Vietnamese; (N) Vietnam 27

In the following glossary, each English entry is separated from its Cambodian equivalent(s) by a colon; multiple entries under a single heading are separated by a semicolon. Grammatical designations are used only when necessary to avoid ambiguity; abbreviations have the same meanings as those listed at the beginning of the Cambodian-English Glossary.

a

a/the . . . one/s (pronominal prefix): qaa-; the maroon one: qaa-chiem-cruuk; which one?: qaa-naa?, qaa-naa-muəy?

abandon, throw away: caol

about (approximately): prɑhael, prɑhael ciə; about (concerning): pii, qampii

abundant (with), full (of): sɑmbou (daoy)

accident: kruəh-tnaq; automobile accident: kruəh-tnaq bok laan

accompany: cuun, qɑɑm, kɑmdɑɑ

according to: taam

account: kɔŋ

accustomed to: tloəp + V, dael + V, quhsaa + V

actor: neəq-leeŋ-lkhaon

A.D. 1953: krɨhsaqkəraac muəy-poən prambuən-rɔɔy haasəp-bəy

address (N): lumnɨw, tii-lumnɨw

adequate, complete: krup-kroən

administer: truət-traa, piinɨt-məəl, krup-krɔɔŋ

advise (tV): prɨksaa

affectionately: daoy meetrəy-phiəp

after, behind: kraoy; back, in back: khaaŋ-kraoy; following after: taam

after that: ruəc pii nuh, bantoəp pii nuh, bantoəp mɔɔk

afternoon (early): rɔsiəl; late afternoon, evening: lŋiəc

afraid (A): phɨy

again (further): tiət; once again: mədaaŋ tiət; back again: wɨñ

against, next to: ptɔəl, ptɔəl nɨŋ; personal, one's own: ptɔəl kluən

age: qaayuq; to be aged . . .: qaayuq . . .; age, period (of history): samay, cɔən, saqkəraac

agree (to): prɔɔm (nɨŋ); willing (to): sok-cət + Verb

agriculture: kaqsəkam; department of agriculture: krɑsuəŋ-kaqsəkam; agricultural products: phallɨttəphal kaqsəkam

air, weather: qakaah

airplane: kəpal-hɑh

alcohol, alcoholic beverage: sraa; distillery: rooŋ-twəə-sraa

all (A, Adv): teəŋ-qah; all of: teəŋ + N, pɨñ + N; all, inclusively: sot-tae; all over, in general: tuə-tɨw; all these: teəŋ-nih; all together: teəŋ-qah kniə

almost: cɨt + Verb; almost, on the point of: stəə-tae, səŋ(-tae) + V

allow: qaoy

alone: məneəq; by oneself: tae məneəq qaeŋ

already: haəy, ruəc-haəy

also, as well: dae

always: ceh-tae + V; ciə-nɨə, ciə-dɑraap

America: qaamerɨc, srok-qaamerɨc, prɑteeh-qaamerɨc; American: qaamerɨkan

ancient, former: bouraan

and: haəy-nɨŋ; and, with: nɨŋ; and then: haəy

and how about . . . ?: coh

anger: kamhəŋ

ankle: kɑɑ-cəəŋ

Angkor: qɑŋkɔɔ; Angkor Wat: qɑŋkɔɔ-woət; Angkor Thom: qɑŋkɔɔ-thom

Angkor Period: samay qɑŋkɔɔ

angry: khəŋ; anger: kamhəŋ

animal, creature: sat

answer (tV): claəy; (N) cɑmlaəy

ant: srɑmaoc

any (indA): qwəy (qəy, sqəy), naa

anyone (indPr): neəq-naa, nɔnaa

anything (indPr): qwəy, qəy, sqəy

anywhere (indAdv): naa, kɑnlaeŋ naa, qae-naa

appendicitis: qapɑŋdisiit

apple: pom

approve: yuəl-prɔɔm; approval, consent: kaa-yuəl-prɔɔm

April: (khae-) meesaa

area (of land): tumhum-dəy

argue: cluəh; argue back and forth: prɑcluəh

arrive (at): dɑl, tɨw dɑl, mɔɔk dɑl

around: cumwɨñ

article, artifact: woətthoq; ancient artifacts: woətthoq-bouraan

artisan, skilled laborer: ciəŋ

as (like): douc; as (being, serving as):
     ciə
as examples, et cetera: ciə-daəm
as well as: dae; prɔɔm-teəŋ (Prep)
Asia: qaazii, qaasii; Southeast Asia:
     qaazii-paek-qaqknee
ask: suə; inquire, ask in marriage:
     dandəŋ; ask for, request: som
assemble, set up: damlaəŋ
at: qae, nɨw; is located at: nɨw qae
at least: yaaŋ təc nah
atmosphere: thiət-qakaah
attach, affix (stamp, etc.): bət; (medal,
     insignia): peəq
attached to, stuck to: coəp
attend, accompany: kamdɑɑ
August: (khae-)səyhaa
aunt (younger sister of either parent):
     miiŋ, neəq-miiŋ; (older sister of
     either parent): qom
automobile: laan; automobile parts:
     krɨəŋ-laan
avoid: ciəh
awaken (iV): pñeəq; (tV): dah
awhile, for awhile, one moment:
     məplɛɛt
a while ago, a moment ago: qambañ-məñ
ax, hatchet: puthaw

b

baccalaureate degree: baasou; first
     baccalaureate degree: baasou
     tii-muəy; second baccalaureate degree:
     baasou tii-pii
bachelor; be single: kamlah
back and forth, reciprocally: tɨn wɨñ tɨw
     mɔɔk
ball: bal
ball up, make into a ball: cmoul
ballet, classical dancing: rɔbam-rɔəm-
     kbac
banana: ceik; banana-tree: daəm-ceik;
     banana-tree bark: sratɔɔp-ceik
bandage (N, tV): paŋsəmaŋ
bank: baŋ, baŋ, thəniəkiə; the National
     Bank: thəniəkiə-ciət
bark (of tree): sambaaq, srataap
bathe (iV): ŋuut, ŋuut-tɨk
bathroom: bantup-tɨk
Battambang (Province, Town): batdambɔɑŋ
battle, war: cambaŋ
be: ciə, kɨɨ
be promoted: laəŋ tnaq
bean: sandaek
beard, mustache: puk-moət
beat (tV): baok, way
beauty, embellishment: lumqɑɑ

because: piprueəh, prueəh; since, because:
     daoy; because of the fact that: daoy,
     daoy saa, haet tae
bed: krɛɛ
bedroom: bantup-keeŋ
beef: sac-koo
beer: byeə
before (Prep): mun; in front of: muk;
     in former times: kaal-mun
beggar: kamsat, smoum
begin (to): cap, pdaəm, cap-pdaəm
behave, act, follow: praprɨt
being, as follows: kɨɨ
believe: cɨə; belief: cumnɨə
beside: kbae
besides, outside of: kraw pii
betray, deceive: kbat
better, improved: krɔən-baə
between: knoŋ canlah (of space);
     knoŋ rɔwiəŋ (of time)
bicycle: kaŋ
birth: kamnaət
bite (tV): kham; bite each other:
     prakham
black: (pɔə) kmaw
blackboard: kdaa-khiən
bland, unseasoned: saap
blood: chiəm
bloom (iV): riik
blow (of wind, air): baq; (a horn): suflei
blue: (pɔə) khiəw; dark blue: khiəw-cah
board: kdaa; low platform or table used
     for sitting, sleeping and eating:
     kdaa-ŋiə
boat: tuuk; motor-boat: kanout; ship,
     steamer: kəpal; boats, rivercraft:
     tuuk-kəpal
body, self: kluən
boil: puh, sŋao; boiled soup: sŋao;
     prawn soup: sŋao-baŋkaaŋ
Bokor (a mountain resort in Kampot
     Province): bokkoo
book: siəwphɨw; specifier for books,
     volumes, or tablets: kbaal
Boppha (common name for girls): bopphaa
border, territorial limit: prum-daen
borrow: kcəy
both: teəŋ-pii; (lit): twii
bottle: dɑɑp
Bouth (personal name): but
box (large): həp; (small): praqap
boy: proh, kmeiŋ-proh; boys: kmeiŋ-
     proh-proh
boys and girls: kmeiŋ-proh-srəy
brave: hiən
bread: numpaŋ
break (shatter): baek; (in two): baq; have
     a fractured skull: baek kbaal; have a

blowout: baek kaŋ; have a broken leg:
   baq cəəŋ; cause to break or shatter:
   bambaek
breakfast (N): baay prɨk
bridge: spiən
bright: plɨɨ; (in color): kcəy
bring: yɔɔk (sthg.) mɔɔk
broken, damaged, spoiled: khouc
broom: qambaoh
brothers and sisters (older and younger
   siblings): baaŋ-pqoun; (full siblings):
   baaŋ-pqoun-baŋkaət
brown (chocolate): (pɔə) sukkholaa
brush (tV): doh; (N): craah; toothbrush:
   craah-doh-tmɨñ
Buddha: put, preəh, preəh-put
Buddhism: puttəsahsnaa, preəh-
   puttəsahsnaa
Buddhist; follower of Buddhism:
   neə̆q-kan-preəh-puttəsahsnaa
build: saŋ, kaa-saaŋ
building, house: qakiə
bunch, hand (of bananas): snət; per
   bunch: məsnət
burn, be on fire: cheh
bus, hired car: laan-cnuəl
business, commercial firm: krom-hun
busy, preoccupied: rɔwuəl
but: tae, pontae
by: taam, daoy; by air: taam kəpal-hah;
   by sea: taam kəpal-tɨk; in the
   provinces: taam khaet
by the way (Idiom): niyiəy qəñcəŋ

c

cabinet, cupboard: tuu; cabinet (of
   ministers) kənaq-roə̆t-muə̆ntrəy
call, invite: haw; is called: haw thaa
Cambodia: kampucciə; prateeh-
   kampucciə, srok-kmae;
   Cambodian (A, N): kmae; Cambodian
   language: phiəsaa-kmae
camera: maasɨn-thaat-ruup
can (mV): V + baan; V + kaət; V + ruəc
can lead to: qaac bandaal qaoy
car, cart: rɔteh; ox-cart: rɔteh-koo;
   train: rɔteh-pləəŋ
cardamom: krawaañ
Cardamom Mountains: pnum-krawaañ
cards (game): biə
careful, take care: prayat
cargo, load: bantuk
carpenter: ciəŋ-chəə
carry (haul): dək; transport: dək-noə̆m;
   carry toward: yɔɔk mɔɔk; carry
   away: yɔɔk tɨw; carry suspended
   from both ends of a shoulder-pole:
   rɛɛk

carve: claq; carving, sculpture: camlaq
cash (a check, etc.): baək
cat: cmaa
catch (tV): cap
cause (tV): qaoy, pkaət, baŋkaət; cause,
   lead to: bandaal qaoy + V
cause to swallow: rumleep
cement: siimaŋ
century: sattəwoə̆t; first century:
   sattəwoə̆t tii-muəy; sixth century:
   sattəwoə̆t tii-prammuəy
certificate: saññaabat
chair: kawqəy
chalk: dəy-saa
chamber, house, assembly: saphiə
Chamcar Mon (a district of Phnom Penh):
   camkaa-mɔɔn
change, replace: plah
cheap, inexpensive: thaok; to cheapen
   oneself: thaok kluən
check: šaek
chemistry: kiimii
Chenla: cənlaa; Chenla Period: samay
   cənlaa
chicken: moə̆n; chicken (meat): sac-moə̆n;
   chicken soup: sŋao-moə̆n; chicken
   salad: ñoə̆m-moə̆n
chief, head: pramuk
child, offspring: koun; children: koun-
   kmeiŋ
China: cən, srək-cən, prateeh-cən;
   Chinese (A, N): cən
Chinese noodles: kuy-tiəw
cholera: qasannərook
Chong (a hill tribe): cɔɔŋ
choose: rəəh, crəəh; select: crəəh-rəəh;
   appoint: crəəh-rəəh taŋ; elect: bah
   cnaot crəəh-rəəh
chop, hack: kap
Christian Era: krɨhsaqkəraac
Christianity: krɨhsahsnaa
cigarette: barəy; cigarette factory:
   rooŋ-twəə-barəy
cinema, movie-theatre: rooŋ-kon; the
   Eden Theatre: rooŋ-qeidaen; the
   Cinelux Theatre: rooŋ-siineluc
circle (N): wuə̆ŋ
Citroën (make of auto): siitroqaen
city: krɔŋ, tii-krɔŋ
civil service: riəcckaa, kaa-riəcckaa
clap the hands: teə̆h-day
clean (A): sqaat; (tV) samqaat, baoh-
   samqaat
clear (distinct): cbah; clear (transparent):
   sralah; (of water): tlaa
clerk: smiən
clever, skilled (at): pukae, prasap, stoə̆t
climb, ascend: laəŋ

cloth (single): kansaeŋ; towel:
    kansaeŋ-cuut-kluən; handkerchief:
    kansaeŋ-day; yard goods: kranat,
    sampuət
clothing: khao-qaaw; clothing worn above
    the waist or on the feet: bampeǝq;
    clothing worn below the waist:
    samliǝq; (lit): samliǝq-bampeǝq
close (tV): bǝt
coal, charcoal: tyuuŋ, kyuuŋ
coat, shirt: qaaw; raincoat: qaaw-pliǝŋ
coconut: douŋ; coconut-tree: daǝm-douŋ
coffee: kafei
cold, chilly: rɔŋiǝ
cold (disease), have a cold: pdahsaay
collide (with): bok
color: pɔǝ, sambao
comb (tV): sǝt; (N): krah-sǝt-saq
come: mɔɔk; come on and . . . : mɔɔk + V
comfortable, pleasant: sruǝl
combine, assemble (tV): ruǝp-ruǝm
commerce: cumnuǝñ
commit adultery, steal another's wife:
    luǝc prapuǝn kee
commune, administrative division: khum;
    commune chief: mee-khum
compare (tV): pradouc
compete (in an exam): pralaaŋ
complete (A): krup-kroǝn, piñ, baaribou,
    qah; completely: krup-sap (haǝy),
    qah (haǝy); complete, get to the end:
    V + cap
compose, write: taeŋ; write a composition:
    taeŋ sǝc-kdǝy
concentrated, strong: cah
concept, faith, principle: latthiq;
    religious belief: latthiq sahsnaa
concerned (with): teǝq-tɔɔŋ (niŋ)
confidence: sǝc-kdǝy-tuk-cǝt
confused (in mind): lap; (of things):
    teeŋ-taaŋ
constitution: rɔǝtthaqthoǝmmǝnuñ;
    constitutional monarchy:
    riǝciǝthippǝtay dael miǝn
    rɔǝtthaqthoǝmmǝnuñ
continent: twiip; the continent of Europe:
    twiip-qǝirop
continually, always: ciǝ-nic
continue (iV): taa; (tV): bantaa; continuing
    on: taa tiw tiǝt
continuously: ciǝ daraap
cook (tV): dam; cook soup: sŋao; cook
    stew, make a stew: slaa; boil: puh;
    cook (N): neǝq-twǝǝ-mhoup, coŋphiw
cool, refreshing: traceǝq, lhaǝy
coolie: kulii
cooperate (at), do together: noǝm kniǝ + V
copper: spoǝn

cops and robbers: qaakiñ-qaacao
copy (tV, N): camlaaŋ
corn (maize): poot
corner: cruŋ
correct (A): trǝw; that's right: trǝw haǝy,
    niŋ haǝy; correct, revise, improve
    (tV): kae
cotton: kapbaah, krabaah; cotton cloth:
    qambah
cough (iV): kqaaq
Council of the Kingdom: krom-priksaa-
    preǝh-riǝc-qanaacaq
country: srok, prateeh; the country-side,
    rural areas: srok-srae; foreign
    countries: prateeh-kraw
cousin (first): cii-doun-muǝy; second
    cousin: cii-tuǝt-muǝy; third cousin:
    cii-luǝt-muǝy
cow, ox: koo
create, cause: pkaǝt, baŋkaǝt
crematorium: pacchaa
crooked, twisted: wiǝc; zig-zagging,
    tortuous: kraŋeik-kraŋaq
cross (tV): claaŋ; across: V + claaŋ + N
crouch, take shelter: crɔɔk
crumble in the fingers: trabaac
cry, wail (iV): yum
cubit: hat
cucumber: trasaq
custard: saŋkyaa
customs, culture: prapiynii, tumloǝp,
    tumniǝn-tumloǝp, cbap, cbap-tuǝnloǝp
cut (tV): kat; chop, hack: kap; cut into
    little pieces: cañcram; cut open:
    weǝh; operate: weǝh-kat

d

dance (tV): roǝm; (N): rɔbam; stylized
    dancing: roǝm-kbac
Dang Raek Mountains: pnum-daaŋ-rɛɛk
dare (to): hiǝn
daughter: koun-srǝy
dawn: qarun, prɔlim; at dawn, early:
    pii prɔlim
day: tŋay; today: tŋay-nih, tŋay-niŋ
death: sǝc-kdǝy-slap
December: (khae-)tnuu
decide: kit, samrac, samrac-cǝt
decree (N, tV): kamrǝt
deep: criw
degree (of temperature): qaŋsaa
democracy: praciǝthippǝtay
dentist: pɛɛt-tmiñ
department, function, duty: krasuǝŋ;
    Department of Interior: krasuǝŋ-
    mǝhaa-ptiy; Department of Tourism:
    krasuǝŋ-teehsǝcaa; Department of
    Justice: krasuǝŋ-yuttǝthɔǝ

depends on: srac-tae
depth: cumrɨw
descend, go down, lower: coh
design (N): kbac
dessert, sweets: baŋqaem
destitute, sad: kamsat
dharma, moral law: thɔə; the Five Rules:
    thɔə pram
diamond, precious stone: pɨc
die (iV): slap; dying: kaa-slap
different: plaek, camlaek; different from
    each other: khoh kniə
difficult: pibaaq, yap
dig (tV): ciik, kaay
dim, dark: qap
diminutive or derogatory prefix: qaa-;
    little Bouth: qaa-but; you thief!:
    qaa-caol; you (derogatory): qaa-qaeŋ
dining room: bantup-ñam-baay
dip up, draw up: daaŋ
diploma (secondary): diiploum
dipper: tralaok; water-dipper:
    tralaok-daaŋ-tɨk
direction: khaaŋ; (lit): tɨh; northern
    direction: khaaŋ-cəəŋ; (lit):
    tɨh-qotdaa
directly: cpuəh; at once, in one operation:
    tae-mədaaŋ
director, manager: caaŋ-waaŋ
dirty: krakwaq
disease: rook, cumŋɨɨ; contagious
    disease: rook-claaŋ
disease prevention: withii-baŋkaa-rook
dish: caaŋ; variety of food: muk
disappear: bat
distance: camŋaay
distillery: rooŋ-twəə-sraa
district: srok
ditch, small canal: pralaay
dive, go under: muc
divide (iV): baek-caek; (tV): caek
division, sector: saŋkat
dizzy: wɨl muk
do: twəə; do numbers, arithmetic:
    twəə-leik; do good deeds: twəə-bon
do without, be without: qat
doctor: pɛɛt, kruu-pɛɛt
dog: ckae
don't: kom + V; kom + V + qəy
don't mention it, it's nothing, you're
    welcome: mɨn-qəy-tee
door, opening: twiə
dozen: lou; one dozen, per dozen:
    məlou
drama, play: lkhaon
drawer: thaat-tuu
dress (tV): sliəq-peăq, riəp-cam kluən,
    twəə kluən

dried and salted: ŋiət; dried and salted
    fish: trəy-ŋiət
drink (tV): phək
drive (a car, etc.): baək; (a nail): bah
drown, strangle: luəŋ-tɨk
drunk: srawəŋ
dry (clothing): sŋuət; (weather, season):
    praŋ; (lake or river): riiŋ
duck: tiə; duck-egg: pɔɔŋ-tiə
dull, worn: rɨl
duration, fixed period, agreement:
    kamnat
durian: thuureen
during: (knoŋ) rɔwiəŋ
duty, function: ŋiə; responsibility:
    phiəreăq
dysentery: (cumŋɨɨ-)muəl

e

each: nimuəy; one by one, the various:
    nimuəy-nimuəy
ear: traciəq
earn a living: rɔɔk-sii, cəñcəm ciiwɨt;
    earning a living: kaa-rɔɔk-sii
east: kaət, khaaŋ-kaət; (lit): tɨh-bou
easy: sruəl, ŋiəy; make easy: samruəl
eat (familiar): ñam; (formal): pisaa;
    (referring to oneself, polite):
    tɔtuəl-tiən; (lit): baariphook; (of
    animals, or condescending): sii;
    (rural): houp; (of clergy): chan;
    (of royalty): saoy
edge, bank: moăt; riverbank: moăt-
    tuănlee; seashore: moăt-səmot
education: səksaa, kaa-səksaa; primary
    education: pathamməsəksaa;
    secondary education: mattyum-
    səksaa
egg: pɔɔŋ; chicken-egg: pɔɔŋ-moăn;
    duck-egg: pɔɔŋ-tiə
eight: prambəy
eight ten-thousands: prambəy-məɨn
eighty: paetsəp
eldest child: riəm
elect: bah cnaot crəəh-rəəh
electricity: qaqkiisənii, pləəŋ; generating
    plant: rooŋ-qaqkiisənii
elephant: damrəy
eleven: dap-muəy
emphatic final particle: nah!, nəh!, wəəy!
end, point: coŋ
endure, withstand: thuăn, qat-thuăn
engineering: wiqswaakaa
English: qaŋglee; England: srok-qaŋglee,
    prateeh-qaŋglee; English language:
    phiəsaa-qaŋglee
enough (to): lmɔɔm + V; reasonable,

rather: V + lmɔɔm; adequate, sufficient:
    krup-krŏən
enter: coul; enter school, begin studies:
    coul riən
enter the monkhood: buəh; become a
    monk: buəh ciə look-saŋ
envelope (N): sraom; (of a letter):
    sraom-sambot
era: samay, cŏən, saqkəraac
erase, rub out: lup; eraser: cɔə-lup
essay: səc-kdəy
establish, set up: taŋ, pdaəm, pkaət,
    prakaət, baŋkaət
euphonic, pleasing to hear: piruəh
Europe: qəɨrop, twiip-qəɨrop
ever, to have ever (done sthg.): dael + V,
    tlŏəp + V
every (in succession): rŏəl, sap; every
    last one of: krup, sap-krup; every
    day: rŏəl tŋay
except (for): ləək-lɛɛŋ-tae
excuse me, I'm sorry: soum-tooh,
    qah-tooh
exhausted, used up: qah; tired, exhausted:
    qah-kamlaŋ; out of cigarettes: qah
    barəy; time-consuming: qah
    peel-weeliə
expel, send out: bañcəñ
expensive: tlay
explain: puənyuəl, qathibaay
explanation: qathaathibaay
export (tV): bañcuun tɨw luəq nɨw
    baarəteeh
expose, spread out: haal; spread out in
    the sun: haal tŋay
extension: damnɑɑ
extinguish (tV): luət
extinguished (A), go out (iV): rɔluət
extract, uproot: daɑq (cəñ)
extremely: peek, kray-peek

f

face: muk
factory: rooŋ, rooŋ-caq; weaving mill:
    rooŋ-dambaañ; automobile assembly
    plant: rooŋ-damlaəŋ-laan; rice-
    mill: rooŋ-kən-srəw
fail to, lack: khaan + V; without fail,
    surely: V + mɨn khaan; fail an
    exam: pralaɑŋ tleəq
fall (iV): tleəq; fell, overthrow: tumleəq
fall asleep: (deik, keeŋ) luəq
fame, renown: lbəy-cmuəh, kei-cmuəh
family: kruəsaa
far, distant: cŋaay
farmer, peasant: neəq-srae
farming: kaa-twəə-srae
fast: liən, liən-liən, chap, chap-chap,
    ñoəp, rɔhah

father: qəwpuk, paa, qəw
father-in-law: qəwpuk-kmeik
fear, be afraid of: klaac, kraeŋ, klaac-
    kraeŋ
fearless: qaqphɨy
feathered projectile: səy
February: (khae-)kumpheəq
feel well: sruəl kluən
female: srəy; (of animals): ñii
fence, hedge: rɔbaaŋ
fertilizer: cii
few: təc
fiber: samləy
field, plain: wiəl
fifteen: dap-pram, pram-dandap
fifth: haasəp
film, movie: kon
filter (tV): traaŋ; (N): damraaŋ,
    kantraaŋ
finalize: V + srac
find: rɔɔk baan, rɔɔk khəəñ; unable to
    find: rɔɔk mɨn baan, rɔɔk mɨn
    khəəñ
finger: mriəm, mriəm-day
finish, complete: bañcap; V + cap
fire, light: pləəŋ
first (original): daəm, dambouŋ;
    (ordinal numeral): tii-muəy;
    (before): mun; (hortatory particle):
    sən; first of all: mun dambouŋ, mun
    baŋqah; at first: kaal-mun; in the
    beginning, originally: kaal pii daəm
fish (tV) with a line: stuuc; (lit): neesaat
fish (N): trəy; smoked fish: trəy-cqaə;
    dried salted fish: trəy-ŋiət; salt-
    water fish: trəy-tɨk-pray; fresh-
    water fish: trəy-tɨk-saap
fish paste: prahok
fish-sauce: tɨk-trəy
fishing: kaa-nesaat-trəy
five: pram
flap (the wings): tɔteəh
float (tV): bandaet
flood (N): cumnuən
floor, level, story: cŏən
flow (iV): hou; cause to flow: baŋhou
flower: pkaa; flower plant, shrub:
    daəm-pkaa
fold (tV): bat
follow: taam; following, according to:
    taam
food: mhoup, mhoup-mhaa, qahaa,
    mhoup-camnəy; priest's food:
    caŋhən; royal food: preəh-sŋaoy
foot, leg: cəəŋ
for (the purpose of): samrap; in order to:
    daəmbəy (nɨŋ); on behalf of (informal):
    V + qaoy; (formal): V + cuun
foreign affairs: kaa-baarəteeh
foreign countries: prateeh-kraw, baarəteeh

forest: prɨy
forget: plɨc
forgive, excuse: qaqphɨy-tooh, qat-tooh
fork (N): sɑɑm
four: buən
fragrant: krɑqoup
France: prɑteeh-barɑŋ, srok-barɑŋ,
  prɑteeh-baraŋsaeh
free (vacant): tumnee; free of charge:
  qət tlay, tɔtee; free (of), clear (of):
  phot (pii)
French (A): baarɑŋ; Frenchman:
  baarɑŋ, mənuh-barɑŋ
frequently: quhsaa (+ V); ñɨk-ñoəp
Friday: tŋay-sok
fried meat and vegetable dish: chaa
friend: puəq-maaq, mɨt
friendship: meetrəy-phiəp
from: pii; from one to another: pii
  muəy tɨw muəy
front, face: muk; in front: khaaŋ-muk
frozen, congealed: kɑɑq
fruit: plae-chəə; fruit tree: chəə-plae
fry, braise: liiŋ, chaa
full: pɨñ; fully (Prep): pɨñ + N; a full
  day, all day: pɨñ mətŋay; the whole
  body, all over the body: pɨñ teəŋ
  kluən; full (satisfied): cqaet
Funan: fuunɑɑn; Funan Period: samay
  fuunɑɑn
funny: kamplaeŋ
furniture: krɨəŋ-tok-tuu; furniture
  salesman: neəq-luəq-krɨəŋ-tok-tuu
further: tiət; tɑɑ-tɨw-tiət

g

game: lbaeŋ
garden: suən; ornamental garden, park:
  suən-cbaa; flower garden: suən-pkaa;
  plantation (other than wet rice):
  camkaa
gasoline: saŋ
gay, boisterous: qɨkkəthɨk
generating plant: rooŋ-qaqkiisənii
gentle, well-mannered: slout, riəpsaa,
  sophiəp-riəpsaa, trəm-trəw
geography: phuumisaah
German: qaaləmɑŋ; Germany: qaaləmɑŋ;
  srok-qaaləmɑŋ; prɑteeh-qaaləmɑŋ
get (tV): baan
gift: qamnaoy, tiən
give (informal): qaoy; (formal): cuun;
  give alms: daq-tiən; contribute (to a
  ceremony): coul bon; present (lit,
  royal): twaay
give birth to, be born: kaət
glass, cup: kaew

glasses (optical): waen-taa
go: tɨw; go ahead and: V + tɨw, V + coh,
  V + nəh; go and come: tɨw mɔɔk; (if
  one) goes anywhere: tɨw naa mɔɔk
  naa
gold: miəh; (color): pɔə-miəh
good: lqɑɑ, lqɑɑ-lqɑɑ; morally good:
  trəm-trəw
good-by: soum liə sən
goodness, beauty: səc-kdəy-lqɑɑ
government: roətthaaphibaal
government service: kaa-riəccəkaa
grade, level: tnaq; final grade: tnaq cɔŋ
  bamphot; 1st grade, secondary (12th
  year): tnaq tii-muəy tumnəəp; 2nd
  grade, secondary (11th year): tnaq
  tii-pii tumnəəp; 3rd grade, secondary
  (10th year): tnaq tii-bəy tumnəəp;
  6th grade, secondary (7th year): tnaq
  tii-prammuəy tumnəəp; 7th grade (6th
  year): tnaq tii-prampɨl; 12th grade
  (1st year): tnaq tii-dɑp-pii
grain, pill: kroəp
gram: kraam
grandchild: caw; great-grandchild:
  caw-tuət; great-great-grandchild:
  caw-luət; great-great-great-grand-
  child: caw-liə
grandfather: taa, look-taa; great-grand-
  father: taa-tuət; great-great-grand-
  father: taa-luət; great-great-great-
  grandfather: taa-liə
grandmother: doun, yiəy, look-yiəy; great-
  grandmother: yiəy-tuət; great-great-
  grandmother: yiəy-luət; great-great-
  great-grandmother: yiəy-liə
grandson: caw-proh
granddaughter: caw-srəy
grape: trapeəŋ-baay-cuu
grass, hay: smaw
grateful: dəŋ-kun; gratitude: səc-kdəy-
  dəŋ-kun
grease (N): klañ
green: (pɔə) baytɑɑn; light green: (pɔə)
  baytɑɑn-kcəy; (pɔə) khiəw
greet, Greetings!: cumriəp-suə; (formal
  or urban): suəsdəy
greet with palms joined: sampeəh,
  sampeəh-suə, baŋkum; greet respectfully with palms joined: twaay-
  baŋkum
grey: (pɔə) prapheh
ground, earth: dəy
group, council: krom; kənaq
grow, come up (iV): doh; (tV): bandoh
guest: pñiəw
gulf, bay: chuuŋ; Gulf of Thailand:
  chuuŋ-səmot-siəm

h

hair: sɑq; get a haircut: kat-sɑq;
    hair oil: preiŋ-liəp-sɑq
half: kɑnlah; peəq-kandaal; (of a sphere):
    cɑmhiəŋ
hall, pavilion: salaa
hammer (N): ñəñuə, qañuə
hammock: qɑŋriŋ
hand (N): day; (tV): hoc
handicraft, fine arts: raccɑnaa
handle (N): daɑŋ; carrying pole: daɑŋ-
    rɛɛk
happen, arise, develop: kaət, kaət laəŋ
happy: sapbaay, sapbaay-cət, treik-qaa;
    happy (well): sok, sok-sapbaay;
    happiness: sɑc-kdəy-sapbaay,
    sɑc-kdəy-treik-qaa
hardly: mɨn-səw + V, mɨn . . . ponmaan
harvest (tV): crout; (N): phɑl, phɑl-
    dɑmnam
have: miən; to have done sthg. (perfect
    auxiliary): baan + V
have a fever: krun; have malaria:
    krun-cañ
have a meal (literally: eat rice): ñam
    baay
have a pain, cramp: cok; have stomach
    pains: cok puəh; have a pain in the
    hand or arm: cok day
have a wedding, get married: riəp-kaa
hall, building, factory: rooŋ
have the goodness to: meettaa + V,
    kaqrunaa + V
have the power to, can: qaac + V; can
    lead to: qaac bɑndaal qaoy
have to: trəw + V, miən-tae + V
Hawaii Hotel: sɑnthəkiə-haaway
he, she, they (polite): koət, kee;
    (condescending): wiə;
    (indefinite): kee
head: kbaal
hear: lɨɨ, sdap lɨɨ; unable to hear:
    sdap mɨn lɨɨ
heart, mind, disposition: cət
heat: kɑmdaw
heaven, Nirvana: thaan-suə
heavy: tŋuən
Hello (formal): cumriəp-suə; (informal):
    məc, tɨw naa nɨŋ?; (lit, urban):
    suəsdəy; (telephone): qaloo
help (to): cuəy; please, help by . . . :
    cuəy; help out in time of trouble:
    cuəy thureəq
here: nih, qae-nih
heritage, honor: kei
hero (of a play): tuə-qaek-proh;
    heroine: tuə-qaek-srəy; principal
    character: tuə-qaek
hey!: qei!

hide (tV): baŋ
high: kpuəh
history: prɑwoəttəsaah
hit: way; come in contact with, hit: trəw
hold: kan; believe, maintain: kan; hold
    in the mouth: biəm
hole: ruuŋ
honor, respect (tV): koorup
hope, intention: bɑmnaaŋ
horn (auto): suflei
hot: kdaw; feel hot: kdaw kluən; inter-
    mittently hot and cold, have chills:
    kdaw-rəŋiə; heat: kɑmdaw
hotel: pteəh-sɑmnaq, hotael; (lit):
    sɑnthəkiə
hour: maoŋ; three hours: bəy maoŋ;
    three o'clock: maoŋ bəy; what time
    is it?: maoŋ ponmaan haəy?
house, shop: pteəh; house and property:
    pteəh-sɑmbaeŋ; hotel: pteəh-sɑmnaq
how? (intAdv): məc?, yaaŋ-məc?; how
    about it, how's it going?: məc +
    phrase
how much, how many (intA, intPr):
    ponmaan?
however much, however many, to whatever
    extent: ponmaan . . . kɑ-daoy,
    ponmaan . . . bɑ-baan
hundred: rɔɔy; one hundred: muəy-rɔɔy,
    mɑrɔɔy
hundred-thousand: saen; one hundred-
    thousand: muəy-saen, məsaen
hungry, hunger (for): kliən
hurry (to): prañap (+ Verb)
husband (N): pdəy; (lit): swaaməy;
    (wife to husband): baaŋ

i

I (context-oriented; see sections 20, B, 1
    and 27, B, 1)
ice, ice-water: tɨk-kɑɑq
ice-cream: kareim
if: baə, kaal-baə, baə-kaal-naa
ill, sick: chɨɨ; have a headache: chɨɨ
    kbaal
illness, disease: cumŋɨɨ
immediately: pliəm
import (tV): tɨñ pii baarəteeh
important: sɑmkhan, thom-dom
in, inside: knoŋ
in abundance: ciə craən
in front of: muk; the front, in front of:
    khaaŋ-muk
in order to: daəmbəy(-nɨŋ)
in that case: baə douccnah, baə qɑñcəŋ
in the matter of: khaaŋ
in the process of: kɑmpuŋ(-tae) + V
including: teəŋ, prɔɔm-teəŋ
increasingly: rɨt-tae, kan-tae + V; V + laəŋ

independent: qaekkəriəc; independence:
    qaekkəriəc; national independence:
    qaekkəriəc-ciət
India: prateeh-qəndiə; Indian (A): qəndiə,
    kləŋ; (N): mənuh-qəndiə, kləŋ
Indochina: qəndoucən; French Indochina:
    qəndoucən baraŋsaeh
industry: quhsaahaqkam
industrious: quhsaa
inflate, pump air into: sap; a pump: snap
information: damnəŋ
inject: caq
injustice: qaqyuttəthɔə
ink: tɨk-kmaw
inner-tube: puəh-wiən
insert (tV): caq, siət; (N): sniət
instrument: kriəŋ, pradap; instruments:
    pradap-pradaa
intend (to): kɨt, paaŋ
interested (in), attracted (by): cap cət
interior (department): məhaa-ptɨy;
    Department of Interior: krasuəŋ-
    məhaa-ptɨy
interjection of surprise or mild
    annoyance: yii!
intersection: pləw-baek
interval, duration: rɔwiəŋ
intervening space: canlah
invite: qañcəəñ, haw
iron, steel: daek
irrigate (the rice-field): baŋhou tɨk
    coul srae
is: ciə; equals: kɨɨ
is possible, does happen: V + kaa-miən
island: kah
Islam: qihslaam ~ qehslaam
it: wiə
Italy: qiitalii, prateeh-qiitalii

j

jack, lift (N): kriip ~ krɨp
January: (khae-)meəqkəraa
Japan: yipun, srok-yipun, prateeh-yipun;
    Japanese (A, N): yipun
Jayavarman: cɨyyeəqwaarəman;
    Jayavarman II: cɨyyeəqwaarəman
    tii-pii; Jayavarman VII:
    cɨyyeəqwaarəman tii-prampɨl
jewelry: miəh-pɨc, kriəŋ-raccənaa
July: (khae-)kaqkədaa
June: (khae-)mithonaa
junior high school: qanuq-wɨttyiəlay
just, only: krɔən-tae + V; (Prep): tae;
    (Adv): ponnoh; just here, right
    here: trəm nih
just now: təəp(-tae)-nɨŋ + V
justice: yuttəthɔə; injustice:
    qaqyuttəthɔə; Department of
    Justice: krasuəŋ-yuttəthɔə

k

kapok: kɔɔ
Kampong Cham (Town, Province):
    kampuəŋ-caam
Kampong-Chhnang (Town, Province):
    kampuəŋ-cnaŋ
Kampong-Speu (Town, Province):
    kampuəŋ-spɨɨ
Kampong Thom (Town, Province):
    kampuəŋ-thom
Kampot (Town, Province): kampɔɔt
Kandal (Province): kandaal
Kêp (a seaside resort in Kampot Province):
    kaep
kick (tV): toət; kicking a feathered projec-
    tile: toət-səy
kill: samlap
kilogram: kilou
kilometer: kiloumaet
kind, variety: yaaŋ, baep, muk
king: sdac, luəŋ, ksat; (lit): preəh-məhaa-
    ksat; (term of reference): preəh-
    kaqrunaa
king's title: preəh-baat; King Norodom
    Sihanouk: preəh-baat nɔrootdam
    siihanuq; King Monivong: preəh-
    baat mɔniiwuəŋ
kingdom: qanaacaq, preəh-riəc-qanaacaq;
    riəc, qaŋkɔɔ-riəc
kitchen: pteəh-baay
knee: (kbaal-)cuəŋkuəŋ
knife: kambət
know (be informed): dəŋ; be knowledgeable,
    educated: ceh; be acquainted with:
    skoəl; know how to: ceh + V
Koh Kong (Island, Province): kah koŋ
Kratie (Town, Province): kraceh
Kuoy, Kuy (a hill-tribe): kuəy

l

lake: bəŋ; lakes, rivers, and streams:
    bəŋ-prɛɛk-stɨŋ-tuənlee
land (under cultivation): srae-camkaa
language: phiəsaa
Lao: liəw; Laos: prateeh-liəw
large: thom; quite large, large and
    numerous: thom-thom; important,
    impressive: thom-dom
late (slow): yɨɨt; late in the morning:
    tŋay nah haəy
launder: baok-qut
law, custom: cbap
lawyer: meethiəwii
lazy: kcɨl, kamcɨl; too lazy to, dis-
    inclined to: kcɨl + V
Le Coq d'Or (name of a restaurant in
    Phnom Penh): ləə-kok-dɔə
lead (tV): noəm, cuun, dək-noəm

leader: neə̆q-dək-noə̆m, prɑmuk
leaf (N): slək; (of paper): sɑnlək; sugar-
     palm leaf: slək-tnaot
learn (study): riən; research: səksaa;
     learn (of): criəp, dəŋ
leather: sbaek
leave, exit: cəñ (pii)
left (side): cweiŋ; (on) the left:
     khaaŋ-cweiŋ; (on) the left-hand side:
     khaaŋ-cweiŋ-day
left over: sɑl; left-over food: mhoup-sɑl
legislation: kaa-twəə-cbap-tməy
legislative (N, A): niqtǝqpaññat
lend: kcəy
length: prɑwaeŋ
lesson: mee-riən
let's, go ahead and: cou + V
letter: sɑmbot; letter-box: prɑqap-
     sɑmbot
letter, writing: qawsɑɑ; letters,
     literature: qaqsɑɑsaah
library: pannaalay
lie, prevaricate: kohɑq
life: ciiwɨt; life, incarnation: ciət; living,
     existence: kaa-ruə̆h-nɨw
light (N): pləəŋ, puə̆nlɨɨ; light in weight:
     sraal; light in color: kcəy; light,
     ignite (tV): baŋkat, dot
like (to): coul-cət; (a person): srɑlañ
like, similar to: douc
liquid: tɨk; tea (liquid): tɨk-tae;
     milk: tɨk-dɑh-koo; ink: tɨk-kmaw
listen: sdap; able to hear, understand:
     sdap baan; unable to hear or under-
     stand: sdap mɨn baan tee
liter: liit
literature: qaqsɑɑsaah
live (be alive): ruə̆h; (reside): nɨw
living room, parlor: bɑntup-tɔtuəl-pñiəw
long (in time): yuu; for a long time now:
     ciə yuu nah mɔɔk haəy; long (in space):
     wɛɛŋ
lose (to), be defeated (by): cañ
loud (of noise): klaŋ; festive, gay:
     qɨkkəthɨk
love (tV): srɑlañ; (N): snae-haa
lubricate: caq preiŋ boum klañ
luggage, things: həp-qəywan; qəywan
lycée: wɨttyiələy, wɨcciəlay, lihsei;
     Lycée Sisowath: wɨttyiələy
     siisouwat
Lycée Descartes: lihsei dekaat

m

meat, flesh: sac; pork: sac-cruuk; beef:
     sac-koo; fish (meat): sac-trəy
meat salad: ñoə̆m; chicken salad:
     ñoə̆m-moə̆n

machine: maasiin, maasɨn
maintain, insist: prɑkan
make (tV): twəə; make, cause to: twəə
     qaoy; make merit, do good deeds:
     twəə-bon; make merit by giving alms:
     twəə-bon-daq-tiən
malaria: cumŋɨɨ-krun-cañ
male: proh; (of animals): cmoul
man: proh, mənuh-proh
mango: (plae-)swaay
mangosteen: muə̆ŋkhut
manners, deportment: dɑmboun-miən
many, much: craən; in abundance: ciə
     craən
map: phaen-tii
March: (khae-)minaa
marked up, disfigured: krɑweem-
     krɑwaam
market: psaa; the Ox-Slaughter Market:
     psaa-kap-koo; the Central Market:
     psaa-kɑndaal; Silep Market: psaa-
     silǝp
maroon (pig's blood): (pɔə) chiəm-cruuk
marry, get married: kaa
mat (woven): kanteel
match (N): chəə-kuh
math: mat
matter: səc-kdəy, rɨəŋ
May: (khae-)quhsəphiə
medicine: tnam; fever medicine:
     tnam-krun; medicine (as a science):
     wɨcciə-pɛɛt
medium, average, middle: mattyum
meet: cuəp; meet together, assemble:
     cuəp-cum; meet by accident:
     prɑteə̆h, cuəp-prɑteə̆h,
     prɑteə̆h-khəə̆ñ
Mekong River: tuə̆nlee-meekoŋ
member: samaaciq, samaacɨk
Meng (a personal name) meiŋ
merchandise: tumnɨñ
merchant, businessman: neə̆q-cumnuəñ,
     cumnuəñ, cmuəñ
merit, good deeds: bon
middle (N, A): kɑndaal; in the middle of:
     kɑndaal + N, peə̆q-kɑndaal + N
Middle Period: samay kɑndaal
milk: tɨk-dɑh-koo
mill (tV): kən; (pound): bok; mill (N):
     tbal; mortar and pestle: tbal-bok
million: liən
mine (possessive Pr): rəbɑh kñom
mine, well: qɑndouŋ; ore mine: qɑndouŋ-
     rae
minister: muə̆ntrəy, niəməɨn; ministers:
     niəməɨn-muə̆ntrəy
minute (N): niətii
miss (tV): tɨw mɨn toə̆n; khaan + V
mistakes: səc-kdəy-kuə-pum-kuə

modern: samay, tumnəəp; modern times:
  paccobən nih, samay paccobən
monarchy: riəciəthɨppətay;
  constitutional monarchy:
  riəciəthɨppətay dael miən
  roɜ̆tthaqthoɜ̆mmənuñ
Monday: tŋay-can
Mondulkiri (Province): muɜ̆nduɜ̆lkirii
money: luy, praq
Monivong: mɔniiwuɜ̆ŋ
monk, priest: look-saŋ, preɜ̆h-saŋ;
  specifier for priests and Buddhist
  images: qaŋ
monk's quarters: kot
Mororom Hotel: santhəkiə-mɔnoorum
month, moon: khae
monument, palace: praasaat
moon: khae; (lit): preɜ̆h-can
more: aV + ciəŋ; more . . . than:
  aV . . . cieŋ + N
morning: prɨk; this morning (past):
  prɨk-nih
mosquito: muuh
most, most of all (Adv): ciəŋ-kee,
  bamphot, baŋqah, tii-bamphot,
  ciə tii-bamphot
mostly, usually: craən(-tae) + V
mother: mdaay, neɜ̆q-mdaay, maq, mae
mother-in-law: mdaay-kmeik
motor: maasiin, maasɨn, krɨəŋ;
  motor-oil: preiŋ-masɨn
mount, ride: cih
mountain, hill: pnum
mouth, opening: moɜ̆t
move, carry: cuɜ̆ñcuun
Mr., Sir: look
Mrs., Madam: look-srəy
much, many: craən; in abundance: ciə
  craən
must: trəw, trəw-tae

n

name: cmuɜ̆h; be named: cmuɜ̆h
national, nationality: ciət
national assembly: roɜ̆t-səphiə
national defense: kaa-piə-prateeh
national museum: saareɜ̆qmuɜ̆ntii-ciət,
  salaa-raccənaa
near: cɨt; nearly: cɨt (nɨŋ) + V
neat: sqaat, trəm-trəw
neck, throat, collar: kaa
necktie: krawat
need (to): trəw-kaa
neighbor: neɜ̆q-cɨt-khaaŋ
nephew or niece: kmuəy
neutralism: qaqpyiəkrət; neutralist:
  qaqpyiəkrət; neutralist policy:
  nəyoobaay qaqpyiəkrət

never (to have done sthg): mɨn-dael
nevertheless: tuɜ̆h-yaaŋ-naa-ka-daoy;
  V + dae
new: tməy
newspaper: kasaet
next (Adv): bantoɜ̆p
night: yup, qatriət; at night: yup; last
  night: yup məň; in the middle of the
  night: peɜ̆q-kandaal qatriət
nightclub, bar: baa
nine: prambuən
ninety: kawsəp
non-human: qaqmənuh
noon, midday: tŋay-traŋ
Norodom Sihanouk: nɔrootdam siihanuq
north: cəəŋ, khaaŋ-cəəŋ; (lit): tɨh-qotdaa
northeast: khaaŋ-cəəŋ-cruŋ-khaaŋ-kaet;
  (lit): tɨh-qəysaan
northwest: khaaŋ-cəəŋ-cruŋ-khaaŋ-ləc;
  (lit): tɨh-piəyoɜ̆p
nose: cramoh
not (negative auxiliary): mɨn + V + tee,
  qət + V + tee, qat + V + tee; (lit):
  pum + V + tee
not at all: mɨn . . . sah (laəy)
not have, not exist: kmiən
not necessary: mɨn-bac-tee
not so very . . . : mɨn . . . ponmaan tee,
  mɨn-səw . . . tee
not yet: mɨn-toɜ̆n . . . tee
November: (khae-)wiccəkaa
now: qəyləw, qəyləw-nih; these days:
  sap tŋay nih; the present, modern
  times: paccobən, paccobən nih
number, figure: leik
nursery plot: tnaal

o

obscure, foggy: sraqap
observe: saŋkeit, saŋkeit-məəl,
  piinɨt-məəl; (lit): tuɜ̆hsəniə
ocean: məhaa-səmot
October: (khae-)tolaa
odor: klən
of: rəbah; (lit): nɨy
of course (+ V): thəy mɨn (+ V)!, miən
  qəy!
often, frequently: ñɨk-ñoɜ̆p; quhsaa + V
Oh!: qou!, qei!
oil (N): preiŋ
old: cah
older brother: baaŋ-proh
older sibling: baaŋ
older sibling-in-law: baaŋ-tlay
older sister: baaŋ-srəy
older sister-in-law: baaŋ-tlay-srəy
on: ləə, nɨw ləə; above, upper part:
  khaaŋ-ləə

on the part of, as for: camnaek
once, one time: mədaaŋ; once and for all:
    mədaaŋ
once in a while: yuu-yuu-mədaaŋ
one: muəy; (before a specifier): mə-;
    e.g.: məneәq, mədaaŋ
oneself: kluən-qaeŋ; alone, by oneself:
    tae mənеәq qaeŋ
onion, garlic: ktɨm
only: tae (Prep); ponnoh (Adv);
    krŏən-tae (Aux)
open (tV): baak; open the mouth: haa
operate (medical): weәh-kat
oppress: biət-biən
or: rɨɨ
orange, citrus fruit: krouc
orange (color): pɔə-slaa-tum
orchestra: wuəŋ-dantrəy
ordinalizing prefix: tii-; first: tii-muəy;
    second: tii-pii; how-many'th?:
    tii-ponmaan?
ore: rae; ore-mine: qandouŋ-rae
originally, formerly: kaal pii daəm
originate: pdaam, pkaət, prakaət,
    baŋkaət
other, different: qae-tiət; other,
    further: tiət, datiy tiət; another:
    muəy tiət
Oudong: qotdoŋ, qutdoŋ
ounce: damləŋ
outside (of): kraw (pii)
oversee, administer: krup-krɔɔŋ,
    piinɨt-məəl
overtake, pass: waa
overthrow: tumlẽәq

p

package, bundle: kañcap
paddy, unhusked rice: srəw; seed rice:
    srəw-puuc; floating rice: srəw-
    laəŋ-tɨk; dry (season) rice:
    srəw-praŋ; broadcast rice:
    srəw-pruĕh; transplanted rice:
    srəw-stuuŋ; wet (season) rice:
    srəw-wuĕhsaa
page (N): tumpɔə
paint, spread on: liəp
pair: kuu; pair off (tV): pkuu
palace: weәŋ, praasaat; royal palace:
    preәh-barommәriәccәweәŋ
pants, trousers: khao
papaya: lhoŋ
paper: kradaah
paralyzed (in the foot or leg): kwən cəəŋ;
    (in the hand or arm): kwən day
parents: qəwpuk-mdaay; qəw-mae
park (tV): caat

part, share, region: paek, pnaek,
    camnaek, phiəq, damban
party, group: kənaq, puəq
pass (an examination): pralaaŋ cŏəp
past, preceding: məñ; yesterday:
    msəl-məñ; last night: yup məñ;
    a while ago: qambañ-məñ
patch (tV): pah
patient, sick person: nеәq-cumŋɨɨ
peanut: sandaek-dəy
pear-like brown-skinned fruit: lmut
pedagogy: kuruq-wɨcciə
pen (for writing): slaap-paqkaa
pencil: kmaw-day
pepper (chili): mteeh; (black): mrɨc
percent: phiəq-rɔɔy
perch (iV): tum; (N): trɔnum
perhaps: prahael, prahael-ciə;
    məəl-tɨw
period (of time): weeliə, peel-weeliə;
    period (of history), era: samay,
    cŏən, kriə, saqkəraac
permission: cbap, qaqnuññaat,
    cbap-qaqnuññaat
permit (N): cbap, cbap-qaqnuññaat;
    (tV): qaqnuññaat (qaoy)
persistent, patient: ceh qat-thuĕn
person, human being: mɔnuh
Phân (personal name): phaan
pharmacy: faamǝsii
Phnom Penh: pnum-pɨñ; tii-kroŋ
    pnum-pɨñ
phosphate: fosfat
photograph (tV): thaat ruup; (N):
    ruup-thaat
pick, gather: beh
picnic: pɨcnɨc
piece, nugget, lump: dom
pier, dock: phae
pierce: caq, mut
pig: cruuk
pile (tV): kɔɔ; (N): kumnɔɔ
pineapple: mnŏəh
ping-pong: peeŋ-poŋ
pink: (pɔə) sii-cumpuu
pitiable, deserving of sympathy: kuə qaoy
    qaanət
pity (tV): qaanət, sdaay, saok; (N):
    sranaok
place: kanlaeŋ, tii; site, establishment:
    sthaan, thaan, tii-kanlaeŋ
plan (to): kɨt + V
plant (tV): dam; (N): daəm + N;
    damnam
plantation (other than wet rice): camkaa;
    rubber plantation: camkaa-kawsuu
plate (N): caan
plateau: dəy-kpuĕh

pleasant: sapbaay, sruəl

please: soum + V, meetaa + V;
   cou + V; please go ahead and . . . :
   qañcəəñ + V

pliers, pincers: daŋkap

plow (N): nuəŋkuəl, qaŋkuəl;
   (tV): pcuə, pyuə

plug, stop up: cok

Pnong; mountain tribes in general:
   pnɔɔŋ

point out, indicate: caŋqol;
   caŋqol-prap

police: poliih, damruət, kɨñ

policy: nəyoobaay

polite: riəpsaa, sophiəp-riəpsaa,
   trəm-trəw

pomegranate: tɔtɨm, kratɨm

poor (A): kraa; poor (at): kamraa + V

population, people: praciə, praciəcuən,
   praciəriəh, puəlləroət

pork: sac-cruuk

porridge: babaa

port, riverine town: kampuəŋ

possible: V + kaa-baan; either . . .
   or . . . is a possibility: kaa-baan. . .
   kaa-baan

postman: neəq-ruət-sambot

post-office: poh, prehsəniiyəthaan

pot, kettle: cnaŋ

potato: damlouŋ

pound, mill (tV): bok

powdered, fine: lqət

power, authority: qamnaac

practice (tV): hat; practice reading,
   reading (N): hat-qaan

prawn, river lobster: baŋkaaŋ

pray: ban

Preah-Bath Monivong Street: pləw
   preəh-baat mɔniiwuəŋ

Preah Chinawong (a Cambodian drama):
   preəh-cɨnnəwuəŋ

Preah-Vihear (Temple, Province):
   preəh-wihiə

precious stone: pɨc, tbouŋ

prepare: riəp, riəp-cam

pretty, beautiful: lqaa, lqaa-lqaa;
   pretty to see, interesting:
   lqaa-məəl

prevent: baŋkaa

Prey Veng (Town, Province): prɨy-wɛɛŋ

price, cost: tlay; value: damlay

primary, first: patham

primary education: pathamməsəksaa

prime minister: niəyuəq-roət-muəntrəy

Prince Sihanouk: samdac siihanuq

probably; likely to: muk-tae

problem: pañhaa, thureəq

product: phal, phallɨttəphal

professor: sahstraacaa

pronounce, read aloud: qaan

proper: sam, kuə, kuə-sam, trəm-trəw,
   sophiəp-riəpsaa

prosper: camraan

protect, defend: kaa-piə

protectorate, protectorship:
   qanaapyiəbaal

provided that, so long as one doesn't:
   kom-qaoy-tae

province: khaet

publicity, information: khoosnaakaa

pull (tV): tiəñ; drag: qouh; uproot:
   daaq; pull off: bout

pump (tV): boum

punch, depress: coc

purple: (pɔə) swaay

purpose, usefulness: prayaoc

Pursat (Town, Province): poosat

put, place, deposit: daq

q

quality, merit: kun

quantity, totality: camnuən

queen: (mɔhaa-)ksattrəyaanii

question (tV): suə, saaq-suə;
   (N): samnuə

question particle (after yes-or-no
   questions): tee?; (after questions
   involving two or more alternatives):
   rɨɨ?; yet?: haəy-rɨɨ-nɨw?; (lit):
   rɨɨ-tee?; (after negative questions):
   tee rɨɨ?

quick: chap; quickly: qaoy chap, qaoy
   chap-chap, ñoəp, rɔhah, qaoy rɔhah;
   quick to, prone to: chap + V

quiet: sŋat, sŋiəm

quit: chup; (of rain): reəŋ

r

race, compete: pranaŋ

race, nationality: saah, sah

Radé (a hill tribe): rədae

railway: pləw-rɔteh-pləəŋ

rain (iV): pliəŋ; (N): pliəŋ

raise, lift up: ləək

rake (tV): roəh; (N): rɔnoəh

rank, grade: tnaq, saq

Ratanakiri (Province): roəttənaqkirii

read (tV): məəl

realize: nɨk khəəñ, kɨt khəəñ

really, truly: mɛɛn-tɛɛn, ciə praakat

realm, kingdom: qanaacaq

Ream-Kerti (Cambodian version of the
   Ramayana): riəm-kei

reason, cause: haet, saa; this is the reason
   that, this is why: haet nih haəy baan ciə

reasonable, moderate: kuə-sam;
   V + lmɔɔm
receipt: prakan-day
receive: tɔtuəl; receive food, eat:
   tɔtuəl-tiən
receiving guests: kaa-tɔtuəl-pñiəw
reciprocally: tɨw wiñ tɨw mɔɔk
red: (pɔə) krahaam
register (a letter, etc.): rɨkkəmandei;
   registered: rɨkkəmandei
regulate, govern: krɔɔŋ, krup-krɔɔŋ
regulation, law: krət, kamrət
reign (tV): saoy-riəc; (N): riəc
related (to): teəq-tɔɔŋ (nɨŋ)
relative (N): ñiət; relatives, family:
   ñiət-sandaan
religion: sahsnaa
rely (on): tuk-cət (ləə)
remain, be left over: sal
remember: cam
rent, hire (tV): cuəl; (N): cnuəl
repair: cuəh-cul; revise, improve: kae
repay, compensate: saaŋ
representative: damnaaŋ; representative
   of the people: damnaaŋ-riəh
request, ask for: som
resist, endure: qat, qat-thuən
respect (tV): koorup; (N): səc-kdəy-
   koorup; respected one: tii-koorup
response particle (polite, masc.): baat;
   (polite, fem.): caah; (familiar,
   either sex): qaə, qɨɨ
rest (tV): samraaq, samraaq-kluən
restaurant: haaŋ-luəq-baay;
   phoocəniiyəthaan
reverse, turn around: tralap
revolve (iV): wuəl; (tV): rɔwɨy
reward, accumulated merit: phal-bon
rice (cooked): baay; uncooked rice:
   qaŋkaa; unhusked rice, paddy:
   srəw; steamed rice: baay-camhoy;
   fried rice: baay-liiŋ; seed rice:
   srəw-puuc; floating rice:
   srəw-laəŋ-tɨk; dry (season) rice:
   srəw-praŋ; wet (season) rice:
   srəw-wuəhsaa; broadcast rice:
   srəw-pruəh; transplanted rice:
   srəw-stuuŋ
rice-farmer: neəq-twəə-srae
rice-field: srae; dry (season) rice-field:
   srae-praŋ; wet (season) rice-field:
   srae-wuəhsaa
ride, get aboard: cih
right (side): sdam; right-hand (side):
   sdam-day; right-hand side:
   khaaŋ-sdam-day
right (correct): trəw, trəw haəy; (true):
   mɛɛn

ripe: tum
rise, get up: kraok (laəŋ)
river (large, wide): tuənlee; tributary:
   stɨŋ; small stream: prɛɛk; the
   Mekong River: tuənlee-meekoŋ
road, street: pləw; paved road: tnal;
   streets and roads: pləw-tnal
room (N): bantup
rose: kolaap, pkaa-kolaap
rotate (tV): rɔwɨy
round: muul
row, range: cuə
royal: riəc, phuumɨn; royalty: sdac
royal anthem: bat qaŋkɔɔ-riəc
royal capital: riəccəthiənii
royal kingdom: preəh-riəc-qanaacaq
royal person (term of reference or
   specifier): preəh-qaŋ
royal queen: mɔhaa-ksattrəyaanii
royal residence: damnaq
royal treasures: krɨəŋ-preəh-riəccətroəp
rub, wipe: cuut
rubber: kawsuu; rubber tree: daəm-
   kawsuu
ruby (N): tbouŋ-tɔtɨm, tbouŋ-kratɨm
ruler, monarch: ksat
run (V): ruət
Russia: ruhsii, srok-ruhsii, prateeh-
   ruhsii; Russian (N, A): ruhsii

S

sacred: preəh-(word prefixed to sacred
   objects or to actions performed by
   sacred persons)
sad: pruəy-cət, kamsat
Saigon: prɨy-nəkɔɔ
salty, seasoned: pray
same: dadael
sapodilla: lmut
sapphire: tbouŋ-kandiəŋ
Saran (personal name): saraan
Sarin (personal name): sarɨn
sarong: saroŋ; dhoti-style sarong:
   sampuət
Sarun (personal name): sarun
Saturday: tŋay-saw
save, collect: sansam
saw (wood, etc.): qaa; sawmill:
   rooŋ-qaa-chəə
say (tV): thaa
scatter (tV): baac
scene, set: chaaq
school: salaa, salaa-riən; technical
   school: salaa-təcnɨc; School of
   Pedagogy: salaa-kuruq-wɨcciə;
   primary school:
   salaa-pathamməsəksaa;

government school: salaa-riəcckaa;
School of Fine Arts: salaa-raccənaa;
pagoda school: salaa-wŏət
science, field of study: wɨccia; higher
education: wɨccia cŏən kpuəh; science
as a field of study: wɨttyiəsaah,
wɨcciəsaah
scratch about: kakaay
screen (tV): baŋ; (N): rɔbaŋ
screwdriver: tuənəwih
sculpture, frieze: kbac-camlaq
scythe, sickle: kandiəw
sea: səmot, sramot; Sea of Thailand:
səmot-siəm
seal, stamp (N): traa
season (N): rɔdəw; hot season:
rɔdəw-kdaw; rainy season:
rɔdəw-pliəŋ; cold season:
rɔdəw-rɔɲiə
secondary education: mattyum-səksaa;
first cycle of secondary school:
mattyum-səksaa tii-muəy; second
cycle of secondary school:
mattyum-səksaa tii-pii
secondary school, lycée: wɨttyiəlay,
wɨcciəlay, lihsei
secretary: smiən
sect: nikaay; liberal sect (of Buddhist
monks): mɔhaanikaay; orthodox
sect: thŏəmməyut
section, fragment: pnaek
see: khəəñ; look at, watch, read:
məəl; see, perceive: məəl khəəñ
seedling, plant: samnaap
seek: rɔɔk
seem (to be), appear (to be): douc-ciə
select, extract: rəəh, samraŋ
sell: luəq; sell abroad, export: bañcuun
tɨw luəq nɨw baarəteeh
send: pñaə; send out, expel: bañcəñ;
send away: bañcuun
sentence, space: kliə
September: (khae-)kaññaa
serious: tŋuən, klaŋ
servant, waiter: bamraə, neəq-bamraə
sesame: lŋɔɔ
set, suite: samrap
seven: prampɨl
seventy: cətsəp
sew: dei
shade (N): mlup
shallow: reəq; quite shallow: reəq-
reəq
sharp: mut; sharpen: samliəŋ
shave (tV): kao
sheaf, handful: kandap
shed, drop off: cruh
shell, skull: rɔliə; coconut-shell: rɔliə-douŋ

shirt, blouse, coat: qaaw
shoes: sbaek-cəəŋ
shop, store: haaŋ; barbershop:
haaŋ-kat-saq; laundry:
haaŋ-baok-qut
shout (tV): sraek; (N): samraek
side, direction: khaaŋ
Siem Reap (Town, Province): siəm-riəp
sign (tV): siññei
silk: sout
silkworm: koun-niəŋ
silver: praq
similar: douc kniə, prahael-prahael kniə
simultaneously: bandaə
sing: criəŋ; song: camriəŋ
sink (iV): lɨc; sink in the water: lɨc tɨk
sit: qaŋkuy; (of clergy): kuən
situated: nɨw, thət (nɨw)
six: prammuəy
six million: prammuəy-liən
sixteen: dap-prammuəy
sixty: hoksəp
size: tumnum
skin: sbaek
sky-blue: (pɔə) ptɨy-meek
slap (tV): teəh
sleep (tV): deik, deik luəq, keeŋ, keeŋ
luəq; (lit): tɔtuəl damneik; (N):
damneik; be hospitalized: deik-pɛɛt;
unable to sleep: keeŋ mɨn luəq,
deik mɨn luəq
slender: skɔɔm; very slender, skinny:
samkɔɔm
slice, cut piece: kamnat
slip, do accidently: cɔluəh
slip off, come off: rɔbout
slow: yɨɨt; slowly, deliberately:
muəy-muəy
small: touc; small and numerous:
touc-touc; small (in quantity): təc
smell (sniff): hət; (receive an odor):
thum
smoke, inhale, suck: cuəq
smoked, roasted: cqaə
snow, frost: tɨk-kaaq
so, accordingly: kaa + V
soap: sabuu
soccer: bal-tŏət
socks, stockings: sraom-cəəŋ
soft: tuən
soldier: tiəhiən; be a soldier: twəə
tiəhiən
some (Pr, Adv): klah
someone (indPr): neəq-naa, nɔnaa
something (indPr): qwəy, qəy, sqəy
sometimes: cuən-kaal
somewhat, a little (Adv): bantəc; a little
bit (Adv): bantəc-bantuəc

somewhere, wherever: naa, kɑnlaeŋ naa,
    qae-naa
son: koun-proh
son- or daughter-in-law: koun-prɑsaa
song (vocal): cɑmriəŋ; (instrumental):
    pleeŋ
soon, in a little while: bɑntɑc-tiət
sound, noise: sou
sour: cuu; sour or pungent food: mcuu;
    pungent stew: sɑmlɑɑ-mcuu
south: tbouŋ, khaaŋ-tbouŋ; (lit):
    tɨh-teəqsən
southeast: khaaŋ-tbouŋ-cruŋ-khaaŋ-kaət;
    (lit): tɨh-qɑqknee
Southeast Asia: qaazii-paek-qɑqknee
southwest: khaaŋ-tbouŋ-cruŋ-khaaŋ-ləc;
    (lit): tɨh-niərədəy
sow, scatter: pruəh, saap
spacious: tuliəy, thom-tuliəy
sparrow, ricebird: caap
speak: niyiəy; speaking: kaa-niyiəy
speed: lbɨən
special, precious: piseh
specifier for long slender objects, such
    as trees, pencils, cigarettes: daəm
specifier for ordinary persons: neəq;
    three persons: mənuh bəy neəq
spend, pay out: caay
spicy, hot: həl
spit (tV): sdɑh
spoon: slaap-priə
sports: kəylaa
spring, mountain stream: tɨk-cruəh
square (A): krɑlaa
stairs: cuəndaə
stamp (N): taem; (tV): bɑh; stamp with
    a seal: bɑh-traa
stand (iV): chɔɔ
starting from, ever since: tɑŋ-pii
state, political entity: rɑət
station, place: sthaanii; train station:
    sthaanii-qayeəqsmaayiən
stationery: krɑdaah-səsei-sɑmbot
stay, reside, remain: nɨw; (of clergy):
    kuəŋ; (lit): sɑmnɑq
steal: luəc
steam (tV): cɑmhoy
steamer, ship: kəpal
stew (tV): slɑɑ; (N): sɑmlɑɑ; pungent
    stew: sɑmlɑɑ-mcuu
still (Adv): nɨw + V; still, up to the
    present: V + nɨw-ləəy
stock, seed, background: puuc
stomach, intestines: puəh
stone: tmɑɑ
stop, cease: chup; stop studying, have a
    vacation (from school): chup riən

story, matter: riəŋ; war story: riəŋ-
    cɑmbɑŋ; comedy: riəŋ-kɑmplaeŋ;
    police story: riəŋ-qaakɨñ-qaacao
stove: cɑŋkraan
straight: trɑŋ
strange: cɑmlaek; stranger: mənuh-
    cɑmlaek
stream, large canal: prɛɛk
street, road: pləw, tnɑl
strength, power: kɑmlaŋ
stroll, amuse oneself, go around for fun:
    daə-leeŋ
strong, hard, extreme: klaŋ; strength:
    kɑmlaŋ
student: koun-səh; (formal): nihsət
study, learn: riən
Stung Treng (Town, Province): stɨŋ-
    traeŋ
stupa, chedi: caetdəy
subject, field of study: wɨcciə, muk-
    wɨcciə; special subject: wɨcciə
    piseh
submerge (tV): crɑmuc
success, increase: cɑmraən
such as: douc-ciə
suddenly: srap-tae
sugar: skɑɑ; sugar refinery: rooŋ-twəə-
    skɑɑ
sugar palm: tnaot; sugar-palm tree:
    daəm-tnaot
suit, clothing: khao-qaaw
suitable, appropriate: kuə, sɑm, kuə-sɑm
Sukkhalay Hotel: sɑnthəkiə-sokkhaalay
sun: tŋay, qaatɨt, preəh-qaatɨt
Sunday: tŋay-qaatɨt
supervisor, chief: cawwaay; provincial
    governor: cawwaay-khaet; district
    chief: cawwaay-srok
support, raise: cəñcəm; support oneself,
    make a living: cəñcəm ciiwɨt; raise
    animals, keep pets: cəñcəm sat;
    support (prop up): tuəl
sure, exact: praakɑt; surely, exactly: ciə
    praakɑt
surface: ptɨy; surface of the earth,
    topography: ptɨy-dəy
surround (encircle): poət; (envelope):
    stɔɔp
Suryavarman: sourəyaawɑɑrəman; King
    Suryavarman II: sdac
    sourəyaawɑɑrəman tii-pii
Svay Rieng (Town, Province): swaay-riəŋ
swallow (tV): leep
sweep (tV): baoh
sweetheart: sɑŋsaa; loved one:
    tii-snaehaa
swim: hael, haəl-tɨk

system, method: rɔbiəp, yaaŋ; system
  of government: rɔbiəp-krup-krɔɔŋ

t

table: tok
take: yɔɔk; take away: yɔɔk (N) tɨw;
  take and bring: yɔɔk (N) mɔɔk;
  take a walk: daə-leeŋ
take care of: thae, reə́qsaa, thae-reə́qsaa,
  thae-thoə́m; treat, care for: pyiəbaal
take leave, say good-by: liə
take off, loosen: dɑh
Takeo (Town, Province): taakaew
tame (A): saŋ; (tV): psaŋ
taste, flavor: ciət
tasty, delicious: cŋañ
taxi: taqsii; taxi-driver: neə́q-baək-
  taqsii
tea (plant): tae; (liquid): tɨk-tae
teakettle: kamsiəw
teach: baŋriən
teacher, master: kruu, kruu-baŋriən;
  (as a title): look-kruu
tear, burst, break (iV): dac; (tV): pdac
telegram: teekekraam
tell, inform (informal): prap; (formal):
  cumriəp
temple: wihiə, praasaat; stupa:
  caetdəy; temple compound: woə́t;
  sacred temple: preə́h-wihiə
ten: dɑp
ten-million: kaot
ten-thousand: məɨn
tender, green: kcəy
term, cycle: kaaŋ
Thailand: siəm, srok-siəm, prateeh-
  thay-laŋ
thank (tV): qɑɑ-kun; thank you: qɑɑ-kun
that (Da, Dp): nuh; (relative Conj): ciə,
  daoy; (quotative Conj): thaa;
  (relative Pr): dael
that's it, you've got it (Idiom): nɨŋ haəy!
thatch (tV): praq; (N): sbəw
then (Conj): haəy, ruəc-haəy; then, after
  which: təəp
there: nuh, qae-nuh; there! (look!): nɑɑ!
therefore: douccnɑh, qəñcəŋ
thermometer: teəmoumaet
these (Da, Dp): nih, nɨŋ
they (polite): koə́t, kee; (condescending):
  wiə; (indefinite): kee
thief: cao
thin: sdaəŋ, very light and thin:
  sdaəŋ-sdaəŋ
thing(s): rəbɑh, qəywan; luggage:
  həp-qəywan; accessory, ingredient:
  krɨəŋ

think: kɨt
thirty: saamsəp
this (Da, Dp): nih, neh, nɨŋ
this way: khaaŋ-nih
those (Da, Dp): nuh, nɨŋ
thought: kumnɨt
thousand: poə́n; one thousand: məpoə́n
thread (N): ceih, qambɑh
three: bəy
three or four: bəy-buən
thresh, mill: kən
throughout, all the way (to): rɔhout (dɑl)
throw (tV): bɑh; throw about, handle
  roughly: bɑh-baok
Thursday: tŋay-prɑhoə́h
thus: douccneh, douccnɑh, qəñcəŋ
ticket: sambot; steamer ticket:
  sambot-kəpal; vote: cnaot
tie, wear (a tie): caaŋ; make a presentation to newlyweds: caaŋ-day
time (era): kaal, samay, coə́n, kriə,
  peel; (occasion): daaŋ, ləək, peel
tired: qɑh-kamlaŋ, ruəy
title for high-ranking royalty: samdac
to (Prep): dɑl; (away from speaker): tɨw;
  (toward speaker): mɔɔk; up to: tɨw
  dɑl; all the way to: rɔhout dɑl, rɔhout
  tɨw dɑl
tobacco: tnam; smoking tobacco:
  tnam-cuə́q
today: tŋay-nih, tŋay-nɨŋ
together: kniə, ciə-muəy kniə
toilet: baŋkuə́n, bantup-tɨk
tomorrow: sqaek
Tonle Sap (Saap River): tuə́nlee-saap
too (in addition): ˑnaaŋ; (as well, also):
  dae
too much, excessive: peek, kray-peek,
  kray-lɛɛŋ
tool, instrument: prɑdap, krɨəŋ;
  prɑdap-cuəh-cul
tooth: tmɨñ
toothpaste: tnam-dɔh-tmɨñ
tough, hard: rɨŋ
tourist, tourism: teehsəcaa
toward: dɑl, tɨw dɑl
trade, exchange (tV): dou, pdou; do trade,
  carry on commerce: luə́q-dou; trade,
  commerce (N): cumnuəñ; trade
  (profession): rɔbaa, rɔbaa-rɔɔk-sii
train, discipline (tV): qap-rum, baŋhat
train: rəteh-pləəŋ, qəteh-pləəŋ; (lit):
  qayeə́qsmaayiən
trample: bañcoə́n
translate: prae
transplant: stuuŋ
trap, snare (tV): teə́q; (N): qanteə́q
traveler, passenger: neə́q-dɑmnaə

tree, plant, shrub: daəm; tree: daəm-chəə;
    coconut tree: daəm-douŋ; rubber-tree:
    daəm-kawsuu; flower-plant, shrub:
    daəm-pkaa; rose-bush: daəm-pkaa-
    kolaap
tremble, shake: ñɔə; to tremble, have
    chills: ñɔə kluən
trip, process: damnaə
trouble, preoccupation: thureəq
truck, van: laan-dək-tumnɨñ
try (to): lɔɔ; try out, try and see: (Verb +)
    lɔɔ-məəl
Tuesday: tŋay-qaŋkiə
turn (tV): bat
twelve: dap-pii
twenty: məphɨy
twenty-one: məphɨy-muəy
twisted: krawiəc
two: pii
type (iV): way daqtilou; way qaŋkulileik;
    typewriter: daqtilou, qaŋkulileik

u

umbrella: chat
uncle (younger brother of either parent):
    puu, look-puu, qəwpuk-miə; (older
    brother of either parent): qom,
    look-qom, qəwpuk-thom
under: kraom; below, downstairs:
    khaaŋ-kraom
understand (hear): sdap baan; understand
    (comprehend): yuəl
understanding, convention: sandap
unhappy, troubled: pruəy-cət, pibaaq-cət
union, confederation: sahaqrɔ̆ət
United States: sahaqrɔ̆ət-qaamerɨc
until: dal, tɔ̆əl-tae
up: V + laəŋ
Upper Khmer, hill-tribes: kmae-ləə
uprooted: rɔdaaq
use: praə; use, put in: daq
useful: miən prayaoc
university: məhaa-wɨttyiəlay
usually: thoămmədaa, taam-
    thoămmədaa, craən(-tae) + V,
    taeŋ-tae + V

v

value: damlay
various, different: pseiŋ-pseiŋ;
    the various: nimuəy-nimuəy
vase: thou
vegetable: banlae
verse, song: bat
very, very much: nah, peek

Vietnam: yuən, wiət-naam, srok-yuən,
    prateeh-wiət-naam; Vietnamese
    (A, N): yuən; South Vietnam:
    prateeh-wiət-naam-khaaŋ-tbouŋ
village: phuum
voice, sound: samleiŋ
volleyball: wallay-bal
vote (iV): bah cnaot

w

wait for: cam
waiter, boy: baoy
wake up (iV): pñeəq; (tV): dah
walk (iV): daə; (tV): bandaə
want (to): caŋ
wash (clothes): baok; (dishes, hands):
    liəŋ; (the face): lup; (the hair): kaq
wat: wŏət; Wat Phnom: wŏət-pnum; Wat
    Onalaom: wŏət-qonaalaom, wŏət
    praloom
Wat Preah-Kaew: preəh-wihiə preəh-
    kaew
water: tɨk; water-fall, spring: tɨk-
    cruəh
waterway: pləw-tɨk
way, method: withii
we: yəəŋ, puəq-yəəŋ
wear (above the waist or on the feet):
    peəq; (below the waist): sliəq; in
    general: sliəq-peəq
weather: qakaah, thiət-qakaah
weaving: dambaañ
wedge, insert: sniət
Wednesday: tŋay-put
week: qaatɨt; per week, in a week:
    maatɨt
weigh (tV): tləŋ
weight: tumŋuăn
well (Adv): lqaa, lqaa nah
well (healthy): ciə; completely well,
    cleared up: ciə sralah; well and
    happy: sok-sapbaay
west: ləc, khaaŋ-ləc; (lit): tɨh-baccəm
wet: tɔtɨk
what (intA, intPr): qwəy?, qəy?, sqəy?;
    what did you say?: look niyiəy qwəy?,
    look thaa məc?; what?(plural):
    qwəy-klah?
whatever (indA, indAdv): qwəy (qəy, sqəy)
    . . . ka-daoy; qwəy (qəy, sqəy) . . .
    ka-baan
wheel: kaŋ; spare wheel: kaŋ səkuə
when (intAdv): kaal-naa?, peel-naa?; (in
    the future): qaŋkal?; (in the past):
    pii-qaŋkal?; (Conj, in the past): kaal;

(Conj, in the future): dɑl; peel dael,
kaal dael

whenever (indAdv): kaal-naa, peel-naa,
qaŋkal; (Conj): kaal-naa, peel-naa

where (intAdv): naa?, kɑnlaeŋ naa?,
qae-naa?; (relative pronoun): dael

wherever (indAdv): naa kɑ-daoy, naa kɑ-baan

which (relative Pr): dael; (intAdj):
naa?; (intPr): qaa-naa?

which one?: qaa-naa?, qaa-naa-muəy?

whichever (indA): naa kɑ-daoy,
naa kɑ-baan

white: (pɔə) sɑɑ

who (intPr): neə̆q-naa?; nɔnaa?;
(relative Pr): dael

whoever (indPr): neə̆q-naa kɑ-daoy,
neə̆q-naa kɑ-baan

why? (intAdv): məc?, məc kɑɑ?; why is
it that . . . ?: haet qwəy baan
ciə . . . ?

wife: prɑpuə̆n; (lit): pheə̆qriyiə

will, about to (Aux): nɨŋ

willing (to): sok-cət + V

win, defeat: cneə̆h; win an election:
coə̆p cnaot

wind (N): kyɑl

window: bɑŋquəc

with: nɨŋ, ciə-muəy, ciə-muəy-nɨŋ;
with, by: daoy; with the fact that,
since: daoy

woman: srəy; women (in general):
srəy-srəy, puəq-srəy-srəy

wonder, reflect: nɨk

wood: chəə; tree: daəm-chəə

word, speech: piəq, sap

work (N): kaa; (iV): twəə-kaa;
work as, follow the profession of:
twəə; work as a soldier: twəə
tiəhiən

worker: neə̆q-twəə-kaa, kamməkɑɑ,
kulii

world: look, piphup, piphup-look

worn, decrepit: cah, rɨc-rɨl

worse, increasingly strong: klaŋ laəŋ

worthy of + V: kuə qaoy + V; worth seeing,
interesting: kuə qaoy cɑŋ məəl

wound (N): rɔbuəh, muk-rɔbuəh;
wounded: rɔbuəh

wrap (tV): kcap

wrench: klei, daŋkap

wrest away, bargain for: tiəm-tiə

wrist: kɑɑ-day

write: sɑsei

wrong: khoh, mɨn trəw tee

Y

year: cnam

yellow: (pɔə) lɨəŋ

yes (masc.): baat; (fem.): caah;
(familiar or colloquial, either sex):
qaə, qɨɨ; repetition of the verb of
the question

yesterday: msəl-məñ, pii-msəl-məñ

yet? (already or not yet?): V + haəy-
rɨɨ-nɨw?

yield, result: phɑl

you: (context-oriented; see sections
20, B, 1, 21, B, 1, and 27, B, 1)

young: kmeiŋ

younger brother: pqoun-proh

younger female first cousin: pqoun-
cii-doun-muəy-srəy

younger first cousin:
pqoun-cii-doun-muəy

younger sibling: pqoun

younger sister: pqoun-srəy

yourself: qaeŋ, kluən-qaeŋ

INDEX OF GRAMMAR NOTES

The following Index provides a quick reference to all the points of grammar discussed under Section B: Grammar and Drills of each lesson. Cambodian words are alphabetized according to the system described in the Cambodian-English Glossary, except that words with initial clusters occur in the position in which they would occur in the normal English alphabetical order. The formula following each topic refers to the lesson, section, and note under which the topic occurs; e.g. 4, B, 8 means Lesson 4, Section B, Note 8.

SOUTHEAST ASIA PROGRAM PUBLICATIONS
Cornell University
LANGUAGE TEXTS

INDONESIAN

Beginning Indonesian Through Self-Instruction, John U. Wolff, Dédé Oetomo, Daniel Fietkiewicz. 3rd revised edition 1992. 3 volume set. 1,057 pp. ISBN 0-87727-519-X

Indonesian Readings, John U. Wolff. 1978. 4th printing 1992. 480 pp. ISBN 0-87727-517-3

Indonesian Conversations, John U. Wolff. 1978. 3rd printing 1991. 297 pp. ISBN 0-87727-516-5

Formal Indonesian, John U. Wolff. 2nd revised edition 1986. 446 pp. ISBN 0-87727-515-7

TAGALOG

Pilipino Through Self-Instruction, John U. Wolff, Ma. Theresa C. Centano, Der-Hwa U. Rau. 1991. 4 volume set. 1,490 pp. ISBN 0-87727-524-6

THAI

A. U. A. Language Center Thai Course Book 1, J. Marvin Brown. Originally published by the American University Alumni Association Language Center, 1974. Reissued by Cornell Southeast Asia Program,1991. 267 pp. ISBN 0-87727-506-8

A. U. A. Language Center Thai Course Book 2, 1992. 288 pp. ISBN 0-87727-507-6

A. U. A. Language Center Thai Course Book 3, 1992. 247 pp. ISBN 0-87727-508-4

A. U. A. Language Center Thai Course, Reading and Writing Text (mostly reading), 1979. Reissued 1997. 164 pp. ISBN 0-87727-511-4

A. U. A. Language Center Thai Course, Reading and Writing Workbook (mostly writing), 1979. Reissued 1997. 99 pp. ISBN 0-87727-512-2

KHMER

Cambodian System of Writing and Beginning Reader, Franklin E. Huffman. Originally published by Yale University Press, 1970. Reissued by Cornell Southeast Asia Program, 3rd printing 1992. 365 pp. ISBN 0-300-01314-0

Modern Spoken Cambodian, Franklin E. Huffman, assist. Charan Promchan, Chhom-Rak Thong Lambert. Originally published by Yale University Press, 1970. Reissued by Cornell Southeast Asia Program, 3rd printing 1991. 451 pp. ISBN 0-300-01316-7

Intermediate Cambodian Reader, ed. Franklin E. Huffman, assist. Im Proum. Originally published by Yale University Press, 1972. Reissued by Cornell Southeast Asia Program, 1988. 499 pp. ISBN 0-300-01552-6

Cambodian Literary Reader and Glossary, Franklin E. Huffman, Im Proum. Originally published by Yale University Press, 1977. Reissued by Cornell Southeast Asia Program, 1988. 494 pp. ISBN 0-300-02069-4

HMONG

White Hmong-English Dictionary, Ernest E. Heimbach. 1969. 7th printing 1997. 523 pp. ISBN 0-87727-075-9

VIETNAMESE

Intermediate Spoken Vietnamese, Franklin E. Huffman, Tran Trong Hai. 1980. 3rd printing 1994. ISBN 0-87727-500-9

———————

To order* any of these titles please contact:

Southeast Asia Program Publications   Tel: (607) 255-8038
Cornell University   Fax: (607) 255-7534
95 Brown Rd. Box 1004
Ithaca, NY 14850-2819 USA

E-mail: SEAP-Pubs@cornell.edu
Visit us online at: www.einaudi.cornell.edu/SoutheastAsia/Publications

* Orders must be prepaid by check or credit card.

CPSIA information can be obtained
at www.ICGtesting.com
Printed in the USA
LVHW020111230623
750501LV00006B/609